Conolly's Guide to Southern Africa

CONOLLY'S GUIDE TO SOUTHERN AFRICA

Denis Conolly

Conolly Publishers CC
P.O. Box 414, Umkomaas
4170 South Africa

Third Edition

© Denis Conolly 1988

Second Edition 1984
First Edition 1982
Preceded by eight editions of *The Tourist in
South Africa* from 1965 to 1978

ISBN 0 620 11993 4

Photosetting and colour reproduction by
Art Plate (Pty) Ltd, Durban.
Printed and bound by
Interpak (Pty) Ltd, Pietermaritzburg.

Cover illustrations

Front: Boshof Gateway gives access to Boshof Avenue at the corner of Paradise Road, Newlands; beautifully preserved, it is perhaps the finest of the few remaining 18th century Cape gateways.
Back: *Erica regia variegata* (Elim Heath) is indigenous to the Western Cape and flowers in the winter.

About this Guide and how to use it

The sequence of *Conolly's Guide to Southern Africa* is that of a tour of each of the areas covered by the fifteen chapters.

In addition to full descriptions of, and directions to, all of the important places of interest to nature lovers and to pleasure and leisure seekers, the 448-page (250 000-word) Guide provides practical background information of geographical, historical, cultural, educational, civic, industrial, commercial, agricultural and sporting interest. In support of the text, the Guide contains 350 full-colour illustrations, a distance table and a 23-page 4-colour road atlas, together with a comprehensive accommodation directory which takes in hotels, caravan parks, public resorts, national parks, game and nature reserves. The exhaustive index provides place-name folios relative to text, atlas and accommodation directory in addition to ready reference to prominent persons in history and to the multiplicity of subjects dealt with in the Guide.

Two examples of how to use the Guide are: (1) After consulting the contents page you may wish to visit Port Elizabeth and the Settler Country, so you turn to Chapter 5 on page 131, and all the information about the area is at your fingertips. If you happen to be making the trip from Cape Town, the direct and indirect routes are provided on the atlas pages 372 to 374. The hotels in the Port Elizabeth area will be found on page 398 and the caravan parks on page 415. The *en route* accommodation information is also easily traceable. (2) Having heard of Nylstroom and not knowing where on earth it is, you turn to the index and find four folio references against Nylstroom. The first number, 274, is the text page, the second, in parenthesis (390 D26), is the atlas page and grid square, and the third and fourth numbers in square brackets, [406] and [421], are those of the accommodation directory; the first the hotels folio and the second that of caravan parks etc. Upon finding Nylstroom in the text (it cannot be missed, since, like hundreds of other place names in the Guide, it is printed in bold type, avoiding the necessity of a frustrating search), not only are you immediately able to acquaint yourself with the interesting facts concerning the town, but you are in the happy position of being able to familiarise yourself with the neighbouring places of interest, without any further cross reference.

New to Conolly's Guide is the schedule of Hiking Trails and Walks, published for the first time in this edition. These trails and walks are numbered and arranged in order of the chapters (not alphabetically). Should you wish to find a particular trail, for instance, the Umfolozi Wilderness Trail, you refer to the index and find the page folio is preceeded by the trail number thus 39/367. On the other hand you may wish to be informed about all the trails and walks in say the Northern and Eastern Transvaal, in which case these walks and trails would easily be found by consulting the Contents page; under Chapter 12 you would soon find the book pages for this information are 368/369.

CONTENTS

McNally

The mountainous Cape Peninsu

...ndowed with majestic natural grandeur.

CHAPTER 1

Cape Town, the Cape Peninsula and the Cape Flats

Civilisation started in southern Africa with the landing of Jan van Riebeeck at Table Bay on 6 April 1652 and from here, in the shadow of stately Table Mountain, where the disa, the protea, the silvertree and carpets of wild flowers flourish, a proud land is announced.

Cape Town, an historic old city of narrow streets and cobble-stone squares unperturbed by its modern adjuncts of high-rise structures and subterranean accesses, is positioned in one of the most beautiful environments of any city on earth; the great backdrop of Table Mountain, flanked by Devil's Peak and Lion's Head, creating a natural sanctuary and forming a dramatic landmark. Rising directly from Table Bay in a sheer precipice of over a thousand metres, the mountainous table-top-front cuts the skyline for three kilometres.

Cape Town has been the seat of government since the earliest times, and with its Houses of Parliament remains the legislative capital of South Africa.

Bordering on Cape Town and within the confines of the narrow Cape Peninsula a number of separate townships have developed over the years. Many of these have united with the mother city; most of the remainder are socially and economically suburbs of Cape Town. The population of the city is 1 042 000, and that of the peninsula, 1 700 000.

Table Mountain

Table Mountain, visible from as far out at sea as 200 kilometres, has always made the anchorage of Table Bay easy to find. This is the beacon of shelter and refreshment – the famed Tavern of the Seas. Land-loving visitors to Cape Town find their bearings by taking a trip to the summit of the mountain; the cable-car journey takes ten minutes and it soon becomes obvious that Cape Town lies on a peninsula; the sea is visible on both sides.

Table Bay, the reclaimed foreshore, its high-rise structures joining with those of the old city centre, other prominent landmarks – the Grand Parade, the Station, the Castle, the residences of the central suburbs spreading up the mountain slope – are all discernible from points near the upper cable station. From the western edge of the plateau the rugged Atlantic coastline is in view over Lion's Head and the Twelve Apostles; stretching from Green Point south as far as Hout Bay, the panorama takes in the charming marine suburbs of Sea Point, Clifton and Camps Bay – all built on the narrow strip between mountain and sea.

The Cape Flats must be viewed from the eastern edge of the mountain plateau. From here the impressive northern urban areas spread out for 16 kilometres to Bellville and the Tygerberg; to the right is D.F. Malan International Airport, and beyond, 50 kilometres away, the high range of Hottentots-Holland, separates the original settlement from the Overberg.

At right angles from the line of the northern

suburbs, starting at the end of Devil's Peak, the southern suburbs cross the plain in a straight line to Muizenberg. Eastwards from here the False Bay resorts, St James, Kalk Bay and Fish Hoek, hug the coastline to Simonstown. To the west of the southern suburbs and in the curve of the mountain are the famous Constantia and Tokai Valleys.

Table Mountain Aerial Cableway consists of lower and upper stations and two single-span cables of over 1 200 metres each. The lower station is in Tafelberg Road, Kloof Nek – the saddle of land linking Table Mountain with Lion's Head. At the upper station there is a tearoom, a post office where your mail will be franked 'Table Mountain' and a television and radio station. The first cableway was built in 1929 and more than a quarter million people use the facility each year. Weather permitting, the cableway is open daily, and on fine evenings in summer it runs until 10.30 p.m. – the signal being the flashing green light from the top station.

There being such a magnificent obstacle literally within a city, it follows that many a climber, whether serious mountaineer or absolute novice, is prompted to accept the challenge of conquering Table Mountain. Some 400 routes of varying grades from easy walks to sheer rockface climbs are available, and the visitor is strongly advised to communicate with the Mountain Club of South Africa before attempting any climb. At the eastern end of Table Mountain, at the summit, 1 086 metres above sea level, is Maclear's Beacon (after the Astronomer Royal), one of South Africa's map survey points. In addition to baboons, dassies and other indigenous animals, Table Mountain supports a herd of Himalayan mountain goats – descended from escapees from Groote Schuur Zoo. *Disa uniflora* (the Pride of ·Table Mountain and a species of orchid), silvertrees (a species of protea) and a host of other indigenous plants including chincherinchees, watsonia, ericas and pelargoniums, thrive on the mountain.

The pure drinking water that was relied upon entirely to replenish the ships that had been at sea for four months and more, came from the springs and streams of Table Mountain. This continued to be the only water supply right up to the end of the nineteenth century.

Although it does not appear so from a distance, the great sandstone mass of Table Mountain is split on the northern face from base to summit by the Platteklip Gorge. Well sign-posted on the Tafelberg Road, one-and-a-half kilometres from the lower cable station, the gorge is one of the easy ascents. Further along the Tafelberg Road, in the rock above a cemented pool, is the bronze plaque of the Monuments Commission proclaiming Table Mountain a natural monument.

Lion's Head

Another strikingly beautiful feature of the Cape is this 669-metre-high sugar-loaf peak on the Atlantic side of Table Mountain, connected to it by the saddle of land known as Kloof Nek. The naming of Lion's Head remains obscure. It is said that the last lion of the Peninsula was shot here. Another version of the origin of its name is that it resembles the head of a lion

with Signal Hill and the connecting ridge forming the rump and body. Its summit can be reached by path and helping chains, and the views of the massive bulk of Table Mountain, the buttresses of the Twelve Apostles, the city and the ocean, are truly stunning.

Signal Hill

Accessible by motor car, Signal Hill is one of the dramatic view sites of the harbour, city and Atlantic foreshore, especially at night. At its 335-metre-high summit is the famous Lion's Battery, used on ceremonial occasions, and the electrically operated noon time-signal gun which is controlled from the Observatory.

Twelve Apostles

Overlooking the Atlantic coast and stretching from above Camps Bay to Llandudno is the impressively steep line of sandstone buttresses that Governor Sir Rufane Donkin named the Twelve Apostles range.

Devil's Peak

A thousand metres above sea level, Devil's Peak flanks the eastern (False Bay) side of Table Mountain and was first named Wind Mountain because of its connection with the Cape south-easter. It acts as the corner-stone in reactivating the wind into its gale force speed of up to 120 kilometres per hour, and takes the name Devil's Peak from the Malay legend. The legend attributes the 'tablecloth' to the smoke-cloud caused by a pipe-smoking contest between an old Dutch Burgher, Mynheer van Hunks, and the Devil. Continuing through all summer, the contest ceases in the winter when van Hunks is stricken with rheumatism and cannot climb the mountain.

The Capetonian accepts the south-easter as a blessing. It blows from October through to February, taking with it the summer smog and pollution, cooling off intense heat and being in fact the 'Cape doctor'. This south-easter is preceded by one of the most splendid natural wonders on earth, the laying of the tablecloth of cloud on Table Mountain. From the point of view of weather the most perfect months at the Cape are March and April, and the period of greatest natural beauty, September to November, when the spring wild flowers abound and the colourful green appearance is surpassed nowhere in the world. From May to August the prevailing north-westerly brings the rain (up to 1 500 mm) without which this paradise would be non-existent.

Table Bay

A great port by any standard, Table Bay was used by the Portuguese navigators a hundred and fifty years before Jan van Riebeeck had landed. Energetic Antonio de Saldanha climbed Table Mountain in 1503 and gave his name to the bay below, Agoada de Saldanha, the name by which it was known until Joris van Spilbergen, the Dutch Fleet commander of the seventeenth century, renamed it Table Bay.

At the age of 33 as settlement leader of one of the bravest expeditions undertaken in history, van Riebeeck and his party, which included his wife Maria and their infant son, arrived at Table Bay. The voyage from Holland had been made in good time, 104 days.

The tiny 200-ton flagship *Dromedaris* was accompanied by the yacht *Goede Hoop* and the flyboat *Reyger*. The ships laid anchor on 6 April 1652. Always seeking promotion, van Riebeeck was made commander at the Cape in 1654, was finally transferred to Batavia (Djakarta) where he became Secretary of the Council of India, and died in 1677. He was not to know that his greatest honour would be in South Africa, where he would be remembered as the founder of a nation.

Table Bay harbour is still the half-way-house between two oceans; it is one of the world's greatest loading ports for fruit and is South Africa's primary port for wine and fish products besides handling huge shipments of wool, wheat and mineral ore. Cape Town has also become a principal container and oil refinery port and its dry dock is one of the largest in the world, able to accommodate giant tankers on the route from the Persian Gulf to the Atlantic.

Foreshore – Roggebaai, Heerengracht – Adderley Street

Cape Town's reclaimed Foreshore led to the unique opportunity for the planning, on a grand scale, of an entire new front to an old city. It originated following the massive dredging of Table Bay during the construction of the new harbour, named Duncan Dock after the South African Governor General, and completed during World War II.

The 145-hectare reclaimed area was once a rocky bay – the name Roggebaai still remains – where today can be seen a built up area in a handsome setting of wide boulevards. Among the many fine buildings is the famous Nico Malan Complex comprising the opera house, theatre and civic offices.

The Heerengracht, the principal thoroughfare, bisects the width of the Foreshore and before joining with famous Adderley Street and the old city it passes the statues of Jan van Riebeeck and his wife Maria and circles three ornamental fountains. The area of the fountains marks the original shoreline before reclamation.

Opposite the fountains on the pavement in front of the Medical Centre is a small but deeply impressive monument – a dedication to Captain Robert Falcon Scott, the British Antarctic explorer who reached the South Pole on 18 January 1912 only to perish in a blizzard on his return. The monument takes the form of a bronze sailing ship inscribed with the moving message from Scott's diary:

> *Had we lived, I should have had a tale to tell of the hardihood, endurance and courage of my companions which would have stirred the heart of every Englishman – these rough notes and our dead bodies must tell the tale.*

Cape Town had served as a base for Scott on his last tragic expedition.

Adderley Street (the original Heerengracht) had its name changed in 1850 to honour Sir Charles Adderley, the British parliamentarian, who successfully opposed the British government's plan to make the Cape a convict settlement.

At the start of Adderley Street, fronted by a beautiful garden, is the modern central railway station and air terminal. Exhibited in the station's main concourse is an historical monument, the oldest rail locomotive in South Africa. It was purchased by the Cape Town Railway and Dock Company from Hawthorne and Leith, Scotland, and arrived with its driver, William Dabbs, in 1859. In 1863 the line from Cape Town to Wellington, via Eerste Rivier, Stellenbosch and Paarl, was completed and the locomotive with its original driver remained in service on this line until 1881. Although the construction of this Cape line started in 1859, it was the second line to come into operation in South Africa – the first, between Durban Central and the Point, opened in 1860.

At about the middle distance of the length of Adderley Street, on the left facing the mountain, is Sanlam's Golden Acre, an imposing high-rise complex with subterranean concourses and suspended pedestrian walk connecting with the railway terminal across Strand Street. Here, during the building operations carried out in 1975, the ruins of Commander Zacharias Wagenaer's reservoir were discovered. Dating from 1663 these ruins were excavated by the South African Museum and preserved in the original position in which they were found. Having preceded the Castle in construction, these ruins are the oldest remaining Dutch structures in South Africa and have been declared a national monument. Opposite the Golden Acre (where Woolworths now stands) is the first trading site in Cape Town.

Beyond the Golden Acre, Adderley Street is connected with Parliament Street by Trafalgar Square which is occupied by the famous flower sellers, and across Parliament Street from the square is the General Post Office. Here on the wall of the vestibule is a fine example of the inscribed post office stones under which the early mariners left their mail for collection by ships going in the other direction. Another post office stone, found during excavations in 1974, is displayed in the Strand Concourse.

Castle of Good Hope

South Africa's oldest building remaining in use, The Castle of Good Hope, had its foundation stones laid on 2nd January 1666 by Commander Zacharias Wagenaer some 220 metres to the east of the site of van Riebeeck's original mud-walled fort. Its construction followed the imminence of maritime war with the Netherlands' trade rival, England. Progress in building was hampered between cessation and resumption of the war and although the Castle was first occupied in 1674 it was not until 1679 that it was completed.

The Castle was designed in accordance with the old defence system of the Netherlands, in a pentagonal shape with five points of the star forming the bastions – the stone walls between bastions 150 metres long and 12 metres high. It was considered to be pretty secure with a powder magazine under each bastion and a 25-metre moat dug around the entire fortification. No attack having ever been launched against the Castle, its strength was never tested.

The five bastions were named after the titles of the

2

1

4

3

1. In the centre foreground Table Bay harbour which has been expanded upon progressively since the inception of sea trade in the 16th century, whilst the mountainous features: Devil's Peak, Table Mountain, Lion's Head and Signal Hill have limited the expansion of Cape Town itself. In the distance the two oceans can be seen, the Indian to the left and the Atlantic to the right, and in the right foreground is Greenpoint Common with the stadium prominent, above Granger Bay.

2. The Kat, balcony-entrance to the palatial Castle residence of the Cape governors, both Dutch and English.

3. Cape Town is one of the great fruit-exporting ports of the world, and its Grand Parade market is unexcelled in the presentation of the season's harvest.

4. The flower sellers of Cape Town's Trafalgar Square charm the buyers in the midst of all this indigenous beauty.

Prince of Orange, the Netherlands' ruler at the time. Buren, the northern bastion, contained officers' quarters and the tollgate, compulsory for all produce dealers entering Cape Town from the interior. The garden in this bastion was much used by Lady Anne Barnard* during the first British occupation of the Cape. Katzenellenbogen, on the eastern side, contained the 'black hole' and other below sea-level dungeons provided for the incarceration of wrong-doers. Nassau, the south-eastern bastion, contained storerooms and offices, and Oranje to the south contained the armoury and gunsmiths' workshop. Leerdam, the western bastion, contained the kitchens and pay office. During the eighteenth century there were approximately one hundred cannon in the fortress in a mixture of 12-, 18-, and 24-pounders.

In the bell-tower over the entrance to the Castle is the original bell, cast in Amsterdam in 1697. The pediment above the entrance bears the United Netherlands' coat-of-arms and on the architrave below are the coats-of-arms of the six Chambers of the Dutch East India Company and the Company's monogram: V O C (Vereenigde Oost-Indische Compagnie).

In 1685 the visiting Dutch East India Company Commissioner, van Rheede, had a defensive wall built diagonally across from Katzenellenbogen to a point midway between Oranje and Leerdam, breaking the enormous Castle courtyard into two. The traverse wall soon became known as the Kat, from the first syllable of Katzenellenbogen. A gate connected the two courtyards now formed and several buildings were· erected against the wall. Adjacent to the gate was the Governor's residence and a large council hall completed in 1695. This hall was used as a church until 1704 when the Groote Kerk was opened, and during the British occupation the spectacular receptions of Lady Anne Barnard were held here.

Much of the Castle was reconstructed between 1782 and 1788. The ornamental balcony entrance to the Governor's residence with its fluted pillars, intricate wrought-iron and carvings, is a striking example of the combined efforts of sculptor Anton Anreith (1755-1822) and architect Louis-Michel Thibault (1750-1815). From this balcony edicts, declarations and government announcements were made. The gracious state rooms today contain a splendid collection of art treasures and antiques of the old Cape, purchased by the State in 1964 from the estate of the Cape Town Africana collector, William Fehr.

The Castle was one of the first South African national monuments to be proclaimed; it remains the

* Lady Anne Barnard was born Lady Anne Lindsay, eldest daughter of the Earl of Balcarres, and at the age of 43 married Andrew Barnard, son of the Bishop of Limerick in 1793. In 1797 she accompanied her husband to the Cape after he had been appointed Secretary for the Colony under Lord Macartney, the first British Governor (General Craig, who accepted the surrender of the Cape in 1795, having acted Governor for two years prior to Macartney's arrival). The Secretary and his wife lived at the Castle and Lady Anne acted as hostess to the Governor whose wife had not been able to leave England. A poet and lady of great charm, history is indebted to her for the many letters she wrote about conditions at the Cape. Her letters became a South African classic, appearing in 1901 under the title *South Africa a Century Ago*, edited by South African author, Dorothea Fairbridge.

military headquarters of the Cape Command and also houses a military museum. Guided tours are conducted and there is a tearoom.

Grand Parade and City Hall

Historically the Parade is older than the Castle; it was in use as the garrison parade-ground before the construction of the Castle was completed and takes its place among our important national monuments. In the seventeenth century it stretched from the Heerengracht (now Adderley Street) and Keisersgracht (now Darling Street) to the Table Bay shoreline. During the eighteenth century it became a green pasture; several streams crossing it on the way to the sea from the mountain, it was further beautified by the oak trees that surrounded it. Building encroachment halved its original size during the nineteenth century but it is nevertheless still Cape Town's largest open area, providing parking space for hundreds of motor cars and being transformed into a colourful spectacle on Wednesday and Saturday mornings when a great variety of merchandise is bargained for in an open-air market.

Facing seaward across Darling Street and the Grand Parade is the City Hall; built of sandstone and completed in 1905, it confronts a statue on the Parade of Edward VII of Great Britain in coronation robes, and symbolises the Imperial grandiosity of the era. Despite the impracticability of its interior design it contains a large hall notable for its fine acoustic quality and has for a long time been the venue for concerts of the famous Cape Town Symphony Orchestra.

Church Square – the Slave Lodge and the Groote Kerk

It could be said that Cape Town was developed around four public squares of which Church Square is the oldest; the other three are Greenmarket, Riebeeck and Stal.

Ironically, Church Square first served as the site of slave markets, and the second building to be constructed in South Africa (after the Castle) was the Company's slave lodge on the south side of the square; this was in 1679. Tradition has it that the slaves were actually sold under a huge pine tree, the situation of which is marked by an inscribed pavement stone on the nearby traffic island of Spin Street.

The lodge was large enough to house some 500 to 600 of the Company's slaves and remained in use as a slave lodge for 130 years. During its long history the building has undergone considerable constructional and functional changes. The most important alterations were carried out in 1810 after the Earl of Caledon ordered that the slaves be sold and the building be converted into government offices. The famous triumvirate, Thibault the architect, Anreith the sculptor and Schutte the builder, produced the dignified building that stands at the top of Adderley Street known today as the Old Supreme Court. Upon completion it housed a number of public services including the Supreme Court, the Attorney-General, the Post Office, the Receiver of Revenue, the Fiscal and the Bank. An enlarged courtroom was added in 1815. The Royal Arms relief by Anreith is in the

Parliament Street pediment. Starting in 1834 the Legislative Council (the precursor of Parliament) under Sir Benjamin d'Urban, sat in the 'record room' of the Supreme Court. The meetings continued here until 1853 when the venue was transferred to the Masonic Banqueting Hall on Stal Plein. Thibault's façade which faces onto Adderley Street was moved back some twenty feet in 1926 to allow for road widening and on this pavement there is a statue of Jan Christian Smuts. The street between the Old Supreme Court and the Groote Kerk is Bureau Street – a significant reference to the onetime government offices. The Old Supreme Court is now the South African Museum of Cultural History. The tombstones of Jan van Riebeeck and his wife Maria de la Quellerie, retrieved from their 17th century places of burial, Batavia and Malacca respectively, are to be seen on a wall of the courtyard.

The Groote Kerk, the second building on the left at the top of Adderley Street, was the first church building to be built in southern Africa. Opened on 6 January 1704, it faced the western side of the open area of slave trafficking that later took the name, Church Square. The steeple, vestry and vaults of the original Groote Kerk were retained in the rebuilding which was completed in 1841 under the supervision of architect and builder Herman Schutte. The design is typical of the great renaissance of building at the Cape at the start of the nineteenth century and contains a mixture of Gothic and Classical styles with a bold and vigorous façade. The famous carved pulpit of Anton Anreith dates from 1779. The vaults of the church contain the remains of six governors of the Dutch East India Company, including those of Simon van der Stel and Ryk Tulbagh. A statue of the Rev. Dr Andrew Murray, a most distinguished divine of the Dutch Reformed Church in the 19th century, is at the Adderley Street entrance.

Church Square, the Old Supreme Court and the Groote Kerk are national monuments. In the centre of the Square is the statue by Anton van Wouw of the Rt. Hon. J.H. Hofmeyr (1845-1909) a great South African and affectionately known as 'Onze Jan'.

Adjacent to Church Square, at 60 Corporation Street, is the renowned three-star Town House Hotel, so conveniently situated it makes a grand base for both business activities and sight-seeing. No hotel in Cape Town offers better value for money.

Greenmarket Square and Old Town House

The late seventeenth and early eighteenth centuries saw a natural development of Cape Town when the first business centre midway between fashionable Sea Street (Strand Street) and the entrance to the Company's garden (the Avenue) came into existence. In what is today Greenmarket Square fresh produce was traded and in this area of commercial activitiy the first Burgher Watch House was built; it was completed in 1716. From here the surveillance of the security of the settlement was conducted and later the civic affairs of the community were administered. During Ryk Tulbagh's term of office the original building was replaced by what is today the Old Town House; the foundation stone having been laid in 1755, it was only completed in 1761 at a cost of some 33 000

guilders.

The Old Town House with its extravagant front elevation is a rare example of the architecture of the era. A Coat of Arms of Cape Town presented by Commissioner J.A. de Mist was added in 1804, and in 1808 the versatile Herman Schutte added the belltower. Beautifully preserved, the building symbolises the development of local government in Cape Town. It served as the city's administrative centre for more than a hundred years, first by the Burgher Council of the Dutch East India Company and later by the Burgher Senate (a true municipal body) of the British occupation. From the time that the senate was abolished in 1828 until Cape Town was granted a municipal council in 1839, the building was used as a magistrate's court. From 1839 until 1905 when the City Hall facing the Grand Parade was opened, the Old Town House remained the chamber of local authority.

In 1916 the building was renovated by architect J.M. Soloman, who transformed the interior to accept the magnificent collection of art presented to the city by Sir Max Michaelis in 1913. Augmented in 1932 by his widow Lady Michaelis, this is the finest collection of old masters in the country and includes 17th century Dutch and Flemish paintings of Rembrandt, Jan Steen and Frans Hals.

The cobble-stoned Greenmarket Square itself and the Old Town House are national monuments. On the square, adjacent to the Old Town House, is the strikingly beautiful Metropolitan Methodist Church which was opened in 1879, four years after the foundation stone was laid. Another national monument is the façade of the inn which looks out across the square that has always been a kaleidoscope of the life of the city itself.

Strand Street — Koopmans de Wet House, Lutheran Church, Martin Melck House and Secton's House

Strand Street, or Sea Street as it was then called, was one of the first thoroughfares of Cape Town; it extended from the Castle along what was then the beach front where the well-to-do merchants of the seventeenth and eighteenth centuries had their homes. One private residence at No. 23 and a unique group of buildings at 96 to 100 Strand Street are preserved today as historical monuments.

Koopmans de Wet House, 23 Strand Street, dates from 1701 when a thatched house was built on this erf granted by Willem Adriaan van der Stel to the affluent mastermariner merchant, Reynier Smedinga. During the surge of prosperity at the Cape towards the end of the eighteenth century a second storey was added, and Louis-Michel Thibault remodelled the front façade to give it the then popular so-called Louis XVI style with its harmonious proportions, fluted columns, panels between lower and upper windows and graceful pediment. In the nineteenth century the house was acquired by the well-known de Wet family and eventually became the property of the influential Marie Koopmans de Wet. She had married a Crimean War officer with the name Koopmans. Today Koopmans de Wet House is part of the South African Museum and contains a priceless collection of Cape Dutch furniture and other antiques.

Two hotels of the Petousis family, each provides a fine blend of historic Cape with the luxury of modern services and amenities and for good measure both have excellent restaurants. At 60 Corporation Street, Town House Hotel is in the midst of the City's activities, and in a perfect Newlands setting in Protea Road, Vineyard Hotel, once the home of Lady Anne Barnard, continues to grace the Cape scene.

3

1

1. Cape Town's famous walk, the Avenue, once divided the first garden in South Africa, started by van Riebeeck.

2. The Lion Gateway (off the Avenue), the work of Thibault and Anreith, once gave access to the Company's zoo and is now the entrance to university property.

3. The towered entrance to the Castle of Good Hope, South Africa's oldest building remaining in use.

17

On the opposite side of Strand Street stretching to the corner of Buitengracht Street is the group of 18th century buildings, Nos. 96 to 100. The centre building, the Lutheran Church, was built in the guise of a warehouse in 1774 by Martin Melck because the Company tolerated only the free worship of the Dutch Reformed Church. This changed in 1779.

The church, which contains Anreith's magnificent octagonal pulpit, was rebuilt to a considerable extent in 1818 and is flanked by the Sexton's House (1779-1783) on the corner of Buitengracht Street and the Parsonage, architecturally the most important of the group. It was built in 1781 soon after Melck's death, and named in his honour Martin Melck House in 1932 when the church authorities restored the building. Thibault was the architect and Anreith provided the moulded architraves, carved front door and the swan (Luther's symbol) on the front of the building. It is a typical example of the Cape town-house with its dormer room or belvedere of four upper windows from which could be surveyed the whole of Cape Town and Table Bay.

Company's Garden and Government Avenue

Van Riebeeck received very definite instructions from the Lords Seventeen, his masters of the United East India Company, to build a fort and a garden and these tasks along with many others he performed creditably. The first plantings were close to the earthern-walled fort. By 1660 however, the entire garden lay west of the Fresh River, the river that ran more or less along the Heerengracht (presentday Adderley Street) to the sea. The garden fronted seaward on Tuin Street (now Church Street) extending toward the mountain. With the choosing of sites for the church and graveyard, the hospital and the slave lodge, the garden was encroached upon from time to time until it finally became established approximately on either side of where the Avenue is today.

In the early days of the settlement the garden was used exclusively for the supply of vegetables and fruit for the needs of ships visiting Table Bay. With the changes brought about after the arrival of Simon van der Stel in 1679, such as availability of produce from the free burghers and the Company's garden at Newlands, the importance of the town garden gradually receded until Simon van der Stel had it converted into a botanical garden. The early botanists (then called master gardeners) Heinrich Oldenland (1692-1697), Jan Hartog (1689-1715) and Johan Auge (1747-1785) assisted in the creation of a botanical garden varied with indigenous and exotic species, sufficient to arouse international attention.

Simon van der Stel built a summer-house in the garden on the site of the State President's present-day residence, Tuynhuys, and during the term of his son Willem Adriaan van der Stel, a zoo was established at the top of the garden. These were the first of many structures to make their inroads upon the Company's Garden. It is now a national monument and the future conservation of the area is protected.

The same national monument protection applies to the Avenue that bisects the width of the garden.

Government Avenue at the top of Adderley Street is a paved walk lined with beautiful old oaks that have replaced the lemon trees of the original garden. Nine hundred metres long, it connects the city with the residential suburb known as the Gardens and is a favourite walk of Capetonians and visitors to the city. It gives access not only to the Botanical Gardens: right here are the Houses of Parliament, the South African Library, St George's Cathedral, the National Art Gallery, the Gardens Synagogue, the South African Museum and the Little Theatre.

Municipal Botanical Gardens

Not quite six hectares of what remains of the Company's Garden is today administered by the municipality. Being as it is in the heart of the city, this is one of the great attractions of Cape Town. Here, amidst some 8 000 varieties of trees and plants gathered from all parts of the world, the squirrels and pigeons are tame enough to be fed from a child's hand. In the conservatories are to be found some 500 species of orchids, foliage plants and ferns. Other botanical features include tropical water lilies, the rose gardens and the scent garden for the blind.

The Slave Bell that governed the working hours of the Company's slaves still stands in the approximate centre of the garden. In this central area is the statue of Cecil Rhodes, pointing northwards and bearing the famous inscription: 'Your hinterland is there.'

Nearby, luncheons and teas are served both indoors and al fresco in the most delightful surroundings. Where the Gardens end, in the open space between the Art Gallery and the Museum, are several monuments on the lawns near the ornamental ponds. Nearest the Art Gallery is the controversial statue of General Smuts; in the centre of the open area are the striking memorials to the South African Gunners and to the South African soldiers who fell at Delville Wood in the First World War; and near the Queen Victoria Street entrance is the statue of Major General 'Tim' Lukin of Delville Wood fame. The statues of Bartholomew Dias (who discovered the Cape) and van Riebeeck's wife, Maria (presented to Cape Town by the governments of Portugal and Holland) previously in this area of the Gardens, now stand on the Heerengracht.

Houses of Parliament

On the left at the lower end of the Avenue are the Houses of Parliament, completed in 1884 at a cost of £250 000, the work of the architect Harry Siddon Greaves, commissioned after the grandiose design of Charles Freeman had to be abandoned.

The building had served for twenty-five years as the seat of government of the Cape Colony before a National Convention, held here in February 1909, provided a draft constitution of the Union of South Africa. There had been two previous conventions, the first taking place in Durban and the second here in the Cape Parliament. The Houses of Parliament have remained the seat of legislative government of the Republic of South Africa, the two houses being the Assembly and the Senate. In 1980 an amendment to the constitution saw the end of the Senate and the incorporation of the President's Council. In May 1983 the constitution was again amended with the introduction of a tri-cameral parliament; the three houses accommodating whites, coloureds and indians. The Houses of Parliament are normally open to the public during recess – July to December. Visitors wishing to attend debates must apply to a member of parliament.

Anglican Cathedral of St George the Martyr
In Wale Street, across the Avenue from Parliament, is St George's Cathedral on the axis of the street with the same name. It stands on the half-hectare portion of the Company's Garden granted by Lord Charles Somerset in 1827 for the construction of an Anglican Cathedral.

Herman Schutte built the original church in 1830 and credit for the design, modelled on that of St Pancras Church in London, belongs to a Mr Skirrow, a British Admiralty Clerk of Works. In 1901 Sir Herbert Baker planned the neo-Gothic cathedral replacement which is taking considerable time to complete. The cathedral contains a memorial to Field Marshal Lord Mountbatten of Burma. Adjoining the cathedral is St George's Grammar School.

South African Library
Adjacent to St George's Cathedral is the South African Library. Opened in January 1822, it is the oldest public library in South Africa.

In front of the library is the oldest statue in South Africa, the figure of Sir George Grey, unveiled in 1864. He was Governor at the Cape from 1854 to 1862. A man born before his time, Sir George Grey visualised the unification of South Africa, was liked by Briton, Boer and Black and had the reputation of being the best governor of all time. He gave freely for the betterment of education and hospitals and presented his personal library to the people of the Cape Colony. His priceless collection, preserved in the museum section of the South African Library, includes a manuscript of the year 900 – The Four Gospels – the oldest book in South Africa. Other incunabula of these treasures are volumes of 1470 and 1482. Another valuable item is a First Folio of Shakespeare, 1623.

South African National Gallery
The National Gallery that had its beginning in 1872 was incorporated in 1895. It grew from the immense help of public spirited citizens and found its home in the spacious 14-gallery premises in the Gardens in 1930. Since then it has housed many important collections and received the continuing support of famous benefactors. The gallery has strength in the English masters and its permanent collection includes works by Gainsborough, Reynolds, Raeburn, Stubbs, Romney, Burne Jones, John and Sickert. French school representation includes Danbigny, Sisley and Pissarro, and the Dutch artists represented are Cuyp, Van Goyen and Van de Velde. Sculpture exhibits of Epstein, Rodin, Greco, Archipenko, Barlach, Giacometti, Lipschitz and Moore provide a commendable display. All major South African artists are represented in the three departments.

South African Museum
The Museum is at the top of the Gardens on the right hand side. It is noted mostly for its collections in the fields of natural history and anthropology. The oldest of its famous 'Post Office Stones' is dated 1614 and a unique collection includes stones inscribed in Dutch, English, French and Danish. Among other outstanding exhibits are Bushman paintings and rock engravings, soapstone objects from the Zimbabwe Ruins and lifelike reconstructions of animals found as fossils in the Karoo meteorites. The extensive structural improvement and refurbishing of 1987 permits improved exhibition, particularly in the marine mammals displayed. The museum now houses a large planetarium.

Government Archives
In Queen Victoria Street, opposite the top end of the Gardens, are the Government Archives. They contain the records of the Cape from the date of van Riebeeck's arrival in 1652. Documents, maps and other objects of great interest are displayed. The outstanding photographic section comprises thousands of pictures from the Elliott and other collections. Photographic prints and copies of documents may be obtained at prescribed rates and students may consult documents and records in the search room.

Gardens Synagogue
A prominent feature at the top of the Avenue, accentuated by the Table Mountain backdrop, is the Gardens Synagogue with its conspicuous marble-white towers. The adjacent building, the Old Synagogue, has a special place in history: it is the oldest synagogue in South Africa and houses a rare exhibition of ceremonial silver and other antiquities relating to South African Jewry.

Lion Gateway, Little Theatre and Egyptian Building
At the south end of the Avenue on the right hand side facing Table Mountain the Lion Gateway marked the entrance to the Company's zoo. Another of the combined efforts of Thibault and Anreith, the gateway was built at the beginning of the nineteenth century during the governorship of the eccentric Sir George Yonge who once actually closed the Avenue to the public. Today the gateway gives access to the Hiddingh Hall Courtyard and a number of buildings which form part of the University of Cape Town. The Little Theatre has a remarkable story of success since its start in the 1930s. A fine record in the blending of amateur, student and professional talent has resulted in its vital contribution to Cape Town's culture. It produces an annual programme of music, drama, ballet and opera, thereby providing a training ground for future stars. Many of South Africa's artists' careers had their beginning at the Little Theatre.

In the courtyard directly opposite the Little Theatre is the so-called Egyptian Building, the oldest building of the University of Cape Town and the first building constructed in South Africa for the purpose of higher education and still in use for that purpose. During the thirties and forties of the nineteenth century the neo-Egyptian style of architecture with its heavy colonnades was very popular, and when in 1838

1

5

4

1. The Mother City's Central Business District below the dominating outline of Devil's Peak and Table Mountain. The freeway system, which connects False Bay with the Atlantic coast, lifts the cross-city traffic above the reclaimed foreshore and the harbour area.

2. Bartholomew Dias rounded the Cape in the fifteenth century. Here his statue, at the foot of the Heerengracht, confronts the twentieth century city.

3. The Groote Kerk, opened in 1704, was the first church building to be built in southern Africa. It faces onto Adderley Street at its top end.

4. This is the oldest statue in the country; it is of Governor Sir George Grey and stands in front of the Southern African Library at the Wale Street entrance to the Avenue.

5. The Houses of Parliament where South Africa's tricameral legislation started in 1984, precisely one hundred years after the first Cape government sitting here. The stone statue of Queen Victoria was unveiled after her death in 1901.

21

Governor Sir Benjamin d'Urban granted part of the land of the then defunct Company zoo to the South African College (now the University of Cape Town), this style of architecture was employed by Col. G.G. Lewis of the Royal Engineers. When the University of Cape Town was inaugurated in 1918, the graduate classes of the South African College fell away and this was then known as the South African College School (SACS) and finally moved to Newlands in 1955. The Egyptian Building, partly concealed from the Avenue by an old white wall of the Company's zoo, is used by the University for sculpture lectures. The Lion Gateway and the Egyptian Building are both historical monuments.

Stal Plein – State President's Residence, Government Printer, Lodge de Goede Hoop and St Mary's Catholic Cathedral

The square which is Stal Plein received its name from the Company's stables which were located there. It is today at the top of Plein Street surrounded by important buildings – a mixture of modern high-rise and historic old – and contains a fine equestrian statue of General Louis Botha whose installation in 1910 as the first Prime Minister of South Africa took place in the Parliament across the way.

The historic buildings near the square all belong to the nineteenth century and an interesting group is in the western corner. Starting on the right: facing onto the Avenue with its separate entrance to Parliament is Tuynhuys, the State President's Residence and offices, built on the site chosen by Simon van der Stel for a summer-house, it is designed in the simple elegance of the English Regency period. To the left of the State President's residential property is the building of the President's Council, inaugurated in 1984. Originally the Masonic banqueting hall, it housed the Cape Legislative Assembly from 1853 until 1884 when Parliament was first opened. From then until 1916 the hall served as the Goede Hoop Theatre, and for many years before conversion to the President's Council chamber it was the premises of the Government Printer. To the left, fronted by a large parking area, is the Masonic Lodge de Goede Hoop.

The masonic order in South Africa began in 1772 when the Lodge de Goede Hoop received its warrant from the Grand Lodge National of the Netherlands. The Freemasons held their meetings in buildings hired and adapted to their requirements until 1800 when they purchased the land and employed three capable Brothers within their ranks to build their Lodge: Louis-Michel Thibault the architect, Herman Schutte the builder and Anton Anreith the sculptor. Although started during the first British occupation the building was only completed after the Cape had been handed back to the Batavian Republic at the Treaty of Amiens. The arrival of the Dutch Commissioner J.H. de Mist at the Cape was a fortunate and great occasion for the Freemasons. De Mist, a Deputy Grand Master National, was able to officiate at the ceremonial opening of the Lodge. He consecrated the Temple on 7 July 1803 and described the new Lodge as the most beautiful in the world.

The Lodge and the Banqueting Hall suffered severely in a devastating fire in February 1892. Of the Lodge, the Master's Room, the vestibule, the waiting room and one other apartment were saved; of the seven statues by Anton Anreith the symbolic figures of Silence, Death and Bereavement remain and these are considered to be the embodiment of the great sculptor at his zenith. The rebuilding was completed in 1893.

Facing the square from Roeland Street is St Mary's Roman Catholic Cathedral, a majestic building, completed in 1851 at a cost of £10 000, double the original estimate made by the architect, Spearman, at the laying of the foundation-stone ten years previously.

Rust en Vreugd

The stately eighteenth-century town house, Rust en Vreugd, in Buitenkant Street is now an art gallery, housing the William Fehr Collection of old water-colours and prints.

Rising in Table Mountain, the Fresh River (once the life and pivot of Cape Town and today controlled by conduit) crossed the extensive grounds that stretched from De Waal Drive to Hope Street on this beautifully sited estate of the notorious Willem Cornelis Boers, the corrupt fiscal who was recalled to Holland six years after he had the mansion built in 1777.

Boers' shameful misconduct notwithstanding, Rust en Vreugd is a rare and beautiful acquisition from its era. Its distinctive feature is the grand façade with architectural woodwork of sculptor Anton Anreith at its best.

During the eighteenth and nineteenth centuries many notable owners enjoyed the grandeur of Rust en Vreugd (Rest and Joy) – Lord Charles Somerset himself choosing it as a town residence. Before being restored to receive the Fehr Collection and the protection of the Historical Monuments Council in 1940, the building was for some time used by the Cape Town High School.

Riebeeck Square and St Stephen's Church

The lateral expansion of Cape Town in the eighteenth century brought into being another famous old square. It was first known as Boeren Plein then Hottentot Plein and finally Riebeeck Square. Situated on one of the outermost streets, Buitengracht Street, the large open area was used by farmers for outspanning their ox-wagons after passing through the toll-gate at the Castle. The adoption of the name Hottentot Plein, although obscure, probably had something to do with the noisy Hottentot wagoners. In the 1860s the square was renamed in honour of Jan van Riebeeck.

The only significant building on Riebeeck Square is St Stephen's Church which was once a theatre. During the first British occupation of the Cape the Governor, Sir George Yonge (an eccentric soon recalled to Great Britain), decided that the settlement, particularly the garrison troops, lacked sufficient entertainment and he started the building of a theatre in 1799. In her letters Lady Anne Barnard records the opening in November 1800.

This first theatre at the Cape, or what the Coloured folk called the 'komediehuis', had limited success and the building soon fell into disuse. In history it is only heard of again in 1838, at the end of the four-year indenture period in the emancipation of slaves. In that year the Presbyterian minister, Dr Adamson, with the support of the Reverend G.W. Stegman of the Dutch Reformed Church opened the premises as a weekday school and a Sunday school for the slaves. From 1857 St Stephen's became a congregation of the Dutch Reformed Church and is the only church in the denomination that bears the name of a saint. It is said that the church took the name of the first martyr after certain citizens stoned the building in protest against its being used for the teaching of slaves. Both the square and the church are historical monuments; the square, today a carpark, is bounded by Buitengracht, Shortmarket, Bree and Church Streets.

Malay Quarter
The first Malays to arrive at the Cape from the East came as political refugees and slaves during the mid-seventeenth century. Nearly two centuries later, at the time of the emancipation of slaves in the 1830s, these Islamic people, many of whom were good artisans, moved into the area known today as the Malay Quarter. They built their mosques with picturesque minarets and their own style of Georgian houses, with a Dutch influence; simple single-storeyed dwellings with high stoeps, flat roofs and colourfully tinted plastered walls to give a special environmental urban character on the steep slopes of Signal Hill.

Through three centuries at the Cape the Malays have founded an identity and a way of life. To preserve their historical, ethnological and architectural contribution, the Monuments Council declared the Malay Quarter a national monument. The properties so protected are those bounded by Wale, Chiappini, Longmarket and Rose Streets and those bounded by Longmarket, Chiappini, Shortmarket and Rose Streets together with numbers 67 to 85 Wale Street.

In inconspicuous and silent places on the peninsula there are to be found the domed tombs of the Muslim holy men of the Malays, and these shrines in accordance with Islamic belief are so placed to encircle Cape Town. One such *kramat*, that of Mohamed Gasan Gaibic Shah, is not far from the summit of Signal Hill on a road on the saddle of land linking Lion's Head with Signal Hill and quite close to a pair of old signal cannon.

Performing Arts, Recreation and Sport
Four of the six principal venues of performing arts on the Peninsula are of special character. Nico Malan Theatre Centre on the Foreshore is among the most modern in the world. There are two auditoriums; the opera house seats 1 214 and is used for opera, ballet and concerts; and the theatre, used for all dramatic presentations, seats 570. Maynardville Theatre in Maynardville Park in Wynberg is the only open-air theatre of its kind in southern Africa and is acknowledged to be one of the most beautiful in the world. The University of Cape Town has two theatres: The Little Theatre at the top of the Avenue serves the city and the country in the field of full training in drama, ballet and opera; and the Baxter Theatre, Concert Hall and Studio on the University's

Rosebank property below the main campus, is the finest complex of its kind in southern Africa.

Cape Town Symphony Orchestra has been maintained by the City Council as a civic amenity since 1914. Symphony concerts are given in the City Hall, the Nico Malan and Baxter complexes.

Goodhope Centre on the Foreshore is the venue for ice skating, boxing, wrestling and indoor tennis.

Playing fields in beautiful natural settings feature prominently in the Peninsula. At Newlands are the internationally famous rugby and cricket grounds and swimming pool. Professional soccer is played at Hartleyvale and Green Point Stadium. There are nine 18-hole and two 9-hole golf courses, club bowling greens in every suburb, and municipal bowling greens and tennis courts at Three Anchor Bay and Lakeside.

The Metropolitan Handicap is held in January at the South African Turf Club course in the suburb of Kenilworth. The Cape Turf Club holds meetings at Durbanville and Milnerton where the principal event in the turf calendar is the Cape of Good Hope Guineas, held on the second Saturday in February.

Cape Town's motor racing track is at Killarney. The Royal Cape Yacht Club at Yacht Harbour, Cape Town Docks, organises deep-sea yacht events as well as sailing-dinghy races in the harbour. The Zeekoevlei Yacht Club caters for smaller shallow-draft yachts. A local angling club should be contacted for details concerning licences, seasons and local conditions for both rock angling and fresh-water angling in the extensive fishing grounds of the Cape Peninsula. The Atlantic Underwater Club is at Green Point. The Mountain Club of South Africa in Hatfield Road advises on climbing.

150-kilometre circuit of the Cape Peninsula
Particularly since the opening up of new boulevards and freeways there are many permutations of routes covering the Cape Peninsula open to the motorist, and no matter which route is taken the scenic value is assured. Take the fast route on the freeway R3 named van der Stel Avenue; in connecting Muizenberg with the city it crosses the Constantia Valley in a straight line and in so doing it exposes previously unseen views of mountain and valley.

An old and tested route in which most of the Peninsula can be traversed in one full day is outward via De Waal Drive and the southern suburbs to the False Bay resorts, thence to Cape Point and homeward via Chapman's Peak and the Atlantic resorts. Many deviations from the 150-kilometre course are made, with a view to familiarising the reader with the points of interest in each area.

Gardens and Oranjezicht
Before reaching De Waal Drive, the route from the city via Long Street passes through the congested mountainside suburbs of Gardens and Oranjezicht – Gardens having once formed part of the Company's Garden, and Oranjezicht being the farm with a fine view of the Oranje bastion of the Castle – a prime region on the slopes of Table Mountain from where the first free burghers played an important role in the early development of the Cape during the latter part

of the seventeenth century. A century later in a fairy-tale resurgence of development, some magnificent mansions were built on these mountainside farms. This was the period in history when the Netherlands joined in the American War of Independence against the British. France, then an ally of the Netherlands, sent a strong fleet and garrison to protect the Cape in 1781, forestalling Britain's intention of occupation and causing a period of great prosperity at the Cape. Some of the historical properties built then remain today and, although privately owned, have been protected by the Monuments Commission. Welgemeend in Camp Street, the well-known home of the Hofmeyr family, Leeuwenhof in Hof Street, the official residence of the Administrator of the Cape Province and Waterhof on the opposite side of Hof Street are among these homes.

On the way to De Waal Drive, the dual carriage-way which is Orange Street passes the columnal portals that mark the driveway entrance to the three-hectare garden of the Mount Nelson Hotel in a sumptuous setting. West of Hof Street there are two reservoirs and De Waal Park, named after a mayor of Cape Town, D.C. De Waal, who saw to it that this open space with its beautiful trees was preserved. Below Molteno Reservoir and opposite the Upper Orange Street boundary of De Waal Park, at the corner of Prince and Sir George Grey Streets, is the Old Pump-house, the only remaining relic of a system of public water supply brought into operation by the Burgher Senate in the early nineteenth century. The mountain stream was led to a well from where slaves worked the pump by swinging to and fro a long handle weighted on the one side; the water issued from a carved wooden lion's head and quantities were recorded on the slate above the carving. This type of pump was the invention of J.F. Hurling, a Swedish colonist. De Waal Park and the Old Pump-house are declared national monuments.

De Waal Drive

De Waal Drive, which was the first of Cape Town's freeways, is named after the man who conceived its construction, Sir Frederick De Waal, first Administrator of the Cape Province. It leads south-east along the slopes of Devil's Peak and from its elevated position the city, Table Bay and the first of the southern suburbs present a breathtaking panorama. Adding splendour to the scene are the islands of indigenous flowers that separate the dual carriage-ways, the first of many such spectacles in Cape Town.

Near to where De Waal Drive joins with the Eastern Boulevard which comes up from the Foreshore, approximately sixty metres above the Drive, is the ruin of the Prince of Wales' Blockhouse, one of three blockhouses built on the mountainside in 1795 as part of the defence system during the first British occupation. Queen's Blockhouse (also in a state of ruin) and King's Blockhouse, a massive stone structure and national monument, are closer to the summit of Devil's Peak and are accessible from Tafelberg Road. Both Table Bay and False Bay can be seen from King's Blockhouse which served as a communications signal station between Cape Town and Simonstown.

Woodstock, Salt River and Observatory

Woodstock, famous for its District Six which has been demolished, was an independent municipality until 1913 when, together with a number of the surrounding municipalities, it amalgamated with Cape Town. Before it became a municipality in 1881 Woodstock was known as Papendorp.

It was here in the Cape Coloured community of District Six that the Coon Carnival had its origin; a vibrant, disciplined festival in an aura of gaiety burst out upon the Cape and became a compelling annual event in celebration of the new year with January 2nd, the 'tweede nuwe jaar' thrown in and soon becoming recognised as an official public holiday in the Cape. It all started in the nineteenth century when these warm-blooded Cape Coloureds, who had very little to be thankful for, were inspired by the American Christy minstrels; they followed closely the minstrel costumes and with their own inborn rhythm, harmony, vernacular songs and banter they have for years entertained Cape Town. It is unfortunate that in recent times they have been prevented from parading in the streets; this was the best part of the carnival when troups of up to 400, brilliantly costumed in their 'satins', tails or short jackets, top hats or 'straw bashers' with saxophones, guitars, drums, whistles, tambourines and jazz singers led by their 'captains', caused a tremendous excitement and the cry went out through the city: 'Die Coons is Uit!' From the street parades they made for the assembly stadiums to be judged in the competitions for trophies and prizes. This is the only remaining part of the carnival and venues are advertised in the press.

Successive military commanders at the Cape realised the strategic inadequacy of the Castle, which would be an easy target for any enemy holding surrounding high ground, so that the defence system eventually stretched from the mouth of the Salt River to Hout Bay. In the 1780s, when a French garrison assisted the Dutch East India Company in protecting the Cape from probable attack from England, a line of redoubts called the French Line was built. Central Redoubt in Trafalgar Park, Woodstock (a national monument), is all that remains of the old French Line.

An old gnarled milkwood tree in Spring Street, Woodstock, marks the site where the Dutch capitulated to the British on January 10, 1806, two days after the Battle of Blaauberg. This was the start of the second and final British occupation, in 1803 the Cape having been handed back to the Batavian Republic after the first occupation of seven years. The site of the capitulation is an historical monument.

Salt River, an industrial suburb with a railway marshalling yard of considerable proportions, takes its name from the river now broken into two canals that encircle another industrial area, Paarden Eiland (island of horses, after the wild horses that once roamed there) before reaching the sea in Table Bay.

Capetonians correct their time daily (except on Sundays) by the noon gun that fires on Signal Hill by electric impulse sent from South Africa's first observatory. What is still called the Royal Observatory, but what is in fact the South African Astronomical Observatory, was established by the British Admiralty in 1821 and sets standard time for the whole Republic. Here in the suburb of Observatory, where the Liesbeek River flows into the Salt River canal, is the extensive recreational club, Liesbeek Park, and adjoining it, Hartleyvale Soccer Stadium.

Mowbray, Rosebank and Rondebosch

Beyond the Eastern Boulevard merger, De Waal Drive reaches a major traffic interchange before it runs into Rhodes Drive and the continuation of the journey to the False Bay resorts. At this junction, with Groote Schuur Hospital complex on the left, a deviation can be taken along Settlers Way (which leads to the Airport and Somerset West), a route that passes through Mowbray and skirts Rondebosch, dividing the fine golf courses of those two suburbs. Mowbray and its southern neighbour, Rosebank, took their names from old estates; Rondebosch received its name from the round thorn bushes that were there in van Riebeeck's time.

In Mowbray, on the left of Settlers Way, is what used to be Coornhoop Farm, where, in the seventeenth century, the so-called free burghers were told to grow corn and where a fort as protection against the Hottentots was built. Here at Coornhoop in 1797, Servaas van Breda built an H-shape Cape Dutch house and a dovecot. Restored by the van der Stel Foundation in 1965, the original dovecot and part of the front of Coornhoop homestead and the adjoining privately-owned Westoe homestead are national monuments.

In Rondebosch, on the right-hand side of Main Road as you proceed toward Newlands, between Burg and Grotto Roads, is Rustenburg House (an historical monument) on a site bound up in the early history of the Cape. Seventeenth century Dutch governors spent their summers in this homestead of an extensive estate, even before the Castle was completed, and entertained their guests here in an area sheltered from the south-easter and surrounded by grain fields and vineyards. When Simon van der Stel occupied the house in 1687 the estate had 100 000 vines in full bearing. After the Dutch forces were dislodged from Muizenberg in 1795, this is where the surrender documents were signed, General Craig accepting the capitulation from the representatives of the Council of Policy who had signed the documents on the same day at the Castle. British rule installed for the first time, Lord Macartney's Lieutenant-Governor, General Dundas (a bachelor), surrendered his quarters at the Castle to Lady Anne Barnard and took up residence here at Rustenburg. During the Batavian Republic regime the owner, Johannes Hoets, built four columns in front of the house to correspond to the then existing pilasters. After its partial destruction by a great fire that enveloped Rondebosch in the middle nineteenth century, Rustenburg House was rebuilt in its present neo-classical style. In 1893 the property was acquired for use as a school for girls and this was the start of the famous Rustenburg School. Beautifully restored in 1977 Rustenburg House contains interesting school relics and is today a functional part of the junior school of some 630 pupils. The high school is in Camp Ground Road. The original belvedere summer-house belonging to Rustenburg was built higher up the mountainside in a good viewing position and, together with its two masonry garden seats on either side, is also an historical monument. The summerhouse is on parkland property of the University immediately below the main campus and is accessible by proceeding up Grotto Road, turning right into Lover's Walk and left into Stanley Road – a very narrow thoroughfare.

Not far from Rustenburg, on the traffic island at the intersection of Main Road and Belmont Road, is a well-known landmark, Rondebosch Fountain – a remarkable example of Victorian ironmongery in the form of a horse drinking trough below a street lantern. As intriguing as the famous Fountain is the story behind its donator, George Pigot Moodie, Surveyor-General of the Transvaal during the epic of the Eastern Line (the construction of the railway linking Pretoria and Lourenco Marques), part-owner and developer of the Barberton goldfields and retired owner of Westbrooke, where he died in 1891.

One of the large open spaces of the Cape Peninsula that has been preserved by the Monuments Commission is Rondebosch Common which is bounded by the thoroughfare of Camp Ground, Park and Milner Roads. The common was utilised in unsettled times by both Dutch and British as a military camping ground, hence the naming of Camp Ground Road on its western side. In 1855 Bishop Gray, the first Anglican Bishop in South Africa, received permission for the Rector of St Paul's Church to use the common to graze the cattle of his parishioners and the pine trees seen on the common today were planted to enclose the graveyards of the Wesleyan and Muslim communities who received concessions in the same year.

Today Rondebosch is a fashionable residential suburb in the midst of fine schools such as Rondebosch Boys High School, Rustenburg Girls Schools, St Joseph's College (Marist Brothers) and Diocesan College (Bishops) founded by Bishop Gray in 1849. A national monument, St Paul's Anglican Church in Church Street was designed by Bishop Gray's wife, Sophy, who was the first Anglican Church architect in South Africa. Her stone-built Gothic Revival churches are to be seen not only here in Rondebosch and Claremont but in many parts of the Cape, including George, Caledon, Ceres and Clanwilliam.

Groote Schuur Estate

This vast estate embraces the whole slope of Devil's Peak and includes the hospital, the medical school, the university, the small zoo and nature reserve, Mostert's Mill and traditional residences of the Prime Minister and the State President. It was bought by Cecil Rhodes in 1891 and was bequeathed to the nation on his death in 1902.

Where the Eastern Boulevard and De Waal Drive merge, to the left is Groote Schuur Hospital which opened in 1938. The world-famous teaching hospital is administered by the Cape Provincial Administration in concert with the Medical School of the University of Cape Town. Here at Groote Schuur in December 1967 the world's first heart transplant was performed by Professor Chris Barnard and his team.

Continuing to skirt the slopes of Devil's Peak, De Waal Drive passes the traffic interchange before it runs into Rhodes Drive which bisects the width of Groote Schuur Estate. To the right, high up on the mountainside, is Rhodes Memorial and to the left is Mostert's Mill, one of the Cape's best known historical monuments and a reminder that one of South Africa's first industries was wheat-milling. The mill, still in perfect working order with its original threshing floor, stands on the Welgelegen farm, first granted to free burgher Cornelis Stevensz Botma in 1676. From the date, 1796, that appears on one of the beams it is apparent that the mill was built by Gysbert van Reenen, who owned the farm at that time. Van Reenen's daughter married a Mostert whose ancestors were the first millers at the Cape. The homestead of present-day privately-owned Welgelegen was rebuilt by Sir Herbert Baker, who masterfully incorporated into the structure the original doors, windows and fanlights. The fine gateway giving access to the homestead is a relic preserved from van Reenen's occupancy and is also an historical monument.

Rhodes Memorial stands alone on the mountainside – a symbol of rugged strength – on a site from where Rhodes enjoyed the sweeping view. Built in 1912 as the nation's tribute, it was designed by Francis Massey and Sir Herbert Baker and has as its centrepiece the famous equestrian bronze, Energy, by G.F. Watts. The bronze lions which flank the stairway and the bust of Rhodes in the granite Doric temple are the work of J.M. Swan. Below the bust are the words of Rhodes' friend, Rudyard Kipling:

The immense and moving spirit still shall quicken and control
Living he was the land and dead his soul shall be her soul

Herds of buck and zebra roam freely on the grass slopes of the mountain where the stone pines, proteas and silver trees provide shade and where arum and other lilies thrive. This is a lovely place to picnic and nearby there is hidden a charming stone and thatch tearoom.

The University of Cape Town has its main campus in Groote Schuur Estate on an unrivalled site below Devil's Peak in full close-up view of motorists using De Waal Drive. Its beginning in 1829 as the South African College makes it the oldest university in the southern hemisphere. The charter under which it functions as the University of Cape Town was granted in 1918 when there were 600 students; in June 1983 the student enrolment was more than 12 000. The University moved from its original premises at the top of Government Avenue in 1928 and has an excellent record of achievement. Its ten principal faculties are: Arts, Commerce, Education, Engineering, Fine Art and Architecture, Law, Medicine, Music, Science and Social Science. The Department of Extra-Mural Studies, open to the public, includes the popular Summer School that requires no entrance qualification.

A mountain road runs behind the University connecting the small zoo at the southern end of the estate with Rhodes Memorial. Rhodes was responsible for the introduction of a number of alien species in South Africa (much to the consternation of the ecologists), including the American grey squirrel that populate the Avenue.

Across Rhodes Drive from the University and the zoo is the private garden (itself an extensive area within a vast estate) of Rhodes' residence. Here Rhodes lived when he was Prime Minister of the Cape Colony. The estate takes its name from the principal residence, Groote Schuur, the unpretentious old home converted from a 'great barn' built in van Riebeeck's time. Rhodes became Prime Minister in 1890 and Groote Schuur was burnt down in 1896; in that year he employed the yet unknown young architect, Herbert Baker, whom he had met on board ship from England, to design and build the present-day mansion and in so doing in the old Cape Dutch style, Baker became the motivating force in the revival of this traditional architecture in South Africa and went on to become famous. Among his most important works are the Union Buildings in Pretoria, South Africa House and the Bank of England in London and the new city of Delhi, India.

Groote Schuur together with two other houses – Woolsack, the summer residence of Rhodes' great friend, Rudyard Kipling, and Westbrooke, once owned by Judge William Westbrooke Burton – stands in a charming informal garden. Since Union, Groote Schuur has been the residence of South African Prime Ministers, and Westbrooke became the home of Governors General and later the State President. During Prime Minister Vorster's time it was decided to turn Groote Schuur into a museum with the Prime Minister taking up residence at Westbrooke and the State President using the residence on Government Avenue, known as the Tuynhuis (summer-house).

Newlands

Beyond Groote Schuur estate Rhodes Drive becomes Union Avenue, where pavement oaks, bordering the mountain forest, and traffic-island wild flowers announce the choice residential suburb of Newlands.

In Simon van der Stel's famous 'instructions' to his son and successor, Willem Adriaan, he recommended the retention of Rustenburg and the continuation of the planting of oaks there, but the strong-headed Willem Adriaan disregarded his father's wishes and followed his own inclination. In 1700 he built a new country residence at 'Nieuweland' and from here in history Newlands prospered in popularity and botanical beauty. Van der Stel's property is Newlands House today, with its prominent entrance gateway facing oak-lined Newlands Avenue. Nearby, opening onto Boshof Avenue from Paradise Road, is the historical monument, Boshof Gateway. It is one of very few of the beautiful gateways to have survived from the eighteenth century, and used to give access to the estate of the well-known Alexander van Breda, where today the wooded area is studded with a number of lovely homes.

On the western side of Boshof Avenue is Fernwood Estate and the delightful cricket ground of the Parliamentary Sports Club. It was near here that Lady Anne Barnard built her cottage, Paradise, and later, in

1799 her residence, The Vineyard, on that prime site in Protea Road in a lush world of garden overlooked by mountain. The elegant hotel there today, well patronised by Capetonians and visitors the world over, has been preserved as a national monument. In recent years, under the direction of the Petousis family, the Vineyard Hotel has established a great reputation for hospitality, comfort and cuisine. South African art and tapestries, by the owner's family, compliment the traditional Cape country antique furniture, altogether a most pleasing and peaceful setting. Alive to the requirements of the social and touring visitors the varied amenities include an à la carte restaurant with live piano music, the coffee shop and Swiss patisserie, a hairstylist, gift and antique shops. In the enchanting 6-acre garden there is a lovely swimming pool.

Not far from The Vineyard are the famous Newlands Cricket and Rugby Grounds, the international swimming pool and Western Province Sports Club at Kelvin Grove. Facing onto Newlands Drive, the South African College School (SACS) is the oldest institution of its kind in southern Africa. As the South African College, in addition to schooling it provided degree classes which later merged with the University of Cape Town. SACS moved from Gardens to Newlands in 1955.

Claremont and Kenilworth

Claremont is notable for its fine shopping complexes and one of the most beautiful public parks to be found anywhere in South Africa, and which is preserved as a national monument. Named to honour its founder, Arderne Gardens, it was originally part of the private estate The Hill acquired by Ralph Arderne in 1840. In the four-hectare parkland facing onto Main Road, protected from the south-easter, the founder and later his son introduced and succeeded in cultivating a remarkable collection of exotic species from widely differing climatic regions of the world; Indian rubber, Norfolk island pine, Atlas Mountain cedar, swamp cypress from North America and rumu from New Zealand are among these, with profusely flowering azaleas, camelias, rhododendrons (their propagation previously unheard of in the Cape), roses, iris and arums providing brilliant colour in the different seasons of the year. Built on land donated by Ralph Arderne, adjoining the park on Main Road is another monument, the Claremont Congregational Church, adding grace to the suburb with its white-washed walls and thatched roof.

Adjacent to Arderne Gardens, facing Herschel Road, is the famous Herschel School for girls, and not far north in the grounds of another school in Grove Avenue, is the Herschel Monument which honours Sir John Herschel (1792-1871), the famous British astronomer, who made many important astronomical discoveries from his home here.

Kenilworth is another popular residential suburb with its famous race course in a most attractive setting. The South African Turf Club, Kenilworth, was established by the British garrison in 1802. In 1863 Queen Victoria presented a 50-guinea prize for a race which became known as 'The Queen's Plate' – this is still run. One of South Africa's classics, the

Metropolitan was established in 1876 and two years later the South African Derby was run for the first time. The race course adjoins the Cape Hunt and Polo Club and Youngsfield, the aerodrome for private aircraft.

Wynberg

Wynberg's history dates back to the seventeenth century but its growth came when the military camp and hospital were established during the first British occupation in the eighteenth century. Wynberg was an independent municipality until its incorporation into Cape Town in 1927. Now the largest suburb of the city, it has retained its old-world character and charm with its congested downtown area noted for its antique and used furniture shops, Little Chelsea the popular residential quarter of artists and Maynardville a charming open-air theatre within a beautiful park. Royal Cape Golf Course which faces Ottery Road was established in 1885 when the Royal Scots Regiment was stationed at the Cape, and Wynberg Park at the commencement of Klaassens Road, Wynberg Hill, is a lovely retreat.

Having deviated to visit the interesting suburbs of Newlands, Claremont, Kenilworth and Wynberg, it is necessary to return to Union Avenue, Newlands, to continue the circuit of the Peninsula. After taking a long sweeping bend, Union Avenue meets a major intersection; turning left here into Rhodes Avenue it takes you through Fernwood Estate to Kirstenbosch.

Kirstenbosch

During the van der Stel era and even before, Kirstenbosch (or Leenderts Bosch as it was known as then) formed an important part of the 'Nieuweland'. It used to be at the end of the 'wagon road to the forest' (before this was extended over Constantia Nek to Hout Bay) and it was excellent for logging here beneath the eastern slopes of Table Mountain. In this, the highest rainfall area of the Peninsula, stinkwood, yellowwood, black ironwood and assegai wood thrived and were felled to provide the main timber requirements of the settlement. Timber was one of the survival factors of the establishment of building at the Cape, but it is unfortunate that some of the timbered areas were stripped bare.

Two centuries later, Cecil Rhodes acquired some 500 hectares in this magnificent setting and from another of his immensely generous gifts the nation inherited this upon his death in 1902. It was not until 1913 that the National Botanic Gardens of South Africa, Kirstenbosch, was proclaimed under its founder and first director, Professor Harold Pearson, with the objects of the preservation, cultivation and study of the indigenous flora of southern Africa, and in this respect Kirstenbosch is unique among the world's great botanic institutions. The area under control stretches from Rhodes Avenue to the summit of Table Mountain (Maclear's Beacon 1 086 metres) including much of the well-watered eastern slopes and embracing the springs that form the source of the Liesbeek River.

The upper region of Kirstenbosch is a wild reserve where the evergreen forests in the kloofs still contain

1

2

1. *One of many beautiful views of Kirstenbosch, a world great in botanical institutions.*

2. *Mostert's Mill can be seen from De Waal Drive. Built in 1796, it still produces flour on special occasions.*

3. *The peafowl are in the zoo that Rhodes started.*

4. *The nation's tribute to Cecil John Rhodes — his memorial on the slope of Devil's Peak, Groote Schuur Estate.*

5. *Part of the extensive campus of University of Cape Town, the core of which (from Jameson Hall to Japonica Walk) is a national monument.*

3

4

5

yellowwood, stinkwood, ironwood and other indigenous trees and where rare disa, nerine and Cape anemone bloom in the krantzes; here too on the hills are the shining silvertrees and other species of protea, masses of erica and a host of bulbous varieties of flora.

The lower region is planted with over 4 000 species of indigenous flora from all parts of the country and laid out in a lovely informal manner. Some of the features that visitors should make a point of seeing include the fine collection of succulents in the rock garden, the dell with its ferns, the natural spring with its exquisite brick-walled bath (said to have been used by Lady Anne Barnard), the splendid collection of cycads grouped in an amphitheatre and the protea garden where hundreds of specimens of the most characteristic Cape family can be seen together. Kirstenbosch is beautiful at anytime of the year, always presenting a spectacular picture of South African trees, shrubs and flowers in a setting unsurpassed anywhere. The most popular season is the spring when there is a brilliant show of annuals, ericas and mesembryanthemums, and the winter is the time for aloes and most of the protea are in bloom then.

The Botanical Society of South Africa has its office in the Gardens which also contain the Compton Herbarium with its 200 000 specimens, and exhibition hall and hot-houses. A fitting tribute to Professor Pearson is the epitaph on his grave in the Gardens:

All ye who seek his monument, look around
Kirstenbosch is open from sunrise to sunset and has a tearoom serving refreshments and luncheons on the stoep, under the oaks or indoors.

Bishopscourt

In the upper valley of the Liesbeek where the select and delightful residential Bishopscourt is today, van Riebeeck once had his farm Boschheuvel; the new name Bishopscourt having been taken from the official residence of the Anglican Archbishop of Cape Town.

Bishopscourt's western boundary, Rhodes Avenue, faces onto Kirstenbosch and along its southern boundary with Constantia, known as Wynberg Hill, runs Klaassens Road. In the 1660s van Riebeeck was plagued with the rustling of sheep and cattle from the Hottentots and decided on a new defence system for the settlement. A thirteen-kilometre-long boundary was formed with military posts strategically positioned in a semicircle from the mouth of the Salt River in Table Bay past the Rondebosch Common, up the course of the Black River and over the Wynberg Hill to Kirstenbosch. In the upper region he planted a boundary hedge, one rood (3,8 metres) wide of bitter almond trees in an attempt to outwit the Hottentot raiders. Part of the hedge is to be seen in Kirstenbosch and other portions are clearly visible at the top of Klaassens Road where the Monuments Commission has marked the site with a masonry bench and bronze plaque. This defence line was the first frontier demarcation in South Africa and what remains of the wild almond hedge is South Africa's oldest living European relic.

Constantia

Opposite Kirstenbosch in a V-shape formed by their meeting, Rhodes Avenue once again becomes Rhodes Drive. Lined with chestnuts and oaks, Rhodes Drive skirts the mountain on its route south-west to Constantia Nek and Hout Bay.

Constantia Nek is recognised by the open-air display of artists pictures and the nearby thatched restaurant in a delightful setting eighteen kilometres from the city. At this point there is a division in the road; to the west the road winds down through lovely avenues of old oak trees to Hout Bay and to the east along Constantia Nek Road is the descent into the beautiful wine-producing valley of Constantia where, with the natural growth of population, the large country estates have given way to conversion into an attractive residential area. Five kilometres from Constantia Nek the approach drive to Groot Constantia is reached; the turn is to the right.

The best known of the Cape Dutch homesteads, commodious Groot Constantia stands on the site of the country home of Simon van der Stel, perhaps the best known of the Dutch governors and certainly the most effective. During his glorious 20-year term of office the settlement at the Cape was transformed from an isolated trading station into a colony. He founded the town of Stellenbosch, he opened up the Drakenstein valley, prospected for copper in Namaqualand and afforded vigorous help to the Huguenot settlers; he started the wine industry and encouraged the planting of trees. In appreciation of his outstanding work he was promoted from Commander to Governor in 1691.

The farm Constantia, much larger than it is today, was presented to van der Stel by the visiting Commissioner H.A. van Rheede tot Drakenstein, Lord of Mydrecht, in 1685 as a reward for van der Stel's services. It was probably named after the Commissioner's young daughter, Constantia. Van der Stel's large but unpretentious house was completed in 1692, but he only took up permanent residence after his retirement in 1699 and he died there in 1712. Within ten years the estate had been planted with more than 8 000 trees, half of which were fruit trees and the extensive vineyard was wine-producing; the red Constantia wine comparing favourably with the Italian Lachrymae Christi of the time. The manor-house was the scene of frequent receptions and the entertainment of dignataries from abroad.

The dividing up of the huge Constantia estate took place four years after Simon van der Stel's death when the main homestead and 192 hectares was transferred to Oloff Bergh and thereafter became known as Groot Constantia; the remaining 570 hectares were bought by Pieter de Meyer and named Bergvliet. In time Bergvliet was subdivided into a number of farms, the best-known of which include Klein Constantia, Hoop op Constantia, Willeboomen and Silverhurst.

Over the years Groot Constantia itself changed ownership a number of times until it came into the possession of Hendrik Cloete. Cloete capitalised on van der Stel's vineyard establishment; he developed the farm and exported his wines to Europe; Red Constantia became famous and Cloete made a fortune. This enabled him during the years 1791 to 1793 to embellish the homestead and wine cellar and in so doing he employed those reliable experts, Louis Thibault, who in replanning the whole building incorporated the elegant main and side gables, and Anton Anreith who created the figure of Plenty in the niche of the main gable and the handsome Rape of Ganymede plaster relief on the pediment of the wine cellar.

And so for three generations Groot Constantia prospered, remaining in the Cloete family until 1860 when the Cape Government bought it for an experimental farm for viticulture. A great tragedy occurred in 1925 when the homestead was destroyed by fire. Upon instructions of the South African government it was faithfully restored under the direction of the architect F.K. Kendall.

Today, under government control and expert supervision, the estate wines of Constantia are still produced in the famous valley and are much sought after. These wines are obtainable from the huge modern cellars on the farm, completed in 1983.

After restoration, Groot Constantia became a museum of period furniture and contains a priceless collection of Cape pieces, old Dutch paintings, Delft and Chinese porcelain. The old wine cellar has been converted into a wine museum and exhibition hall.

A short walk through an avenue of oaks, past the modern cellars, leads to an ornamental swimming pool, also dating from the 18th century. There are two restaurants; one, in a picturesque outbuilding, graces one side of the forecourt, and on the opposite side is a low white-washed wall from where there is a fine view of the famous vineyards.

Groot Constantia was one of the first historical monuments to be proclaimed.

Easy to find from Wynberg over Alphen Hill on a turnoff right, from Constantia main road, marked 'Alphen – Hohenort' is another national monument in the famous Constantia Valley. This is Alphen, established by a branch of the large Cloete family in the 1830s and a name associated with good estate wines ever since. The historic homestead is today part of the elegant Alphen Hotel.

From Alphen, should you follow Hohenort Avenue you are sure to reach The Cellars on the left of the road, high above the Constantia Valley – this is the historic home of Lyn and Jonathan Finnis, converted into the most delectable Country House you could imagine. And if you seek comfort, charm and contentment, you have surely reached your destination. The Cellars Country House was reconstructed in 1950, having been a successful winery for some 250 years. It stands in a beautiful wooded garden in one of the loveliest residential areas in all the Cape with views on to Table Mountain. Famed for its cuisine (non-resident guests can reserve a table for dinner), with such attendant variations as log fires in the winter and special Cape breakfast under the oaks in summer, it is easy to be pampered at The Cellars.

Tokai

From the start of the Groot Constantia approach drive, the right-hand turn onto Constantia Road joins with Ladies Mile which if followed proceeds through the orderly residential suburbs of Meadowridge and Bergvliet and meets Main Road, Retreat, on a direct route to Muizenberg. If from Ladies Mile the right turn into Spaanschemat River Road is taken, this continues as Orpen Road into the Tokai Valley and a pleasant world of country estates. Taking Tokai Road in the direction of the Constantiaberg the Tokai Forest Reserve is reached.

This was the foundation forest for the South African re-afforestation plan put into effect in the 1880s and today a substantial area of the slopes of the Constantiaberg is covered with pine forests. Between Tokai Road and Orpen Road there are shady picnic places, sheltered from the wind and open to the public until sunset. At the end of Tokai Road is the old Tokai Manor House dating back to 1795 and a national monument. Its elegant façade and high stoep are attributed to Thibault. The estate was named after the Tokai hills in Hungary, a wine-producing area.

During the winter months, when there is a decrease in the fire hazard, permits are obtainable from the forester to enter the main forest, and the walk up to the radio mast on the Constantiaberg is a rewarding experience.

Ou Kaapse Weg and Silvermine Nature Reserve

Crossing the Steenberge from Tokai to Noordhoek is the Ou Kaapse Weg, a spectacular road which climbs to the top of the Silvermine plateau from where there are extensive views over the southern suburbs to False Bay and right across Cape Town to Lion's Head.

This is a favourite area for mountain walkers; places to explore include the Silvermine Nature Reserve with its winter flowering giant proteas, the old reservoir surrounded by tall pine trees, the waterfall and picnic spots along the Silvermine stream and the old silvermine where unsuccessful prospectors sunk a shaft in 1687. There is, however, manganese in the area. Here at Silvermine is the South African Navy strategic communications and surveillance centre which is linked with Simonstown.

Retreat, Zeekoevlei, Rondevlei and Sandvlei

Returning to Tokai to continue the circuit drive, Orpen Road runs into Steenberg Road which passes the Westlake Golf Course before meeting Main Road, Retreat.

East and south of Retreat there are a series of lakelets formed by the mountain streams as these reach the sandy region on the verge of the Cape Flats. The largest is Zeekoevlei where there are yachting and rowing clubs and a caravan park. Rondevlei is the site of the famous bird sanctuary and ornithological field station of international reputation. Numerous species of birds including flamingoes and pelicans inhabit the 105-hectare area and can be seen from observation platforms, the best months being January and February. Sandvlei is popular with the local people for picnics, canoeing and relaxation on the lawns under shade trees. The amenities include a tearoom and caravan park. On the eastern side is Marina da Gama, a residential waterfront marina of some 600 hectares.

After holding the British for some time, it was from Retreat that the Dutch finally fell back before capitulation in the Battle of Muizenberg in 1795, and it was from here that thousands of allied troops were re-assembled in transit during the two World Wars.

When in Cape Town a lovely place to stay — The Cellars Country House is positioned in a beautiful environment high above the Constantia Valley with views on to Table Mountain, and enjoys the highest reputation for comfort and cuisine.

Groot Constantia: the main gable entrance to Simon van der Stel's homestead, now a national monument.

Boyes Drive

From Retreat, Main Road continues to Muizenberg and on the boundary of Retreat and Lakeside a fork road to the right leads to Boyes Drive which follows the slopes of the Muizenberg mountain to Kalk Bay and which to a large extent has relieved the congestion of traffic on the narrow coastal road. On the mountainside are proteas and other wild flowers and from the view sites the vast stretches of False Bay can be enjoyed. Mountain walkers will find pathways at the back of Boyes Drive which lead up the Muizenberg and Kalk Bay mountains and on to the Steenberge – the whole region renowned for its many caves.

Muizenberg

False Bay received its name when the early mariners sailing from the east mistook Cape Hangklip for the Cape of Good Hope. The False Bay inlet is thirty kilometres wide and at about midway in the inlet is Muizenberg, one of the best known and safest seaside resorts in the world. Its fame rests entirely with the glory of its splendid surfing beach, gently sloping and without backwash or current. On a fine summer's day vast crowds are attracted to Muizenberg where a colourful scene is presented with its scores of private bathing boxes, canvas cubicles and umbrellas. On the lawns which front the long raised promenade, entertainments are arranged and a special children's playground is provided. When the beach is exposed to the south-easter (an accepted Cape hazard) the crowd congregate in the sheltered area of seasand behind the bathing boxes to sunbathe in what the locals call the 'snake pit'.

Muizenberg took its name from Sergeant Wynand Willem Muys, the commander of a small military outpost sited there in 1743 after the road linking Cape Town and Simonstown was completed. In 1825 Farmer Peck's Inn was the popular halfway house between the two towns and in 1883 the railway line to Muizenberg was opened. Muizenberg, which included Kalk Bay, became a municipality in 1893 and was absorbed by Cape Town in the general merger of 1913. Its fame as a seaside resort started when it became a convalescent centre for British soldiers during the Anglo-Boer War of 1899 to 1902 – the built-up area today has changed little from its Victorian heyday.

Rhodes Cottage faces the sea on the main coast road between Muizenberg and St James. When Rhodes acquired it in 1899 he named it Barkly Cottage after the constituency, Barkly West, for which he was the member of the Cape Parliament. At the end of 1899 war broke out and Rhodes was in Kimberley when it was besieged. After the siege was raised in 1900 he returned to his cottage rather than to Groote Schuur. Again in 1902 upon his return from England, when he was very ill, he drove down from Groote Schuur in the Wolseley he had brought back with him, to rest at his cottage. In conditions of intense heat (the cottage had an iron roof then) he had to give evidence against the notorious Princess Radziwill who had defrauded him of a very large sum of money. In the evening of March 26th, 1902, he died here in his beloved cottage. Rhodes Cottage is an historical monument and is maintained as a memorial museum containing interesting personal belongings and a diorama of the Matopo Hills south of Bulawayo in what was then Rhodesia and is now Zimbabwe, to where his body was carried by train to rest.

From Muizenberg the road which follows the False Bay coastline, eastwards, leads to Strandfontein and the Coloured peoples housing estate of Mitchell's Plain. Opposite Muizenberg's East Beach is the start of Prince George Drive which connects with the city, and along this Drive is the access to the beautiful Marina Da Gama, an Anglo American development.

St James

A kilometre beyond the Rhodes cottage is St James, named after the church built there in 1874. This is a charming resort where lovely residences look down from the mountainside upon the warm ocean, an intimate, wind-protected beach with a tidal pool, and little beach huts, painted all the colours of the rainbow.

Here on the mountainside, fitting unobtrusively into the pretty scene, is the famed and long established St James Hotel. Recent extensive refurbishing and upgrading to four stars has enhanced the distinguished character of elegance and tranquillity – ingredients which have caused visitors from all over South Africa and abroad to return to the St James year after year. In every way the new St James is an improvement on the old – an absolute joy is the comfort and decor of the wide range of bedroom accommodation, standard, deluxe, suite, duplex and cottage. Cuisine, cellar and service are key-words in the directorate policy. New amenities include a tennis court, solar heated pool and an extended car park. See pages 36 and 394.

Kalk Bay

Seventeen kilometres from Cape Town is a picturesque little fishing harbour, Kalk Bay. It has two swimming pools and a sandy beach and during the summer months a launch takes visitors to Seal Island, densely populated with the mammals.

Excitement is high in Kalk Bay during the snoek season, June and July, when catches of as many as 40 000 of the silver fish are landed. 'Kalkbaai', the original name, means 'lime bay'. In the 17th Century, lime for the painting of buildings was made here by burning sea shells in kilns.

Sandwiched between Kalk Bay and Fish Hoek, where the Silvermine stream reaches the sea, is the residential area of Clovelly with its Country Club. From here a road leads back to the Atlantic side of the Peninsula via Noordhoek.

Fish Hoek

The separate municipality of Fish Hoek, on the electric railway to Simonstown, is 29 kilometres from Cape Town and claims the uniqueness of being the only teetotal town in the Republic. Under the original title deed granted by Lord Charles Somerset to Andries Bruins in 1818, Fish Hoek was to have no 'public winehouses' and the ban is still maintained; there are no licensed hotels or bottle stores within the municipal boundaries. Fish Hoek has a safe bathing beach, extremely popular in the summer, and it is noted for good catches in net fishing. In terms of an old law which still applies, fishing here is free of licence.

The main road out of the town to the south divides at a traffic circle; the right-hand branch passes through the Fish Hoek Valley on its way to the lonely white sand dunes of Noordhoek and the Atlantic coast. Along this road there is a signposted track which ends at Brakkloof forest station. From here there is an interesting short walk through the dunes and up rocky outcrops to the famous Peer's Cave, named after Victor Peer and his son who discovered the fossilized skull of the Fish Hoek Man in 1927. Near the summit of the ridge is the Tunnel Cave and beyond this at the beacon the view over the whole of the Fish Hoek Valley is superb.

Simonstown

Beyond the left-hand branch at the Fish Hoek traffic circle the road winds along the edge of the sea around the slopes of Elsies Peak (305 metres) and in so doing passes Sunny Cove, from where there is a sweeping view of False Bay, and reaches Else River Valley. A road up this valley leads past holiday camps of the Moths and Rotary and the farms of Welcome and Oaklands, owned in the nineteenth century by the famous Brand family – Sir C.J. Brand was the first Speaker of the Cape Parliament and his son Sir J.H. Brand was President of the Orange Free State for three successive terms. Beyond the farm is the Da Gama Park, the housing estate for South African Navy personnel. Opposite the mouth of the Else River is Glencairn, a residential suburb of Simonstown. Before the coastal road enters Simonstown a road to the right climbs Red Hill and continues in a drive to the Atlantic coast via Scarborough.

Simonstown, the principal base of the South African Navy, lies on Simon's Bay, an inlet of False Bay, at the foot of the Simonsberg (601 metres). Its history goes back to 1671 when the captain of the Dutch East Indiaman *Isselsteijn* reported to Governor Simon van der Stel his discovery of this sheltered bay which could be used in the winter when Table Bay was exposed to the dangerous gales. Although the port was later named in honour of the governor and was to a limited extent used, it was not until 1742 after further tragic losses in Table Bay that Simon's Bay became the second harbour at the Cape. Under the first regime the British recognised the strategic value of the harbour and in 1796 built a Martello tower as a defence against the French. Large developments began after the second British occupation in 1806, and from 1814, when Admiralty House was acquired, it became the headquarters of the Royal Navy South Atlantic Command. This command ceased in 1957 when the South African Navy took control of Simonstown.

With its dockland, narrow winding streets and quaint pubs, Simonstown has the distinctive nautical flavour of an old English seaport and this has been savoured through its 143 years of Royal Navy occupation. A number of its historical buildings have been preserved by proclamation of the Monuments Council and most of these are to be found in or off St George's Street (the main thoroughfare) where the town, sandwiched between sea and mountain, has had limited means of expansion.

The Martello tower, now a maritime museum, is near the southern-most point of Simon's Bay and among its interesting exhibits is a landscape, *Simon's Bay in 1840* by Mauritz Hattingh. The painting shows the commanding position of the tower and includes three of the best-known remaining residences, all built towards the end of the eighteenth century. On the left is the present-day Palace Barracks; in existence since 1798, it was acquired by John Osmond, the shipwright who amassed a fortune and was nicknamed King John – his home of course became the Palace. In the centre is the Admiral's Residence (Admiralty House), built in the 1790s and bought by the navy in 1814. In the right-hand corner is Studland, built as a wine house or tavern in 1797 by J.P. Eksteen, who, in making the highest bid, received the wine licence monopoly.

Probably the first example at the Cape of an English cottage is now the clubhouse of the Simonstown Yacht Club. This exquisite example of the simple dwelling of the time was built by Alexander Tennant between 1799 and 1801.

The foundation stone of the Dutch Reformed Church was laid by the Commander of the Royal Navy, the Honourable Henry Dundas Trotter, in 1855. In the adjoining parsonage, the Reverend M.L. de Villiers (who came from Wellington) composed the music of the national anthem in 1921.

The oldest Anglican parish in southern Africa is that of Simonstown. In what is today the Church of St Francis of Assisi, a tablet records the names of the Colonial chaplains and rectors of the Anglican Church and heading this list is the Reverend J.E. Atwood 1795 – 1797 (the time of the first British occupation). In 1814 the church was named St George's. When a new church building was completed in 1837 it received the name St Frances in recognition of the fund-raising services of Governor Sir Lowry Cole's wife, Frances. In 1862 the building was remodelled in the Gothic style and was again altered in 1875. Not until 1958 was the name changed to St Francis of Assisi. The church contains some unique memorials revealing the historical Royal Navy connection with Simonstown.

Tombstone epitaphs in the naval cemetery on the hill unfold some amazing stories of seafights, privateers and pirates in the early history of the Cape.

Apart from the activities of the South African Navy, Simonstown is an important commercial fishing harbour and the base of a substantial fleet of ocean-going yachts and motor launches whose private owners seek sailing pleasure and the adventure of big game fishing for marlin and tunny off the Cape of Good Hope.

The hotel in this seafaring town bears no less appropriate name than the *Lord Nelson*. There are two caravan parks at Froggy Pond, two to three kilometres south of the town.

Continuing the route to Cape Point, the coastal road passes the Simonstown Country Club and thereafter a host of little seaside places.

Seaforth, The Boulders and Froggy Pond

There is much to explore at Seaforth with its picnic spots, sheltered swimming beach, bungalow accommodation and tearoom. Once a whaling station, evidence of the blubber melting pots remains. The coastline between Seaforth and The Boulders is only accessible on foot. The Boulders has enormous

1. Four-star St James Hotel, much loved by overseas visitors and South African holiday makers alike, has an elevated position overlooking False Bay.

2. St James beach, directly opposite St James Hotel, is protected from the winds and the privately-owned cubicles add a touch of colour to the lovely seascape.

3. and 4. Part of the snoek fleet moored at Hout Bay jetty.

5. The Cape of Good Hope, at the southernmost tip of the Cape Peninsula, is well known to mariners as one of earth's stormiest capes.

3
4

5

37

granite rocks and a maze of vivid blue and emerald green channels of seawater ideal for underwater swimming and fishing – completely wild with no amenities.

At Oatland Point are the two caravan and camping parks in an area known as Froggy Pond.

Miller's Point

Occupying a superb site at Miller's Point (once a whaling station) is the caravan park maintained by the Cape Divisional Council. The sites have been developed on terraces enjoying magnificent views of the sea and mountain. Green lawns, wild flowers, playgrounds, picnic places, a tidal pool, clear pools with sandy floors, sea urchins, anemones, shoals of fish, sea shells and ultimately a good restaurant, set the scene. Miller's Point has always been a good fishing spot, particularly at night. Adjoining a recreational area is Rumbly Bay where the Cape Boat and Skiboat Club has its headquarters.

Cape of Good Hope Nature Reserve

From Miller's Point the road winds up the mountainside reaching a plateau 150 metres above Smitswinkel Bay where fishermen's shacks cluster at the water's edge. The road swings inland and then forks – one branch backs across to the Atlantic coast and the other continues southwards for the final twelve kilometres along the narrowing spine of the Peninsula to the cul-de-sac at Cape Point. Beyond the fork the traveller enters the gate of Cape of Good Hope Nature Reserve, open from sunrise to sunset.

A proclamation of the Cape Divisional Council dated 11 April 1939 embraced the entire southern tip of the Cape Peninsula, some 7 680 hectares of wilderness, as a nature reserve. In this windy region of coastal scrubland, stunted trees, everlastings and other seasonal wild flowers, baboons and small wild creatures live with an interesting variety of birdlife including ostrich, plover, Cape francolin, cormorant, gull, yellow-billed duck and sugar-bird. The rugged coastline of some 40 kilometres provides dramatic scenery and excellent fishing opportunities. Attractive picnic places have been developed at Buffelsbaai and Olifantsbosch; Buffelsbaai has a tidal swimming pool and boat-launching facilities. Beyond the turnoff to Buffelsbaai there is a restaurant in what used to be a farm homestead. Fishing for yellow tail from the rocky ledges at Rooikrans is reputed to be the most favourable on the entire coast.

At the end of the Cape Peninsula there are three heads. Furthest south and first seen by ships approaching from the north, is the Cape of Good Hope; in the centre is the small promontory of Cape Maclear (named after the astronomer) and at the extreme tip is the dramatic cliff, Cape Point. Bartholomew Dias discovered the Cape of Good Hope in 1488 and because of the rough seas he encountered he called it 'Cabo Tormentoso', or the Cape of Storms. King John II changed the name to 'Cabo de Boa Esperança', the Cape of Good Hope. Although King John's hope was justified by later events, ironically enough Dias lost his life in a shipwreck off the peninsula in the year 1500. There is no doubt that the early mariners referred to the whole

mountainous end of the Peninsula as the Cape of Good Hope as indeed we do today. Sir Francis Drake called it 'the most stately thing and the fairest cape we saw in the whole circumference of the earth'.

From the parking area at the terminus of the tarred road, a path takes you to the tip of the Cape of Good Hope and the pretty little Dias Beach. A concrete road leads up to the summit of Cape Point (243 metres) and to the old lighthouse, erected in 1857. From here there are breathtaking views of the ocean, the Peninsula, False Bay and the Hottentots-Holland Mountains. The modern lighthouse, far below, some 87 metres above the sea, is at the tip of Cape Point and can be reached by zig-zag path and many steps. Controlled by automation, the powerful beam ($19\frac{1}{2}$-million candle power) penetrates for more than 35 kilometres, often during the intense fog which obscures the summit. Visitors have the choice of walking to the summit or of going by bus. There is a refreshment kiosk at the parking area.

Although geographers mark the meeting place of the Atlantic and Indian Oceans as Cape Agulhas, which is the southernmost point of Africa, there is no doubt that in the summer months the warm Moçambique current of the Indian Ocean flows into False Bay and the Cape of Good Hope becomes the line of demarcation of the two oceans. So it is that in the summer surfers and bathers enjoy the warm waters of the False Bay side of the Peninsula whilst the waters of the western or Atlantic side, influenced by the Benguella Current, remain pretty cold.

Smitswinkel Bay, Perdekloof, Scarborough, Witsands, Slangkop, Kommetjie and Noordhoek

Returning to the nature reserve entrance gate to follow the circuit tour, the road to the left is taken to cross the Peninsula. This road meets the road from Simonstown at Perdekloof farm where the Cape Divisional Council has created a recreational area of lawns and shade trees. Three kilometres further on, the road passes Scarborough with its weekend cottages and a huge rock in the shape of a camel. Beyond Scarborough the road hugs the coastline, passing picnic places and camping sites and the stark-white sandy bay of Witsands, and after climbing the face of the cliff it reaches the Slangkop lighthouse from where there is a fine panorama of Kommetjie, Noordhoek and the distant Hout Bay.

The little village of Kommetjie surrounds a large tidal pool in the natural inlet of the coast. Off Long Beach the rollers provide surf riders with all the thrills. Eight kilometres north of Kommetjie the main road joins with the road that crosses the Peninsula from Fish Hoek and a short distance beyond the junction it enters the farming settlement of Noordhoek.

Chapman's Peak Drive

Noordhoek marks the southern entrance of Chapman's Peak Drive, rated among the world's most spectacular marine drives. Cut out of the mountainside surrounding the 592-metre-high Chapman's Peak, it winds along a magnificent scenic route; new vistas open up on each bend with sweeping views of the white sands of Chapman's Beach (with its history of shipwrecks), sheer cliffs of the most brilliant colours, and the bluest of blue seas with fascinating white streaks of current and waves battering the granite of the lower slopes. On the opposite side wild flowers and forests of pine reach down to the road; and finally, the road descends with a deep sweep into the little fishing harbour of Hout Bay with its Sentinel, a strikingly beautiful cliff that falls a sheer 300 metres to the beach below.

Chapman's Peak Drive, a remarkable engineering feat, was the brain-child of Sir Nicholas Frederick De Waal, first Administrator of the Cape and after whom De Waal Drive was named. Work commenced in 1915 and the drive was opened in 1922. Although the origin of the name Chapman's is obscure, two theories are advanced; one is that it is a corruption of Kaapmans, the name which the early Dutch applied to the Goringhaiquas, a tribe of Hottentots then living in the area; the other is that it comes from an incident in history when in the early seventeenth century an English sailor, John Chapman, was sent ashore to explore the area to ascertain whether a harbour existed.

Hout Bay

It would seem that the name Hout Bay is not really the Anglicized version of the Afrikaans Houtbaai (wood bay) but rather a shortening of the original Dutch 'Houtbayken'. Be that as it may, the name is derived from what Jan van Riebeeck recorded in his journal after his visit to the place in July 1653: 'The forests were the finest in the world and contained timber as long, thick and straight as one could wish'. However, mountainous terrain and other road-building hazards accounted for the delay until 1693, in the extension of the 'wagon road to the forest' from Kirstenbosch to Hout Bay.

Successive Dutch and British colonists were interested in Hout Bay; not only did it provide a vital supply of timber and offer alternate anchorage when in the winter months of gale force conditions Table Bay was unsafe, but it had to be protected against its being used for the landing of hostile troops. Batteries of cannon were laid first by the Dutch (assisted by their French allies) in 1780 during the American War of Independence, on the western side of the bay at the foot of the Sentinel, and then by the British when General Craig erected a blockhouse with a battery of five 18-pounders on the eastern side of the bay in 1796. The ruins of the batteries are important relics in our military history and have been declared historical monuments.

Manganese used to be mined in the surrounding mountains and the remains of the old manganese jetty can still be seen on the eastern side of the bay. Today Hout Bay is the headquarters of the crayfishing fleet which provides a rich export trade and the centre of much activity during June and July when the catches of snoek are brought in and sold on the quayside. Also on the eastern side, mounted on the rocks overlooking the bay, is the fascinating bronze leopard of Ivan Mitford-Barberton; he used to have his studio in the village.

The delightful hillside residential area, a good school, an interesting local museum, bowling green, two hotels, a village shopping area and waterfront holiday bungalows all go to make Hout Bay very attractive. The lovely sandy beach is notable for trek fishing when heavily laden nets are dragged ashore. The water at Hout Bay is generally cold, although the beach is protected from the north-wester by the huge headland, Karbonkelberg and from the south-easter by the Noordhoek mountain and Chapman's Peak.

In the village, on the main road, the fine old Cape Dutch homestead, Kronendal, dates from 1800; it used to be part of a large farm and is today a popular restaurant and historical monument. Another interesting building of circa 1820 is the manor house of Groot Moddergat, situated between Hout Bay and Constantia, it is part of Cape Grande Tours.

Llandudno and the approach to Cape Town's Atlantic suburbs

Outside Hout Bay village the marine drive meets with the road from Constantia Nek and then climbs the slopes of Little Lions Head, affording fine views of the valley of the Disa River. The road reaches its highest point at the saddle connecting Little Lions Head with the Twelve Apostles, and from here there is another rewarding view, with the houses of Llandudno lying far below.

At the turnoff to Llandudno the marine drive (which from this point is named Victoria Road) commences its descent across the cliffs and a few kilometres further on the road bends westward to unfold a most splendid view across a magnificent stretch of sea to Lion's Head. Close at hand, on the land side, the great buttresses of the Twelve Apostles dominate the residences of Camps Bay and Bakoven. And here at Bakoven, suburban Cape Town ends abruptly, giving way to open countryside and the beautiful coastline where the rollers crash against the huge granite boulders and where sun revellers, fishermen and picnic lovers seek out their favourite places among the many coves and inlets. About four kilometres before reaching Bakoven a curious community of Coloured families live in the honeycombed caves at the place called Hottentots Huisie. Further along the drive is the imposing farmhouse Oudekraal which belonged to the Van Breda family, and less than a kilometre before entering the built-up area, hidden on the slopes of the mountain, is Bellsfontein Kramat, the Malay tomb sheltering the remains of their holy man, Nureelmobeen.

Bakoven, Camps Bay, Glen and Clifton

A part of Camps Bay, Bakoven gets its name from a large hollowed-out rock on the coast, in the shape of an oven.

Camps Bay was originally the farm Ravensteyn and became known as 'Die Baay van von Kamptz' in 1778, after the invalid sailor Frederich von Kamptz married the widow, Anna Wehrnich, who owned the farm. The farmhouse stood where the Rotunda Hotel is today. A suburb of affluent society, Camps Bay extends well up the mountainside of the Twelve Apostles. It has a shopping centre, library, civic centre with a theatre auditorium, a tennis club, recreation hall and cinema and a bowling club known throughout South Africa. A wide lawned promenade with palm trees faces the

Bantry Bay International Vacation Resort (an Ovland Timesharing project), occupying this prime position right at the water's edge on the Cape Peninsula Atlantic coast, is rated among the ten best timesharing resorts in the world.

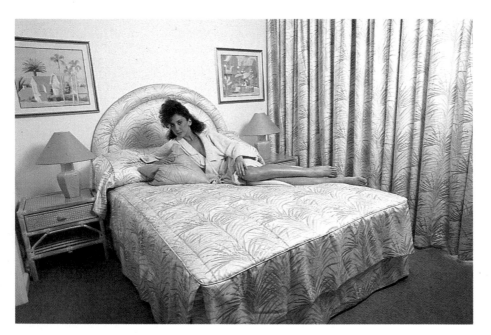

spacious white beach where the ocean is inclined to be cold. There is a safe children's seawater pool and across the road from the beach are the covered warm water sea baths. Surf riders use the Glen Beach in the cove adjoining Camps Bay.

From Camps Bay there are two roads over the mountainside which join at Kloof Nek before entering the city. Camps Bay Drive branches off opposite the pavilion and passes many beautiful homes and gardens en route. High above the drive is the Pipe Track, one of the most popular mountain walks in the Cape. The track is a service path which follows the water pipes from the reservoirs on Table Mountain, to Kloof Nek. The other road, Kloof Road, branches from Victoria Road at the Camps Bay High School and takes the route through the stone pine trees along the slopes of Lion's Head and passes the Glen picnic sites and the historic Round House, once the shooting lodge of Lord Charles Somerset and now a restaurant. Open from Tuesday to Sunday for luncheon and dinner, the Round House specialises in the classical cuisine of the Cape, and has a fine cellar of more than 150 estate wines. It is essential to book during times of inclement weather when Capetonians are denied their obsession for outdoor life. During fine weather every beach and mountainside picnic place is inhabited and the restaurants are neglected by the local population.

Returning to the marine drive, beyond the high school (conspicuously positioned on the headland north of Camps Bay) is Clifton, famous for its four sheltered beaches, the parade of pretty sunbathers and the fashionable cottages built right at the seashore. Originally erected as temporary structures during the housing shortage of the First World War, these cottages have become an attractive permanent part of the scene. The area between the sea and Victoria Road from Fourth Beach, Clifton, to Glen Beach, Camps Bay, has been preserved by the Monuments Commission as a nature reserve.

Bantry Bay

From Clifton through Bantry Bay, Victoria Road takes a precarious winding route cut out of the spurs of Lion's Head, the mountain reaching right down to the water's edge. Although heavily built-up, the area here is picturesque, where many of the houses and flats are built on high stilts and where massive mountain boulders often take the place of the normal garden.

Here on the seaward side of Victoria Road, right at the edge of the ocean on the sweep of this exclusive bay is Bantry Bay International Vacation Resort (members of resort Condominium International), rated among the best timesharing resorts in the world, it was opened by Ovland Timesharing in 1987. Ovland has devised a unique fifty per cent return of investment after ten years (underwritten by a large insurance company); called 'Prime Time' the scheme's strong attraction is that buyers retain ownership in perpetuity after the return of half their initial investment. In this highly fashionable locality the Resort emphasis is on luxury – of the 38 self-contained apartments there are spectacular penthouses, spacious one- and two-bedroomed units and delightful studio apartments. Excellent amenities include individual sun decks,

swimming pool with leisure deck and own off-street and under-cover parking.

Sea Point

Victoria Road ends at the boundary of Sea Point and you have the choice of three roads to the city. On the slope of Signal Hill, High Level Road traverses Fresnaye (a distinctly French part of Sea Point) and a portion of Green Point (where from the elevated position there are fine views) entering the city in Strand Street. Regent Road, which is the continuation of Victoria Road, later becomes Main Road and is the central route; it divides the three-kilometre-long shopping and business centre of Sea Point whilst Beach Road follows the coast, flanked on the land side by a continuous line of tall luxury apartments and hotels. Within the compass of these three thoroughfares is the most densely populated area of the Peninsula, a cosmopolitan region with many restaurants.

The handsome Sea Point promenade with its wide lawns and neat gardens, children's playground, pavilion, aquarium and immense seawater bath is a colourful sight during any summer season; and the late sunsets up to nine o'clock are the most dramatic to be seen anywhere. Crying seagulls, huge rollers crashing on the sea wall and the tang of the salty breezes add to the charm of this popular resort.

The rock formation below the sea wall at the extreme southern end of Beach Road is of significance to geologists. Here the relationship between sedimentary and igneous rock is exposed by a remarkable occurrence where slate has been penetrated by a network of granite veins. This was first recorded by Clark Abel in 1818 and has been visited by many eminent geologists and naturalists including Charles Darwin in 1836. Above the rocks and fronted by spacious lawns is the five-star President Hotel, once the Queen's Hotel and originally the Heeren Huis; established in 1766 as a gentleman's country club, it was the first building in Sea Point. Ten years later members of Captain Cook's Australian expedition encamped at Sea Point to avoid the smallpox epidemic in Cape Town. This recalls the epidemic of 1713 when smallpox, brought in by a merchantman from India, resulted in the worst disaster in the history of the colony; a quarter of the white population died and the Hottentot race was decimated.

Green Point, Three Anchor Bay, Mouille Point and Granger Bay

Green and Sea Point had been an independent municipality since 1839 and became part of Cape Town in the general merger of 1913.

In 1657 Jan van Riebeeck was granted the farm where Green Point Common is today. The area was found to be unsuitable for cultivation and the Commander started his successful farm Boschheuvel, now Bishopscourt. In the eighteenth century the crowds were drawn to the common for two reasons. Gallows Hill Road at the northern boundary is a reminder that public hangings took place here and continued well into the nineteenth century; and we read of Lady Anne Barnard 'in a splendid vehicle drawn by eight Spanish stallions' arriving at South Africa's first ever race meeting held here in 1797. Toward the end of the nineteenth century boating regattas were held on the vlei that used to be there and the Common was used by the military for reviews and during the Anglo-Boer War as a prisoner-of-war camp.

Today, in addition to the large open area for free use by the public, Green Point Common contains many sports fields including a stadium for soccer, athletics and cycling, the 9-hole course of the Metropolitan Golf Club and the Three Anchor Bay sports complex of tennis courts and bowling greens.

On the coast is the tiny inlet, Three Anchor Bay, where chains strung across the water for protection against invaders were secured by three anchors. Along Beach Road, little more than half a kilometre north of the bay at the north-west point of the promontory, is Green Point and near it the Green Point Lighthouse built in 1824, well-known for its foghorn. A further one-and-a-half kilometres eastwards is Mouille Point where Governor Swellengrebel constructed a mole in 1743 in an attempt to develop a harbour; the huge stone blocks cut out by slaves having long since disappeared. The whole of this coastal front is built up with residential apartments facing the sea across Beach Road and a wide lawn and is known as Mouille Point; hence the often-heard erroneous reference to Mouille Point Lighthouse instead of Green Point Lighthouse.

After Beach Road passes the nautical academy at Granger Bay and the New Somerset Hospital (a national monument), a road to the left enters Cape Town dockyard whilst to the right, Portswood Road connects with Main Road into the city to end the 150-kilometre circuit of the Peninsula. Via modern freeways the western (Atlantic) suburbs are directly connected with the southern suburbs without the necessity to enter the city.

Cape Flats

Between the Peninsula and the mountain ranges of the Boland and flanked by the shores of the two bays, Table Bay and False Bay, is the wide stretch of low lying sand known as the Cape Flats. Sir John Montagu, Colonial Secretary at the Cape from 1843 to 1853, overcame the problem of the drifting sand of the Cape Flats when he imported and planted the sand-loving Port Jackson wattles from Australia. This alien vegetation reclaimed the ground from the sand and the wind which enabled the establishment of modern towns with fertile gardens. Two national routes, N2 to Somerset West and the Garden Route, and N1 to Paarl and the north, cross the Cape Flats and in between the two routes the long thoroughfare, Voortrekker Road, divides the heavily built-up suburbs and independent municipalities referred to generally as the Northern Suburbs.

Maitland

The suburb of Maitland was named after Sir Peregrine Maitland who was governor at the Cape from 1843 to 1847. It became a municipality in 1902 and joined Cape Town when most of the other independent municipalities did in 1913.

There are important industries in Maitland and at the next station on the railway north is Woltemade where Cape Town has its main cemetery. The station was named after a South African hero, Wolraad Woltemade, who lost his life near here on 1st June 1773. The ship *de Jonge Thomas* was wrecked at the mouth of the Salt River in a violent storm and Woltemade, the Company's zoo keeper, made seven trips on horseback, each time rescuing two men, until finally on the eighth trip he and his horse were drowned. Opposite the Woltemade Cemetery is the Wingfield military aerodrome.

Pinelands

South of Maitland is Pinelands, a flourishing municipality of beautiful thatched homes and gardens with a population of 12 000. The town was laid out on the farm Uitvlugt where the Zulu King, Cetshwayo, was imprisoned after the Zulu War of 1879. At Mutualpark is the huge building complex which forms the head office of the Old Mutual, South Africa's biggest life assurance institution.

Goodwood

The municipality of Goodwood, which incorporates Vasco, has a population of 35 000 and is a bustling town with modern residential development. The adjoining industrial development at Elsies River is administered by the Cape Divisional Council. The Western Province Agricultural Society has its showground at Goodwood where the annual Cape Show is held in February. When it was first established in 1905 it was intended that Goodwood should become a major horse racing centre, hence its having been named after the famous racecourse in England. Near Goodwood are the Black townships of Nyanga and Langa.

Parow

Parow, sixteen kilometres from Cape Town, was named after the shipwrecked German sea captain, Johann Parow, who settled in the area in 1865. It became a municipality in 1939 and has a population of 71 000. Among its important industries is Cape and Transvaal Printers Limited, the largest printing works in southern Africa. The town has a handsome civic centre and extensive residential suburbs, including Tiervlei where the Tygerberg Hospital and Medical Faculty of the University of Stellenbosch are situated.

Bellville

The rapid industrial and residential growth of Bellville resulted in its becoming a municipality in 1940 and a city in 1979. It received its name to honour the surveyor-general of the Cape, Charles Bell, in 1861. This new city of 101 000 inhabitants possesses a fine civic centre and theatre complex and the well-known Karl Bremer Hospital. Sanlamhof, the handsome head office building of Sanlam, one of South Africa's best known and largest insurance companies is here at Bellville. The municipal recreational facilities include an Olympic-standard swimming pool and cycle track.

Bellville is laid out on the slopes of the Tygerberg, a range of hills with a highest point of 415 metres. This

1. A vista from Chapman's Peak Drive looking across the Atlantic at the Sentinel, standing guard at the entrance to Hout Bay.

2. A section of cosmopolitan Sea Point, dominated by Lion's Head.

1

1. *A section of the glorious Atlantic seaboard. The clean wide beach of Camps Bay with the development of the suburb reaching the lower slopes of the mountain. Between Lion's Head and Table Mountain (with the upper cable station clinging to the edge) is* the Kloof Nek saddle and the Hottentots Holland range looming in the background.

2. *In a magnificent setting, Glen Bowling Club.*

3. *Sea Point's fabulous seawater swimming pool.*

2

3

summit is accessible from the suburb of Welgemoed from where the easy walk is approximately four kilometres to a position of superb views. It is said that the early settlers named the Tygerberg from the patchwork of vegetation which resembled the markings of the tigers (a mistaken identity, they were actually leopards) that were in the area.

Durbanville and Killarney
The pleasant rural town of Durbanville was previously called Durban and originally Pampoenekraal. In 1836 the name was changed to Durban, after the Governor Sir Benjamin d'Urban, and to avoid confusion with the city of Durban in Natal, it changed to Durbanville in 1888. It lies ten kilometres to the north of Bellville which was originally named Durban Road. Horse racing is held at Durbanville on Wednesdays in an attractive garden setting. The road which connects Durbanville with Killarney follows the lovely Elsjeskraal River valley and to the north of the Tygerberg hills it passes a number of historic farms, some dating back to the early eighteenth century. The motor racing circuit is at Killarney.

Kuils River
Formerly De Kuilen, Kuils River was a cattle post of the Dutch East India Company in the seventeenth century and is today an industrial town with a population of 25 000.

Milnerton
The drive along the eastern shores of Table Bay passes Paarden-Eiland which lies between the two mouths of the Salt River, now channelled into canals, and reaches Milnerton where there are 6 500 inhabitants. The municipality having incorporated Table View and Bothasig, the total population is 40 000. Milnerton was founded in 1902 and named after the Cape Governor, Lord Milner.* It has among its assets some lovely homes and gardens, the Dieprivier lagoon for boating and water-skiing, a championship golf course, a well-patronised bowling club, the Ascot racecourse, and a natural sanctuary for birds at Rietvlei in an area notable for wild flowers.

Bloubergstrand
In the whole of the Cape there is no sightseeing vantage point to match that from the seaside village of Bloubergstrand. Across the bay from here the magnificence of Table Mountain comes into dramatic perspective and if you are fortunate enough to witness this when the south-easter is laying the table-cloth, there is then no view more spectacular in the circumference of the world.

Bloubergstrand is reached along the coastal road due north of Milnerton. It is a favoured area for picnicking, fishing, shell collecting, sunbathing and, despite the chilly waters of the Atlantic, surf-riding. During the spring the whole neighbourhood is carpeted in wild flowers, the daisies and mesembryanthemums thriving even in the white sand dunes. On a clear day Robben Island, eight kilometres away, appears remarkably close to the mainland. The island is so named because of the seals (Afrikaans 'robbe') which once inhabited it.

To the west and overlooking the village is the Blouberg, rising to 230 metres; the scene of the short battle on 6 January 1806 which resulted in the Dutch surrendering the Cape to the British.

Melkbosstrand
To the north of Bloubergstrand is Melkbosstrand which takes its name from the milky euphorbia which grow there. Fishing is excellent in the cold waters and there is a free lobster-catching season in the summer months, with a limit of five lobsters per person a day. Every year on the day after Christmas farmers arrive at the wide sandy beach to take part in the strenuous 'Boere Sports' – the tug-of-war being the principal contest. It was here in the cove called Losperds Bay that the British force landed to engage the Dutch in 1806.

* Lord Milner, born Alfred Milner in Bonn in 1852, was of part German origin. As Sir Alfred Milner he became Governor of the Cape Colony in 1897. His negotiations, on behalf of the British government, with Presidents Kruger and Steyn in 1899 to avoid war with the Transvaal and Orange Free State Republics, broke down largely because of his arrogance and uncompromising attitude. Following the eventual British victory over the Boers and the annexation of the two republics, Milner became Governor of both Transvaal and the renamed Orange River Colony. During his regime he did much to alienate the Afrikaner people but was nevertheless acknowledged to be an able administrator and was confronted with the enormous task of repatriating some 200 000 white and 100 000 black refugees. In the end Milner had established highly efficient Civil Service departments and personally assisted in the successful development of the entire country. In 1905 when he returned to Great Britain much of the war damage had been repaired. During the First World War, Lord Milner was a senior member of the British Cabinet. He died in 1925.

CHAPTER 2

The Western Cape

The Western Cape is the beautiful Mediterranean region of majestic mountains and intensely cultivated valleys, orchards, wheatlands, vineyards, gabled homesteads and wild flowers, its world-renowned fishing grounds providing a wealth of seafood.

Embraced by the rugged coastline of two oceans, the Atlantic and the Indian, it is bounded in the north by the semi-desert region of Namaqualand; to the north-east the great mountain ranges cut it off from the arid Karoo and to the east it merges with the southern coastal belt of the Garden Route.

For convenience the Western Cape is divided into four sub-regions commencing with:

The North-western coastal belt from Cape Town to Velddrif-Laaiplek

Mamre

The drive from Cape Town to Melkbosstrand is described in the first chapter. From Melkbosstrand the traveller has the choice of two routes for part of the way to Velddrif-Laaiplek: the magnificent coastal road R27 and the old road via Mamre and Darling.

Thirty-one kilometres north of Melkbosstrand the old road passes through a 20-kilometre-long avenue of eucalyptus trees, two kilometres after which there is a gravel turnoff to the Moravian Mission Station of Mamre.

The mission was founded in 1808 in the fertile Groene Kloof with its three pure-water springs where a military cattle-check post stood from the early 1700s, and takes its name from the Biblical plain of Israel where Abraham built an altar. The Moravian Society is a Protestant sect which accepts the Bible as the only source of faith and was founded in Saxony by emigrants from Moravia (now part of Czechoslovakia). Its missionaries in the Cape had impressed the governor, the Earl of Caledon, in their good work at Genadendal, to the extent that he encouraged the establishment of this second mission amongst the Hottentots of the area. Of the 2 000 predominantly Coloured people at Mamre today, there are about 100 descendants of the Hottentot tribes.

The Mission Station is a national monument; its oldest building, a relic of the military post days, is the 18th century 'langhuis', that served as soldiers barracks, situated behind the present-day parsonage. The thatched church was dedicated in 1818, the date seen on the front pediment; the water-mill, built in 1874 to grind from 20 to 24 bushels of corn a day and restored to working order by the Rembrandt Group in 1973, the quaint mission store, bakery, acorn store and rows of white-washed houses, present a unique architectural complex.

It was here in the Groene Kloof that the wool industry in South Africa had its start in 1789 when Colonel Gordon* imported the first Merino ewes and rams and put them to breed.

Koeberg

At the coast south-east of Mamre and south of Bokpunt is Koeberg, the site of South Africa's first nuclear power station; the first phase providing Escom with the total-projected energy needs of the Cape Peninsula and pumping about 1 000 megawatts into the national system.

Darling

This little municipality of 2 000 people was founded in 1854 and named in honour of the lieutenant-governor, Sir Charles Henry Darling, who as acting-governor opened the first Cape Parliament in the same year.

The centre of a rich dairy-farming area, Darling is also notable for the export of chincherinchees and lupins and its wild flower show held in September. The Tinie Versfeldt Wild Flower Reserve is twelve kilometres beyond the town on the road to the coast.

Ysterfontein

At the coast, and once a fishing port with its own canning factory, is Ysterfontein, today a favourite seaside resort in an area noted for its wild flowers. The long jetty is now used only by anglers and acts as a lee for surfers who ride the huge rollers. There is a caravan and camping park.

Langebaan Lagoon, its western bank and Langebaan Village

A gravel road runs the length of the narrow peninsula which forms the western bank of the great Langebaan Lagoon and leads to Donkergat at the northern tip of the peninsula. From the southern end this road passes the farming and fishing settlements of Churchhaven (where the graveyard headstones bear the names of mariners from many lands) and Schryvershoek (named after Ensign Izaak Schryver, commander of the seventeenth century Dutch garrison) and reaches the sheltered Kraalbaai and the site of the first military outpost of Saldanha Bay, established during van Riebeeck's time and known as Oupos, where today antelope, hares and ostriches inhabit the privately-owned Postberg Nature Reserve.

Donkergat, at the cul-de-sac of the road, is so named because of the exceptionally deep water off the coast at this point where there are to be seen the remains of the old whaling station in a picturesque setting. From Donkergat there is a track leading to Salamander Bay named after the Dutch ship *Salamander* which took shelter there when its crew was stricken with scurvy. A melancholy atmosphere

---

* Colonel Robert Jacob Gordon, soldier-explorer-artist, was Commander of the Cape Garrison from 1780 until 1795 when he committed suicide after surrendering to the British at the Battle of Muizenberg. This was when Commissioner Sluysken and the Council of Policy were governing the colony for the Dutch East India Company. Gordon was born in Holland of Scottish emigrants and did part of his soldiering in a Scottish regiment under Colonel Dundas. He reached the Cape in 1777 when, as second in command of the garrison he began his travels. During 1778, with Governor van Plettenberg, he visited the Eastern Frontier and in 1779 he discovered the river to the north of the colony and named it the Orange River in honour of the Stadholder of the Netherlands, the Prince of Orange.

1

2

3

1. At rest — fishing trawlers in Lambert's Bay and cormorants on Bird Island.

2. Children gather outside the Mamre mission store — directly opposite is the plaque of the Monuments Commission.

3. Peach blossoms and an old thatched Cape Dutch dwelling — indicative of the tranquillity in Clanwilliam's main street.

prevails amidst the ruins of ill-fated fishing and whaling concerns, wrecks of vessels and the small cemetery with tombstones of seafarers of the last century; although deep-sea yachtsmen still use the bay from where there is a fine view of the islands of Jutten, Marcus and Malagas at the entrance to Saldanha Bay. From the high points all along this narrow strip of land the views are spectacular.

Langebaan Village lies at the head of the lagoon and comprises a number of lagoon-side cottages and a good stretch of firm beach, comfortably negotiable in a motor car. It provides anchorage for power boats and yachts and is popular with those who enjoy fishing and aquatic sports.

Sea birds, herons, flamingoes and wild flowers all go to make Langebaan an enchanting little place to sojourn. Quite close to the charming lake-side Hotel Panorama with its jetty of privately-owned boats is the South African Naval Rescue Base, *S.A.S. Flamingo.* Visitors facilities include bungalows for hire and the caravan and camping sites.

The permanent population at Langebaan is mainly connected with fishing and the oyster-shell industry. The recovery of oyster shells is from the extensive deposit lying in a bed 5 metres deep and covering an area of 10 square-kilometres. It is said that the deposit amounts to some millions of tons and although guesses have been made, the cause of the oysters dying remains a mystery. The shells are used in the making of lime and poultry food.

The lagoon has remarkable dimensions; great length and breadth, 16 kilometres by 5 kilometres by 5 kilometres, but averaging only 6 metres deep. Translated, 'langebaan' is 'long channel'. Schaapen Island partially blocks the lagoon where it joins with Saldanha Bay, and at this point the long iron-ore wharf has been constructed from the mainland.

Langebaan National Park

In August 1985 the Langebaan Lagoon, including the intertidal and admirality zones, and the islands Malgas, Jutten, Marcus and Schaapen, were proclaimed a national park. In 1987 some 1 850 hectares of adjoining farmlands was, by agreement, incorporated in the park, marking the first instance of a national park being expanded substantially with the co-operation of private landowners.

The connecting routes between Langebaan village and Saldanha

To reach the town of Saldanha from Langebaan village one can rejoin route R27 or take the old road which meets route R45 about midway between Hopefield and Vredenburg. At the junction of the old road and R45 is the railhead, Langebaan Road, where there is an Air Force station and a large phosphate quarry. Apart from wild flowers, Flanders poppies have somehow been introduced to lend a nostalgic note to any traveller who has been in France or Italy and witnessed the sight of this delicate blood-red bloom intermingled with the golden wheat.

Hopefield and the Saldanha Man

A Major Hope and a Mr Field established Hopefield in 1852. It lies east of Saldanha Bay and is the centre for the farming district known as the Voorbaai, meaning 'before the bay'. The area is noted for wheat farming and the production of honey. Fifteen kilometres west

of this little town of 2 000 people is the farm of Elandsfontein, since 1951 a world-famous site of pre-historic findings. Here in a sand-dune area thousands of fossil bones and stone implements have been found. The most notable of these are fossils of the Neanderthal-type human, the Saldanha Man, and a variety of extinct animals. Hopefield has an hotel.

Vredenburg

With its meaning 'town of peace', Vredenburg belies the atmosphere in which it had its beginning. The place was originally known as Prosesfontein (the fountain of lawsuits) because of the quarrelling that went on between the first owners of the two farms (on which the town now stands) over the water rights of the spring on the boundary separating their farms.

Since its establishment in 1875 it has been known as the centre for the Agterbaai, the prosperous sheep-and wheat-farming district to the rear of the bay. Upon its centenary in 1975 it amalgamated with Saldanha. Vredenburg has two hotels. The population of Vredenburg-Saldanha is 26 000.

Saldanha Bay

Saldanha Bay was originally the name applied to present-day Table Bay, after the Portuguese admiral, Antonio de Saldanha, who anchored his fleet there in 1503. It kept the name for nearly a century until, in 1601, the Dutch renamed it Table Bay and, in some navigational error, the name Saldanha Bay was applied to its present position. Had it not been for the lack of drinking water, Saldanha would have superseded Cape Town in its importance, Saldanha Bay being far better sheltered and a good deal larger than Table Bay.

Lying due south of the entrance is the island Vondeling and at the entrance are the islands Jutten, Marcus and Malagas. In 1976 Marcus Island was joined to the mainland by causeway. Deep channels between the islands permit the passage of large ships into the bay. In the bay, at the commencement of the shallowing of the waters near the Langebaan Lagoon, are the islands of Meeu and Schaapen.

Strategically important, Saldanha Bay has been the scene of a number of naval engagements in the time of its long and colourful history and it has been the site of one or two large money-making scoops.

Before van Riebeeck sent his exploration party up the coast, shortly after his arrival at the Cape, French adventurers were taking rich hauls of seal skins and oil from the islands in Saldanha Bay. It is known that in 1653 one French vessel alone loaded no less than 4 800 skins and many casks of oil. Rivalry over the possession of the bay between the Dutch and the French continued even after the Dutch set up a garrison at the watering point called Oupos on the west bank of the Langebaan Lagoon in 1666, until finally the Dutch East India Company took control. In 1702 one of the Company's ships, the *Merestyn,* was wrecked off Jutten Island and a considerable treasure of ducatoons was salvaged some twenty years later. There are tales told of pirate ships surprised whilst taking shelter in the bay in these early times, and the Dutch, themselves, were caught at anchor by a British squadron in 1781. The *Middelburg* and five attendant ships were captured, although the *Middelburg* was scuttled by her crew before the British could take possession. Many other ships have been sunk in the bay in contest or in bad weather and relics are to this day washed up on the shores.

Considerable fortunes were made at Saldanha Bay after the European countries discovered the use of guano as a fertiliser. The fantastic rush for the enormous deposits of this 'white gold' left on the islands by the vast numbers of gannets, cormorants and jackass penguins, resulted in there being three hundred ships at anchor in Saldanha Bay in August 1844. On the tiny island of Malagas, guano, accumulated over the centuries, measured up to 8 metres deep. It is known that over 200 000 tons were removed from the islands of Saldanha Bay and with the selling price in Europe at £7 a ton, the financial scoop was in the region of one-and-a-half million pounds sterling.

The Confederate States 1 000-ton commerce-raider, the *Alabama*, used the shelter of Saldanha Bay during her escapades in South African waters from 1862 to 1864 and, as is well known, her memory is preserved in the Cape-Malay song 'Daar kom die Alabama'.

Saldanha Bay is one of the great natural ocean harbours of the world and with its fresh-water problem having been overcome by piping from the Berg River, 43 kilometres away, it was selected for the creation of a modern iron and steel port to serve Iscor at Sishen Mine (the greatest producer of high-grade haematite in South Africa). Sishen, in the far Northern Cape (51 kilometres north of Kuruman), is 861 kilometres from Saldanha and had to be connected to it by special railway, completed in 1976 as part of the enormous R1 000-million scheme.

Modern developments apart, Saldanha is a fishing port of considerable significance with its fish canneries processing the catches of lobsters, pilchards and anchovies. An interesting industry at Saldanha is the harvesting of seaweed for agar-agar, the gelatinous substance used in meat canning, as a stabiliser for chocolate and a colour base for synthetic fabrics. The islands continue to yield guano and certain edible eggs and the age-old drying of mullet and mackerel for 'brokkens', the staple food of farm labourers in the district, continues as well.

From the aspect of a resort, Saldanha remains unspoilt and is a most delightful place for those who prefer a holiday in the free and easy manner; in a world of maritime wonder amidst fishing-craft, from the row-boat type to sizeable trawlers and pleasure-craft from canoes to launches. This is a romantic world for those who love the sounds of sea birds and lapping waters and the noises of seafarers bringing in the catch.

Saldanha has a Naval Gymnasium and a Military Academy (a faculty of the University of Stellenbosch) in the vicinity of which there are fine playing fields including a 9-hole golf course and all-weather tennis courts. The municipality has developed caravan and camping sites and bungalows can be hired. There are two licensed hotels.

The municipalities of Vredenburg and Saldanha merged on 1st March 1975 when the farms in the 13 kilometres between the towns together with Paternoster and its surrounding area were all embraced in a single municipality of Vredenburg-Saldanha with a total population of some 26 000 people.

Paternoster, Cape Columbine and Tieties Bay

From Vredenburg the road to Paternoster passes through wheatlands with strangely shaped outcrops of granite. Paternoster is a picturesque fishing village of white-walled cottages and a lovely white-beached bay. It has a lobster factory and a small hotel and received its name from the survivors of a shipwreck who said the Lord's Prayer in thanksgiving.

Three kilometres south is Cape Columbine; its nine million candle-power lighthouse has a range of 37 kilometres and is the first light seen from ships approaching South Africa from Europe by the western route.

Not far along the track beyond the lighthouse is Tieties Bay, named after a Coloured fisherman who was drowned there. This is a peaceful cove in a rugged seascape where wild flowers spread across the countryside down to the beaches. The fishermen's track carries on for some distance along the coast.

St Helena Bay

St Helena Bay stretches in a great curve of 20 kilometres from Stompneus Point to the mouth of the Berg River. It was here that Vasco da Gama rested in 1497 on the day of the saint, 7th November. This is the principal area of South Africa's multimillion-rand marine products industry where, in the cold Benguela Current, shoal fish thrive and huge hauls of pilchards, maasbankers and anchovies are brought to the jetties of a dozen or more processing factories established along the shores of this huge bay. For those contemplating an overnight stop there is a licensed hotel.

Velddrif-Laaiplek

The municipality combining these two settlements has a population of 3 000 and the town is built on the north bank of the Berg River.

Velddrif was once the fording place a little way up the river and Laaiplek the loading place at the river mouth. Modern improvements have made considerable changes to the town. A breakwater offers the important fishing fleet safe anchorage at the river wharfside from where the lobster cannery and meal processing plant are supplied. From here the Berg River is navigable in small boats for 60 kilometres in an area notable for prolific birdlife. Velddrif is the finishing post of the 280-kilometre Berg River canoe marathon that starts at Paarl and is held each year in August.

From Laaiplek a coastal road leads northwards to Dwarskersbos where there is a caravan park administered by the Swartland Divisional Council.

National road N7 from Cape Town through Swartland to the entrance of Namaqualand

It is said that van Riebeeck named the territory lying north-west of Cape Town, Het Zwarte Land (Swartland or black country) from the colour of the soil, but if you go there at ploughing time you will find the soil is red. A more likely reason for the name is that in its wild state, the countryside (which was then semi-desert) was covered in a very dark scrub, which in certain light looked quite black. Patches of the natural scrub still remain, otherwise the scene has been transformed into a sea of wheatfields, emerald green in the rainy winter and golden brown at reaping time.

Malmesbury

In the early times the small settlement where the town of Malmesbury now stands was simply referred to as Het Zwarte Land until 1829 when Governor Sir Lowry Cole visited the place and renamed it in honour of his father-in-law, the Earl of Malmesbury. It became a municipality in 1896.

Malmesbury today has a population of 15 000 and is the most important town of this, the richest wheat-producing district in South Africa, which is also noted for oats and milk production. In the somewhat awkwardly planned town are the enormous storage silos and flour mills and a sulphur spring in a five metre square fenced area. The spring was discovered in 1744 and was popular enough for the construction of a small sanatorium; unhappily it fell into disuse. Malmesbury's recreational facilities include golf, bowls, and a fine swimming pool. There are three licensed hotels.

There is an interesting dialect in pronunciation, peculiar to the Afrikaans-speaking people who come from this area, the main feature of speech being the guttural 'r'. General Smuts, who was born in the district, spoke with the Malmesbury accent.

Riebeek-Kasteel and Riebeek-Wes

A short deviation from national road N7 to the north-east in the setting of wheatfields and vineyards, and separated from one another by a few kilometres, are the sister villages of Riebeek-Kasteel and Riebeek-Wes. They lie near the middle reaches of the Berg River on the slopes of the solitary 940-metre-high Kasteelberg.

Outside the post office of Riebeek-Kasteel is an old gun, a reminder that this was one of a number of frontier outposts of the Dutch East India Company. The guns were sited on prominent hills and used as a signal to farmers, either of the arrival of ships in Table Bay, or as a warning of an impending attack by Hottentots.

The district has the distinction of having been the birth-place of two South African Prime Ministers: Dr D.F. Malan was born on the farm Allesverloren, which adjoins Riebeek-Wes, and General J.C. Smuts on the farm Ongegund (or Boplaas as it was also called) where the old farm-house is a national monument and can be reached by proceeding from Riebeek-Wes for about six kilometres along the road north to Moorreesburg. Here in an industrial area is a deep quarry of a large cement factory and on the edge of the quarry is the long, narrow house with a thatched roof. Although the farming character of the area is lost, the modest dwelling is true to its period.

South-east of Riebeek-Kasteel on route R44 is the rural centre, Hermon, and 10 km north of this village is the extensive dam at Voëlvlei. Fed by a canal from the Little Berg River, the dam supplies users as far apart as Cape Town in the south and Saldanha and Velddrif in the north. Voëlvlei is popular with fishermen and yachtsmen.

Moorreesburg

As in the case of so many South African towns, Moorreesburg had its beginning with the building of the Dutch Reformed Church. The settlement, founded in 1882, was named after the Rev. H.A. Moorrees. With its present-day population of 6 000, Moorreesburg is a thriving centre of rich wheatlands and sheep farms. The interesting museum is devoted to the history of the cultivation of wheat. The town has good recreational facilities in the form of golf, tennis and swimming and there are two licensed hotels. On the outskirts of the town is the government experimental wheat farm.

Piketberg

Three kilometres south of Piketberg at the place named De Hoek, is the huge open cast limestone mine of the Cape Portland Cement Company.

Piketberg with its beautiful church (a national monument) lies at the foot of the steeply-rising Piketberg range in the surrounds of vast wheatlands. The town has a population of 5 000 and there are two licensed hotels.

In the 1670s when the marauding Hottentot, Gonnema, was causing so much trouble, the Dutch East India Company placed a military picket at the foot of the mountain to check cattle rustling.

The drive up Versfeld Pass to the surprisingly wide plateau at the top reveals a rural scene of intense cultivation in deciduous fruit and wheat, orchards and wheatfields enclosed by avenues of tall pines. The farms, dominated by the 1 459-metre Zebra Kop, date from the early nineteenth century and have some lovely old homesteads. From the corkscrew bends of the pass, where wild flowers grow on the mountainside, there are sweeping views across the valley.

Porterville

South-east of Piketberg on route R44 is Porterville; the centre of a mixed farming area, it dates from 1863 and was named after the attorney-general, William Porter. Another of the Dutch East India Company's signal guns is to be found outside the magistrate's court.

Some ten kilometres to the east of Porterville, in the Olifantsrivierberg, there is a rich concentration of Bushmen caves in spectacular mountain scenery. These caves are decorated with some fine examples of their paintings.

From Porterville route R44 leads south-east for 37 kilometres to Gouda.

Piekenierskloof Pass

From Piketberg, national road N7 heads north-east across a vast plain of wheatlands hemmed in by the Piketberg and Olifants River ranges. Piekenierskloof Pass, the fine motor road over the Olifants River mountain, was completed in 1950 and replaces two previous passes. The original Piekenierskloof Pass used by the early explorers follows the course of the gorge.

In 1685 Simon van der Stel used this route when

These pictures depict the rich ambience to be found at D'Ouwe Werf Country Inn, 30 Church Street, Stellenbosch, and match the genuine Cape hospitality and fine cuisine provided by its charming host, Gerhard Lubbe.

he took his great cavalcade of wagons and soldiers in search of the famed copper mountains of Namaqualand.

Below the line of the present pass it is possible to trace the course of the pass built by Thomas Bain in 1858 and named Grey's Pass after Governor Sir George Grey.

The name 'Piekeniers' comes from the pikemen introduced by the Dutch to do battle in this area against the Hottentot, Gonnema. The first whites to enter the area comprised a 14-man expedition led by Jan Danckaert. Assisted by Bushmen they crossed the mountain in December 1660, and it is said they came upon a great herd of elephants on the banks of the river.

Citrusdal

Today groves of citrus cover the fertile valley of the Olifants River, and the small town of Citrusdal, perfectly situated with its mountainous backdrop, marks the entrance to the beautiful valley; its oranges, of the very sweetest variety, are sought-after throughout the world, the citrus co-operative exporting more than a million cases each year. Visitors to the town during the packing season may witness the speed in which the great harvest of the golden fruit is wrapped and packed by country girls. The record for one girl is 177 000 oranges packed in 46 working hours.

Citrusdal, with its licensed hotel and municipal caravan park, is a good base for the visitor wishing to explore the scenic wonderland of the district. The town was founded in 1916 and has a population of 2 500. Farming goes back a good deal further; Modderfontein has been farmed since 1725 and Karnmelksvlei since 1767. The farms Hexsrivier to the north and Valhalla to the south are the most beautiful citrus estates.

Below Valhalla on the western bank of the Olifants is The Bath where the mineral waters at a temperature of 45°C are reputed to be radioactive and of considerable benefit to persons suffering from rheumatic ailments. The springs lie in a well-wooded ravine which joins with the main valley. The facilities consist of an open pool, a number of enclosed private baths, a variety of sleeping accommodation and a tearoom. Preserved rock inscriptions dating from the eighteenth century demonstrate that 'the waters were taken' in those times.

The area is rich in Bushman paintings; those on the koppie of the farm Vlakrug, 7 kilometres from the town, are easily accessible by motor car.

To the south-east of Citrusdal a spectacular scenic route over the Kouebokkeveld mountain leads, via the Buffelshoek and Gydo Passes, into the Ceres Valley to Prince Alfred's Hamlet and on to Ceres, a distance of 110 kilometres.

Olifants River

National road N7 to Clanwilliam follows along the west bank of the Olifants and the way is particularly charming during orange blossom time, late September and October. The road along the east bank, essentially a farm road, passes closer to the majestic Cedarberg range in superb scenery. Because the orange is prince of this province other important production is likely to be overlooked. High quality dry wine is produced here and deciduous fruits are also packed and exported; wheat is grown and there are some fine dairy farms. The Olifants is well stocked with black bass and yellowfish and the sight of the sandfish migration at spawning time has been likened to the salmon of Canada.

Cedarberg range

Twenty-seven kilometres north of Citrusdal a gravel turnoff to the east leads through the precipitous Kriedouw Krans over Nieuwoudt Pass in magnificent rugged mountain scenery into the valley of the Rondegat River and to the forestry station of Algeria, dominated by the Middelberg ridge and so named by its founder, the first forester, George Bath, because the gnarled cedar trees growing on the mountains reminded him of the North African Atlas Mountains.

Ramblers and climbers will find Algeria to be an ideal base for excursions into the Cedarberg range. There is a fine caravan and camping site amongst the trees near the river and with the help of the forester, pack donkeys and guides may be found. This is a resort for nature lovers with its wide variety of places of beauty and fascination – superb view sites, waterfalls, caves, astonishingly weird rock formations, twisted cedars, wild geraniums, ericas, blood red pincushion proteas, pure white snow proteas and the magic of the mountain air.

There is a rest hut on the Middelberg ridge and from here are found the walks to Crystal Pools, Sneeukop (1 931 metres) and the strange rock formation of Wolfberg Arch. In the vicinity are the Tafelberg and Langeberg peaks, both rising above 1 800 metres. The aromatic leaves of the Buchu shrub are collected in the kloofs and used medicinally.

From Algeria there is an interesting direct route northwards for 31 kilometres to Clanwilliam. To the south-east another road finds its way over Uitkyk Pass for 36 kilometres to the farm Kromrivier, where bungalows may be hired. From here the 2 027-metre Sneeuberg may be climbed or the less strenuous walk to the famous 10-metre-high Maltese Cross may be made. Five kilometres beyond the farm is the turnoff right which leads for another three kilometres to the amazing collection of caves named the Stadsaal (town hall). Beyond the Stadsaal turnoff the road from Algeria continues south to join with the Citrusdal-Ceres road.

Clanwilliam and its District, including Wupperthal Mission Station

At the foot of the Cedarberg in the well-watered valley of the Jan Dissels River, lies the little town of Clanwilliam. The place was first known as Jandisselsvleidorp until January 1814 when Sir John Cradock, the governor, renamed it in honour of his father-in-law, the Earl of Clanwilliam.

The district was settled by a small group of Irish immigrants at the time of the 1820 settlers. Today there are about 3 000 people in this pleasant old-world town with its wide concreted main street and thatch roofed houses. It serves a prosperous mixed farming community producing citrus, deciduous and sub-tropical fruit, cereals, timber, tobacco, jersey cattle, sheep and rooibos tea. The thriving rooibos tea industry started when Dr L. Nortier (the local physician) discovered a method of propagating the shrub which grows wild in the surrounding mountains. The herb tea, free of tannin and rich in vitamin C, is in fairly wide use in South Africa and is exported to Germany, America, Israel and Australia. Dr Nortier and the poet, Dr Louis Leipoldt, were great friends. Their memory is preserved in the Leipoldt-Nortier Memorial Library in the town where a fine selection of books, personal belongings of Dr Leipoldt and paintings of Hugo Naudé and other artists may be seen.

Irrigation of the vast area of farmland in the district has been made possible through the harnessing of the Olifants River at the Bulshoek Dam, 22 kilometres north of the town and the Clanwilliam Dam a kilometre to the south of the town which also provides an excellent stretch of water for all manner of aquatic sports, fishing and swimming. The eastern shore of the dam has been proclaimed a Nature Reserve and there are camping grounds.

Boskloof and Kranskloof, beauty spots close to the town, are ideal for picnics and swimming. Clanwilliam has always been strong in competitive tennis and rugby and there is a nine-hole golf course.

The town has a licensed hotel and municipal caravan park and attracts many visitors during the spring when the wild flowers are profuse. In the Citrusdal-Clanwilliam area there is a greater number of species than in Namaqualand where there is usually a far greater density of a particular species. One of the best places to see the wild flowers is to the east of Clanwilliam in the Bidouw Valley; this is not far from the mission station at Wupperthal and the journey to these places is full of interest. The road to Calvinia is taken and the distances are 60 and 70 kilometres respectively. Along this route, in the Pakhuis Pass, 14 kilometres from Clanwilliam and near to the roadside in the shelter of a Bushman cave, is the grave of Dr C. Louis Leipoldt (1880 to 1947). This is the countryside the renowned poet and naturalist loved so much and an exciting place to stop awhile and look around, where the mountainside is a fantastic assembly of the most extraordinary rock formations. At 38 kilometres from Clanwilliam you leave the road to Calvinia and take the branch road to the south (the junction is marked by a British soldier's grave under a large tree) and proceed over the Bidouw Pass to the fork at Mertenhof. The road due east leads to the valley of the Bidouw River with its flowers (at their best during August and September) and the road to the south winds through another pass of steep gradients to a cul-de-sac and the Rhenish Mission Station at Wupperthal.

The mission lies in the deep valley of the Tra-Tra River dominated by the Vaalheuning and Krakadouw spurs of the eastern Cedarberg. It is a completely isolated and very beautiful oasis cast in an eerie wilderness of massif and chasm. Founded in 1830, the settlement is predominantly of Coloured folk who live in a village of white-walled, thatched cottages so typical of the Cape. They labour in the irrigated fields and produce many kinds of fruit and vegetable, rooibos tea, tobacco and grain. Jersey cows graze in the meadows and the mission keeps up its tradition of producing excellent footwear of the *velskoen* type. There is a fine gabled church and the people of Wupperthal are well known for their choir singing.

Heerenlogement

There is a tarred highway from Clanwilliam to Lambert's Bay, a distance of 58 kilometres. The railhead, Graafwater, with its large school is midway between the two towns. Thirty-two kilometres north of Graafwater on the gravel road to Vredendal, in somewhat bleak surroundings, is the historical cave, Heerenlogement, or 'gentlemen's lodgings'.

Used as a shelter by travellers who journeyed northwards from Cape Town, the cave was close to the old main road to the Koperberge (copper mountains) and there is evidence of it having been in use during the 17th, 18th and 19th centuries. Many have carved their names or initials on the walls during the years. The first known traveller to visit the cave was Pieter van Meerhof in 1661, although he did not record his name. The first names to be recorded are those of Kaje Jess Slotsbo and two others in 1712. Slotsbo, a member of the Dutch East India Company's Council of Policy, was accompanying an expedition of 181 persons to take action against Namaqua Hottentots. Ensign I.T. Rhenius, 1712, C.P. Thunberg the botanist in 1774 and Hendrik Swellengrebel on 19th January 1777 are other names amongst the early visitors. Swellengrebel wrote an account of the cave and mentioned the old wild-fig or milk tree growing out of a crevice at the back of the cave, which remains there today.

Lambert's Bay

Rear-Admiral Sir Robert Lambert, commander of the Cape Station from 1820 to 1821, gave his name to Lambert's Bay. It is the harbour for a large fishing fleet and the site of important fish processing and lobster canning factories. During the lobster season hundreds of small rowing boats leave the harbour for the fishing grounds several kilometres along the open coast.

Connected to the harbour by concrete pier is Bird Island with its colonies of gannets and cormorants, wide variety of other sea birds and penguins. In great numbers the birds can be inspected at very close quarter. The guano yield from the tiny island is over 300 tons annually. A licensed hotel, attractively situated, overlooks the harbour; nearby is the municipal caravan park.

Leipoldtville, Wagendrift, Elands Bay and Baboon Point

On the coastal road to Leipoldtville in a series of pans at Steenbokfontein and Wagendrift, large numbers of water birds, including flamingoes, find sanctuary. Further south is Eland's Bay, the surfer's Mecca, where the summer south-easter provides great waves for long rides from a convenient headland starting point. Primitive Bushman drawings decorate the walls of the cave in the cliffs of Baboon Point on the southern side of the bay.

1

2

5

3

4

1. Stellenbosch, in the valley of the Eerste River, nestles below the Simonsberg.

2. La Gratitude, with its all-seeing Eye of God looking down upon the townspeople, is in Dorp Street.

3. St Mary's Anglican Church is the only building on the Braak.

4. The Dutch Reformed Theological Seminary stands on the site of the first Drostdy of Stellenbosch.

5. Paul Roos Gymnasium, on the south bank of the Eerste River, is a famous Stellenbosch school for boys.

National road N1 from Cape Town to the entrance of the Great Karoo

The Boland (upland) area of the Western Cape encompasses the magnificent mountain ranges and fertile valleys that stretch in a great arc from the Cedarberg in the north to the Langeberg in the south.

The famous deciduous fruit and wine producing valleys are those of the Eerste, Berg, Breede and Hex rivers and the high-lying Palmiet river-basin southeast of the Hottentots Holland range. From 300 million vines 60 000 tons of table grapes and 700 million litres of wine are produced annually and thousands of tons of choice apples, peaches, pears, plums and apricots are exported.

Four Passes Drive

The 210-kilometre-circuit from Cape Town into the Boland takes in its route the passes of Helshoogte, Franschhoek, Viljoen's and Sir Lowry's and the towns of Stellenbosch, Franschhoek and Grabouw. It can be accomplished in a day and is one of the most beautiful and varied scenic drives of the Western Cape.

There are two exits from Cape Town to reach the start of this Drive. National road N2 turns off into Stellenbosch Road (R310) just before Faure, and continues past The Pigeon House at the farm Meerlust on the right (see page 83), over-looked by the striking Helderberg. Eight and a half kilometres from Stellenbosch the R310 passes Drie Gewels Hotel at Lynedoch on the left and 1½ km further on the very popular Spier Restaurant and cellar on the right. National road N1, via Bellville and Kuils River, turns off into the attractive Polka Draai Road (R306) that makes a stupendous bend around Ribbokkop. The two routes meet 2 km short of the turnoff left to Devon Valley, 1½ km outside Stellenbosch.

Stellenbosch

The landscape setting of the environment of Stellenbosch is surely the most beautiful of all our inland towns and with the preservation of its original planning of oak-lined streets, clear water furrows and classic architecture, the town itself is among the most charming of urban areas in the whole of South Africa. Stellenbosch is surrounded by vineyards and orchards as indeed it is by mountains; the peaks of the Simonsberg rising to 915 and 1 390 metres present a particularly spectacular sight.

Soon after his arrival at the Cape in 1679 Simon van der Stel undertook expeditions to open up the interior. In November 1679 he entered the valley of the Eerste River and made camp on a site near an indigenous forest which he called Stellenbosch. Within a month of his discovering the broad valley, free burgher families were making the Cape's second settlement 48 kilometres from Table Bay. By 1685 Stellenbosch was the seat of the frontier landdrost and remained the only inland magistracy for the next hundred years.

The architectural style which came into being during the latter half of the 18th century and early 19th century, and known today as Cape Dutch, is derived from simple vernacular European pitched roof homesteads and evolved gradually to suit not only the warm climate of the Cape, but also the needs of the hospitable agrarian settlers. Of necessity, the buildings were simple structures built with the available materials – timber from the local forests (invariably the beautiful indigenous yellowwood) provided for floors, windows, doors and roofing. The roofs were covered with thatching grass and walls (invariably massive) were of stone, mud, green brick or rubble, covered with lime plaster obtained by burning coastal shells. As a protection against the rain, the walls were lime-washed at regular intervals, and it is this unifying white that makes the style so distinctive. The widths of rooms depended entirely upon the lengths of ceiling and flooring joists available, and this accounted for original barn-shaped houses (never more than seven metres wide) having wings added to form the L-plan, T-plan and H-plan structures. The easily-worked lime plaster allowed freedom of expression for the mouldings of pilasters, urns, cornices and the embellishment of gable faces.

Many of the fine old Cape Dutch-style homesteads with their highly inflammable thatched roofs miraculously survived the disastrous fires of 1710, 1803 and of Victorian times.

Stellenbosch was proclaimed a municipality in 1840 and in 1987 the population was 46 180.

University of Stellenbosch

Stellenbosch has been a leading educational centre since the first school opened in 1683. A gymnasium and a theological seminary were set up in 1859 by the Dutch Reformed Church and in 1866 the gymnasium became Stellenbosch College. In 1887 it was renamed Victoria College to honour Queen Victoria in the year of her Golden Jubilee. A number of South Africa's leading figures studied at Victoria College, among these were the three prime ministers, General Smuts, General Hertzog and Dr Malan.

By Act of Parliament in 1918, Victoria College became the University of Stellenbosch. The eight faculties in Stellenbosch are Agriculture, Arts, Commerce and Administration, Education, Engineering, Law, Science and Theology. The faculties of Medicine and Dentistry are at Tygerberg, Parow; the faculty of Military Science is at Saldanha and the Graduate School of Business is at Bellville.

Opened in 1886 the 'Ou Hooggebou' (old main building) is a national monument. The University has 11 000 students nick-named 'Maties'.

Sport and Recreation

Stellenbosch is the largest rugby club in the world with 1 400 players. It has produced well over 100 internationals, 10 international captains and many famous names in rugby since the club's origin in 1880. The university sports ground, with its D.F. Malan Centre and Danie Craven Stadium, is in a splendid setting at Coetzenberg on the south bank of the Eerste River.

At the Van der Stel sports grounds north of the Braak, there are bowling greens and tennis courts, and the very interesting 18-hole golf course is just outside the town on the Strand Road. The Eerste River is one of the finest trout fishing rivers in southern Africa.

The visitor to Stellenbosch will be well rewarded by taking a walk through what has been aptly described as an open-air museum. The majority of historic buildings including many national monuments are to be found in Drostdy Street, van Ryneveld Street, Dorp Street and around the village green, the Braak.

Drostdy, Van Ryneveld and Church Streets

The east side of Drostdy Street is unspoilt with three historic buildings preserved in fine condition. First, on the left approaching from Plein Street, is Grosvenor House, a typical double-storey Cape Dutch town house. In its original design, built by C.L. Neethling in 1782, it was a single-storey gabled and thatched house on the H-plan. The upper floor, flat roof, fluted pilasters, pediment and straight moulded cornice were probably added after the conflagration of 1803, and demonstrate the neo-classic influence of the era. Today, as part of the Stellenbosch Village Museum (comprising four homesteads), it houses articles illustrating the history of and life in Stellenbosch. The next, the centre building of the three, is the Gothic-style Moederkerk of the Dutch Reformed denomination. Completed in 1863 by architect Carl O. Hager, it incorporates walls of the original church built in 1722, contains burial vaults of old Stellenbosch families and stands at the head of Church Street. The third building, Utopia, dating from 1799, is the church house on the Dorp Street corner. With its four identical gables and completely symmetrical façade it is the perfect example of the H-plan design. The classicist centre gable was added in 1815. The three buildings are national monuments.

Facing Dorp Street at the head of Drostdy Street, the Dutch Reformed Theological Seminary stands on the foundations of the first Drostdy (the home and office of the landdrost) which was built in Simon van der Stel's time, when present-day Drostdy Street was the avenue of approach.

Two houses on the west side of Drostdy Street which form part of the Village Museum are Blettermanhuis, circa 1789, home of Hendrik Lodewyk Bletterman, the last Dutch East India Company landdrost, and Murray House which was originally the home of O.M. Bergh, circa 1850.

West of and parallel with Drostdy Street is van Ryneveld Street, where two interesting houses (probably the first to be built in Stellenbosch and now national monuments) have been restored. Schreuder House, a modest pioneer house said to date from 1710 and Morkel House with a wine cellar dating from 1693.

At No. 30 Church Street, near the corner of Andringa Street, on a site where the archaeological remains of a Church circa 1687 – 1787 were excavated in 1981, is D'Ouwe Werf Country Inn. Quite unique in its setting, furnishing and hospitality, it is recommended without hesitation. Pictures appear on pages 52 and 53.

Dorp Street

Dorp Street is the oldest and most typical street of the old village; its ancient oaks, some probably dating back to 1760, intertwine to form a natural archway. Stellenbosch has often been called 'Eikestad' (city of oaks) and the oaks of Dorp Street, between the railway line and Parsonage Street, and those in The Avenue between Parsonage Street and van Riebeeck Street, have been proclaimed historical monuments.

The houses of Dorp Street (the old wagon road to Cape Town) go to make up the most interesting collection of vernacular domestic architecture to be seen anywhere in South Africa. In turning into Dorp Street from van Ryneveld Street, on the left-hand side of Dorp Street you are confronted with a splendid street frontage of five adjoining houses. Absolutely without uniformity the splendour of the scene lies in the variety of the buildings themselves. These houses, postal numbers 159 to 151 are: Saxenhof, converted by the famous Stellenbosch medical man of the nineteenth century, Dr J.H. Neethling, from its original single-storeyed H-shape to a double storeyed town house with a unique balcony; Loubser House (No. 157), built in the early 1800s and bearing the name of its twentieth century occupant, Bob Loubser, the Springbok rugby wing of 1906 and MP for Stellenbosch; Meuwes Bakker House (No. 155) where from 1798 Bakker started a school for slave children; Hauptfleisch House (No. 153) with its triangular gable, built by Frederick Hauptfleisch in 1812 and the Corner House (No. 151) on the corner of Helderberg Street. Numbers 159 to 153 are national monuments.

La Gratitude, close to the pavement at No. 95 Dorp Street (between Piet Retief and Hamman Streets), is perhaps the best known of the magnificent Cape Dutch homes of Stellenbosch. This well-preserved, gracious old homestead with its splendid classicist gable, was designed on the U-plan and built by the erudite Reverend Meent Borcherds in 1798 and remained his parsonage until his death in 1832. The profound faith of the man is manifested in the name he gave his home, La Gratitude, and the all-seeing Eye of God which is placed in the surround of an aureole above the window of the gable.

Across Dorp Street from La Gratitude is another charming group of national monuments; they number from 120 down to 100. The Gymnasium (No. 120) was completed in 1866 and was the first home of both the University and of present-day Paul Roos gymnasium the famous boys high school on the south bank of the Eerste River. The lovely cottage, Voorgelegen (No. 116) with its Batavian floor tiles, adjoins the four neo-Georgian houses, all similar and beautiful in their simplicity. On the same side of Dorp Street, higher up, between Mill and Bird Streets is the old Lutheran Church, now the University of Stellenbosch Art Gallery. No permanent art collection is housed here but interesting exhibitions are held of the art of university students and others.

Continuing westwards down Dorp Street, on the same side as La Gratitude, is Vredelust (No. 63), a charming Cape Dutch house and national monument, which stands concealed behind a white wall in an extensive garden. The H-shaped dwelling and adjoining wine cellar were built in the eighteenth century; the beautiful front gable with its four pilasters (each with a vase on top) was added in 1814. Little Vredelust, to the left of the main building, was probably built at the time as farm buildings and was restored in 1970.

At 33 Dorp Street, forming an impressive entrance

1. The main entrance to Oude Libertas, the head office of Stellenbosch Farmer's Winery — surrounded by vineyards and overlooked by the Helderberg range.
2. and 3. SFW Centre and Amphitheatre, across Adam Tas Road from the head office of SFW.

4. Famous Lanzerac, an hotel renowned for gracious living, superbly positioned beneath the Jonkershoek Mountains.

3

4

to Stellenbosch from Cape Town (N2) and from the Somerset West – Strand road, is a fine group of buildings of the old farm Libertas Parva, restored by Historical Homes of South Africa Limited and proclaimed historical monuments at the same time as Vredelust, in 1970. Libertas Parva was built on the H-plan by Lambertus H. Fick, probably in 1783. It is a striking mansion with its four concave-convex end gables. The front gable, two front doors and Georgian windows were added in circa 1819. The property was purchased by J.D. Krige in 1869 and it was here that General J.C. Smuts courted and married Sibella Margaretha Krige (affectionately known as Isie).

Today Libertas Parva is the Rembrandt van Rijn Art Centre and houses a fine collection of South African art including oils by Irma Stern, line cuts by Pierneef, sculpture by Anton van Wouw, as well as a famous collection of sculpture by the German expressionists, Ernst Barlach and Käthe Kollwitz. Italian Giacombo Manzu is represented by the large bronze *Guantanamera*.

The wine cellar at Libertas Parva is now the Stellenryck Wine Museum. Amongst the interesting collection of articles associated with viticulture and the history of wine are three wine amphoras, approximately 2 000 years old, recovered from the depths of the Mediterranean Sea near the islands of Giglio, Montecristo and Elba. These two-handled vessels were used by the Greeks and the Romans for transporting their wines. The old wine press outside the museum is from Germany and dates from circa 1790.

Old Strand Road

Across the Eerste River along the Old Strand Road from the wine museum are a group of buildings; humble in origin, these labourers' cottages were designed by that illustrious architect, Sir Herbert Baker. They have been preserved to excellent advantage. Here today is De Volkskombuis aan de Wagenweg (the people's kitchen of the wagon road to Cape Town) which was in 1977 voted the South African Restaurant of the Year. Other cottages have become the Oude Meester Brandy Museum with more than a thousand valuable exhibits in distillation, maturation and blending of brandy.

The Braak

Bounded by Bird, Market and Alexander Streets, is this village common, a unique historical asset of Stellenbosch, named the Braak in Dutch East India times. (Braak being short for 'braakland' meaning 'fallow land'). Itself a proclaimed national monument, it is surrounded on three sides by no less than a dozen other monuments, and over the centuries of its history it has withstood numerous attempts to spoil its 'open space' character. From the beginning, during the Dutch occupation of the Cape, it was used for the parading of the local burgher militia, and for festivities such as the celebration of Governor Simon van der Stel's birthday on 14 October. From the start of the British occupation the Braak was put to different use when cricket, rugby and athletic games were all held here.

The militia drew their arms and ammunition from the Kruithuis (Arsenal) which overlooks the Braak on the western side. This is a quaint little double-storey building with walls 66 centimetres wide and the monogram of the Dutch East India Company, 'V.O.C.', engraved on one of the gables. The building dates from 1777 and the pedimented bell-tower and surrounding wall were added later. Today the Kruithuis houses a small military museum.

The only building on the Braak itself is the charming little thatched Anglican Church, St Mary's-on-the-Braak; built in 1852 in a mixture of Dutch and English styles, it has beautiful stained glass windows. The other buildings are around the village green.

Opposite the Anglican Church, on the western side, is the Burgher House, built in 1797 and expertly restored by the Town Council. It has been furnished in period style and is maintained by the Rembrandt Tobacco Company who use certain rooms as offices. This H-plan house has a perfectly proportioned front gable and is the only surviving part of what was once a complex of Cape Dutch houses of superb beauty.

Across Alexander Street on the northern side of the Braak is the Coachman's Cottage (1790) with its charming 'leg of mutton' dormer gable. Neighbouring the Coachman's Cottage is the Georgian town house, Laetitia (circa 1820), the building of the Divisional Council (1935), and the Drostdy Inn (no longer occupied as an inn). The façades of the Divisional Council and Drostdy Inn have been declared national monuments to ensure against the encroachment of modern style architecture around the Braak.

At the southern end of the Braak, at the commencement of Market Street, is the Rhenish Mission Church; consecrated in 1823, it has a unique pulpit made by master-carpenter, Londt (a pupil of Anreith), and presented to the mission by the Dutch Reformed Moederkerk, Drostdy Street, in 1863.

Around the corner from the Rhenish Church is the P.J. Olivier Children's Art Centre. Previously the Rhenish Institute, it was originally built as a private dwelling in 1785 and brought into use as a girls school and hostel in 1862, making it the first girls boarding school in South Africa. The upper storey to the Rhenish Institute was added in 1872. Next to the Art Centre is the Rhenish primary school, built in 1905 to supplement accommodation for the Institute.

The Rhenish Complex

Behind the Rhenish Institute and the Rhenish primary school, approached from Market Street, is a magnificent cluster of houses set in a spacious area of lawns and old oaks behind a white ring-wall. Here is the H-shaped old Rhenish Parsonage with its beautiful classicist western gable and Leipoldt House with its east facing gable. The buildings of this complex were there before the arrival in Stellenbosch of the remarkably fine men and women of the Rhenish mission, and date from circa 1817. This is the most extensively restored complex in South Africa and was undertaken by the Cape Provincial Administration.

Market Street and Herte Street

Constructed on a curve, Market Street connects Dorp Street with the Braak and has some historical houses on its western side. Of particular interest is Van der

Bijl House on Van der Riet Square. Standing behind four splendid oaks, it has been well restored and is the administrative headquarters of the Stellenbosch Museum.

Herte Street runs from Dorp Street northwards to the top of the curve in Market Street. On the western side of its northern end is a row of 19th century semi-detached houses and a slave lodge (Slavenhuis 1841).

Plein Street

East of the Braak, it is a pleasant walk up Plein Street, which is the principal business thoroughfare of Stellenbosch. On the lefthand side is the handsome Town Hall, completed in 1941; its design is of traditional Cape Dutch style, with its marble and woodwork frieze by Mitford-Barberton commemorating the arrival of the French Huguenots. On the same side as the Town Hall, at number 30 Plein Street, is the Visitors Information Bureau.

In Plein Street, approximately opposite the Town Hall, there is preserved a beautiful gateway, an excellent example of the plaster style of circa 1780, and all that remains of the Baroque splendour that once characterized parts of Stellenbosch. This narrow little gateway was the entrance to the churchyard of the first church in the village, which was gutted by fire.

Proceeding in an easterly direction, Van Riebeeck Street is a continuation of Plein Street and passes the Stellenbosch University Botanical Garden; notable for its indigenous succulents, insectivora and orchids.

Lanzerac and Old Nectar

Beyond the Botanical Garden, Van Riebeeck Street runs into Jonkershoek Road and one of the most spectacular drives in the Western Cape. The area was named after Jan de Jonker an early settler. Approximately three kilometres out of the town at the corner of Neethling Street there is a turnoff to the right which leads to the historic wine farm Lanzerac. Built in 1830 the stately old Cape Dutch homestead and its group of ancillary farm buildings have been expertly converted by David Rawdon into the now famed Lanzerac Hotel. The route to Lanzerac is clearly indicated by road signs at regular intervals marked: HOTEL →

Continuing on the way to Jonkershoek, the road winds up the valley passing beautiful farms; one of these is the historic Nectar, on the lefthand side of the road. Built in 1780, Nectar, like Lanzerac, is a national monument. It is surrounded by one of the most beautiful rose gardens in the Country and is the home of General and Una van der Spuy.

Jonkershoek

Ten kilometres from Stellenbosch, at the foot of the 1494-metre Twin Peaks, the road enters the Jonkershoek Nature Reserve. Within the reserve are the famous hatcheries of the Department of Inland Fisheries. Although previously engaged in the breeding of exotic trout and bass these hatcheries now concentrate on the recovery of our indigenous species, such as yellow-fish, with a view to the protection of the ecology. The forestry reserve covers some 5 000 hectares of magnificent mountain scenery,

and climbers and hikers are admitted during the non-hazardous autumn and winter seasons upon application at the Forestry Office. Many rare varieties of protea are to be seen in the adjoining Assegaaibos Reserve for indigenous fauna and flora.

Stellenbosch Wine Route

The lover of good table wine is provided with the wonderful opportunity of touring a region where wine-making has a history of 300 years in the surroundings of most beautiful countryside studded with lovely old homesteads – an integral part of the cultural heritage of the Cape.

On the route there are three giant producers (Stellenbosch Farmers' Winery, Distillers Corporation and Gilbeys), five co-operative wineries and twelve estate wine cellars all within 12 kilometres of Stellenbosch. The promoters, Stellenbosch Wine Route Co-op, publish an illustrated guide to some of the cellars and restaurants on the enchanting route. The Wine Route office is at Doornbosch, Strand Road (R44), telephone 4310. Here at Doornbosch, KWV maintains a restaurant, taphouse and cellar.

Stellenbosch Farmers' Winery (SFW)

South Africa's largest wine and spirit producer-merchant, Stellenbosch Farmers' Winery, has an annual turnover in excess of R850-million accounting for a major contribution to the wine and spirit market of southern Africa, and is one of the biggest operations of its kind in the world. In assessing the strength of SFW in the industry it should be remembered that it has been longer in the field than any of its competitors (more than 60 years), and has resolutely continued the production and marketing principles of its founders: 'Good, healthy, honest products with strong trademarks sold at the most reasonable price'. A remarkable feature of SFW has been its retention of a proud independent corporate image despite its financial control having passed to SA Breweries in 1960 and in 1979 to Cape Wine and Distillers (jointly owned by SAB, KWV, Rembrandt and the wine farmers). Other important factors in the build up of its greatness have been: in 1950 the incorporation of the wine firm of V.H. Matherson, in 1966 the absorbing of the family concern of Monis Wineries of Paarl which brought the magnificent Nederburg Estate into the group, and in 1970 the acquisition of a former arch rival Sedgwick Tayler with its top selling cane spirit, Mainstay. Since 1980 SFW has been a major exporter in South African wines and spirits.

A true adventurer started Stellenbosch Farmers' Winery. William Charles Winshaw was born in Kentucky, USA, in 1871. At the age of twelve he ran away from home and, in the company of an old hobo, he made his way down the Tennessee River in a canoe. Later he came to know the legendary 'Buffalo Bill' (Colonel William Frederic Cody), and in 1893 he was fighting as a Texas ranger in the Yaqui War on the Mexican border. In his mid twenties Winshaw entered Tulane University, New Orleans, to study medicine. After qualifying he set up a practice in New Mexico, and it was here that Dr Winshaw met Lieutenant McGuiness who was buying mules for use by the British in the Anglo-Boer War. The ever restless

1. Looking across the wine farms at the Helderberg from Devon Valley.

2. The vineyards stretch right up to the Simonsberg.

3. The 'Ou Hoofgebou', University of Stellenbosch, completed in 1886.

1

2

1. A beautiful rainbow adds to the already magnificent spectacle of Boschendal manor house backed by the towering mass of the Groot Drakenstein range.

2. Boschendal luncheon restaurant, one of the finest in all the Cape, renowned for classic cuisine and famous Boschendal wines.

Winshaw persuaded McGuiness to give him the job of delivering some 4 000 mules to the army at the Cape, and sailed with this cargo on board the *Laringa*. The animals duly delivered, Winshaw joined the British forces and saw action at Modder River and elsewhere.

After the war Dr Winshaw practised his profession for some time in Cape Town, and then in 1905 he rented from a dentist friend a small farm in the Stellenbosch district for £6 a month. Here he started his wine making and was soon supplying a 'processed hermitage'. In 1909 he opened the Stellenbosch Grape Juice Works and by 1919 Winshaw was a highly respected wine producer. However, excessive over-buying from the farmers caused the collapse of his operation in 1921. Undaunted, in 1923 he joined G.J. Krige who operated a distillery and wine business from Oude Libertas, the northern section of the farm Libertas. Completely rehabilitated by March 1924 and backed by his friend Oubaas Markötter (the attorney and famous Stellenbosch rugby player) Winshaw purchased Oude Libertas from Krige for the sum of £5 500. Then, with the full blessing of his many farmer friends, he established Stellenbosch Farmers' Winery with a capital of £10 000. His two sons Jack and Bill (who later became the chief executive) were brought into the business and Dr Winshaw remained at the helm of SFW until 1962 when at the age of 92 he retired. He died shortly after his 96th birthday.

The farm Libertas has a colourful history. It was granted by Simon van der Stel in 1689 to Jan Cornelius van Ouderlingenland who transferred it to Hans Jurgen Grimpe in 1690. Grimpe died a year later and his widow married Adam Tas, who by the law of the time, acquired the farm. Adam Tas is remembered in history for his confrontation with Governor W.A. van der Stel and his subsequent imprisonment, and although it is purely coincidental that his name was part of the farm name, legend has it that Tas named the farm Libertas (liberty) as a pun on his own name upon being set free from prison. There are other good reasons why the name Tas will long be remembered: the cellar he built in 1706, named Adam Tas Cellar, remains in use at Stellenbosch Farmers' Winery, and some of their finest wines include the name Tas, these being Tasheimer, Tassenberg, Oom Tas. With many changes of ownership after Adam Tas, the farm Libertas altered considerably in size and shape until 1869 when G.J. Krige purchased Oude Libertas, the section north of the Eerste River, which he sold in 1924 to Dr Winshaw and where Stellenbosch Farmers' Winery has its headquarters and major wine cellars today. This is one kilometre out from Stellenbosch on Adam Tas Road (R310 to Cape Town). The southern section of the farm (which is today called Libertas) with its old homestead across the Eerste River, is approached from Strand Road (R44) and has for many years been in the ownership of Robbie Blake, affectionatley known as the stawberry king.

Across the Adam Tas Road (R310) from the SFW main entrance gate is the SFW Centre, situated below the Papegaaiberg, it comprises the restored Cape Dutch homestead Mon Repos, a restaurant connected to a cellar containing thousands of bottles of red wine laid down for maturing, a training centre, visitors' reception, and the Oude Libertas

Amphitheatre. Visitors to SFW are taken, by appointment, through the cellars at 10.30 am and 2.30 pm Monday to Thursday and at 10.30 am on Fridays. Telephone 73-400 (02231). The amphitheatre was opened in 1977 and is a fine asset for the performing arts. The three-month season is during the summer from the end of November to mid-March, when ballet, Spanish dancing, symphony and theatre are performed. Six Sunday afternoon concerts of light classics and jazz are very popular – so much so that when filled to capacity (432 persons) the overflow surrounds the theatre in the open lawns, a colourful sight with picnics under umbrellas. At one Gerry Bosman show there were 2 500 present.

The Papegaaiberg and Devon Valley

The Berg Kelder of Distillers Corporation is on the slopes of the Papegaaiberg. The hill received its name in the early days when the militia practised shooting there, using a wooden parrot (papegaai) as a target. From the Papegaaiberg there are fine views of Stellenbosch, Somerset West, Strand and the sea.

The eight-kilometre drive up Devon Valley, to the west of Stellenbosch, leads to the charming Devon Valley Hotel, amongst the vineyards and adjacent to Bertrams Estate (a part of the Gilbey organization). Close by is the 25-hectare nature reserve, Protea Heights, with its priceless collection of proteas, ericas and the rare painted lady (*Gladiolus blandus* and *Gladiolus devilis*). The reserve overlooks the town.

Ida's Valley, Helshoogte Pass and Pniel

In following the route of the Four Passes Drive from the entrance to Devon Valley, it is necessary to proceed to the northern exit of Stellenbosch along Banhoek Road which leads into Helshoogte Road and winds past the built-up township of Ida's Valley. From here there is a deviation worthwhile taking; it is the turnoff left that leads for four kilometres into the rural Ida's Valley, environmentally and historically interesting, where a dozen or more farms with their Cape Dutch homesteads were proclaimed national monuments in 1976. At one of these monuments, Schoengezicht, Cape Prime Minister John X. Merriman farmed, and at High Rustenburg is the well-known health hydro.

Leaving Ida's Valley township, the main road leads into the pass known as Helshoogte (precipitous heights) in rugged mountain scenery. Eight kilometres from Stellenbosh the summit (366 metres) and a superb viewsite are reached. The bulk of the Simonsberg is close-in on the left, the sharply pointed Botmaskop seemingly touchable to the right, and beyond it the grand massif of the Groot Drakenstein and Franschhoek ranges. Surrounded by mountains directly ahead, is the glorious Drakenstein Valley with the flat-topped Wemmershoek Tafelberg at the far end. In the days of wild animals in the vicinity of the pass summit the area became known as Banhoek, a corruption of 'Banghoek', meaning fearful corner. Here the Banghoek Kombuis is a stop known for its delicious teas and luncheons. Less than 2 km on the northern descent, is the turnoff right to the fine old farmstead Zeven Rivieren and other farms beautified by orchards and vineyards.

Further down the northern descent the road divides the picturesque Coloured people settlement, named by the German missionaries, Pniel (the face of God) and established by them in 1843. Today the Dutch Reformed Church and attendant church bell can be seen on the left of the road; the Simonsberg forming a dramatic backdrop. Most of the population of Pniel, some 1 500 people, work on the farms of the Drakenstein Valley.

Drakenstein Valley

This part of the immense Berg River valley was named Drakenstein (dragon rock) by Simon van der Stel when he explored the area in 1687. The name he applied was that of the great estates of the Lords of Mydrecht in Holland, and here in that year he settled 23 free burghers and their families. A year later these pioneers were joined by 176 French Huguenot refugees who brought their skills in viticulture and wine-making. This was the start of the romantic story of this fertile valley, where on a single estate, wines of notable difference in flavour and bouquet are grown, and where many of the lovely old farmsteads have been restored and remain in perfect condition.

A number of the historic farms of the famous valley are the property of Anglo American Farms Limited, and these include Bethleham, Languedoc, Rhône and Boschendal; the ownership having been directly descended from that remarkable enterprise, Rhodes Fruit Farms, created by Cecil Rhodes at the end of the 19th century and managed by the man who became known as the father of the South African deciduous fruit industry, Harry Pickstone. From Pickstone's labours as a dedicated nurseryman, magnificent orchards of peaches, pears, plums and apricots were cultivated. Today from the 21 farms, 10 000 tons of fruit and grapes are produced each year and 60 per cent of the crop is exported. In addition over 25 000 tons of canned fruit and juice concentrate are processed annually.

Proceeding from Pniel and before reaching Groot Drakenstein station, on the right of the road are the two farms, Boschendal and Rhône.

Boschendal

Of the distinguished historical farmsteads of the Drakenstein Valley, Boschendal certainly has the prime setting – the whitewashed walls and gables of the traditional H-shaped Cape Dutch manor house, strikingly simple in architecture, are perfectly set off by the dark towering irregular mass of the Groot Drakenstein mountains – the whole scene (invariably complemented by the lush green of the surrounding vineyards) prompting the viewer with the irresistible urge for further exploration. And no one passing Boschendal need be denied the opportunity to satisfy that urge – the rewards are manifold. Within the limits of this fine estate there is much to see and enjoy, and visitors are made very welcome.

The manor house is open to the public between 11 am and 4 pm Monday to Sunday, and groups wishing to arrange to be guided through the house should dial 02211-41031. The visitor will marvel at the magnificent main gable, the accurate restoration of the interior, the acorn adorned friezes, the yellowwood floors and ceilings, the authentic period furniture, and the priceless Ceramic (including the world famous Kraak porcelain collection). Across the yard from the manor house, one of the Cape's most sought after restaurants, is housed in the cellar. Here in an atmosphere of exquisite decor buffet luncheons are served daily, and on the lawns in the shade of stone pines packed French picnic baskets (le piquenique) can be enjoyed in season. The high popularity of the place makes reservation essential. Dial 02211-41252. In the shop near the restaurant there is a fascinating variety of souvenir gifts.

Wine sales are conducted from the Taphuis. The cellar for wines sold under the Boschendal label is in fact on the adjoining historical farm La Rhône, and here in the Taphuis these famous estate wines (red, white and sparkling) can be tasted, and purchased. Taphuis wine sales are Monday to Friday 8.30 am to 5 pm, and Saturday 8.30 am to 12.30 pm. Vineyard tours, with audio visual presentation, are conducted Monday to Friday at 11.00 am and in season again at 3 pm. Group tours are arranged only in advance. Dial 02211-41031.

Boschendal means 'wooded vale' and was originally spelt Bossendaal, which was the name given by the first owner, the Huguenot, Jean Le Long, who farmed here from 1685. For 164 years from 1715 to 1880 members of the great South African family, bearing the name De Vlliers, were the owners of Boschendal. The manor house was built in 1812, during the occupancy of the farm by Paul de Villiers. Restoration of the manor house and ancillary buildings was completed in 1976 and on 5 November of that year Boschendal was declared a national monument.

Groot Drakenstein and Simondium

Anglo American Farms Limited offices are at Groot Drakenstein station, and a short distance north of Groot Drakenstein station is the village of Simondium, named after the first pastor and leader of the Huguenots, Pierre Simond. There is an hotel in the village and in the vicinity is the old farm Bien Donné, now an experimental grape farm of the Fruit and Food Technology Institute.

North of Simondium are a number of nurseries specialising in roses and not far from the national road to Paarl on the banks of the Berg River is Campers' Paradise, a caravan park and resort of high repute.

Backsberg

A kilometre from Simondium on the road to Paarl there is a turnoff left to Klapmuts and 3 km from the turnoff is the entrance gate to Backsberg wine estate, one of the finest vineyards of the Paarl Valley. Named after Charles Back who purchased the farm in 1916, Backsberg wines are sought after to the extent that most of its production is sold direct from the cellar to the public. The guided tours include a closed circuit television illustration on wine making. Open Monday to Friday 8 am to 6 pm and Saturday 8 am to 1 pm.

1
2

1. The Huguenot Memorial lies at the foot of the Franschhoek mountains in a lovely formal garden. 2. One of many spectacular views of the Franschhoek valley seen from Franschhoek Pass.

The lovely holiday hotel, Swiss Farm Excelsior, in its strikingly handsome Franschhoek mountain setting. Completely refurbished in 1987, it is also a firmly established convention centre.

Bellingham and Wemmershoek Dam

Returning to the junction of roads at Groot Drakenstein station to continue with the Four Passes Drive, the turn east is taken into the Franschhoek road which is flanked with vineyards and orchards stretching up to the mountains.

Three kilometres beyond the Dwars River bridge is the entrance to Bellingham, one of South Africa's largest wine-producing farms, renowned for its excellent range of estate wines. A little further on is Waterval caravan park and camping ground on the bank of the Berg River.

After crossing the Berg River, the road reaches a junction. The left turn sweeps around the Klein Drakenstein mountain on its way to Paarl. Along this road is a turnoff to Wemmershoek Dam which supplies Cape Town and many other towns of the Western Cape. It is 52 metres deep in places and the view across this 300-hectare stretch of water is particularly beautiful in the winter when the surrounding mountain peaks are under snow. Permits to visit the dam are obtainable from the municipal offices of Cape Town, Stellenbosch, Paarl, Strand, Bellville, Hermanus, Franschhoek and Wellington. There are picnic places at the dam and there is good trout fishing to be had. Near the dam is the popular holiday resort, De Hollandsche Molen, with its camping and caravan park, bungalows and restaurant.

La Motte Forestry Station and the source of the Berg River

Continuing on the road to Franschhoek, on the right-hand side of the road at La Motte is the forestry station. Above this where the Jonkershoek, Groot Drakenstein and Franschhoek mountains meet, is the source of the Berg River with its numerous mountain-stream tributaries and an area of nature reserve and extensive afforestation. Permits must be obtained from the forestry station to enter this rugged wilderness which abuts the Jonkershoek Reserve.

Just before reaching Franschhoek town, the road passes the entrance, on the left, to the historic La Provence farm.

Franschhoek

The Franschhoek mountains close the end of the Drakenstein Valley and below the range is the little town of Franschhoek, first settled by the French Huguenots in 1688. Its population numbers 1 600 inhabitants and it became a municipality in 1881. In the town is the popular Huguenot Hotel and on the opposite side of the main road, the Dutch Reformed Church is a national monument. There is a municipal caravan park and the Franschhoek Wine Cellars Co-operative is here.

Huguenot Memorial and Museum

At the head of Franschhoek's main road and the foot of the Franschhoek Pass is the impressive Huguenot Memorial. Set in its own formal garden with a splendid mountain backdrop, it was started in 1938 to mark the 250th anniversary of the arrival of the Huguenots. The work is of Paarl granite and was designed by J.C. Jongens. The centre figure of a woman symbolising freedom from religious oppression was sculptured by Coert Steynberg. She holds a Bible and a broken chain. At her feet is the globe of the spiritual realm; the pool of water below her represents spiritual tranquillity and the three tall arches behind her stand for the Trinity.

In the extensive grounds of the memorial is the Huguenot Museum; opened in 1967, its exhibits are housed in replica buildings of the stately home Saasveld, built on the outskirts of Cape Town in 1791 by architect Louis Michel Thibault for Baron van Rheede van Oudtshoorn. The old homestead and its ancillary buildings were demolished in the 1950s. Primarily concerned with research, the Huguenot Museum covers the history and genealogy of the Huguenot families. Interesting early documents and very fine 18th-century Cape furniture are among the many relics.

Swiss Farm Excelsior

Before it actually reaches the Huguenot Memorial, the main road divides. The right-hand turn leads to the southern cul-de-sac of the valley and the lovely holiday hotel, Swiss Farm Excelsior, in its strikingly handsome mountain setting. In the vicinity are the famous farms, La Dauphiné, Burgundy, Champagne and Robertsvlei.

Franschhoek Pass

The left-hand turn at the memorial is the main road out of the town and almost immediately, it commences to climb the Franschhoek Pass. The pass was first called Oliphantspad, when early travellers used the way over the mountain beaten out by elephants and other herds of wild animals. A new pass was built in 1930 and improvements were made in 1965. From both the engineering and scenic aspects this is one of the finest mountain roads in South Africa. At the 750-metre summit, the western view over the valley is superb. In the pass Petite Femme Restaurant serves delightful teas and luncheons. On the eastern side of the pass the road twists and turns in its difficult 8-kilometre descent in the region of the Riviersonderend headwaters.

The road reaches a junction in the Sonderend Valley, ten kilometres from the bottom of the pass. The turn to the left leads to Villiersdorp and on to Worcester; the right turn crosses the Riviersonderend on the Four Passes journey.

Villiersdorp

The short deviation to Villiersdorp is worthwhile. The small town was named after Field Cornet P.H. de Villiers who was responsible for its establishment in 1843. It is the centre for the processing and marketing of the fruit, grapes, grain and onions of the district and lies in the picturesque Elands Valley, sheltered by the surrounding mountains; Aasvoël-berg, 1 644 metres to the west and Olifantsberg, 1 603 metres to the east, are the highest peaks.

The foundation stone of the De Villiers Graaff High School (named after its benefactor, Sir David de Villiers Graaff) was laid in 1907 by 'Onze Jan' Hofmeyr. The town has an hotel.

Viljoen's Pass

Returning to the Four Passes Drive, having crossed the Riviersonderend, the road divides again. The left turn leads to Caledon; the right-hand branch follows a course close to the Franschhoek mountains with orchards on either side of the road. In front lies the commencement of Viljoen's Pass. This is a short, scenic pass notable for the forest reserve at the summit and the deep gorge of the Palmiet River, a dramatic picture as it makes its way southwards to enter the sea near Kleinmond. In the pass is the Eikenhof Dam which supplies irrigation water to over 100 surrounding farms.

Elgin and Grabouw

From the summit of Viljoen's Pass the descent is gradual, through beautiful farmlands down to Elgin, a household name for apples and one of the most important transportation centres in South Africa. From here during the apple-picking season (January to May) the packhouses, employing the ultra modern electronic methods (grading by size and colour) grade and pack millions of apples which after being pre-cooled are transported to Table Bay Harbour. Forty per cent of the country's apples come from Elgin.

Across the Palmiet River is Grabouw, the commercial centre of the district, where in addition to apples, pears, peaches and timber are produced. The town was named after the birthplace in Germany of its first settler, W. Langschmidt, who is reputed to have arrived in 1856 with 23 children. Municipal status was attained in 1956 and the population is 4 000. This is where Appletiser Pure Fruit Juices are produced. There is an hotel in the main thoroughfare.

At the crossroads of Settlers Way (N2), Grabouw-Elgin and Highlands forestry station is the well-known farm stall of Peregrine (67 km from Cape Town). Delicious fruit juice, fresh produce and farm made products are offered for sale.

Grabouw is not far from the last of the Four Passes.

Sir Lowry's Pass

The original Sir Lowry's Pass was constructed at a cost of £3 000 after lengthy argument between the intrepid Governor at the Cape, Sir Lowry Cole, and the British Government (who could not understand the need) and was opened in 1838. Prior to 1838, traders and other travellers crossed the magnificent Hottentots Holland range, to and from what was known as the Overberg (the country on the other side of the mountain) at considerable risk of damaging or losing their wagons by following the course beaten by migrating herds of wild animals.

Approaching the summit of Sir Lowry's Pass from the east, as we do in our Four Passes Drive, the climb is not steep. The mountain here is notable for its weird rock formation in shapes of fantasy. In the forests on the plateau ferns are in abundance. On the roadside and in the open veld daisies, ericas and everlastings flourish.

There is a turnoff to the left to the Steenbras Dam and a short two kilometres further on is the viewsite of the summit. From an elevation of 452 metres the spacious panorama embraces the whole sweep of False Bay from Cape Hangklip to Cape of Good Hope – one of the most dramatic of the view points at the Cape.

The route down the western side of Sir Lowry's Pass is another example of remarkable engineering.

The road is wide and beautifully graded in its steep descent, yielding spectacular views on the entire journey to the valley below. And here on the mountainside nature has provided an unspoilt wilderness with ericas and proteas of several varieties. The view of the Hottentots-Holland from the bottom of the pass is worth stopping for. It is said that the Hottentots so praised the grazing lands at the foothills of the mountains that the early pioneers jocularly called the area the Hottentots' Holland.

Ahead lies Somerset West and the splendid freeway back to Cape Town. This ends the Four Passes Drive.

The Berg, Breede and Hex River Valleys and neighbouring areas

As the name implies, the Berg River is surrounded by mountains. From its source, high up in the Franschhoek Mountains, it flows north and then north-west on its 210-kilometre course to reach the Atlantic Ocean at the fishing port of Velddrif-Laaiplek. Where it passes the towns of Paarl and Wellington it forms a broad, fertile valley, one of the richest farming areas of the Cape with fine estates of orchards and vineyards.

The Breede (meaning 'wide' and sometimes referred to as the Breë River) together with its many tributaries (including the Hex River) forms the largest of the three principal wine and fruit producing valleys of the Western Cape. It has as its source the beautiful Ceres Basin, enclosed by the ranges of Skurweberg and Witzenberg, where such headwater streams as the Koekedou, Dwars, Skaap and Witels finally join up to burst through Michell's Pass and become the Breede River. In making its way south-east to reach the Indian Ocean at Port Beaufort it passes through the magnificent deciduous fruit and grape producing valley close to the towns of Worcester, Robertson, Ashton and Bonnievale.

The Hex River rises in the Kwadousberg and on its 40-kilometre journey to join with the Breede it takes a spectacular route through a mountain pass into the famous table-grape valley.

Paarl

Toward the end of van Riebeeck's time at the Cape, in 1657, the Secretary of the Council of Policy, Abraham Gabbema, led an expedition into the interior in search of meat, when he came upon the Berg River Valley. It is said that when Gabbema saw the glittering granite domes that dominate the middle reaches of the valley he likened them to giant-size pearls and so named the valley 'Paarlvallei'. The original name of the valley still remains in the name of the town. Thirty years after its discovery, in 1687, Simon van der Stel granted farms in the valley to certain free burghers from Table Bay and a year later they were joined by a number of refugee French Huguenot families.

Paarl is the second largest town of the Western Cape and the largest inland town of the Cape Province. Its population is over 75 000. The town lies on the banks of the Berg River and is protected by the Paarl and Drakenstein Mountains (a beautiful sight after snow fall). Huguenot and Daljosafat, east of the Berg River, are within the Municipal boundary.

1

1. The elegant Cape Dutch manor house at Nederburg — the best known wine estate in southern Africa.
2. Maturation of wine taking place in the cool cellar at Nederburg.
3. Grapes of the cultivar Cabernet Sauvignon from which the noble red Nederburg Cabernet Sauvignon wine is produced.

2

Mountain Shadows manor house, a national monument in the shadow of the striking Klein Drakenstein, where discerning people can spend a delectable holiday in the true Cape environment.

3

Close to Paarl, on both sides of the Berg River, there are wine farms; eight estates and eleven co-operatives supporting the industry. Other important industries in the town include Rembrandt Tobacco, Berg River Textiles and All Gold Jams. There are six licenced hotels in the town and two caravan parks in the district. Visitors can participate in golf, bowls and tennis and there is fishing in the dams and rivers. Paarl has a nationally famous cycle track and is the start of the Berg River canoe marathon held annually in August. The Visitors Information Bureau is in the Civic Centre which faces Berg River Boulevard at the end of Market Street, telephone 24-842 (02211).

Much of the atmosphere of dignity and charm created by the early settlers is retained in Paarl, with its oak-lined streets and graceful buildings surrounded by orchards and vineyards. Overlooking the town from its western side, Paarl Mountain is given a distinctive appearance by the three enormous granite domes: Paarl Rock (closest to and dominating the town), Bretagne (after the French province and the highest of the three domes, 729 metres) and Gordon Rock (probably named after Colonel Robert Jacob Gordon the Cape garrison commander).

Starting at the turnoff from national road N1, Paarl's Main Street runs south to north (approximately with the Berg River) for some twelve kilometres and eventually connects with the road to Malmesbury. Many of the interesting places in the town are in this street or start from it.

Two kilometres along Main Street from the south there is a turn to the west sign-posted Jan Phillips Drive. This is a pleasant 11-kilometre gravel circuit up the mountainside to the Wild Flower Reserve and the picnic site near the mill-stream used to drive an early grain mill. The drive gives access to Paarl Rock and the higher twin domes of Bretagne (sometimes called Britannia) and Gordon's Rock, all three of which may be climbed. From the drive itself and from the summits of the Rocks there are spacious views of the vineyards, the town and the whole valley. The drive was built in 1929 and named after a wagonmaker who subscribed a large portion of the cost of its construction. His trade is a reminder that the very best of wagons and Cape carts came from Paarl and its district.

Several dams have been constructed on top of Paarl Mountain to supplement the town's water supply. The geological, botanical and zoological aspects have interested travellers and scientists from as early as 1772 when Francis Masson, on a Royal mission from England came to collect seeds and plants and reported back on the remarkable geological occurrence which resulted in Dr William Anderson and Sir William Hamilton visiting the rocks soon after. In 1836 the famous naturalist, Charles Darwin, on his journey round the world, paid a special visit to Paarl Mountain. To ensure its preservation the mountain was proclaimed a national monument in 1963.

Two kilometres north along Main Street after the mountain drive turnoff on the eastern side is La Concorde, of considerable architectural interest and head office of K.W.V. (Ko-operatiewe Wijnbouwers Vereniging or Co-operative Wine Growers Association). Founded in 1918 to bring stability to the wine industry, it is today the national co-operative of South African wine producers and one of its principal functions is the export of quality wine and brandy. The pressing cellars, distillery and winery complex occupies 15 hectares facing Kohler Street, where the cellar storing capacity is 1 400 000 hectolitres and the complex is among the largest in the world. Of approximately 30 million litres of wine and brandy exported annually, sixty per cent reaches the United Kingdom and the rest is shipped to thirty different countries. During the highly interesting guided tours which last about an hour and a half, visitors are shown the historical oak vat 'Big Bill', the Cathedral Cellar with its superbly hand-carved vats, the Criadera and Solera technique in the sherry cellar and an exhibition hall where the story of wine-making is told.

Across Main Street from K.W.V. head office is their recently acquired Laborie Estate (a national monument) with its lovely old manor-house and historic wine cellar, wine-house and restaurant.

On the same side of Main Street, a little north of K.W.V. is the beautiful Dutch Reformed Church of Suider Paarl. Known as the Strooidakkerk (thatched church) and rich in historical associations, it was completed in 1805. It is the oldest church building still in use in South Africa and is the church of the third oldest congregation in South Africa. Proclaimed a national monument, its notable features are the cruciform plan and graceful gables, the church bell, tall cypress trees and fine gabled vaults in the churchyard. In the interesting custom known as the 'etiquette of pews', young girls were required to occupy seats at the back of the church and young men took their places along the side. With the passing away of the elders, so the girls moved forward until in old age they sat in the coveted front seats beneath the pulpit. The men always remained in the side seats.

Opposite the Strooidakkerk, at 144 Main Street is the Parsonage Museum.

Once part of a farm, Vergenoegd Homestead at 188 Main Street is another of Paarl's architectural gems. Built in circa 1800, although altered over the years, the original windows and beautiful stinkwood and yellowwood doors have been retained. During the middle 1800s the property was rented by the authorities as a residency, courthouse and magisterial offices and was therefore the first Drostdy of Paarl. The lovely old oaks, cobbled yard and remarkable old well enhance the attractiveness of this fine property which in recent times was bought by Historical Homes of South Africa Limited and is administered by the Dutch Reformed Church as a home for the aged. It is a national monument.

Heading northwards, at about half the length of Main Street (six kilometres), before reaching the intersection of Lady Grey Street (the principal shopping centre) there is a cluster of interesting buildings. On the eastern side, at the intersection of Main and van der Lingen Streets, is the conspicuous landmark, the handsome Noorder Paarl Dutch Reformed Church with its 57-metre spire – the reason for the church being known as the Toring Kerk. Built in 1905 it can seat a congregation of 1 500.

Behind the Toring Kerk, on the corner of Pastorie Avenue and Loop Street, is the Oude Pastorie Museum on the site of the original parsonage of the Dutch Reformed Church of Suider Paarl. The original building constructed in 1715 was replaced by the present one in 1786. A complete restoration was carried out by the Paarl Town Council in 1939 to receive what was then named the Huguenot Museum. During restoration the front gable had to be rebuilt and is a true reproduction of the original. The side gables were replaced by concave-convex gables. A national monument, the museum contains some fine exhibits of Cape Dutch furniture and of Cape silver, copper and brassware.

On the western side of Main Street, directly opposite the Toring Kerk, is another national monument, Paarl Gymnasium. The famous school for boys formed the basis of Paarl's educational system and is inseparably associated with its ecclesiastic founder, the Reverend G.W.A. van der Lingen. The Gymnasium was opened in 1858 in the year that the stately building of neo-Egyptian architectural style was completed. Its walls are decorated with symbolic Egyptian figures such as the scarabs, symbolising Time and Eternity, which surround the clock, and the sphinxes that pour Learning into a vase. This style of architecture was the vogue in the mid-nineteenth century and the only other remaining building of its type in South Africa is that of the University of Cape Town's original campus at the top of the Avenue.

The Reverend van der Lingen, who served as minister of the Dutch Reformed Church of Suider Paarl for 38 years, opposed the school authorities of the colony at the time because of inadequate religious tuition and exclusivity of instruction in the English medium, and in his exceptional predilection for the Dutch language, appointed only Hollanders as teachers. Ultimately, and only after his premature death in 1869, his school became a base for the start of the Afrikaans language. One of the men he imported from Holland, Arnoldus Pannevis, a teacher of classical languages, became involved in the construction of this fascinating new language and he attended the founder-member meeting of an Afrikaner Society held at the home of Gideon Malherbe in August 1875. It was Pannevis who had a profound influence in shaping the character of the language movement.

To the south of the Toring Kerk, in Pastorie Avenue, is Gideon Malherbe House where Gideon Jozua Malherbe, a prominent wine farmer, lived from 1860 to 1921. He was one of eight founder-members who met here on 14th August 1875 to establish the 'Genootskap van Regte Afrikaners' (the society of true Afrikaners) which laid the foundations of the Afrikaans language and the printing of the first Afrikaans newspaper, Die Afrikaanse Patriot. The printing press used for the first newspaper is a national monument and is one of the exhibits of the Afrikaans Language Museum now housed in Gideon Malherbe House.

Paarl was the venue of a congress held in 1896 to celebrate the twentieth anniversary of the founding of the 'Genootskap van Regte Afrikaners' and discuss the further promotion of Afrikaans. The first professor of Afrikaans at the University of Stellenbosch, J.J. Smith, was a product of Paarl Gymnasium. Although attempts at Afrikaans literature began with the Reverend S.J. du Toit of Paarl (often referred to as the founder of Afrikaans) as early as 1875, it was not until after the Anglo-Boer War of 1899-1902 that national interest was aroused with the emergence of real Afrikaans literature from the great triumvirate, Jan Celliers, J.D. 'Totius' du Toit (son of Rev. S.J. du Toit) and C.L. Leipoldt. These great poets were followed by C.J. Langenhoven with his considerable and genial works. It was Langenhoven who was responsible for an epoch-making event in 1914, when as Provincial Councillor he succeeded in having Afrikaans replace Dutch as the second language for Cape schools. However it was not until 1925 that Afrikaans replaced Dutch as one of the two official languages.

Afrikaans Language Monument – Paarl

The only language monument in the world, the monument to Afrikaans, was completed in 1975 under the guidance of its architect, Jan van Wijk. Occupying a superb three-hectare site on the southern slopes of Paarl Mountain, it is constructed of Paarl granite and hammered concrete; its great mass and bold outline contribute to its being visible from considerable distance on all sides.

The architect has stated that his symbolic concept was inspired partly by the nature of the site and partly by words of the great authors, van Wyk Louw and C.J. Langenhoven. To appreciate the significant features of the monument it should be faced from the approach steps. A series of three columns close together on the left or west side symbolise the contribution to Afrikaans of the Western languages and cultures; a podium with three round shapes on the right or east side symbolise the contribution of African languages and cultures, and the Malayan language and culture is represented by the wall on the steps. In the centre, the main column, 57 metres high, represents the growth, evolution and achievement of Afrikaans. Light from the hollow main column illuminates a life-giving fountain below, which symbolises new ideas. A smaller column (to the right of the main column, also drawing sustenance from the fountain) symbolises a free Republic of South Africa, having two languages and cultures but being one nation, deeply conscious of the presence of an omniscient being to guide its destiny.

The Language Monument is accessible by turning off national road N1 and taking the specially constructed tarred approach drive, or via the Jan Phillips Drive in Paarl.

Nederburg

Of all the wine estates of the Western Cape Nederburg holds pride of place as the most prestigious.

In 1792 when the German immigrant, Philip Wolvaart, was granted some 700 hectares on the eastern side of the Berg River Valley at the foothills of the Klein Drakenstein mountains he named the farm after the chief advocate of the Dutch East India Company, Sebastian Cornelis Nederburgh. By 1800

Wolvaart had completed building the H-plan homestead with its elaborate gables, thick walls and wide stoep. Today this remains one of our most beautifully preserved homesteads, a fine example of traditional Cape Dutch style architecture.

The story of Nederburg as a highly successful wine producing estate only began in 1937 when another German immigrant, Johann Georg Graue, purchased the farm. A dedicated pioneer, his painstaking efforts started with developing stock and strengthening cultivars; he then went on to perfect a method of cold fermentation, to become the first winemaker in South Africa to assimilate the delicacy and fruitiness of the wines of the Rhine. The cornerstone of Nederburg tradition started with Graue who had the philosophy: 'Good wine starts in the vineyard – not in the cellar'.

Graue was succeeded in 1956 by a compatriot, the brilliant cellarmaster, Günter Brözel, who, whilst carrying on a tradition, created a legend of his own, and under his management Nederburg has become the best-known wine estate in southern Africa. Nederburg wines consistently receive Superior rating from the South African Wine and Spirit Board, and at home and abroad have won over 900 gold medals and awards. In 1979 Nederburg Edelkeur won the double gold at the Club Oenologique, the highest tribute any wine can receive.

In keeping with its tradition Nederburg is constantly improving its range and variety in wines, and important farms such as Groenhof, Plaisir de Merle and Lanquedoc have been acquired and developed in addition to the establishment of a research nursery at Ernita where selection, grafting and the techniques of viticulture are explored.

1975 saw the introduction of a new tradition in South African wine industry when the first Nederburg Wine Auction took place. Now an annual event conducted by the international auctioneers, Sotheby's, it is attended by connoisseurs and wine buyers from all over the world, and has become the most important single event of the South African wine calendar. Rare and special wines of Nederburg and other top producers are offered; the public may watch but bidding is confined to the trade. The Johann Graue Centre (comprising the hall and ancillary buildings) was completed in 1979 to cater for these auctions and other functions.

Nederburg is open to the public from Monday to Friday and offers a number of daily tours. It is essential to make an appointment, telephone 62-3104 (02211). To reach the estate from Paarl, proceed to the western end of Lady Grey Street (in so doing you cross the Berg River and the railway at Huguenot Station). Beyond the station turn left into Jan Van Riebeeck Drive (the main thoroughfare to Wellington) which leads through the industrial area of Daljosafat. Some 3 km along Jan Van Riebeeck Drive there is a turnoff right (westwards into the Klein Drakenstein mountains) which leads for 2 km to Nederburg gate.

Schoongezicht and Kleinbosch at Daljosafat

On the road to Wellington from Paarl, about three kilometres out of town and just past the right-hand turn to Nederburg, is another turnoff right that leads past Schoongezicht to Kleinbosch. These are two national monuments under the Klein Drakenstein Mountains.

Schoongezicht farm dates from 1694 when it was granted to the Huguenot, Abraham Viviers. Its present homestead, although considerably altered over the years, was built in circa 1770; the front and rear gables are neo-classic and iron has replaced the thatched roof. The Voortrekker leader Sarel Cilliers was born at Schoongezicht in 1801, and the Reverend S.J. du Toit, one of the founders of Afrikaans, lived here from 1901 to 1906.

Today Schoongezicht is a restaurant famed for traditional Cape dishes. The farm is in an area not suited to wine production but it is famous for its production of an Afrikaans delicacy, waterblommetjies, a vegetable from which a soup of distinctive flavour is made.

The particular interest in Kleinbosch farm is its historical presence. In 1692 the farm was granted to Francois du Toit, the Huguenot ancestor of the du Toit family in South Africa. Three of the founders of the 'Genootskap van Regte Afrikaners' lie buried in the farm cemetery: the Reverend S.J. du Toit, D.F. du Toit and P.J. Malherbe, and there are also the graves of Martha Retief, a sister of the Voortrekker Piet Retief, and D.P. du Toit the Afrikaans author.

Wellington

A national monument in Berg Street in the heart of Wellington places more emphasis on history than architecture. The subject is the old T-shaped house, changed in character from its original Cape Dutch glory; a galvanised roof has replaced the thatch, sash windows the multipane casements. The old house nevertheless retains the aura of the dignified era of its construction. This is the homestead, Twist Niet, and its history is important. It was built in 1811 on part of the 25-hectare farm Champagne on the Spuit River, granted to the French Huguenot, Hercule Verdeaux, in 1699. In 1713 it was transferred to another Huguenot, Etienne Crognier (Cronje), and after a number of further changes of ownership in 1768 it became the property of Daniel Retief, an uncle of Piet Retief. When the farm was divided into two in 1801, this portion was bought by Herman le Roux and in 1811 he built Twist Niet. Thirty years later in 1840 the town of Wellington was planned around this part of the farm Champagne on the wagon road to the north.

When the urban settlers asked the Governor at the Cape, Sir George Napier, for a name, he sent a curt reply, 'Call it Wellington. It is a disgrace that no town in the colony bears that name'.

Wellington's progress was stimulated first with the opening of Bain's Kloof Pass toward the end of 1853 and again when the town was connected with Cape Town by railway in 1863, the first 70 kilometres of line laid in the colony. It prospered considerably during the Kimberley diamond rush of the 1870s, particularly in the supply of wagons.

Today Wellington has a population of 23 000. It is only 12 kilometres down the Berg River from Paarl and like all Boland towns, in its own valley it takes up a position unable to escape the beauty of the surrounding mountains. Limietkop, 1 032 metres, the

1. The Afrikaans Language Monument, built on a commanding viewsite on the southern slopes of Paarl Mountain.

2. At the foot of Paarl Mountain, the Parsonage Museum is directly opposite the Strooidakkerk.

Groenberg, 941 metres and Hawekwaberg, 1 398 metres, all rise steeply from the floor of the valley which the early settlers named Limietvallei, because they regarded this the outpost, the 'limit' of colonization. In the nineteenth century, during the Kimberley diamond rush, the name changed to the appropriate Wagenmakersvallei.

The Dutch Reformed church with its tall spire was built when the town started. In the churchyard is the statue of the Reverend Dr Andrew Murray junior, moderator of the church and son of the pioneer minister of Graaff-Reinet. He went to Wellington in 1871 and served in the parish there until 1906. He died in Wellington in 1917. Through his influence the famous Huguenot Seminary (later the Huguenot University College) was founded in 1874. This first institution in South Africa for higher learning of women was based on Mount Holyoke College in the United States of America and had two American ladies from that institution as its first teachers; they were Miss Abbie Ferguson and Miss Anna Bliss. The Seminary was patronised by leading South African families and soon gained a high reputation. From 1951 the institution became Huguenot College, where students are prepared for diploma and university degrees (in co-operation with Unisa) relative to social workers and missionaries of the Dutch Reformed Church.

Wellington Teachers College, established in 1896, is the oldest teacher training institution in South Africa.

Wellington serves over 200 fruit and wine farms, many of which are of great historic interest. It is the centre of the South African dried fruit industry and has the largest piano factory in the country. Piet Retief, General Hertzog and the Reverend M.L. de Villiers who composed the South African national anthem, were born in the district.

The town has two hotels; there is a golf course and a modern caravan park adjoins the swimming pool. The Berg River is renowned for its trout fishing. Wellington is the headquarters of Boland Rugby Union.

In 1901 when Lord Kitchener took command of the British forces in the Anglo-Boer War, he introduced a series of blockhouses to protect bridges and other strategic points to counter the guerilla tactics of the republican forces. On the historic farm Versailles, just north of Wellington railway station, there is a perfectly preserved stone blockhouse (another type was built of corrugated iron) which guarded the railway bridge over the Berg River. It was the most southerly in the system of thousands of blockhouses that by 1902 encompassed the two Republics, Natal, Bechuanaland (now Botswana) and the Cape Colony. Proof of the effectiveness of the blockhouse network is that during Kitchener's command, not a single bridge was destroyed by the republican forces. The Wellington blockhouse is a national monument and may be reached from the road to Hermon. Three kilometres along the Bovlei road (which branches off the main road through Bain's Kloof) there is a national monument, the Wagenmakersvallei Church. Built in 1820, it played an important role in the history of missionary activities of the Dutch Reformed Church in South Africa. As was the custom in missionary churches, it was always referred to as the 'Gesticht' (the Institute).

Mountain Shadows

For those who would like, during a sojourn, to be part of the Cape scene, and who would truly enjoy being pampered by two lovely people in a genuine Cape Dutch manor house with all its beautiful appurtenances, Mountain Shadows could well be the place to visit.

Basie and Sandy Maartens, who own Mountain Shadows, have a magic concept of what a real holiday is all about and they have this magnificent home (in the surrounds of their vineyard and orchard beneath the striking Klein Drakenstein mountains) from which to entertain their guests.

Your holiday starts in this perfect atmosphere but if you wish your hosts will personally conduct your Cape safaris in a thrilling itinerary of wine tours, big game fishing, sea cruises and many other outdoor pursuits, planned to suit your mood.

Mountain Shadows manor house, a proclaimed national monument, was built in 1823 and has been magnificently restored and refurbished in period style. Basie Maartens is the well-known professional hunter and his wife Sandy is a gourmet well practised in the culinary arts, particularly the traditional Cape delicacies. They have a fine cellar of Cape wines. Their farm is quite close to D.F. Malan Airport and they will gladly meet your aircraft. To reach Mountain Shadows by road from Cape Town, proceed on the national road N1 towards Worcester. After bypassing Paarl and before ascending Du Toit's Kloof the N1 crosses the Berg River. A short distance beyond the crossing take the turnoff left marked 'Klein Drakenstein' and proceed 300 metres to take the turnoff right to Drakenstein Noord. Follow this road for 2 km to reach Mountain Shadows signboard on the right. See page 73.

Bain's Kloof Pass and Du Toit's Kloof Pass

Two mountain passes today connect the valleys of the Berg and Breede Rivers. The old pass of Bain's Kloof which traverses the formidable barrier where the Slanghoek Mountains join with the Limietberg, was conceived and constructed in 1853 by the famous South African road engineer, Andrew Geddes Bain (the father of Thomas Bain).

Bain's Kloof Pass follows the course of the white-stoned Witrivier (an upper tributary of the Breede) and used to carry all the traffic to the north. It was constructed in the days when the preservation of scenery caused engineers to take the longer route rather than destroy a natural feature. The 30-kilometre pass with a summit of 595 metres is spectacular and in some places precipitous. It is an area renowned among hikers and climbers for the clear mountain streams and pools for both swimming and fishing, the delightful waterfalls, the interesting rock formations, the indigenous forests and wild flowers (here the rare disa can be seen growing out of the rock face), the thrilling views of the Hex River Mountains under snow and the good camping grounds. Before exploring the area it is necessary to obtain the permission of the forester at Bainsberg

Forestry Station, which, travelling south to north, is on the tortuous descent of the pass some eight kilometres beyond Bain's Kloof Lodge. A camping and caravan site adjoins the lodge and the Forestry Department has camping facilities at the Station which is on the site of the old Toll House.

Although several previous attempts were made to build a pass over the saddle and into the gorge of the Drakenstein Mountains, it was close on a century before the second pass connecting the valleys of the Berg and Breede Rivers was constructed. This is along national road N1 between Paarl and Worcester and is the Du Toit's Kloof Pass which takes its name from the seventeenth century Huguenot, Francois du Toit, who was the first farmer in the area.

Du Toit's Kloof Pass took six years to complete and was opened in 1949. As originally constructed, in its 45-kilometre journey it climbed to an 820-metre summit and traversed a 225-metre tunnel before making its precipitous descent into the valley. The 4-kilometre-long motor road tunnel to eliminate the steep gradients and high summit started in 1976 in the construction of a pilot tunnel which was completed in February 1984. Contractors are now heavily involved in the completion of the final work.

Du Toit's Peak rising to 1 995 metres dominates the scene and is particularly beautiful when snow-capped. This is a popular area with climbers, and the rivers Krom, Elandspad and Molenaars offer opportunities for trout-fishing and swimming. Protea Park Hotel is in the pass and the Mountain Club of South Africa has built huts at strategic points.

Michell's Pass

Opened in 1848, Michell's Pass was named after Colonel Charles Michell, surveyor-general at the Cape. Its famous engineer, Andrew Geddes Bain, in constructing the fine mountain road, followed the spectacular course of the Breede River which, having gathered sufficient force from the many streams of the Ceres basin, breaks through the narrow gorge at the confluence of the Witsenberg and Hex River Mountains. Adding to the dramatic scene, the Witels River meets the main water concourse at about midway in the pass and presents anglers, climbers and lovers of the open air with easy access to an abundance of opportunity.

At the southern entrance to the pass is the 2 033-metre double peak named Mosterthoek Twins after Jan Mostert who farmed in the area during the eighteenth century.

Ceres

Everything grows well in Ceres and the town is aptly named after the Roman goddess of agriculture. It has oak-lined streets, riverside willows, fine forests, deciduous orchards and beautiful flower gardens.

The perennial Dwars River (a tributary of the Breede) runs through the town which has a year-round fine climate with snow in the winter, warm summer days and a consistent 1 000 millimetres a year rainfall. To add to the perfection of climatic conditions, it is cut off from the Cape south-easter; the Witsenberg, Skurweberg and Hex River Mountains encircle the town.

Established in 1854, Ceres received municipal status ten years later. It is the centre for the rich deciduous fruit-growing district of the Warmbokkeveld, a well-watered plateau of some four to five hundred metres above sea level. The population of 7 000 is increased by the large weekend and school holiday-period influx.

In the setting of the municipal recreational area, with a mountain-stream swimming pool in a pine forest, cottages, rondavels and sites for caravanners and campers have been provided. Other visitor accommodation includes a number of guest farm establishments and the popular two-star New Belmont Hotel.

Ceres has a modern sports ground complex with athletics track and pavilion and an attractive 9-hole golf course. The mountains around Ceres, and especially the Hex River Mountains, do on occasion provide sufficient snow slopes for ski-runs. Here on the Matroosberg, 2 251 metres high, the Cape Town Ski Club has a hut.

Prince Alfred Hamlet and Gydo Pass

The railway terminus of the Ceres basin is Prince Alfred Hamlet from where considerable quantities of peaches, pears, plums and potatoes are despatched to the markets of the Republic and abroad. Twenty kilometres beyond the hamlet, in the Skurweberge, is Gydo Pass, from the summit of which there is a rewarding view of the Hex River Mountains. This road continues northwards to Citrusdal.

Tulbagh

When you enter re-built Tulbagh it is not difficult to appreciate that it was first settled in 1699, so beautifully have the buildings and setting been restored. It remains the cherished centre of an historic fruit and wine producing district that was named 'Het land van Waveren' to honour the Waveren family in Holland with whom Governor Willem Adriaan van der Stel was connected.

In their penetration deeper into the interior and what is now the Tulbagh basin, the early pioneers came through the Roodezand Kloof (red sand kloof), where the first church was built in 1756. The town itself had its start in 1795, and when a landdrost was appointed in 1804 it was named in memory of the much loved and respected Ryk Tulbagh who had been governor at the Cape for 20 years from 1751.

Disaster in the form of an earthquake struck the north-western part of the Western Province on the evening of 29 September 1969 killing nine people and destroying a large part of Tulbagh. Soon after the catastrophe a restoration committee was formed under the auspices of the government and the whole of Church Street was restored to its original nineteenth century character. Some thirty houses and the mission church were rebuilt to form the largest complex of national monuments in South Africa.

Since the earthquake a number of historical Cape Dutch farm homesteads of Tulbagh district have been proclaimed national monuments and these include Klipfontein, Wolwefontein, Schoonderzicht, Montpellier and Schalkenbosch. And in the town itself the old Church Museum, De Wet House and the Public Library are all monuments.

1

3

2

4

1. Strand's fine stretch of beach and the gentle waters of Milk Bay are protected by the Hottentots Holland Mountains.
2. On the road to Hangklip, looking back at Gordon's Bay with the Hottentots Holland range dominating the scene.
3. One of many beautiful views in the Du Toit's Kloof Pass in the Klein Drakenstein Mountains.
4. The Dutch Reformed Moederkerk overlooks Worcester's Garden of Rememberance in the centre of town. In the background are the Hex River Mountains.

Tulbagh is encircled by mountains; the notable range is Witsenberg, where the slopes are covered in vineyards.

The town acquired municipal status in 1861 and has a population of 2 000. There are two hotels and a municipal caravan park.

Near the railway station at Tulbagh Road, on the bank of the Little Berg River, is an Anglo-Boer War blockhouse which formed part of the British defence line between Wellington and Beaufort West.

South-west of Tulbagh is Gouda, where there is an hotel.

Wolseley

At a railway junction south of Tulbagh Road and Ceres, is Wolseley, established in 1893 and named after that distinguished British soldier and administrator, Field-Marshal Sir Garnet Wolseley (1833-1913) who in the course of his illustrious career, captured Cetshwayo, became Governor of Natal, and then as Governor of the annexed Transvaal, put an end to the long-drawn-out Sekukuni War. After other important military missions including Egypt, the Sudan and Ireland, in 1895 he finally became Commander-in-chief of the British Army. He is probably best remembered by old soldiers in the expression 'its all Sir Garnet' referring to his emphasis on the meticulous order of things.

Fruit farms surround the little town of 2 000 inhabitants noted for its fruit canning and table grapes.

Goudini

In the Breede River Valley on national road N1 between Du Toit's Kloof Pass and Worcester, cross-roads are reached; the turn to the right leads to the village of Rawsonville, where there is an hotel, and the turn to the left to the thermal baths and Goudini Spa.

Worcester

Principal town of the fruit- and wine-producing Breede River Valley, Worcester was founded in 1820 and named after the Marquis of Worcester, elder brother of the governor, Lord Charles Somerset. It lies at the entrance to the Hex River Mountain Pass, 244 metres above sea level. The surrounding mountains rise to 1 600 metres above the floor of the valley, providing a background of unusual beauty.

Worcester received municipal status in 1842 and is today one of the most important industrial towns of the Cape with distilleries, canneries, woollen mills and the large Hex River Power Station. The population is 46 000.

The first landdrost, Captain Charles Trappes, receives the credit for the building of the handsome Drostdy completed in 1822 and for the layout of the town with its broad, water-furrow-edged streets and spacious public squares.

The Drostdy building now forms part of the Drostdy Technical High School and is a national monument. The yellowwood beams came from the Knysna forest and in the grounds is the burial place of Captain Trappes. The Drostdy faces the western end of High Street, the principal thoroughfare.

Church Street is quite the most attractive street of Worcester with its numerous gabled houses dating from the middle 1800s. The street is dominated by the white spire of the Dutch Reformed Church; known as the 'Moederkerk' and now a national monument, it was completed in 1832, although the spire was erected in 1927.

A pleasant feature of the town is the Garden of Remembrance which is on Church Square, another national monument. The garden was designed by Hugo Naudé, the famous landscape and portrait artist who was born in the district in 1869 and made his home in Worcester where he died in 1941. In the garden is the War Memorial, and here cairns to commemorate historical events are placed from time to time; these include: Worcester Centenary 1820-1920, the 250th anniversary of the Huguenots arrival 1688-1938, 'Ossewatrek' upon the centenary of the Great Trek 1838-1938, arrival of Jan van Riebeeck tercentenary 1652-1952, Republic Festival 1960, Worcester 150th anniversary 1820-1970 and 'Afrikaans Taalfees' held at the inauguration of the Afrikaans Language Monument on Paarl Mountain in 1975.

Hugo Naudé House at 113 Russell Street (parallel with High Street and near the corner of Adderley Street) was designed by the artist and completed in 1904. Here he lived and had his studio until his death. The house contains a collection of his work.

Among the other historical buildings in Worcester, the Divisional Council building, the Rhenish Church complex, the first gaol (near the Drostdy) and St James' Anglican Church are all national monuments.

Worcester Museum occupies a delightful complex on the corner of Church and Baring Streets. The complex comprises two thatched and gabled cottages, Beckhuis and the smaller Afrikaner Museum (both nineteenth century and national monuments) and the iron roofed Stofberghuis, known as the annexe. The exhibits include Cape furniture, domestic utensils, fire arms, the Jean Welz collection of art and the Worcester local archives. Hugo Naudé House is part of the Worcester Museum and so is the Agricultural Museum at the Show Grounds, adjacent to Kleinplasie, to the east of the town, off the Robertson main road.

Kleinplasie is part of Roodewal farm, which with Langerug farm made up the total area of Worcester as allocated in 1818 by the colony for the formation of the town. K.W.V. has restored the manor house and provided a wine house and restaurant. This is the oldest surviving homestead in Worcester municipality, where the first landdrost, Charles Trappes, lived until his Drostdy was completed in 1822.

Kleinplasie is the pivot of the Breede River Valley Wine Route which follows the river from Tulbagh to Swellendam and comprises some thirty-five co-operatives and estates producing a selection of fine table wines. Route details are available at Kleinplasie.

The Brandvlei Dam, known as Lake Marais, a few kilometres south of the town, provides a fine stretch of water for yachting and is the irrigation dam for the dry region of the valley to the south-east. The dam is notable for the hot springs in the southern corner.

Worcester's main water supply comes from Stettyn's Kloof Dam, in a magnificent scenic area between the Du Toit's and Wemmershoek Mountains, 32 kilometres to the south-west. Lake Marais is stocked with small-mouthed black bass; Stettyn's Kloof Dam, the rivers and mountain streams, are noted for trout. Angling advice should be sought from the Worcester Trout Anglers' Association.

Worcester is renowned for its schools for the deaf and the blind, founded in 1881 by the Dutch Reformed Church. The handcraft workshop of the blind in Church Street (where purchases can be made) is well worth a visit.

In the town there are two hotels and the Burger Park municipal caravan park adjoins the lovely swimming pool on the corner of Roux and De La Bat Roads, north-east of the railway station. Sporting activities are centralised at Boland Park where there is a modern stadium. Bowling greens are floodlit for night play and there is an 18-hole golf course, approached from Rainer Street at the west end of the town. University of Cape Town Ski Club has huts and lifts on the Brandwagberg and Waaihoek Peak.

Off the national road three kilometres to the north of the town, is the Karoo Garden, a national botanical garden; devoted to the cultivation of the succulent flora of the Karoo, it occupies some 115 hectares at the foothills of the Brandwagberg. Interesting at all times of the year, the garden is especially beautiful in the spring.

Hex River Valley and De Doorns
The word 'hex' is Dutch for 'witch' and legend tells of the witch that haunted the river below the massive mountain barrier that screens the fertile Western Cape from the arid Great Karoo. The Hex River finds a tortuous passage between the Kwadouw and Hex River Mountains to enter the magnificent valley where more than six million vines produce the bulk of the total export harvest of South African dessert grapes. The Hex River Valley is famous for its hanepoot and barlinka grapes and presents a particularly beautiful spectacle in the autumn and early winter when the brilliant scarlet of the barlinka vine is backed by the snow capped mountains.

The valley has been farmed since the early 1700s when it was covered in thorn bush, the browsing and grazing-place of large numbers of antelope and the hunting ground of the lion and bushman. So it is that the principal centre of the valley was named De Doorns (the thorns), and this municipality with its schools, church, railway station and hotel has a population of 4 000.

The northern end of the valley is dominated by the 2 248-metre dome of the Matroosberg, the highest peak of the range. The Hex River Mountain Pass winds its way for ten kilometres along the escarpment to the summit 964 metres above sea level. Here the road reaches the central plateau of southern Africa and enters into the arid wastes of the Great Karoo (see chapter 4).

Robertson and Silverstrand
Robertson is situated south-east of Worcester on the road to Swellendam and had its beginning in 1852 when the Reverend Dr William Robertson came from Swellendam to open the first Dutch Reformed Church. It is the centre of the irrigated region of the Breede River Valley, famous for its fruit and wine farms, notably muscatel.

The town has a population of over 8 000 and is the site of the huge pot still house of K.W.V. and of the Koo canning plant. There are three hotels.

Robertson is situated amidst spectacular scenery and is a popular starting point for climbs into the Langeberg range, especially to Dassiehoek and De Hoop, where the beautiful flora nerine can be seen in its natural habitat.

Three kilometres from the town the municipality has developed a resort at Silverstrand on the banks of the Breede River. The amenities comprise caravan and camping sites, apartments, rondavels and cottages, restaurant and a 9-hole golf course, all in the vicinity of a wide, sandy beach.

Thirteen kilometres from Robertson on the road to the village of McGregor, is the Predator Control Research farm, Vrolijkheid, where jackal-hounds, greyhounds and terriers are bred and trained to hunt jackal.

Ashton
On the road between Robertson and Swellendam is Ashton, at the foot of the Langeberg range at the point where the Cogman's Kloof Pass leads up to Montagu, ten kilometres to the north.

In 1940 the Langeberg Koöperasie Beperk commenced the erection of its giant canning and food-processing plant, which is today the largest of its kind in the southern hemisphere and well worth a visit. In addition to the district's importance in fruit and vegetable farming it is notable for its rose nurseries.

Ashton became a municipality in 1956 and has a population of 3 000. There is an hotel in the town.

Sheilam, a unique farm of more than 3 000 varieties of cactus and succulents, is near Ashton.

McGregor
The little town of McGregor, 20 kilometres south-east of Robertson, has a Scottish flavour, lying as it does in the foothills of the Langeberg. It was first called Lady Grey when it was founded in 1861 and because of the confusion with the Eastern Cape town, in 1906 it took the name of the Dutch Reformed Church minister, Andrew McGregor, one of the Scots clergy who played such an important role in the formation of the Afrikaans church. The municipal offices and Dutch Reformed Church are national monuments.

McGregor is noted for fruit, grapes and whiphandles, Nearby Boesmanskloof is a place of scenic beauty.

Cogman's Kloof
North of Ashton is the pass through Cogman's Kloof, built by Thomas Bain and opened in 1877. Although it is only six kilometres long, the scenery is most attractive; the twisted and contorted volcanic strata covered with lichen are vividly colourful after rain or heavy dew. The pass follows the course of the Cogman's Kloof River and there is a short tunnel at

the summit. Halfway through the pass, in the Keur Kloof, there are picnic sites near the reservoir that supplies Montagu's water.

Montagu and Koo
The town of Montagu, named in honour of the popular Colonial Secretary, Sir John Montagu, lies in the valley of the Langeberg range where the Boland, the Little Karoo and the south-western districts meet. The outstanding scenery, tonic climate, mineral springs and sporting facilities attract large numbers of holidaymakers especially in the winter months. The thermal radio-active springs are at the municipal Montagu Baths Hotel, 3,5 kilometres from the town.

There are many beautiful walks through the various kloofs. Bath Kloof leads from the mineral baths to the town through the picturesque Lovers Walk. An interesting nature garden, famed for its mesembryanthemums, adjoins the town and there are opportunities for visitors to play golf, tennis and bowls. There are two hotels in the town.

Montagu Museum has an interesting local history section with fine examples of locally made furniture of stinkwood, yellowwood and other indigenous timber. The museum is housed in the old Dutch Reformed Mission Church at 15 Long Street which is a national monument. There are other attractive old buildings in Long Street and numbers 13, 24 and 38 are all national monuments. Yet another national monument in Rose Street is the Dutch Reformed Church Parsonage, built in 1911 for Dr D.F. Malan when he was the local minister.

Part of the district is notable for its muscatel grape- and apricot-growing and in the famous Koo valley to the north of the town are the prosperous pear and apple farms.

Montagu was founded in 1851 and became a municipality in 1895. The population is 6 000.

Bonnievale
Halfway between Robertson and Swellendam is Bonnievale. When it was founded in 1902 it was named Vale. The name changed in 1917 and municipal status was granted in 1953. Famous for its outstanding muscatel wines, sherries and Bonnita cheese, it also produces table wines, brandy and excellent clingstone peaches and apricots, mainly for canning. Some fine race horses have been bred in the district including Excise, a July Handicap winner. The population is 2 000 and the town has an hotel.

Swellendam, at the southern end of the Breede River Valley, on national road N2, is described further on in this chapter.

National road N2 from Cape Town to Albertinia and the entrance to the Garden Route, with deviations along the coast

From Cape Town, national road N2 has been named Settlers Way and is probably the oldest route out of the city. It leads directly to the east, crossing a section of the Cape Flats where the Port Jackson wattles have tamed the shifting sands. Only in very recent times have the road engineers overcome the problem of these shifting sands and a splendid dual motorway now connects Cape Town with Somerset West.

Eighteen kilometres from Cape Town there is a major junction; the turnoff to the right leads to the Black townships of Nyanga and Guguletu; the turnoff to the left to D.F. Malan International Airport and beyond the airport is the University College of the Western Cape, for the Coloured race. On the right of national road N2, past the turnoff roads to Muizenberg and Swartklip (a fishing spot on the False Bay), is the modern building of the Southern Universities Nuclear Institute.

Faure and Meerlust
A further major junction is reached near the village of Faure (32 kilometres from Cape Town) where one road leads off to Stellenbosch and another back to Bellville. A short distance from this point, along the Stellenbosch road, is an unusual national monument, the Pigeon House on the farm Meerlust, perfectly preserved, and one of the few remaining Cape outbuildings of the eighteenth century. In those times the pigeon house was elaborately designed and formed an artistic feature among the buildings around the erf of Cape homes. As much care was devoted to the design and construction of its gables as to those of the homestead itself.

Meerlust has belonged to the Myburgh family for many generations. Its first owner Henning Huysing (the large-scale cattle farmer) received the farm from Governor Willem Adriaan van der Stel in 1701. However the Governor's generosity did not pay off; during the burgher agitation which ended in van der Stel's dismissal in 1707, Huysing was one of his chief opponents.

Macassar and the Kramat of Sheik Yussuf of Bantam
Near Macassar beach where the Eerste River finds its way into False Bay is the *Kramat* of the Muslim holy man, Sheik Yussuf of Bantam. This tomb is one of several holy places of the Muslims at the Cape and is frequented by many pilgrims. The sheik was exiled to the Cape by the Dutch in 1694 and died five years later.

From Macassar there is a spacious view of the False Bay area, stretching from the Hottentots Holland range to Table Mountain.

Firgrove
At Firgrove, situated in well-wooded grounds, is the explosives and fertilizer factory started by Cecil Rhodes in 1902. Local people continue to refer to the factory as 'De Beers' although it is now owned by African Explosives and Chemical Industries.

Somerset West
The setting of Somerset West is one of the loveliest at the Cape. It is not that the one-street business centre has any distinction; the town's attractiveness is its rural atmosphere; graceful old homes and estates in a valley protected by the Helderberg and Hottentots-Holland ranges.

Historical interest in the area dates from 1700 when the farm Vergelegen (far away) was granted to Governor Willem Adriaan van der Stel by the visiting

Commissioner Wouter Valckenier. The governor thereupon took upon himself to indulge in the greatest extravagance ever to be seen at the Cape. He set about the construction of the luxurious Cape Dutch residence and numerous ancillary buildings; enlarged his farm to 527 hectares by purchasing adjoining farms that he had only just granted to his subordinates and planted the land with grainfields, orchards and a half-million-vine vineyard.

The burghers, believing that the governor's farming activities threatened their rights, petitioned the Dutch East India Company. Van der Stel reacted by imprisoning the petition leaders but finally lost the battle and was dismissed in 1707. The directors of the Company ordered that the homestead be demolished but the order was never carried out. In the course of time it has undergone numerous alterations, and is for this reason, not a national monument. However, five enormous camphor trees which stand in front of the house are centuries old and were proclaimed in 1943.

Another fine old farm house in the area is that of Parelvallei (pearl valley), occupied by the governor's brother, Frans, who was also compelled to quit the Cape. A number of settlers had followed the Van der Stels to the district and a number of their lovely Cape Dutch homes have been preserved; perhaps the best known of these are Morgenster (morning star) and Weltevreden (contentment).

The building of the town itself started in 1820 and it was named in honour of the Governor, Lord Charles Somerset. Somerset West attained municipal status in 1903.

At the south-eastern end of the main street is the Lourens River and the historical old stone bridge, constructed in 1845. Colonial Secretary Sir John Montagu, who began the first road building programme at the Cape, made the first task that of the construction of a hard road from Cape Town across the Cape Flats and over the Hottentots-Holland Kloof (Sir Lowry's Pass), ensuring for the first time satisfactory communication between Cape Town and the interior. In this plan two bridges had to be built, one over the Eerste River and the other over the Lourens River. So it is that the Lourens River Bridge is a milestone in the history of South African communications and a proclaimed national monument.

Five kilometres beyond the Lourens Bridge is the railway marshalling yard and the village of Sir Lowry's Pass, at the foot of the famous pass.

Helderberg Nature Reserve occupies 245 hectares on the slopes of the Helderberg (clear mountain), a spur of the Hottentots-Holland. It is a sanctuary for the preservation of local indigenous flora from where, with the permission of the ranger, it is possible to reach the highest point in the spur, Helderberg Dome, a breathtaking view-site.

Somerset West is a favourite place for retired people and businessmen who commute with Cape Town, using the fast electric train which takes 50 minutes. The town is fortunate in having a very fine country club, fully licensed, with sections for golf, bowls and tennis. There are four hotels and the population is 24 000.

Strand

Across national road N2 from Somerset West and linked by an almost continuous line of houses is Strand. In False Bay, it used to be the seaside suburb of Somerset West and was first named Somerset Strand. It soon outstripped its parent and became a municipality in its own right in 1897. Strand is today a modern town with good shopping facilities, a healthy industrial sector and a population of 21 000. This number increases considerably in the summer season when the two hotels, various guest establishments and the large camping and caravan sites are filled to capacity.

The holiday attraction to Strand is the warm sea and a superb three-kilometre stretch of bathing beach in Milk Bay, said to be the safest swimming area in South Africa. The long coastline in False Bay is renowned for its fishing possibilities and Strand has a launching ramp for small boats. Added attractions are the 18-hole golf course, tennis courts and bowling greens.

Marine Drive from Gordon's Bay via Cape Hangklip to Betty's Bay and on to Hermanus (a deviation from national road N2)

Starting from Gordon's Bay is the celebrated coastal road round Cape Hangklip to Hermanus – a striking coastline where the mountains crowd in onto the edge of the ocean, a fisherman's paradise and a coast of spectacular seascape scenery where proteas and other wild flowers abound.

Gordon's Bay

This enchanting little resort, six kilometres south-east of Strand, lies in a protected cove at the base of the Hottentots-Holland Mountains.

Colonel Robert Jacob Gordon of the Dutch East India Company, a traveller of some note during his time, gave his name to the place when he explored the coastline in 1778. The village became a municipality in 1961 and the population is 1 000.

The sheltered harbour is well-constructed with two moles and provides anchorage for pleasure and fishing craft. Once the training college for merchant officers of the famed General Botha (now moved to Granger Bay), the facilities are used by the Naval Academy.

Although a little rocky, the beach shelves gently and bathing is safe at Gordon's Bay where sea temperatures average 23°C in the summer months. The municipal caravan park and an hotel front the beach.

Steenbras River Dam

From Gordon's Bay a road leads off the marine drive and ascends steeply up the mountain for four kilometres to reach the summit and the filtration plant of the Steenbras River Dam.

Beyond the filtration plant the road crosses a final ridge to reach the 380-hectare dam, one of the scenic show-pieces of the Western Cape. This reservoir of Cape Town and several other towns has been developed into a charming recreational area of wild flower gardens, forests, grassed picnic places and thatched rondavels that can be hired.

Twelve hundred hectares of pines have been

On this spectacular site overlooking Walker Bay, the Marine Hotel, Hermanus, is famed for comfort, décor, cuisine, and the touch of genius that belongs to David Rawdon.

planted and the brilliant flowering gum has also been introduced. The gardens are especially rich in varieties of the protea family and at the different seasons, red disas, nerines, watsonias and daisies make a colourful display. An attractive waterfall spectacle occurs during the wet winter months when the reservoir overflows. Permits to enter the area are obtainable at the municipal offices of Cape Town, Strand, Gordon's Bay and Grabouw.

Immediately above Steenbras River Dam is Steenbras II, a hydro-electric scheme of the Cape Town municipality.

Beyond the dam the road continues for 5 kilometres to join national road N2 at the summit of Sir Lowry's Pass.

Steenbras River Mouth, Koeëlbaai and Rooi-els River Mouth

Continuing on the marine drive from Gordon's Bay, the road has been cut into the cliffs of the Hottentots-Holland range and follows a most spectacular course of natural beauty; one minute you are motoring high above the waves of the ocean and the next you are descending to the very shores of the beach.

Fishermen say this is without doubt the finest rock angling coast of the whole of the Western Cape and they agree that it is also the most dangerous. The danger arises from the sudden surge of the water up the rocks and the deadly backwash. The Western Province Anglers Union has marked the recognised fishing spots with lifebuoys. The catches are of great variety; geelbek, yellowtail, elf, red roman, red stumpnose, mussel-cracker and steenbras are all taken with regularity and in quantity.

The road passes the Steenbras River Mouth, where there is a tearoom and a camping ground; it climbs and then descends again at Koeëlbaai with its attractive long beach where swimming is dangerous. The Koeëlberg (1 219 metres) stands back from the bay and takes its name from its shape, that of a bullet (koeël). At the southern end of the bay is the Blousteenberg, which indicates manganese in the mountain, and the remains of the old jetty where the boats used to load the ore is still to be seen.

At Rooi-els River Mouth there is a camping ground and another attractive beach, but it is inadvisable to attempt bathing.

Cape Hangklip, Pringle Bay, Silver Sands and Stony Point

After crossing the Rooi-els River the road swings inland and the stretch of countryside from here to the turnoff to Pringle Bay is famous for the abundance of wild flowers, especially protea and heath.

The road skirts the back of the 452-metre Hangklip – the landmark that gives its name to the cape at the eastern end of False Bay. The turnoff from the marine drive to Pringle Bay continues to Cape Hangklip and to the automatic lighthouse there, controlled by radio from the lighthouse at Cape Point.

The bathing is quite safe at Silver Sands and at Stony Point, made melancholy by the ruins of an old whaling station.

Betty's Bay

A beautiful feature of Betty's Bay is the Harold Porter Botanic Reserve; it stretches up the mountainside to the waterfall at Disa Kloof in an area noted for the magnificent orchid *Disa uniflora*.

Betty's Bay is a sleepy little village of holiday cottages, the haunt of nature lovers and fishermen. Furnished chalets and cottages can be rented.

Kleinmond

Two rivers reach the sea at Kleinmond (small mouth), the Bot and the Palmiet, forming lagoons, safe for bathing. The resort has a permanent population of 800 and is very popular with caravanners and campers. The hotel, holiday bungalows and three caravan and camping establishments are all packed to capacity in the summer season. The surrounding scenery is pleasant and the proteas outstandingly beautiful in the winter and spring.

In February 1988 the hotel at Kleinmond is being completely refurbished and decorated, details appear on page 395.

Onrus River

The pounding of the seas on the rocky coast gave Onrus (restless) its name. The little resort lies at the mouth of the Onrus River where the lagoon, sandy beach, natural bathing pool in the rocks and fishing are the attractions. The municipality administers large camping grounds and there are other caravan parks.

Hermanus

The picturesque town of Hermanus lies between the Kleinrivierberge and the sea and stretches for six kilometres along the north shore of Walker Bay. Celebrated for its coastal beauty, wild flowers, angling, yachting and fine beaches, Hermanus is one of the premier holiday resorts of the country. The holiday season ranges through spring and summer to autumn – approximately from September to May – and during this period the population is increased from five to fifteen thousand. The S.A.R. luxury motor coach service connects Hermanus with Cape Town via the scenic coastal route.

Rotary Way is a gravel drive which runs along the top of the mountain behind the town. From Rotary Way all of Hermanus can be seen with a sweeping view to Cape Point and to the mountain peaks of the far distant Franschhoek and Swartberg ranges.

Some sixteen kilometres of walks have been constructed in Fernkloof Nature Reserve on the slopes of the mountain. The reserve is notable for the waterfall and a display of protea and veld flowers. Here on the mountainside the Department of Nature Conservation has, for some considerable time, carried out experiments in the propagation of the rare marsh rose, *Orothamnus zeyheri,* and by using *Leucospermun cordifolium* as root stock there has been a measure of success.

Hermanus had its beginning in 1855 when the fishing village was named Hermanuspietersfontein after Hermanus Pieters, a local teacher-shepherd. The abbreviated form was adopted at the time when it became a municipality in 1894. The town has a modern shopping area, a Visitors Bureau, two caravan parks and 3 hotels including the Marine which occupies a prime site facing Walker Bay. The Marine is owned by the famous David Rawdon, and, as one would expect, it has exceptional charm and comfort, and is highly recommended. Not only is Hermanus recognised as one of the best fishing resorts in the world, there is a fine 18-hole golf course and excellent bowling greens. At Die Mond, the lagoon at the mouth of the Klein River, there is boating, skiing and swimming. Hermanus Yacht Club, at the head of the lagoon, offers harbour, slipway and storage facilities. Grotto and Voëlklip are delightful beaches on the eastern side of Hermanus where there are bathing booths and where surfboards, chairs and sun umbrellas may be hired. Along the coast there are many small coves with safe, sheltered rock pools.

From the New Harbour, boats are chartered for the deep sea tunny and marlin catches. The highlight of the fishing season is the kabeljou run from November to March. During the same season, yellowtail are caught from the jetty by trolling. In its main function the New Harbour provides anchorage for the fleet of sole trawlers and diving craft and for the visitors there is an opportunity for the excitement of witnessing the ships returning from the Agulhas Banks to off-load tons of fish and perlemoen (abalone) – the South African shellfish delicacy.

The atmospheric Old Harbour, for years the scene of tricky ship berthings, is the favourite subject of photographers and artists. It was here that the world record rod-and-line catch was made by Bill Selkirk in 1922. After a tremendous battle lasting more than five hours he landed a shark with a mass of 988 kilogrammes and a length of more than 4 metres. The Old Harbour is a national monument and a museum has been made on its slipways where there is a collection of the small fishing boats (some over a hundred years old) that reaped the rich harvest of Walker Bay.

The most southerly region of the Western Cape

South-east of Hermanus lies the coastal promontory of the most southerly region of the Western Cape, and indeed of the continent of Africa, and in the little-known resorts on this seaboard is preserved an unspoilt, flowering plant countryside and some of the most delightful scenery in southern Africa.

From Hermanus fine roads lead to this region. At the start the road (R45) follows a scenic route for 12 kilometres between Hermanus mountain and the lagoon (Kleinriviersvlei), and reaches Stanford after 24 kilometres.

Stanford

This little town lies on the junction of roads and was named after Captain Robert Stanford on whose farm it was laid out in 1856. Stanford is the centre of a farming district noted for wheat. Seventeen kilometres from the turnoff route R326 is Salmons Dam Nature Reserve with its flowering wild plants, small game species, mountain viewpoint and caravan and camping park.

Die Kelders

Here there is a 'healing cave'; the mineral spring within the cave is said to have effected many cures.

This is one of a series of caverns known as Die Kelders (the cellars) and is electrically illuminated. The others are completely submerged in water. From the cliffs above the caves there is an hotel among the assortment of bungalows, and a sweeping view of Walker Bay.

Gansbaai

Named after the wild geese in the area, Gansbaai is a quaint fishing village from where there are sweeping views of this rugged stretch of coast. A favourite amongst artists and photographers, the harbour shelters a fleet of boats that fish in Walker Bay and along the Agulhas Bank. A fish-processing factory, its smoke billowing in season, adds to colourful picture. There is an hotel in the village and caravan and camping parks at Uilenskraal and Pearly Beach.

Danger Point and the Birkenhead

It is a worthwhile 10 kilometre byway journey from Gansbaai to Danger Point. At the base of the powerful Danger Point lighthouse is the tablet commemorating the wreck of the *Birkenhead*. She struck a reef near Danger Point on 26 February 1852. The story of the heroism of the soldiers who stood in line under their officers while the women and children were helped into the boats is well known. The vessel parted almost immediately it struck, and 357 soldiers and 87 of the crew perished.

The gravel motor road ends at the lighthouse gate from where a fishermen's path leads down to the coast. Here a blow-hole is linked with the sea by an underground chasm. Jets of water, sometimes 10 metres high, are forced through the blow-hole during rough seas.

Franskraalstrand and Kleinbaai

On the peninsula south-east of Gansbaai are the two ideally situated resorts of privately-owned cottages, Franskraalstrand and Kleinbaai, which overlook Vandyks Bay.

Uilenskraal

The mouth of the Uilenskraal (owl's corral) River is reached by turning off from the main road 2 km south of Franskraalstrand. The resort at this mouth is notable for its good fishing and swimming and there is a large caravan park and camping ground. Offshore lie the two small islands Dyer and Geyser, inhabited by seals and penguins.

Pearly Beach

Some 14 kilometres south-east of Uilenskraal, in an area beautified by flowers of the veld, is Pearly Beach with its huge sand dunes. Popular with fishermen and hikers, Pearly Beach has fine facilities for camping and caravanning.

Elim

On the road from Gansbaai to Bredasdorp is the Moravian mission station, Elim, with its charming atmosphere from the past, where sheep graze at the doorsteps of thatch-roofed white-washed cottages. The farmhouse, built in 1796, the church with its old clock and the watermill are fascinating features. Probably the last of its kind in South Africa, the watermill was erected in 1828 and was in use until 1972. In 1974 the millhouse was converted into a museum – the key is kept at the church.

Bredasdorp

On the right-hand side of the main road as you enter Bredasdorp from the north are two unusual national monuments.

The second building, with the thatch roof, is the older of the two. This is where the rector of the Anglican Church lived after the town was laid out on the farm Langefontein in 1838. It was originally the homestead of the old farm and although built on the traditional U-plan there are signs that its builders were not artisans – the 50 centimetre mud-brick walls are irregular and opposite walls are not parallel. Other interesting features are the skew lintels and roof beams taken from the wrecks along the coast. The building is still known as the Rectory.

Next to the Rectory is the dignified old slate roofed neo-Gothic style Independent Church which was built in the 1860s. The founding of the church had to do with an unfortunate period in the history of the Dutch Reformed Church in Bredasdorp when the independent congregation broke away from the mother church and continued as such until 1875.

The Rectory and the Independent Church both form part of an interesting local history museum with shipwreck exhibits which unfold the story of the nearby treacherous Agulhas Bank.

Bredasdorp was named after the Hon. Michiel van Breda, Member of the Legislative Council. It became a municipality in 1917 and has a population of 9 500. The district is known for its prosperous wool and grain farms and wild flowers are cultivated on a large scale. The wild flower show is held in August. There are two hotels and a 9-hole golf course.

To the north-west of Bredasdorp on the road to Caledon is the small town of Napier, named after Governor Sir George Napier.

Cape Agulhas

The most southerly point of Africa is Cape Agulhas; its meridian 20°E is the recognised geographical dividing line of the Atlantic and Indian Oceans, although in fact the warm currents of the Indian Ocean reach False Bay.

The Portuguese name Agulhas signifies needles and refers to the saw-edged reefs and sunken rocks which are so dangerous to ships hugging the land too closely. The shallow Agulhas Bank (60 fathoms deep) extends for 80 kilometres from the coast and is one of the world's most prolific commercial fishing grounds.

Agulhas lighthouse was built in 1849 and in modern times strengthened to 18 000 000 candle-power with a range of 27 kilometres.

Struisbaai

The fishermen's cottages roofed with straw gave Struisbaai its name. Three of these old cottages have been restored and proclaimed national monuments. The handsome bay has been formed by an 11-kilometre curve in the coastline where fishermen, bathers and shell collectors are attracted. Struisbaai has an hotel, caravan park and rondavels are rented.

Arniston (Waenhuiskrans)

On Marcus Bay, Arniston was named after the East Indiaman wrecked there in 1815 with tragic loss of life. The name Waenhuiskrans comes from the enormous cavern which is two kilometres south of the village, eroded into the cliff, it is big enough to house several wagons together with the teams of oxen. The cavern can be explored at low tide.

Several fishermen's cottages on the headland of Kassiesbaai are national monuments. Bungalows can be rented at the caravan park and at the comfortable Arniston Hotel with its distinctive decor, delicious meals are served.

The site of the foundered *Arniston* was proclaimed South Africa's first underwater national monument after discovery of the vessel in January 1983.

Skipskop and De Hoop Nature Reserve

Prior to the news-leak in March 1983 that Armscor was to develop a missile-testing facility in the southern Cape to replace the range at St. Lucia, on the Natal north coast, De Hoop Nature Reserve was practically unheard of by the South African general public – simply because it is not spectacular from either a wild animal or scenic point of view. Overnight De Hoop became a household name and conservationists, ecologists and nature lovers were in an uproar.

Six kilometres to the north of the tiny fishing settlement at beautiful Skipskop beach is the 18 000 hectare De Hoop Nature Reserve, which lies as an enclove between the coast and the intensively cultivated wheat-lands of the south-western Cape. It had its start as an experimental wildlife farm when the Cape Department of Nature Conservation bought the historic De Hoop farm, with its old Cape Dutch homestead, in 1956.

The reserve is a unique sanctuary incorporating coastline, duneveld and De Hoop Vlei, a landlocked freshwater lake (fed by rivulets and springs) 14 km long and averaging ½ km in width. The upper half of the vlei is flanked by a series of limestone cliffs, grotesquely eroded and forming numerous caves. The area, with its ideal conditions for roosting and breeding, is the habitat of thousands of waterfowl and is proclaimed an international wetland (an area used by migrant birds). De Hoop supports a rare combination of aquatic and terrestrial birds. Of the 220 recorded species waterfowl predominate, and the largest population, 24 200, is that of the red-knobbed coot – often seen in flocks of from 2 000 to 5 000 individuals. Other large counts are the yellow-billed duck, 4 626, the Cape shoveler, 3 004, the Egyptian goose, 2 166, the lesser flamingo, 1 715, the greater flamingo, 1 473, the South African shelduck, 896 and the maccoa duck, 895. Other interesting aquatic species are the white pelican, spurwing goose, red-billed teal, Cape teal, southern pochard, white-backed duck, black stork and Caspian tern, all of which can be seen in good numbers. The milkwood trees growing at the edge of the vlei provide ideal nesting places for the fish-eagles that occur here. Although they prey largely on the tilapia introduced in the vlei, fish-eagles can often be seen taking coot. Of the large terrestrial species the majestic Stanley's bustard and the reptile eating secretary bird occur.

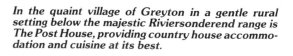

In the quaint village of Greyton in a gentle rural setting below the majestic Riviersonderend range is The Post House, providing country house accommodation and cuisine at its best.

The Cape is the richest area in the world for land tortoises, and here in the reserve there are five species including the attractively marked geometric tortoise (Psammobates). The Potberg, a 1983 acquisition of the reserve, marks the southernmost breeding colony of the Cape vulture, an endangered species, and the remarkable system of limestone caves are the breeding grounds of five species of insectivorous bats.

The apparent blessing is that despite the construction of the Armscor range ecological interference will be minimal.

Houw Hoek Pass and Bot River

National road N2 from Somerset West continues eastwards to reach Sir Lowry's Pass and Grabouw which are described in the Four Passes Drive.

Between Grabouw and Bot River the national road winds through the Houw Hoek Pass in strikingly beautiful mountain country with protea and heath close to the road. Near the summit a gravel road leads off to the left, down to Houw Hoek railway station and the old Cape coach inn secluded in the trees of the lovely Houw Hoek Valley. This used to be the second staging post of coaches from Cape Town and the old-world character has been preserved notwithstanding its popularity as a modern-day hotel.

Below the pass there is a protea farm and cross roads; the right-hand turn is to Hermanus and the left-hand turn leads to the village of Bot River where there are houses, trading stores, a petrol service station and an hotel.

From Bot River the traveller enters the Overberg and the magnificent wheat country of the South Western Cape.

Caledon

In 1715 the first white settler, Ferdinand Appel, obtained permission from the Landdrost of Stellenbosch to start gardening at what was then called Swartberg (after the mountain behind the town). In 1813 the place was renamed in honour of the Earl of Caledon (governor from 1807 to 1811). It became a municipality in 1884 and has a population of 7 000.

The town lies 38 kilometres from the coast and is famous for the chalybeate baths and the wild flower reserve. The baths have been used since the days of the Dutch East India Company; at the fountainhead there are six thermal springs with a temperature of 50°C, and one cold spring. During the Victorian era a sizeable hotel was built at the site but this was gutted by fire in 1946 and was never reconstructed. Since 1961 the baths have been under the control of the municipality, and a caravan and camping ground has been laid out in the area.

The 10-hectare wild flower reserve is at the entrance to Venster Kloof, so named after a curious rock which forms 'the window' (die venster). Through the careful planning of the reserve, wild flowers in great profusion are presented to their best advantage. A flower show is held in September.

Caledon has a 9-hole golf course, bowling greens and three hotels.

Genadendal and Greyton (a deviation from N2)

Between the towns of Caledon and Riviersonderend

several roads lead off national road N2 northwards to Genadendal and Greyton which lie within 5 kilometres of each other under the peaks of the Riviersonderend Mountains.

In this dramatic setting in 1737, George Schmidt, 'the Apostle of the Hottentots', founded South Africa's first mission station in the Baviaanskloof (baboons' kloof). Forbidden to administer baptism and generally hampered by the Dutch authorities, Schmidt returned to Germany in 1744. The Moravian Society resumed the missionary work in 1792 and made considerable progress after the British occupation in 1795. In 1806 the mission station was named Genadendal (valley of grace).

In the village there are the church and manse, a water mill, lovely old oaks, and the cherished eighteenth-century relic is the old church bell. Now a national monument, the bell has survived a remarkable history. It was brought into the precinct of the mission station in 1793 when the Reverend Meent Borcherds controlled the large Dutch Reformed Church parish of Stellenbosch. During these early days of colonization 'foreign' churches were jealously guarded against. It will be remembered that the Lutheran congregation at the Cape had a long struggle for recognition and when they eventually obtained permission to build their own church, a church bell was prohibited. Similarly, the Reverend Borcherds complained about the bell brought to Genadendal, saying that it could be heard in Stellenbosch! And he made representations to the Council of Policy to have the Genadendal church suppressed. For a long time after this the ringing of the mission bell was allowed only after permission was first obtained from the authorities. When Lord Macartney came to the Cape, he gave permission for the bell to be used to call the congregation to church. Thus the famed bell was built into a bell-cage and from 1798 the missionaries rang the bell for every conceivable reason, usually nine times a day.

The beautifully situated little municipality of Greyton lies in an area rich in wild flowers where there are opportunities for bass fishing and delightful walks into the mountains. In this peaceful environment the town is made picturesque by its thatched homes, and for those who seek the very best in country house accommodation there is The Post House, pictured on the previous page. Details appear on page 395.

Riviersonderend

The small town of Riviersonderend takes its name from the river without end and serves a rich wheat farming community of the river valley. The river in fact belies its own name since it ends where it joins with the Breede, north of Stormsvlei. The town lies astride the national road; it was established in 1925, became a municipality in 1940 and has a population of 2 000. There is an hotel in Riviersonderend and one at Stormsvlei, 24 kilometres eastwards, on the way to Swellendam.

Swellendam

After Cape Town and Stellenbosch, Swellendam was the third settlement to be founded by the Dutch East India Company.

On 12th November 1743 the Council of Policy nominated separate members for the country court of the Lower Breede River, and on 31st August 1745 a new district was proclaimed. The building of the Drostdy was completed in 1747 and in the same year the new district was named Swellendam in honour of Governor Hendrik Swellengrebel and his wife, Helena ten Damme.

The Drostdy, a national monument, is the only eighteenth century drostdy building that has been preserved in its original form. It stands on the eastern side of the town on the bank of the Koringlands River (cornfields river) close to the Groote Wagen Weg or Cape Wagon Road, the route of early expeditions to the interior. This part of the route is now Swellengrebel Street.

The yellowwood timbers used in the construction of the Drostdy were brought from the southern slopes of the Langeberg. The landdrost dwelling was the section furthest from the river. Closer to the river were three large rooms: the court room, the landdrost office and the office of his secretary. The man responsible for its siting and construction was the first landdrost, J.T. Rhenius.

By the winter of 1795 the burghers of Swellendam had had enough of the misrule of the Dutch East India Company and on 17th June, lead by their strong man Commandant Delport, they stormed the Drostdy and ejected Landdrost A.A. Faure. The burghers proclaimed an independent republic and installed Hermanus Steyn as president. The pocket-size republic (comprising some twenty families) was short-lived; it faded out when the British took the Cape three months later and reinstated the landdrost.

Eventually the Drostdy became privately owned and in 1856 it belonged to P.G. Steyn. It escaped the disastrous fire of 1865 and remained the property of the Steyn family until 1939 when it was bought by the State, restored and converted into the Drostdy Museum. Today it stands in a lovely formal garden that sets off its charming architectural features and it houses a fine collection of pieces associated almost exclusively with the history of the Swellendam district.

The stately avenue of old oak trees on both sides of Swellengrebel Street provide an attractive entrance to Swellendam from the east. The original oaks date from the eighteenth century and the avenue of today has been proclaimed a national monument.

Second only to the Drostdy as the oldest building is the Old Gaol, obliquely opposite the Drostdy across Swellengrebel Street. A national monument, it has been restored and converted into a dwelling for the curator of the museum.

Next to the Old Gaol is a small thatched-roof house (also a national monument) still known as the Old Post Office. It was originally the residence of the gaoler who also filled the postion of postmaster.

From the reign of George IV, his brother William IV, and well into Victorian times and before the fire of 1865, Swellendam, as administrative centre of the rich Overberg wool producers, experienced an amazing boom period. These were the days of the commercial empire of Barry and Nephews, the merchants who dominated the scene issuing their own bank notes and trading their own ships from

Cape Town to Port Beaufort near the mouth of the Breede River, 60 kilometres down river from Swellendam.

A few buildings remain from those days of prosperity and some of these are among Swellendam's national monuments that are in the main thoroughfare, Voortrek Street. It is convenient to explore these from the south-west to the north-east of the street. On the corner of Moolman Street is the Old Boys' School; an H-plan gabled homestead built in circa 1825 and converted into a school for boys in 1870. After it fell into disrepair, Historical Homes of South Africa purchased and restored the old building which is today occupied by Olyfkrans College, a remedial school for boys. In the centre of the town, on an island at the corner of Nelson Street, is the Meeting House, a little gabled building built in 1838 for prayer and educational meetings; it is now used as the visitors information bureau. Partly hidden by beautiful oaks, on the corner of Rhenius Street, is the Auld House, bought in 1826 by Joseph Barry, head of the famed empire and still owned by his descendants. Across Voortrek Street from the Auld House is an interesting historical group; it comprises a row of Tuishuise – traditional town houses used by farmers when they came to town on such occasions as 'nagmaal', and in this case so conveniently situated close to the Dutch Reformed Church – the Cottage, the permanent dwelling of an urban owner in the nineteenth century, and, to complete the group, the Little Square, around which the buildings are arranged. It is interesting that in 1845 Joseph Barry bought the land and built the Tuishuise as an investment. The north-eastern end of Voortrek Street becomes Van Oudtshoorn Street and on the right (where the street in climbing the hill makes a bend), in a wall-enclosed garden with a dramatic Langeberg backdrop, is the town residence that Thomas Barry built in 1839. Thomas, one of Joseph's two nephews, took care of the affairs at Port Beaufort and lived there. He needed a town-house because he frequently came to Swellendam on business. After Thomas Barry's death, the Cape Government purchased the house for the use of the heemraden (council of the landdrost) and later it was used by the magistrate and so it is today known as Heemraden House or the Old Residency. Another of the assets of Historical Homes of South Africa, it was beautifully restored in 1969.

Swellendam continues to be a busy centre of a thriving agricultural district notable for wheat and wool and the largest output of youngberries in South Africa. Municipal status was received in 1904 and the population is 8 500. The town occupies a scenically superb situation in the Breede Valley at the foot of the Langeberg range where the four conspicuous peaks known as 10 o'clock, 11 o'clock, 12 o'clock and 1 o'clock form natural sundials by which early farmers told the time.

The Swellengrebel Hotel, 91 Voortrek Street (the main thoroughfare) rates with the best country-town hotels in the republic. There are two other hotels in Voortrek Street and two municipal caravan parks. Besides golf, bowls and tennis there is angling in the Breede River.

1. *A prominent landmark in Voortrek Street, Swellendam, is the Dutch Reformed Church built in 1911.*
2. *The Old Residency in Van Oudtshoorn Street,* *Swellendam, was built in 1839 as a town house for Thomas Barry. 3. One of the Cape's most cherished monuments, the Drostdy in Swellendam, was built in the 18th century.*

1

2

1. and 2. Two-star Swellengrebel Hotel, Voortrek Street, Swellendam, adequately fills the need of a first-rate hotel in this historic environment.

In amongst the forests of indigenous trees and veld of wild flowers interesting foot trails into the Langeberg lead to the Clock Peaks and such places as Hermitage Kloof and Nooitgedacht Kloof. A permit must first be obtained from the Forester, from whom advice should also be sought. The office of the Forester is reached by proceeding from the centre of the town along Andrew Whyte Street northwards in the direction of the mountains. The office is 3 kilometres from the town; the road passes the golf course and is sign posted Swellendam State Forest. A Forester's permit must also be obtained to visit the 430-hectare Marloth Flower Reserve which is accessible by motor car.

Bontebok National Park

The entrance gate to Bontebok National Park is across the national road, south of Swellendam, approximately 6 kilometres from the town. The establishment of the sanctuary has ensured the revival of this once endangered species. In addition to bontebok there are several other antelope species in the park which occupies 2 786 hectares on the banks of the Breede River, overlooked by the impressive Langeberg range.

The park is open throughout the year, refreshments are obtainable at the rest camp and in addition to picnic places, there are camping and caravan sites on the river bank.

In 1931 the bontebok were established near Bredasdorp, but owing to poor grazing, in 1960 the Parks Board was obliged to capture the herd and re-establish the park at its present site which has proved to be ideal. The bontebok was orignally found only here in the South Western Districts of the Cape. Its average mass is 90 kilogrammes, height 101 centimetres and record length of horns 43 centimetres.

The bontebok is closely related to the blesbok. In the bontebok the white blaze is undivided and the rump, legs and belly are white, the rest of the body being dark brown to black. In the blesbok there is a prominent division in the blaze, the legs, belly and rump are a lighter colour than the rest of the body. The natural habitat of the blesbok is the highveld.

When the park was established, grey rhebuck, steenbok, Cape grysbok and duiker were already in the area. In addition to bontebok, the Parks Board re-introduced springbok and bushbuck. The veld here, chiefly grass and scrub, provides the correct grazing and open country for easy viewing of the game. The river banks, lined with indigenous trees such as yellowwood, wild olive, Karoo acacia, milkwood, round-leaf kiaat and candle-wood, complete the typical South African game park scene.

Witsand and Port Beaufort

At the mouth of the Breede River, Witsand and Port Beaufort are accessible from roads that lead off the national road from Buffelsjagsrivier and from four kilometres west of Heidelberg.

Witsand, right at the mouth of the estuary overlooking the bay of St Sebastian, is a fine fishing area with wide, white beaches. On the estuary and up-river for a considerable distance conditions are ideal for power boats. Conveniently sited are the hotel and caravan park with camping sites.

Port Beaufort, three kilometres up-river, takes its name from the family of Lord Charles Somerset and was the scene of much activity at the wharfside warehouses of Barry and Nephews in the nineteenth century. The Barry Church carries a bronze plaque of the Historical Monuments Commission and is a memorial to the busy industry that once flourished there. In those days the merchandise was transported up-river for 30 kilometres to Malgas, where today the old pont still carries the traffic across the river on the roads to Swellendam and Bredasdorp.

Suurbraak

From Swellendam there are two routes to Heidelberg; the much used national road and the road via Suurbraak. For the quiet road shortly after crossing the Buffelsjagsrivier (buffalo hunt river) where there is overnight accommodation, the turnoff to the left is taken, to reach Suurbraak (sour marsh) site of the mission station of the London Missionary Society.

Tradouw Pass and Barrydale

North of Suurbraak the Tradouw Pass carries the road over the Langeberg. Constructed in 1873 by the famed Thomas Bain, the pass follows the gorge made by the Tradouws River (from the Hottentot 'river of the women').

At the top of the pass is Barrydale, which evokes the success story of Barry and Nephews. However, Barrydale was founded in 1882 by another generation of the Barry family, long after the unfortunate collapse of the Barry empire. Deciduous fruit and grapes are grown in the district also renowned for brandy distilling and mesembryanthemums. Barrydale has an hotel and a caravan park.

Heidelberg

This market town and rail centre for a prosperous wheat and wool district was named after the ancient German city. It is attractively situated on the bank of the Duivenhoks River (dovecote river) and has two hotels, a caravan park, golf course, bowling green and tennis courts. The population is 4 000.

Riversdale

Part of the highly-productive coastal wheat-belt, Riversdale is at the foothills of the Langeberg (that very long mountain range), close to the Kafferkuils River. It was founded in 1838 and named after the Hon. Harry Rivers, the Civil Commissioner and later Colonial Treasurer.

Riversdale became a municipality in 1849 and today has a population of 6 000. There are three hotels and a caravan park where rondavels can be rented. Near the town is a small game reserve.

This is a district notable for the delicious honey produced from heath and other flowers of the veld, and for the aromatic *Agathosma* shrub that gives off an antiseptic-like perfume.

J.E.A. Volschenk (1853-1936), the South African landscape artist, was born in the district. Some of his

Cape mountain scenes, which convey the typical hazy air, can be seen in the local Julius Gordon Africana Centre.

Garcia Pass
To the north of Riversdale the road to Ladismith and the Little Karoo crosses the Langeberg by way of the Garcia Pass, a picturesque motorway in a rural setting with colourful sandstone cliffs and ravines filled with wild flowers.

A.H. Garcia, who was Commissioner of Riversdale, personally followed the course of the Kafferkuils River on horseback to investigate the possibility of constructing a road. The pass was eventually completed by the famed engineer, Thomas Bain, and opened in 1877.

The toll-house, an historical monument at the summit (some 19 kilometres from Riversdale), is one of the last remaining in South Africa. The old building, situated within the Kristalkloof Forest Reserve, is in the tranquil surroundings of shady oaks and tall cypresses.

Puntjie
At the coast, south of Riversdale, is Puntjie, a unique complex of seventy reproductions of the 18th century kapstylhuise.

After the covered wagon, the kapstylhuis was the first dwelling constructed by the trek-boers. The technique having been passed down through the decades came into vogue at Puntjie in the 1920s when this resort settlement grew. The land, part of the farm Kleinfontein, belonged to a Bredasdorp owner who permitted the people of Vermaaklikheid and Brakfontein to build their resort dwellings on his property on the basis that they paid him a nominal annual rental, the equivalent of 50 cents per annum. This resulted in most participants building the kapstylhuise that remain today and which form the basis of an important proclamation by the Monuments Commission to preserve these structures as an intrinsic part of the architectural history of South Africa. The building technique has a history in Europe that dates back to 500 A.D.

'Kapstyl' is literally 'truss-style' and the structure consists solely of a thatched roof carried on a series of trusses that reach down to the ground. Each of these modest dwellings has a floor space measuring about 8 × 5 metres with a simple screen dividing living room from bedroom. Each dwelling has a separate small cookhouse of the same style. In the 18th century cooking was done outside on an open-fire.

Puntjie lies at the mouth of the Duivenhoks River on a small point (puntjie) in St Sebastian Bay where the coastline is rugged with cliffs and caves and the bathing beach is sandy and safe.

To reach Puntjie, take the turnoff to the coast opposite Riversdale sign-posted Vermaaklikheid. It is an hour's drive to the village of Vermaaklikheid, singularly old-world in life-style, from where it is 10 kilometres to Puntjie.

Stilbaai
In the summer season the farmers of the southern Cape (in their hundreds) pack up and make for Stilbaai where the opportunities for a carefree holiday in the traditional manner are ideal: splendid bathing and surfing at a magnificent beach, where there are sea shells in abundance, boating on the broad estuary and up river for a number of kilometres, and varied fishing – deep sea, surf, estuary and river. Competitive games such as tug-of-war and jukskei are followed by braaivleis and dancing to concertina bands with the merriment continuing into the early hours of the morning. Most of these happy-go-lucky people have their own shack, bungalow or cottage and this type of accommodation can be rented; in addition there is a large caravan and camping park and a small hotel.

Stilbaai is divided by the estuary of the Kafferkuils River, with most of the resort buildings on the east bank and the fishing harbour on the west bank. A bridge connects the two banks. The area is renowned for its oysters and eels.

Along the coastal road 10 km to the west of Stilbaai is Grootjongensfontein, a resort with a large caravan park.

Albertinia
An important grain centre with huge silos at the railhead, Albertinia was named after the Reverend J.R. Albertyn who pioneered the establishment of the Dutch Reformed Church there. The town was laid out in 1900 and became a municipality in 1920. Its population is 2 000.

The substantial deposits of yellow ochre in the district provide South Africa's principal output. The clay is recovered by opencast methods and after processing the ochre is despatched to local and overseas markets for use as a pigment in the colouring of cement products, linoleum and paint.

This is a popular stopping place on the national highway. The town has an hotel and a 9-hole golf course.

Gouritz River Bridge and Gouritsmond
Fourteen kilometres east of Albertinia the national road crosses the Gouritz River. The spectacular parallel road and rail bridges which span the deep ravine (65 metres deep and 75 metres wide) are worth stopping to view. The new road bridge, longest of its kind in the Southern Hemisphere, was opened in 1977 and replaced the one constructed in 1892.

A short distance beyond the ravine is the turnoff to Gouritsmond where there is a licensed hotel, a caravan and camping site and excellent fishing on a fine stretch of coastline.

1. *The little resort at Herold's Bay, another of nature's beauty spots, is eight kilometres from George Airport.*

2. *The area of the Post Office Tree and spring, where Bartholomew Dias came ashore at Mossel Bay.*

1. St Mark's Anglican Cathedral, a landmark in York Street, George.

2. The George General Post Office fronted by the wide pavement of York Street, and backed by George Peak in the Outeniqua range.

3. and 4. Glentana and Victoria Bay two little Indian Ocean resorts, each in its own enchanting setting, along the coast from Mossel Bay to Wilderness.

3

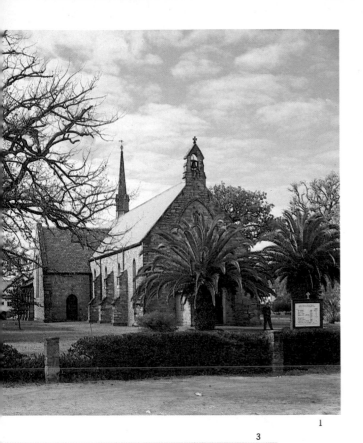

2

1

4

CHAPTER 3

The Garden Route, the Little Karoo and the Long Kloof

Beyond the Gouritz River Bridge the traveller moves out of the Mediterranean region of the Western Province into the southern coastal belt and the celebrated Garden Route, which is the area between the Indian Ocean and the Outeniqua and Tsitsikamma Mountains, stretching approximately 225 kilometres from Mossel Bay to beyond the Storms River. It is characterised by rainfall at all seasons and an equable climate. The inland town of Oudtshoorn and the famous Cango Caves although not in the same climatic region are part and parcel of the Garden Route.

The whole of the route is a tourist attraction of national significance, providing scenery that is beautiful and varied: flowers, ocean beaches, mountains, lakes, rivers, ravines and forests.

The Garden Route attracts visitors throughout the year. The more popular periods are during spring-time, when the veld is a profusion of wild flowers, there being over 2 000 varieties, and the summer months, when glorious sea bathing, boating and fishing are the main attractions. Within the region there are golf courses, bowling greens, tennis courts and yachting waters.

P.W. Botha Airport, George, is a scheduled stop of South African Airways and Plettenberg Bay, George and Oudtshoorn are scheduled stops of Air Cape. The area is connected with Cape Town, Port Elizabeth and Johannesburg by S.A. Transport Services motor-coach tours.

National road N2 — Mossel Bay to Jeffrey's Bay

Mossel Bay

A colourful hillside town and port, Mossel Bay lies on the sloping promontory of Cape St Blaize, overlooking the spacious bay with a backdrop of the Outeniqua range. The harbour has berths for coasters, a lighter handling service for larger vessels that stand off in the roadstead and a submarine pipeline that permits discharge from oil tankers.

Mossel Bay holds the distinction of being the first part of South Africa to be seen by Europeans. Bartholomew Dias, after doubling the Cape of Good Hope, sailed into the bay on 3rd February 1488. He saw Hottentots with their cattle and called the place *Angra dos Vaqueiros* (bay of the cowherds). Dias disembarked and found a good spring to replenish his water supplies near an old milkwood tree, but the Hottentots were unfriendly. This happened fifteen years before the first ship entered Table Bay. Since Dias had landed on the day of the Saint, the Portuguese subsequently changed the name to *Aquada de São Bras* (watering place of Saint Bras).

Nearly ten years after Dias, on 20th November 1497, Vasco da Gama landed here and made friends with the Hottentots, purchasing a bull for a few trinkets and thus carrying out the first known commercial transaction in South Africa. The

transaction was most acceptable to both parties and legend tells that da Gama was thereafter entertained by the Hottentot reed-flute players.

After da Gama, ships frequently took shelter in the bay. Water was replenished from the perennial spring and fresh meat bargained for from the Hottentots. The milkwood tree marked the place where messages were left to be delivered by those voyaging in the other direction. In 1501 João da Nova found a message here, left by Pedro d'Ataide the year before. In thanksgiving, da Nova erected a shrine, the first place of Christian worship in South Africa. Some messages were carved into rocks and an example of one can be seen in the local museum.

So it was that the milkwood tree became known as the Post Office Tree. The tree and the spring are national monuments, still to be seen in an area attractively laid out with lawns and flowers. Old cannon, a copy of a Portuguese padrão, a handsome plaque and a letter box in the shape of a navigator's boot are all in keeping with the simple setting. Letters posted here bear a special postmark. This historic feature of Mossel Bay is opposite the inlet named Munro's Bay, where Dias and others came ashore.

Mossel Bay received its present name in 1601 when the Dutch navigator, Paulus van Caerden came upon a great collection of mussel shells in a cave at the headland of Cape St Blaize. The name of the cape is apparently a corruption of the Portuguese São Bras. When Mossel Bay became a separate magistracy in 1848 an attempt was made to change the name to Aliwal South to commemorate the success of Governor Sir Harry Smith, in the Battle of Aliwal in India prior to his coming to the Cape – but the name Mossel Bay stuck. Mossel Bay became a municipality in 1852 and today has a population of 29 000.

Mossel Bay the resort is best known by the Karoo farmers and their families; year after year in the summer season they return to the expansive beaches, gently sloping and safe for bathing. Deserted for nine months of the year, the camping and caravan sites become an enormous tent city. The classic example of the Cape farmers holiday resort, Mossel Bay, like Stilbaai and Kleinmond, is for the season a scene of absolute carefree fun in the sun, with the traditional competitive games, singsongs, braaivleis, traditional concertina and guitar music and dancing. Die Bakke beach, with its hundreds of seaside bungalows, was named after the water-trough that stood there; Santos Beach opposite the hotel, takes its name from a Spanish ship wrecked there, and the Poort with its enormous, natural tidal pool adjoins the caravan and camping park at the Point. The sporting facilities are golf, bowls, tennis, yachting and fishing.

During the summer holidays boat trips are arranged to Seal Island where thousands of the fascinating mammals can be seen at close quarter.

On the crown of Cape St Blaize is the picturesque lighthouse with its twenty thousand candle-power beam, and Bat's Cave where van Caerden found the floor covered with mussel shells. Mossel Bay remains famous for its mussels and its oysters and some of the biggest catches of tunny and black marlin are made on its coastline. Tunnel Cave, a 60-metre passageway through the headland, emerges on a stretch of wild coast, where the surf thunders against a cliff. The beaches are notable for the variety of sea shells and the local shell museum is an outstanding contribution to conchology.

In Victorian times the port shared with Oudtshoorn the prosperity of the ostrich-feather boom. In 1931 alone, R6 000 000 worth of feathers were exported. Today ships load yellow ochre, fruit, wool and grain.

Voorbaai is a model industrial suburb east of Mossel Bay where there is one of the most modern chocolate factories in the world. By contrast, to the west of the town, there is a primitive but nevertheless thriving industry carried out by the Coloured people, who hand-crush and boil aloes to produce the bitter medicinal juice.

Positive indications of vibrant growth in the quiet town of Mossel Bay follow successful ocean gas tapping in 1987 which is expected to make a substantial contribution to South Africa's fuel requirements.

Hartenbos
A few kilometres beyond Voorbaai is the turnoff coastwise to Hartenbos; its name comes from the bush growing there on the river banks. It is the resort of the Afrikaans Taal en Kultuurvereniging (ATKV) whose Voortrekker Museum is there. The resort has two hotels, bungalows and a caravan park with camping sites.

Robinson Pass and Ruitersbos (Eight Bells)
Beyond Hartenbos, trunk route R328 leads off to the left and over the spectacular Robinson Pass northwards for 80 km to Oudtshoorn. The pass is a reconstruction of the one completed by Thomas Bain in 1869 and named after the Commissioner for Roads, M.R. Robinson. It is a fast, easy highway with sweeping views from the summit, 860 metres above sea level. Proteas, heath and other flowers of the veld all along the roadside add to the scenic splendour.

At 35 km from Mossel Bay is Ruitersbos and the most delightful stop-over and holiday hotel in the region – two-star Eight Bells Mountain Inn, off the right side of the highway.

Little Brak River and Great Brak River
Continuing on the route to George, the road crosses the Little Brak River and the small resort of that name with its cluster of bungalows at the river mouth and a motel close to the national road.

A short distance further on, the road bridges the Great Brak River with another little resort built on the island of the lagoon. Upstream on the left of N2 is the industrial empire of Searles Limited, the well-known footwear manufacturers. It had its beginning in 1859 when Charles Searl, a recent immigrant, took up his position of toll-keeper of the bridge. He made the toll the centre of one enterprise after another and today almost the entire permanent population of Great Brak River, over 2 000, is connected with the Searles organisation.

There is a lovely scenic drive north of the village to Ernest Robinson Dam in the Jonkersberg. The dam is the principal reservoir of Mossel Bay.

Glentana
From Great Brak River there are two routes to George; the one hugging the coast passes several seaside villages, including Glentana, from where there is a steep climb of eight kilometres back to the inland route to George. The coastal road continues to George airport.

Outeniqualand
After leaving the low-lying Great Brak River, the inland route to George makes a steep climb up the coastal plateau, rewarding the traveller with a magnificent view back over the entire sweep of Mossel Bay, and forward, there is a complete change of scene with the whole range of the Outeniqua mountains looming over the rolling plains of Outeniqualand. Outeniqua was the name of a tribe of the Hottentots; translated it is 'men laden with honey' – certainly typified by the bee hives that thrive in this land of heather.

Herold's Bay
The coastal cliffs of the Garden Route are occasionally accessible from the land side and this is so at Herold's Bay, where the road makes a steep descent to the sea to discover this secluded cove with its sandy beach. This approach road passes George Airport from where it is eight kilometres to the resort.

A ridge, built-up with holiday homes, overlooks the bay with its tidal swimming pool and tiny church, built on the rocks. Indigenous coastal vegetation softens the whole scene. The first minister of the Dutch Reformed Church in George, the Reverend Tobias Herold, gave his name to the resort where the Divisional Council has provided bungalows and caravan and camping sites. There is also an hotel.

George
At the junction of two important trunk routes, the town of George is built astride national road N2 at the southern terminal of route R29. It is positioned amid majestic scenery on the high coastal plateau on the seaward slopes of the Outeniqua Mountains, and is dominated by George Peak which rises 1 146 metres above the plateau. Despite its close proximity to the sea – only 8 kilometres away – the town enjoys a year-round gentle climate with equable rainfall and little or no humidity. The surrounding countryside is perennially green.

George was the first new magistracy to be established after the second British occupation of the Cape. The district was proclaimed on 23 April 1811 when the governor, the Earl of Caledon, named the place George Town, in honour of the reigning king of England, George III, and appointed A.G. van Kervel as the first landdrost. In accordance with the custom, the first landdrost was responsible for the laying out of the town, and van Kervel accomplished this with merit in providing wide, oak-lined thoroughfares. One of the fine old oak trees, thought to have been planted in his time, stands in the library garden in York Street (the main street) and is a national monument.

In 1837 George became a municipality and in 1850 the metropolitan bishop, Robert Gray (who founded

Eight Bells Mountain Inn, on a 200-morgen farm at Ruitersbos, is an excellent stop-over and a lovely place for holidays for the whole family — the recreational amenities are outstanding. The Inn is situated in the foothills of the Outeniqua at the commencement of the Robinson Pass, trunk route R328, between Mossel Bay (35 km) and Oudtshoorn (50 km).

1. *One of the best coastal views in South Africa, Wilderness beach from the northern head of Kaaiman's River mouth.*

2. *The Kaaiman's River mouth, skirted by the national highway and crossed by the railway — an immutable feature of the Garden Route.*

the famous Diocesan College for boys in Cape Town and many other ecclesiastical institutions in South Africa), consecrated St Mark's Anglican Cathedral. During its centenary in 1911, George was established as the centre of a new Diocese, stretching east to west from Plettenberg Bay to Swellendam and north to Uniondale and Graaff-Reinet. To mark the occasion, King George V presented a Royal Bible and Prayer Book to St Mark's Cathedral, which was at the time the smallest cathedral in the world. The Roman Catholic Church of St Peter and St Paul was erected in 1843 and is the oldest existing Roman Catholic Church in South Africa. The Dutch Reformed Church in Courtenay Street is the oldest church in George; it was completed and inaugurated on 9 October 1842.

The town is the centre for a rich agricultural district where there are extensive forestry undertakings, concentrated fresh vegetable cultivation and it is the only district in South Africa that produces hops, being the closest to the equator anywhere in the world where hops is grown. George is an important educational centre and the sporting amenities are of the highest standard. The George Country Club is the venue for the Cape Province Amateur Golf Championships. There are fine bowling greens and tennis courts and the sports stadium seats 4 000.

Gramophones, musical boxes, cameras, telephones and typewriters collected by Curator C.D. Sayers form a unique part of the historical museum of George in the Drostdy which is in Courtenay Street on the axis of York Street. Here in the restored Drostdy the visitors information bureau is also housed.

P.W. Botha Airport, 10 kilometres south of the town, is close to national road N2. This is a scheduled stop of S.A. Airways and Air Cape and there is an active flying club.

George has a population of 42 000 and is a popular place of retirement.

There are 7 hotels including the well-appointed 2-star Mayfield Park Hotel, off national road N2, 8 km from George on the same side as and near the turnoff to Victoria Bay. The municipality administers a tourist camp at the Cape Town entrance to the town, where there are caravan sites, rondavels and all facilities.

Outeniqua Pass

Trunk route R29 to the north of George is carried over the mountains for 21 kilometres by the Outeniqua Pass.

There are fine view sites at strategic positions and one in particular six kilometres up the seaward slope where there is ample parking space and an interesting plaque built at a vantage point to identify the various historic passes in the range. The pass used by the Voortrekkers, laid down in 1812 by A.G. van Kervel, the first landdrost of George, and named Cradock Kloof in honour of the governor, Sir John Cradock, is a precipitous route identified by white beacons. Montagu Pass, winding like a huge brown serpent as it follows the Malgas River Kloof, was completed in 1847 and is still in use. It was named after John Montagu, Colonial Secretary of the Cape who programmed the construction of the first trunk roads of South Africa and was responsible for the building of this pass. The railway line, cut out of the mountainside runs high above the Montagu Pass. Completed in 1913 this line, still carrying steam locomotives, connects George with Oudtshoorn on one of the world's most dramatic railways.

The splendid Outeniqua Pass itself has a uniform gradient of one in sixteen and reaches the summit, 800 metres above sea level, after 14 kilometres from George. It presents the traveller with one of the scenic highlights of the district. On the northern descent the road reaches a fertile valley of fruit farms, especially beautiful in blossom time, and at the bottom, the junction of routes R62 and R29, R62 swinging hard right in an easterly direction and R29 continuing northwards to Oudtshoorn and the Cango Caves which are described further on in this chapter.

Serious hiking enthusiasts wishing to explore the Outeniqua region should apply to the Department of Forestry, Private Bag X93, Pretoria, for Pamphlet 194 which provides an excellent guide and indispensable maps.

The Routes from George to Knysna

There are several routes from George to Knysna. Early travellers went via Cradock Kloof (now Montagu Pass) and the Long Kloof. By 1882 the famed Thomas Bain had completed what is today called the Passes Road; it avoids the coast and follows the inland plateau terrace. The national road N2, a masterpiece of engineering over this section, follows the coast and skirts a number of lakes (unique in South Africa). A most delightful experience is to take the 67-kilometre three-hour 'Puffing Billy' trip – the narrow-gauge line traverses coastal cliffs, tunnels through mountains, passes through forests, crosses lakes and deep gorges, ending the journey in a final dramatic crossing of the Knysna lagoon.

The Passes Road — Kaaiman's River, Touw River, Swart River, Karatara River, Homtini Pass, Millwood and Phantom Pass

For the Passes Road you leave the national road N2, three kilometres out from George, and the first river it crosses is the Swart. An equal distance beyond the crossing, where the road rises through the forest, on the left-hand side are two large gate posts, framing a dramatic picture of the Outeniqua Mountains. This is the entrance to the State-owned Saasveld Forestry College. From the plateau the road winds down to the Kaaiman's River (Hottentot for crocodile), rises again and descends to the bridge of the Silver River all in a matter of a kilometre or so, in lovely wooded surroundings. Bain avoided the notorious Kaaiman's Gat (crocodile hole) which formed part of the old ox-wagon trail.

Further on, at the little settlement of Ginnesville there is a branch road leading down to Wilderness, the first of a number of connections with the national road. This is known as White's Road, after Montagu White, son of the builder of Montagu Pass, and was for a long time the only route to Wilderness. The next pass is the ravine crossing of the Touw River (a corruption from the Hottentot word meaning a maiden's ford). At the eastern summit of the pass the road reaches the Olifantshoek settlement where another branch road leads to the south.

After crossing the Kleinkeur River there is a turnoff left to the important forest station at Woodville, from where, upon the permission of the forester, an interesting circular drive can be taken to Bergplaas and Kleinplaat forest stations. Two kilometres north-west of Woodville there is a large yellowwood tree (one of a number of 'Big Trees' in the forests ahead of you). Beyond Woodville another branch road joins the national road at Rondevlei.

The Passes Road continues its relentless journey through valley after valley; twisting and turning, it crosses the Diep or Swart River, passes Lancewood and then the Hoogekraal River, up the plateau again and past Karatara, where there is another forestry station and the Social Welfare forestry workers rehabilitation settlement. To the east of the Karatara River is Barrington (where Henry Barrington had his farm) and to its north the forestry reserve of Farleigh. To the south, another road leads off to meet the national road at Ruigtevlei.

Leaving Barrington, the Passes Road makes its tortuous journey through the primeval forest of the Homtini Pass. It winds in short curves right down to the bottom of the impressive gorge, the Homtini River itself a spectacular amber-coloured torrent. This is one place where it is possible to gauge the density of the indigenous vegetation that once covered the entire Knysna region. For those who are fascinated by relics of the past there is a turnoff to the left beyond the eastern summit of the pass; it leads to the abandoned goldfields of Millwood and the ghost town of that name. In the late 1880s there was an excited rush to Millwood when first nuggets, then alluvial gold and finally gold-bearing reefs were discovered. By 1887 there were established six hotels, twenty shops, three newspapers, a magistrate's court, banks and a Post Office. But nothing came of the great expectations. In the years that followed the primitive building structures disappeared and the great forest repossessed the land, and today little remains other than the ghost of the once optimistic gold rush. In the vicinity east of the old gold diggings is Jubilee Creek, a beauty spot with another Big Tree.

After the forestry settlement of Rheenendal the road forks. The continuing tarred road is not part of the Passes route. The left-hand, gravel road through the Phantom Pass is taken. Despite its eerie name, the Phantom Pass is an easy motor road, although the descent is steep, presenting lovely vistas of the Knysna River Valley. The name comes from the phantom moths found in the area. You come out of the pass two kilometres above the national road causeway, where the Passes route divides and you have the choice of following either the east or west bank of the Knysna River to connect with the national road.

National road N2 — George to Knysna
Returning to George to continue the journey eastwards on national road N2, at approximately opposite the Passes Road turnoff there is another branch road leading to the coast.

Victoria Bay
The branch road leads in twists and turns for five kilometres to reach the coast at Victoria Bay – a cove enclosed by cliffs. The little resort comprises a number of cottages clustered around the water front and an all-facility caravan park. The gently-sloping beach makes bathing safe and big waves from far out give surfers a long ride – although the water is invariably cold. Inland from the bay there is a hutted camp and tearoom.

Kaaiman's River Gorge
Thirteen kilometres east of George the national road dips down into the Kaaiman's River Gorge in some of the loveliest scenery imaginable. The road crosses the gorge on an elegantly curved concrete bridge revealing the deep river and two sheer, wooded headlands. Further on the 'Puffing Billy' railway makes its spectacular crossing high above the river mouth. At the end of the eastern headland there is another splendid view from a considerable height above the ocean, where the relentless rollers wash the clean white sands of Wilderness beach.

Wilderness
Although the national road divides Wilderness it has done nothing to spoil its profound beauty, in fact if anything the separation of the 8-kilometre-long beach from the village fringing the lagoon produces a special charm and the road provides accessibility to view sites to take in the scenic delights.

Accommodation at this renowned resort is at three hotels, Wilderness, Fairy Knowe and Holiday Inn and a number of caravan and camping parks.

At Wilderness the Touw River forms a lagoon from where boats can be taken upstream for sixteen kilometres leading to the lakes and Ebb and Flow Nature Reserve, a sanctuary of woodland streams, waterfalls and prolific bird life.

The Lake District
Beyond Wilderness is a chain of five lakes. The national road passes four of these on the inland side: Upper and Lower Langvlei, Rondevlei and Swartvlei. Groenvlei or Lake Pleasant is on the seaward side. The Serpentine River connects the Langvleis with the Touw River at the Ebb and Flow, making it possible to reach Wilderness by boat, and this is a very pleasant way to spend a morning or afternoon. Rondevlei is a sanctuary teeming with bird life. A gravel road cuts in between Rondevlei and Lower Langvlei, affording a circular drive around the two Langvleis. Swartvlei, the largest of the lakes, is directly connected with the sea and is the scene of yachting and other water sport.

Groenvlei, the freshwater lake, is stocked with blue-gill and black bass; on its banks is the recommended two-star Lake Pleasant Hotel in the surroundings of the Goukamma Nature Reserve, it is a resort within itself for fishing, boating, bird watching, swimming and tennis. Elegant comfort and excellent catering are this hotel's best advertisement.

There is a varied assortment of holiday accommodation along the banks of all of the lakes, ranging from camping and caravan parks, rondavels and bungalows, to the romantic boat houses.

Sedgefield
The inland section of the village of Sedgefield lies astride the national road; in this built-up area is the

1

2

3

4

1. *King Edward's Tree — one of many giant yellowwoods to be seen in Knysna forest.*

2. *Lake Pleasant is an exclusive holiday hotel in the beautiful lake district of the Garden Route.*

3. *Belvidere Church, erected in 1851, remains a jewel in a remote environment.*

4. *Buffalo Bay as seen from the road to Brenton.*

turnoff to Sedgefield beach. A fine beach this, where the Swartvlei enters the sea, and a popular resort with its array of attractive cottages.

Buffalo Bay

At the Goukamma River, where arum lilies grow in profusion on the roadside, there is a branch road of ten kilometres to Buffalo Bay. On its way to the sea the road passes the Buffelsbaai Provincial Nature Reserve.

Buffalo Bay is a secluded resort of private cottages and a Divisional Council caravan and camping park, where the wild flowers flourish in the sand dunes that adjoin a broad, white ocean beach.

Belvidere and Brenton

Just before the national road crosses the Knysna River, at the junction of the Passes Road and national road N2, there is a turnoff on a gravel road that leads under the bridge to another fork. The left fork leads to Belvidere and the right to Brenton.

Belvidere, a lagoonside estate, was acquired by Captain Thomas Henry Duthie when he married Caroline, the daughter of George Rex. The road passes the homestead and the pretty little Holy Trinity Church, a private chapel erected by Duthie in 1851 in memory of his descendants. When Bishop Gray consecrated the miniature Norman-style church on 5 October 1855, he commented 'by general consent the most perfect church as yet in the Diocese'. Indeed it remains a jewel in a remote environment. In the adjoining graveyard there lie buried Thomas and Caroline Duthie, some of their children and grandchildren and the Honourable Henry Barrington, a friend of both Rex and Duthie. Brenton Estate, notable for the variety of heaths there, occupies the peninsula of hilly country on the western side of Knysna from where there are extensive views of the river, the lagoon and the town.

At Lake Brenton there is a holiday camp of rondavels and caravan sites, and at Brenton-on-Sea an hotel, a caravan park and good fishing and surfing.

Knysna

George Rex, the founder of Knysna, has few rivals in South Africa for legendary glory, and when you consider his noble bearing and indeed his background, the manner in which he made his entry upon the scene, his ability to influence people in high office and not least of all his name, it would seem logical (particularly in those days at the start of the nineteenth century) that it should become widely accepted that this man was of royal descent. Modern research does not agree with this conclusion and there is no record of Rex himself having made such a claim.

Upon his arrival at the Cape in 1797 (during the first British occupation) Rex was appointed marshal of the vice-admiralty court, notary public to the governor and advocate for the Crown. Seven years later, in 1804, having married a widow with four children, he journeyed to Knysna with his family. He arrived in a coach bearing his coat of arms and drawn by six horses. The large retinue of friends and servants completed the royal image. The legend is that he was the son of George III of England by morganatic marriage to the Quaker beauty, Hannah Lightfoot, and that he was banished into exile when his father unexpectedly became heir to the throne.

Rex bought the farm Melkhoutkraal and rebuilt the homestead which had been razed by the Xhosas during its Dutch owner's occupancy. The farm was expanded by some 10 000 hectares bordering the lagoon as far as the Heads. He founded the first settlement which he named Melville, in honour of Viscount Melville, First Sea Lord at the time, and with the help of the Admiralty he established the port.

Little is known of the Rex family except that by the time they took occupation of Melkhoutkraal there were four more children. The daughter Caroline was married in 1832 to Thomas Henry Duthie, an officer of the Highland Regiment, and they settled at Belvidere. George Rex died in 1839, and in 1842 the Honourable Henry Barrington, twelfth son of Viscount Barrington and friend of Duthie, settled in the area. In 1845 Colonel John Sutherland bought the remains of the Melkhoutkraal estate from the descendants of Rex and founded the village of Newhaven adjoining Melville to the east.

In 1870 the Norwegian family, the Thesens settled, started a timber business and Thesen's Shipping Line that served Knysna for many decades. The hamlets of Melville and Newhaven merged in 1882 to form the municipality of Knysna. The derivation of the name Knysna is uncertain but it is probable that it comes from a Hottentot word meaning 'the wood there'.

During the romantic years of George Rex, many people of great esteem were entertained in his home. Visitors to Melkhoutkraal included the Earl of Caledon in 1811, Lord Charles Somerset in 1817 and later another Cape governor, Sir Lowry Cole. The early explorers, Burchell, Thompson and Steedman were his temporary guests. That he was respected by all and sundry during his 35 years in Knysna, there is no doubt. He was buried near the site of the old homestead of Melkhoutkraal. The epitaph on the tombstone (enscribed in modern times) reads:

In memory of George Rex Esquire, proprietor and founder of Knysna, died 3rd April, 1839.

The grave is in a stone-walled enclosure off the national road, a kilometre beyond the turnoff to the Heads, from the west. Within the enclosure are two tall pine trees and the graves of George Rex junior and his wife Jessie. There are no remaining descendants of the male line of the Rex family in Knysna.

The naval brig, *Emu*, was the first vessel to attempt entrance of the Knysna lagoon; this took place on 11 February 1817 and ended in disaster – the wreck is still visible at low tide. In May of the same year the *Podargus* (sent to salvage the *Emu*) made a perfectly safe entrance and exit. In 1831 Rex launched his own brig, the 140-ton *Knysna;* made of stinkwood, she traded between South Africa and Mauritius and carried the expedition that added East London to the Cape in 1836. East London was originally named Port Rex. For many years thereafter the *Knysna* did stout service as a collier on the English coast.

Despite the hazards of crossing the shallow bar, shipping continued throughout the sail and steam eras for 120 years; virtually the only link between Knysna and the outside world. In 1928 came the railway and the end of the seaport.

Knysna is built on the banks of the Knysna Lagoon, a landlocked estuary fed by the Knysna River and connected with the sea between two great sandstone cliffs, the Knysna Heads. It is an atmospheric town and the area in which it is sited is one of the lovely places on earth. The town has a population of 30 000 and is famous for its stinkwood, the most prized and beautiful South African indigenous wood. It is the centre of the timber industry of the great Knysna and Tsitsikamma Forests. Furniture craftsmen produce fine articles in stinkwood, yellowwood, white alder and blackwood and a thriving boat-building industry continues, using modern techniques in fibre-glass construction. Oyster production is carried out on a large scale.

The waters of the Knysna River, in common with all other rivers south of the Outeniqua range, are a deep wine colour and this is no sign of impurity; it is due to oxide of iron and vegetable matter. Close proximity of the mountains is the cause of the rivers in the region rising rapidly in rainy weather.

The old St George's Anglican Church, consecrated in 1855, stands adjacent to the new church in a peaceful, wooded garden off Main Street. A dwelling house preserved from the goldrush days (late 1880s) has been removed to Queen Street and is now the Millwood Museum.

There is a large variety of holiday accommodation in Knysna and this includes six hotels and eight caravan parks apart from bungalow, rondavel and cottage establishments. Golf, bowls, tennis, yachting, boating and water skiing are well provided for and there are some 27 varieties of fish to be taken from rock, jetty and boat. An airfield adjoins the town.

The scenic drives in and around Knysna have a special appeal. On the road to the Heads (called George Rex Drive) a concrete causeway connects the mainland with Leisure Isle, a charming residential suburb with its art gallery, safe lagoon bathing and opportunities for fishing and boating; and in this serene setting is the well-known two-star Leisure Isle Hotel, a fashionable meeting place and ideal base from which to explore the region.

At the Heads there is an excellent vantage point for rock anglers. Whales often cross the bar into the estuary, the scene of a dozen or more fatal ship-crossing attempts in bygone days. In this enchanting setting there is a licensed restaurant and a quaint tearoom.

Between the causeway turnoff to Leisure Isle and the lagoon mouth there is another turnoff left to the summit of the eastern Head. The road is steep but the journey should not be missed. The tang of the fresh sea-breeze, the flower bedecked veld and the spacious views make this a memorable short drive. On the reverse side of the promontory a concrete strip road leads through Coney Glen Nature Reserve to the rugged coastline of the Indian Ocean; a place of beauty and tranquillity.

The western Head is accessible only by boat and special cruises are arranged to the privately owned Featherbed Nature Reserve by the two licensed cruiser organisations, Lagoon Charter and Lightleys.

For the Salt River Road scenic circuit, it is necessary to take the national road back in the direction of George. The Salt River flows into the Knysna Lagoon about two kilometres west of the town. Just before it is reached there is a turnoff to the right along a gravel road that follows the bank of the river, sweeping up the valley in enchanting rural and forest scenery, and then climbing sharply up the hillside. From the top of the hill the view of Knysna River is magnificent. Further on at the junction of roads, the branch to the right leads back into Grey Street, Knysna, to complete the 8-kilometre circuit.

Noetzie River Mouth
The way of the national road between Knysna and Plettenberg Bay is very pleasant and there are a number of interesting diversions. Beyond the Heads turnoff and outside the limits of Knysna town, the next turnoff from the national road to the right is a gravel road that winds seawards through a pine forest and ends on a cliff high above the ocean. From the cliff there is a steep descent along a private road of concrete strips to the splendid wide beach of Noetzie River Mouth, closed in by indigenous forest dotted with seaside houses, several designed like Spanish castles.

Brackenhill Falls
From the national road the next turnoff to the right is another forest road that leads to Brackenhill Falls, a series of lovely cascades of the Noetzie River.

Knysna Main Forest — Prince Alfred's Pass to Avontuur
Today's road engineering makes it possible for the traveller to penetrate what Sir John Barrow described as impenetrable – the depths of the Knysna Forest. If you take the road that turns off from the national road opposite the Noetzie turnoff, signposted 'Uniondale', you will reach the main forest. The same road continues over Prince Alfred's Pass to Avontuur (adventure), a town in the Long Kloof. The whole distance is 80 kilometres, altogether a scenically rewarding drive.

The first portion of the drive passes through pine and gum plantations along a tarred road and enters the virgin forest as a gravel road. In the heart of the main forest a signpost diverts the visitor to a 'Big Tree', a giant yellowwood known as King Edward's Tree. It is between 600 and 800 years old (previously but nevertheless erroneously calculated to be between 1 700 and 2 000 years old), over 41 metres tall from ground to bole and more than 7 metres in circumference.

This densely wooded area is traditionally the feeding ground of a herd of large elephants and it affords shelter to small game and many birds. The Knysna loerie (*Tauraco corythaix*), a large bird of green and red plumage, is strikingly beautiful – to quote Roberts, 'the sight of a loerie in flight is almost a tourist attraction'. The Knysna elephants, in modern times

1. The famous two-star Leisure Isle Hotel, situated in a romantic atmosphere surrounded by the Knysna Lagoon, is visited by guests from all over the world.
2. Flat-bottomed vessels still cross the shallow bar between the Knysna Heads to enter the Knysna Estuary. Leisure Isle, the town, and the Outeniqua range can be seen in the background.
3. Arum lilies growing on the roadside near the turnoff to Buffalo Bay from the N1.
4. The grave of George Rex, founder of Knysna, in a stone-walled enclosure off the N1 a kilometre east of the Heads turnoff.

1

3

2

1. *Fuchs Kraal on the eastern side of Prince Alfred's Pass in the Outeniqua range. See pages 105 and 110.*

2. *Nature's Valley, as seen from the Grootrivier Pass. See page 111.*

3. *Bloukrans Pass, crowded in by tall yellowwood and stinkwood trees festooned in moss. See page 111.*

made legendary by the South Africa authoress Dalene Matthee's novels, *Circles in the Forest* and *Fiela's Child* (translated into 13 languages and causing world attention to Knysna), having been reduced to three in number by 1987, has brought about the reintroduction, by State environmental authority, of three young females, with the hope of successful breeding.

Over 50 species of trees have been marked by the forestry department for easy identification. Of special interest are the two types of stinkwood, two types of yellowwood, ironwood and bastard ironwood, white red and thorn pear, wild gardenia, red and white alder, wild chestnut, Cape ash and Cape teak, saffron and bastard saffron, Cape beech and Cape plane, candlewood and swarthout (not to be confused with the alien blackwood used in furniture manufacturing).

Two kilometres beyond the 'Big Tree' sign post is the Diepwalle Forest Station from where the Elephant Walk commences. Arranged by the Department of Forestry, this is an 18-kilometre nature trail through the indigenous forest and an opportunity that should not be missed. Permits, obtainable at the forest station, are issued free of charge and the visiting hours are 6 am. to 6 pm. The whole route, 18 kilometres, takes about six and a half hours and there are two shorter walks: 8,9 kilometres taking three hours and 14,3 kilometres taking five hours.

Opposite the turnoff to Diepwalle Forest Station another road leads to the delightful 15-kilometre drive to Gouna Forest Station.

Continuing northwards through the main forest, the road passes the turnoff right to the Kransbos Forest Station then traverses the lovely dale of giant ferns – Dal van Varings – where there are picnic sites and pleasant walks. Six kilometres beyond here is the famed Spitskop View Site. From the Buffelsnek Forest Station the road descends steeply to the valley of the Kruis River and the little settlement of Kruisvallei. Here the road forks. The road to the left continues northwards and the road to the right branches eastwards and back to Plettenberg Bay. Seven kilometres along this road to Plettenberg Bay is Paardekop with its fabulous view over mountain and valley right through to the coast.

Back on the way to Avontuur the road crosses the Keurbooms River to commence its spectacular assault of the Outeniqua Mountains by way of Prince Alfred's Pass. The two South African road engineer stalwarts, Andrew Geddes Bain and his son Thomas, were both involved in the construction of this pass. Father planned the route in 1856 and son carried out the work, completing the pass in 1867. It was named in honour of Queen Victoria's son, Prince Alfred, the Duke of Edinburgh, who, in company with members of the Rex family had hunted elephant in the Knysna forest in 1864.

Substantially the same as when constructed, no attempt should be made to hurry the journey in this mountain crossing; the road was not built for present-day speeds and the scenic splendour of the entire route encourages a meandering pace. In negotiating the narrow passage known as Reed's Poort, the road crosses the Fuchs Kraal, far below. It then climbs over the saddle, known as Voor die Poort, before the final

complicated 12-kilometre climb to the summit, 1 045 metres above sea level. The 5-kilometre descent to Avontuur and the fruit-producing Long Kloof is fairly straightforward.

Garden of Eden
Returning to national road N2, sixteen kilometres from Knysna, on the left, the road passes a part of the indigenous forest that has been named the Garden of Eden. It makes a convenient short stop to walk in the forest. The forestry authorities have attached identification tags on the various species of indigenous trees.

Harkerville and Kransview
Not far beyond the Garden of Eden, on the right of the national road, are the signposts to Harkerville and Kransview, beautiful forest reserves that reach down to the rugged cliff-bound coast, where there are delightful places to picnic.

Plettenberg Bay
The Portuguese navigators named this Bahia Formosa, and it certainly is a beautiful bay. The deep inlet, protected by Cape Seal (the western peninsula better known by its Afrikaans name, Robberg) has the magnificent backdrop of the converging Outeniqua and Tsitsikamma Mountains. Its three sheltered beaches, stretching over eleven kilometres, provide the main attraction for summer holidays, when the influx of people increases the population from 10 000 to 30 000.

The bay received its present name in 1778 when Governor Joachim van Plettenberg made his visit during his tour of the forests and timber cuttings. To mark the place a possession of the Dutch East India Company, he erected a monolith bearing the arms of the Company. Some years after van Plettenberg's visit an attempt was made to establish a port. A stone timber house of considerable dimensions (62 metres by 6,5 metres) was constructed and ships did call and load, but the harbour was never a success and the building fell into disuse. The monolith and the ruins of the timber house are national monuments, although the original monolith was removed by the Historical Monuments Commission to the South African Cultural History Museum in 1964 and replaced with a replica.

The rocky islet called Beacon Island is separated from the mainland by the estuary of the Piesangs River and takes its name from the navigational beacon set up in 1772 and used for checking chronometers. The beacon was twice renewed in the nineteenth century. The Piesangs River (banana river) is so named from the wild bananas (*Strelitzia alba*) that grow on its banks. Beacon Island was the site of the headquarters of a Norwegian whaling company which commenced operations in 1912 and closed down in 1920. The whales still come into the bay to calve in the spring. Today a luxury holiday hotel occupies this spectacular site.

A lovely resort of equable climate, Plettenberg Bay is particularly popular with up country people who own cottages. It is a schedule stop of Air Cape and the S.A. Transport motor-coach tours, and has a modern shopping area, a fine golf course, four hotels and four caravan parks.

Robberg Nature Reserve

The mountainous peninsula south-west of Plettenberg Bay is a nature reserve and an angler's paradise. Robberg (seal mountain) was so named because the area was once inhabited by the mammals.

Paths criss-cross the 240-hectare reserve. A gravel motor road across the peninsula leads to a parking area high above the ocean where there are spacious views of steep cliffs, a beautiful stretch of white beach and a small island. The peninsula is divided into two sections and at 'the gap' a path leads down to the beach. On the southern section there is a huge cave where heaps of sea shells indicate the one-time presence of prehistoric Strandlopers.

The resort at Robberg provides the visitor with bungalow accommodation and pleasant sites for caravans and camping.

Keurbooms River and Keurboomstrand

An extension of Plettenberg Bay that provides fine opportunities for boating and water sport is the area of the pretty Keurbooms River and the broad lagoon formed where the Keurbooms and Bitou Rivers join, north-east of the town. A short distance up the river is the public resort of cabins and caravan sites in a magnificent wooded nature reserve setting. In the upper reaches, in such places as Whisky Creek, the indigenous trees form a canopy over the river in strikingly beautiful areas.

Keurboomstrand lies on the rocky coast south-east of the river where there is a wide variety of caravan, cottage, bungalow and shack accommodation that adjoins another fishermen's beach and mounds of sea shells said to be thousands of years old. The local hotel is pleasantly situated and is filled with antiques.

Grootrivier Pass, Nature's Valley and Bloukrans Pass

After crossing the Keurbooms River the traveller enters Tsitsikamma country (from the Hottentot word meaning 'clear water') and from here to the Storms River Bridge is an especially beautiful section of the Garden Route.

The old national road substantially follows the road completed by Thomas Bain in 1885 and in so doing traverses two spectacular river gorge passes. Grootrivier Pass descends steeply losing some 200 metres before reaching the floor of the gorge, the river mouth lagoon and the lovely seaside settlement of Nature's Valley.

Six kilometres after climbing out of the Grootrivier Pass is the commencement of Bloukrans Pass where the road winds down in a series of hairpin bends to cross the Bloukrans River and then rises steeply again to reveal delightful views back at the coastline.

The great forest closes in on both of these passes and at the roadside are giant yellowwoods festooned in moss, arum lilies mixed with ferns and the pink and mauve blooms of the wild chestnut trees. There are several places to picnic in the passes and there is a tearoom in Nature's Valley.

What is known as the Tsitsikamma Highway (national road N2) follows a straightened course and takes in three magnificent high level bridges over the river gorges, and was opened in June 1984. This is South Africa's first toll road in modern times.

Tsitsikamma Forest and Coastal National Parks — Storms River

This magnificent national park lies to the east of the above-mentioned passes and consists of two sections: the indigenous forest on the northern side of national road N2, west of the Paul Sauer Bridge (this is 100 kilometres east of Knysna and 84 kilometres west of Humansdorp) and a narrow strip of coast, 76 kilometres long, stretching from Eersterivier estuary (west of Humansdorp) to Grootrivier estuary (east of Nature's Valley).

In the centre of the park is the Paul Sauer Bridge (Storms River Bridge) which crosses the Storms River gorge in a single span of over 138 metres, 129,5 metres above the river bed. At the bridge there is a tearoom and restaurant, a shop and a caravan and camping site.

The beautiful rugged coastal section is a very popular angling resort and skin diver's paradise, the rock pools having a wide variety of fish and other marine life. Spearfishing is not permitted.

Storms River Mouth is 11 kilometres from the national road. In the Parks Board camp there are ocean facing cottages, huts, caravan and camping sites, restaurant and shop. Remarkable for any national park, the Otter Trail commences from Storms River Mouth. The walking time of the 62 kilometre trail is approximately 24 hours. There are sleep-over huts with the trail ending at Grootrivier, Nature's Valley. Enquiries should be made at the Storms River Mouth restaurant.

A few kilometres after the turnoff to Storms River Mouth is another turnoff to the coast to Storms River village and the secluded Tzitzikama Forest Inn, a romantic stop-over. From here arrangements can be made for trail riding and picnics and this is an ideal centre for the Tsitsikamma System of Hiking Trails, a convenient base for those wishing to take advantage of overnight comfort whilst completing sections of the trail.

Continuing on the national road for a further kilometre after the Storms River village turnoff, on the left (north side) of the road, is the entrance to the indigenous forest region, De Plaat, where there are a number of giant yellowwood trees.

Kareedouw Mountains and Pass

Across the Storms River, national road N2 enters open country where the Tsitsikamma range reaches its eastern end and the less impressive Kareedouw Mountains commence. Eighteen kilometres west of Humansdorp the Long Kloof road dips through Kareedouw Pass to join with national road N2.

Humansdorp

Before being by-passed by national road N2, Humansdorp was a convenient stop for Garden Route travellers. It is a busy town serving an agricultural district and is at a junction of roads serving the resorts of St Francis Bay. The town is on the romantic 'apple express' narrow gauge railway between Port Elizabeth and Avontuur and has four hotels and a municipal caravan park.

Humansdorp was founded on the farm of Matthys Human in 1849 and became a municipality in 1906. The population is 5 000.

1. *A view of Plettenberg Bay — the converging Outeniqua and Tsitsikamma ranges providing the magnificent backdrop.*

2. *Ruins of the 18th century stone timber house in use when Plettenberg Bay was a harbour.*

3. *Moorings of the boating club on the Keurbooms River, north of Plettenberg Bay.*

4. *Storms River Mouth, with its crystal clear water and lovely beach.*

5. *Tzitzikama Forest Inn, placed in a restful setting with a magnificent mountain backdrop — an ideal base from which to explore the exciting Storms River region.*

2

1

4
5

3

St Francis Bay

The huge bay stretches from Cape St Francis in the west to Cape Recife in the east and contains several beaches world famous among professional and amateur surfers. The principal resorts of the bay are the village of St Francis Bay (previously Sea Vista), Paradise Beach and Jeffrey's Bay. Of the several rivers that reach the sea in the bay, the Gamtoos, its mouth about halfway between the two capes, is the largest. Reached by road via Humansdorp, St Francis Bay resort has a marina in the Krom River estuary surrounded by elegant white-walled thatched homes and the charming, two-star Hotel Cape St Francis. The three-kilometre stretch of flat beach attracts bathers, anglers, surfers and shell-collectors. Other recreational facilities include yachting and tennis and there is an airstrip for light aircraft. At Seal Point the 36-metre-high lighthouse has a range of 25 kilometres.

Paradise Beach

The little resort of privately-owned holiday houses is on the western bank of the lagoon formed by the Swart and Seekoe rivers where they reach the sea. The lagoon is the sanctuary of a large variety of water birds including flamingoes and swans.

Jeffrey's Bay

A little municipality with a population of 1 500, Jeffrey's Bay was once a port for coasters. It is a popular resort of anglers and surfers and the beaches are renowned for a wide variety of sea shells. The town received its name from the nineteenth century trader, J.A. Jeffrey.

Oudtshoorn and the Little Karoo

Two of the most prominent tourist attractions in South Africa belong to Oudtshoorn. Its world fame centres around the Cango Caves and the ostrich-feather boom during the Victorian and Edwardian eras.

The town is situated astride the Grobbelaars River on the fertile plain known as the Little Karoo, which lies between the great Swartberg and the forest-clad Outeniqua Mountains. Only 67 kilometres from the coast, Oudtshoorn is at an altitude of 305 metres and enjoys a healthy climate with invigorating dry winters and humidity-free hot summers. The annual rainfall average is 250 millimetres.

Oudtshoorn was founded in 1847 and became a municipality in 1863. Its name commemorates Baron Pieter van Rheede van Oudtshoorn, an appointed governor of the Cape who died at sea in 1773 before he could assume office.

The population of Oudtshoorn is 48 000. It is the principal centre of the Little Karoo, a prosperous farming district notable for the production of ostriches, lucerne, tobacco, grain, fruit, wine and cheese. There are three hotels and two motels. N.A. Smit Memorial Park provides first-rate tourist camp facilities, including furnished rondavels, caravan and camping sites and a fine swimming pool. There is a Divisional Council camping site at Schoemanspoort.

A modern Civic Centre, theatre, library, sports stadium (which is the venue for South Western Districts Rugby) and bowling greens (which are floodlit for night play) are all in Baron van Rheede Street. An interesting 18-hole championship golf course fringes the town and is approached from the far end of Voortrekker Street. Squash courts adjoin the golf club-house. There are two tennis clubs and a flying club. Oudtshoorn is a scheduled stop of Air Cape. Visitors to Oudtshoorn are made welcome at all sporting clubs. A free information service is available at the Visitors Bureau at the Voortrekker Street entrance to the Civic Centre.

Arbeidsgenot, the home of Senator Cornelius Jacob Langenhoven, (1873-1932) is in Jan van Riebeeck Road, near the corner of Church Street, and is a national monument. Langehoven, perhaps the most popular of all writers in Afrikaans, was a great poet and champion of the Afrikaans language. In 1918 he wrote *Die Stem van Suid-Afrika* which was set to music by the Reverend M.L. de Villiers and became the South African National Anthem. The modest old house is a museum of Langenhoven's personal belongings which include a number of carvings of his literary creation, the elephant Herrie. In the garden there is a sundial designed by Langenhoven in 1926.

The C.P. Nel Museum contains an interesting collection of local antiquities illustrating life in the Oudtshoorn district during the ostrich feather boom and before. There is a representative collection of firearms and the vehicle section includes an ox-wagon made in 1837 and a chain-drive motorcar of 1898. There are also archaeological and geological exhibits and a collection of stuffed birds. The museum is housed in the original building of the Boys' High School; established in 1881, it is opposite the Civic Centre. The façade of the building is considered the finest stone-masonry workmanship in South Africa.

Ostrich farms and the ostrich feather industry

The ostrich farms of the Little Karoo are unique in the world since in no other place can the ostrich be reared as successfully. Oudtshoorn, as the centre of this district, used to be 'the ostrich feather capital of the world'. Fortunes were made following the discovery that these strange birds could be domesticated, bred and plucked at regular intervals. This important discovery happened in 1869 when a Mr A. Douglas perfected an incubator for ostrich eggs that led to hatching control, lucerne feeding and induced egg laying. Suddenly it was found that ladies fashion houses in Europe were prepared to pay large sums for quality ostrich plumes and high society developed such a taste that prices soared to dizzy heights, prime plumes fetching £115 a pound.

By 1880 the ostrich feather industry was yielding greater profits than any other farming activity in the country. Affluent farmers built the 'ostrich baron castles', birds changed hands for as much as £1 000 a pair and Oudtshoorn remained the most important town in the Cape Midlands for forty years. During the renewed boom in 1913, £3 000 000 worth of feathers were exported.

With the first World War came the slump and fashion conscious women had presumably had enough of feathers, for there was no revival when the war was over.

Today the ostrich industry is firmly established to meet a smaller but nevertheless steady demand. Regular auctions are held in Oudtshoorn and approximately 55 000 kilograms of feathers are marketed annually at prices which vary between R400 and R20 per kilogram, depending on grade and quality.

Although the ostrich is not a gregarious species, most of the birds on farms are raised communally in paddocks. To enable plucking, the bird is caught at the neck with a hooked stick, put into a triangular wooden plucking box and masked by the placing of a sock over the head. Each bird produces one kilogram of feathers every nine months. The white wing and tail feathers of the males are sold to the fashion houses; the rest of the male plumage, which is black, and that of the females, which is grey, are made into feather dusters. The plumage deteriorates after fifteen years and generally, birds are slaughtered at this age. The tender portions of the meat are used for biltong. Handbags, wallets, belts and shoes are made from the leather, novelty ashtrays from the feet, bone-meal for chickens from the skeleton, soap from the fat and fertilizer from the remains. The fertilizer is used on the lucerne fields which provide the main ostrich diet and so the cycle is completed.

The farmer selects pairs of birds for breeding in the spring. The male courts a female by first giving a booming call and he then proceeds to bend his knees and spread out his beautiful plumage; whilst he does it, he sways from side to side in a rhythmic dance – altogether a fascinating performance. The male kicks a depression in the ground in which the female lays a clutch of from 12 to 15 eggs and duties are shared by both birds during the six weeks of incubation. A nest temperature of 45°C is generated by their sittings. For three months after hatching the chick is delicate but thereafter growth is very rapid. Birds reach maturity at 18 months and a breeding ostrich may be productive for 40 years.

The oldest known ostrich to have died of natural causes at Oudtshoorn was 81. The grown males are often very vicious having a powerful forward kick with a downward stroke, the single toenail being very dangerous. The domesticated ostrich lives on lucerne and swallows numerous small stones and other objects to assist digestion and can exist for months without water. Although flightless, a mature ostrich runs at a speed of over 50 kilometres per hour for short distances.

Some of the ostrich farms are organised as show establishments. A few kilometres from Oudtshoorn on the road to Mossel Bay are Safari and Highgate Ostrich Show Farms where conducted tours are held daily. Interesting, informative and really amusing, all stages of the development of the ostrich, the largest living bird in the world, are explained by an expert during the 2-hour tour, with a finale of the handlers competing in an ostrich race.

A number of the mansions built during the boom periods are still to be seen in Oudtshoorn and among these is Pinehurst in Jan van Riebeeck Road. Completed in 1911, it was built under the direction of the eminent architect, J.E. Vixseboxse, who designed President Kruger's house in Pretoria. An historical monument, the building is now part of the Teachers'

Training College. It was during the 1913 boom period that the suspension bridge over the Grobbelaars River was built by engineers from London in a single span of 91 metres. Approached from Church Street, the bridge is also a monument.

Cango Crocodile Ranch
This well-run show farm is close to town on the road to the Cango Caves and has over 200 crocodile specimens which range in size from 35 centimetres to 4 metres. During the one-hour conducted tour the expert will tell you (among many other interesting facts) that the female lays 45 eggs, the crocodile can measure 6 metres and weigh 300 kilograms, he can remain submerged for 2 hours and does not feed for 4 to 5 months during winter. This is an excursion filled with fascination and excitement. An additional feature is the lion enclosure. There is a restaurant providing light refreshments.

Cango Caves
Acknowledged to be one of the most beautiful calcite caverns in the world, the Cango Caves are situated 30 kilometres north of Oudtshoorn in the limestone formation at the base of the great Swartberg range. The caves were proclaimed a national monument in 1938 and are controlled by Oudtshoorn Municipality.

In recent times, after the discovery in 1972 of what was then called the Wonder Cave, spelaeologists continuing with explorations had by July 1978 uncovered another 2 200 metres and in so doing had extended the explored distance of 800 metres to 3 kilometres. The caves have now been numbered: Cango 1 (the original known length of 800 metres) Cango 2 (the Wonder Cave) and Cango 3 and 4 (the latest additions to the explored area). In the new discoveries conservation for scientific research is vital and because spelaeologists fear uncontrolled public access could cause dire damage (mainly through change of atmosphere), the newly discovered caves have not been opened to the public.

Cango 1, open to the public, is a series of 80 caverns and corridors lighted by electricity, where fantastic formations of innumerable stalactites (hanging columns) and stalagmites (growing upwards from the floor) are revealed in sparkling brilliance. There are weird patterns in most delicate colours, some of which resemble easily recognisable objects such as the Pulpit, Canopied Bed, Throne, Leopard, Madonna and Child and Organ Pipes. A fascinating Sonet-Lumière presentation of approximately 48 minutes duration in the Van Zyl's Hall and Botha's Hall caverns, forms part of the guided tour; the sound, light and oratory subtly combine to create an impressive experience.

The constant filtration through the earth of water containing carbon dioxide has, over a great period of time, caused these colossal caverns of stalactites and stalagmites. Van Zyl's Hall measures 107 metres by 54 metres and is 17 metres high; its roof is of a series of beautiful symmetrical folds of grey limestone. Cleopatra's Needle, the 10-metre-high pillar in this cavern has formed over a period of 150 000 years – a cubic centimetre for every 100 years. The completed column (where stalactite has united with stalagmite) measures 12,65 metres. The roof of the Devil's Workshop is 32 metres above the floor at the highest

1

2

1. The Organ Pipes at Cango Caves, a subterranean wonderland of stalactites and stalagmites.

2. Contrasting landscape in the Little Karoo — male ostriches approaching a lucerne field.

3. A Cape-cart enters
Meiringspoort, the spectacular
21-kilometre pass over the
Swartberg.
4. A handsome example of a
feather baron's mansion is
Pinehurst, built in Oudtshoorn
in 1911.
5. Having fun at an ostrich show
farm, Oudtshoorn.

117

point. These are but a few of the remarkable features of the Cango Caves. There are several versions of the manner and circumstances in which the original discovery took place. The popular belief is that in 1780 farmer Van Zyl followed a wounded bushbuck and was lowered by his farm labourers into the cavern, which today bears his name.

The four-storey cavemouth building complex has been designed to cater for every need of the visitor. The facilities include self-service restaurant, à la carte grill room, roof garden, curio shop, dance floor, cocktail bar, crèche and kennels. Over 100 000 people visit the caves annually.

The fully guided tour of the Cango Caves takes about two hours.

Schoemanspoort, Oude Muratie Valley, Rus-en-Vrede and Kamanassie Dam

The drive from Oudtshoorn to the Cango Caves is in itself a pleasant experience; the perfectly constructed tarmac road follows the valley of the Grobbelaars River and winds through Schoemanspoort in fine mountain scenery. At the northern end of the poort, 21 kilometres from Oudtshoorn, is the gravel turnoff through the Oude Muratie Valley, a wild kloof formed by the Le Roux River, to Rus-en-Vrede (rest and peace), the town's main water supply, where there are ideal picnic places and a lovely waterfall with a drop of 61 metres.

Twenty-four kilometres south-east of Oudtshoorn the Kamanassie Dam (14 kilometres long and up to 2,5 kilometres wide) is an important irrigation dam that also provides opportunities for water sport.

Meiringspoort

Separating the fertile Little Karoo from the Great Karoo is the 200-kilometre-long Swartberg range – a magnificent spectacle rising to 2 133 metres at its highest point. Over this formidable barrier there have been constructed some of the most spectacular mountain roads of the sub-continent. Starting at the hamlet De Rust (where there is an hotel) is the southern entrance to Meiringspoort, a pass that carries the eastern fork of trunk road R29 for 21 kilometres through a vertical cleft in the mountains, crossing the Meirings River 32 times. Hemmed in by gigantic precipices of twisted and contorted volcanic strata, at each bend the road reveals a different and more beautiful scene. Wild flowers abound on the roadside and the pass is alive with dassies.

Fourteen kilometres out from the southern entrance a memorial tablet has been erected to C.J. Langenhoven's literary character, Herrie the elephant. Three kilometres beyond the tablet and reached by footpath from the road, a 55-metre-high waterfall plunges into a deep, clear pool.

Meiringspoort was opened in 1858 and was named after Petrus Meiring who owned the farm De Rust. It was he who gave Andrew Geddes Bain, the famous road builder, the idea of linking the Great Karoo and Little Karoo by way of the ravine north of his farm.

At the northern end of the pass is Klaarstroom and en route to national road N1 is Seekoegat. Route R29 meets national road N1 near Beaufort West (Chapter 4).

Swartberg Pass and Gamka Kloof (The Hell)

The western fork of trunk road R29 traverses the mighty range over the Swartberg Pass in a pattern reminiscent of the game of Snakes and Ladders. The scenically beautiful 10-kilometre southern climb to the summit, 1 577 metres above sea level, is followed by the dramatic 13-kilometre northern side descent. The pass was opened in 1888, seven years after Thomas Bain commenced construction. The mountain slopes are invariably covered with protea, watsonias and other flowers of the veld. Winter snowfalls are heavy enough to provide sufficient snow for ski-runs.

Some three kilometres from the summit on the northern side of the pass, a track leads off westwards for 33 kilometres to Gamka Kloof (also known as The Hell), an eerie canyon of the Gamka River, where a strange clan of white people, descendants of the early trek-boers (nomadic farmers), who speak a peculiar language of their own making, have shut themselves off from civilisation in this lost valley. Gamka is the Hottentot word for lion.

Prince Albert

Directly north of the Swartberg Pass is the attractive rural town of Prince Albert, notable for its peaches, apricots and grapes. Founded in 1842, it was subsequently named in honour of Queen Victoria's husband, the Prince Consort. Municipal status was acquired in 1902 and the population is 4 000. There is an hotel and a municipal caravan park. An old watermill in the town has been declared a national monument.

The road to the north forks outside the town; the eastern branch joins with national road N1 at Kruidfontein and the western branch, at Prince Albert Road (Chapter 4).

Calitzdorp

A fine road connects Oudtshoorn with Calitzdorp and the route is made unique by the flocks of ostriches feeding in the lucerne fields.

Calitzdorp was founded in 1845 and laid out on the farm Buffelsvlei which was owned by the Calitz family. In 1913 it became a municipality and the population is 3 000. The district is notable for ostriches, lucerne, tobacco, grapes and other fruit. There is an hotel in the town. At Calitzdorp Warm Baths Public Resort, 22 kilometres from the town on the old road to Oudtshoorn, there are mineral springs, bungalows and a caravan park. Calitzdorp is connected with the Cango Caves by way of an attractive scenic road through Coetzeespoort.

Huisrivier Pass

After crossing a tributary of the Gamka River, a few kilometres north-west of Calitzdorp (where the Divisional Council has provided a caravan park in the lovely riverine setting), the road commences the crossing of a spur of the Swartberg by way of the spectacular Huisriver Pass. In the middle of the pass the Gamka River itself is crossed and the summit is reached at an altitude of 664 metres.

Zoar

The South African Missionary Society established the mission station at Zoar in 1816. It lies beyond the Huisriver Pass on the road to Ladismith and is noted for irrigated cultivation. The name comes from the quotation in the Bible: 'Like the Garden of the Lord, as thou comest into Zoar'.

Seven Weeks Poort

From Zoar there is a branch road north-east to Prince Albert through yet another remarkable pass, the Seven Weeks Poort. Dominated on the east side by the 2 335-metre Seven Weeks Poort Mountain, the highest peak in the Swartberg range, this is one of the scenic wonders of the sub-continent with its colossal, orange-coloured sandstone cliffs overhanging the road. The origin of the name is obscure but it probably refers to the everlasting flowers which abound in the pass. Here too is the habitat of the rare *Protea aristata*.

Ladismith

The little town of Ladismith, with its Victorian era houses, lies in a superb setting at the foot of the western end of the Swartberg, beneath the towering peaks – 2 200-metre Toorkop and 2 189-metre Toringberg. Named after the beautiful Spanish-born wife of Governor Sir Harry Smith, the town had its beginning when the Dutch Reformed Church was built in 1852 and became a municipality in 1862. Ladismith shared the ostrich feather boom of the 1800s and early 1900s and suffered severely when the crash came in 1914. Today it is the centre of a farming district that produces dairy products, fruit, lucerne and ostriches, and has a population of 3 000. There are two hotels and a caravan park.

The road to the north-west joins national road N1 at Laingsburg (Chapter 4).

Long Kloof

Hemmed in by the unbroken Outeniqua range to the south and the parallel Kamanassie hills to the north, the Long Kloof stretches nearly due east to west without interruption for approximately 240 kilometres. A fine tarmac road runs down its length and the traveller along this road can be in no doubt as to the fertility of this handsome valley. Its principal product is fruit, notably apples. After Elgin, this is the second largest apple-producing region of South Africa.

From the east the Long Kloof road, which is R62, branches off national road N2 seventeen kilometres west of Humansdorp and joins with trunk road R57 seven kilometres west of Avontuur. Avontuur, Haarlem, Misgund, Joubertina and Kareedouw are the main centres for fruit despatch along the valley and there are hotels at Joubertina and Misgund and one 3 km from Kareedouw. There is a picturesque Dutch Reformed Church in Kareedouw, and here in the churchyard South Africa's 7th Prime Minister and 4th State President, John Vorster, was laid to rest on 13 September 1983.

A charming relic of a bygone era is the narrow gauge railway which runs from Port Elizabeth and serves the Long Kloof, its principal function being the transportation of fruit from the farm packers to the port. During the summer season excursions are offered on this diminutive 'Apple Express' which passes through some of the finest scenery in the Eastern Cape. Details of these excursions can be obtained from the Port Elizabeth Visitors Bureau.

CHAPTER 4

The Great Karoo

The name Karoo is a Hottentot word meaning 'land of thirst', an apt description of this vast area of more than 250 000 square kilometres forming the heartland of South Africa, characterised by dry climate, scanty soil, rocky outcrops, sparse vegetation and the most vivid sunsets.

Treasure-house of reptile and mammal fossils and unique for its flora, the Karoo was the scene of the greatest animal migrations known to mankind – the dramatic springbok migrations when the lithe and beautifully-marked little antelope congregated in their hundreds of thousands and swarmed across the plains from drought-stricken areas to find better grazing.

Where subterranean water is found and irrigation made possible the soil is highly productive and as a result there are innumerable windmills in the Karoo. On the rare occasion when rain falls an amazing variety of wild flowers come into bloom. The Karoo is of course one of the principal sheepfarming areas of South Africa.

The Cape and Orange Free State are connected by trunk routes that traverse the Great Karoo. National road N1 takes the motorist from Cape Town to Beaufort West and on to Colesberg near the border. Meanwhile trunk route R57, having started at Uniondale (near Oudtshoorn and George), follows a course through Willowvale, Graaff-Reinet and Middelburg and merges with national road N1 at Colesberg, from whence N1 continues through the Free State and Transvaal as the Great North Road.

National road N1, after crossing the Hex River Mountains, enters the Great Karoo.

Touws River

A rail junction and marshalling yard, Touws River was first named Montagu Road and received its present name which means 'pass river' in 1883. It became a municipality in 1962 and has a population of 5 000. The town has an hotel and a caravan park.

Behind the old Douglas Hotel there is an astronomical relic that bears witness to pioneer work in this field in South Africa. A national monument, two concrete pillars commemorate the observation of the transit of Venus on 6 December 1882.

Matjiesfontein

The story of the development of Matjiesfontein (bulrush fountain), an insignificant railway stopping place, is one of the most remarkable episodes in the history of South Africa. It starts in 1876 when James Douglas Logan, a young seaman of 19 years, the son of a Scottish railwayman, left his Australian-bound ship at Simonstown and got a job as porter on Cape Town railway station. Promotion was rapid and at 21, Logan was District Superintendent of the Hex River – Prince Albert Road section of the line.

Persisting with an inclination that he could make his mark in the catering world, Logan persuaded the authorities to allow him to open a restaurant on the platform at Montagu Road (now Touws River). This was before the time of dining cars on trains and

success at Touws River led to his getting the refreshment room concessions from Cape Town to Bulawayo.

Jimmy Logan found that the warm sunshine and dry, invigorating air of the Karoo had cured the chest ailment from which he had long suffered and he determined to establish a health and holiday resort here. In 1883 he bought up large tracts of ground at Matjiesfontein where he built an hotel, a fine house which he named Tweedside Lodge and a number of ancillary buildings to make up a Victorian village and the headquarters of his extensive business enterprises. Soon he was known everywhere as 'the Laird of Matjiesfontein'.

Socialites and the aristocracy came from far and wide to enjoy his hospitality and the health-giving air of the Karoo. Among the visitors to Matjiesfontein were Lord Randolph Churchill, the Sultan of Zanzibar, Cecil Rhodes, Edgar Wallace and Lord Hawke and his cricket team, while Olive Schreiner returned many times to occupy her favourite cottage.

At the age of 36, J.D. Logan was a member of the Legislative Assembly of the Cape Parliament. Upon the outbreak of the Anglo-Boer War, Matjiesfontein became the site of the British Remount Camp of over 10 000 troops and 20 000 horses. The hotel was converted into a military hospital where officers of such famous regiments as the 17th Lancers and Coldstream Guards convalesced and where the turret of the building was used as a lookout post.

When Logan died in 1920, Matjiesfontein was no longer the fashionable resort it had been. Ownership of the village passed through the hands of several members of the family until it was sold in 1968 to Mr David Rawdon (of Nottingham Road and Lanzerac), who completely restored the major part to its original Victorian glory.

The lamp posts which Logan imported from London still light the main street; flags fly from the masts of the Lord Milner, an elegant hotel in the true tradition; next door is the Laird's Arms, a gay English country pub followed by the Post Office, the Standard Bank, The Coffee House and Logan's Masonic Hotel, now called the Losieshuis – in all an obvious place to stay awhile on this harsh, arid route through the Karoo.

From Matjiesfontein a branch road leads northwards through the Verlatekloof and Rooikloof passes to Sutherland and the North Western Cape. (Chapter 14).

Laingsburg

The next town on the national road N1 is Laingsburg, which had its start in 1881 and became a municipality in 1904. It was named after a government official, John Laing. The population is 6 000 and there are two hotels and two caravan parks. The town lies on the main railway line and is the centre of the sheep and wheat district of the Buffalo River. In common with other regions of the Karoo, pomegranates, figs and quinces flourish.

Little change has taken place since the establishment of the town in the Victorian era and it remains the classic example of the South African dorp.

Restored to its original Victorian glory, Matjiesfontein Village, a delectable oasis in the arid Karoo, with its gracious-living Lord Milner.

Fourteen kilometres north of the town at a point where the national road and the railway cross a tributary of the Buffalo, is one of the best preserved of the Anglo-Boer War blockhouses, a symbol of the three-year struggle between the British and republican forces. This double-storey building is an historical monument.

Prince Albert Road
Eighty-four kilometres north-east of Laingsburg is the convenient stop, Prince Albert Road, with its garages, tearoom and hotel. The village lies on the crossroads of national road N1 and the road which leads northwards for 43 kilometres to Merweville (where there has been an exploration for uranium) and southwards for 45 kilometres to Prince Albert (Chapter 3).

Leeu-Gamka
Fraserburg Road has been renamed Leeu-Gamka – a combination of the Afrikaans and Hottentot names for lion, so that the name translated is lion-lion. It is a railhead 39 kilometres north-east of Prince Albert Road and lies on the junction of the road to Fraserburg, 114 kilometres to its north.

Fraserburg
In a bitterly cold part of the Karoo, Fraserburg often has snow in the streets during winter and is an isolated centre in an extensive wool-producing area. Established in 1850 it was named after the Reverend Colin Fraser, father of the much loved Tibbie Fraser, wife of the sixth and last president of the Orange Free State.

Beaufort West
Entering Beaufort West with its pear-tree-lined streets, green playing fields and pretty gardens is a refreshing experience after a long drive through the flat, hot, dry Karoo. It is what its citizens call it, 'the oasis town'. It lies between two rivers, the Kuils and the Gamka, but there is seldom any water in the river beds; the town's lifeline is the Gamka Dam, a great reservoir built in the catchment area, high up in the Nuweveld Mountains, 10 kilometres to the north.

In 1836 Beaufort West was the first town to take advantage of the Cape ordinance which permitted elective municipal councils and thus has the distinction of being the first municipality in South Africa. However, it does not have any particular distinction in its name. When it was founded in 1820 it took the family name of Lord Charles Somerset who also named Fort Beaufort and Port Beaufort, apart from Somerset East and Somerset West. A fine painting of the 5th Earl of Beaufort (Charles Somerset's father) is above the mayoral seat in the town's Council Chamber.

Upon the introduction of merino wool sheep to the district in the 1850s, prosperity came to Beaufort West and during those early years of progress it had among its citizens J.C. Molteno, the wool trader and champion of responsible government. Known as the 'Lion of Beaufort', he became the first prime minister of the Cape and it was he who founded the first bank in Beaufort West in 1854. The town's weekly newspaper *The Courier* was established in 1869 and

has been published continuously ever since that year. Beaufort West became a locomotive depot and marshalling yard when the railway reached there in 1880. In addition to the famed merino wool farms there are important karakul farms and racehorse studs in the district, which is under exploration for uranium deposits.

In the centre of the town, at the corner of Church Street and Donkin Street (the main thoroughfare), a cluster of buildings lend unmistakable character to the environment. Among these buildings there are three national monuments. Closely related to the history of the town is the Old Town Hall, the construction of which was started in 1865 and completed in 1867. Typical of the flamboyant Victorian era in which it was designed, the bold, whitewashed building carries a distinctive and somewhat elaborate clock tower canopied in bronze. It once housed (at one and the same time) the offices of the local authority, the magistrate's court and library, and during an emergency when the dam above the town broke its walls, it served in addition as post office, school and mission church. Military authorities used part of the building during the Anglo-Boer War. Facing the three buildings from Donkin Street, on the right is the red-roofed Mission Church, built in 1872 and now a museum, and on the left across Church Street, the Dutch Reformed Church; inaugurated in 1830 it is a prominent landmark with its white tower 45 metres tall.

Beaufort West has a population of 25 000 and to cater for the influx of visitors in the winter season there are four hotels, a motel with caravan park, a municipal caravan park, and holiday farms in the district. Recreation facilities include the 18-hole golf course, two bowling clubs, numerous tennis courts and a swimming pool. There is a modern airport and active flying club.

Seven kilometres from Beaufort West is the Karoo National Park; opened in 1979 for the preservation of indigenous flora and fauna, the park is over 20 000 hectares in extent. To reach the approach road, turnoff into Church Street opposite the Dutch Reformed Church.

Rosesberg and Molteno Passes – Loxton
The road to the north of Beaufort West leads through the Rosesberg and Molteno Passes for 126 kilometres to Loxton.

Loxton, a road-junction town in the heart of a sheepfarming district, was named after the Dutch Reformed Church minister, the Reverend A.E. Loxton, who was responsible for the building of the church in 1899. The population is 2 000.

Three Sisters
Continuing on the N1 route, after passing the tuberculosis sanatorium at Nelspoort, the road reaches the well-known landmark called the Three Sisters, three almost identical dolerite-capped hills. This is the point of the continuation of trunk road R29 to Johannesburg via Kimberley – the southern terminal being George.

Victoria West
Sixty kilometres along route R29 is Victoria West, another old-world Karoo town with a population of

4 000. It had its beginning with the building of the Dutch Reformed Church in 1843. It was named in honour of the British Queen and became a municipality in 1858. The town is the centre of a rich wool-farming district and has an hotel and caravan park.

Hutchinson, 13 kilometres to the south, used to be called Victoria West Road and is the mainline railhead for Victoria West.

Britstown
Another important centre on trunk road R29 to Kimberley is Britstown, which is half-way between Cape Town and Johannesburg. It lies on the junction of trunk road R32 which is the main route to South West Africa – Namibia. Apart from sheep-farming in the district, wheat and lucerne crops flourish in a large area under irrigation from the Smartt Syndicate Reservoir. In the town is the two-star Trans Karoo Hotel and a municipal caravan park.

Vosburg
Forty-eight kilometres due west of Britstown, on the way to Carnarvon (Chapter 14) is Vosburg where there is an hotel and Bushman paintings.

Richmond
After Three Sisters, national road N1 reaches Richmond, an orderly little town with shade trees and pretty gardens. Named in honour of the Duke of Richmond, father-in-law of the Cape governor, Sir Peregrine Maitland, it was founded in 1844 and today has a population of 3 500 serving a rich sheep-farming district.

The scene of several battles during the Anglo-Boer War, it was the birthplace of the South African medical pioneer Dr Emil Hoffa, founder of the science of orthopaedics.

Richmond has two hotels and a municipal caravan park. It is the junction of a number of subsidiary roads which lead off northwards to Victoria West, Britstown and De Aar and in a southerly direction to Murraysburg, Graaff-Reinet and Middelburg.

Hanover
From the platteland (rural) towns of South Africa have come many of the citizens that influenced its history. Hanover is one of those small towns. The Reverend T.F. Burgers, the second president of the South African Republic (Transvaal) was a preaching minister of the Dutch Reformed Church in Hanover, and a controversial one at that – he had caused a stir in expressing his disbelief in the literal truth of the Bible – when the burghers summoned him to Pretoria in 1873 and he was elected president by a large majority.

Hanover was named after the town in Germany and lies on the junction of national road N1 and trunk road R32. In the heart of the wool-producing Karoo, it has a population of 2 500 and there is an hotel and caravan park.

De Aar
An historic railway town, De Aar, in the middle of nowhere, is the most important country junction in the whole of the South African railway system. As a railway marshalling yard it is superseded only by Germiston which is the heart of the intense Witwatersrand railway complex. De Aar has 110 kilometres of track and a traffic rate of 92 trains a day. This is where the lines from the Western Cape, the Eastern Cape, the Orange Free State, Transvaal and South West Africa meet. It is a huge trans-shipment depot and the crack passenger trains, the Blue Train, Orange Express, Trans-Karoo and Drakensberg change crews here.

De Aar (the vein) was the name of the original farm with an underground watercourse and the settlement there was started in the 1870s by the Friedlander brothers. Municipal status was granted in 1904. Today De Aar has a population of 29 000 and there are two hotels and a caravan park. The town is well-known for its extreme winter and summer temperatures.

In the house where Olive Schreiner lived for a number of years the Historical Monuments Commission has placed a bronze inscription:

In this house the well-known authoress Olive Schreiner (1855-1920) and her husband S. Cronwright-Schreiner lived from 1908 to 1913. Here she completed her book 'Woman and Labour' and wrote two articles for special occasions entitled 'Thoughts about Women' and 'Closer Union'.

Trunk Route R57 from Uniondale to Colesberg

Uniondale
At the southern terminal of trunk route R57 is Uniondale which was founded in 1856 when two rival rural settlements united. It used to be famous for its wagon building and is today the centre for sheep and general farming operations. Municipal status was granted in 1881 and the population is 3 000. The town has an hotel, caravan park, some very interesting 19th century buildings, an historical fort and an old watermill.

Willowmore
A district noted for its wool and mohair production and famous breeding studs of sheep and angora goats supports the town of Willowmore. The Beervlei flood control dam, 29 kilometres north of the town, is an interesting feature and pleasant place for a picnic lunch. There is an hotel and caravan park in this town of some 4 000 people.

From Willowmore there is a road leading south-east through the magnificent Baviaanskloof to Patensie and Port Elizabeth, a total distance of 288 kilometres.

Aberdeen
Laid out in 1856 by the Dutch Reformed Church, Aberdeen was named after the birthplace in Scotland of the famous Dutch Reformed minister, the Reverend Andrew Murray. The Kamdeboo Mountains form a backdrop to the town which has a population of 6 000. The district is noted for its sheep

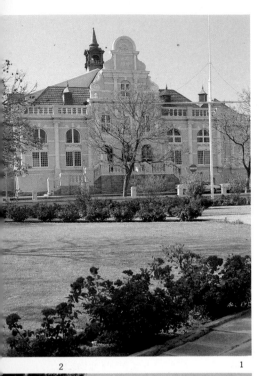

Graaff-Reinet, an historic Karoo town, restored and preserved.
1. The Town Hall, built in memory of Queen Victoria.
2. John Rupert Theatre, once a mission church.
3. Grootkerk, a near replica of Salisbury Cathedral.
4. Reinet House, a parsonage for a century, now a museum.

*The Drostdy, Graaff-Reinet —
not only an exquisite showpiece
but a well-managed present-day
hotel with every amenity. Do not
miss an opportunity to stay
here.*

and cattle farms. The town has an hotel and a municipal caravan park.

Kudu signs on the roadside are a reminder that these browsers migrated from the eastern Cape and, having reached as far north as Middelburg, are frequently seen in the Graaff-Reinet area.

Graaff-Reinet

One of the historic towns of South Africa, Graaff-Reinet has a population of 38 000. Its steady prosperity in the course of its 200 years of existence and present-day serene atmosphere successfully hide its beginning as a frontier outpost plagued with turmoil, insurrection and war. At the same time it is one of the country towns of the republic where its people have taken care to preserve their heritage and so it is that nostalgia persists there.

On 19 July 1786 the Dutch East India governor at the Cape, Cornelius Jacobus van der Graaff, proclaimed a new eastern frontier district which he named Graaff-Reinet after himself and his wife whose maiden name was Cornelia Reinet. Moritz Hermann Otto Woeke, a man from Stellenbosch, became the first landdrost and it was he who chose the fine site in the valley formed by the horseshoe bend of the Sundays River from which to administer the vast, newly-created district that stretched from the Gamtoos River to the Great Fish River, an area of over 77 000 kms. Woeke had the unenviable task of maintaining law and order in the sparsely settler-inhabited district where wild animals and marauding tribes were the hazards of the day.

The second landdrost, Andries Stockenström Snr. (father of the controversial lieutenant-governor), was unceremoniously removed from office when, in 1795 the local burghers took matters into their own hands. They were dissatisfied with the handling of frontier disturbances and concerned with the instability of the Company and simply declared an independent republic installing one of their number, Commandant Adriaan van Jaarsveld, as president. The isolated republic lasted a few months, ending in 1796 not long after the British took possession of the Cape.

The Reverend Dr Andrew Murray, who together with his family had a great influence on the people of Graaff-Reinet and for that matter upon the whole of the Cape Province, arrived in the town in 1824. He was born in Aberdeenshire, Scotland, in 1794. After qualifying for the Presbyterian ministery (closely allied with the Dutch Reformed Church) he answered a call of the London Missionary Society, upon representations of Lord Charles Somerset, to make up the shortfall of clergy in the Dutch Reformed Church in the Cape. His arrival in Graaff-Reinet marked the commencement of a remarkable example of family unification of the two major European communities in South Africa, and which persists among the English and Afrikaans speaking peoples of Graaff-Reinet to this day.

At the age of 28 Andrew Murray married 16-year-old Maria Stegman who was of Lutheran-Huguenot ancestry and they occupied the old parsonage, now known as Reinet House, for some 40 years; and here their large family grew up. Five of the six sons entered the church: John was the first professor of the

theological Seminary at Stellenbosch; Andrew (also the Reverend Dr.), one of the greatest spiritual leaders in South Africa, whose work in Bloemfontein, Worcester, Cape Town and Wellington led to his being elected six times Moderator of the Dutch Reformed Church; William founded the Institutes for the Blind and the Deaf in Worcester; Charles followed his father as minister at Graaff-Reinet and he occupied Reinet House for a further 40 years, and George served at Willowmore, Swellendam, Oudtshoorn and Worcester.

Reinet House was so named by Helen Murray (a daughter of the Reverend Dr Andrew Murray) when she was principal of the Midland Seminary and the building was used as a hostel for girls training to become teachers. Prior to this, since its construction in 1812, it had been in continuous use as the parsonage of the Dutch Reformed Church and it is interesting to note that it was built at the expense of the government. Today the old parsonage is Graaff-Reinet Museum. Proclaimed a national monument, it is the perfect example of Cape Dutch architecture and houses a remarkable collection of eighteenth and early nineteenth century Cape furniture of the typical contrasting combination of yellowwood and stinkwood and is one of the finest period house museums in South Africa. The classical H-plan, thatched and gabled Cape Dutch building has lofty yellowwood ceilings and wide front and back stoeps. An enormous basement covers the whole area of the house.

At the back of the house is a unique double curved stairway (added in 1820) with the entrance to the cellar between the flights of steps. Here too is the famous grape vine of the Black Acorn variety, until 1983 when it became necessary for survival reasons to be severely pruned, it was reputed to be the largest grape vine in the world. It was planted by the Reverend Charles Murray in 1870 and had a girth of 2,38 metres at 1,5 metres above the ground and covered an area of 123 square metres.

Parsonage Street, the thoroughfare of approach to Reinet House, has many interesting buildings including some of the vernacular Karoo-style architecture and there is a strong intention ot have all of these restored.

On the right of Parsonage Street, diagonally opposite Reinet House is another Cape Dutch H-plan homestead, apparently built sometime between 1819 and 1831. From the time of its acquisition by the government in 1916 it served as the magistrate's residence and so became known as The Residency. Declared a national monument in 1962, it has, since 1978, became an annexe of the museum and houses one of the finest collections of sporting rifles in the country – the excellent Jan Felix Lategan Memorial Gun Collection, which includes a unique collection of Botha hunting rifles.

Careful restoration and ingenious conversion has provided a delightful asset for the town. This is another nineteenth-century building in Parsonage Street, about midway down the street on the same side as The Residency – it was a mission church for more than a hundred years and is now the John Rupert Theatre. Donated by Dr Anton Rupert to the

Town Council in perpetual trust, the name honours Dr Rupert's father.

The building which housed the first library in Graaff-Reinet, on the corner of Church and Somerset Streets, is now the Reinet Museum and contains the Lex Bremner collection of Karoo reptile fossils (under the curatorship of the South African Museum, Cape Town), the Rykie Pretorius clothing collection and the Rembrandt van Rijn collection of paintings by Townsley Johnson (being reproductions of rock paintings).

One of only three remaining churches in South Africa designed in the traditional cruciform plan is the Dutch Reformed Mission Church in Church Street, near the corner of Parsonage Street. It dates from 1821 and is a national monument. Another donation to the Town Council, it was restored in 1965 by the Rembrandt Group and converted into an art gallery. It bears the name Hester Rupert Art Museum in memory of Dr Anton Rupert's mother. The gallery is devoted entirely to contemporary South African art and contains a fine representative collection.

Strikingly beautiful, the Grootkerk, complete with 'ringmuur' (traditional encircling wall) stands in a commanding position at the head of Church Street. It was the fourth Dutch Reformed Church to be built in Graaff-Reinet and the third on the site. The inaugural sermon was delivered by Professor de Vos on 11 September 1887, during the ministry of the Reverend Charles Murray. The architect, J. Bisset of Cape Town, employed local stone for construction in the early Gothic style – a near duplication of Salisbury Cathedral in England. The church can seat a congregation of 1 500 and possesses a fine collection of ecclesiastical silver – most of Cape origin dating from 1768 and 1810. Also known as the mother church, this is a national monument.

Approached from Bourke Street, between Middle and Somerset Streets is the historical monument, Drostdy Hof, Stretch's Court, a picturesque complex of mid-nineteenth century cottages restored in 1970. The story of the cottages goes back to 1855 when Captain Charles Lennox Stretch, an Irishman from Limerick and noted soldier, land surveyor and Member of the Cape Legislative Assembly, acquired a large piece of land comprising seven erven at the rear of the Drostdy which faced Church Street at the foot of Parsonage Street. Stretch sub-divided the land and a number of transfers were effected, many of these were to Coloured labourers. Early diagrams of the area bear the name Vrystraat (free street) as the name of the present-day Stretch's Court, a cul-de-sac connected with Church Street through the gardens of the Drostdy by way of a narrow path. It is not certain whether the name Vrystraat referred to the free passage which linked with Church Street or whether it was associated with the freed slaves living there.

Drostdy Hotel stands in Church Street on the axis of Parsonage Street, the site of the original Drostdy, designed by Louis Thibault and erected in 1806. Restored by the Oude Meester Group of Companies during the mid 1970s the hotel embraces the cottages of Stretch's Court. The whole complex is a national monument and the Drostdy is rightfully regarded as one of South Africa's finest country hotels.

On Magazine Hill, to the north of the town near the Panorama Hotel, there is an old powder magazine, a reminder of the arduous lives of the frontiersmen in this nineteenth century outpost of civilisation. The magazine was built in circa 1831 by a firm of merchants who had to carry large supplies of gunpowder used for blasting in road construction and for firearms in protection against savages and wild animals. The Old Magazine has been restored and is an historical monument.

Graaff-Reinet is certainly the most interesting town in the Karoo and situated as it is with the surrounding heights providing catchment for the Sundays River, it has adopted the nickname *Gem of the Karoo* – which fits the plan of things; a gracious, old-world town almost encircled by a river, the irrigation furrows (serving every home) that follow streets lined with an assortment of trees; cypresses, oaks, pines and jacarandas providing the shade and palms lending the oasis touch – all placed in the heart of an arid tableland.

There is a handsome Town Hall on Church Square constructed in 1910 in memory of Queen Victoria. Graaff-Reinet has a fine record as an educational centre, its parallel-medium Teachers' College, the co-educational boarding school, the Union High School and Die Hoër Volkskool (the first Afrikaans medium school to be established in the Cape), founded in 1917, 1919 and 1922 respectively, are acknowledged throughout the country for their achievements.

Blended with the modern facilities of shops and hotels is Graaff-Reinet's old-world charm. Fortunately it did not escape the surge of the neo-Georgian-style architecture so popular in the Cape during the 1850s. The addition of an upper storey and the simple lines of the façade introduced an interesting variation of the single storey, thatch-roofed Cape Dutch-style. A classic example of this is at No. 24 Caledon Street. Although the building was previously used for other purposes, a typical Victorian chemist shop has continuously traded at this site since 1870. An unusual national monument, the present-day Graaff-Reinet Pharmacy occupying these premises proudly displays its Honduras mahogany shop fittings, teak door and show windows, gold inlaid dispensing bottles, stone jars with brass taps, china jars and Victorian scales. In Victorian times the chemist manufactured and sold 'aerated water'.

The sporting and recreational attractions lie to the north of the town. Rugby is the traditional game. The sports field and bowling greens adjoin the park on the western side. A little farther afield is the attractive Urquhart Park on the banks of the Sundays River, where the municipality has laid out first-rate facilities for caravanners and where bungalows may be rented. Beyond the caravan park is the Van Ryneveld Pass Dam in the Sundays River. This is the town's water supply and it provides irrigation for over 2 500 hectares of farmlands. The dam is a fine spectacle when overflowing and is a popular water-sport venue in the summer.

Graaff-Reinet used to be a centre of the ostrich feather industry but now draws its prosperity from a rich district of Merino sheep, Angora goat, cattle and

Bizarre natural erosion — the Valley of Desolation. In this picture, Spandau Kop, which is a considerable distance from the Valley, is brought close-in by the magic of the telephoto lens.

horse stud farms, and the fruit and other produce of the irrigation schemes.

To the north-east on the Middelburg road, the statue of Andries Pretorius (by sculptor Goert Steynberg), is a reminder that he and Gerrit Maritz led hundreds of families from the district in the Great Trek. Beyond the statue is the golf course, with its licensed clubhouse, and the turnoff to Lakefield Aerodrome.

Valley of Desolation

Graaff-Reinet is the obvious starting point for a visit to the Valley of Desolation. The 16-kilometre drive along a tarred road is in itself a scenically rewarding experience with sweeping views of the town and the encircling Sundays River. The most spectacular time to visit is sunset.

The exit from Graaff-Reinet is on the road to Murraysburg (R63). Past Urquhart Park the road skirts Van Ryneveld Pass Dam. A short distance beyond the dam is the signpost indicating the turnoff to the west. This tarred approach road makes a steep climb to the mountain summit, 1 400 metres above sea level and 600 metres above the town. The road leads to a clearing where there are picnic places and whitewashed stones indicating footpaths leading off to the view sites.

The Valley of Desolation presents a scene that is at once awesome and attractive. The extreme example of erosion, cliffs and rock pinnacles of many grotesque shapes (some rising 120 metres above the valley floor) have been carved out of the dolerite-capped shale and sandstone massif by erosive forces of 200-million years. And beyond this confused grouping is the seemingly endless plain of the Great Karoo. The Valley of Desolation forms part of the extensive Karoo Nature Park (with its amazing variety of flora, including the rare elephant-foot tree) and is a natural monument.

Spandau Kop

From high points in Graaff-Reinet and from the view sites of the Valley of Desolation, the conical mountain, Spandau Kop, is conspicuous. A Prussian soldier, Werner, who settled in Graaff-Reinet gave it the name Spandau Kop because its inaccessibility likened it to a fortification and so he named it after the old fortress and arms manufacturing town 12 kilometres from Berlin.

Murraysburg

The town of Murraysburg lies on route R63 at the crossroads: Graaff-Reinet – Victoria West and Nelspoort – Richmond, and when founded in 1856 was named after the Reverend Dr Andrew Murray and the owner of the original farm, J. Bruger. It became a municipality in 1883 and has a population of 4 000. There is an hotel in the town and a caravan park on the outskirts.

New Bethesda

From Graaff-Reinet, trunk route R57 heads northwards reaching a branch road after 30 kilometres that leads west to the mission town of New Bethesda, established in 1886. The little town lies at the foot of the 2 404-metre peak, Compassberg, in the Sneeuberg range and is the highest point in the Cape Province apart from some peaks of the southern Drakensberg, close to the Lesotho border. The peak received its name in 1778 during the visit of Colonel Jacob Gordon and Governor van Plettenberg, because the neighbouring country could be surveyed from there. At Bethesda Road, the railhead, there is a motel. Continuing, R57 negotiates first Naudesberg Pass and then Lootsberg Pass (a favourite haunt of the eagle) and eventually joins with R32 as it enters the municipality of Middelburg.

Middelburg

In 1852 Middelburg was founded as the middle point of the circle formed by the older towns: Cradock, Graaff-Reinet, Richmond, Hanover, Colesberg and Hofmeyr. It lies in mountainous country on the banks of the Little Brak River in a rich sheep-farming district. Grootfontein Agricultural College (once a British military cantonment) is three kilometres from the town. The population of Middelburg is 17 000 and there are two hotels, a municipal caravan park and golf course.

Rosmead

A rail junction, Rosmead lies in a group of Karoo hillocks 10 kilometres east of Middelburg on route R56 to Steynsburg. Rosmead has an hotel.

Steynsburg

The municipality of Steynsburg with its population of 7 000 is situated in a well-watered area in typical landscape of dolerite-capped hillocks of the vast Karoo.

Some 20 kilometres north of Steynsburg on the road to Venterstad (Chapter 6) at the foot of the Suurberg, is the farm Bulhoek, where the Historical Monuments Commission has placed a bronze plaque in honour of President Paul Kruger's mother, Elsie Steyn. (Steynsburg was named after a relative of hers). For more than two decades from the 1930s there was a bitter dispute as to the birthplace of the President, with strong contention that he was born at Bulhoek, but in 1958 it was established that he was born at Vaalbank on the Brak River in the Colesberg district.

Noupoort

An important railway centre that handles as many as 100 trains a day, Noupoort was founded in 1852 and is 40 kilometres north of Middelburg. The reason for the name 'narrow passage' relates to the kloof in the Carlton Heights through which the railway passes. The population is 8 000 and there are two hotels. This part of the Karoo is bitterly cold in the winter.

Colesberg

Trunk route R57 converges with national road N1 just outside Colesberg, another old-world Karoo town which serves a famous horse and sheep stud district, the stock thriving in the crisp dry air. The 1 707-metre Coleskop, a prominent landmark, remarkably symmetrical and conspicuous on all sides from long distances, was known by the early travellers as Tooverberg (magic mountain) because it is always deceptively close.

The town lies approximately halfway between Cape Town and Johannesburg and, although off the highway, is a recognised stopover.

Colesberg was named after Sir Lowry Cole, the governor at the time of its establishment in 1830. It became a municipality ten years later. The concrete thoroughfares, Victorian era houses and graceful churches provide the nostalgia experienced in a number of the old Karoo towns. Of the churches the two reformed churches, Nederduitse Gereformeerde Kerk and the Gereformeerde Kerk, were built in the 1860s and are national monuments; the Anglican Church, built in 1854, was designed by Sophy Gray (wife of Bishop Gray) and is beautifully decorated with stained glass window, carved oak lectern, oak pulpit and font.

An incident in the identification of the first diamond to be found in South Africa is unique to Colesberg. This concerned one John O'Reilly who brought the diamond (not yet identified) into the town. He showed it to the magistrate, Lorenzo Boyes, in the premises of the wholesale merchants, Draper and Plewman. The magistrate tested the stone by scratching the letters 'DP' on a window pane. The diamond had been found by a child in Hopetown in the last days of 1866 and the window pane is now a treasured exhibit in the Colesberg Kemper Museum. The name of the museum honours the donor of a fine collection of Boer War relics. The building of the museum, which is in Murray Street, dates from 1860. Built for Colesberg Bank, later absorbed by Standard Bank, it was for years the Town Clerk's office.

Bell Street, Colesberg, is worth investigation. Here, there is the last remaining horse mill in the country, in working order, and a complex of six houses, numbered 26 to 32, a fine representative selection of the vernacular Colesberg-Karoo architecture, some with the 'brakdak' (mud roof) waterproofed by special technique of the time of construction in the 1800s. The mill and residential complex are national monuments.

The house named Coniston in Sarel Cilliers Street was built in 1838. It recalls another singular incident in history. This was where Lord Loch, the moderate British governor at the Cape stayed when he came to meet President Paul Kruger – halfway between Cape Town and Pretoria, to discuss the 'Klein Vrystaat' (the incorporation of a part of Swaziland into the Transvaal) in 1891.

Paul Kruger was born on the farm Vaalbank on the Brak River in the Colesberg district in 1825.

About 16 kilometres south-west of Colesberg, on national road N1 to Hanover, is the farm Quaggasfontein. Here, near the Seekoe River, is the site of a beacon placed by Governor van Plettenberg who took a considerable interest in exploring the colony during his term of office from 1774 to 1785. The stone beacon was engraved with the Company's monogram, the governor's name and arms and the date, 1778. It marked the farthest point reached on his journey and the north-eastern limit of the colony. Portion of the stone is preserved in the South African Museum, Cape Town.

Hendrik Verwoerd Dam

Thirty kilometres north of Colesberg, national road N1 in leaving the Karoo crosses the Orange River at Norvalspont (where there is an hotel) and enters the Orange Free State (Chapter 13).

Upstream to the east of the crossing is the Hendrik Verwoerd Dam, an irregularly shaped man-made lake, more than 100 kilometres long and 15 kilometres wide, part of the gigantic Orange River Scheme and one of the great projects of world engineering. The scheme involved the construction of the huge P.K. Le Roux Dam, downstream, and two tunnels – one 82 kilometres long connecting the Orange and the Fish Rivers and the other 58 kilometres long connecting the Fish and the Sundays Rivers.

CHAPTER 5

Port Elizabeth and District and the Settler Country

Port Elizabeth

The second city of the Cape Province, Port Elizabeth stretches some sixteen kilometres along the shores of Algoa Bay at the foot of a 75-metre plateau. It has a population of 617 000.

Algoa Bay (named by the early Portuguese) was visited by the Dutch in 1690 and again in 1752 when a beacon of possession with the arms of the Dutch East India Company was erected at the mouth of the river they named the Baakens (after the beacon). Very little use was made of the bay and its shores remained uninhabited by Europeans until 1799 when the British built Fort Frederick. Named after Frederick, Duke of York, the Commander in Chief of the British Army, it was garrisoned by an officer and 350 soldiers.

It was not until 1820 when 4 000 British settlers landed that the town was founded. The acting governor, Sir Rufane Donkin, named the town after his wife, Elizabeth, who two years previously had died tragically in India at the age of 28. As a tribute to her memory he erected a stone pyramid seen on the hill near the lighthouse. The pyramid bears a plaque with the memorial inscription:

One of the most perfect of human beings who has given her name to the town below.

Port Elizabeth is a major ore, wool and mohair port and it pioneered the establishment of the automobile industry in South Africa. Samcor (previously Ford) and Delta (previously General Motors) have plants here.

The city enjoys a temperate climate and has many attractions for the visitor. Apart from its famous beaches it has fine golf courses, bowling greens, tennis courts and sports fields. Port Elizabeth Turf Club at Fairview on Cape Road and St Andrew's Racing Club at Arlington on the Skoenmakerskop road hold meetings throughout the year.

The Visitors Information Bureau is in the library building on the Market Square and enquiries regarding tours should be made here. Port Elizabeth has a unique under-cover bus terminal, approached through Traduna House at the top of Main Street. The city's system of express motorways is another example of South Africa's phenomenal progress in road engineering. The air terminal is in South Union Street and H.F. Verwoerd Airport is only three kilometres south-west of the city, near the suburb of Walmer. Conveniently situated, in 10th Ave, Walmer, is the recommended 2-star Walmer Gardens Hotel.

Fort Frederick

On the western side of the now conduit Baakens River, overlooking the harbour, are the ruins of Fort Frederick, a national monument. The fort is at the southern end of Belmont Terrace; from White's Road the turnoff is in the opposite direction to that of the Donkin Reserve. The original walls and old cannon may still be seen and the strategic siting of the fort will be appreciated. Outside the northern wall of the fort, in the tranquil surroundings of well-kept lawns, is the grave of Captain Francis Evatt of the 21st Regiment of the Light Dragoons. Commandant of the fort from 1817 until his death in 1850 he is affectionately remembered as the father of Port Elizabeth; it was he who supervised the landing of the settlers in 1820.

Donkin Memorial and Reserve

Reached from the city by taking White's Road up the hill and turning right into Belmont Terrace, the Donkin Memorial and surrounding four-hectare reserve is a national monument. This preserves the order of Sir Rufane Donkin that the reserve 'not be alienated, encumbered, or built upon'. The lighthouse beside the pyramid has been in use since its construction in 1861, and the building at its base houses a military museum.

Built on a steep hill in Donkin Street on the northern side of the reserve is a row of double-storey houses integrated into a single unit to form a typical Victorian era terrace. The whole street was proclaimed by the Historical Monuments Council, thus preserving the traditional appearance of the vicinity of the famous reserve.

What is today called the Old Grey Institute faces onto the Donkin Reserve from across Belmont Terrace at its northern end. From the date of its structural completion in 1859 until 1914 it housed the famous Grey High School which outgrew the premises and moved to Mill Street. The school was named in honour of Governor Sir George Grey who played a major part in the revival of higher education in the Cape during his term of office, 1854 to 1861. Although altered by such changes as the addition of the clock tower the building is a pure example of the revival of Gothic-type architecture peculiar to the nineteenth century. Now a Teachers' Centre, the Old Grey Institute is an historical monument.

In Belmont Terrace, facing the Donkin Reserve, between White's Road and the Old Grey Institute is The Edward Hotel. A prominent landmark and indeed part of the city's heritage, it was built in 1900 under the expert eye of the famous London architect, Victor Jones, who brought the *Art Nouveau* style to Port Elizabeth, and to this day the hotel retains the distinctive atmosphere of Edwardian times. Its central Palm Court (once a covered access for horse-drawn carriages); its restaurant, The Causerie; its three bars, Edd's Inn, The Terrace and Place Belmont; its comfortable bedrooms and master suites, all provide the visitor with that peaceful feeling of another era.

Campanile and Harbour Area

At the foot of Jetty Street, near the original harbour landing for rowing boats, stands the 52-metre-tall Campanile, built in 1923 as a memorial to the 1820 settlers. It remains a significant reminder of the 4 000 British pioneers of the Eastern Cape who lived with one hand on the plough and the other on the gun. For those who undertake the 204-step spiral climb to the top, the view is rewarding. The Campanile contains a carillon of 23 bells which ring changes every day at 8.32 a.m., 1.32 a.m. and 6.02 p.m. The modern freeway system has obstructed the much photographed view of the Campanile and pedestrian access is under the paved deck covering what was Jetty Street. Close to the Campanile are the railway station and customs house, relics of the Victorian era.

1

2

1. Port Elizabeth's Donkin Reserve overlooks Algoa Bay. The stone pyramid was erected in memory of Elizabeth Donkin after whom the city was named.

2. The first inhabitants of the future city were the garrison of Fort Frederick; built in 1799 it commanded the mouth of the Baakens River and now overlooks the busy port.

3. and 4. Two views of the historic Port Elizabeth Market Square: on the left the City Hall with the Post Office to its left rear, and on the right the Public Library at the foot of White's Road.

In Flemming Street on the harbour side of the Market Square is the old Harbour Board Building; known as the White House, it is one of the few examples of the *Art Nouveau* style of architecture in South Africa, its interior being lavishly adorned with fine wood sculpturing. The corner-stone was laid in 1904 and the building is a national monument.

Castle Hill
Parsonage House, 7 Castle Hill, is the oldest remaining private dwelling house in Port Elizabeth. Built in 1827 for the Reverend F. McCleland, the first Colonial Chaplain, it is a fine example of the type of town house built in the Eastern Province during the early nineteenth century. It has been converted into a domestic museum and contains a collection of furniture and household appliances which aptly illustrate the way of life of the pioneer settlers. Parsonage House and the Sterley Cottages, Numbers 10 and 12, on the opposite side of Castle Hill, have recently been restored. All three buildings are historical monuments. Sterley was an 1820 settler and the first constable of the town. His appointment dated from 1822 and he apparently had a sizeable family because both cottages were used to accommodate its members.

Market Square
The City Hall, a national monument, faces the historic Market Square, at the head of Main Street and was opened in 1860. It was partly destroyed by fire in 1977 and has been completely restored. The square has for long been the focal point of the city. Being close to the original ships' landing place, this was where farmers' products were first marketed and where the people assembled for meetings. A central bell announced the arrival of a ship, called the people to the market and served as a fire alarm.

A replica of the Bartholomew Dias Cross stands on the Market Square. This was the cross that Dias erected at Kwaaihoek (q.v.) in Algoa Bay at its northern end, to mark the most easterly point of his historic voyage in 1488.

An extension of the activities on the Market Square came about in 1883 when the Feather Market Hall was completed. At first it was used exclusively to house and auction feathers during that incredible ostrich-feather boom of Oudtshoorn and other districts of the Karoo and later it coped with the auctions of wool, hides, skins and fruit. In 1886 the South African Exhibition was held here. The Feather Market Hall is close to the Market Square, across the street from the Post Office, and is still used for exhibitions as well as for other functions.

A distinctive building facing the square and another national monument is the Public Library. Its architectural style known as *Gothic Revival* was the vogue in England during the nineteenth century. The stucco façade was manufactured in England, sent out in numbered pieces and assembled on the site. The library was opened in 1902 and the stone statue of Queen Victoria was placed at its entrance in 1903. Following upon her death in 1901 many replicas of this finely sculptured image were distributed throughout the Empire. The library has a fine collection of Africana.

Churches
Among the lovely churches of Port Elizabeth are St Mary's Anglican Church which dates from 1897 and is opposite the library facing its own terrace above Main Street; St Augustine's Roman Catholic Church, built in 1886, is across White's Road from the Opera House; the Presbyterian Church, close to the northern end of the Donkin Reserve, was consecrated in 1865, and St John's Methodist Church in Havelock Street at the intersection of Lawrence Street was opened in 1896. Lower down in Havelock Street at the corner of Whitlock Street is the Holy Trinity Anglican Church, rebuilt in 1897 after the pyromaniac, Miss Livingstone Johnstone, had destroyed the previous building. At about the same time she attempted to burn down the newly-built St Mary's Church above Main Street; the altar alone was damaged. Before ending her days on Robben Island, Miss Johnstone nearly succeeded in burning down the government offices.

Horse Memorial
Probably unique anywhere in the world is Port Elizabeth's Horse Memorial which stands in Cape Road, near the junction of Russell Road. It is the work of Joseph Whitehead and was erected by public subscription in recognition of the services of innumerable horses which perished in the Anglo-Boer War of 1899-1902. The memorial bears the inscription:

The greatness of a nation consists not as much in the number of its people or the extent of its territory as in the extent and justice of its compassion.

St George's Park
The 73-hectare park (completely encircled by Park Drive) dates almost from the beginning of Port Elizabeth and remains the main recreational centre. The history of its playing fields is unchallenged in the number of firsts in South African sport. In 1843 the first cricket club in South Africa was established here and in 1880 the first athletics club; this was followed by the first cycling club in 1881 and the first bowling club in 1882. In 1889 the South Africa versus England Test was the first cricket test in this country and in 1891 this was the venue for the first rugby test.

This famous park also contains a fine botanical garden, a swimming pool and steam baths, the Mannville Open Air Theatre, the Cenotaph and Memorial to the fallen soldiers of the famous local regiment, Prince Alfred's Guard, dating back to 1877 and the Pearson Conservatory named after Henry Pearson, one of the city's most remarkable personalities; he served sixteen terms as Mayor, became a Member of the Cape Legislative Assembly then Treasurer General of the Cape in 1880 and finally Colonial Secretary in 1889.

The main entrance to St George's Park is at the end of Western Road on the central hill. The buildings of the King George VI Art Gallery and the Fine Arts Hall flank the entrance gates. The gallery has permanent collections of South African, British and Oriental works of art and the hall is used for special exhibitions.

Settler Park

Another considerable asset of Port Elizabeth is its Settler Park, a 54-hectare sanctuary on the banks of the Baakens River. In this well-wooded, tranquil setting a variety of indigenous flora has been re-established, and a collection of buck, wildebeest and water-fowl introduced.

Victoria Park, near the Airport, is the home of the South African Dahlia Society.

Opera House

The state-owned Opera House in White's Road is the headquarters of the Cape Performing Arts Board in the Eastern Cape. Regular performances of drama, symphony, opera and ballet are staged in the beautifully equipped theatre.

University of Port Elizabeth

Opened in 1965, the University of Port Elizabeth has faculties of arts, science, education, law and economic sciences. Its 850-hectare campus on the Marine Drive, beyond Summerstrand, is a tremendous asset to the city. This is the only dual-language medium university in South Africa. The campus of the Port Elizabeth Technikon is near the university.

Humewood

Situated so as to afford glorious swimming and surfing in the safest conditions and where the water is always clear, Port Elizabeth is a popular summer resort. The mild waters of the Indian Ocean with temperatures ranging from 16°C to 23°C make bathing most enjoyable. At night the whole of the two-kilometres-long esplanade is ablaze with coloured lights.

Less than 3 kilometres to the south of the city centre is Humewood, famous for its fine beaches, Humewood Beach and King's Beach (where the British Royal family swam during their 1947 visit). The resort has been imaginatively developed with wide promenades, children's pools with fountains and a water-chute, miniature railway, amphitheatre, gardens, putting courses, car parking facilities, restaurants, change rooms, hot seawater baths, a tidal bath surrounded by lawns and a skating rink.

On the Humewood beachfront is the famous Port Elizabeth snake park, museum and oceanarium. The museum houses exhibits of settler and natural history. The snake park, known the world over for research in serum, has a large and fascinating collection of reptiles, including crocodiles, pythons and hundreds of deadly-poisonous snakes. During three demonstrations in the mornings and two in the afternoons, the attendant handles the live snakes and explains the habits of the various species. The adjoining nocturnal animal section is a fascinating addition to the park.

The tanks of the oceanarium contain a wide and colourful variety of fish and other marine life. The huge central tank is occupied by three bottle-nosed dolphins who, with the assistance of their trainer, provide the most delightful half hour of entertainment to be had anywhere. This great variety show of tricks and display of almost human intelligence takes place twice a day. A baby dolphin was born here in captivity.

Adjoining the oceanarium and overlooking the sea is a delightful tea-garden.

One of the most pleasant experiences is to take a stroll into Happy Valley, where there is a fairyland of flowers, lawns, lily ponds and winding paths.

On the Marine Drive here at Humewood, directly opposite the famed Hobie beach, is Beach Hotel, Port Elizabeth's social rendezvous, ideally situated for holiday makers and short stay visitors alike. "The Beach", as it is called, has all the attributes for high recommendation.

Other amenities at Humewood are a number of other hotels, the Humewood Bowling Club, Humewood Golf Club, Boet Erasmus Rugby Stadium and a magnificently positioned caravan and camping park. From Humewood the drive south-westward passes the seaside suburb of Summerstrand.

Popular drives from Port Elizabeth

Marine Drive via Humewood to Skoenmakerskop and return via Victoria Drive and Walmer is a 40-kilometre drive along the picturesque rockbound coast which returns through the residential garden suburb of Walmer. There are attractive picnic spots all along the coast where good catches are made throughout the year of musselcracker, poenskop and elf. Bait is easily obtainable at low tide. Worth remembering on this drive is the very attractive two-star Walmer Gardens Hotel with its lovely pool and so convenient for H.F. Verwoerd Airport.

At the Willows (18 kilometres) there are rondavels for hire, a caravan park and tearoom. One-and-a-half kilometres further along at Willow Grange are camping and caravan sites. Skoenmakerskop has no beach but it does have natural swimming pools. Five kilometres beyond Skoenmakerskop is the turnoff to Sardinia Bay, which has a beautiful beach.

Seaview (30 km) is best reached via the N2 to Cape Town. Here there are delightful picnic places and fishing spots bordering close to the road. The little resort is famous for gully fishing where large catches of galjoen, blacktail and hottentot are made, and there is a tidal pool, golf course and an hotel. Another asset of the area is Seaview Game Park, inland 2 km from the sea.

Van Staden's River Mouth

On the dual highway (national road N2 to Cape Town) a short distance beyond Greenbushes is a turnoff to the coast and Van Staden's River Mouth which is approximately 30 kilometres from the city.

The extensive lagoon, tall sand dunes and the expanse of grass and wooded hills all go to make this a place of beauty. The beach abounds with sand mussels and the fishing for steenbras and musselcracker is excellent. The holiday amenities are furnished bungalows, camping and caravan sites and tearoom. The river is navigable in small boats up to the gorge.

Van Staden's Pass

A spectacular bridge now carries national road N2 high above the Van Staden's River gorge and it is no

Two hotels that grace the Port Elizabeth scene. 1. 2. and 3. Historic Edward Hotel (part of the local Heritage Trail) overlooking the Donkin Reserve and Algoa Bay. 4. 5. and 6. Beach Hotel, Humewood, directly opposite the famous launching pad for Hobie-catters — here Gino's restaurant 'The Bell' is the most popular of the city's rendezvous. So close to safe bathing and recreational activities, Beach Hotel is an obvious choice for holidays.

4

5

longer necessary for motorists to negotiate the Van Staden's Pass. However the old road through the pass remains a very popular and lovely drive and there are opportunities for picnics in the wooded gorge and bathing in the river pools.

Just before reaching the pass from the Port Elizabeth side there is the Wild Flower Reserve, open from sunrise to sunset and ideal for walks and picnics. The Eastern Cape is notable for a wide variety of flora; watsonias, ericas and proteas are some of these. A short distance beyond the pass there is an hotel at Thornhill.

Gamtoos River Mouth

A great resort for fishermen, Gamtoos River Mouth is approximately 65 kilometres west of Port Elizabeth. The turnoff from national road N2 is just before the Gamtoos River bridge is reached. Built in the days when the river was crossed by ferry, is the hotel, a kilometre upstream from the bridge. The River takes its name from a Hottentot tribe that once inhabited the area.

Baviaanskloof and Gamtoos Valley – Hankey, Patensie and Loerie

Comparatively remote, the Baviaanskloof (baboon gorge) and Gamtoos Valley region is probably more beautiful than any other region of the Eastern Cape and is easily accessible from Port Elizabeth. At about 53 kilometres west of Port Elizabeth on national road N2 there is a turnoff inland leading to Hankey and a further 150 kilometres of stunning scenery. This is a memorable drive and takes a full day to complete.

The road follows the course of the Gamtoos and Couga Rivers, for part of the way keeping company with the narrow gauge railway. It passes through the little towns of Hankey and Patensie, centres of this rich citrus-, vegetable- and tobacco-producing valley with tremendous views of the forest-covered Grootwintershoek range crowding-in to the north. The highest peak in the range, the 1 759-metre Cockscomb, is also the highest mountain in the Eastern Cape. Before reaching Hankey there is a turnoff to the right to the picnic spot, Yellowwoods and a forest of the magnificent indigenous trees. Beyond the little town a signpost on the left hand indicates the road to the historic Dr Philip's Tunnel, a national monument. Missionaries and their Hottentot charges dug this tunnel in the mid-nineteenth century to enable irrigation of their lands. Above the tunnel is the geological curiosity, 'Die Venster' (the window), from where there are fine views of the Baviaanskloof mountains.

The Kouga Dam, beyond Patensie, is worth turning off the route to see. From here onwards wilder country is reached and the untarred road negotiates several gorges and mountain passes in the Baviaanskloof where orange-coloured sandstone cliffs, aloes, proteas, pelargoniums, arums, wild fig and other indigenous trees, contribute to varying scenes of great beauty. At about 30 kilometres short of Willowmore the road emerges from the Baviaanskloof and enters the Karoo.

There are many attractive camping sites and picnic places along the route but there are no hotels between Patensie and Willowmore. Baviaanskloof

has been declared a natural monument.

Returning to Hankey, from where a road leads due east for 27 km to the railway village of Loerie, a picturesque stopping place of the 'Apple Express'. This is the site of an important water storage dam of the Port Elizabeth municipality and the centre of the limestone quarries of the Eastern Province Cement Company, with its interesting ropeways.

Swartkops, Redhouse and Amsterdam Hoek

Eleven kilometres to the north of Port Elizabeth is Swartkops which lies near the mouth of the river of that name. That is the venue for important regattas – sailing, rowing and power-boating. The water-side clubhouse is architecturally unique, and the hospitality of the club members is acknowledged throughout South Africa. The river abounds with a variety of sporting fish.

Upstream some four kilometres is the riverside suburb of Redhouse where there is yachting, boating, fishing, golf and an hotel. This is a much favoured place for picnicking.

The enchanting hamlet of Amsterdam Hoek is close to the river mouth. Here a narrow road skirts the water's edge where colourful landing stages and jetties help create an authentic Dutch atmosphere.

St George's Strand

Beyond the Swartkop River bridge is the comparatively new suburb, Blue Water Bay, and further on the turnoff to St George's Strand where there is a vast stretch of white beach and good surfing. Its other attractions are the picnic places, camping sites and splendid views of the islands in Algoa Bay, including Bird Island with its gannet colony, the largest in the world.

Colchester

At Colchester, 43 kilometres north of Port Elizabeth, national road N2 crosses the Sundays River near the mouth and here in a desert-like setting of enormous sand dunes, a popular summer weekend resort has developed. The resort is notable for the large cob caught in the river, aquatic sporting facilities in the extensive estuary and the unusual recreation of sand-skiing on the dunes. Furnished bungalows can be rented and there are camping and caravan sites.

Uitenhage

Founded in 1804, Uitenhage was named in honour of Commissary-General J.A. Uitenhage De Mist of the Batavian Government who came to the Cape to take-over from the British in 1802. In 1803 he carried out an extensive tour of the colony and increased the number of districts from four to six by adding Uitenhage and Tulbagh. The first landdrost was Captain Ludwig Alberti, a German-born soldier who was a mercenary of the Batavian Government. Prior to taking up his appointment of landdrost he commanded Fort Frederick at Algoa Bay. When the British recaptured the Cape in 1806 he was sent to Holland where he wrote a book in German entitled *The Kaffirs on the South Coast of Africa* which remains one of the most enlightening early accounts.

In 1806 Major Jacob Glen Cuyler (he was later promoted to colonel and finally general) was appointed landdrost. He was born in Albany, New

York, where his father was mayor. His family sided with the British during the American War of Independence and that was how he came to enter the British Army. During his term of office the entire eastern frontier was administered from Uitenhage. He had the unenviable task of officiating during the Slagtersnek Rebellion of 1815 and was responsible for the welfare of the 1820 settlers whose frontier region was named Albany after his native town.

Uitenhage was proclaimed a municipality in 1841 and the railway connecting it with Port Elizabeth was opened in 1877, by which year several wool washeries were functioning.

The town is pleasantly situated on the banks of the Swartkops River at the foothills of the Winterhoekberg. Its wide streets are shaded by jacaranda and oak trees and there are many attractive gardens. The population is 150 000. Uitenhage has a significant industrial output, the major share coming from the motor industry; Goodyear and Volkswagen have the largest plants.

In this well laid out town a number of beautiful old buildings have been preserved. In Caledon Street, the main thoroughfare, the Old Drostdy, built for Landdrost Cuyler in 1806, has recently been restored to receive the Africana Museum. Amongst the collection of clothing, household utensils and furniture gathered together from the pioneer days of Uitenhage there are some particularly interesting items; these include the De Mist Bible, donated by the founder of the town to its inhabitants, the ceremonial dress of Adriaan van Kervel, Governor of the Cape in 1737, and personal relics of Landdrost Cuyler (1806-1828).

Also in Caledon Street is the Dutch Reformed Church, built in 1817 in graceful and simple lines. It is today used as a church hall.

The delightful Old Railway Station dates from 1875 and houses a railway museum which includes two vintage steam locomotives. This old station, which is a museum piece itself, is in Market Street.

On the corner of Caledon and Church Streets is the beautifully preserved and much-photographed Victoria Tower. Completed in 1899 it once housed the magistrate's courts and post office. It was customary in the country towns of the Cape for these government departments to share premises. The building is still being used by the state.

Uitenhage's Town Hall, opened in 1892, faces onto Centenary Square, part of the Old Market Square.

Cuyler Manor, the elegant Cape Dutch homestead of Landdrost Cuyler, was completed in 1814 and remained the home of his family for 150 years. It is situated where the general had his farm, 4 kilometres out from the town on the Port Elizabeth road and now forms part of the Uitenhage Museum. The old watermill is an added attraction.

The Drostdy, Railway Station, Cuyler Manor and another homestead in Baird Street, Blenheim House, have all been declared national monuments.

The central Magennis Park approached from Church Street, is noted for its many beautiful flowers, especially dahlias, and for its aviaries. The caravan sites in the park are positioned amongst the trees. At Cannon Hill there is a succulent and cactus garden and a fine view of the town.

Ten kilometres to the north of Uitenhage is the Springs Recreation Park and Reserve. The famed artesian 'eyes' deliver between three and four million litres of crystal water a day. Here there are places to picnic, tennis courts, a swimming pool and a children's playground. A nature trail follows the crest of the hills that encircle the Reserve.

Uitenhage has five hotels, an 18-hole golf course and several bowling greens.

Despatch

Between Uitenhage and Port Elizabeth is Despatch, a residential municipality with a population of 36 000 and an hotel. Bethelsdorp, between Port Elizabeth and Van Stadens, is a Coloured peoples township within the Port Elizabeth municipality.

Sundays River Valley and Kirkwood

To the north of Uitenhage lies the famous Sundays River Valley and its principal centre, Kirkwood. Reached by tarmac road, Kirkwood is 51 kilometres from Uitenhage and 80 kilometres from Port Elizabeth.

The Sundays River rises in the Sneeuberg range near the peak, Compassberg, and flows through Graaff-Reinet and Jansenville before breaking through the Suurberg to be harnessed at Lake Mentz from where the fertile valley is irrigated. The drive up the valley past magnificent farms, notably citrus, is a memorable experience.

Pioneers in the Sundays River Valley venture include the unfortunate J.S. Kirkwood from Port Elizabeth who went bankrupt after years of endeavour in promoting an irrigation scheme in the 1880s and Sir Percy Fitzpatrick, financier, politician and author of *Jock of the Bushveld* who was instrumental in bringing the construction of Lake Mentz (named after the Minister of Lands) to conclusion in 1922. The origin of the name of the river is obscure but it was probably named after a Boer family, Zondag, who lived in the valley in the eighteenth century.

Situated on a high promontory that forms the right bank of the Sundays River some six kilometres from the co-operative centre, Hermitage, is the Look Out, burial place of Sir Percy and Lady Fitzpatrick and their two sons. From this vantage point there is a superb view of the extensive valley of citrus growers. The site is an historical monument. To reach the Look Out you turnoff the main road to Kirkwood to the right opposite Sunland railway siding (this is about 2 kilometres north of Fitzpatrick Library in the village of Hermitage) along a gravel road that crosses the main canal from where the direction is signposted.

Kirkwood is the principal centre of the Sundays River Citrus Co-operative and in the winter picking season its packhouses and juice processing plants are the scene of perpetual activity. The valley produces about twenty-five percent of South Africa's citrus output – exporting ten million cases of oranges. (A case of oranges has a mass of 15 kilograms). A lovely time to visit this beautiful valley is in October when the air is heavy with the perfume of orange blossoms. Kirkwood has a population of 6 000, it was founded

1. *Families crowd a watering point in Addo Elephant National Park.*

2. *The diminutive 'Apple Express' crosses the Van Stadens River gorge by means of the highest narrow-gauge bridge in the world.*

140

1. Dias Cross and environment at Kwaaihoek, an isolated headland in Algoa Bay.

2. The famed Port Elizabeth Oceanarium is across the road from Humewood's main beach.

3. Hobie beach is between Humewood main beach and Summerstrand.

in 1913 and received municipal status in 1950. The town is noted for its roses and jacarandas and has an hotel.

Addo Elephant National Park

In the village of Addo there is an hotel and here at the commencement of the Sundays River Valley the road forks: to the left is the branch to Kirkwood and to the right the branch road leads to the Addo Elephant National Park, situated in the heart of dense bush along the foothills of the Suurberg range.

The park is 7 450 hectares in extent and the elephant camp which occupies 4 000 hectares is completely fenced and encircled by motor road. The construction of the Armstrong fence, named after the ranger who carried out the work with steel lift-cables and tram-line posts, was completed in 1954, and finally secured the safety of elephant from man and man from elephant. Because of the destruction caused to farms in the Sundays River Valley the authorities had attempted to liquidate the entire Addo elephant population. In 1919 the big game hunter, Major Pretorius, shot and killed over a hundred elephants before a halt was called. The fate of the few remaining elephants and the continuing destruction of farms hung in the balance until the area was proclaimed a national park in 1931.

The impenetrable wilderness that Pretorius called 'a hunter's hell' makes the ideal sanctuary for the elephant who thrives on the spekboom, the predominant vegetation that is interwoven with melktou, tree-fuchsia, sneezewood, gwarri and a variety of other trees and creepers providing a luxuriant denseness, supported by other interesting plants such as aloe, mesembryanthemum and crassula.

The elephant population in the Addo Bush has increased from 17 in 1954 to 100 in 1985. They differ in certain respects from other African bush elephants, probably as the result of isolation and inbreeding. The tusks of the Addo herd are smaller (females are often tuskless) and the ears tend to be smaller and more rounded.

When Addo was proclaimed a National Park there was a small herd of Cape buffalo and this has increased to some 250 head. This very shy animal is seen mostly in the early morning or late afternoon. The buffalo and the reintroduced black rhino can be seen in the same areas as the elephant. The Parks Board has cleared a portion of the bush and reintroduced species of antelope indigenous to the eastern Cape: these include eland, kudu, bushbuck, red hartebeest, grysbok and duiker. There are also bush pig, antbear, vervet monkey and jackals in the park and the bird species number about 170.

Accommodation is offered in self-contained rondavels (without cooking facilities). The caravan and camping park has an ablution block and braai facilities. There is an à la carte restaurant, shop and petrol and oil station. The Suurberg Inn is 16 kilometres north of the park.

Settler Country

Before entering the Settler Country it is fitting that a short explanation be made regarding the numerous wars fought out by the pioneers who endeavoured to bring civilisation to the eastern area of the Cape Colony which was generally referred to as the Zuurveld.

Historians have recorded that nine major encounters took place on the Eastern Frontier over a period of a hundred years from 1779 to 1879. These wars they thought fit to call the first to ninth Kaffir Wars and sometimes the Kaffir Frontier Wars or simply the Frontier Wars. The first two wars involved Dutch burghers against the Xhosa, and the other seven, British soldiers and settlers against various tribes of the Xhosa. Nowadays there is a tendency to call these wars the Xhosa Wars. Except in quotations, throughout this book these wars are referred to as the Frontier Wars.

The First Frontier War took place in 1779-80 when the laager was used for the first time; the Second in 1789; the Third in 1799; the Fourth in 1811; the Fifth, the Battle of Grahamstown, in 1819. The Sixth Frontier War was from 1834-35 and the Seventh, known as the War of the Axe (because it was triggered off when a petty chief stole an axe from a trading store) from 1846-48; the Eighth from 1850-53 and the Ninth and final campaign was from 1877-79.

In between the periods of named wars, skirmishes, cattle thieving raids and farm razing were frequent occurrences.

National road N2 from Port Elizabeth to Grahamstown and trunk road R72 from Ncanara to Alexandria and Port Alfred

The northern exit from Port Elizabeth on the magnificent freeway close to the shore of Algoa Bay is carried over the mouth of the Swartkops River by the Settlers Bridge and continues as national road N2. The road passes the evaporation pans of the Salnova Salt Company near the mouth of the Colega River and crosses the Sundays River just before the settlement at Colchester. Fifty kilometres from Port Elizabeth at a place called Ncanara is the traffic interchange where trunk road R32 commences its journey northwards to Middelburg (Chapter 4) and trunk road R72 branches off to the coast making an interesting alternate route to Grahamstown or East London.

Alexandria

Named after the Reverend Alexander Smith of the Uitenhage Dutch Reformed Church, Alexandria lies in open country south of the Richmond hills, 16 kilometres from the sea. It is the railhead centre for flourishing dairy and pineapple farming and the only district in South Africa in which chicory is grown on a large scale. It is the headquarters of the Chicory Control Board. The population is 4 000, municipal status was obtained in 1940 and there is an hotel and a caravan park.

From Alexandria the circular coastal drive is well worth exploring. The road leads through a small but nevertheless magnificent indigenous forest and passes the paddocks of a number of superb dairy farms and a rugged coastline with tall cliffs that meet with the pounding ocean. This 45-minute drive reaches the little resorts of Cannon Rocks and Boknes Strand on the banks of the Boknes River, before turning inland to complete the circle on the eastern side of Alexandria, from where the journey to Port Alfred may be continued along route R72.

Dias Cross

Approximately two kilometres before reaching the junction of the circular drive and route R72 (described above), there is a turnoff on the lefthand side (facing the direction of Boknes Strand) and a dilapidated sign post indicating the route, seawards, to the Dias Cross. This leads along a track for two kilometres (passing lovely meadows and three farm gates) ending at the coastal forest reserve fence. From the stile, a footpath through the narrow belt of coastal bush comes out on a fairly high plateau overlooking a sea of sand dunes, and in the far distance the Dias Cross. The reward for making the pretty stiff hike across this kilometre-wide miniature desert will be experienced when the site is reached.

Here on a headland above a 28-metre-high cliff Bartholomew Dias set up the cross or padrão dedicated to St Gregory on 12 March 1488. This was one of three stone crosses which he carried on his great voyage of exploration. His expedition was the first to double the Cape of Good Hope. Because of the unwillingness of his men to continue the voyage to India, Dias had to turn back, and this for all practical purposes marked the farthest point of his voyage.

The isolated headland where the cross was placed was known to the early Portuguese as the *Penedo das Fontes* (rock of the fountains) probably because of the huge spray caused by the high seas lashing the cliffs here. The Dutch named the site Kwaaihoek, referring to the 'angry' coastline in a deserted 'corner'. The English name, False Island, certainly fits the scene from the landward side from where the bright green scrubland of the isolated headland stands out like an island surrounded by white sand.

The Dias Cross was lost track of after the sixteenth century and it was not until 1938, during the systematic search made under the direction of Dr Eric Axelson that the first signs of the historic cross were unearthed. Numerous fragments, some of which were found buried deep in the shifting sands and others in the sea at the foot of the cliff were recovered and sent to the University of Witwatersrand where the reconstructed cross, the oldest relic associated with European activity in South Africa, is in safe keeping.

A number of replicas were thereafter made. One was set up at the original site by the Monuments Commission and unveiled on 20 June 1941, another was presented to the Portuguese Government, others may be seen in museums in Cape Town, Grahamstown, Pietermaritzburg, Pretoria and Johannesburg and one stands on Market Square, Port Elizabeth. The cross is 2,134 metres high and is made of coarse and hackly white limestone. It bore an inscription (now illegible) and the royal arms of Portugal. The original padrão was proclaimed a national monument in 1939 and the site on which it stood and the replica there were proclaimed in 1945.

The second Dias Cross, the padrão of St Philip, was erected at Cape Point on 6 June 1488 and no trace of this has ever been found. At Luderitz Bay, Dias erected the third padrão of St James on 25 July 1488. Fragments are preserved in Cape Town, in Lisbon and in Auckland, New Zealand – taken there by the Cape governor, Sir George Grey, in 1861.

It is possible to reach the site of the Dias Cross by four-wheel drive vehicle from Bushman's River Mouth, described below.

Bushman's River Mouth

The resort of Bushman's River Mouth lies on the west bank of the river and comprises a number of cottages and bungalows and is a hive of activity in the summer season when the local farmers and their families assemble for fun in the sunshine. Fishing, boating and bathing are the main attractions.

Kenton-on-sea

Situated between the estuaries of the Bushman's and Kariega Rivers, Kenton-on-sea is a delightful seaside resort. There are long stretches of sandy beach that slope gently to the Indian Ocean and a number of rocky coves that form clear pools. The two rivers are navigable for small boats for 65 kilometres in all and the banks of the middle reaches are well wooded and very beautiful. The climate here is ideal for holidays and this little resort offers swimming, fishing, boating, skiing, bowls, tennis and many fine walks. The hotel is conveniently situated.

Port Alfred

With its riverine setting, 1820-settler atmosphere and favourable climate, Port Alfred is perhaps the most charming of the seaside resorts of the Eastern Cape Province. The town is sited on the banks of the beautiful Kowie River estuary and has a permanent population of some 12 000 people.

Port Kowie (the original name) dates from 1821, in which year the schooner *Elizabeth* crossed the bar and entered the river. In 1825 the place was renamed Port Frances after Frances Somerset, the wife of the frontier commandant, Colonel Somerset (son of the governor). In 1860 it was again renamed Port Alfred in honour of the visit to the town of Prince Alfred, second son of Queen Victoria. Prince Alfred toured the Cape, Orange Free State and Natal and it is interesting to note the enormous enthusiasm with which he was received wherever he went. The town became a municipality in 1894.

Early government attempts to establish a port failed. However, by 1841 William Cock (later the Hon. William Cock, Member for Albany of the Legislative Assembly), an 1820 settler and wealthy printer from Cornwall, had developed a private harbour at considerable personal expense by changing the course of the Kowie River where it entered the sea. By 1843 he had floated the Kowie Navigation Company that owned a fleet of ships, plying as far afield as Mauritius and St Helena, exporting wool and beef. His home, Cock's Castle (which still overlooks the river) fortified with cannon, was the scene of much activity during the Frontier War of 1846.

The government gave renewed assistance to the harbour development in 1857 and by 1863 the port was flourishing, dredging of the bar was taking place and a tug had been put into commission. The mailships of two companies, the Union Line and the Castle Line, called regularly. Port Alfred went into decline as a port after 1881 when the privately-owned railway to Grahamstown was completed and the traffic was

1. *The classic example of a river meander, where the Kowie River reaches the Bathurst Nature Reserve.*
2. *Port Alfred has this glorious stretch of bathing beach.*
3. *The Royal Port Alfred Golf Course is considered to be among the best links in the country.*
4. *The Nico Malan Bridge carries the R72 trunk route across the Kowie River near its mouth.*

1

2

3

Kowie Grand Hotel, commanding a magnificent view of the Kowie River, the Indian Ocean and the whole holiday scene at Port Alfred. The Grand has a reputation for fine fare, comfort and hospitality for the whole family.

coupled with Port Elizabeth. In the 1890s Port Alfred ceased to function as a fiscal port.

The Kowie River, 72 kilometres long, rises near Grahamstown and is navigable for small craft for 30 kilometres from its mouth. The middle reaches are well wooded and especially beautiful at the horse-shoe bend, near Bathurst. At the mouth there is a spacious beach, once famed for its large variety of sea-shells, including the rare nautilus, which seem to have disappeared. The beach is safe for bathing and renowned for surfing. The river is bridged about two kilometres upstream and near the mouth by the Nico Malan Bridge, opened in 1972 and forming part of the fabulous coastal road R72 connecting Port Elizabeth with East London. There are ample stretches of water suitable for speed boats, skiing and yachting with mooring and launching facilities available for visitors – regattas are held in season. For the fisherman there is the river, beach, rock and deep-sea, and it is common to have great bags of cob (kabeljou), galjoen, shad (elf), steenbras, leervis, musselcracker, Jan Bruin, grunter, blacktail, zebra and moonfish. This is also the place for goggle-fishing and sole spearing. Oysters, prawns and crabs are plentiful in season.

The Royal Port Alfred Golf Course is rated among the famous golf links. It is laid out in rolling green countryside with outstanding views of the coastline and ocean. The club welcomes visitors. It received its royal charter through the Duke of Connaught in 1924 and the course is of championship standard.

Visitor accommodation is well provided for by three hotels, a number of guest and apartment establishments and three caravan parks. On the western side the first choice is Kowie Grand Hotel in a prime position high above the Kowie River Estuary it commands stunning views of the river, the Indian Ocean and the whole holiday scene. And rest assured this is a holiday hotel for the entire family – good fare, comfort and hospitality have a real meaning here, and timesharing holidays are on offer as well. On the eastern side of the river, magnificently situated with fine views is the Victoria Hotel, of long standing high reputation, offering fine cuisine, comfort and service close to the holiday activities. Visitors are made welcome at the bowling and tennis clubs, and there are municipal squash courts. The town has a visitors information bureau and an airfield.

A well-preserved remnant from the beginning of Port Alfred is close to the main road as it leaves Port Alfred on the way to East London. Opposite the Shell garage is the turn left (inland) to the Settlers Church of the Methodist denomination, a lovely church built of local stone in a well-kept churchyard shaded by huge fig trees. It bears the bronze plaque of the Monuments Commission and an inscription tells part of the grim story of the pioneers:

This Church was erected in the year 1825 by the British settlers of 1820. It was twice destroyed during the Kaffir Wars and rebuilt.

Coastal road from Port Alfred to East London

Port Alfred is equidistant from the two coastal cities, Port Elizabeth and East London, approximately 170 kilometres from each.

On its way from Port Alfred to East London, this route R72 crosses ten rivers, revealing some of the most beautiful estuary and river-mouth scenery in the Eastern Province. The Great Fish, 40 kilometres from Port Alfred, and the Keiskamma, 70 kilometres from East London, are the largest rivers. Ten kilometres from Port Alfred, the Ciskei government has developed a most enchanting marine resort at Mpekweni.

Bathurst

The tiny municipality of Bathurst (it has little more than 250 inhabitants), at an altitude of 274 metres, is 14 kilometres from Port Alfred on the road to Grahamstown. It is an attractive little 1820-settler town, notable for its kaffirbooms and wild fig trees and the centre of a district famous for its pineapple cultivation and cattle-raising. Named after Lord Bathurst, Colonial Secretary at the time of its foundation in 1820, it was for a brief period the magistracy of the district of Albany with Captain Charles Trappes of the Seaforth Highlanders installed as deputy landdrost. The main thoroughfare of Bathurst and the valley to the north were named after him.

In 1821 the administrative headquarters for Albany were transferred to Grahamstown because of its superior military position. However, Bathurst continued as a rural settlement and its brave inhabitants withstood some brutal attacks by the Xhosas during the Sixth and Seventh Frontier Wars.

The Wesleyan Chapel, opened in 1832, and St John's Anglican Church, started in 1834 and completed in 1837, are both historical monuments. Before the roof of St John's was completed it became a refuge for women and children in December 1834. Early in 1835 the Chapel was besieged and fierce attacks were repelled until military relief arrived from Grahamstown. During the war that started in 1846 the two churches, now linked by earthwork defences, again became a strong-point whilst the rest of the countryside was being ravaged. The Wesleyan Chapel (in York Street, opposite the inn) contains the Goldswain family bible and St John's Church (opposite the town hall on Donkin Terrace) is unique in having two pulpits.

The Pig and Whistle Inn on the corner of Trappes Street and Kowie Road, had its start in 1831 when the settler Thomas Harley opened an inn adjoining his blacksmith's forge. The inn survived the ravaging and looting of the Frontier Wars and accommodated the governors, Sir Henry Pottinger in 1846 and Sir Harry Smith in 1848. Jeremiah Goldswain, the settler diarist who provided historians with a unique picture of early colonial life in his journal 1819 to 1858, bought the inn for his son-in-law in 1853. It is regarded as the oldest inn in the Eastern Province.

On the side opposite that of the Wesleyan Chapel, higher up in York Street, is the site of the Drostdy built by Captain Trappes but never used for the functions of the deputy landdrost. Although the foundation stone was laid by Frances Somerset in 1820, the fourteen-roomed building was not completed until 1824. In the interim, Lord Charles Somerset, having returned from England, resumed the governorship. He countermanded the orders of the acting governor, Sir Rufane Donkin, and removed the administrative offices of the district of

Albany from Bathurst to Grahamstown. Through the years the drostdy building has been so considerably altered that it is no longer recognisable as a nineteenth-century structure.

From the Pig and Whistle Inn, Trappes Street continues as a gravel road and runs into Horseshoe Road which leads to the Bathurst Nature Reserve and the view site of the horseshoe bend of the Kowie River. Here there is the classic example of a meandering river, a remarkable sight in itself, placed in the environment of one of the earth's richest floral regions. The Eastern Cape coastal region is botanically unique; it lies between two distinctly different rainfall area – the wet winter western and the wet summer eastern areas – and it is the meeting ground of four major groups of flora, resulting in the mixture of a great number of species – an occurrence unknown elsewhere in the world. Of the sub-tropical flora there is the vivid orange and blue crane flower, the graceful Phoenix palm, the delicate blue plumbago, the coral-coloured kaffirboom and the primitive cycad. Western Cape flora is widely represented with protea, heath, gladiolus, watsonia and pelargonium. Karoo flora occurs in the form of a variety of succulents such as aloes, crassula, euphorbia and mesembryanthemum – the massed irridescent blooms forming carpets of colour. Grassland flora, prevalent before cultivation of the lands, persists and tambuki, turpentine and thatch grasses can still be seen with a variety of tuberous-rooted plants in addition to the bulbous plants of the amaryllis and lily families.

On the way to the nature reserve is the sign posted turnoff on the right hand side leading to the wool mill of the versatile Samuel Bradshaw, a weaver from Gloucestershire who arrived with the 1820 settlers and built both the Wesleyan and Anglican churches. He started the mill in 1822, building a millrace and waterwheel connected to a weir in the river. By 1827, having imported the spinning jenny and loom from England, he started producing rough woollen blankets and Kersey cloth, much needed by the settlers. His mill continued in production until it was set on fire by the Xhosas in 1835, and it symbolises the modest start of South Africa's flourishing wool industry, and was probably South Africa's first textile factory.

The wool mill was restored by the Simon van der Stel Foundation in 1963 and is a national monument. The key to gain access is kept at the Pig and Whistle Inn.

Colonel Jacob Cuyler, the Uitenhage landdrost, was responsible for settling the British pioneers of 1820 and he chose to do this by pitching camp on an eminence two kilometres to the east of Bathurst and personally directing each party to the farm allocated.

In carrying out a survey of the eastern districts in 1859, Captain W. Bailey of the Royal Engineers, erected a beacon on the old camp site. This beacon has been incorporated in a toposcope dedicated as part of the National Memorial commemorating the arrival of the 1820 settlers. On the low stone wall that surrounds the beacon there are 57 bronze plaques, each inscribed with such details as the party leader's name, the number of its members, the name of the ship in which they sailed, the distance in miles from

the toposcope to the land allocated and an arrow indicating the direction of the land. The panorama form the toposcope encompasses most of the Settler Country including its historic coastline which stretches from the Great Fish River to Kwaaihoek.

The site of the toposcope is a national monument and it is best reached by proceeding along Nico Malan Avenue which starts at the Town Hall.

A small powder magazine, another relic from the Frontier War era, can be seen on what is today known as Battery Hill. The magazine, a national monument, is accessible from Gradwell Street near the Grahamstown entrance to Bathurst.

Sidbury and Alicedale

Returning to the traffic interchange at Ncanara, national road N2 on its way to Grahamstown crosses the Bushman's River 24 kilometres further north in undulating country farmed originally by the 1820 settlers, where aloes flower in the early winter. Roads branch off to Sidbury, a settler village and to Alicedale, a railway junction where there is an important weaving industry. This district is noted for merino sheep.

Salem

Thirteen kilometres south-west of Grahamstown a road leads due south for 11 kilometres to Salem, an 1820 settler village so named from the Hebrew word in Psalm 76 meaning peace. This was the area assigned to the largest party of the pioneers, that of the leader, H. Sephton; the party numbered 344 settlers and among them was the Wesleyan divine, the Reverend William Shaw. Here on the Assegaaibos River he set up the first Methodist church in South Africa in 1822. It was replaced by a more substantial building in 1832 and this became a fortress church during the Frontier Wars. In the church academy that was established, Theophilus Shepstone and Mary Moffat received education. The building bears a bronze plaque of the Monuments Commission.

A rugged stone bearing another bronze plaque is placed on a hill that overlooks Salem. It commemorates the heroic deed of Richard Gush, a Quaker and man of peace who, unarmed, confronted a 500-strong impi of Xhosa warriors during the Sixth Frontier War in 1835 and saved the settlement from certain annihilation. Fearlessly Gush confronted the chief warrior and 'expostulated on their great wickedness'. When the chief explained that his men were hungry Gush returned to the settlement and delivered to the impi a quantity of bread, 10 lbs of tobacco and 25 pocket knives. The Xhosas kept their part of the bargain and the settlement was left in peace.

Grahamstown

In 1811 Colonel John Graham commanded a mixed force of troops of the 21st Light Dragoons, the 23rd Foot, his own Cape Regiment and Boer Commandos and succeeded in driving back from the Great Fish River frontier some twenty thousand Xhosa marauders. This was the Fourth Frontier War which temporarily secured the safety of Algoa Bay and the districts of Uitenhage and Graaff-Reinet. The site that

Graham chose for a military outpost in 1812 was named in his honour, Grahamstown, by the governor, Sir John Cradock.

It was not until the arrival of the settlers of 1820 that Grahamstown took on the proportions of a town and in 1861 it acquired municipal and city status under the Cape, Act No. 29 of that year.

Cathedral city, seat of the Supreme Court and principal educational centre of the Eastern Cape Province, Grahamstown has a population of 74 000. It is situated on the wooded slopes of the Suurberg range at the source of the Kowie River, 50 kilometres from the sea, and enjoys a healthy, equable climate. Prominent features of the city are its wide, tree-lined streets, beautiful gardens and handsome buildings. Twentieth-century Grahamstown presents a scene of serenity and culture in complete contrast with its turbulent nineteenth-century history.

Grahamstown grew from the frontier situation already described and it soon became the garrison town for the defence of the Settler Country. A year before the arrival of the British pioneers the small garrison of some 350 soldiers, under Colonel Willshire, received a severe test in the Battle of Grahamstown. On 22 April 1819 Makanna, the Xhosa witchdoctor (who exercised a powerful spell over the chiefs), had joined with Chief Ndlambe (Gaika's Uncle and rival) to lead the 9 000-warrior attack at about one o'clock in the afternoon. The huge impi swept down in the dreaded crescent formation upon the small band of redcoats who held an improvised line in the open valley. The defenders, under strict discipline, waited until ordered then fired their muzzle-loading flintlocks and two cannon at point-black range. The result was a rout, the Xhosas broke in disorder leaving a thousand dead on the battlefield. The garrison lost three killed and five wounded. Makanna's Kop, the hill to the north-east of the town, marks the place where the Xhosas mustered, and the garrison line is accepted as having been between present-day York and Barrack Streets. The command post, Fort England, was where the mental hospital is now. A sequel to the battle was Makanna's surrender and internment on Robben Island. He drowned in the surf while attempting to escape but so profound was his influence on the Xhosas that for half a century they refused to believe he was dead.

The other large-scale encounters that threatened Grahamstown were the Sixth, Seventh and Eighth Frontier Wars. From 1834 to 1853 these wars raged in the vicinity of the town and the defiles of the Amatola Mountains to the north.

It was in 1827 that the rule against trading with the Xhosas was relaxed and a surge of prosperity came to Grahamstown by way of ivory and skin trading and by 1830 the boom was considerably increased with the trade of wool from Albany sheep farms.

Grahamstown became the seat of an Anglican bishop in 1853 – the second bishopric (after Cape Town) in South Africa. The Cathedral of St Michael and St George stands on Church Square on the site of the original St George's Church. The south wall of the nave is part of the old church built in the 1820s and is the oldest surviving piece of Anglican church architecture in the southern hemisphere. The prominent tower and spire, 45,7 metres tall, was designed by Sir Gilbert Scott and completed by his son in 1878. The cathedral contains a number of memorials to those who fell in the Frontier Wars, and the regimental colours of local units. Other items of special interest are the bishop's throne, locally carved, Reuben Sayer's copy of Leonardo da Vinci's *Virgin of the Rocks* and a copy of Perugino's *Crucifixion*. A monument to Colonel Graham stands near the west door.

There are some fine churches in Grahamstown. The Methodist Commemoration Church in High Street faces the South African War Memorial at the junction of Bathurst Street. It was built to mark the Silver Jubilee of the settlement and was opened in 1850 by the Reverend William Shaw. Built by troops of the Inniskilling regiment, St Patrick's Catholic Church, on the corner of Huntly and Hill Streets, was completed in 1844. In Bathurst Street near the junction of Huntly Street is the Baptist Church, opened in 1843. The denomination had its start in South Africa here in Grahamstown when the chapel opened in Bartholomew Street in 1823. Both the chapel (now called Chapel House) and the church are national monuments.

The little Wesley Chapel on the corner of Market and York Streets possesses a much-treasured relic in the history of Grahamstown; this is the precious Hill organ. When Colonel Somerset and his wife Frances left Grahamstown for India in 1852 they presented the organ to the Methodist Church. The colonel had imported it for his wife from William Hill of London where it had been made sometime between 1832 and 1837. There is no doubt that it was the first pipe organ to be brought into the Eastern Province and it is believed to be the only unaltered Hill organ in existence. Proclaimed a national monument in 1960 the organ measures 3 metres high, 2 metres wide and 1 metre deep.

Grahamstown attracts students from all over southern Africa. The history of its schools follows closely on its establishment as a religious centre. The first of the great schools of Grahamstown, St Andrew's College, at the intersection of Somerset and Worcester Streets, was founded in 1855 by Bishop Armstrong who modelled it on the famous English public school principle of Christian citizenship. Higher up in Worcester Street, the Diocesan School for Girls, founded in 1874, is the sister school to St Andrew's. Further along on the opposite side is St Paul's Theological College which became the Anglican college for the whole of South Africa in 1911. In 1876 the Jesuits opened St Aidan's College in Milner Street. Kingswood College in Burton Street was established by the Methodist Church in 1894 – members of its brass band still wear scarlet Guardsmen's uniforms. In the same year that Kingswood was founded Victoria Boys High School (founded in 1873) changed its name to Graeme College. At the Port Elizabeth end of Beaufort Street (which is the route of national road N2) are Graeme College, Victoria School for Girls and the Assumption Convent. Further on, Grahamstown Training College (for female student teachers) was opened by the

1

2

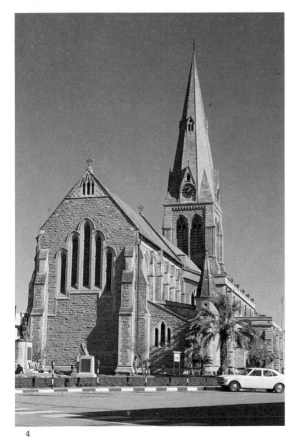

3

4

Grahamstown is a city filled with memories of the 1820 settlers.

1. The 1820 Settlers' National Monument stands on Gunfire Hill, overlooking the city.
2. Once a military prison, the old Provost stands in the Botanical Gardens.
3. The old gateway to the Drostdy is now the entrance to Rhodes University.
4. Cathedral of St. Michael and St. George dominates High Street, the principal thoroughfare.

Anglican sisterhood in 1894 and is now merged with Rhodes University. The oldest school building in Grahamstown and probably the first Anglican school in South Africa is a fine example of English Gothic Revival architecture – it is the school in Huntly Street. Although the foundation stone was laid in 1844 progress in construction was interrupted by the Eighth Frontier War and it was not opened until 1849. In 1857 it became the St George's Cathedral Grammar School and since the closing of that school in 1911 the building has been used for various educational purposes, and is today the Good Shepherd School for Coloured Children. A fine modern school is the Afrikaans medium Hoërskool P.J. Olivier, which overlooks Somerset Street from its south-eastern end – the handsome building was completed in 1956.

Rhodes University was founded in 1904 as Rhodes University College and attained full status in 1951. Approximately 2 700 students are accommodated. The extensive campus, with fine playing fields and modern theatre, is bounded by Lucas, Somerset and Prince Alfred Streets. Sir Herbert Baker designed the handsome main building in 1911 and it was erected in stages from 1913, taking the place of the Drostdy which was being demolished. The works were completed in 1935 with the right wing of the Drostdy being retained and incorporated into the university building. Parts of the Drostdy barracks also remain.

Piet Retief, a very energetic and active man, was born in Wellington in 1780 and moved to the Grahamstown district in 1814 where he bought several farms including Mooimeisiesfontein (part of his farm is now Riebeek East) and remained in the area until 1836 when he led his party of Voortrekkers in the Great Trek. He lived for a considerable time in Grahamstown while he was engaged in his business as a building contractor.

One of the building contracts that Retief undertook was the construction of the Drostdy in 1822 which apparently fell into disuse after one sitting of the Circuit Court. In 1833 Sir Lowry Cole ordered that it be renovated for conversion into the town's public offices – the Sixth Frontier War intervened and Cole's orders were never carried out. In 1835 Sir Benjamin d'Urban selected the sight for a 'fortified barracks establishment' in a defence system to include redoubts to be built on the hill to the south. Only one redoubt was known to be built and that was Fort Selwyn. Sir George Napier, Governor d'Urban's successor, made drastic cuts in the military expenditure with the result that only a portion of d'Urban's original project was completed. In 1842, Major Selwyn R.E. constructed the substantial gateway with attendant sentry boxes as the entrance to the fortified barracks. This is today the Drostdy Gateway; a national monument, it faces Somerset Street on the axis of High Street, and is the main entrance to Rhodes University.

During the 1860s there was a strong movement in the Cape Legislative Assembly to separate the eastern and western Cape into two provinces, and as a token of his support for the secessionists the governor, Sir Philip Wodehouse, convened parliament in Grahamstown on 28 April 1864, where a full session lasting three months was held. The governor's opening ceremony took place in the Shaw Hall at the lower end of High Street (opposite the present-day Grand Hotel) and thereafter the members of the Assembly rode up High Street in procession and passed through the Drostdy Gateway to attend Parliament in a building converted from the one-time military hospital in the Drostdy grounds. From all accounts the ceremony was a grand and colourful spectacle. Shaw Hall, named in honour of the Reverend William Shaw, was built as the Methodist Church in 1832 to seat 800 people and its use changed when the Commemoration Church was completed in 1850. Both the military hospital and Shaw Hall bear plaques of the Monuments Commission. The building of the old military hospital, close to the Botanical Gardens, now forms part of the Department of Botany in Rhodes University.

Across Lucas Street from the old military hospital, standing in the Botanical Gardens is the Old Provost, a national monument. Built in 1838 as the military prison of the Drostdy barracks it was designed to enable the warder (whose quarters were in the circular tower) to see into each of the cells which fanned out in the shape of a quadrant below him. After the Company Garden in Cape Town, Grahamstown's Botanical Gardens, laid out in the 1850s, were the second to come into being in South Africa.

The Albany Museum is one of the foremost general museums in South Africa and had its beginning when a Literary, Scientific and Medical Society was formed in Grahamstown in 1855. Establishment in the present building in the historic Drostdy grounds took place in 1900. The Albany Museum, although general in character, has a strong leaning towards natural history. The almost complete series of birds of the Eastern Province, the fresh water fishes, the representative collection of rocks and minerals and the herbarium (which includes material commencing with Burchell of 1813 to the present day) are all fine exhibits. The ethnographical displays include African wood-carvings, ornaments, utensils, masks, musical instruments and ceremonial dress, and a fascinating collection of dolls carried by the women of certain tribes to ensure fertility. The pre-history collection dates from the first palaeolithic stone implements found in 1858 by Thomas Bowker near Bathurst.

Also facing Somerset Street, across Lucas Street, the 1820 Settlers' Memorial Museum was opened in 1965 and houses the extensive cultural history material previously included in the Albany Museum. In the 1820 Settlers' Gallery (one of eight galleries in the museum) 150 settler families are represented by the relics of their descendants. There is a costume hall, armoury hall, and a pictorial art and map hall where interesting works by early South African artists such as Thomas Baines are displayed.

Lucas Street climbs up Gunfire Hill in a zig-zag route to reach Fort Selwyn. In 1835 when Sir Benjamin d'Urban converted the Drostdy into fortified barracks it was part of his strategy in the defence of Grahamstown to construct redoubts along this hill that commands the town on its southern flank. Before the completion of the fort, d'Urban was succeeded as governor by Sir George Napier and as far as is known no further fortification of the hill took place. The fort was named after Major C.J. Selwyn, commander of the Royal Engineers responsible for its construction. It is recorded that when the newly-appointed Lieutenant-Governor of the Eastern Cape, Andries Stockenström, arrived in Grahamstown in 1836, the Selwyn battery fired a 17-gun salute in his honour. From 1841 to 1868 the fort served as an Artillery Barracks and it was during the 1840s that a semaphore mast was erected in a link-up with Fort Beaufort and Fort Peddie via a series of semaphore towers, two of which, Governor's Kop and Fraser's Camp are still to be seen. Fort Selwyn remained under army control as a magazine and guardhouse until 1870 and has recently been restored to form part of the Albany Museum. The naval 9-pounder cannon in the fort date from about 1800 and bear the royal insignia of George III of England. These peices were extensively used in the Eastern Cape during the nineteenth century. For Selwyn is a national monument.

It is here on Gunfire Hill, adjacent to Fort Selwyn, that the 1820 Settlers' National Monument in the form of a conference centre and sumptuous 950-seat theatre was opened on 13 July 1974, and where a performing arts festival is held annually in July. Opposite the Settlers' Monument is the entrance to the Settlers' Inn Motel, a stop-over highly rated by its many patrons, secluded yet conveniently close to national road N2.

What is known as the Yellow House is near the top end of High Street, on the left as you face the Drostdy Gateway. Its construction for use as a gaol started in 1814 and it is probably the oldest remaining building in the city. It is further significant for the reason that the government surveyor, Baron Knobel, who laid out the town in that year, took the northern wall of the gaol as the line of High Street and commenced his survey from that point. In 1824 a new gaol was built on the corner of Somerset and Prince Alfred Streets and the Yellow House was used successively as a school, public library and functions hall. It bears a bronze plaque of the Monuments Commission.

A press in the form of the *Grahamstown Journal* was established in 1831 and there was a substantial output of books from publishers of the town in the following fifty years. The Public Library in Hill Street (between High and Huntly Streets) was founded in 1842 and contains many rare South African books.

Established in 1919, the South African Library for the Blind is near the top end of High Street on the corner of Hemming Street. In 1962 its founder, Miss Josie Wood, was made the first Freeman of the city. The library serves the whole of South Africa and besides braille and moon books it supplies books recorded on discs and tape. This was the third library in the world outside Britain to stock the cassette tape book.

In High Street, below the cathedral (which incidentally stands on a triangular site and not a square), there have been preserved in the main shopping area some beautiful examples of Victorian commercial architecture. On the opposite side of the street is the City Hall, its impressive memorial clock-tower dating from 1870 — the year of enthusiastic jubilee celebrations commemorating the landing of the British settlers. The halls, ante-chambers and other rooms were added as an afterthought and the completed City Hall opened in 1882.

An esteemed citizen of Grahamstown who had received part of his education there and later returned, was William Guybon Atherstone, D.D., F.R.C.S., F.G.S., who is remembered in South African history for two outstanding achievements. In 1847 he performed the first operation in South Africa (the amputation of a leg) using ether as an anaesthetic, and in 1867 he identified the first diamond found in South Africa. After medicine, Atherstone's second love was geology which originated from his meeting Andrew Geddes Bain, and his interest was stimulated when he formed a geological society in Grahamstown, the other foundation members being Henry Carter Galpin, a jeweller and watchmaker, Professor Peter Macowen, the distinguished South African botanist, and the Catholic Bishop, James David Ricards, the Irishman who brought the first nuns to South Africa in 1849 and who founded St Aidan's College. The diamond, found by a child, Erasmus Jacobs, on a farm outside Hopetown, was sold to a travelling peddler, John O'Reilly, who took it to Lorenzo Boyes, the Colesberg magistrate. Boyes posted it to Dr Atherstone for identification (apparently in an unstamped ordinary envelope). In his laboratory, Atherstone established beyond doubt that it was a diamond and passed it on to his three colleagues for confirmation. Using his jeweller's scale, Galpin determined the weight of carat. The sequel to this amazing story is that O'Reilly sold the diamond to Sir Philip Wodehouse for £1 000 (the value Atherstone had attached to it) and the governor had it shown at the Paris Exhibition. Later the stone was cut into a 10,73-carat brilliant and it became known as the *Eureka* although in South Africa it continued to be called the *O'Reilly*. It then changed ownership and when it became the property of Peter Logan he exhibited it at the Ageless Diamond Exhibition in London. The *Eureka* was returned to South Africa when, in 1966, it was purchased by De Beers Consolidated Mines. It was shown at the Johannesburg Diamond Pavilion before De Beers presented it to the Parliament of South Africa in Cape Town.

H.C. Galpin was an enterprising businessman with scientific leanings. His home and watchmaker's shop in Bathurst Street, near the corner of Huntly Street, was built in 1850 and by the huge clock in its prominent tower the people of Grahamstown set their watches. The Tower House also contained a camera obscura on the roof which for a long time entertained the townsfolk. It was in these premises that Galpin (at the request of Dr Atherstone) determined the weight of the Hopetown diamond. So it is that through the good offices of De Beers Consolidated Mines Limited that the premises (and the home of Dr Atherstone at 87 Beaufort Street) were restored during the years 1979 to 1983, and presented to the Albany Museum to form part of its Cultural History Division. Today Galpin's home, watchmaker's shop complete with the unique clock tower and obscura go to make up The

Observatory Museum.

A unique architectural quality of Grahamstown is its possession of original settlers' houses and a fine concentration of these occur at the intersection of Cross and Bartholomew Streets below the national road which is Beaufort Street. The area has been named Artifercers' Square and at least twelve of its houses and cottages have been declared historical monuments. It is an area well worth visiting – three interesting churches, Chapel House, St. Bartholomew's and the Dutch Reformed Church are close at hand and not far off is the 1819 battlefield region.

Opposite the golf course on the road to Cradock, west of the city, is the famed Bible monument (probably unique as between the two white language groups of South Africa). The monument marks the outspan where in 1837 British settlers presented the departing Voortrekkers led by Jacobus Uys with a Dutch Family Bible.

Grahamstown was the terminus of two heroic rides each of 900 kilometres. The reason for the first ride, that of Colonel Harry Smith in 1834, was the tremendous gallantry of the soldier dedicated to duty. As Chief of Staff he rode to the scene of hostility to personally take command. He took 6 days from Cape Town to Grahamstown. The second was a ride of mercy in 1842 for the relief of a beleaguered garrison made by the civilian, Dick King, whose compassion urged him on. In his desperate ride from sub-tropical Durban he crossed fifty rivers and arrived in Grahamstown 10 days later.

Thirteen kilometres out of Grahamstown on the national road to Port Elizabeth is the picturesque Howieson's Poort Reservoir, a water sport venue adjoining the Thomas Baines Nature Reserve.

A fine natural asset of the city is its 17-kilometre Mountain Drive which climbs up to the ridge, Dassie Krantz, a nature reserve from where there are superb views.

Cricket, rugby and tennis are played at the City Lords grounds and bowls at the Fiddlers Green. Grahamstown Golf Club has an interesting 18-hole course and there are seven hotels. The Cathcart Arms in West Street facing the market was opened by the settlers, William and Ann Trotter, in 1830, and is the oldest hotel in South Africa still using the original premises. There is a municipal caravan park.

Grahamstown has rich clay deposits and there is a thriving pottery industry. The surrounding district is devoted to agriculture, the main crops being pineapples and citrus.

National Road N2 – Grahamstown to King William's Town

To the east of Grahamstown national road N2 climbs the slopes of Makanna Kop (named after the Xhosa witchdoctor who led the attack on Grahamstown in 1819) and 17 kilometres from the town it reaches the two radio and telecommunication towers sited on Governor's Kop.

Governor's Kop, Fraser's Camp and the Great Fish River Valley

From Governor's Kop, a height, 848 metres above sea level, there is a spacious view across the Great Fish River Valley, scene of much fighting during the Frontier Wars. Governor's Kop Tower, a national monument, was built in 1843 as part of the system of signal towers which were invariably rendered useless by the early morning mists. Each of these towers had two rooms, one above the other, accommodating a sergeant and five men.

In the valley below, just west of the Great Fish River, on the farm Tower Hill (where a roadside kiosk provides the traveller with delicious refreshment in the form of iced pineapple juice) national road N2 passes Fraser's Camp Tower (after Colonel Fraser) another tower of the alarm system and also a national monument.

Peddie (Ciskei)

Across the Great Fish River is the Ciskei and the small town of Peddie, built on the site of Fort Peddie, one of the most important military posts of the eastern frontier. It comprised an eight-pointed-star-shaped structure of earth walls with trenches on the outside, constructed when the Frontier War of 1834-35 ended. The fort was named after Lieutenant-Colonel John Peddie of the Seaforth Highlanders. Some distance away from where the fort was built is the sturdy stone-walled watch tower (a national monument) probably added to the defence system in 1841. The fort was used for the protection of 16 000 Fingos (refugees from the area of present-day Transkei) with their 22 000 head of cattle, and in 1846 it was beseiged by a strong force of Xhosas.

The Monuments Commission has erected a bronze plaque under the large Milkwood Tree in Peddie, recording the assembly of the Fingo People at this proximity after their entry from 'the country beyond the Kei', and the Fingo people's declaration of loyalty to God and the King in the presence of the Reverend John Ayliff, the Methodist missionary who was partly responsible for the resettlement of the Fingo tribe. He carried out most of his work in the territory of Chief Hintza where he exercised considerable influence, and he translated part of the New Testament into the Xhosa language. The Old Milkwood Tree is venerated by the Fingos who gather there for Remembrance Service each year on 14 May.

Important as a trading centre, Peddie serves an agricultural area noted for pineapples.

Beyond Peddie national road N2 crosses first the Keiskamma (sparkling water) and then the Buffalo River to reach King William's Town (Chapter 6).

Hamburg (Ciskei)

From Peddie a branch road leads east to the village of Bell and to Hamburg, a holiday resort at the mouth of the Keiskamma River, from where there is a road along the coast through Kidd's Beach to East London.

Trunk road R32 from Ncanara to Cookhouse and branch road R63 from Somerset East to King William's Town

Returning once again to the traffic interchange at

Ncanara, trunk road R32 commences its journey northwards to Middelburg.

Paterson, Olifantskop Pass, Middleton and Golden Valley
At Paterson (also known as Sandflats) branch roads lead off west to Addo Elephant National Park and east to Alicedale. Trunk road R32 traverses the wooded slopes of the Suurberg range through the Olifantskop Pass where there are splendid views from the summit. Beyond Middleton, a rural centre with an hotel, are the irrigated farmlands of the upper valley of the Great Fish River and before entering the settlement of Golden Valley (so named from the apricots that used to flourish there), the road passes a memorial to Slagtersnek.

Slagtersnek
The insurrection of 1815, the Slagtersnek Rebellion, followed the prosecution of Frederik Cornelius Bezuidenhout who farmed on the Baviaans River, north of Cookhouse, and was charged with illtreating a native servant. After he had ignored the summons to appear in court a military escort, comprising Lieutenant Frans Rossouw and twelve Hottentots, was sent to arrest him. He fled and hid in a cave where he was found and shot dead. Over his grave Jan Bezuidenhout swore that he would not rest until he had avenged his brother's death.

A band of some sixty angry farmers formed up and skirmished along the frontier but broke when confronted with organised force. Jan Bezuidenhout barricaded himself with his wife and eleven-year-old son to fight out the last action of Slagtersnek. He was killed and five other ring leaders were brought to trial in Uitenhage and sentenced to death. The hanging, carried out in public with considerable clumsiness, added to the disgust and indignation among the pioneers at the whole affair and will probably never be forgotten.

Cookhouse
Two kilometres before reaching the town of Cookhouse, on the righthand side close to the road, there is a small stone pyramid erected on an historic site of the farm Roodewal (red bank). It commemorates the passing through here in 1820 of the group of Scots with their settler leader, Thomas Pringle. They rested here for two nights. This was the same military post from where, five years previously, Lieutenant Frans Rossouw and his Hottentot soldiers set out to make the arrest of the unfortunate Frederik Bezuidenhout of Slagtersnek. At this stage of the journey the Scottish party of the 1820 settlers were not very far from their destination – they settled in the Baviaans River Valley and played a valued part in the development of the Cape Colony.

Cookhouse is an important rail and road junction and has an hotel. The unkind derivation of the name 'that the soldiers of the military outpost there gave it the appropriate name because of the extreme heat' is apparently untrue. It was in fact a sought-after place by the soldiers because the kitchen or 'cookhouse' was situated there.

Farmers of the district have benefited extensively by the irrigation facilities provided by the enormous Orange River Scheme. Half-way between Cookhouse and Somerset East is the headquarter office of the Fish-Sundays section and nearby the Cookhouse Tunnel, an integral part of the scheme. Lucerne occupies sixty-five percent of the irrigation farms, and there are also crops of maize, fruit and vegetables. The area has always been noted for merino wool and mohair from the angora goats.

Somerset East
An attractive town situated at the foot of the 1 615-metre Boschberg, Somerset East lies on the branch road R63 which connects East London with the Karoo and is 24 kilometres west of the junction, Cookhouse. The town was laid out in 1825 on a farm which Lord Charles Somerset had bought ten years before to produce fodder for the frontier garrisons. The town became a municipality in 1884 and today has a population of 14 000.

Somerset East has oak-lined avenues, beautiful rose gardens and a fine recreation ground, Victoria Park. The surrounding countryside comprises pastoral land, orange groves, wooded mountains and a veld covered with wild flowers. The district is noted for its sheep stud-farms and wool production.

The 25-kilometre Auret Drive should not be missed. In leading to the summit of the Boschberg from where there are splendid views of the town, the road passes a beautiful golf course and the delightful Besterhoek where the municipality has laid out a caravan park with camping sites among the pines. Neighbouring dams and rivers have been stocked with trout and bass and there are some lovely walks to the numerous mountain waterfalls and to the indigenous forests. Bowls, tennis, swimming and a pleasant climate are the other attractions that entice visitors from the coast to come here for holidays.

Many well-known South Africans have studied at Gill College. It was established in 1867 as a result of the considerable endowment left by the philanthropist, Dr. William Gill, who came to Somerset East in the 1820s and gained a fortune outside his medical practice as a wool grower before he died in 1863. The college opened as a high school and university training college for boys. The graduate side fell away in 1904.

A cultural asset of the town is the Old Parsonage at the foot of the Boschberg. It has been restored to receive the local-history museum. Dating from the mid-nineteenth century, the Parsonage and the Dutch Reformed Church are national monuments.

Branch road R63
East of Cookhouse on the branch road R63 a number of historic frontier towns string out in the line of the route to King William's Town.

Bedford
Laid out in 1854, Bedford formed part of the farm Maaström, owned by Sir A.J. Stockenström, the controversial lieutenant-governor of the Eastern Province, who named the town after his great friend, the Duke of Bedford. Municipal status came two years later in 1856.

Bedford lies at the foot of the wooded Kaga Mountains in a district renowned for livestock breeding. The annual gymkhana is a major event of the South African horse-riding calendar. The town has a population of 8 000 and there is an hotel.

Baviaans River Valley

The Scottish Party members of the 1820 settlers preferred to remain an entity, and in choosing their destiny they trekked further inland away from the other British pioneers. Blessed in strength of leadership – that of the Pringle family, · notably Thomas Pringle, they finally made camp in the Baviaans River Valley. Many descendants of the party, including the Pringle family, farm in the valley today; their nineteenth century homesteads and churches are intact and the place names bear unmistakable witness of the district's pioneers.

In the valley 29 kilometres from Bedford on the road to Tarkastad is the settlement at Glen Lynden (called Baviaansrivier before the settlers arrived) where there are two churches, both national monuments. The smaller, stone church was built in 1828 by the Cape government at the instigation of Thomas Pringle, to serve both the Presbyterian and Dutch Reformed congregations. It is designed in the T-plan, favoured in Scotland at the time, and the massive buttresses on the western side were added in 1834. The larger church was built for the Dutch Reformed denomination in 1874 and became the mother-church for the Bedford and Adelaide district. The little church continued as the Presbyterian church until 1958 when the Scottish 1820 Memorial Church was built at Eildon, higher up the Baviaans River.

On his farm Eildon, 24 kilometres from Glen Lynden on the Tarkastad road, Thomas Pringle built what he called in a poem his 'Emigrant's Cabin' – a hut in the shape of a beehive. Here he lived until 1822 before handing over his farm to his brother and moving to Cape Town. In the city, with his friend John Fairbairn, he established the *South African Journal* which brought him into conflict with Lord Charles Somerset. He eventually gained the freedom of the Press. Thomas Pringle's principal fame rests on his poems with South African themes, the better known being *Afar in the Desert* and *The Lion Hunt.* His best-known prose work was entitled *Narrative of a Residence in South Africa.*

The Monuments Commission has placed a bronze plaque at the site of the 'Emigrant's Cabin' and Pringle's remains have been brought from Scotland and reinterred in a vault of the Memorial Church here at Eildon farm.

John Pringle, the elder brother of Thomas, was granted a farm in the Macazana Valley, which he called Glen Thorn, and here he built a stone church in 1840. Since then the building has been in uninterrupted use by the Presbyterian Church and is a national monument. Glen Thorn is best reached from Adelaide, from where it is 26 kilometres along the road to Tarkastad. Before taking up his farm, John Pringle was for four years the superintendent at Somerset Farm.

Adelaide

Named after the wife of William IV of England, Adelaide has grown out of a military post that was established on the banks of the Koonap River at the start of the 6th Frontier War in 1834. It lies to the south of the magnificent Winterberg range which rises to an altitude of 2 371 metres.

Municipal status was granted in 1896 and the population of 10 500 is supported by a district producing wool, mohair, citrus and grain.

Our Heritage Museum was originally a parsonage built in 1855 and is arranged as a living home of the mid-nineteenth century. Among the fine exhibits is the outstanding Ash collection of glass, porcelain and silver. The old building is one of a number that still grace this charming country town.

Visitor amenities include golf, bowls, tennis and fresh water angling. There is a caravan park at the Bedford entrance to the town and two hotels including Midgley's, a highly rated country hotel which is opposite the central gardens.

Fort Beaufort

The attractive town of Fort Beaufort was named after the Duke of Beaufort, the father of Governor Lord Charles Somerset, long before it emerged as an urban area. It lies on the left bank of the Kat River and is almost encirlced by the combined waters of the Kat and Brak Rivers. In the early days of colonisation the locality was chosen as ideal for defence against the continuous hostility of the marauding Xhosas. The important consideration was not so much the planning of a place to do battle as it was a case of refuge for the families of the pioneer farmers. As a part of the general protection plan of the frontier, a military post was established in 1822 on the flat land between the two rivers.

An earthworks fortification withstood the onslaught in 1834, at the start of the Sixth Frontier War, and at the end of the conflict, under the plan of Governor Sir Benjamin d'Urban, Fort Beaufort was strengthened by permanent emplacements built in the vicinity of the present-day Law Court. In the same year, 1837, the town was laid out and the first plots were granted to the people. At the same time construction of the strategic Queen's Road, connecting with Grahamstown, was commenced.

Although there is some uncertainty about the date of the construction of a Martello Tower as part of the fortification it is apparent that it dates from 1847, which places its completion during the 7th Frontier War – the War of the Axe, triggered off right here in 1846 when a petty chief was accused of stealing an axe from a local trading store, and was arrested. This Martello Tower, remaining today in perfect condition, is one of two constructed in South Africa, the other being at Simonstown. It is a massive circular building of dressed stone and today faces Bell Street. In the open turret a small swivel gun on a wooden mounting can be rotated in a full circle. A key to enter the tower can be obtained from the Town Clerk.

The name is a corruption of Mortella, a cape in Corsica where the defenders of a tower of this design held off a superior British naval attack in 1794. The British were so impressed at the prolonged resistance offered that they erected similarly designed towers along the coast of England and put them into use in the colonies.

Adjoining the tower in Bell Street are the military barracks; built in the nineteenth century they have undergone restoration for conversion into a military museum.

The museum in Durban Street used to be the Officers' Mess in the frontier war days. Entirely devoted to the history of the district, the museum contains a good collection of firearms, household equipment, early prints, photographs and documents. An oil by Thomas Baines, a watercolour by l'Ons and a small but unique library of the history of the area are of special interest. The famous sandstone sundial which had stood in the grounds of the Residency in Seymour since 1839 has recently been moved to the safety of the museum. The two nine-pounder cannon at the entrance bear the date 1814 and the insignia of George III of England, and were probably used in the defence of the town.

Fort Beaufort's population is over 13 000, its recreational facilities include golf, tennis, bowls, squash, swimming and angling and there is a municipal caravan park. There are three hotels including the well-appointed, airconditioned, two-star Savoy Hotel, opposite the museum in Durban Street.

Starting from Campbell Street, a winding road leads for 10 kilometres to the technical institute run by the Methodist Church at Healdtown. This is a worthwhile drive in English downs-type country, the institute itself being sited on what appears to be an inaccessible promontory.

Queen's Road through the Great Fish River Valley – Fort Brown and the Ecca Pass

From Fort Beaufort, route R67 leads to the south to join national road N2 six kilometres east of Grahamstown and provides an interesting 77-kilometre drive through the Great Fish River Valley. This road follows substantially the strategic military road instigated by Sir Benjamin d'Urban and built by Andrew Geddes Bain in the years 1837 to 1842. It was named Queen's Road to honour Queen Victoria who was crowned in the year the construction commenced.

The road passes the turnoff to the popular sulphur springs, ten kilometres out of Fort Beaufort, and after a winding route through undulating country it is eventually carried across the Great Fish River by the fine stone bridge built by Bain. Fort Brown commands the river crossing from the southern side (50 kilometres from Fort Beaufort and 27 kilometres from Grahamstown) and is now a police post. The site was first established as a military post by Lord Charles Somerset in 1817 and was then known as Hermanus Kraal. When Sir Benjamin d'Urban had it converted into one of the strongholds of the frontier the fort was named after its commander, Lieutenant Brown of the 75th Regiment. Construction was started in 1835 and completed in 1838, and it withstood several determined attacks during the frontier wars that followed. The gun tower and adjoining walls are preserved as a national monument.

Renowned for its infinite variety of vegetation, the Great Fish River region is botanically of international importance. Route R67 traverses a part of the large region passing dense bush where aloes, euphorbias and many other succulents thrive. Ten kilometres beyond the river crossing, the road is carried over the Ecca Heights by means of the Ecca Pass, revealing some outstanding views of the expansive valley.

At the top of the pass (within 15 kilometres of Grahamstown) on the right of the road is the monument to the great South African pioneer road-engineer and geologist, Andrew Geddes Bain. The monument is in the form of a simple cairn with a commemorative bronze plaque of the Monuments Commission, recording some of the accomplishments of this most remarkable and talented man. There could not have been a better choice for the siting of the monument. The construction of Queen's Road was Bain's first assignment as Superintendent of Military Road Construction – Major Selwyn of Royal Engineers, Grahamstown, having recognised his capability. The most difficult part of the construction was the pass through Ecca Heights and to be perpetually on site in the accomplishment of this task, Bain built a house in the heights. It was from this base that he studied geology and during the construction of the road from the Ecca heights to the Katberg that he made the observations of the successive geological formation, naming the shales and mudstones that he found at the bottom of the pass the *Ecca Series*, which became acknowledged world-wide as the origin of the coal bearing deposits of South Africa. His simultaneous discovery of a series of Karoo fossils was not previously known to science and exposed the vast palaeontological wealth of the Karoo System. In 1852 Bain compiled the first geological map of South Africa and is remembered as the father of South African geology.

Before he died in 1864, Andrew Geddes Bain (who was born in Scotland in 1797) traded as a harness maker in Graaff-Reinet from 1822, journeyed twice to Kuruman and the Molopo River between 1825 and 1834 (keeping accurate records and leaving interesting accounts), helped build the privately-financed Onderberg Pass, supervised the construction of Graaff-Reinet's Van Ryneveld Pass, completed the military road from Grahamstown to the Katberg, built the Michell's Pass over the Hex River Mountains to Ceres, completed the Bain's Kloof Pass over the Drakenstein range and had nearly completed the Katberg Pass. To add to his distinguihsed achievements he found time to create the humourous literary character, *Kaatjie Kekkelbek*, written in what was called Hottentot-Afrikaans.

Alice (Ciskei)

The next town on branch road R63 is Alice, named after Queen Victoria's daughter when it was founded in 1847. It lies on the west bank of the Tyumie River and has a population of 12 000.

The town was built up around the Lovedale Missionary Institution which was founded in 1824 and named Incehra and was later renamed to honour Dr. John Love, Secretary of the Glasgow Missionary Society. The mission was twice abandoned during the Frontier Wars of 1834 and 1846. Lovedale came into prominence after Fort Hare was built on the east bank of the Tyumie River, with the development of schools and a hospital, and has been continuously active since then. Institutions with a high reputation today are Lovedale High School, Lovedale Hospital (where nurses and midwives are trained) and Lovedale Press

1. 2. 3. and 4. In an enchanting setting, providing good fare and cellar and every comfort, is Hogsback Inn — a delightful holiday resort hotel in all seasons of the year. 5. and 6. Interdenominational church services are held in the tiny chapel of St Patrick's on-the-hill, and at Christmas and Easter worshippers sit on logs placed across the roadway of Oak Avenue. Both scenes typify the tranquil beauty of the Hogsback. 7. Mountain zebra in the national park near Cradock.

5

6

4

7

3

(which produces educational books). Also in the town is the Federal Theological Seminary of Southern Africa comprising colleges of Anglican, Congregational, Methodist and Presbyterian denominations.

Fort Hare was built in 1847 at the end of the War of the Axe, and the ruins of the fort, a national monument, can be seen on the campus of Fort Hare University which was established in 1916. The fort was named after the distinguished soldier, Lieutenant-Colonel John Hare who commanded the First Division against the Xhosas in 1846 – during 1838 he acted as Lieutenant-Governor of the Eastern Province.

Five kilometres north of the town is the prominent feature, Sandile's Kop, favourite rallying point of the warriors of Chief Sandile (1850-1878). Here the Lantern Tower of dressed stone is a memorial to the Rev. Dr. James Stewart of the Free Church of Scotland, the famous principal of Lovedale, who together with his wife is buried there. The hill overlooks Fort Hare, Lovedale and Alice.

From Alice the road R63 crosses the Keiskamma River, passes through Middledrift (a Ciskeian irrigation centre) and continues on its 65-kilometre journey to King William's Town (Chapter 6).

Hogsback

The road to the north of Alice follows the valley of the Tyumie River into the Amatola Mountains in superb scenery and 39 kilometres from Alice on the eastward slopes of the range is situated one of the most delightful holiday resorts in South Africa. This is the Hogsback, overlooked on the east side by three similar mountain heights each resembling the bristly-backed wild hogs of the local forests. In the final eight kilometres from Alice the road winds in a 600-metre climb through the primeval forest to reach the rustic settlement with its two hotels, caravan park and holiday cottages dotted over a wide area of vegetation. The village is at something over 1 200 metres above sea level and the neighbouring mountain peaks rise from 600 to 750 metres above the resort level.

Hogsback can be reached via Cathcart without traversing any part of the Ciskei.

The summer days at Hogsback are pleasantly warm, the evenings cool and bracing – a generous rainfall, 1 000 millimetres a year, mainly in this season, provides a luxuriant vegetation. Autumn brings crisp days and colder nights and contrasting vegetative colours. The first heavy snowfalls can be expected from May – the winter days are generally gloriously sunny and the nights sharply cold. In the spring and early summer the gardens of Hogsback, both natural and man-made are truly beautiful.

People go to Hogsback for the magic of the mountain air, for gentle walks along the country lanes and into the forests where giant yellowwoods mix with fern and wild flowers; they go there for easy climbs where waterfalls, mountain streams and singing birds abound; they go there to enjoy swimming, bowls, tennis and trout fishing, and for the simple pleasure and comfort of log fires, congenial company, cards, music, good food and rest. The permanent white inhabitants number little more than one hundred and there are some 1 500 blacks engaged in the forestry department.

Climbing at Hogsback is perfectly safe provided that the natural warnings of mist and fog are observed. Experienced walkers can take in a dawn to dusk walk of Gaika's Kop (1 954 metres), Tor Doon (1 565 metres) and the main Hogsback peak (1 820 metres).

The famed Hogsback Inn, in co-operation with Department of Forestry, has for many years provided a real service to visitors wishing to explore the area. The routes are defined by various markers, using the Inn's hog emblem in the basic colours of red, green, yellow and blue. The corresponding and indispensable 'Piggy Book' guide is obtainable from the hotels and shops.

Among the lovely waterfalls are the Madonna and Child, Swallowtail, Bridal Veil and the fascinating Kettlespout where the water forces its way through a natural spout at the top of a cliff – most beautiful when a strong wind blows the water back to resemble an emission of steam some ten metres high. Oak Avenue, a short walk from the village, is a delightful retreat. The old trees were planted in the 1880s and the avenue is used for open air interdenominational church services at Christmas and Easter when worshippers sit on logs placed across the roadway. In the vicinity metre-high ferns grow in a forest dale. A twenty-minute walk from the main road through indigenous bush lead to the Eastern Monarch, a giant yellowwood said to be the oldest and largest in all the Cape. Other trees indigenous to Hogsback include stinkwood, white ironwood, Cape chestnut, assegai, camdeboo, red currant and red pear.

Hogsback is one of the few places in South Africa where berries do well. Apart from the wild blackberries to be seen everywhere, the cultivated varieties include red, white and black currants, raspberries, loganberries, English gooseberries, Booysen berries and strawberries. The area is also notable for its hazel nuts, chestnuts and walnuts.

There are clay deposits in the Hogsback area and its Xhosa name is Qabimbola (where they paint the clay) and this refers to the time-honoured custom of painting the face with red and white clay. On the approach roads to the resort young Xhosas will be seen offering for sale their unfired clay models of animals (particularly horses) – this is an art handed down for generations.

In this tranquil setting it is difficult to imagine the plunder that took place during the nineteenth century in the defiles of these magnificent mountains and in the lovely valley below. This was the stronghold of Gaika the Xhosa warrior-chief, and typical of the dramas witnessed here was the bloody start of the 8th Frontier War in 1850. On 24th December of that year, 700 British soldiers fought their way out of a Xhosa ambush in the Boma Pass to reach Keiskammahoek and in so doing lost 25 men killed. On the following day, Christmas Day, four settlements of the valley were completely wiped out and all of the men, some eighty of them, were massacred. In 1848 it had been the idea of the governor, Sir Harry Smith, to settle discharged soldiers in the valley to strengthen the frontier. Three of the ill-fated settlements were named after towns in England with which Sir Harry had been associated – Auckland, Ely and Woburn, and the fourth he named Juanasburg, after his Spanish-born wife Lady Juana. Back on the road to Alice where a mission church overlooks the valley, a stone monolith, erected by the Toc H in 1903, commemorates the disaster that Christmas Day in 1850.

The military outposts nearest to where the resort is today were Fort Mitchell where traces of the old earthworks can still be seen on the plateau abutting Tor Doon peak, and Fort Cox, built on a peninsula formed by a loop of the Keiskamma River. These forts together with Fort Willshire were daringly forward positions guarding the so-called ceded territory which Lord Charles Somerset had gained in his peaceful co-existence negotiations with Gaika in 1819. It was from Fort Cox that Sir Harry Smith had a miraculous escape at the end of 1850.

Seymour, Balfour, Fort Armstrong and Post Retief (Ciskei)
West of Hogsback lies the valley of the upper Kat River where in 1829 the Kat River Settlement was established by the Colonial Government and supervised by the Reverend Robert Read of the London Missionary Society who strove to settle and teach farming and industry to a large group of vagrant Hottentots. Good progress was made and by the mid-1830s there were some 3 000 Hottentots and Coloureds employed. The settlement broke up upon the outbreak of the 8th Frontier War in 1850, when the Hottentots rebelled.

North of Fort Beaufort a magnificent highway leads along the Kat River Valley, today a tranquil rural area of irrigated citrus farms, past Blinkwater, Tidbury's Toll with its quaint inn and Seymour (once an atmospheric town with an historic little hotel), into the Elandsberg. The road is carried through that range by means of the Nico Malan Pass (in fine cattle rearing country) and eventually it reaches Queenstown (Chapter 6), 152 kilometres from Fort Beaufort.

Before reaching Seymour, at approximately 46 kilometres from Fort Beaufort, within a short distance of each other, two by-roads lead off into Balfour – the first is tarred and the second is of gravel. Taking the gravel turnoff, the farm approach road leading to Fort Armstrong is passed on the left; this is just before reaching the school and railway in the hamlet of Balfour.

Fort Armstrong was built in 1835 at the close of the 6th Frontier War and named after its commander, Captain A.B. Armstrong. In January 1851, during the 8th Frontier War, it was seized and occupied by the Hottentot rebels and on 23rd February it was attacked by a combined force of burghers and regulars. Fierce fighting ensued, the fort itself was demolished by artillery fire and the surviving main tower had to be taken by hand to hand fighting until the last nine defenders were killed. The tower, today a national monument, is preserved in the peaceful surrounds of farming country and is a conspicuous landmark, clearly visible from the main Fort Beaufort-Queenstown road.

It was from another fortress, Post Retief, 50 kilometres north west of Fort Armstrong that the retaliatory force had assembled and set out to recapture the fort. They had just relieved the Post from heavy investment by another large force of rebel Hottentots. Post Retief was named after the famous Voortrekker leader. Here on the plateau of the magnificent Winterberg, Retief had his last home in the Cape and he received this honour from a great British soldier and governor, Sir Benjamin d'Urban, who wrote: 'when in 1836 I caused a military post to be established in the Winterberg, I named it Retief... The gentleman, Mr Retief, is the same whom in the latter end of 1835 I appointed Field Commandant, for his active and judicious conduct at a period of difficulty and danger'.

Katberg (Ciskei)
Due north of Balfour at the confluence of the Winterberg and Elandsberg ranges the Katberg Pass carries the road through one of the most dramatic drives in the Eastern Cape, the scenery varying widely between the lush indigenous vegetation of the southern ascent and the weirdly beautiful barren sandstone shelf of the Devil's Bellows Nek on the northern descent. At the southern entrance to the pass is the Katberg Hotel. Further on in the pass is a caravan park and near the summit, the Forestry Station.

Whittlesea and Sada (Ciskei)
Beyond Devil's Bellows Nek, on the road to Queenstown (Chapter 6) is the rural village of Whittlesea, named after the birthplace in Cambridgeshire of Sir Harry Smith. From here permits can be obtained from the magistrate to visit Sada, a resettlement town for people from the Transkei and already famous for its handwoven rugs, table-cloths, stoles and other articles.

Trunk road R32 from Cookhouse to Cradock

From Cookhouse trunk road R32 continuing northwards leads for 89 kilometres through the Daggaboersnek up the valley of the Great Fish River to Cradock.

Cradock
This is a spacious, busy country town with a population of 36 500. It is the centre of a rich agricultural valley stretching some 100 kilometres north to south and watered by three large irrigation control dams – Grassridge, Lake Arthur and Kommandodrift, and linked with the giant Orange River project which involved the construction of the 82-kilometre-long Orange-Fish tunnel, the longest irrigation tunnel in the world. The valley is noted for its wool and mohair production, its fine cattle ranches and for fruit, poultry and lucerne.

A frontier outpost was established in 1812 (after the Fourth Frontier War) where Cradock now stands, with Andries Stockenström installed as deputy landdrost. This was in the time of the soldier-governor of the Cape, Sir John Cradock, after whom the town was named. In 1873 it received municipal status.

Cradock has some very attractive features. The beautiful Dutch Reformed Church, built in 1866, is a replica of St. Martin's-in-the-Field, London; this is a national monument and so is the Old Parsonage and Wagon House. It is interesting to note that Paul Kruger, who was born on the farm Vaalbank, near Colesberg, appears in the Cradock Dutch Reformed Church baptismal register in 1825.

The spacious Municipal Park comprises lovely gardens with shade trees, swimming pool, tennis courts, rugby field encircled by an athletic track with a pavilion to seat 2 000 and a caravan park. Van Riebeeck Karoo Garden with its succulents, wild pomegranates, heaths, flag-stoned walks and pergolas is a quiet retreat. Lake Arthur, a splendid stretch of water is ideal for all types of water sport. There are two hotels and opportunities for bowls and golf.

Four kilometres to the north of the town are the municipal Karoo Sulphur Springs and open air swimming pool where the temperature of the water is 38⁰C. Adjoining the baths is a caravan park with all facilities and bungalows can be rented.

On the summit of buffelskop (1 500 metres) to the south of the town is a memorial cairn, in the shape of an African hut, to Olive Schreiner, author of *The Story of an African Farm* and many other South African books. She had lived in Cradock for a number of years.

Mountain Zebra National Park
This sanctuary for the mountain zebra is situated in the Great Karoo, 27 kilometres west of Cradock on the northern slopes of the Bankberg range. The turnoff to the park is 5 kilometres along the road to Graaff-Reinet (R32, R61).

The Park was started in 1937 when the National Parks Board bought the farm Babylons Toren with its small herd of six of this very rare species. Adjoining farms were later acquired and through the years the herd has increased to over 200 head. In recent years a further 196 mountain zebra have been relocated in 19 other reserves.

The Cape mountain zebra *(Equus zebra zebra)* stands about 1,25 metres high and is the smallest of all zebra species. It is ideally adapted to its mountainous environment, the striped coat blending with the dull grey of the karoo hillocks. It has a more compact frame than other zebra and moves about the rocks of the mountainside with the sure-footed agility of the klipspringer. It differs from other zebra in that there is a definite dewlap present; the beautiful black and white stripes are sharply defined with no shadow stripes, but there is a reddish tinge; the stripes do not meet on the underside of the body and

unlike other zebra the stripes encircle the legs, extending right down to the hooves.

The Park covers an area of 6 536 hectares on a scenically beautiful plateau, 1 200 metres above sea level. The rock formations are sandstone, siltstone and mudstone from the Lower Stage, Beaufort Series of the Karoo System and post Karoo dolerite intrusions. The interesting vegetation differs from the less mountainous karoo areas. There are thick patches of sweet-thorn *(Acacia karoo)* with a variety of karree species, mostly along the Wilgerboom River bed, and in the high ravines dense groves of wild olive *(Olea africana)* occur, as do white stinkwood and kiepersol. After the slightest rainfall many flowering shrubs and carpets of mesembryanthemum and blue tulips come into bloom.

Other game species which originally occurred in the area have been reintroduced. Among these are springbok, eland, blesbok, black wildebeest, red hartebeest, kudu, duiker, steenbok and mountain reedbuck. Predators include, black-footed cat, caracal (African lynx), African wild cat, black-backed jackal, bat-eared fox, Cape fox and aardwolf. Of the birds that abound in the sanctuary, 206 species have been recorded – the large birds are ostrich, Stanley crane, secretary bird, bustard and lapwing.

A R2,5 million rest camp was opened in 1982. Accommodation (completely self-contained) comprises 20 two-bedroomed, 6 five-bedroomed and 12 four-bedroomed chalets. In addition the old Doornhoek farmstead (a national monument) completely refurbished, is now the show-piece guesthouse. The caravan park has every necessary facility. Other features of the camp are fully licensed à la carte restaurant, swimming pool, petrol station and well-stocked shop (liquor, fresh meat and bread sold).

Walking is permitted in the Park, and the Mountain Zebra hiking trail a 3-day hike with 2 night stops in huts, is popular.

Hofmeyr and other routes from Cradock
The R390 from Cradock leads for 64 km north-east to Hofmeyr, a town of 3 000 inhabitants notable for salt production. It was named after 'Onze Jan' Hofmeyr, champion of Afrikaans-English equality.

The R61 from Cradock leads to the east, and via Tarkastad it links with Queenstown (Chapter 6).

Ninety-eight kilometres from Cradock, route R32 having merged with R57 from Graaff-Reinet, reaches Middelburg (Chapter 4).

1

2

4

3

1. Buffalo River small boat harbour, East London.
2. East London's famous Orient Beach adjoins Buffalo Harbour with its cranes, huge grain elevator and freighter funnel in view.
3. The beautiful reef which separates the Orient and Eastern beaches, East London.
4. British Kaffrarian Savings Bank, King William's Town, has been continuously in business here since 1860.

CHAPTER 6

East London and the Border, North-eastern Cape and East Griqualand

The history of the Border area of the Eastern Cape is both eventful and colourful. The Xhosa warriors, Macomo and his brother Tyali with their 12 000-strong impi, swept across the border in December 1834 and laid waste the country from the frontier to Somerset East. This was when Colonel Harry Smith (then Chief of Staff) rode from Cape Town to Grahamstown (a distance of 900 kilometres in six days) to personally take command. He was followed by reinforcements and the governor himself.

D'Urban and Smith pressed a counter attack beyond the Kei and annexed the territory from the Keiskamma to the Kei, a buffer state, which was named the Province of Queen Adelaide. Hintsa, the great chief of the Xhosas, whom d'Urban believed was responsible for the invasion, was shot whilst attempting to escape captivity and Macomo was captured and sent to Robben Island. At the close of this the Sixth Frontier War, Smith rode to the coast to investigate the possibility of a landing port at the mouth of the Buffalo River to supply the Province of Queen Adelaide. However it was only after the new Province had been abandoned, upon the instructions of the Colonial Office, that the brig, *Knysna*, on 19 November 1836 anchored off the Buffalo River mouth to trade there. John Baillie, an ex-naval officer, went ashore, explored the area and hoisted the Union Jack on the summit of what is today known as Signal Hill on the east bank near the entrance to the harbour. Baillie named the place Port Rex in honour of George Rex of Knysna, who owned the brig.

There is no record of any further activity at the mouth of the Buffalo until the outbreak of the War of the Axe. In 1847 the famous vessel *H.M.S. Beagle*, in which Charles Darwin voyaged round the world, was engaged in surveying the area. The entrance was found to be suitable and troops and supplies were landed. At this time Harry Smith, now Major-General Sir Harry Smith, returned to the Cape from his victorious campaign in India, as governor, and at the end of the War of the Axe, on 23 December 1847, he once again annexed the territory from the Keiskamma to the Kei, proclaiming a separate colony, the Province of British Kaffraria, with King William's Town as the capital. A few days later on 28 December, by government notice, the settlement at the Buffalo mouth was renamed East London.

During the period 1848-1849, Fort Glamorgan was built on the west bank of the river.

At the close of the Crimean War in 1857, members of the German Legion who served in the British Army were settled in British Kaffraria. Some 2 400 men, women and children landed in East London and thereafter greatly influenced the growth and development of the district. Many well-known South African families are descended from these colonists and many of the place names in what is today known as the Border are of German origin.

East London

One of South Africa's most pleasant residential cities, East London is a reputed family holiday resort. Its fine year-round climate, its ideal setting and splendid beaches are the foundation of its reputation. Throughout the year visitors can expect seven and a half hours of sunshine each day and warm sea temperatures varying from 17°C to 23°C.

The only South African river harbour of commercial importance, East London is built on the banks of the Buffalo River. It is the export centre for the district forming the Border area of the Cape Province and is most conveniently situated to handle the cargo of the Orange Free State Goldfields and the extensive areas of the Ciskei and Transkei.

East London occupies an area of 93 square kilometres and has a population of 142 000. A large percentage of the 180 000 Blacks who live in Mdantsane, work in East London. The Black town, part of self-governing Ciskei, is 17 kilometres away on the road to King William's Town. Beacon Bay, a residential municipality and close neighbour of East London, has a population of 12 000.

East London's principal thoroughfare is Oxford Street, 5 kilometres long. The main shopping centre, General Post Office, City Hall and Information Bureau are all in Oxford Street. The Air Terminal is in Terminus Street. Ben Schoeman Airport is on the West Bank, 12 kilometres from the city via the fine John Vorster Bridge over the Buffalo River.

The powder magazine, a substantial building of stone, is all that remains of Fort Glamorgan on the west bank of the Buffalo River, overlooking East London harbour. It is a national monument. The naming of the fort was intended to honour Colonel Henry Somerset (son of Lord Charles) in acknowledgement of his services during the War of the Axe. The Colonel was the grandson of the Duke of Beaufort who also bore the title Earl of Glamorgan. The first troops to occupy the fort were the 73rd Regiment (Black Watch). The fort housed quarters for one officer, 20 cavalrymen, 300 infantrymen, a commissariat, the powder magazine and a small hospital.

A memorial to the German immigrants can be seen near the beach front. It commemorates their arrival in 1857. In the same year on 28th November, 153 Irish colleen immigrants were put safely ashore from the chartered 583-ton tea clipper *Lady Kennaway*. They came to marry the German legionnaires. Five days after the landing the ship, lying in the roadstead, was wrecked in a heavy storm.

There are three beaches within the city limits. The Esplanade stretches for approximately two kilometres from the harbour's eastern breakwater (which forms a promenade pier) to the mouth of the Blind River. The promenade pier overlooks the famous Orient Beach (named after the Russian sailing ship *Orient* wrecked there in 1907) with all the modern beach facilities including a restaurant and theatre. To the east is the Aquarium, with its penguins and sea lions, and Eastern Beach noted for its surfing rollers.

Facing the sea a number of good hotels string out along this rugged coastline where ocean liners and freighters pass close inshore upon entering or leaving the river port. The hotel restaurants provide a variety in night life ranging from cocktails, discothèque and inexpensive fare to sophisticated cabaret, poolside dancing and smörgasbord.

The City Council has laid out a spacious, all-facility caravan and camping park above the Eastern Beach and adjoining this amenity is Marina Glen with its well kept lawns, gnarled shade trees, miniature railway and SANTA tearoom – altogether an attractive feature in a delightful coastal setting.

Nahoon Beach and River Mouth, six kilometres to the north-east of the city centre, is a completely natural bathing and fishing beach where the lawns and shade trees reach down to the white sands and provide the ideal place for picnics, caravanning and camping. Nearby there is an hotel and bowling club.

Wool, maize, pineapples, citrus, meat and dairy products are the principal exports from Buffalo Harbour. There are pre-cooling facilities for perishable products, bulk petrol and fuel oil tanks, a modern graving dock and one of the country's largest grain elevators. The lighthouse at Hood Point on the west bank is 55 metres high and has a light range of 30 kilometres.

Most of East London's factories are concentrated on the west bank where the original settlement was established and the products of these industries include textiles, confectionery, pharmaceuticals, stockings, batteries, leather goods, soap, furniture, plastic goods, clothing and motor cars.

The 34-hectare Queen's Park (a national monument) is a botanical garden and zoo that lies between the main shopping centre and the Buffalo River. A motor road traverses the park where there are over a thousand animals, birds and reptiles with many interesting trees and shrubs and a tearoom.

East London Museum is near the top end of Oxford Street. General in scope, the museum is particularly devoted to South African natural history, ethnology, pre-history, archaeology and local history, and contains some fine exhibitions and study collections. The first gallery exhibits the famous coelacanth genus of primitive fish, which was trawled off the Chalumna River near East London on 22 December 1938. The museum houses one of the most complete Karoo reptile fossils as well as a collection of marine fossils. The bird gallery contains a dodo egg, brought from Mauritius in 1846 and reputed to be the only one in existence. The ethnological gallery has interesting ornament, implement and beadwork exhibits of Xhosa, Fingo, Tembu and other tribes. In the historical gallery emphasis is laid on the German colonists of 1857 in a similar way as in Grahamstown's museum, where the main topic is the British settler of 1820.

Gately House, a well preserved Victorian period house, once the home of John Gately – 'the father of East London' – was opened to the public in 1967 as a department of the East London Museum. John Gately came to the Cape to serve in the Frontier War of 1850 and became East London's first mayor in 1880. The building is a national monument.

Adjacent to the Museum is the Guild Theatre, well-known among the intimate theatres in the country. On the opposite side of the street is the War Memorial.

Ann Bryant Art Gallery, on the corner of Oxford Street and St. Lukes Road, is notable for its collection of contemporary pictures, especially of Betty Cilliers-Barnard, Walter Battis and Jean Weiz. Of the older schools represented there is a fine original of Pierneef. In the sculpture gallery are the bronze heads of two local sports idols: Joan Harrison, the first South African to win an Olympic gold medal, and Basil Kenyon, the Border player who captained the Springbok rugby sides of 1949 and 1951-52. There is also a fine model of the brig *Knysna*, the first vessel to trade at the Buffalo River mouth.

Jody Schechter, the 1979 Grand Prix champion, came from East London where South Africa's first Grand Prix circuit was built on the west bank. Races still take place there during winter and summer seasons. The Buffalo River is famed for the summer regattas of yachting, rowing and power-boating. Jan Smuts and Border grounds in Recreation Road are the venues for cricket, rugby and soccer. The East London Golf Club at Nahoon and the Alexander Country Club on the west bank welcome visitors as do a number of bowling clubs in the city.

Some of the most attractive rock angling in South Africa is to be had in East London and along its neighbouring coastline. Close to the city Flat Rocks and Bat's Cave are popular fishing spots, and when the west wind is blowing the Reef provides particularly fine sport.

East London's neighbouring coastal resorts

To the north-east and south-west of East London, stretching from the mouth of the Great Kei to the estuary of the Keiskamma lies an enchanting seaboard. In this region numerous clear-water rivers form beautiful lagoons and estuaries before reaching the sea and there are lovely bays, sandy beaches, majestic headlands and secluded coves. The many little resorts along this coastline extending 100 kilometres on each side of East London provide excellent opportunities for bathing, fishing, boating and shell collecting.

Eastern Resorts

For the Eastern Resorts the exit from East London is at the top of Oxford Street and into the Transkei road, which is national road N2. Turnoffs to the resorts are clearly marked on this highway.

Bonza Bay, part of the municipality of Beacon Bay, has an attractive beach at the lagoon formed by the Quenera River. At the resort, where the fishing is good, there is an hotel, caravan park and a bowling club.

Gonubie, on the mouth of the river of that name, is a municipality with a population of 5 000 and has excellent resort amenities in the safe tidal pools, shady caravan park, tennis courts, bowling greens, lagoon boating, heavy tackle fishing at the river mouth and an hotel.

Between Gonubie and Bulugha are a number of interesting picnic, camping and fishing spots, such as Rainbow Valley, Sunrise-on-sea and Kwelera Mouth. What is known as the Fisherman's Cove area at the mouth of the Bulugha River is a year-round resort with the Yellow Sands Caravan Park and the Glen Muir Holiday Resort offering cottage accommodation.

North of the mouth of the Bulugha are Queensberry Bay, Krauses Beach, Cintsa and Kefani and at each of these unspoilt resorts there is a variety of caravan, cabin, bungalow and cottage accommodation.

Haga-Haga, at the foot of two hills, is a seaside village with a holiday hotel and caravan park with cottages. The fine beach at the river mouth is notable for good fishing and a wide variety of sea shells.

Morgan Bay is a holiday resort placed in a singularly beautiful part of this enchanting coastline. It lies on the south bank of the lovely lagoon formed by the Nchara River and has an hotel, holiday flats and a caravan park. There are fine walks along the beach and in the area called Double Mouth, a lagoon formed by two small rivers. The area is famed for its sea shells. In the forest four kilometres north-east of the village are the workings of Cape Morgan Titanium Mine.

Kei Mouth with its two hotels and caravan park is particularly well liked by rock fishermen. Its other attributes are the splendid beach and interesting walks in the coastal forest.

Across the Kei River is Transkei, described in Chapter 7.

Western Resorts and the coastal road R72 from East London to Port Alfred

For the Western Resorts the exit from East London is over the handsome John Vorster Bridge that spans the Buffalo River upstream from the original road and rail bridge.

At Shelly Beach there are fishermen's bungalows, camping sites and a tearoom. Fuller's Bay has a fine stretch of beach with good fishing spots. Hickman's River has holiday cottages and a caravan park and is popular for boating, river and sea fishing. Cove Rock and Rockclyffe are famous fishing spots where there are bungalows and cottages. At the river mouths of Igoda and Gulu there are resort establishments with caravan parks and camping sites and opportunities for boating, fishing, bathing and horse riding.

Kidd's Beach at the mouth of the Mcantsi River was named after Charles Kidd, a mayor of King William's Town in the 1860s, and is a favourite holiday resort of the people of that town. It comprises a sandy beach and rocky shoreline with a tidal pool. Its facilities include an hotel, bowling green, tennis courts, holiday cottages and 3 caravan parks.

Christmas Rock, Kayser's Beach and Chalumna Mouth are all fishermen's haunts.

Pleasantly situated overlooking the estuary of the Keiskamma is the resort village of Hamburg (Ciskei). Established by the German Legion immigrants in the 1860s, it has a population of about 1 200. The spacious beach, bathing and organised fishing trips are the principal attractions. There is an hotel and caravan park.

Beyond the turnoff to Hamburg the road R72, after passing the turnoff to the Wesley mission station, swings back to the coast and continues on the very beautiful route to Port Alfred. Before reaching the Great Fish River bridge the road crosses a succession of rivers and these are the Gqutywa, Bira, Mgwalana, Mtati and Mpetweni – each lagoon crossing appears more beautiful than the last, all as yet in settings unspoilt by development. Beyond the Great Fish River there are many more lagoon crossings before reaching Port Alfred (Chapter 6).

National road N2 from East London to King William's Town

The portion of national road N2 that links East London with King William's Town is a pleasant 60-kilometre drive in rural landscape. The exit from East London by-passes the eastern suburb of Cambridge (named after the Duke of Cambridge who was the British Commander when the German Legion left the scene of the Crimean War).

After a third of the way to King William's Town the road passes Berlin, a small town founded by the settlers from the German Legion, where there is an hotel and a caravan park. The area is being industrialised as part of the Ciskeian development plan.

King William's Town

Situated on the banks of the upper reaches of the Buffalo River, King William's Town has retained the pleasant country-town atmosphere of the booming place it was a hundred years ago. In the last quarter of the nineteenth century it rose to great prosperity as a military, administrative and trading centre, with several large business institutions having their head offices there. Today the town has a population of 25 000.

King William's Town originated as a mission station established by the Reverend John Brownlee of the London Missionary Society in 1826. At the time that the redoubtable soldier-governor, Sir Benjamin d'Urban, proclaimed the Province of Adelaide (which he named in honour of the wife of the reigning monarch of Britain, William IV) in May 1835, he also created a new town as its centre at the site of the mission station, naming it in honour of the monarch himself. Before the close of that year the new province was abandoned but the small settlement continued.

In the War of the Axe, King William's Town was overrun by the Xhosa and upon the termination of the war in 1847, Governor Sir Harry Smith (another fine soldier) revived the idea of a separated province and proclaimed the Province of British Kaffraria with King William's Town as its capital.

During 1857 the area was settled by more than 2 000 immigrant German legionnaires who played a major part in the growth impetus of King William's Town, and after the visit of Prince Alfred on 13 August 1860 the status of 'Royal Borough' was conferred on the town. Upon the peaceful consolidation of the frontier in 1878, British Kaffraria was annexed to the Cape. It remained a garrison town for imperial troops until the first World War and still bears much of the character of its military history.

After the War of the Axe the Buffalo River became

the central line of occupation and Fort Murray, on the western side of the river nine kilometres to the south of the town, was completed in 1848. This was the second fort to bear the name, the first having been constructed at Mount Coke, seven kilometres further south, as part of the defences of the Province of Queen Adelaide and was abandoned in 1836. The second fort which is now in ruins is a national monument. The large outpost was jointly a fort and a barracks for infantry and cavalry – built of stone with a thatched roof. A large house near the fort was occupied from 1848 to 1862 by Colonel John Maclean, Chief Commissioner of British Kaffraria and afterwards Lieutenant-Governor of the province. In 1858 the fort was used for the detention of the two youthful prophetesses, Nongquase and Noxosi, whose ridiculous prophecy caused the disastrous famine of the Xhosas – a people highly sensitive to superstition and witchcraft.

In what became known as the Cattle Killing Delusion of 1856, these young women preached that the day was near when the white people and all those of the Xhosas who disobeyed orders would be driven into the sea by a great wind. Dead chiefs would rise, cattle kraals and grain pits would be filled to capacity and upon the sacred day the sun would rise blood-red, illness and old age would disappear and fields would stand ready for reaping. To bring about these things it was first necessary to kill every head of livestock in the possession of the Xhosa nation and destroy all grain and other produce. Despite the protests and efforts of the British authorities the destruction began and could not be halted.

A quarter of a million head of livestock were killed, special kraals and grain pits were built to house the new cattle and harvest, and houses were strengthened to withstand the great wind. The day set down for the miracle was 18 February 1857. When the sun rose in the normal manner and nothing extraordinary occurred the Xhosa people realised that they had been duped and a dreadful famine descended upon the nation. The official population figures of British Kaffraria fell from over 104 000 to 37 000 between the period 1 January and 31 July 1857, and this put an end to the military power of the Xhosas.

The Kaffrarian Museum in Albert Road was established in 1884 by the local Natural History Society and is housed in a fine old building constructed in 1898. It contains one of the world's largest collections of African mammals – 25 000 specimens assembled mainly by the former director, Captain G.C. Shortridge (1920-1949). A favourite among the exhibits is the mounted figure of Huberta, the hippo that endeared itself to the entire country during its two-and-a-half year wanderings of a thousand kilometres. Appearing in Zululand toward the end of 1928 she travelled south with diverse deviations, turning up at the most unexpected times at the most unusual places (including an escapade in the middle of the city of Durban). Her adventures came to a tragic end in April 1931 when she was accidentally shot by a farmer in the Keiskamma River. At first the famous hippo, considered to be a male, was given the jocular name of Hubert and was posthumously renamed Huberta.

The clock tower and brass tablet of the Magistrate's Court and Post Office are a memorial to the Reverend John Brownlee who founded the mission at the site of the town. In front of the building which is in Alexandra Road and is a national monument, is a memorial to Major-General Henry Timson Lukin, the South African soldier of Delville Wood fame, who spent much of his time in the Border area.

The old railway station built in 1877 in Alexandra Road is now occupied by the School Board and is a national monument.

Within the handsome building of the Town Hall on the Market Square is an excellent concert hall. The library in Alyff Street was established in 1861 and contains a valuable collection of Africana. British Kaffrarian Savings Bank on Maclean Square dates from 1860; the building, recently restored, was completed in 1908. In the centre of Maclean Square in the surrounds of a pretty garden is a bronze of Queen Victoria; provided by public subscription, it commemorates her diamond jubilee in 1897. The Town Hall and Savings Bank are national monuments.

In the northern part of the town, in Reserve Road (the road that continues as R30 to Stutterheim) is the Residency; rebuilt in 1847 after the War of the Axe, it was occupied by Sir Harry Smith during his visit and is today a national monument. Here in Reserve Road is the Holy Trinity Anglican Church, built of stone by soldiers of the British Garrison of 1850.

It is fitting that the country's only museum devoted to missionaries should be in historic King William's Town which had its start as a mission station. The Methodist Church in Berkeley Street, built in 1855, is now the South African Missionary Museum. The church and adjoining manse are both national monuments.

King William's Town is renowned for its good schools, notably Dale College, which was founded as the Diocesan Grammar School in 1861 and renamed in 1877 after Sir Langham Dale, Superintendent-General of Education, who greatly improved the school system of the Cape Colony. Sutton House, a hostel of Dale College, in Queen Street, dates from 1877.

Grey Hospital in Lonsdale Street, a charming old building in a sylvan setting was erected by Sir George Grey and is a national monument.

Laid out on six hectares on the left bank of the Buffalo River is the Botanical Garden with its fine conservatories.

King William's Town has seven hotels, a municipal caravan park with all facilities on the right bank of the Buffalo River (opposite the Botanical Garden), a golf club, bowls and tennis clubs and flying club and public swimming baths. At East London's water supply, Laing Dam, near Mount Coke, there is a yacht club and trout fishing is to be had there and at Rooikrans and Maden dams to the north of the town where the Pirie trout hatcheries are located. The turnoff west, to the dams and hatcheries is 15 kilometres along trunk road R30.

Over the years King William's Town has developed into an industrial centre of some importance. It is of course ideally situated for future development in co-operation with Ciskei.

King William's Town is an important road junction. In the areas already described, national road N2 from Grahamstown approaches the town from the south and turns due east to link with East London. Due north trunk route R30 starts its journey via Aliwal North to Bloemfontein. Due west road R63 leads off to Alice and Fort Beaufort and to the south-east is the road to Mount Coke and Kidd's Beach. The continuation of road R63 is to the north-east of the town; it completely bypasses East London and joins with national road N2 south of the Kei River Pass.

Mount Coke

Off the road to Kidd's Beach, 20 km south of King William's Town, is Mount Coke Wesleyan Methodist Mission Station. Founded in 1825 the mission was twice destroyed in the frontier wars and restored in 1848. From 1852 to 1876 a number of Xhosa publications were printed on a press there, including a translation of the Bible.

Zwelitsha and Bisho (Ciskei)

To the south of King William's Town is Zwelitsha, the principal industrial town of Ciskei. Most of its Xhosa population of some 30 000 are housed in the extensive estate of Good Hope Textile Corporation. Bisho, the capital of the Republic of Ciskei, adjoins the northern boundary of King William's Town on route R63 to Kei Road. The houses of parliament, the independence stadium and the Amatola Sun Hotel and Casino are passed along the route R63. Ciskei has a population of 660 000 and another 500 000 Ciskeians live and work in the RSA. Independence was granted in December 1981.

Kei Road and Komga

The East London bypass along route R63 from King William's Town is scenically pleasant and passes through the villages of Kei Road and Komga in each of which there is an hotel. Komga has a municipal caravan park, delightful golf course, bowling green and a school with fine playing fields. It was near Komga on 29 December 1877, during the Ninth Frontier War, that Major Hans Garret Moore (Connaught Rangers), while commanding a patrol of the Frontier Mounted Police, won the first Victoria Cross to be earned on South African soil. From Kei Road a road leading north-west to Stutterheim passes Amabele, a railhead with a trading store and hotel.

Trunk route R30 from King William's Town to Aliwal North

Stutterheim

Forty-two kilometres due north of King William's Town is Stutterheim, a municipality with population of 18 000 inhabitants established by the German Legionaires who settled there in 1857. They named their town after their commander Major-General C.G.L.W.J. Von Stutterheim, a Prussian baron. He came to South Africa with his men but later returned to Germany.

Stutterheim lies in well-watered forest country on the slopes of the Kologha Mountains, a spur of the Amatola range, and it serves a district rich in timber, sheep, cattle and citrus. There is an agricultural research institute at Dohne, 8 kilometres north of the town.

Stutterheim has two hotels and a municipal caravan park. There are several guest farm establishments in the area and holiday-makers come to enjoy the mild climate, the beautiful mountain forest scenery (where waterfalls, ferns and wild flowers abound) and for trout fishing and boating in the winding Kubusie River. There are also tennis courts, bowling greens and a golf course.

Sandile's Grave, Bethel Mission and Fort Cunynghame

Several historic sites near Stutterheim draw attention. Six kilometres to the south on road R30 is a turnoff west to the grave of Sandile, warrior-chief of the Gaikas (tribe of the Xhosas) who was killed in June 1878 during the ninth Frontier War.

On a gravel road to the north of the town is the Bethel Mission. The church there, built in 1865, is on the site of the first Berlin Mission Station in the Eastern Cape, chosen in 1837 by Ludwig Döhne. A bronze plaque of the Monuments Commission reveals that 'Albert Kropf, serving here, was the chief translator of the Xhosa Bible and compiler of the Xhosa-English dictionary published respectively in 1887-1889 and 1899'.

On the right hand side of road R30, eleven kilometres north of the town are the ruins of Fort Cunynghame, built during the Ninth Frontier War and named after General Sir Arthur Cunynghame who was in command of the British troops in South Africa in 1876. Overlooking the fort is Dohne Peak, 1 456 metres.

Keiskammahoek and Gaika's Grave (Ciskei)

From Stutterheim there is a scenic road to the west through the Dontsa Pass to Keiskammahoek that joins with the King William's Town-Alice road near Debe Nek. Gaika's Grave is at Keiskammahoek – warrior-chief and founder of the Gaika tribe, he lived from 1776 to 1829.

Cathcart

On trunk route R30, forty-eight kilometres north of Stutterheim, is Cathcart at the foot of the Windvoëlberg in a district famous for wool. It started as a military post in 1858, became a municipality in 1881 and was named after the soldier-governor, Sir George Cathcart, who was killed at the Battle of Inkerman in 1854, having been governor at the Cape from 1852. The population is 4 500 and there is an hotel and caravan park.

Queenstown

The governor, Sir George Cathcart, founded Queenstown in 1853 as a military outpost and named it in honour of Queen Victoria. It received municipal status in 1879 and is today a prosperous town with a population of 60 000 people. Situated between the Katberg and Stormberg ranges on a well-watered broad plain 1 070 metres above sea level it enjoys a healthy climate. This is the administrative centre for one of the richest concentrations of sheep and cattle farming areas in South Africa.

A unique feature of Queenstown is its street planning, laid out as a stronghold with a hexagonal open area from where the six thoroughfare approaches could be commanded by artillery. Today a fountain plays in the garden of the Hexagon, a national monument, and the centre of this busy, amiable town.

Coming off the Hexagon to the north-east, Shepstone Street divides the Public Gardens from the Cultural Centre. The Public Gardens make a delightful retreat and its centre-piece is the memorial for those Queenstown citizens who fell in the Moorosi Rebellion of 1879 and the Basutu War of 1880-1881. The Queenstown and Frontier Museum and the Municipal Art Gallery (housed in a lovely stone building dating from 1897 and once a school), and the Public Library (the 3 000 volumes include the collections of Sir Bissett Berry and the South African philologist the Reverend Charles Pettman) are part of the attractively laid-out Cultural Centre where there is a beautiful Victorian drinking fountain and a fine example of a British-built class 15AR steam locomotive, at rest after 60 years of mainline service.

Cathcart Road (running in the direction south-east to north-west) is the main thoroughfare of Queenstown and is part of the trunk route R30 which connects East London with Bloemfontein. In crossing the Hexagon it forms two of the six radiating streets and in the south-eastern section are many handsome offices and stores. The Town Hall, in this street, is a graceful stone building dating from 1882; the clock tower was added in 1897 to commemorate Queen Victoria's Diamond Jubilee.

At the East London entrance to the town the Walter Everitt Sunken Garden has been developed and with its artistic landscaping, ornamental shrubs and trees, colourful flower beds, and lovely ponds attracting aquatic birdlife, it is indeed a pleasant introduction to Queenstown. Close to the gardens on the south bank of the Komani River is the all-facility municipal caravan park and adjoining drive-in cinema. The town is notable for its roses.

Well worth visiting is the gallery of shell work assembled by Miss R. Lock at No. 1 Lamont Street, in the south-western part of the town, just below the railway line and near the Bloemfontein exit. Miss Lock started this remarkable collection in 1941.

For a country town, Queenstown has an enviable record as an educational centre. The famed Queen's College, in College Avenue to the north of the railway station, was founded in 1858. The old buildings of the college have been declared a national monument.

Due north of the town and approached via Kingsway and Hangklif Road is the Queenstown Nature Reserve occupying some 700 hectares on the slopes of Madeira Mountain. The 7-kilometre drive to the top of the mountain provides spectacular views of the town and surrounding countryside and opportunities of seeing a number of antelope species including the graceful springbok. Indigenous plant life is both varied and interesting. Peculiar to the region is the tamboekie thorn (*Erythrina acanthocarpa*); well-known in the jocular vernacular as the 'wag-'n-bietjie

doring', it produces masses of red and yellow flowers during the spring and early summer (October to November). In the winter (July and August) the red-orange *Aloe ferrox* is in full bloom. The region is also notable for cycads and six kilometres south of the town the species *Encepholartos fridirichi-guiliemix* are to be seen at Fincham's Nek.

The recreational amenities, in keeping with the general high standard of the town, provide for golfers, bowlers, tennis players and swimmers. The Bongolo Dam, 5 kilometres out of the town on the Lady Frere road, has been stocked with bluegill and black bass and is the site of the yacht and power boat club. The Queenstown-Fort Beaufort road skirts the Water-down Dam 52 kilometres from Queenstown and supplements its water supply. Large by any comparison, its earthwall is 40,6 metres high and 256,6 metres long and its capacity 38,19 megalitres and it covers an area of 7,2 sq. kilometres. This dam is well stocked with trout. Bushman paintings are to be seen near the dam site.

Queenstown has seven hotels and an airfield with scheduled connecting flights with East London's airport.

Tarkastad
Sixty-four kilometres due west of Queenstown on route R61 is Tarkastad; a sheep farming centre founded in 1874, it has a population of 4 000. The Dutch Reformed Church Parsonage is of historical interest and there is an hotel in the town.

Sterkstroom and Molteno
These two towns north-west of Queenstown were coal-producing until the rich Natal and Transvaal coalfields put an end to production there. Today these towns serve a prosperous wool-growing district and each has a population of about 4 000. Molteno was named after Sir John Molteno, the first Prime Minister of the Cape Colony. There are two hotels and a caravan park in Molteno and an hotel in Sterkstroom.

Penhoek Pass and Jamestown
After the turnoff to Sterkstroom, trunk road R30 is carried across the Stormberg range by Penhoek Pass where the summit is 1 830 metres. Beyond the pass the road reaches Jamestown, on the northern slopes of the mountain, an old time staging post and now the terminus of a branch railway from Molteno. There is an hotel in the town and a caravan park to the north on the road to Aliwal North. The population is 6 000.

Aliwal North
The two powerful thermal springs which originate at a depth of 1 280 metres and deliver through artesian pressure over three million litres of water to the surface every day, have made Aliwal North famous. At the site of these hot mineral springs, 3 kilometres from the town, the municipality has built a modern complex of baths, buildings and playgrounds spread over an area of 12 hectares to provide the most elaborate spa in the Republic.

Surrounded by well-kept lawns there are five open-air pools. The Olympic Pool varies in depth from one to four metres and holds over two-and-a-quarter-million litres of water at a temperature of 27°C, making it an ideal year-round swimming pool. Built in the eye of the main spring is the Wonder Pool; completely enclosed, its gas-impregnated water bubbles out at a temperature of 34°C providing a champagne bath. A special seat in the waterfall (created by the overflow of the main bath) allows the bather to have the water fall on the body, and those who take the waters say that this is as good as a massage. These springs are highly regarded for their curative properties by sufferers of the rheumatic complaints.

Among the exceptional amenities at the spa are a 90-metre-long water slide, two warm pools for children, turkish baths, cabanas comprising room with divans, private toilet, hot and cold shower and balcony with chairs, cafeteria, restaurant, shop and recreation room.

In the year that Sir Harry Smith became Governor of the Cape, 1848, he annexed the territory north of the Stormberg and sent his secretary, J.C. Chase, as civil commissioner and magistrate to establish an administrative centre for the territory. Chase chose the De Wet family farm Buffelsvlei, on the south bank of the Orange, as the site for the new town which was founded in 1849 and named Aliwal North to commemorate the victory (three years earlier) of Sir Harry Smith over Runjeet Singh and his Sikhs at Aliwal in India. Mr. Chase, a freeman of the Worshipful Company of Founders in London, obtained the permission of the Company for Aliwal North to use its armorial bearing and motto *God the only Founder.*

Aliwal North became a municipality in 1882 and prospered considerably when the railway reached the town in 1885. Before the Frere Bridge was built in 1880 a pontoon served the traffic across the Orange River into the Free State. Upon the construction of the Hertzog Bridge in 1937 the old Frere Bridge was demolished but its stone buttress remains on the south bank of the river next to the new bridge.

Today Aliwal North has a population of 25 000 and is a well laid-out town with wide, tree-lined streets and every modern amenity. It has the beautiful Juana Square Garden, named after the governor's Spanish wife Lady Juana Smith, and fine recreation grounds at Sauer Park. Visitors are welcomed at the golf club and the bowling club. The local angling club should be consulted regarding fishing spots along the Orange and Kraai Rivers. There are five hotels in the town, and two hotels and the well known two-star Umtali Motel at the spa. There is a municipal caravan park and bungalow accommodation at the spa.

Aliwal North lies on a splendid agricultural plateau, 1 370 metres above sea level and has a fine bracing climate. The district is noted for its wheat, barley, maize, dairy, beef and wool farms. The huge Bokomo mill with its sixteen grain elevators and extensive bakery is sited on the Burgersdorp road to the south-west of the town. Products from other industries of the town are cheese and butter, meat and poultry, furniture, mineral waters, monumental stones and bricks.

The convention between the Basotho chief, Moshesh, and the governments of the Orange Free State and the Cape Colony was signed in Aliwal North in 1869 and a copy can be seen in the Town

Clerk's office. Aliwal North has always been considered a strategic point and it was occupied by the Boer forces during the Anglo-Boer War for the period from 13 November 1899 to 11 March 1900. After its relief by the British a number of blockhouses were built in the area under Kitchener's defence plan. Two of these remain and are national monuments. One is to be seen on an eminence overlooking the town from the eastern outskirts and is reached by proceeding to the eastern end of Barkly Street. Next to the blockhouse is the beautifully laid-out Garden of Remembrance with its 122 tombstones of British soldiers killed in the heavy fighting that took place around the town. Here in the open country a small game park has been developed. The second blockhouse is on raised ground at the approach to the Spa (reached by taking Levy Street from the town) and adjoins the De Wet Monument and homestead.

Among its citizens, Aliwal North has had such famous people as Commandant Lourens Wepener who was killed in leading the attack on the Moshesh stronghold, Thaba Bosiho, in 1865, and John X. Merriman, Prime Minister of the Cape Colony from 1908 to 1910. The building of the market hall in Barkly Street with its iron pillars and handmade trellis ornamentation was at one time the Dutch Reformed Church, and here President C.R. Swart was baptised.

Fourteen kilometres south of the town on the road to Queenstown are the famed Bushman rock paintings at Kalkoenkrans. Cave No. 1 is a national monument and contains a *White Lady* very similar to the treasure of the Brandberg range in Namibia. To visit the caves it is necessary to be accompanied by a guide arranged at the spa office.

From Aliwal North trunk road R30 crosses the Orange River over the Hertzog Bridge (named after South Africa's third Prime Minister) to enter the Orange Free State (Chapter 13).

Route R58 from Colesberg to Elliot and route R56 from Maclear to Dordrecht

Route R58 commences at Colesberg (Chapter 4) on its journey eastwards to the Witteberg range. In the first 70 kilometres it skirts the Orange River and Verwoerd Dam (Chapter 4) to reach Venterstad.

Venterstad
A municipality with a population of 3 000, Venterstad was named after the owner of the farm there, Johannes Venter, when it was laid out in 1875. It lies close to the gigantic Hendrik Verwoerd Dam in a tourist resort area.

Burgersdorp
In the sheltered valley of the Stormberg River, close to the Stormberg range, is the town of Burgersdorp with its 23 000 inhabitants. The centre of a farming district devoted mainly to sheep, it was established by the Dutch Reformed Church in 1846. The town has an hotel.

There are several national monuments in Burgersdorp. The Taal Monument was erected in 1893 to commemorate the recognition of the Dutch language in the Cape Parliament. Its composition is that of a marble figure of a woman pointing to a tablet which she supports with her left arm. The tablet is inscribed 'De Overwinning der Hollandsche Taal'. The figure stands on a massive granite pedestal with inscriptions on the base and is placed in a prominent position on the Market Square.

A stone blockhouse to the north of the town, on a Koppie aptly named Brandwag (sentry), formed part of the system which Lord Kitchener introduced when he took command of the British forces early in 1901. This blockhouse formed part of the line that stretched from Queenstown through Molteno, Burgersdorp, Aliwal North and Bethulie, across the Orange River.

Burgersdorp's third monument is the outbuilding of the Old Parsonage of the Dutch Reformed Church, where plans for the Potchefstroom University were made. In recent times the old Gaol and the parsonage of the Gereformeerde Church in Retief Street have been declared national monuments.

Lady Grey

East of Aliwal North route R58 leads for 48 kilometres to Lady Grey which is placed in one of the most spectacular positions for a built-up area. Completely dominated by the Witteberg range, this delightful little town is flanked by the Witteberg Peak to the north and Spioenkop to the south – the whole scene particularly beautiful after snow. To the north of the town there is a scenically rewarding drive in wooded country to the reservoir at the head of a gorge. The area around the dam is a nature reserve and the easy but sharp walk up the mountainside to the viewsite overlooking the dam is worthwhile. From the dam the road continues over rugged country by way of Joubert's Pass to join with the Lady Grey-Barkly East road.

The town of 3 000 inhabitants was founded in 1858 and named after the wife of the governor, Sir George Grey. The town has an hotel and a caravan park.

Barkly East

In this very beautiful mountainous country at an altitude of 1 800 metres is Barkly East, one of the coldest towns in South Africa where snowfalls are frequent. Highly rich pasture lands have made this one of the finest stock-farming areas in the country.

The town of 5 000 inhabitants was named after its founder, Governor Sir Henry Barkly. It was established in 1874 and became a municipality in 1881. There is an hotel and a caravan park in the town.

The railway from Lady Grey to Barkly East is by means of a 1 in 36 gradient and eight reversing stations.

Barkly Pass

The 64-kilometre drive from Barkly East to Elliot through the Barkly Pass is a spectacular scenic adventure. Route R58 heads southwards along the floor of the Kraai River valley passing magnificent stock farms overlooked by enormous sandstone buttresses. The road reaches the 2 000-metre-high summit of the pass from where there are majestic views, particularly the western view of the great wall of the Drakensberg.

Elliot

This town with a population of 6 000 lies at the junction of roads R58 and R56 in a lovely valley with a dramatic backdrop of massifs of the Drakensberg. It was named after the Tembuland chief magistrate, Sir Henry Elliot.

Ugie

Fifty-three kilometres north-east of Elliot on route R56 is the little town of Ugie. The strange sounding name comes from Scotland and the birthplace of an early missionary, the Reverend Newnay. Ugie lies in a picturesque setting on the bank of the Inxu River and has an hotel.

Maclear, Naude's Nek Pass and Rhodes

From Ugie, route R56 heads northwards along the foothills of the Drakensberg in majestic scenery with sandstone massifs and bright green slopes. After 21 kilometres this road reaches Maclear, the terminus of the railway from Sterkstroom. It was established in 1875 and named after Sir Thomas Maclear, His Majesty's Astronomer at the Cape from 1833 to 1879. The town of 4 000 inhabitants lies in beautiful country notable for trout fishing. It serves a rich farming district producing dairy products of the highest standard. Maclear has two hotels.

Maclear lies on a junction of roads. Route R56 which continues north-east across Transkei to Matatiele (East Griqualand) and a subsidiary road leading south-east to meet national road N2 near Tsolo (Transkei) and in the other direction, north-west along a breathtaking route through Naude's Nek Pass to Barkly East. The pass reaches its summit at 2 620 metres and the scene is dominated by the splendid 3 000-metre Ben Macdhui. After the pass, on its way westwards to Barkly East, this road passes through the village of Rhodes, founded in 1893 and named after Cecil Rhodes. The stone pine trees sent by Rhodes as a gift are the only remaining relics of its hectic early twentieth century days when horse racing, other gambling and drinking were the order of the day.

Indwe

Returning to Elliot, route R56 continues to Dordrecht and after 66 kilometres reaches Indwe which gets its Xhosa name from the blue cranes in this area of the southern extremity of the Drakensberg range. Mines at Indwe have been worked for low grade coal. The town has an hotel and the population is 3 000.

Dordrecht

Close to the Stormberg at 2 128 metres, Dordrecht is celebrated as the coldest town in South Africa in the winter. It was founded by the Reverend Andrew Murray in 1857 and was named after the town in Holland, well known in the early history of the Dutch Reformed Church. The population is over 3 000 and there is an hotel in the town.

East Griqualand (Natal)

East Griqualand was until 1 August 1978 a part of the Cape Province. Its incorporation into Natal Province followed upon the independence of Transkei and the realisation that it would be beneficial for East Griqualand to be administered by Natal.

National road N2 crosses the Transkei frontier into East Griqualand and in so doing the road climbs through the pass at Brooks Nek (after the trader named Brooks) on the slopes of the 2 012-metre Nolangeni Mountain, and ten kilometres out of the pass there is a turnoff west to Kokstad. National road N2 continues from this point, via Harding to reach the Natal south coast at Port Shepstone (Chapter 8).

Kokstad

Kokstad has a population of 19 000 and lies in the elevated valley of the Umzimhlava River at an altitude of 1 335 metres. It is dominated by Mount Currie which rises to 2 224 metres and was named by the Griquas to honour Sir Walter Currie, of Cape Mounted Rifles fame. A year after Sir Walter's visit in 1861 to what was known then as *No-man's-land*, some 2 000 emigrant Griquas under Adam Kok III were settled in this unoccupied but fertile highland area. The territory they occupied became known as East Griqualand and Kokstad was made the capital.

The Griquas, a race of mixed origin (European and Hottentot) were nomads until the early 1800s when the London Missionary Society settled them at Klaarwater (which became Griquatown) in the Northern Cape. The Griquas eventually threw off the missionary influence and established their independence. Thereafter they fought among themselves and split into two sections, one section following the Koks descended from their first chief, Adam Kok I, and the other under Andries Waterboer. Those with Kok emigrated to Philippolis in the Orange Free State and from there made their final trek to what is today known as the Mount Currie District. With their 300 wagons and 20 000 head of cattle they suffered untold hardship in crossing the Drakensberg. The biggest tragedy was that in the end they failed to establish a lasting community. They became involved in brawls with the Blacks and sold off their farms to Europeans for ready money. The unstabilised position was getting out of hand when the territory was annexed to the Cape Colony in 1874.

Adam Kok III died in 1875 and an obelisk memorial marks his burial place next to the police station in Hope Street, the main thoroughfare. The Griqua National Independent Church, also in Hope Street (at the Market Square) was opened in 1877 and bears a plaque of the Monuments Council. Kokstad's unique little Town Hall is fronted by a bandstand and memorial to the historic Cape Mounted Rifles, which played a major part in establishing the authority of the Crown in the whole border area.

Kokstad became a municipality in 1892 and owes its prosperity and significance as a social centre to the rich farming community it serves. Many magnificent farms surround Kokstad, the district being notable for stock raising, dairying and horse breeding. The annual rainfall varies between 750 and 1 000 millimetres with fairly heavy snowfalls in the winter. On the outskirts of the town there is a large cheese factory.

Polo is the main recreational pursuit of Kokstad and there are bowling greens, tennis courts, an 18-hole golf course and an angling club. There are two hotels and a municipal caravan park in Kokstad and a motel and caravan park at its southern entrance from national road N2.

Mount Currie Nature Reserve

The Monuments Council has provided a bronze plaque on a stone pillar to mark the place where Adam Kok III and his followers made their first laer (camp). Here on the slopes of Mount Currie is the 1 600 hectare Mount Currie Nature Reserve, in the care of the Natal Parks Board. Opened in 1983, it is part of the original municipal commonage and contains the Crystal Dam for bass, bluegill and trout fishing, and boating. The ideal place for picnics, walkers and climbers are likely to come upon blesbok, springbok, mountain reedbuck, grey rhebuck and duiker. To reach the reserve, 5 kilometres north of the town, proceed along the Franklin road and take District road D623 turnoff left, and follow the sign posts.

Ingeli

From Kokstad national road N2 traverses the top of the 'toe' of the Natal 'boot' and passes through the Weza and Ingeli forests (well-stocked with bushbuck and duiker) below the Ingeli Mountain, before meeting with trunk route R56 which crosses the northern section of Transkei from Umzimkulu. In Natal, just off national road N2 amongst the plantations of Ingeli, is the comfortable stop-over, Ingeli Forest Motel, with its excellent table and hospitality and its own petrol service station.

Franklin and Swartberg

A rural village 32 kilometres north of Kokstad, Franklin used to be the terminus of the railway from Pietermaritzburg until the lines were extended to Kokstad and Matatiele. North-west of Franklin, in a beautiful mountain setting, is the railhead, Swartberg.

Matatiele

On its 75 kilometre journey from Kokstad route R56 passes Cedarville, in a dairy-farming district, on its way to Matatiele.

Translated from the Sotho, Matatiele means 'the ducks have flown' and probably refers to their going when the marshes in the vicinity dried out. The town of 4 500 inhabitants lies in a valley with the splendid background of the Drakensberg range.

Being close to the Lesotho border Matatiele had its start as a tough gun-running, cattle-rustling outpost. The two hotels in the town (one was destroyed by fire in 1984) are relics of the old days and hair-raising stories have been told of tough customers riding into the bars on horseback to gamble, drink or brawl according to what was going on.

Today this amiable little town supports the recreational amenities of a country club and polo grounds and is the centre of a district rich in dairy, wool and polo-pony stud farms.

Transkei and its Wild Coast

A self-governing state, Transkei occupies an area of 42 870 square kilometres; an extensive and beautiful tract of undulating pastoral country (studded with whitewashed, thatched rondavel huts) that lies north to south between the Umtamvuna-Umzimkulu rivers and the Great Kei River and east to west between the Indian Ocean and the Drakensberg-Stromberg ranges. It embraces the tribal territories of the original Transkei, bounded by the Kei and Bashee rivers; Tembuland, bounded by the Bashee and Umtata rivers; Pondoland, bounded by the Umtata and Umtamvuna rivers and the magnificent stretch of coastline called the Wild Coast.

Concerned mainly in pastoral and agricultural activities, there are approximately two-million people living in the Transkei. They are the descendants of the various tribes of the Xhosas (an offshoot of the Zulus) who in the nineteenth century migrated south at the time that the Europeans of the Cape were moving north. The constant clashes between white and black led to the battles of nine Frontier Wars and the eventual annexation by the Cape Colony government of the Transkeian territories in 1879.

Over the years the people of the Transkei were encouraged by the South African government to administer their own affairs. In 1931 the various councils of the territory amalgamated to form what the Xhosas call the *Bunga* (the United Transkeian Territories General Council). In May 1964 this became the Legislative Assembly of the Transkei and in October 1976 complete sovereign independence was declared. Parliament sits in the *Bunga* building in Umtata, the capital.

In recent times re-construction of the N2 through Transkei has improved the route considerably.

Original Transkei – the area between the Kei and the Bashee Rivers

Butterworth (Gcuwa)
After negotiating the cuttings through the Great Kei River-gorge (decorated with aloes blooming in winter and acacia blooming in summer), national road N2 reaches Butterworth; the oldest town in Transkei, it has a population of some 28 000 people and lies on the banks of the Gcuwa River.

The town had its start when the Wesleyan Mission was established in 1827. Its founder, the Reverend W.J. Shrewbury, named the station after Joseph Butterworth, treasurer of the Wesleyan Missionary Society. It is recorded that this remote outpost of civilisation received a regular postal service from Grahamstown as early as 1832. During the mid-nineteenth century the mission was destroyed by fire on three separate occasions.

Today Butterworth is a bustling trading town and is notable for its fine hospital, a prominent building on the hillside. On the outskirts of the town important advancement has been achieved in the construction of housing schemes on a large scale close to a huge industrial area which is under development.

The district is scenically attractive. The Bawa Falls on the Qolora River has a sheer drop of 91 metres and the cascades on the Gcuwa River are quite as spectacular. There is an hotel in Butterworth.

Idutywa
Thirty-four kilometres from Butterworth along national road N2 the small river with the unpronounceable name of Nqxakaxa is crossed and this is remindful of the many words in the Xhosa language with the strange 'click' sound, apparently copied from the speech of the Hottentots whom the Xhosas encountered during their great migration to the south at the start of the seventeenth century.

Idutywa lies two kilometres north of the Nqxakaxa River. The town's name 'the restless place' originates from the inter-tribal disorder there in the 1850s which led to the Cape government establishing a police post in what was called the Idutywa Reserve. On the railway line connecting Umtata with the Cape Province, Idutywa is today an important trading and distributing centre. The population is 3 000 and there is an hotel.

Gcalekaland – Kentani (Centane) and Willowvale (Gatyana)
The area to the south-east of Butterworth and Idutywa is named Gcalekaland after Gcaleka, the chief of the Xhosa tribe of the same name. In this district the two magisterial districts at Kentani and Willowvale were demarcated in 1878 after the last battle of the ninth and final frontier war was fought out. This was a sad day for the Xhosas who had been duped by the renowned witchdoctor Xito who had convinced the two great warrior chiefs Kreli (of the Gcalekas) and Sandile (of the Gaikas, of their invulnerability to bullets of the white man. In a makeshift fort at Kentani the colonial force of some 400 British and 500 Fingos commanded by Captain R. Upcher won a decisive victory over the 5 000-strong impi who in making a frontal attack were literally mowed down.

Today Kentani and Willowvale are trading centres with hotels and are recognised staging posts for a number of Wild Coast resorts.

The Wild Coast from Qolora Mouth to Qora Mouth
This rugged, sub-tropical, magnificently beautiful coastline, broken by the waters of numerous splendid rivers with their deep gorges and spacious lagoons is completely unspoilt and truly wild. This is a veritable fisherman's paradise and is quite incomparable with any other part of southern Africa.

Qolora Mouth
The most southerly of these resorts is at the mouth of the Qolora River. On the road to this resort, 27 kilometres from Kentani is a deep pool at a place called Gxara where the medium, Nongquase, claimed to have held communion with the ancestral spirits of the Xhosas that promised the destruction of the white man. It resulted in the Cattle Killing Delusion and the disastrous famine of 1857 that followed.

At Qolora Mouth there are the well known resorts, Sea Gulls and Trennery's, with golf, tennis, boating, surfing and a superb stretch of fishing ground between the Qolora and the Kei. The name Qolora refers to the steep banks of the river gorge there.

Wavecrest

Another resort reached from Kentani is Wavecrest. It lies at the beautiful lagoon formed by the two rivers Nxaxo and Nqwasi. This is a sanctuary for a variety of birds, including the crested crane, and there is a fine beach between the lagoon and sea. There is an hotel and simple facilities for caravanners.

Mazeppa Bay

Reached via either Kentani or Willowvale, Mazeppa Bay is an outstandingly beautiful part of the coastal area of Transkei. The resort was named after the *Mazeppa*, a coaster that did some illegal trading along this coast in the 1930s. The three beaches, First Beach, Second Beach and Shelly Beach have varied attractions with superb fishing and bathing possibilities and a great number and variety of shells. The area is notable for its oyster beds. There is an hotel and Forestry Department caravan site with simple facilities. The road to Mazeppa Bay skirts the magnificent Manubi Forest.

Qora Mouth

This resort is best reached via Willowvale from where the road to the coast reveals spectacular views of the river with its deep gorges in the surrounds of forest country. There are opportunities in the area to view and purchase the fine beadwork and handcraft of the Gcaleka tribeswomen, traditional experts in arts handed down for generations. At the river mouth there is an oyster bed, a lovely lagoon and a beautiful beach. The name of the hotel, the Kob Inn, is indicative of the fish caught there.

Tembuland – the area between the Bashee and Umtata Rivers

Viedgesville, Mqanduli and Elliotdale (Xhora)

Returning to national road N2, it will be found that it continues in its general northward direction to reach first the Mtentu Cuttings and then the trading post of Viedgesville (named after a German trader). From this point there is a branch road to the trading centres of Mqanduli and Elliotdale, the Xhosa name for which is Xhora. This is the area of the Bomvana people who took their name from the tribal chief, Bomvu. There is an hotel at each of these centres which are on the route to another scenically dramatic part of the Wild Coast and more resorts.

The Haven

At the mouth of the Bashee River, this resort is placed in a superb setting with a magnificent beach and the dense, indigenous vegetation of the Dwessa Forest reaching right down to the golden sands. In addition to the famous fishing ground there is an hotel, tennis, boating, bathing and the sheer pleasure of being in a coastal wilderness.

Along the road from Elliotdale to Bashee river mouth there is a turnoff to the renowned River View of the *Colley Wobbles*, an extraordinary series of twists in the Bashee River. Its jocular name arose when Lieutenant G.P. Colley, special magistrate of the Idutywa Reserve, visited the Bashee River area on an inspection during his term of office (1858-1860). He came upon this remarkable river meander and exclaimed to one of his party 'how the river wobbles' and received the quick-witted reply, 'Yes sir, it Colley Wobbles'.

Coffee Bay

A cask of coffee beans washed ashore is said to have given Coffee Bay its name. The resort, in the lovely setting of a wide bay with a long beach backed by green hills, has two hotels, a caravan park, golf, bowls, tennis, riding, bathing, boating and fishing.

A remarkable feature on the coast, 8 kilometres south of Coffee Bay, is the Hole-in-the-wall, or as the Xhosas call it, esiKhaleni, the place of the sound. This prominent freak of nature is a gigantic rock island with an enormous hole tunnelled through its base by the perpetual pounding of the sea, and has for long served as a navigational landmark for seafarers. There are no accepted holiday facilities at the Hole-in-the-wall except outstanding possibilities for camping, and the fishing in this secluded area is excellent on this famous fishing coast.

Umtata

The capital of Transkei, Umtata takes its name from the river that runs through the town, and the river was so named after the sneezewood (umtata) trees that once grew in abundance on its banks.

Umtata has a population of 40 000 and is practically in the centre of Transkei. The town is a trading and communications centre of considerable importance being the terminus of the railway from the south and the junction of national road N2 and trunk route R61.

The first Europeans to settle in the area were farmers who came in the late 1860s to take up grants offered by the Tembus on the one side of the river and by the Pondos on the other side. The chiefs of the two sides, in forming this buffer strip of Europeans, hoped to put an end to the continual faction fighting between their respective peoples.

When Tembuland was ceded to Great Britain in 1875 the territory was divided into four magisterial districts and it is recorded that when the magistrate, Major J.F. Boyes, arrived, he pitched his tent in the area of the Cicira River, 9 kilometres to the west of where Umtata is today. In 1877 Bishop Henry Callaway, who was also a medical practitioner, took up his seat of Anglican Bishop of the new Diocese of St John's. He acquired the land known as 'The Mission' and immediately established a hospital (the precursor of the substantial present-day Sir Henry Elliot Hospital), a church and a school. By 1880 a township was laid out and in 1882 Umtata became a municipality.

Umtata has some imposing buildings including the one which houses the Bunga (parliament) which dates from 1929, the Town Hall, built in 1908 and fronted by a beautiful garden, and the Anglican

2   3   1

1. Second Beach, Port St Johns, is one of the loveliest bathing beaches in southern Africa.

2. and 3. Young Pondo women, near Umtata, engaged in their relaxing and joyful ceremonies — 'face making up' on the left, and 'grinding of the maize' on the right.

Cathedral. In recent years development in the capital has been remarkable, with the construction of architecturally handsome high-rise administrative blocks, the completion of the University of Transkei (founded in 1977) at the town's southern entrance and a cluster of official residences which overlook the university.

Umtata's recreation amenities include bowling greens and a golf course and there are six hotels including the fashionable Holiday Inn at the southern entrance. Here too is the municipal caravan park in a pleasant setting. K.D. Matanzima Airport is on the outskirts of the town.

Engcobo and Cala

West of Umtata, on trunk route R61 is the trading town of Engcobo, situated in the middle of the afforestation in the Kumba Mountains, 975 metres above sea level. Near the village is the All Saints

Mission, founded in 1869.

From Engcobo a branch road joins with trunk road R56 north of Cala Pass where the summit is 1 460 metres. Cala has a population of 3 500 and is notable for its unusual sandstone buildings.

Pondoland – the area from the Umtata River to the Umtamvuna River

North of Umtata national road N2 enters the territory of two closely related tribes, the Pondo and the Pondomisi. A noticeable change is the dress of the people. Although the fashion is similar the colour scheme changes from the orange-red favoured by the Xhosas and Tembus to a pale blue used by the Pondos. In this region as in most other parts of Transkei it is not unusual to see youths and young women whose faces are weirdly masked with white and red clay. These young people are at some stage of initiation into adulthood in the ceremonies known as *Abakwetha* for the males and *Ntonjaan* for the females, still practiced among the more conservative and primitive peoples.

Along this route there are a number of small trading towns.

Tsolo, Qumbu, Mount Frere (Kwabhaca), Mount Ayliff (Maxesibeni) and Mount Fletcher

Tsolo, which is off the main highway, takes its name from the pointed hill, a conspicuous landmark. Qumbu is near the beautiful Tsitsa Falls. Mount Frere, named after the governor, Sir Bartle Frere, is halfway between Durban and East London and has an hotel.

Mount Ayliff was named after the Reverend John Ayliff who was largely responsible for settling the Fingos near Peddie.

North-west of Qumbu on route R56 is Mount Fletcher, named after the Reverend John Fletcher upon its establishment in 1882. It is a trading centre near the Tina River and close to the massive rock peak, the 2 315-metre Castle Rock. The town has an hotel.

Umzimkulu

Beyond Mount Ayliff national road N2 climbs out of Brooks Nek into East Griqualand (Natal) near Kokstad, from where in swinging eastwards it crosses Transkeian territory again before entering Natal, again at the 'toe' of its 'boot', passing the Ingeli Forest near Weza before once again entering Transkei to cross that country's most northern precinct to the border town of Umzimkulu (home of the rivers). Here on the bank of Umzimkulu River there is much trading activity, an hotel and the immigration and customs check posts of Transkei and South Africa.

North-east of Umtata is the magnificent Pondoland coastline.

Port St Johns (Umzimvubu)

In one of the most beautiful environments in all the world is Port St Johns, a town of 3 000 inhabitants. Even in times of modern road engineering, in the drive down to the coast it is not difficult to assess that one of the reasons Port St Johns did not flourish as a port was the difficult access from the hinterland. For nature lovers this is a godsend since this enchanting part of the spectacular Pondoland coast has been preserved in all its natural glory.

On the way the road follows the Umzimvubu as it cuts its gigantic cleft in the coastal mountains to reach the sea between two precipitous sandstone cliffs. The headlands form the Gates of Port St Johns. They rise some 360 metres above the sea and were named Mount Thesiger (west bank) and Mount Sullivan (east bank) after General Thesiger and Commodore Sullivan who arrived to hoist the Union Jack after the area of the river had been ceded to Britain by the Pondo chief, Nqwiliso in 1870.

The manner in which Port St Johns received its name is obscure. There are those who believe that the early Portuguese navigators named it after their galleon, the *Sao João*, wrecked on this coast in 1552;

others say that the eastern headland, Mount Sullivan, strongly resembles the figure of a robed apostle (as portrayed by the old masters) and that upon seeing it a priest on board a Portuguese ship exclaimed 'Sao João'.

In November 1878 two officials, the first magistrate and collector of customs, and the harbour master and pilot, arrived to administer the St Johns River Territory. A wharf was built and a garrison was established at Fort Harrison. All this put a stop to the smuggling and gun-running that preceded the British occupation. In 1884 the district was annexed to the Cape Colony. Considerable trading in both imports and exports took place at the port. In fact small coasters were able to voyage some 16 kilometres upstream to load the produce of the Pondos there. Over the years the entrance to the river silted up and it was not an economical proposition to build a proper harbour. The last coaster to call was the *Border* in 1944.

From vantage points along the walks to the headlands of Mount Thesiger and Mount Sullivan and at Eagle's Nest there are uninterrupted views of the lay-out of the town. The density of the indigenous tropical forest enclosing the three sides of the town can be appreciated and superb vistas of the river and the beaches are revealed. Here in the shelter of some of nature's loveliest sanctuaries are the wild harebells, tree orchids, succulents and fern, and a profusion of birdlife.

Second Beach is five kilometres from the centre of the town along a motor road that passes banana plantations and the picturesque holiday resort, where brightly coloured huts reflect in a small stream. On the right of the road are lawns which front a charming teagarden, and directly opposite, there is an opening in the shady indigenous trees which fringe this lovely beach.

Some of the best fishing in southern Africa can be had from the rivers and rocks at Port St Johns and the neighbouring coastline. The rivers in the region are well known for catches of kabeljou, spotted and pig-nose grunter and river bream. The river mouths and beautiful reaches of the Umzimvubu, the Umngazi, the Intafufu and the Umgazana are renowned for sport. Along the numerous beaches there are some fine fishing grounds; protected gullies and deep water for both light and heavy tackle, some spots rather difficult to reach and others easy to get at; places famous for shark fishing, where hammer-heads are caught in large numbers; other spots where good fun can be had landing kabeljou, garrick, black and silver steenbras; and pan-fish-grounds where blacktail, bronze bream and damba are readily caught in season. Apart from fishing and bathing, which are the big attractions, Port St Johns offers a variety of recreational opportunities to the visitor. There is golf, bowls, tennis and boating. The town has three hotels and the population is 3 000.

Umngazi Mouth and Mngazana Mouth

South of Port St Johns a narrow road, crowded in by the indigenous forest, follows the Umngazi River for 11 kilometres to where it ends in a spacious lagoon and a sandy beach, and here in an unspoilt wilderness is the haunt of fishermen from all over southern Africa – the Umngazi Bungalows Hotel. South of the resort is the huge cliff face known as Brazen Head and beyond it the mouth of the Mngazana River where it is intended to develop a harbour for Transkei.

Umzimvubu River
The Umzimvubu River has its source high in the Drakensberg range and all along its course it is surrounded by magnificent scenery of a green ruggedness. It has created one of the most splendid valleys in the whole country. The name Umzimvubu means 'home of the hippopotamus', and although this species had not been seen along the long length of the river for many a year, by strange coincidence, the most famous of all hippos, Huberta, spent a six-month vacation there during her long walk from Zululand to the Keiskamma River.

Three kilometres up the river from Port St Johns the road to Lusikisiki crosses the Pondoland Bridge into Eastern Pondoland. The scenery on the way to Lusikisiki is spectacular and varied. There are turnoffs to the coast for the fishing resorts of Mntafufu and Embotyi. On the Embotyi road there is a turnoff to the Magwa Falls. A stream running beside the Magwa Forest feathers in a thin cascade over the edge of a chasm, dropping 140 metres to the ebony rocks below. Further along the Embotyi road are the three cascades of the Fraser Falls.

Lusikisiki and the wreck of the Grosvenor
The strange name Lusikisiki is said to be taken from the sound made by whispering wind blowing through the reeds. The village here bustles with the activity of blue-blanketed Pondo tribesmen on horseback who come to the trading stores, the labour recruiting office and the magistrate's court. Not far from the village is Qawukeni, the Great Place of the paramount chief of the Pondo people.

About 15 kilometres out from Lusikisiki on the way to Flagstaff, the road passes Mount Nelson, the blue-painted mansion, once the home of Pondoland's millionaire medicine man, herbalist Khotso Sethunsta. The old eccentric kept his 24 wives garmented in long orange-coloured robes. In his old age (he was considered to be 90 when he died) his wives were still producing his off-spring (he had over 200 children) and he boasted that a secret potion called 'umangalala' accounted for his virility.

The district of Lusikisiki will always be linked with the most celebrated of all South African shipwrecks – the British ship *Grosvenor* that foundered off this coast in 1782. Homeward bound from India with a great wealth of gold and gems she struck the treacherous submerged reefs opposite the cove known as Lwambazi. Only 14 of the 150 aboard the ship were drowned with the wreck, but a lesser number than those that drowned ever reached civilization.

Many have been the elaborate schemes to recover the reported immense treasure that went to the bottom of the ocean, but all have been abandoned with little or no success. The last venture gave up in 1952. Some 3 000 gold and silver coins and four cannon are some of the comparatively meagre spoils.

A cannon from the wreck is to be seen outside the Royal Hotel, Lusikisiki, two in the Umtata Museum and one at Durban's Old Fort.

A few kilometres up the coast from Lwambazi is Port Grosvenor, where an abortive attempt was made to build a harbour in 1885.

Flagstaff (Siphageni) – Mkambati
Forty-five kilometres north of Lusikisiki on the way to national road N2, the road R61 reaches Flagstaff, a trading village in a beautiful district. It received its name from two enterprising traders who had difficulty in persuading the Pondos in the area that there could be no trading on Sundays. They struck upon the idea of erecting a flagstaff from which a white flag was flown on Sundays. The conspicuous sign could be seen by the tribesmen from a long way off and they respected the message it conveyed.

The Holy Cross Mission with its large hospital is 20 kilometres south-east of Flagstaff on the road to the coast. It was founded by the Anglican missionary, Robert Callaway, in 1911. On the same road at the coast where the Msikaba River reaches the sea is the Mkambati Nature Reserve and the famed Mkamabati Palms (Jubaeopsis caffra), a botanical rarity. This species belongs to the same family as the coconut palm, with globular fruit about the size of a walnut, but without 'milk'. This is one of the four genera of palms known to be indigenous to southern Africa and has been recorded at only two other situations on the sub-continent. Its nearest ally is a South African palm of the genus Jabaea. In the 8 000 hectares of the reserve various species of antelope have been re-introduced. This was, for over 50 years, the site of a leprosy institution.

In making its way to the sea the Msikaba River forms a dramatic gorge, densely wooded. In the vicinity, the Mateku Falls take a plunge 120 metres from the Mateku stream into the Msikaba River.

Flagstaff to the Natal border
The road from Flagstaff through the village at Tabankulu (the big mountain) joins national road N2 between Mount Frere and Mount Ayliff and is a scenic drive that passes the spectacular horse-shoe bend in the Umzimhlava River – another classic example of a river meander.

The road northwards from Flagstaff forks just before reaching Magusheni (the place of the sheep) and refers to an incident when a large flock of sheep were struck by lightning and killed. Continuing past Magusheni the road winds through the hills to meet national road N2 at the foot of Brooks Nek. The fork that branches right before Magusheni leads down to the trading centre, Bizana (the small cooking pot), near the Natal border.

From Bizana there are two crossings of the Umtamvuna River into Natal, and in reaching these from Bizana the road reveals spacious views of the great Umtamvuna Valley. The first crossing is at Mpunzi Drift and the other is at the coast over the magnificent bridge near Port Edward (Chapter 8). In Transkei, near the coastal crossing of the Umtamvuna is the site of the Wildcoast Sun International hotel-casino.

The centre of Durban from the air — one of the most attractive maritime cities in the world.

Durban and District and the Natal coastal resorts

Durban

The combined attributes of Durban make its rise to fame unusual if not unique. It is one of the most beautiful maritime cities of the world and surely the cleanest. Not only is it South Africa's principal harbour with its own considerable industrial output, but it is, with its all-year-round sunshine season, the country's major holiday resort. With a history filled with romance and adventure, its background is as colourful as its cosmopolitan population of today.

The first Europeans to explore the coast of Natal were the survivors of shipwrecks during and after the discovery by the Portuguese navigators of the sea route to India. Vasco da Gama, in 1497, was the first to sight this coast, and being on Christmas Day, he called it Natal (nativity), and the great lagoon, which is Durban Bay today, the Portuguese thereafter called Rio de Natal (river of the nativity). After its discovery three centuries passed before any Europeans purposely set out to reach the river of Natal with any idea of permanent settlement, and it happened at the time when Shaka, the despot but nevertheless great Zulu king, was employing his magnificent impis in the conquering of all the other tribes of the territory.

Lieutenant Francis George Farewell, R.N., is the acknowledged founder of Durban. He, with another officer of the Royal Navy, Lieutenant James Saunders King, were on a private trading survey of the eastern seaboard during November 1823 when by a stroke of luck they discovered the protected bay. Their brig *Salisbury* and sloop *Julia* lay at anchor close to the entrance to the river of Natal when a squall got up and the *Julia* was blown across the sand bar into the sanctuary of the landlocked bay. Excited about the possibilities of trade from this natural harbour they returned to Cape Town to canvass the support for the setting up of a trading settlement at this ideal base. King, who went to England to seek the favours of the Admiralty, had his proposal rejected and returned to Natal later. Meanwhile Farewell organised backers in Cape Town and two parties set sail for Natal; one party under the young man of 21, Henry Francis Fynn, a true pioneer who was destined to leave his mark on the history of Natal, and the other party under Farewell himself.

In May 1824 Fynn, in a party of 26 men, anchored the *Julia* in the bay and landed on the wild and lonely foreshore of primeval bush. These were the men who cut the clearing in the bush opposite St Paul's Church and built their first house (12 feet square) of wattle and daub. Some days later Farewell and the second party of 30 people arrived aboard the *Antelope* with horses and cattle. It must be remembered that this small band of pioneers consisted of traders and hunters engaged in private enterprise (not backed by the Cape government) in search of the ivory and skin wealth of the prosperous Zulu territory. These were adventurous men of remarkably tough stature, prepared for the hard and precarious life that followed.

Farewell with his Dutch father-in-law, Petersen, Fynn and their interpreters made the long journey to accomplish the historic meeting with Shaka which resulted in the signing of a document on 7 August 1824 which gave Farewell all the land around Port Natal from the Umdloti River in the north to the Umbogintwini River in the south.

Eleven years later in 1835, after the arrival of the first missionary, Captain Allen Gardiner (also retired R.N.), the settlers named their settlement in honour of the popular soldier-governor at the Cape, Sir Benjamin d'Urban.

With the advent of the Great Trek, the first of the Voortrekkers arrived in Natal in 1838 and after the tragedy of the murder of their leader, Piet Retief, and his party, the small band of Britons at Port Natal came under the protection of the short-lived Voortrekker Natalia Republic.

In May 1842 troops under Captain Thomas Smith were sent from the Cape to take control. Another of the dramas of South African history was about to be enacted. The Voortrekkers resisted and besieged the British garrison in what is today known as the Old Fort. Dick King made his heroic 10-day 900-kilometre ride to Grahamstown to obtain the relief of the garrison. The British withstood the siege for 34 days with relief coming on 26 June 1842. Two years later, in May 1844, Natal was proclaimed a British Colony and annexed to the Cape of Good Hope. Durban reached municipal status in 1854 and was proclaimed a city in 1935.

Durban's population of 790 000 does not include the Black townships KwaMashu and Umlazi, 17 kilometres north and 18 kilometres south of Durban respectively. The population of KwaMashu is estimated at 300 000 and that of Umlazi 550 000 and a high percentage of these people work in the city. The two townships are administered by the selfgoverning KwaZulu. During peak holiday periods Durban's population increases by 200 000 and at these times the daytime population of the city is over 1,5 million.

The Durban Publicity Association has its Visitors Bureau in Church Street, close to where Fynn built the first European house of wattle and daub. The bureau is adjacent to St Paul's Anglican Church and opposite the historic Post Office. The site of the Fig Trees in the bureau garden near where the Indian flower sellers have their stalls, is a national monument. Apart from the extensive free information service available from the bureau, sight-seeing tours and holiday accommodation reservations are arranged.

Louis Botha International Airport is situated 13 kilometres south from the city centre, over the southern freeway. The S.A. Airways Air Terminal is at Shell House, cnr. Smith and Aliwal Streets. The Municipal Airport at Virginia flanks the main road to the North Coast and accommodates non-scheduled flights, civil and private aviation. Durban's modern Railway Station opened in 1980, is approached from Umgeni Road.

General Post Office
Facing West Street, the General Post Office overlooks Francis Farewell Square, and is bounded on the other sides by Gardiner, Pine and Church Streets. The architect, Philip Dudgeon, designed it as Durban's

Town Hall; the foundation stone was laid in Febraury 1883 and it was officially opened in October 1885 The postal authorities took over when the present City Hall was completed in 1910. From the front steps on 23 December 1899, Winston Churchill, War Correspondent, delivered his historic speech after his escape as a prisoner of war of the Boer forces, and this has been commemorated by a bronze plaque at the Church Street corner of the building. Here in the old Town Hall the National Convention met from 12 October to 5 November 1908 to discuss the terms of Union between the British Colonies and the Boer Republics. The General Post Office is a national monument.

City Hall – Durban Museum and Art Gallery
With its magnificent copper domes, figured architraves and beautiful statuary, the City Hall occupies an extensive area and is of fine architectural proportions. Built by architect Philip Dudgeon, it is a near replica of Belfast City Hall and took five years to complete, the opening taking place on 12 April 1910. The City Hall fronts on Francis Farewell Square (across Church Street) and is bounded by West and Smith Streets for almost the entire block from Church Street to Aliwal Street; its surrounding off-pavement gardens being particular joy to both citizen and visitor.

The City Hall contains a spacious concert hall and houses municipal offices, the mayoral suite and the council chamber, as well as the library, museum and art gallery.

The Durban Museum dates from 1887 and is the oldest as well as the largest municipal museum in the country. Occupying several floors of the City Hall, it is largely concerned with natural history and has amazingly realistic displays and exceptionally fine collections of birds and insects.

The Durban Art Gallery is the second largest institution of its kind in South Africa comprising good collections of European painting and a fine collection of non-South African applied arts including Chinese, French and Turkish ceramics, Chinese and Japanese ivories, English, Peruvian and Persian silver and the glass of various European countries.

Durban's City Hall is a national monument.

The Natal Playhouse
Opposite the City Hall in Smith Street stands The Natal Playhouse, a unique amalgam of a most modern theatre with the atmospheric old Tudor style Playhouse and the Moorish style Colosseum. Home of the Natal Performing Arts Council, it opened on 12 April 1986 and houses the magnificent performing venues – 1 272-seat opera house, 489-seat drama theatre, The Loft 146-seat experimental theatre, The Studio 300-seat recital room/recording studio, The Cellar intimate supper-theatre, and has the additional facilities – Legends Restaurant, Alhambra Room, souvenir shop and pavement café.

Francis Farewell Square
This is the garden square formed by West, Church, Smith and Gardiner Streets where life-sized statues and a number of glazed-tile plaques tell the story of Durban from its early days. On the Gardiner Street side of the square the Gates of Memory (opened by King George VI in 1947) lead to the Cenotaph, an

impressive monument to the sons of Durban who fell in the two world wars.

Francis Farewell Square was formerly known as the City Gardens; the renaming took place during the 150th Anniversary celebration in 1974 and a year later it was declared a national monument.

Local History Museum and the Old House

The Local History Museum and the Junior Library are housed in the Old Court House which adjoins the City Hall and faces onto Aliwal Street. This was the first public building to be erected in Durban and is now a National Monument. Construction started in 1865 and the building was opened on 26 April 1866 as the Court House and Post Office. The museum forms part of the Durban Municipal Museum and contains relics relevant to the history and development of Natal and Durban in particular.

The Old House at 31 St Andrew's Street forms part of the Local History Museum and is a modest 19th century settler residence containing furniture and domestic materials typical of the era.

Old Fort

This is the fort in which the British garrison withstood the 34-day siege by the Voortrekkers. It is perfectly preserved; the grounds having been transformed into a beautiful garden and the magazine converted into a small interdenominational memorial chapel (where many Durban weddings are held). The adjoining Warriors' Gate, designed on the lines of an old Norman gateway, is the general headquarters and first shrine of the Memorable Order of Tin Hats (Moths), an order founded in Durban in 1927. Here there are trophies from battlefields all over the world and relics of Natal. The Old Fort is on the corner of Old Fort and Jelf Taylor Roads, next to the famous Kingsmead Cricket Ground.

Dick King Statue and da Gama Clock

Natal's traditional hero, Dick King, whose remarkable feat saved the British garrison, is remembered by a fine equestrian bronze on the Esplanade at the foot of Gardiner Street. The bronze, designed by H.H. Grellier, is known to Durban citizens as Dick King Statue. Also on the Esplanade, approximately at the foot of Aliwal Street, is the da Gama Clock. It originally stood at the Point where it was erected in 1897 to commemorate the discovery of Natal by Vasco da Gama in 1497.

University of Natal

The Durban campus of the University of Natal is on the hill overlooking the city, above the suburb of Glenwood which is in the southern part of the Berea. It is sited in this magnificent position as a result of the generous donation by a Durban citizen, Mr T.B. Davis, who gave £50 000 in 1930 in honour of the memory of his son, Howard, who had fallen in the Battle of the Somme in the First World War. The University College dates from 1910 and full status was granted in 1949. The student enrolment for Durban and Pietermaritzburg is approximately 11 700 and there are nine faculties.

Killie Campbell Africana Library and William Campbell Museum – Muckleneuk

The magnificent contributions of rare books and furniture bequeathed to the University of Natal by the members of the famous Durban family are housed in their elegant home, Muckleneuk, 220 Marriott Road, Berea. The library's principal collections are of Natal and Zululand history and of ethnological books.

It was here at Muckleneuk, under the direction of Miss Killie Campbell, of a brick red shade, was propagated bougainvillaea, of a brick red shade, was propagated and called *Killie Campbell*.

Central Durban and its historical street names

Down town Durban is a compact, uncomplicated area of exceptionally wide main streets and numerous side lanes and arcades providing shopping opportunities of variety ranging from western departmental stores to eastern emporiums and market places.

The city main streets, parallel to one another leading from the bayhead westwards, are: the Esplanade, or more correctly Victoria Embankment, named after the British Queen. Smith Street, in past decades traditionally reserved for banks, building societies and insurance companies, was named after Major Thomas Charlton Smith, the commander of the British garrison during the siege. He is better remembered as Captain Smith and he retired with the rank of general. West Street, traditionally the principal shopping thoroughfare, was named after Martin West, Lieutenant-Governor of Natal from 1845 to 1849 and the first but not very successful civilian administrator of the sub-colony which was still under Cape rule. Pine Street was named after the very popular Lieutenant-Governor, Sir Benjamin Pine, who was in office from 1849 to 1856 and returned during the time that Natal was a full colony to be governor in 1873.

The principal streets which cross the city centre from east to west commencing at the beach end are: Prince Alfred Street which honours Queen Victoria's son who visited South Africa in 1860. Stanger Street was named after Dr William Stanger, first surveyor general of Natal. Aliwal Street received its name to honour the gallant Sir Harry Smith for his victory over the sikhs at Aliwal in India. Gardiner Street was named after Captain Gardiner, Natal's first missionary. Field Street was named after Durban's first magistrate, William Field. Grey Street was named after Earl Grey, Secretary of State for Colonies, and Russell Street after the British Prime Minister, Lord John Russell.

Durban bay and harbour

A geological feature common along the Natal coast is the lagoon, fed by one or two small rivers and enclosed by sandspits. Durban bay is the typical large-scale example of this feature. The big land-locked lagoon the Zulus called eThekwini was fed by the Umbilo (the bubbler) and the Umhlatuzane (the forceful little one) and enclosed by the huge sandspits known today as the Bluff and the Point.

The making of this great port could never have

179

1

3

2

5

4

Gardens are the essence of Durban's sub-tropical splendour, and these surround the public buildings of the city centre.
1. The General Post Office, from Pine Street.
2. The City Hall from West Street.
3. Medwood Gardens, a haven in the heart of the metropolis.
4. Francis Farewell Square, with its statues and memorials, is also a sanctuary for hundreds of pigeons.
5. and 6. The equestrian bronze of Dick King and the ornamented Da Gama Clock are on the Victoria Embankment.

6

been achieved had the silting up problem of the narrow harbour entrance not been overcome. The crossing of the bar (the narrow entrance) was for many years a precarious procedure. In the 1850s the bar had a low-water depth of 2 metres and the bay had a water surface of 34 hectares. Through constant dredging – the removal of millions of tons of sand and river debris – and the construction of the north and south breakwaters (335 and 700 metres long respectively) the harbour has today a 183-metre-wide entrance channel with a low-water depth of 12,8 metres and a harbour water surface of 892 hectares at high tide or 679 hectares at low tide, and the distance around the harbour is 21 kilometres.

In 1850 cargo had to be discharged into small boats, which were beached through the surf and then transferred to ox-wagons. Recent records achieved by Durban harbour provide some idea of its present-day greatness. In one financial year 7 246 vessels totalling 165 217 237 gross tons called at the port. On 23 March 1975 the *Olympic Progress* shipped a record 14 916 tons of bulk maize in twelve hours and twenty minutes, and on 2 May in the same year the *St Asimi* completed the shipment of 40 026 tons of coal. On 20 October 1976 the *Ashdod* entered port from Eilat and 240 containers were handled on and off the vessel's four 20-ton derricks.

In November 1823 the 25-ton sloop, *Julia*, was the first vessel to enter Durban bay. In recent years the harbour has admitted such tankers as the *Fina Brittania* with a length of 330 metres, a beam of 49 metres, a loaded draft of 26 metres and deadweight of 230 284 tons. The port has also accommodated two of the world's largest passenger liners: s.s. *France* with a length of 316 metres, a beam of 34 metres, draft of 11 metres and passenger capacity of 2 033, and the s.s. *Queen Elizabeth* (Q.E.2) with a length of 294 metres, a beam of 32 metres, draught of 10 metres and passenger capacity of 1 970.

Durban harbour is ranked ninth in the world; it is the largest harbour in Africa and handles more cargo than the other ports of the Republic together. This does not include the new ore ports, Richards Bay and Saldanha Bay. During the financial year 1977/78 Durban harbour handled over 35-million tons of cargo.

South Africa's first railway line in use connected the Point with the city. Opened in 1860, it covered a distance of 3½ kilometres. Today harbour rail tracks cover a distance of 290 kilometres (the rail distance from Durban to Colenso).

In 1870 an 81-metre-long timber wharf was completed near the present A berth. Today the port is equipped with over 15,50 kilometres of wharfage with 72 berths and shed storage accommodation of over 340 000 cubic metres, its facilities being among the most modern in the world. At the head of the bay are the Floating Dock and the Prince Edward Graving Dock. The two-berth graving dock has an overall length of 352 metres and width of 42 metres and is one of the largest dry docks in the southern hemisphere. The grain elevator has a storage capacity of 38 100 tons; the intake capacity is 1 000 tons per hour and a shipping capacity of 1 422 tons per hour. The bulk-loading appliances at the Bluff for coal, iron

and other ores are electrically driven and the two dumpers have a capacity of 1 220 tons per hour.

From the South African Sugar Terminal, Maydon Wharf, where the sugar storage capacity is 520 000 tons, up to 850 tons per hour can be shipped.

Durban Harbour Container Terminal is at No. 2 Pier in the south-western precinct of the bay. Occupying a 125,7-hectare site it provides for five deep-sea and two coastal berths with eight giant ship-to-shore cranes each with a capacity of 40 tons, a deadweight of 650 tons and a height equivalent to a 15-storey building. Containerization became operative in South African ports in mid-1977 and about 70 percent of cargo imports are shipped in container vessels.

South African Co-Operative Citrus Exchange Ltd owns and operates the citrus pre-cooling terminal. This modern terminal, opened in 1986, handles sixty per cent of the South African citrus exports of from 24 to 28 million cartons per annum. During the peak of season a million cartons can be shipped in a week. Covering a floor area of 2,65 hectares, the terminal is located on T Jetty and involves berths O and P.

Commissioned in 1962, the Ocean Terminal is one of the most modern passenger terminals in the world, two telescopic gangways providing an enclosure between liners and the reception hall. In addition to the long established service between the Point and Bluff, the harbour ferry service now links the Point with Pier No. 1, the Container terminal and the Gardiner Street Jetty, and the service is open to the public.

From Dick King Jetty at the foot of Gardiner Street, harbour and deep sea pleasure cruises operate at regular intervals. The Small Craft Basin is approached from the Esplanade approximately opposite Field Street. In close proximity are Royal Yacht Club, Point Yacht Club and Durban Rowing Club.

Durban beaches and adjacent attractions

Durban's popular holiday scene is attributable to a combination of the warm waters of the Indian Ocean (ranging from 17°C in winter to 25°C in summer), the provision of first-rate holiday amenities (accommodation, entertainment and sport) and the prevailing carefree, do-as-you-please atmosphere. The climate, hot from December to March, is warm throughout the year with near perfect weather from April to July.

The expansive foreshore extends for 8 kilometres from the harbour entrance in the south to the Umgeni River in the north. Its famous Golden Mile of hotels, restaurants, holiday flats and pleasure amenities, occupies the centre of this foreshore with easy access to the safety protected beaches and all the attendant facilities: change rooms, umbrellas and deck chairs for hire, restaurants, tearooms, and the Little Top variety show on the sands.

At the foot of West Street is a fascinating marineland. The huge oceanarium tank contains sharks and turtles and over 1 000 species of brilliantly coloured tropical fish. At 11 a.m. and 3 p.m. the scuba diver enters the tank to feed the fish population by hand. On the opposite side of West Street is the Dolphinarium where daily shows of performing dolphins and Cape fur seals can be seen.

At the children's play centre there are graded pools with chutes and cascading fountains, powered boats to steer through winding courses, vintage model car rides and a go-kart track in addition to 'the caves of terror', dodge-em car enclosure, slides, swings and an overhead cable car. The open air swimming bath is exceptionally large with sunlawns and change rooms.

The Amphitheatre Garden, situated behind North Beach, is a delightful sanctuary in the midst of all the holiday activity. On the last Sunday of each month it is the venue for a craft and collectors flea market.

Minitown is an attractive project sponsored by the Round Table and Rotary Club, designed to provide a permanent source of funds for charitable organisations through the establishment of an attractive amenity for Durban. Minitown does not represent any particular city, but embodies typical South African city life. Scale models of durable materials incorporate ships docks, an airport, railway system and commercial, industrial and residential buildings. A tea terrace overlooks the 'city'. Minitown is particularly attractive at night.

At Fitzsimon's Snake Park, famous the world over for research in serum, there is a large and fascinating variety of reptiles including crocodiles, pythons and hundreds of deadly-poisonous snakes. New and little-known species also provide an enormous source of interest. The snake park is situated at the northern end of the lower Marine Parade.

Forming part of Kings Park, on opposite sides of the new North Coast access road, approximately opposite the Country Club Beach are Nick Steyn's R30-million Water Wonderland (where artificial river rides and criss-cross slides tumble down into 3 huge swimming pools) and Durban's R40-million Olympic pool (covered with 7 000 square metres of fibre-cement, it can seat 1 000 people).

From the Blue Lagoon, Umgeni River Mouth, there is a splendid view of Durban's beachfront. This is a popular fishing spot and there is a convenient restaurant. Water-skiing, pedal boating, canoeing, speedboat rides and trips up the river in the 'Swan' are the other attractions. In the vicinity are the go-cart circuit, model yacht pond and putt-putt course.

The North and South Piers which stretch into the Indian Ocean at the harbour entrance are the favourite spots of the big game fishermen, and in the right season it is a thrilling spectacle to watch the catching and landing of deep sea fighters such as sharks and barracuda. Special fishing piers have been constructed near the main bathing beaches. Deep sea fishing boats leave from the fishing jetty at the city end of Maydon Wharf. The ski-boat base, Vetch's Pier, south of Addington Hospital and adjacent to North Pier, is a hive of activity just before sunrise any morning of the year when the boats set out for the offshore waters.

Sport
There are municipal bowling greens immediately above the South Beach and at Victoria Park, 24 Gresham Place, behind the Pavilion Hotel. In Umgeni Road near the Umgeni River is the municipal 18-hole golf course, Windsor Park; here clubs can be hired. Golf clubs within easy reach of the city include: Amanzimtoti Country Club, Beachwood Golf Club, Circle Country Club, Durban Country Club and Royal Durban Golf Club.

The venue for Currie Cup and international cricket is historic Old Kingsmead ground, corner Old Fort and Jeff Taylor Roads. Important rugby matches are played at King's Park Stadium, Walter Gilbert Road and in the same road is New Kingsmead where professional soccer is played. There are public tennis courts at Westridge Park, Jan Smuts Highway, where national and international tournaments are held.

The city has two attractive turf clubs and the highlight of the winter season is the Rothmans July Handicap, held at Greyville Race Course (in the centre of the city's limits) on the first Saturday of July, attracting top-class racehorses from all over southern Africa. 'July Fever' is an ailment which sweeps through the country every winter when people (even from the remote parts of the country) who would never consider gambling at other times, have a small 'flutter' on the July, as it is called, and for the ladies the event gives cause for a fashion parade. Clairwood Turf Club, 11 kilometres from the city centre, is reached by car via the Southern Freeway.

Parks, gardens, drives and views sites
Durban is enriched by many beautiful parks and gardens splendidly laid out in sub-tropical settings. Medwood Garden adjoining the swimming bath opposite the City Hall in West Street is a haven for busy shoppers right in the heart of the metropolis. Albert Park at the west end of the Esplanade has a restaurant from where meals and refreshments are served al fresco. The Botanic Gardens on the lower slopes of the Berea and entered from Sydenham Road, started out in 1849 as an agricultural society and were administered by a botanical society from 1882. Within 20 hectares there is a fine collection of tropical and sub-tropical trees and flora and the famed orchid house. High up on the Berea and adjacent to one another are Jamieson Park, bounded by Musgrave and Nimmo Roads and noted for its roses, and Mitchell Park, with its beautiful trees and well-kept lawns containing aviaries, small fauna and an open-air tearoom and restaurant. The Amphitheatre on the Marine Parade with its sunken garden and lily ponds and the Japanese Garden, reached from Northway, Durban North, with its waterfalls and pagodas, are both places of beauty.

Beachwood Mangroves Nature Reserve of 76 ha on the north bank of the Umgeni River mouth is a unique nature conservation centre.

Motoring anywhere within the 390 square kilometres of this beautiful city is in itself a pleasure. An outstanding feature of the city is its wealth of flowering trees, shrubs and climbers, and among the better known of the exotic flora are: flamboyant, tibouchina, golden shower, cassia, spathodea, poinsettia, frangipani, bougainvillaea and hibiscus. Burman Drive winds for approximately 3 kilometres through a densely wooded nature reserve (with its large population of monkeys) on the northern extremity of the Berea and connects Umgeni Road with North Ridge Road. In the lower section of the reserve there are particularly fine picnic places. The Bluff Marine Drive is reached by way of the Southern Freeway, turning off left at Edwin Swales V.C. Drive and again left at Bluff Road and continuing to Lighthouse Road. From here a circular tour can be

1

2

1. *Docked at Durban's Marine Terminal, QE II, dwarfing all other vessels in the harbour.*
2. *The yacht basin, Victoria Embankment, provides shelter for the craft of two Durban yachting clubs that hold regular off-shore regattas.*
3. *Symbol of 'Durban the fun city' the ricksha puller is seen here on the Lower Marine Parade.*

3

made. The view site at the end of the Bluff was closed to the public in 1977.

Some vantage points from which to enjoy the series of breathtaking vistas of the city, the bay and the ocean include: the Berea and particularly from the viewing site in Currie Road near the corner of Sydenham Road, and from the garden of Caister Hotel in Musgrave Road; the gardens of the University of Natal; the front terrace at Athlone Hotel. A fascinating panorama of shipping is to be seen from the parking ground, North Pier, at the harbour entrance. The pier is reached by proceeding along Point Road.

Umgeni River Bird Park
Well worth visiting, this privately owned amenity is situated on the northern bank of the Umgeni River, across Riverside Road (M21) on the corner of Buttery Road. Beautifully planned with ponds, waterfalls and natural walk-through aviaries, there are both indigenous and exotic birds. Open every day from 9 am to 5 pm. Homemade teas and lunches are served at the tea-garden.

Indian Market, Hindu Ceremonies and Zulu Dancing
Although the Indian Market in Warwick Avenue is only a token of what it used to be, its oriental fascination remains. Aromatic odours of pungent curry powders and fragrant spices still drift between stalls laden with brassware, basketware, ivory, novelty curios, strangely-carved wooden masks, intricate silverware and a wealth of semi-precious jewellery.

Several ceremonies take place during the year which are enacted by the various religious groups that make up Durban's colourful population. Fire walking and *Karvadi* (the piercing of the skin with fish hooks and needles by penitents) ceremonies occur at chosen Hindu temples usually during March and April. The annual procession of the colourful and gaily bedecked pagodas to the Umgeni River during the *Moharrum* festivities takes place around July and August.

Zulu dancing is held regularly on Sunday afternoon at King's Park athletic stadium, Walter Gilbert Road.

Despite the objections of traffic authorities the Zulu ricksha puller remains very much a part of the Durban visitor scene. resplendent in his lavish costume, he attracts the attention of a likely fare with bell, whistle, hissing noises and high jumps into the air. Rickshas were introduced to Durban from Japan in 1893 by the sugar industry pioneer, Sir Marhsall Campbell (Natal Estates Limited, Mount Edgecombe). Sir Marshall, who sat in the Natal Parliament and was knighted in 1815, was an authority on and much revered by the Zulu people. The large Black township to the north of Durban was named Kwa Mashu (the place of Marshall) as a tribute to him.

Industrial Durban
After the Witwatersrand, the Durban-Pinetown industrial complex is the second largest in the Republic. A number of Durban's industrial giants attract and welcome visitors. The Sugar Terminal with its three massive silos, has a capacity of 520 000 tons and the holds of bulk carriers are fed direct from the silos at 850 tons an hour. Conducted tours of the terminal are held and the Visitors Bureau should be consulted about these and also about visits to Corobrick, Lion Match and South African Breweries.

Natal Coastal Resorts
The traditional seaside resort of thousands of South African families is Natal's evergreen coastline, stretching from the Tugela River, 88 kilometres to the north of Durban, to the Umtamvuna River, 169 kilometres away to the south. Served by a fine coastal road there are more than fifty marine towns and villages offering carefree holidays of year-round sunshine, golden sands, ocean and lagoon bathing, surfing, fishing, boating, aquatic sports on the rivers, and golf, bowls and tennis amidst delightful surroundings. Sea temperatures average 20°C.

The summers are hot but seldom excessively so, the warm Moçambique current of the Indian Ocean which sweeps these shores ensures a pleasantly warm winter. The good summer rainfall promotes the luxuriant vegetation common along the whole of the Natal coast and the wild scene is in places encroached upon by long stretches of soft green sugar-cane. The evergreen indigenous belt (in places two kilometres wide from the sea) comprises a rich variety of flora; many of the 4 826 named species of Natal flourish in this region and these range from the flowers of tall trees to the earth-bound tiny wild violets.

Prominent is the ubiquitous wild banana (*strelitzia nicolai*) seemingly never without its boat-shaped twin spathe giving off clusters of delicate flowers pollinated by sunbirds and white eyes – sometimes in forests on their own and often in clumps mixed with ilala palms, date palms, kaffirbooms, aloes and primeval bush. Forest trees, beloved by the vervet monkeys (whose population, despite cultivation and urbanisation of the area, seems never to diminish), are the magnificent wild figs, in fruit twice a year in spring and autumn, and the monkey-apple trees, in fruit in winter. Also of the forest is the majestic umkhuhlu or thunder tree with its huge spreading branches of dark green satin leaves – the Zulu strips its bark for use as an emetic and its fruit produces scores of giant-size red and black 'lucky bean' seeds. On the banks and mud flats of the rivers the beautiful umdoni tree is crowded with bulbuls and thrushes when its fruit ripens in the spring. A favourite among the many shrubs is the amatungulu with its dark green leaves, starry white flowers and milky bright-red edible fruit – the whole plant system protected by a strong two-pronged thorn system. In the less hurried days of eras past, children would gather the amatungulu fruits and mothers made delicious jelly jams, and the v-shaped hardwood branches were the best for schoolboy catapults. Of the smaller plants ferns, orchids and lilies such as the ifafa lily, flame lily, snake lily, fire lily and arum lily beautify the open veld during the various seasons, while canary creepers and morning glory drape shrubs and trees with their yellow and purple blooms from Easter onwards into winter.

Among the exotic flowers that grace the man-made

gardens, poinsettia, bougainvillaea and golden shower are the most popular. Sub-tropical fruit is plentiful – this is not only 'banana country'; here are to be found the delicious pawpaw, litchi, avocado, mango and pineapple.

The 'Sardine Run', usually from mid-June to the end of July, is the annual migration when the waters are teeming with the small fish followed by game fish – an event eagerly awaited by anglers in Natal.

South Coast

The southern exit out of Durban is along the Esplanade and over the Southern Freeway which continues past Louis Botha Airport as national road N2.

Amanzimtoti

The first resort to the south of Durban is Amanzimtoti. It was here at the river from which the town takes its name that Shaka's impi paused a while and the great Zulu king, after being served water from the river, exclaimed 'kanti amanza mtoti' (so, the water is sweet).

The river, Civic Centre, railway station, principal business area and bathing beaches of Amanzimtoti lie some 27 kilometres to the south of Durban. Amanzimtoti became a municipality in 1962 and its growth in recent times, particularly in high-rise buildings, has been remarkable. There are a number of apartment complexes and the massive Sanlampark in Beach Road is the largest building on the entire South Coast. The population (entirely white) is 18 000.

Adjoining Louis Botha Airport, at the northern limit of the municipality, is its industrial suburb, Prospecton, where there is a colossal Hyperama, and on the hill south of Prospecton is the residential suburb, Athlone Park, with a perfect view of the sea. The Indian municipality of Isipingo is divided by Prospecton with Isipingo Rail on the west and Isipingo Beach on the east side. Isipingo comes from the Zulu word siphingo, an intertwining shrub that grows on the banks of the Isipingo River.

Offshore nets protect Amanzimtoti's bathing beaches: Inyoni Rocks, (Inyoni meaning the place of the bird) where there is a tidal pool and children's paddling pools, and Chain Rocks, where the surfing is very good. All along this coast there are good opportunities for rock and surf fishing. A wide, kilometre-long promenade connects the Amanzimtoti River lagoon area with Inyoni Rocks. Boats may be hired at the landing stage at the lagoon and taken upstream for about two kilometres to the tea-gardens. The wooded banks of the middle reaches of the river are particularly beautiful.

Hutchinson Park, off Riverside Road on the southern bank of the Amanzimtoti River, provides for a variety of games. In this well laid out park are bowling greens, tennis courts, playing fields for soccer, rugby, hockey and cricket. Here on this bank of the river are the prominent slate-roofed buildings of the municipal complex, comprising the town hall and supper room and one of the most modern libraries in Natal. Across the river on the north bank is the Civic Centre.

Visitors are welcomed at the two 18-hole golf courses: Amanzimtoti Golf Club on the bank of the Umbogintwini River and the Umbogintwini Club in the village of Umbogintwini, where the huge Kynock explosives factory is sited. The correct Zulu spelling for this name is emBokodweni and means 'the place of the stones'.

Ilanda Wilds, at the junction of Riverside Road and Old Main South Coast Road, is a 26-hectare nature reserve beautified by the Amanzimtoti River, with over 120 species of trees and shrubs and a rich variety of birdlife. The Bird Sanctuary, west of the national road, off Umdoni Road, is a 4,5-hectare sanctuary where peafowl parade and ducks, geese and other water birds use the small dam in the surrounds of such indigenous trees as the kaffirboom, umdoni and strelitzia – a very pleasant place to picnic.

Amanzimtoti has a large number of blocks of holiday flats and three hotels including the very popular Beach Hotel, right at the beach and famed for its sea foods.

Kingsburgh

The name Kingsburgh honours Dick King, who passed through this area at the commencement of his heroic ride to Grahamstown, and this municipality of 10 000 people embraces five popular seaside resorts: Doonside, Warner Beach, Winkle Spruit, Illovo Beach and Karridene. Most of these have caravan parks, camping sites and hotels, and the recognised bathing beaches are protected by offshore nets.

Doonside is characterised by its tree-fringed beach and quite amazing residential flat development. The name was taken from the title of R.D. Blackmore's classic novel.

Warner Beach is an attractive village across the Little Amanzimtoti River from Doonside and is notable for good surfing, tidal pool bathing, surf angling, lagoon bathing and boating. The village was laid out in 1910 and was named after the surveyor, T.A. Warner.

At Winkle Spruit the indigenous trees and grass reach down to the sands and there are lovely walks through shady natural woods. The beach with its rocky outcrops presents a picturesque setting and provides for surf and tidal-pool bathing and good fishing spots. The contention that the first part of the name Winkle Spruit is a misspelt version of the Afrikaans word 'winkel' (a trading store) is by no means valid. The founders of the village in the early twentieth century were of English origin and seeing the many small snail-like shellfish burrowing at the tide's edge they mistook these for the English winkle or periwinkle. They added the South African word spruit (pronounced the English way, 'sproot') from the nearby small watercourse which was invariably almost dry. The name is in two words Winkle Spruit and should not be joined together as normal in the Afrikaans language.

Illovo Beach and Karridene are close neighbours and lie beyond the Illovo River (the name is derived from the trees which the Zulus call Mlovo, which grow on the banks of the river). This is a district of intense sugar cultivation, the plantations stretching far inland. Upstream from the road and rail bridges is the Illovo Sugar Mill, established in 1890.

1

2

4

5

3

1. Looking across South Beach at Durban's famed 'golden mile' of hotels and apartment blocks — an all-year-round pleasure resort.
2. At the children's play centre, North Beach, there is a variety of rides, chutes and safe pools.
3. Board sailing and ski-boat launching from Durban's Addington Beach.
4. and 5. Up-country visitors and local residents crowd Durban's beaches on a sunny day. In the top picture the Bluff is in the distance.

Karridene was named after Lt. Col. Walter Karri-Davis who built the home there for miners suffering from phthisis, and is at the mouth of another river, the Umzimbazi where a pretty lagoon affords opportunities for boating. The area is notable for walks along the beach and through the indigenous bush.

Umgababa

South of Karridene is the Umgababa River tidal lagoon with the typical Natal coastal feature of a sandspit forming the southern bank. To the north of the lagoon, off the R102, are two colourful handcraft and sub tropical fruit markets. At the time of their settlement in the area, the river became known to the Luthuli tribe of the Zulus as Umgababa (the place of jealousy) in reference to their fertile valley being the envy of other tribes. North of the lagoon, where a titanium extract plant was forced to close through sea pollution, there is an African tourist centre. Umgababa beach is notable for its cowries.

Umkomaas

This municipality takes its name from the river on the banks of which it is built. Zulu tradition tells us that the river was named by their great king, Shaka. When he and his impi were fording the mouth they came upon a number of female whales with their calves, and Shaka exclaimed 'umKhomazi' (the river of the cow whales). The town of 3 000 inhabitants (many of whom are retired people) is the centre for the cellulose factory, Saiccor. The recreational facilities include a championship golf course and bowling greens which overlook the ocean and tennis courts adjacent to a park of indigenous trees. There are two hotels, a well-supported Italian restaurant, and a caravan park at Widenham. Surfing and fishing here are good and there is a large tidal pool.

Clansthal and the Aliwal Shoal

The notoriously dangerous Aliwal Shoal with a minimum depth of only 1 1/2 fathoms (2,7 metres) and scene of several shipwrecks, lies off the coast between Umkomaas and Scottburgh and was first reported in 1849 by James Anderson, captain of the *Aliwal*. A 240 000-candlepower lighthouse erected at Greenpoint in 1905 marks the shoal. Below the lighthouse, unobserved from the main road, R102, sheltered by the indigenous vegetation, is Clansthal, its unobtrusive homes and beach cottages facing a beautiful stretch of sandy beach and unusual formations of coastal rock. Here marine life abounds and an unspoilt tranquillity prevails. Clansthal was originally Clausthal, a farm so named by Bernard Schwikkard after the town in Germany. To add to the confusion the railway siding is Claustal. Above the railway and close to the national road is an all-facility caravan park. The majestic breakers at Greenpoint are known internationally amongst surfers.

Renishaw

To the north of Scottburgh, on the Crookes Brothers sugar estate at Renishaw, a R2-million crocodile farm was started in 1984. It occupies 30 hectares on the banks of the Amahlonga River (named after the Hlonga tribe of the Zulus).

Scottburgh

By the summer of 1860 the first township south of Durban had been laid out and named Scottburgh in honour of Sir John Scott, Lieutenant-Governor of Natal. In its early history, with the development of the sugar industry in the region and the excellent fishing off the Aliwal Shoal, Scottburgh was for a time used by coasters and trawlers but the experiment was soon considered too hazardous. The town's development was however stimulated by the construction of a railway line from Durban which was opened on 1 December 1897. Municipal status was granted in 1964.

Scottburgh is built on a prominent headland overlooking the Indian Ocean on a rugged section of the coastline where pools, rocky inlets and stretches of sandy beach create delightful places for bathing and fishing. It is a residential town of some 7 000 people and a holiday resort of enchanting character. At Scott Bay, the main bathing beach, the surf is protected with offshore nets, and here the picturesque grassed banks merge with the golden sands. The tidal pool with a cascading fountain is the delight of all children and so is the miniature railway.

Scottburgh golf course is among the best coast courses in the country. At the civic centre with its three hectares of parkland in the heart of the town there are two greens of Scottburgh Bowling Club and the all-weather tennis courts. There are four hotels, other holiday accommodation including several blocks of holiday flats and a caravan park ideally situated on the seafront.

Park Rynie and Umzinto

Only three kilometres south of Scottburgh is Park Rynie which was the terminus of the first railway south of Durban. Today it is a seaside resort with a bathing beach protected with offshore nets, two hotels and a caravan park with cottage accommodation. The strange name comes from an early developer, John Hoffman whose wife's name was Catherine Renetta Hoets and he called her Rynie and so named the newly acquired farm after her when this was purchased in 1857. The breakwater built for the whaling station during the First World War is today used by fishermen.

Inland 8 kilometres to the west is Umzinto, an important sugar milling and rail centre where the first imported Indian indentured labourers who arrived in Durban on the *Truro* in 1860, started work. The name Umzinto, which is taken from the Zulu *umezi wezinto* (important place of things), might refer to the village of shipwrecked survivors which existed there between 1600 and 1650. Nothing came of the gold prospecting that took place here in the 1880s.

Pennington and Umdoni Park

This little resort gets its name from the original owner of the estate who came to a tragic end after being attacked by a leopard in 1865. His two sons continued to run the estate and opened a wagon-building shop.

A portion of the estate was subsequently sold to Sir Frank Reynolds and was named Umdoni Park after the Zulu name for the water myrtle trees which are prolific in this region where two rivers, the Nkhomba and Nkhombana, flow through this natural parkland. The two rivers the Zulus named after the magnificent palms that also thrive here. Here at Umdoni Park, Sir Frank donated a holiday residence for the use of the Prime Ministers of South Africa. At the time of his failing health in 1952 an invitation was extended to King George VI by the then prime minister, Dr Malan, offering the King the use of Umdoni Park, and a visit was being planned just before he died.

The coastline here is unspoilt and the dense vegetation and sandy beaches are a particularly restful scene. There are two caravan parks.

Sezela

Famous in the sugar industry of Natal the Reynolds brothers, Frank and Charles, established the sugar mill at Sezela in 1914. The Sezela River gets its name from the legendary crocodile said to have had the ability to 'smell out' its victims no matter where they forded the river. When Shaka arrived at the river and heard of the crocodile he ordered that it be hunted down and it was eventually killed but the name Sezela (the one who smells out) remains the name of the river and the place, and yet another memory of the warrior-king whose escapades seem to have been endless. There is good fishing and an hotel at Sezela.

Ifafa Beach

The lovely lagoon at the mouth of the Ifafa River is the site of the resort, Ifafa Beach, much favoured by anglers. There is good bathing at the offshore protected beach, skiing on the lagoon and canoeing for a considerable distance upstream. The Zulu word 'ifafa' describes the shimmering surface of the water. There is a non-licensed hotel at the beach and bungalows are hired at the middle reaches of the river.

Hibberdene

A popular family seaside resort Hibberdene is identified by the rows of whitewashed rondavels of Rondalia holiday camp, which overlooks the town from its southern end. At the wide beach near the mouth of the Umzimai, bathing is protected by offshore nets. The fishing at Hibberdene is said to be excellent and the resort has an 82-metre-long tidal pool. There are several guest establishments, an hotel, three caravan parks, a light aircraft club and a bowling green. The resort was named after C. Maxwell-Hibberd, one-time Postmaster General of Natal, an early settler in the area.

Umzumbe

Between the Umzumbe and Ingambili Rivers, five kilometres south of Hibberdene is Umzumbe which incorporates the well-known Pumula Beach with its popular hotel. This is a delightful little resort for carefree days, basking in the sun, bathing, fishing or walking along the tranquil unspoilt coast or inland where the coastal forest is particularly beautiful. Offshore nets protect the beach.

The scene today is far removed from when Shaka, on his coastal manoeuvre of 1828, practically wiped out the Hlongwa cannibals who preyed upon others from their stronghold here in the valley of the Umzumbe (the bad kraal). Ten kilometres west of Umzumbe along district road D453, and another 500 metres walk up a well-worn pathway to the top of a ridge, there is to be found a relic from Shaka's attack upon the Hlongwas in the form of a huge pile of pebbles, and this isivivane (good-luck cairn) is much revered by the Zulu people. From this eminence overlooking the valley Shaka carried out an ancient ritual of atonement with his ancestral spirits to ensure success in the battle into which he was about to lead his army. Using the toes of the left foot he picked up a pebble then transferred it to the right hand, spat on it and dropped it at the side of the path. Following him in single file, each and every man of the impi carried out the same ritual and so formed the mound of pebbles to be seen there to this day.

Bendigo

An amalgamation of the four seaside villages, Sunwich Port, Anerley, Southport and Sea Park, Bendigo is the name of the original farm that occupied the entire area.

The lovely coastal stretch is favoured by retired people; the rates are said to be the lowest along the entire coast. Sunwich Port has a caravan park, Southport has a licensed hotel and two bowling clubs and the bathing beach has offshore net protection. Sea Park, at the southern boundary of the township has a ten-storey block of holiday flats. Here, at the estuary of the Umtentweni River, there is boating and river fishing.

Umtentweni

The municipality of Umtentweni lies between two beautiful rivers, the Umtentweni (after the Umtente, a long grass with a sharp point that grows in the area) and the Umzimkulu (the great home of rivers).

Pleasantly situated in undulating terrain, this resort north of Port Shepstone has for long been a place of retirement; its environment certainly encourages relaxation. The extensive beach shelves gently from grass covered dunes down to the sea, and a feature of this beach is the children's playground and tearoom in a natural parkland of lovely shade trees. There are offshore nets protecting bathers and some good vantage points for fishing. The two hotels, bowling and tennis club are near the beach, and the caravan park is on the south bank of the Umtentweni River.

Port Shepstone

Its administrative and commercial sector built high on the south bank of the Umzimkulu River, Port Shepstone dates from the Victorian era. It was first settled in 1867 and named Shepstone after the Natal statesman, Sir Theophilus Shepstone. When the town was laid out in 1882, over 200 Norwegian immigrants settled there in the belief that a successful fishing harbour could be maintained and to a limited extent they were rewarded when a fiscal port was established in 1893 and the name was changed to Port Shepstone. For a number of years coasters

2

1

Two Ovland Timesharing hotels situated in prime positions on Natal's South Coast — both have outstanding holiday amenities, comfort, service and excellent restaurants.

4

1. and 2. St Michael's Sands, with its own private golf course, is right on the beach.
3. and 4. Glenmore Sands has suites equipped for self catering and is right on the beach.

3

Quite unique in its situation and amenities is San Lameer, on the Natal South Coast between Ramsgate and Port Edward. A completely self-contained resort with both villa and hotel accommodation, a first-rate restaurant, a private ocean beach and opportunities for golf, fishing, windsurfing, boating, tennis, bowls, squash and walking, all within this superb sub-tropical property.

traded between Durban and Port Shepstone but despite financial support from the Natal government the harbour was never a success because of the perpetual silting up of the river entrance. When the railway reached Port Shepstone in 1901 the port fell into disuse. Municipal status was granted in 1934 and when the bridge upstream was washed away during the heavy storms of 1959, a modern road and rail bridge was constructed at the mouth of the Umzimkulu, finally sealing the fate of the port. A lighthouse on the south bank still serves as a beacon to shipping.

Port Shepstone is the southernmost terminal railhead of the South Coast. It is the seat of the Magistrate's Court and here are sited the Provincial Hospital and regional Water Supply Corporation. The town has five schools and is the centre of a large sugar and sub-tropical fruit farming community. The principal industry is the exploitation of the valuable limestone and marble some distance up the Umzimkulu River. Natal Portland Cement has an important factory at Simuna in the valley.

With the separation of Marburg, a town of some 8 000 inhabitants (mostly Indian) on the south-western boundary, Port Shepstone's population decreased considerably in recent times, although an additional 1 000 whites was added to the population with the incorporation of Oslo Beach to the south-east. The population of Port Shepstone is now 4 000 whites. Its black workers commute with the neighbouring KwaZulu territory in which Gamalakha is a large township.

Positioned in a splendid setting on the north bank of the Umzimkulu is Port Shepstone Country Club with its fine 18-hole golf course, bowling greens and tennis courts, and a good stretch of estuary water for yachting and speed boating. The Umzimkulu is navigable in small craft for 8 kilometres. The sandspit formed on the southern side of the river mouth is renowned for its big catches in surf fishing. Beach facilities include a tidal pool, change rooms and pavilion. The municipality maintains beachfront camping and caravan sites and there are four hotels including the 2-star Bedford Hotel facing the national road. At Oslo Beach chalets can be rented.

Oribi Gorge Nature Reserve
Oribi Gorge (approached along the N2 to Harding), some 24 kilometres north-west of Port Shepstone, is one of the most remarkable of nature's features to be found anywhere in southern Africa. Here the Umzimkulwana River, a tributary of the Umzimkulu, has carved out of the face of the earth a fantastic cleft, 24 kilometres long, 5 kilometres wide and 366 metres deep. The scenic drive through the gorge should not be missed by visitors to the lower south coast and they should set aside at least half a day for the excursion.

Some of the most spectacular viewing points are to be seen by taking the turnoff to Oribi Gorge Hotel, in the privately-owned parkland of Fairacres Estate where tourists are welcome. The famous views of Echo Valley, The Pulpit, Oribi Heads, Ola's Nose, Lehr Falls, Horseshoe Bend and Baboon's Castle and also views of the distant Umzimkulu Valley are all to be

seen from Fairacres Estate which overlooks the Oribi Gorge Nature Reserve of some 1 783 hectares. The reserve received its name from the antelope, oribi, once prevalent in this area and still seen on occasion, as are the duiker, bushbuck and other creatures of the forest.

For details of hutted camp accommodation in the Oribi Gorge Nature Reserve itself, application should be made to Natal Parks Board, P.O. Box 662, Pietermaritzburg.

Shelly Beach
The first resort south of Port Shepstone is Shelly Beach, appropriately named because of the quantity and variety of sea shells at its coast. At the wide sandy beach there are offshore nets and a number of renowned fishing spots. Across the main road from the beach there is a drive-in cinema near the large caravan park and shopping complex. The assortment of other holiday accommodation includes cottages, flats, chalets and an hotel.

St Michael's-on-Sea
The northern boundary of St Michael's-on-Sea is formed by the pretty Umhlangeni River and at its mouth is the secluded St Michael's beach. The Umhlangeni, which is the Zulu word for 'the place of the reeds', follows part of the magnificent 9-hole golf course and just across the road is the St Michael's Sands Hotel, perfectly situated. Redesigned and refurbished in 1987, St Michael's Sands is an Ovland Timesharing development, and here there are excellent opportunities for happy holidays. See pictures on page 192.

Near St Michael's beach there is a macadamised parking area. The tidal swimming pool is floodlit at night and adequate change-room facilities are provided. The bathing beach is fully protected with offshore nets and lifesavers are in attendance during the seasonal months. Across the lagoon is a tearoom where canoes and paddle boats may be hired. The bowling club has its greens at the hotel.

Uvongo Beach
The Zulu name for the river – Ivungu, refers to the 'murmuring noise' of the waterfall, and Uvongo is a corruption.

The beautiful Ivungu River cuts a deep ravine on its way to the sea. Just past the main road it takes a plunge of 23 metres forming a lovely waterfall. At the coastal lagoon two sheer headlands of rugged rock protrude high above the indigenous bush to complete another of nature's scenic wonders. On the southern side of the lagoon is the main bathing beach and above the beach, built on a spectacular site, is the hotel. Below at La Crete Point and across the river mouth near the tidal pool and paddling pond, good fishing is to be had. Here there is ample parking. a tearoom and change rooms. The bathing beach is protected with offshore nets and there are lifesavers in attendance during seasonal months.

Uvongo Beach is a sophisticated resort that has everything for the holiday maker. Apart from the hotel, there are a number of boarding houses, modern holiday flats, three caravan parks and chalets.

It was the original township owner, the surveyor and great fisherman Thure Lilliecrona, who set aside teen hectares of land on the bank of the beautiful vungu River as a public sporting amenity. The Uvongo Bowling Club has three greens and the Uvongo Tennis Club has four all-weather courts here. In addition there are squash courts and boating on the river. Uvongo Angling Club welcomes visitors and there are particularly good fishing spots at Orange Rocks, Beacon Rocks and La Crete Point, where there is a fine pier.

Uvongo Beach municipality dates from 1954 and embraces St Michael's-on-Sea and Manaba Beach. The population is 6 000.

Manaba Beach

The village of Manaba Beach is at the original northern boundary of Margate and the name comes from the Zulu word meaning 'spreading out or growing'. Places of interest are Shad Bay where the fishing is excellent, the tidal pool where there are change rooms and a refreshment kiosk and the delightful pools and rock enclosed private beaches.

Margate

For a resort town, Margate has had an unusually high growth rate and gets its unimaginative name from the original farm that changed hands for £466 in 1919. The buyer, Mr Hugh Ballance, planned a township to be named Inkongweni (where the bushbuck are) after the river that flows through Margate, but the development failed. Ballance sold out to a New Zealander by the name of Erasmus and in the early 1920s (after the publicity of the so-called Margate monster, washed up on the beach) the place started to grow. The first local authority in the form of a health committee was established in 1932 and municipal status was granted in 1948. Today the borough has a permanent population of 8 500 which of course multiplies considerably during seasonal periods.

Margate has one of the finest and safest bathing beaches along the entire coast. Its great attraction to the younger set is that it is the centre of organised entertainment. In season there is around the clock activity, dancing to first-rate bands, discotheque, talent contests, stag nights, concerts and the Miss Margate beauty contest.

The beach is protected by offshore nets and a full-time beach superintendent and lifesavers are on duty daily. The amenities include change rooms and showers, tearooms and restaurants, all right on the beach. A feature of Margate beach is the entertainment area, attractively laid out on lawned terraces shaded by tall palm trees where the Little Top variety shows are held. In this area there is a super paddling pool with cascading fountains and chutes. A fine fishing pier has been constructed south of the main beach and is reached by way of the lovely marine drive.

Margate has six hotels, three caravan parks, a number of fine blocks of holiday flats and a variety of other holiday accommodation.

Margate Country Club, three kilometres inland from the centre of the town, welcomes temporary membership. The amenities include golf, tennis, bowls, billiards and a licensed clubhouse. Margate Bowling Club is close to the centre of the town on the northern side.

From the modern airport, $2^1/_2$ kilometres west of the town, Citi Air (Durban) arrange flights to and from Louis Botha Airport except on Saturdays and Sundays. Comair provide schedule flights to Jan Smuts, Johannesburg, via Pietermaritzburg, daily except on Saturdays and Sundays.

Ramsgate

The main coast road reaches a tranquil scene when it dips down to Ramsgate's Blue Lagoon; the teahouse, the reeds, the sleepy lagoon with its paddle boats, the green indigenous bush meeting the golden sands of the ocean beach and the neat homes with lovely gardens clustering the hillside. Across the river bridge the dramatic ship's figurehead marks the entrance to the famous Crayfish Inn filled with maritime treasures.

Ramsgate has a fine bathing beach, fully protected with offshore nets, and a car park that permits bathers to drive right onto the beach. The fishing spots are 'Little Billy' and 'Blue Boy'. Ramsgate bowling Club has greens near the village.

Southbroom

Remembered mostly for its fine 18-hole golf course, Southbroom, although considered to be a built-up area, has retained a wild coast aspect. Its natural inheritance is the contrasting rock-bound coast enclosed at each end by the sandy beaches of river lagoons. From the main road all of this is hidden by the indigenous layer of coastal scrub forest.

Southbroom golf and bowling clubs welcome visitors. The main bathing beach, at the mouth of the Imbezane River, is protected with offshore nets. Here there is a tearoom and the rock and lagoon tidal pools are quite safe. Black Rock is well known to fishermen. At the estuary of the Umkobi River there is a tea-garden and small boats can be hired. A caravan park fronts the lagoon and flats and cottages can be rented.

Marina Beach

For sheer unspoilt spaciousness the view across Marina Beach is surely one of the best along the

1. *The glorious beaches of Margate as seen from the rocks at Manaba Beach.*

2. *Among the scenic delights of Oribi Gorge, The Ledge, one of a number of viewsites in Fairacres Estate.*

3. *The Crayfish Inn, Ramsgate, an hotel known far and wide for its décor, hospitality and good fare.*

196

1

2

3

entire coast – 180 metres wide it is uninterrupted for a distance of 5 kilometres. Lush sub-tropical vegetation massed with aloes (flowering in the winter) reaches down to the coast to complete another of nature's surprises. The bathing beach is net-protected and has a tearoom right on the sands. Excellent fishing prospects prevail all along the coast and there is an hotel overlooking the whole scene.

San Lameer
Grand by any measurement, this magnificent resort comprises first-rate hotel or handsome villa accommodation, securely enclosed in an extensive nature reserve right at a private ocean beach. Its exceptional recreational facilities include golf, squash, tennis, bowls, fishing, windsurfing, canoeing and swimming (both pool and ocean). The villas provide for full self catering and there is a fine restaurant with international cuisine.

Trafalgar and Palm Beach
South of San Lameer the main road passes through emerald green countryside of ilala palms, banana farms and sugar plantations, with turnoffs to a number of unspoilt little seaside resorts. Trafalgar and Palm Beach each have caravan parks.

Glenmore Beach
This is a delightful seaside resort with offshore net protection, a picturesque beach and lagoon fringed with indigenous bush and several vantage points for fishermen. The protected inlet on the coast here permits the launching and beaching of ski-boats.

The garden of Glenmore Sands Hotel borders the glorious ocean beach. In a setting ideal for relaxing holidays this Ovland time-sharing project has first-rate facilities including *en suite* bedrooms with complete self catering, á la Carte restaurant, action bar with entertainment, and a sparkling pool.

Glenmore Beach is a part of Munster which is administered by a health committee and the post office of the region is Voortrekkerstrand. This is the site of the newspaper *Rapport* children's resort, Kinderstrand, where the anchor of the shipwrecked *Nightingale* of 1933 can be seen in the garden.

Leisure Crest and Leisure Bay
To the south of Glenmore Beach are the villages of Leisure Crest and Leisure Bay on the picturesque coastline of huge boulders and crystal clear pools.

Port Edward
The most southerly of the coastal resorts of Natal is Port Edward. The village lies five kilometres north of the Umtanvuna River (the reaper of mouthfuls) which forms the boundary between Natal and Transkei.

The little town was established in 1924 by T.K. Pringle who planned to 'strike the banner' here for retirement. Originally he called the township Kennington, based on his Christian name Kenneth, but subsequently changed the name to Port Edward to honour the Prince of Wales, later the uncrowned Edward VIII and finally the Duke of Windsor.

There is a hotel in the village and adjoining the ocean beach is the S.A. Police Holiday Resort, a resort of large proportions laid out in the surrounds of shade trees with tarred roads throughout and well-kept lawns fronting the chalets, cottages and rondavels. The resort is open to the general public. The beach is net-protected and the fishing is very good.

Overlooking this peaceful scene is Tragedy Hill, a sandhill in the shape of a pyramid and named by the tribespeople Isandlundlu (that which is shaped like a hut). In 1831 this was the scene of a massacre of a party of refugees comprising followers of Frank Fynn (the son of Henry Francis Fynn) and Langeni tribespeople who were fleeing from and caught by the Zulus. It is said that until recent times the hill was littered with the bones of the victims.

Umtamvuna Estuary and Nature Reserve
The Umtamvuna, once crossed by pont, is now spanned by a handsome bridge and the scenery surrounding the river is superb. The wide estuary is particularly beautiful and ideal for ski-boats. From the south bank (which is in Transkei) the nearby Wild Coast Sun hotel-casino hires out boats.

Upstream at the old pont site there are picnic places and a caravan park controlled by the Port Edward municipality. In this setting of magnificent indigenous trees, where the apricot-coloured blooms of the wild clivia make a fine display in the springtime, is the entrance to Umtamvuna Nature Reserve, administered by the Natal Parks Board. Botanists rate this a unique sanctuary with trees that occur nowhere else in the world, among these the *Syzigium pondoenis* (lost for 100 years) has been rediscovered. Along the walking trails antelope likely to be encountered include the blue and grey duiker, reedbuck, bushbuck and albino bushbuck – white, with slightly pink hooves and horns. Nesting in the kloof overlooking the river is one of the last breeding colonies of the Cape vulture, and Bushman paintings have been found in the caves. The reserve itself has no overnight accommodation.

North Coast
The most attractive exit out of Durban for the north coast is along the Snell Parade, across the mouth of the Umgeni (river of the acacia trees), spanned by the Leo Boyd Bridge, and through the seaward side of Durban North (where cannas and other flowers in the roadside gardens make a brilliant display) past the Virginia Airport onto a coastal highway and a superb scenic route.

Umhlanga
Although one of the youngest boroughs in Natal (proclaimed in 1970) Umhlanga is one of the most affluent and fashionable places to live and to holiday. Among its hotels there are to be found some of the finest in South Africa and its residential suberb, La Lucia, with its 'millionaire's mile', possesses many beautiful homes. The permanent population is 13 000.

Within the area of recreation at Umhlanga Rocks (the original name) is the attractive beach, part rocky and part sandy, a number of sheltered pools of the beachfront hotels, caravan parks, tennis courts, bowling greens, a mashie course and a small park of exotic birds. The resort is notable for its specialist seafood and other restaurants and for its gay night life.

There are seven hotels in all, including the famed Oyster Box Hotel right on the sea front and within its own extensive sub-tropical garden – its history going back to 1869 when the Oyster Box, the first cottage of Umhlanga, was built there.

The other assets of Umhlanga include modern shopping and commercial complexes and residential and holiday apartments. All this expansion has happened in a matter of a few years and has, rather sadly, transformed what used to be a dreamy little village by the sea. The original township surveyed in 1926 used to be part of Natal Estates Limited, owned by the famous Campbell family, of which Sir Marshall Campbell was the head.

At the town's northern limit the Umhlanga lagoon with its surrounding coastal forest area (Hawaan Forest) has been declared a nature sanctuary. The bird fauna here is quite remarkable. Umhlanga takes its name from this river, the Zulu 'river of the reeds'.

In Umhlanga Rocks Drive (between Mount Edgecombe and Umhlanga), close to Huletts head office complex, is the Natal Anti-Shark Measures Board, the only institute of its kind in the world. From these headquarters a field staff either service or supervise the servicing of 306 shark nets in the water off 42 beaches of the Natal coast (including Durban), stretching from Richards Bay in the north to Port Edward in the south, a distance of some 400 kilometres. On Wednesdays at 2.30 p.m. the public receive free instruction on sharks in the form of a conducted tour of the laboratories, a film and lecture. The Board was established in 1964.

Umdloti Beach
This is a little resort with a lovely beach and a spacious rock-enclosed tidal pool. Its built-up area consists of a number of seaside cottages and two hotels. The name Umdloti is taken from the river the Zulus called 'of the wild tobacco'. The beach is net-protected.

Westbrook Beach (formerly Tongaat Beach)
Another little restful resort with cottages in amongst the casuarina trees, close to the beach. The well-patronised Westbrook Beach Hotel is ideally situated right on the beach, with no roads to cross. The Tongaat River forms a pretty lagoon north of the resort; the Zulus gave the river its name because of its meandering course. The bathing beach is net-protected.

Ballito
On a delightful part of the coast, Ballito became fashionable with up-country people who built substantial residences there. Recently timesharing developers have competed in constructing cabana type apartments, one of these is La Montagne with its full hotel facilities.

The older established Willard Beach adjoins Ballito, and the beaches are protected with offshore nets.

Shaka's Rock
At Shaka's Rock the hotel overlooks a rock-enclosed tidal pool and a secluded stretch of beach, altogether a peaceful holiday setting. It is said that Shaka used this beach when, towards the end of his life, he established his main kraal at Stanger.

Salt Rock
Thirty minutes drive from Durban is the Salt Rock Hotel and Timeshare Resort, also known as Salt Rock Palms, a development of the Hulett family in association with Ovland Timesharing. The resort occupies a restful situation on this rugged and wooded coastline, with excellent opportunities for fishing from specially constructed towers and piers, and the tidal swimming pools are among the largest on the coast. The country club facilities include tennis and bowls. There is golf at Umhlali, not far from the resort. See page 201.

Sheffield Beach, Blythdale Beach and Zinkwazi Mouth
National road N2 continues northwards on a scenically beautiful course with turnoffs leading to Sheffield Beach and Blythdale Beach, little resorts with caravan parks and chalet-type accommodation. At the mouth of the Zinkwazi, the river the Zulus named after the white-headed fish eagles there, there is a caravan park with all facilities. These bathing beaches are all protected with offshore nets.

Tugela River Bridge, Fort Pearson, the Ultimatum Tree and Fort Tenedos
Eighty-eight kilometres from Durban, national road N2 reaches the Tugela River, the traditional boundary between Natal and Zululand and a neighbourhood rich in historical interest. On the Natal side, 5 kilometres south of the handsome bridge that carries the road across the Tugela, there is a turnoff to the river mouth with its narrow beach and fishermen's bungalows.

The historical interest starts less than two kilometres along this road to the mouth. On a low hill commanding the wagon drift of the old Zululand road is the ruin of Fort Pearson built in 1878, just prior to the British invasion of Zululand. The fort was built by the men of the Royal Navy from *H.M.S. Tenedos* and *H.M.S. Active,* under the supervision of Colonel Pearson of the Buffs, commander of Lord Chelmsford's coastal columns in the march to Zululand. A large military base camp was developed here on the south bank of the river.

A kilometre or so below the fort, where the ferry was formerly situated, is the Ultimatum Tree. This is an old fig tree and beneath its branches a large tent was pitched for the meeting, on 11 December 1878, of the respective envoys of the British governor, Sir Bartle Frere, and the Zulu king, Cetshwayo. Ranged on the British side where John Wesley Shepstone, Charles Brownlee, Henry Francis Fynn and Lieutenant-Colonel F.W. Forestier-Walker. On the other side were three chieftains and eleven indunas (headmen). On both sides there were many interested onlookers, among these on the Zulu side was John Dunn, an Englishman 'gone native' who was one of Cetshwayo's chiefs.

Here under the fig tree on this fateful day the Zulus

Known to guests from all over the world, three-star Oyster Box Hotel at the water's edge at Umhlanga Rocks. The Oyster Box is notable for gracious living in an atmosphere of complete relaxation.

For completion in 1988 on this stunningly beautiful coastline, Salt Rock Hotel and Timeshare Resort — developed by the Hulett family in association with Ovland Timesharing.

were given the British ultimatum which for the proud Zulu race made war inevitable. In a long list of complaints and demands the Zulu envoys were informed that Cetshwayo must accept the British demarcation of the boundary between Zululand and the Transvaal (then under British rule) and he was required to deliver up the murderers of certain Zulu women who were abducted on the Natal side of the Tugela; to break up the Zulu military system to enable men to be free to marry when they wished; to ensure a fair trial of every accused person; to permit the return of missionaries to Zululand; and to receive a British Resident. He was ordered to reply within 30 days. All that was received from Cetshwayo was a request for extension of time. This request was ignored and British troops crossed the Tugela on Sunday, 12 January 1879 to begin the Zulu War, and they were to meet with disaster before they finally crushed the might of the redoubtable warrior-king.

Opposite the Ultimatum Tree, on the north bank of the Tugela, the British built Fort Tenedos during the Zulu War, and this with Fort Pearson was the twin guardian of the Lower Tugela Ferry. The sites of the two forts and the fig tree are national monuments.

The continuation of national road N2 and the territory of Zululand are described in Chapter 9.

Old North Coast Road

The original main north coast road followed the sugar cane country and found its exit from Durban along Umgeni Road crossing the Umgeni River over the Connaught Bridge, some distance upstream from the mouth. Just before Avoca, an Indian residential area, the road forks; the branch leading north-west is to Duffs Road and the Black township of KwaMashu (with its 300 000 inhabitants, a part of self-governed KwaZulu) and on into the green hills of the magisterial district of Inanda at the eastern end of the scenically superb Valley of a Thousand Hills.

Sugar Industry of Natal

From the turnoff to Inanda, all the way to Stanger, the old north coast road follows the sugar belt with an almost continuous ocean of green, rolling canefields.

The sugar industry in Natal had its beginning in 1851 when Edmund Morewood built a crude mill at his farm Compensation (so named because it had been awarded him in lieu of another farm). In 1855 J.B. Miller and H. Milner introduced the crushing of cane by steam power, and a further advance was made in the industry when the labour problem was overcome by the introduction of Indian immigrants in 1860. Real stimulation came about through the efforts of Sir Liege Hulett in opening new areas in Zululand. In 1909 production stood at 87 000 tons of sugar. In the 1979-80 season, 17 mills produced more than 2 000 000 tons of sugar from approximately 18 400 000 tons of cane. These results came from 370 587 hectares of farmlands under cane and 218 101 hectares harvested.

Mount Edgecombe

Huletts Corporation Limited (of which Natal Estates Limited is today a part) has spacious sugar estates at Mount Edgecombe and the extensive sugar mill there can be visited from May to December. The estate has a splendid garden setting with beautiful trees, bougainvillaea, hibiscus and cannas providing a beautiful show. Here at Mount Edgecombe is an experimental station with its approach drive of majestic palms and the Huletts Country Club, a recreational extravaganza of clubhouse, cricket oval, golf course, bowling greens and tennis courts.

An unusual national monument is to be seen at Mount Edgecombe. It is the small Ganesha Hindu Temple, built in 1899 by Mr Kristappa Reddy. A Dravidian-style deep sculpted sikhara, complete with stucco sculptures of Nanda the Bull, Shiva and other deities, surmount the central freestanding cella. The temple was proclaimed in 1977.

Verulam

The third oldest town in Natal, Verulam was founded in 1857. It was established in the valley of the Umdloti River by British settlers under the patronage of the Earl of Verulam and is today inhabited by the Indian community who date back to the indentured Hindu labourers imported in 1860 by the sugar industry. The municipality has an all-Indian council, the first elections having been held in 1975. Near Verulam at Hazelmere Dam water skiing championships are held.

Tongaat

The fascinating oriental stores at Tongaat are a big attraction to visitors. Away from this scene, to the north of the town, the Tongaat Sugar Estate has its mill, offices and self-contained township for its employees, beautifully laid out with recreational amenities including an 18-hole golf course in a lovely setting.

Compensation, Umhlali, Shaka's Kraal and Groutville

At Compensation there is a memorial to Edmund Morewood, the pioneer sugar producer, in the form of a replica of his first mill. Umhlali has a cluster of trading stores and a popular golf course and takes its name from the river, 'where the monkey apples grow'. Shaka's Kraal was the site of one of a number of kraals occupied by the warrior-king where today there is a sugar mill and some trading activity. At Groutville the first American Board Mission was started in 1836 by the Reverends George Champion and Aldin Grout.

Stanger

Across the Umvoti River (named after the headman Mvoti Ncashange) 72 kilometres from Durban, is the town of Stanger which was established in 1873 and named after Dr William Stanger, first Surveyor General of Natal. It became a municipality in 1949 and has a population of 17 000.

Stanger is surrounded by extensive sugar cane plantations that reach down to the sea 8 kilometres away. It is the rail and magisterial centre for these estates and for other important agricultural activities in the district. An asset of Stanger is the unique tambuti-wood furniture factory of the Singh family.

The town was built on the site of Dukuza, the principal kraal of Shaka, the great warrior-king and founder of the Zulu nation, and it was here on 23 September 1828 that Shaka was murdered by his two half brothers, Dingaan and Mhlangana, assisted by the trusted bodyguard, Mbopha. Marking the spot where he died and the place traditionally respected as his grave, a monument was erected in 1932 from funds collected mostly from the Zulu people. It was proclaimed a national monument in 1939.

Kearsney

North of Stanger the old north coast road joins with national road N2 which links Durban and Zululand. To the west of Stanger a road passes through Kearsney where Sir Liege Hulett, the sugar pioneer, built his home in the 1880s and called it after his birthplace in Kent. The climate was found to be suitable for tea and Sir Liege developed extensive plantations and a tea factory. In more recent times the tea industry proved to be uneconomical and sugar has replaced the tea. Upon his death in 1928, Sir Liege Hulett's homestead was converted into a school for boys and as Kearsney College it later moved to Botha's Hill. In 1944 the house passed into the hands of the Spiritual Healing Homes of Africa.

From Kearsney the road passes interesting tribal territory on its way to Mapumulo and Kranskop (Chapter 10).

Old main road from Rossburgh to Sarnia

One of the suburban areas to be developed early in the history of Durban lies on a ridge beyond the Umbilo River . Rossburgh is the junction of the railway lines to the Bluff, the South Coast and the main line to Johannesburg. A road to these suburbs follows the main line, and from Rossburgh takes a pretty steep course known as Jacobs Ladder. The Durban suburbs on this old main road are Sea View, Bellair and Hillary.

Queensburgh

A number of residential settlements sprang up beyond Hillary and in 1924 Cavendish, Malvern, Escombe, Moseley and Northdene amalgamated. In 1954 municipal status was granted this amalgamation in the name of Queensburgh. The houses in the area are generally of the older type in a picturesque sylvan setting. The population is 20 000. From Northdene the narrow old main road continues to Sarnia which is part of the municipality of Pinetown. Within the municipal limits of Queensburgh is the 52-hectare North Park Nature Reserve, proclaimed in 1968.

Kenneth Stainbank Nature Reserve

To the south of Queensburgh and north of Yellowwood Park (a suburb of Durban) lies the magnificent 214-hectare wilderness donated by Mr Kenneth Stainbank in 1963. Once a Zulu military outpost named Ndaba Nkhulu (the big discussion), in 1847 it was part of the farm Bellair, belonging to Robert Dunn, and was in turn acquired by the Stainbank family in 1857. The walking trails lead through lovely wooded areas where there is prolific birdlife, a variety of antelope including duiker, bushbuck, impala and nyala, in addition to zebra and giraffe.

The Stainbank Nature Reserve is best reached via the southern suburb of Yellowwood Park, taking Kenyon Howden Road as far as Kingfisher Avenue from where the signs are followed.

National road N3 from Durban to Pietermaritzburg and old main road from Hillcrest to Cato Ridge

National road N3 leads out west of Durban and is a dual freeway to Pietermaritzburg. It passes the international tennis courts, Westridge Park, and the suburbs of Mayville and Sherwood. Beyond 45th Cutting (constructed by the 45th Regiment in 1838 and no longer part of the national road) it reaches the boundary of Westville. On the right of the road some distance away, high up on the Cotswold Hills, is the huge complex of the University of Durban-Westville for Indians on a magnificent campus of 162 hectares and fronting Durban's Indian residential suburb of Reservoir Hills.

Westville

This is an extensive residential municipality of 28 000 inhabitants, with beautiful homes, gardens and fine schools. The name honours Martin West, Natal's first governor. Westville has a hotel with a well-patronised restaurant.

Cowies Hill

Mainly to the right of the national road, Cowies Hill is a fine residential suburb of Pinetown with lovely homes and spacious gardens. Paradise Valley Nature Reserve of 24 hectares is at the source of the Umbilo River; proclaimed in 1963 it is now overlooked by a huge residential complex. The name of the suburb honours William Cowie who arrived in Natal with the Voortrekkers.

Pinetown

When Archibald Murray built the Wayside Hotel as a staging post in 1850, he had part of this 550-hectare estate surveyed for a township and named it after Sir Benjamin Pine, Natal's governor at the time. In 1871 Canon J.S. Crompton took transfer of the balance of Murray's estate and this land forms the centre of Pinetown today on both sides of Crompton Street. The town experienced a temporary boom in 1876 when the railway from Durban reached here. With the continuation of the line beyond Pinetown its importance as a railhead fell away.

Pinetown has a colourful history starting with the Zulu War of 1879 when many British regiments were stationed here. Among these were the 6th Inniskilling Dragoons, the 7th and 13th Hussars, the 60th Rifles and the Bengal Lancers. The famous soldiers associated with these regiments were Lord Baden-Powell, Sir Baker Russell, Lord Allenby, Lord Chelmsford, Captain Pennefather, Major Bromhead, V.C., a hero of the 24th Regiment that defended Rorke's Drift and Captain J. Malone, V.C. a hero of the immortal Six Hundred of Balaclava. Captain

The enchanting three-star Rob Roy Hotel, famous for weekend and longer holidays and functions of every description — in an invigorating atmosphere overlooking the Valley of a Thousand Hills at Botha's Hill.

1

3

2

4

*1. 2. and 3. Floral
decoration on the road from
Botha's Hill to Drummond:
poinsettias, sunflowers, and lion's
tail.*

*4. An early morning view as
the mist rises — Valley of a
Thousand Hills.*

Malone died at the Rugby Hotel (then the officers' mess) and was buried in St Andrew's Churchyard. Pinetown became a great place to convalesce and one English newspaper named it 'the healthiest spot in the British Empire'. Being 330 metres above sea level it is without the humidity of the coastline.

During the Anglo-Boer War (1899-1902) Pinetown again became an important military base and the avenue of oaks along the old main road was planted in memory of those who fell in that war.

Pinetown's situation on the trunk and rail routes to the hinterland, only 24 kilometres from the port of Durban, is ideal for the siting of industry. With the incorporation of added areas the town's population is 100 000. It became a borough in 1948. Pinetown has 4 hotels. It is the home of caravan manufacturing in Natal.

Mariannhill

Within the municipality of Pinetown and south-west of the town is the extensive Roman Catholic Mission of Mariannhill. Founded in 1882 by Abbot Franz Pfanner it was, to begin with, run by the Trappist monks but changed to the Order of the Mariannhill Missionaries in 1909. It contains a monastery, cathedral, convent of the Sisters of the Precious Blood, a modern hospital, an orphanage and St Francis College. Education is provided for Blacks from infancy to high school and in addition there is teacher training. The weekly paper *Um-Afrika* is printed and published here. Visitors are welcomed to be shown over this remarkable institution. Enquiries should be made to the Durban Visitors Bureau regarding tours.

New Germany

North-east of Pinetown is the industrial town of New Germany, with its population of 6 000. It had its start in 1847 when Jonas Bergtheil received permission to settle some 200 German immigrants in the area. They attempted to produce cotton and coffee but this failed and the place was later developed industrially. New Germany became a municipality in 1960 and contains the Umgeni Power Station and a number of important industries, including the textile mills of the Frame Group. The Circle Country Club golf course is at New Germany.

Toll Road

Before reaching Pinetown in its north-westward journey, national road N3 divides, the left-hand fork as the new toll road, completely avoiding the notorius Field's Hill and Kloof village. The right-hand fork is now R613.

Kloof

The borough of Kloof, proclaimed in January 1961, spreads over valleys and hills at an altitude of 548 metres, 27 kilometres to the west of Durban, and lies largely on Richmond Farm No. 999, granted to W.S. Field by the British Government on 1 October 1851 (before the area was tamed of its elephants and lions) in reward for his services as first Magistrate and Collector of Customs of Durban. His descendants still live in the area.

The assets of Kloof are its wooded, shrub-covered home gardens (blazoned with the colour of the blooms of poinsettias, bougainvillaea, azalea, hydrangea, abelia and lasiandra and invariably containing the fruits of the avocado, mango, pawpaw, guava, litchi and banana), a magnificent country club in the heart of the borough, and the close proximity of the 11-kilometre-long 447-hectare Krantzkloof Nature Reserve with its beautiful waterfall. The population of Kloof is 15 000; it has fine schools and two hotels.

Gillitts-Emberton

As in the case of Kloof the magnificent residential area of Gillitts-Emberton is divided by trunk road R613.

Hillcrest

At Emberton a flyover bridge crossing the R613 carries the subsidiary road to Hillcrest, an old-world village on the old main road to Pietermaritzburg. Highbury, the famous school for boys, is at Hillcrest and there are beautiful homes with lovely gardens and a wayside hotel.

Botha's Hill

From Hillcrest the old main road takes a climbing, meandering course in its loop to join with national road N3 at Cato Ridge and for most of the distance of 30 kilometres it skirts the Valley of a Thousand Hills with a variety of wild flowers (especially lion's tail, kaffirboom, species of cassia and sunflowers) on the roadside and opportunities of viewing the amazing spectacle of nature from vantage points along the way.

At Botha's Hill, where General Botha's grandfather once lived, the road passes the imposing entrance to Kearsney College, a famous school, set in magnificent grounds. Beyond the school on the right of the road is the Rob Roy, an enchanting hotel with a reputation for fine fare and every comfort, and further on the same side of the road is the attractive pheZulu Tourist Boutique with its viewsite of the famous valley and authentic Zulu village where tribal life can be witnessed.

Drummond

At Drummond there is the Valley View Restaurant and curio shop overlooking the valley and from here there are opportunities to see and photograph tribal life in the surrounds of bee-hive huts. Drummond has two hotels including the well-known Thousand Hills Hotel occupying a prime site and catering for overnight stops as well as holiday makers in this remaining unspoilt and beautiful part of inland Natal.

The Valley of a Thousand Hills and the Umgeni River

This majestically spectacular phenomenon of nature could not have received a more descriptive name. On a clear day, when the innumerable small hills and valleys which surround the main valley of the twisting Umgeni River stand out in a three dimensional panorama, it requires quite an effort to take in the whole scene at once. If you could get close enough to the scene as the mists rise in the early morning you might first hear the long shrieking cries of the tribesmen sending their distant messages from one hill to another and then, with the mist lifting a little more, the beehive shaped huts would be revealed on the slopes and in the valleys – for this is the protected territory of the Debe tribe of the Zulus who fled to this less accessible terrain, in the face of cannibals, little more than a century ago.

Indeed the Umgeni is well named (the river of the acacia trees) for here the entire great valley is covered in the tree of the yellow bloom. Tracing its course, this short river is found to make a spectacular journey. Its source and catchment area is a large vlei surrounded by the Impendle hills (the highest point of the hills having received the unimaginative Voortrekker name Spioenkop, not to be confused with the Spioenkop of Anglo Boer War fame, north-west of Bergville), south of the Kamberg Nature Reserve; it feeds the Midmar Dam before providing the spectacle at each of Howick Falls and Albert Falls; lower downstream it feeds the Nagle Dam, and then makes its tortuous way through the Valley of a Thousand Hills to empty itself in the Indian Ocean at Durban's Blue Lagoon. The Umgeni provides part of the arduous route of the annual canoe race along the Umzimduzi and Umgeni Rivers from Pietermaritzburg to Durban.

Supporters and riders of the Durban-Johannesburg motor cycle race of the 1920s and 1930s will remember the section of the route from Hillcrest to Cato Ridge to have been one of the most testing parts of their gruelling race, and it remains the well beaten track of those untiring athletes who year after year compete in the Durban-Pietermaritzburg *Comrades Marathon*.

Inchanga and Harrison
From Drummond the old road passes Inchanga with a caravan park, and Harrison in a farming region, to reach the junction with national road N3 at Cato Ridge.

Nagle Dam and Natal Table Mountain
Just before reaching Cato Ridge, the old main road meets the road coming up from Nagle Dam. The dam lies at the foot of Natal's Table Mountain in picturesque surroundings, in an area notable for interesting succulent plant-life. The impounding of the waters of the Umgeni has provided a lake with a surface area of 162 hectares at an average depth of 30 metres. In the catchment area opportunities arise to see tribal life. The dam contributes to Durban's water supply.

Shongweni and Summerveld
Shongweni is the site of another Durban municipal dam and it is also the name of the river (a tributary of the Umlaas) given by the Zulus because the waters in falling over a precipice create a long misty spray resembling a high column of smoke which they in fact call 'ntshongwe'. Here at Shongweni there is a fine polo ground where international games are played. Adjoining the grounds is the Polo Pony Hotel.

Nearby at Summerveld is the South African Jockey Academy, fast becoming the world's biggest training centre. Unlike other racing centres notably Newmarket in Britain and Chantilly in France, the vast complex at Summerveld is confined to a compact region.

Assegai
At the same turnoff as that to Shongweni a road leads in the opposite direction to connect the national highway with the old main road and this road leads in a winding course through Assegai, a delightful wooded area of small holdings.

Cato Ridge
Originally the estate of G.R. Cato, the Natal pioneer and first mayor of Durban, Cato Ridge is an important rail centre and site of the ultra modern abattoir serving Durban and Pietermaritzburg. The wattle chip factory there is engaged in important export business. Cato Ridge has a hotel.

Camperdown
Camperdown marks the commencement of the extensive breeding and broiler farms of Rainbow Chicken Farms, the long low whitewashed structures surrounded by beautifully kept lush-green lawns fringed with herbaceous borders.

The settlement was named by the first owner of the land, John Vanderplank, an Englishman of Dutch extraction, and commemorates the naval Battle of Camperdown, where the British defeated the Dutch in 1787. It was Vanderplank who planted the first Australian black wattle seeds that pioneered the wattle bark industry in Natal. There is an hotel in the village.

Umlaas Road
This railhead takes its name from the Umlaas River (the river that looks like whey). At this point a fly-over bridge across national road N3 divides on the southern side, with signposts marking the direction of roads to the South Coast and to the Transkei and Cape.

The district road to the South Coast is used by up-country people who wish to avoid the traffic congestion of Durban.

Eston, Umbumbulu and Adams Mission
Route R78 continues to the South Coast through Eston, the small centre of a farming community, and Umbumbulu (the place of the round knoll) to join national road N2 at Kingsburgh on the South Coast. Umbumbulu in KwaZulu is the site of Adams Mission School, named after its founder, Dr Newton Adams, one of six American missionaries who arrived in Natal in 1834.

Natal Lion and Game Park
Beyond Umlaas Road another turnoff to the left leads to the Natal Lion and Game Park. This deviation is well worth taking; the signpost is at 58 kilometres from Durban and there is a further 7 kilometres of pleasant tarmac journey to the gates of this privately-owned, beautifully situated park. It spreads over 240 hectares of well-wooded, undulating terrain in the upper region of the Valley of a Thousand Hills providing fine scenic views. Separated by adequate fencing from the magnificent lion specimens (to be seen at close quarter) are giraffe, zebra, a variety of antelope, crocodile and rhino. There is also very interesting bird fauna in the park including blue crane, crowned crane and flamingo. Barbecue facilities are provided in the picnic area and light refreshments and curios are sold at the shop. The park is open from 7.30 a.m. until dusk. A motel adjoins the park.

The interesting Natal Zoological Garden is a short distance beyond the motel.

The turnoff to the Lion Park is 16 kilometres from Pietermaritzburg, described in Chapter 10.

Zululand and Northern Natal

Zululand (KwaZulu)

Zululand was incorporated with Natal in 1897. The territory, which is 27 000 square kilometres in area, lies north of the Tugela River and extends northwards to the Transvaal's wedge between Natal and Swaziland, and to the Moçambique border. Zululand has a low-lying sub-tropical coastal strip of luxuriant and wild vegetation, part of which is intensely cultivated with sugar-cane, and an interior of rolling hills and wide valleys where maize and sorghum are grown.

The Zulus are a proud people and have a natural charm and dignity. Descendants of a powerful warrior nation, today they are a peaceful people living in picturesque kraals. They have a large measure of self-government, the most recent development being the establishment of KwaZulu.

Eighty-eight kilometres from Durban, national road N2 reaches the Tugela River, the traditional boundary between Natal and Zululand, in an area rich in historical interest surrounding the places and events at the commencement of the British invasion of Zululand in 1879 described in the previous chapter.

The Coastal Region and the Game Reserves of Zululand (Natal Parks Board and other accommodation details appear on page 418)

The Tugela (the startling one) is today spanned by a handsome bridge named in honour of the youthful Natal hero, John Ross Bridge. In the year 1827, John Ross, at the age of 15 years, walked from the lagoon which is now Durban bay to Lourenço Marques (now Maputo) to fetch urgently needed medical supplies for his comrades.

Mandini and Amatikulu

Near the John Ross Bridge at Mandini (in the water) Sappi Kraft (Pty) Ltd has its paper mill, and at Amatikulu (big water) on the northern bank of the river of that name is a sugar mill of Huletts.

Gingindlovu

The rail and road junction of Gingindlovu marks the place where Cetshwayo established a kraal after defeating his brother Mbulazi in the struggle for leadership of the Zulu people, and so it was that Gingindlovu (the swallower of the elephant) received its name.

It was here, some years later, in April 1879, that a British force under Lord Chelmsford, on its way to relieve Eshowe, was victorious in a battle against the Zulus and the British soldiers interpreted the name as 'gin gin I love you.'

The road from Gingindlovu to Eshowe climbs 450 metres in 24 kilometres in scenically beautiful sugar-cane country.

Eshowe

The old traditional capital of Zululand, and a very pretty one, is Eshowe. It takes its name from the sound made by the breezes through the forest trees and at 500 metres it escapes the intense humidity of the coast. The forest to which the Zulus referred is that of Dlinza (the grave-like place of meditation), a 160-hectare nature reserve within the municipal limits – a place of peace and beauty with lovely walks, waterfalls, abundant birdlife and small game species. A clearing in the forest is called the Bishop's Seat; the name commemorates a former Bishop of Zululand who conducted open air services there.

Eshowe had its beginning in 1860 when Cetshwayo (who then completely dominated his aging father, the king Mpande) moved from Empangeni to the cooler situation and built his main kraal which he called Eziqwaqeni (the abode of the robbers). At the same time the Norwegian Mission under Pastor Ommund Oftebro moved its headquarters to the site which the Zulus called KwaMondi (the place of Mondi, their pronunciation of the pastor's first name 'Ommund').

It was here (after the Isandhlwana disaster), near the Norwegian Mission Station, KwaMondi, on the eastern outskirts of Eshowe, that Colonel Pearson, in command of some 4 000 British in the coastal column of the invasion of Zululand, was besieged by the Zulus for ten weeks until relieved by Lord Chelmsford on 3 April 1879. After the departure of the military forces their laager was used by the Norwegian Mission as a cemetery. Ommund Oftebro was later buried there. The old cemetery and the military entrenchments are still there and the site has been proclaimed an historical monument.

At the close of the Zulu War in 1880, Sir Melmoth Osborn took up his seat in Eshowe as the Resident Commissioner (a post known throughout the colonial empire in that era as the British Resident). In 1887 Sir Melmoth was appointed Chief Magistrate, and Eshowe was proclaimed the capital of Zululand. Sir Melmoth remained in office until 1893, a year after Eshowe was established as a town.

Fort Nongqayi, the Beau-Geste type fort two kilometres from the town, was built in 1883 and manned by a force of Zulu police, known as the *Nongqayi* (the restrainers), raised to protect the British Resident. The fort, a national monument, was established as a museum in 1961 and houses interesting Zululand relics.

Eshowe is an attractive, amiable town with a population of 8 000. Its recreational amenities include a magnificent swimming pool and caravan park adjoining the Dlinza Forest, a fine 18-hole golf course and the 1 600-hectare Ocean View Game Park on the Gingindlovu road entrance to the town.

The social event of the year attracting visitors from throughout Natal and Zululand to Eshowe is the Zululand Agricultural Show held in May or June. Eshowe has two hotels.

Mtunzini and Port Durnford

Eighteen kilometres north-east of Gingindlovu there is a turnoff from national road N2 to the magisterial village and resort of Mtunzini (the shady place) at the mouth of the Umlalazi River where there is good fishing, lagoon boating and the 900-hectare Umlalazi Nature Reserve. Near the Mtunzini railway station, a small grove of raffia palms (*Raphia vinifera*) is a national monument. Common in Malawi and Moçambique these palms owe their origin here to a one time magistrate Mr C.C. Foxon who brought the seeds from Kosi Bay, the most southerly natural occurrence. These palms attain a height of over 18 metres with leaves, some 9 metres in length, said to be the longest leaves known in the plant kingdom. There is resort accommodation at the lagoon and a caravan park near the nature reserve.

Some 20 kilometres along the beach north of Mtunzini is the 6 000 candle power lighthouse at Port Durnford, an open anchorage used occasionally during the Zulu War of 1879 for putting ashore British troops and supplies. It was named after Colonel A.W. Durnford of the Royal Engineers who was killed at Isandhlwana.

Three kilometres north of the turnoff to Mtunzini on national road N2 is the Forest Inn Hotel. Past the hotel is the Port Durnford Government Forest and beyond the afforestation on the left of the road is the University College of Zululand.

Felixton
At Felixton there is a sugar mill of the Hulett group and the plant of Ngoye Paper Mills Limited, surrounded by plantations of pine and gum.

Empangeni
The first Norwegian Mission Station in Zululand started at Empangeni in 1851 but later moved to Eshowe. The railway reached Empangeni in 1903, a township was established in 1931 and the borough was proclaimed in 1960.

The town is the principal centre of the sugar industry in Zululand with a mill of Huletts sited there. The other products of the district are cattle, cotton, timber and pineapples. The population is 20 000 and there are two hotels and an 18-hole golf course.

Eucalyptus trees (originating in Australia) were planted in the first Natal government experimental farm near Empangeni in 1905 and success led to the present-day forests of the Zululand coastal belt.

Empangeni is an important rail junction on the main line between Durban and Golela (Swaziland border) and traffic to the huge coal harbour at Richards Bay.

The origin of its Zulu name is uncertain; Empangeni could have been derived from the words meaning 'to seize' or 'the place of important people' or from the type of tree that grows on the banks of the Empangeni River.

Enseleni Nature Reserve
Off the national road 15 kilometres north east of Empangeni is the 293-hectare Enseleni Nature Reserve on the banks of the Enseleni River, a sanctuary with a nature trail through mangroves, papyrus and ferns, alive with water birds and the home of several species of antelope.

Richards Bay
Used for the landing of stores and troops during the Zulu War of 1879, Richards Bay was named to honour a great British sailor, Sir Frederick William Richards, who was in command of the Cape and West African Station of the Royal Navy at the time, and later became Admiral of the Fleet. The presence of his naval brigade in Natal largely averted the danger of an invasion by the Zulus after their victory at Isandhlwana.

This great natural bay has always been a favourite resort of fishermen and nature lovers – the 3 000-hectare lagoon of the Mhlatuze River having been populated with game fish, sharks, hippos, crocodiles and a great variety of aquatic birds. It is believed that Huberta, the famous hippo, started her long walk to the Keiskamma River in the Eastern Cape, from here. The largest recorded crocodile to be found in South Africa (6,7 metres long) was shot in the lagoon by John Dunn in 1891.

With the opening of the harbour in 1976 and the construction of the largest coal terminal in the world, the scene at Richards Bay has changed. A specially-built electric railway links with the Transvaal coalfields and an oil pipeline is connected with the Witwatersrand. Other huge enterprises are Alusaf, the aluminium smelters, Tisand, where (17 kilometres inland from the port) titania slag, low manganese, pig iron, zircon and rutile are mined from the sand, and the R600-million pulp mill of Mondi (Anglo American).

Only a portion of the Richards Bay Game Reserve remains and is not accessible to the public. Bait is still obtainable from the Natal Parks Board office there. There are two good hotels overlooking the bay, and a municipal caravan park.

Richards Bay has a population of 22 000 and most of the work force commute with the nearby KwaZulu towns, Ezikhaweni and Nseleni where the combined population is some 100 000.

Kwambonambi
National road N2 passes the gum plantations of Kwambonambi, the place of Bonambi, a tribe famous as blacksmiths. Other tribesmen shunned the place because it was known that the smiths used human fat to temper their blades. It was Ngonyama, 'the lion', a highly respected Bonambi smith, to whom Shaka went to have his short stabbing spear forged.

Today Kwambonambi is notable for its saw mills.

Mtubatuba
Across the fine bridge that spans the Umfolozi River is the turnoff eastwards to Mtubatuba which was named after a tribal chief who, at birth, had to be kneaded from his mother's womb ('ukutuba' to knead). Mtubatuba is a busy trading centre and there are two hotels in the village.

St Lucia Lake
St Lucia Estuary lies 29 kilometres east of Mtubatuba and stretched out north of the estuary in a most irregular shape is St Lucia Lake; covering a surface of 36 000 hectares, it is 40 kilometres long and on average 10 kilometres wide. Two cliffs are formed on the western shores of the northern reach and between the cliff is Hell's Gate, a treacherous passage of water that opens out into False Bay, 26 kilometres long and 3

kilometres across. The average depth of the whole water system is less than 2 metres. The reed-covered Bird Island and Lane Island are in the northern reach and Fanies Island, midway, separates the southern reach. The system is fed by the sea and the six rivers flowing into the lake.

The 36 000 hectares of water surface is a proclaimed game reserve and so are the surroundings covering some 14 000 hectares that make up St Lucia Park and False Bay Park.

Although the silting up of the Umfolozi River mouth at the lake estuary and evaporation caused by the hot climate has from time to time presented salinity problems (much improved by the floods of 1984) affecting the fish, bird and animal population of St Lucia, this is one of the most magnificent of South Africa's parks. Great shoals of mullet, bream, grunter and salmon inhabit the waters of the lake and are followed by sharks and big game fish, offering the best angling opportunities imaginable. Numbers of crocodiles have their haunts here, especially at the mouths of the various rivers, and hippos in their hundreds wallow in the water and bask on the banks. Huge flocks of flamingoes, pelicans, ibis, herons and duck provide splendid spectacles, and the cry of the fish eagle will forever be remembered. On the shores are a wide variety of antelope with bushbuck, nyala, impala, reedbuck and duiker the main species.

Mapelane Nature Reserve
Approached along a sandy road, Mapelane is 40 km from the Kwambonambi lighthouse signpost off the N2 and lies at the coast due south of St Lucia Estuary. Rising up to 200 metres directly from the seashore, the Mapelane Dunes are the highest forested dunes in the world, and the reserve is certainly the finest example of dune forest in South Africa. Of great scientific interest is the fact that this is the southernmost limit of distribution in Africa for many rare and beautiful trees, birds, reptiles and insects. The proclamation in November 1984 has prevented exploitation of the known deposits of illmenite, zircon and rutile in the area. The Natal Parks Board has a caravan and camping site here and there are furnished log cabins.

Umfolozi Game Reserve
Directly west of Mtubatuba is Umfolozi Game Reserve; 47 000 hectares in extent, it is famed as the sanctuary that protected and revived the very nearly extinct species, the white (square-lipped) rhinoceros. So successful has the conservation exercise been that after retaining the estimated safe capacity of the reserve at approximately 1 000 of the species the surplus is, each year, made available to other game parks and zoological gardens.

Umfolozi Game Reserve occupies an area of undulating wilderness in the great basin enclosed by the White Umfolozi and Black Umfolozi Rivers. Apart from the rhinos there is an interesting animal population of buffalo, giraffe, zebra, wildebeest, kudu, waterbuck, nyala, steenbuck, reedbuck, duiker, bush pig, baboon, cheetah, leopard and hyena. A most incredible story of game conservation surrounds the lions that roamed this far from Moçambique, the first

a black maned male arriving in October 1958.

Famous for its three-day wilderness trails, the reserve is open throughout the year and there is hutted camp accommodation. Only petrol, film and curios are sold in the camp.

Hluhluwe Game Reserve
North-east of Umfolozi, Hluhluwe Game Reserve is the best known of all the Natal reserves. Its 23 000 hectares surround the deep valley of the Hluhluwe River. The Zulu name comes from the monkey ropes that grow in the area. The variation in terrain, from 60 to 600 metres, provides unexpected and thrilling opportunities to see the game animals at close quarters. There are areas of forest, dense bush, open grasslands, secluded stream crossings and a fascinating variety of animals and vast numbers of birds. This is the home of the irritable black rhino as well as the more docile white rhino and there are giraffe, buffalo, zebra, wildebeest, waterbuck, nyala, kudu, impala, bushbuck, steenbuck, duiker, warthog, monkey, baboon, leopard, cheetah, hyena and crocodile. Occasionally lion are to be seen.

Hluhluwe is open throughout the year and there is hutted accommodation. Only petrol, film and curios are sold in the camp.

Mkuze Game Reserve
North-west of St Lucia Lake is Mkuze Game Reserve; it takes its name from the Mkuze River which forms the northern and eastern boundaries of the reserve before meandering off southwards to empty itself into the lake. The Zulu name 'Mkuze' refers to a 'a chorus master of singing and dancing'.

Mkuze lies on a tree-covered plain beneath the Ubombo Mountains, a magnificent wild parkland and a sanctuary densely populated with impala, nyala, bushbuck, reedbuck, duiker, steenbuck, wildebeest, zebra, warthog, black and white rhino and birds of numerous species. Cleverly-designed hides provide fine opportunities for seeing and photographing the game at the watering places.

There is a hutted camp in the reserve and a caravan park at the entrance. The reserve is open throughout the year and the approach is from national road N2; the turnoff on the right (east) is well marked, 9 kilometres south of the village of Mkuze.

Mkuze and the Ghost Mountain
The trading village of Mkuze is dominated by the 528-metre peak of the Ubombo range named the Ghost Mountain from legendary tales of the local tribespeople. Here the Ghost Mountain Inn, offering traditional hospitality, is a popular stop-over.

Malachite Camp
This 2 400-hectare game reserve, owned by Michael Rattray, opened to the public in August 1987, and is hidden in the Zululand bush beneath the Ghost Mountain, 8 kms south-east of Mkuze village.

To stay in this intimate camp in the wilds for a few nights is a delectable experience. In the four thatched double bungalows (each with bathroom en suite) every comfort-care has been taken. In fine weather, breakfast and lunch is served in the delightful outdoors, and dinner takes place beneath the stars in the reed-walled boma where an atmosphere of no rush prevails.

Game viewing is well arranged – the importance of good ranger-to-guest relationship is there, and the use of an open landrover to deliver you close to the white rhinoceros, giraffe, zebra or antelope, is always exciting. Bird-fanciers will be in their element with close to 400 species and a trained tracker to guide you through the bush on foot.

Anglers will delight in the opportunity to use the Camp's boat at the Jozini Dam, a 20-minute drive away.

Sordwana Bay National Park
A few kilometres north of Mkuze there is a turnoff east to Ubombo, and from this magisterial village a road leads for 90 km to the coastal strip, proclaimed in 1950 the Sordwana Bay National Park. Little more than 400 hectares in extent, the area of forest-clad sand dunes is inhabited by small game species and a great variety of birds, including the Zulu batis and Rudd's apalis, and is a popular winter camping site of fishermen and those who love the wilds. During the summer it is intensely hot and humid. Anti-malarial precautions should be taken. Petrol, provisions, including perishables and ice are available at the camp.

Jozini and J.G. Strijdom Dam
From the village of Ubombo a road leads for 23 kilometres up the mountainside to Jozini (named after a tribal headman) and the J.G. Strijdom Dam (named after the South African Prime Minister of 1954) in the Pongola Poort – one of the largest irrigation dams in the country. The village of Jozini, with its Jozini Ho-Motel, overlooks the dam which impounds the waters on the Pongola River. Legend has it that the river was so named, meaning 'like a trough', by the migrating Nguni tribe when they found it to be so long and so deep with very few crossing places. Good angling is to be had.

Ndumu Game Reserve
The Great Usutu River forms the northern boundary of the Ndumu Game Reserve and the frontier between South Africa and Moçambique. The reserve lies in the northern precinct of Maputaland. It covers an area of 10 000 hectares and contains a primeval forest in a riverine setting of infinite beauty. Within this superb sanctuary, although sometimes difficult to see in the denseness of the indigenous vegetation, there is a wild animal population in great numbers of nyala, bushbuck, impala, reedbuck, suni (Livingstone antelope) and bush pig. Black and white rhino have been reintroduced.

In the numerous lakelets or pans fed by the overflow of the Pongola and Usutu Rivers, there is birdlife such as cannot be equalled anywhere in South Africa. Notable examples of the 390 recorded species are the aquatic birds: black heron, dwarf goose, bat hawk, fish eagle, crested guineafowl, water dikkop, jacanas, fishing owl, white-eared barbet, broadbill and nicator. The reserve is the southern limit of the range of many tropical East African birds.

A particular feature of Ndumu is its large crocodile population. In the crocodile breeding station, after the eggs are hatched, the young are protected for three years before being released into the waters. In the rivers and pans there are also some 400 hippos.

Of the prodigious number of trees which flourish in the area the wild fig, marula, sycamore and fever trees are of the most majestic specimens to be seen anywhere.

There is a hutted camp in the reserve but there are no caravanning or camping facilities. Confirmed bookings are essential. Anti-malarial precautions should be taken.

The reserve is open throughout the year but is excessively hot and humid in the summer months. The route to Ndumu is through Jozini, from where there are two roads for part of the way. The high road along the side of the Ubombo Mountains (called Lebombo in Swaziland) reveals outstanding views of the Pongola Valley but local advice regarding the route to take should be sought at Jozini. After 50 km from Jozini along the high road, a junction is reached. The turn left (westwards) leads to the magisterial village of Ingwavuma from where there is access (following the course of the Ingwavuma River) over the spectacular Cecil Macks Pass into Swaziland. The districts of Ubombo and Ingwavuma form part of what is today known as Maputaland (previously Tongaland).

Kosi Bay Nature Reserve (KwaZulu)
At the coast east of Ndumu, Kosi Bay Nature Reserve consists of 20 hectares contiguous to the Kosi Bay lake system. The largest of the chain of these magnificent lakes is Lake Hlangwe, eight kilometres by five kilometres and forty-five metres deep. The wealth of interesting marine life can be seen in the crystal clear water. The area abounds with gulls, terns, waders, and a variety of other aquatic species. One of the duties of the game ranger at Kosi Bay is the conservation of the loggerhead and leatherback turtles which nest on the beaches. The leatherback, the world's largest marine turtle, has a mass of 500 kilograms and is 2 metres long.

It is not advisable to attempt a visit to Kosi Bay unless a four-wheel drive vehicle is used. There are several tracks to the park including one from Ndumu. The accommodation at Kosi Bay is restricted to camping sites with simple facilities. Visitors must take all necessary equipment and food. Depending upon the route used, petrol must be taken at either Ubombo or Jozini.

From 1984 administration of Kosi Bay Nature Reserve is controlled by the KwaZulu homeland government.

Pongola
In the narrow wedge of Transvaal territory that separates Natal from Swaziland is the small town of Pongola; it lies on route N29 to Piet Retief (described in Chapter 12) and is the centre of the extensive sugar-cane and subtropical fruit plantations irrigated by the Pongola Government Water Scheme, of which the J.G. Strijdom Dam is the focal point. The Pongola Hotel has a good table and is a comfortable stop.

1

2

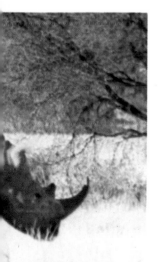

Two species common to Zululand game reserves:
1. The square lipped or so-called white rhinoceros is the second largest land mammal and has a mass of up to 5 tons.
2. The giraffe goes through a series of jerky movements to get into this incongruous position to enable it to drink but is able to return to its normal posture very quickly if suddenly alarmed.

3. A little gem among the privately owned game reserves is Malachite Camp hidden in the undulating knobthorn wilderness of northern Zululand, a short distance from Mkuze. If you are looking to be spoilt in an unspoilt camp, this is for you. Malachite is owned and directed by Michael Rattray.

The Inland Region, Kings' Kraals and Battlefields of Zululand, and Northern Natal

Bulawayo Kraal and Coward's Bush

On the secondary road between Eshowe and Empangeni, where Zulu tribal huts and red aloes mingle on the hills overlooking the splendid valley of the Mhlatuze River, 27 kilometres from Eshowe on the lefthand side of the road, a monument marks the area of Shaka's principal kraal, which he called KwaBulawayo (place of the persecuted). In naming this kraal, Shaka was apparently referring to the treatment meted out to him by his father, Senzangakhona. In about 1826 one of Shaka's generals, Mzilikazi, broke away from the king, formed his own tribe, the Matabele (the refugees) and established his own Bulawayo kraal which is the city in Zimbabwe today.

Approximately two kilometres beyond the site of the Bulawayo kraal there is a prominent kei-apple tree known as Coward's Bush, where Shaka tested those accused of cowardice in battle, and put to death those who flinched.

Route R68 Eshowe to Melmoth

This scenic route provides today's motorist with dual enjoyment – the luxury of a fine highway and the superb example of Zulu tribespeople country. In the surrounds of a great valley the road descends to the floor of the Mhlatuze River before passing the railhead at Nkwalini. From the northern side of the river there are breathtaking views of the Zululand hills (once the hunting grounds of the Zulu kings), as the road makes its ascent to reach the summit outside the town of Melmoth.

Melmoth

When it was founded in 1887 Melmoth was named after the British Resident and First Magistrate of Zululand, Sir Melmoth Osborn. It is a magisterial seat and the centre of a district notable for cattle and wattle. Natal Tanning Extract Company has a factory there.

Some 5 kilometres outside Melmoth the main highway to the north divides, the left fork to the north-west, R68, continues to Babanango and Nqutu, whilst the right fork, after proceeding some 25 kilometres divides once again, the left fork here is R34 to Vryheid and the right fork, R66, continues to Ulundi and Mahlabatini.

Ulundi and Mahlabatini

Mahlabatini (the white sands) is a trading and magisterial centre close to Ulundi or Ondini (the heights), once the great capital kraal of Cetshwayo, the Zulu king. The kraal was built in the great bowl formed by the White Umfolozi, known as the Mahlabatini Basin, which is overlooked by the heights.

A few kilometres from the kraal, on 4 July 1879, the advancing 5 000-strong British force commanded by Lord Chelmsford was attacked by Cetshwayo's 20 000 warriors. The British formed the traditional battle square, the spear proved to be no match for the gun-fire and when the attackers broke in disorder they were set upon by the 17th Lancers. Some 1 500 Zulus were killed and the British loss was 15 killed. The great Ulundi Kraal was burnt to the ground by the British, marking the end to the Zulu War and the power of the Zulus as a nation.

Built in 1873 when Cetshwayo became king, the royal kraal covered about 60 hectares on the bank of the White Umfolozi; Cetshwayo's personal hut was 9 metres in diameter. Fireplaces and hut floors (baked hard by the fire) may still be seen. The areas of the kraal and the battlefield are national monuments. Four whitewashed stone cairns mark the position of the British square and there is a small cemetery where 15 of the British force were buried. A monument in honour of the dead on both sides was erected at the site and unveiled in June 1943. Three kilometres from the memorial are the administrative buildings of the capital of the KwaZulu government, transferred there from Nongoma in 1976. Nearby is the two-star Holiday Inn.

Nodwengu

Mpande's Kraal Nodwengu (turmoil), situated about a kilometre north of the Ulundi battlefield, was, according to custom, destroyed before Cetshwayo, Mpande's son and successor, laid out his new kraal at Ulundi. Only the grave, surrounded by trees, remained on the site which was proclaimed a national monument. Mpande (Panda) was the youngest of the three sons of Senzangakhona who occupied the Zulu throne; his illustrious brothers were Shaka and Dingaan (Dingane). The kraal was built in 1845 and covered 40 hectares.

Nongoma

Continuing north from Mahlabatini, after 50 km, route R66 reaches Nongoma at the crossroads of R66 and R618 from Mtubatuba.

Strategically important, Nongoma (the diviner or wizard) was the scene of bitter fighting between the rival chieftains, Dinizulu and Usibebu in 1888, ending in the withdrawal of the British military escort and the burning down of the village of Nongoma by Dinizulu's impi. Dinizulu eventually surrendered to the authorities in Pietermaritzburg when he and his accomplices were tried, found guilty of high treason and sent to serve long sentences on St Helena Island.

Nongoma is today the residence of the South African Government Commissioner General of KwaZulu. In the district is Mcwayizeni, Zulu Royal Kraal of the Paramount Chief, Bekuzulu College for the sons of chiefs and headmen, Nhlopenkulu Methodist Missionary Institute, the Benedictine Mission Hospital and St Alban's Convent.

Route R68 Melmoth to Babanango and Nqutu

Returning to Melmoth to take the R68 to the north-west, approximately 19 kilometres from the town there is a turnoff left which leads along a gravel road to Nkandla.

Nkandla

Translated Nkandla is 'mountain of fatigue', and here a dense natural forest is to be found on the sides of a precipitous cliff. Here in the deep gorge of the Mome stream Cetshwayo was buried in April 1884. The Nkandla Forest was the scene of the end of the Bambatha Rebellion when the petty chief Bambatha and 500 of his followers were killed in the bitter fight of June 1906.

Babanango
Surrounded by wattle trees, Babanango lies at the foot of the mountain feature that gave the trading and magisterial centre its name. the translation from the Zulu is 'father, look there it is'.

Emakosini and Mgungundlovu
East of Babanango lies the valley of the perennial Mkumbane, a tributary of the White Umfolozi. This valley, much revered by the Zulu people, is known to them as Emakosini (the graveyard of the kings). Here most of the early rulers are buried, and in 1829 Dingaan built his royal kraal and capital on the ridge overlooking the sacred valley. He had successfully completed his secret plot to assassinate his half-brother, Shaka, and ever mindful of the spiritual attachments of Shaka's royal kraal, he left the scene of his gruesome crime to start afresh in the valley of the old kings.

Dingaan called his kraal Mgungundlovu (the secret conclave of the elephant) referring to the conspiracy against Shaka. Here the many rows of round huts, in two concentric hedges, formed the oval kraal encompassing an area of 60 hectares. Up to 200 000 warriors occupied the 2 000 huts. At the upper end stood the king's *isigodlo* (personal quarters). Specially guarded, these quarters included his own hut and those of his mother and his many wives and servants. Anyone attempting to enter the women's quarters was put to death. Other important appendages of the capital were the royal slaughter kraal and the washing kraal.

This was where Dingaan received Piet Retief in November 1837 and again in February 1838. Before being brutally murdered, Retief, describing Dingaan's private hut, wrote: 'the mud floor shone like a mirror, the interior being supported by twenty-four pillars entirely covered in beads.'

After the Battle of Blood River, Andries Pretorius reached Dingaan's Mgungundlovu kraal on 20 December 1838 to find that it had been razed to the ground by fire and abandoned. Pretorius found the remains of Retief and his party and had them buried in a common grave. Among the remains Retief's leather knapsak (containing the treaty) and a water-bottle were found. The grave is in the valley about a kilometre from the kraal. In 1922 a memorial above the grave was unveiled.

Dingaan's Kraal area and the Piet Retief grave are national monuments, and the Monuments Commission has placed a bronze replica of the treaty between Retief and Dingaan at the spot where it was signed on that fateful day, 6 February 1838. Bronze plaques have also been placed on the graves of the Zulu kings: Zulu (the founder of the nation whose name translated means 'heaven'), Ndaba, Phunga, Jama, Nkosinkulu, Mageba and Senzangakhona. There is also a plaque at Emtonjaneni (the place of the little fountain), the source of the Mfule River

where Dingaan had his drinking water drawn.

Of interest to visitors to Rorke's Drift is the Zulu Arts Centre, where pottery, drawings and woven carpets (all products of fine quality) are on sale.

Nqutu
The magisterial and trading village of Nqutu lies in a part of Zululand where the landscape is scarred by the dongas of soil erosion. It is close to the Buffalo River (often dried up) in an area of three historic battles.

Isandhlwana
The battlefield of Isandhlwana is reached by taking the branch road to the south-west, 14 kilometres south of Nqutu.

On 20 January 1879 the advancing British columns under Lord Chelmsford made camp here on a hill. On 22 January when the commander was away carrying out a reconnaissance, a 20 000-strong Zulu impi, commanded by Nthsingwayo Ka Mahole Khoza, surrounded the British camp. Making use of the cover afforded by the deep gashes into the red earth of the soil erosion, the practised warriors crept up onto the hill to completely surprise the unsuspecting British who believed the position they held commanded every attack.

The British force under Colonel A.W. Durnford was annihilated; killed were 52 officers (including Colonel Durnford), 806 men and 471 black helpers. Isandhlwana translated is 'second stomach of a cow' and apparently the shape of the hill resembles this organ.

Today whitewashed boulders mark the position of units engaged in the battle. At a point higher up the hill in the small museum overlooking the battlefield there are maps and a relief model of the scene. Shields used by the different Zulu regiments and the badges and uniforms of the British units involved complete the display.

Rorke's Drift
Rorke's Drift is 16 kilometres due west of Isandhlwana and can be reached by road directly from Nqutu or from the main Dundee – Vryheid road.

The buildings of James Rorke's trading store at the Buffalo River fording place had been taken over by the Swedish Mission. The drift formed part of the strategy of Chelmsford's invasion of Zululand. Encamped here close to the mission, using the church as a storeroom and the parsonage as a hospital, was a small British garrison of some 130 men of the 24th Regiment under Lieutenant Bromhead and a detachment of the Natal Native Contingent under Lieutenant Chard of the Royal Engineers.

After 3 o'clock on the afternoon of 22 January 1879 a carbineer galloped in with the news of Isandhlwana, riding on immediately to Helpmekaar. Meanwhile two Zulu regiments, some 4 000 strong, under command of Dabulamanzi, disengaged from the victory of Isandhlwana to pursue fugitives and were accidentally led to Rorke's Drift. Eleven Victoria Crosses were awarded to gallant defenders of Rorke's Drift and the entire garrison is remembered for its heroic stand that day and night. They were attacked continuously that afternoon and by the light of the

1. Dancing participants of the May Festival in Richards Bay
Nature Reserve.
2. Roadside market near the Tugela Ferry.

3. and 4. The married woman in Zululand is a person of
standing. Until betrothed, girls wear a brief kilt and their hair
is braided. After marriage a woman wears a long full skirt, a
draped shawl and many beads and anklets. Her hair is built
up into an elaborate 'isocolo' and these differ between the
different districts. Bead patterns also signify the area from
which the wearer comes.

Natal Spa, the renowned all-year-round holiday resort with its health beneficial mineral water pools and many other recreational facilities, lies between Vryheid and Paulpietersburg.

burning hospital throughout the night until finally Dabulamanzi withdrew his regiments and the battle was over. The Zulu casualties numbered 400 dead; the British lost 15 men and each of the survivors was wounded to some degree.

Blood River
Between Dundee and Vryheid, 26 kilometres from Dundee and 47 kilometres from Vryheid, there is a turnoff leading east for 21 kilometres to the Blood River battlefield. In the tranquil rural scene as it presents itself today, with the river crossing a flat meadowland, there is only a memorial, a replica of the trekker wagon, to identify the site of the bloodiest battle ever fought in South Africa.

On 7 December 1838 Andries Pretorius with his 465-stong commando set out on the long overdue punitive expedition against Dingaan to avenge the murder of Piet Retief and his followers. With Pretorius was Sarel Cilliers (a deeply religious man and diarist) who worded the vow in their prayer to the Almighty that should victory be granted, the day of such victory would henceforth be kept sacred.

The afternoon of 15 December 1838 saw the commando making camp here on the bank of the river, using the river, which ran deep for 1 400 metres, as their front (east), and a steep, wide donga, which joined with the river and could not be scaled, as the protection on the left flank. A tight laager was drawn up on this triangular peninsula; ladders joined one wagon to another; wheels were covered with rigidly stretched oxhide and horses remained saddled up. At dawn on the morning of the 16th the sentries gave the alarm. The Zulu impi, 10 000 strong, under command of Ndlela, coming up from the east, had found the camp.

In his story of the battle Sarel Cilliers tells us that in a period of two hours, the warriors, with great courage, made four separate frontal attacks in an attempt to storm the laager and that the impi would not respond to their commander who wished them to attack for the fifth time. When the attack ceased the trekkers jumped to their horses to pursue the warriors, now broken in disorder. Three thousand Zulu corpses choked the river and the donga and the beautiful little watercourse was henceforth to be called Blood River. Four of the commando, including Pretorius himself, were wounded but there was no loss of life on their side. And so it is in South Africa that we celebrate 16 December as the Day of the Vow.

Vryheid
It could be said that Vryheid had a glamorous start. It was founded as the capital of the New Republic, a territory that included part of northern Natal and a great slice of Zululand, with a Zulu prince as its vassal king.

After the defeat of Cetshwayo in 1879, the British plan of dividing Zululand into thirteen little kingdoms did not succeed. In fact chaos set in and the British tried to restore order by reinstating Cetshwayo, but the king's turbulent opponents would have none of it and he died of fatty disease of the heart in February 1884.

At this time some 800 men who farmed in and near Zululand (Boer republicans and British colonists) under Lucas Meyer, set out to restore order for themselves. They secured the person of Dinizulu (Cetshwayo's son and rightful heir) and crowned him king of the New Republic in exchange for half of Zululand. Of course this started an international scene involving Britain's immediate annexation of St Lucia (which territory the New Republicans were about to sell to Germany). This in turn involved Pretoria, Berlin and Paris, with Bismarck eventually renouncing his claim to St Lucia in exchange for concessions in the Cameroons. Dinizulu's tie to the New Republic soon came to an end when he became involved with the British and was exiled to St Helena. Although shorn of its seaboard and its rule over all Zululand, the Vryheid government was recognised by Britain in 1886.

The end of the New Republic was not as colourful as its start. Lucas Meyer, fearing defeat in the coming elections, had his country incorporated with the Transvaal Republic on 9 September 1888. This incorporation lasted only twelve years; at the end of the Anglo-Boer War, Vryheid, with Utrecht and part of Wakkerstroom, was annexed to Natal.

Vryheid has a population of 18 000 and became a municipality in 1912. It lies in a broad valley at the foot of the Zungwini Mountain (1 713 metres). There are a number of coal mines around the town including some of high grade anthracite. Wattle, maize, beef and dairy products otherwise contribute to the prosperity of the town. There are two hotels, including the two-star Silwater Motel on the road to Dundee, and a municipal caravan park. Vryheid's national monuments are the Dutch Reformed Church, the Old Town Hall and the historical police station in Landdrost Street.

Hlobane
Some 27 kilometres east of Vryheid is the flat-topped mountain and village, Hlobane (the beautiful place), in an area rich in coal deposits. Two deeds of heroism in South African history took place in this vicinity. On 11 April 1838 the 14-year-old Dirk Uys, seeing his wounded father surrounded by chanting warriors, went back alone and from his father's body shot and killed three Zulus before he too was killed. And this was where General Redvers Buller won the V.C. in the Zulu War of 1879.

Paulpietersburg
The small town of Paulpietersburg, 48 kilometres north of Vryheid, was named after President Paul Kruger and Commandant-General Pieter Joubert.

Natal Spa
Between Vryheid and Paulpietersburg, the Natal Spa makes the ideal holiday resort, particularly for those wishing to take the waters. These hot springs contain what is known as *triple water* with notable presence of chlorides, sulphates and carbonates. The water temperatures in the seven pools vary from 44°C to cold, providing ideal conditions for year-round swimming. The two-star hotel with its tennis courts, squash courts, bowling green and riding horses is set in a spacious garden overlooking the mineral baths.

CHAPTER 10

Pietermaritzburg, Natal Midlands, Natal Coalfields and Drakensberg Resorts

Pietermaritzburg

Capital city of the Province of Natal, Pietermaritzburg is surrounded by green hills and lies in a beautiful bowl, 677 metres above sea level, 80 kilometres inland from the port of Durban.

In October 1838 the Volksraad (people's council) of the Voortrekkers selected this site in the valley of the Umzinduzi River for the capital of their Natalia Republic and for the next two years they continued to live in the area under temporary laager conditions. Committed to avenge the murder of Piet Retief and his party and the massacre at Bloukrans which took place in February 1838, their commando under Commandant-General Andries Pretorius, before setting off on the punitive war, made a vow to the Almighty proclaiming that if victory be granted, that day would henceforth be observed for thanksgiving as of the sabbath, and a church would be erected in honour of God. Notwithstanding Pretorius's resounding victory at the Battle of Blood River on 16 December 1838, the Church of the Vow was not completed until 1840 when the Volksraad appointed the Reverend Daniel Lindley of the American Board of Missions the first minister, and he took up office in January 1841. It was also in 1840 that a hall was built on the site of the present City Hall, where from then on the quarterly assembly of the Volksraad took place. The Voortrekkers named their new capital in honour of their two hero leaders, Pieter Retief and Gert Maritz who had died of natural causes a year after Retief was murdered.

With the collapse of the Natalia Republic, in 1843 the British garrison constructed and occupied the small stronghold, Fort Napier, on an elevated position overlooking the town and in 1845 Martin West was installed as the first Lieutenant-Governor of the sub-colony of Natal. On 23 November 1853 the District of Natal was created a Diocese of the Church of England with the controversial John Colenso the first bishop. So it was that Pietermaritzburg became a cathedral city before it received borough status, which came on 15 May 1854.

Bishop Colenso, who had gained the friendship of the Zulus, caused an uproar by refusing to compel polygamous Zulus to divorce their surplus wives. When confronted with difficult questions put to him by his converts he wrote articles challenging the literal truth of the Scriptures. Charged with heresy and excommunicated by his Metropolitan, Bishop Robert Gray, he took the matter to court and finally the British Privy Council confirmed him in his office as bishop. Colenso wrote the first Zulu grammar, dictionary and reading books. His tomb is in front of the altar of St Peter's Church in Church Street, which was originally his cathedral. The colours of the famous local regiment, *The Natal Carbineers*, are deposited in St Peter's for safe keeping. In recent times the Cathedral of the Holy Nativity (on a site at the rear of St Peter's) has been consecrated.

In 1856 Natal was created a separate colony by Royal Charter and on 23 March the following year the first Legislative Council of the colony sat in Pietermaritzburg. With the movement towards Natal gaining responsible government, the building of a suitable council chamber received attention and to commemorate Queen Victoria's jubilee on 21 June 1887 the foundation stone was laid by the governor, Sir A.E. Havelock, at the site in Longmarket Street. Responsible government was achieved in 1893 with a constitution providing for a parliament comprising the upper house, a Legislative Council of eleven nominated members, and a lower house, the Legislative Assembly of 37 elected members. The latter body took occupation of the council chamber started in 1887 and this became known as the Legislative Assembly Building. Continuation of adjacent work to provide a chamber for the Legislative Council (or Senate) resulted in the laying of the foundation stone for that building by the governor, Sir Walter Hely-Hutchinson on 12 September 1898, and it was completed in 1900. Since the Act of Union in 1910, the Assembly Chamber has been in continuous use as the council chamber of the Natal Provincial Administration and the Legislative Chamber is used during cession as offices for members. These buildings symbolise the constitutional development of Natal and provide magnificent architectural examples of public buildings of the era in which they were built.

The old transport riders were fast disappearing when the railway line from Durban reached Pietermaritzburg in 1880. By 1891 it was commissioned as far as Charlestown on the Natal border with Transvaal and was completed to Johannesburg in 1895.

Disaster struck Pietermaritzburg in 1898 when the City Hall was destroyed by fire. During his visit to the city in 1901 the Duke of York (later crowned George V) opened the rebuilt City Hall in its grand Renaissance style, much favoured in Edwardian times. An integral part of the character and charm of Maritzburg (as it is often called) are the bright red bricks used in the construction of its old buildings and the many lanes which link the principal streets. Fine examples of architectural usage of the local brick are to be seen in the City Hall and the old Supreme Court (1871) in the garden across Commercial Road from the City Hall. No longer in use as a court the building now houses art exhibitions.

Among the fine statues and memorials in the Court Garden are the monuments to the fallen of four wars: the Zulu War of 1879, the Anglo-Boer War, World Wars I and II and a handsome marble statue of Sir Theophilus Shepstone who retired to the city after an illustrious civic career. He was venerated by the Zulus who called him 'Somtseu' (the mighty hunter). In the adjacent Carbineers Garden are the Langalibalele Rebellion Monument and the Sherwood Foresters Monument.

The market used to be behind the City Hall, between Longmarket and Church Streets. When it was moved to the complex at Mkondeni (to the south-east of the city) in 1972 the open area was

1. The marble statue of Sir
Theophilus Shepstone and the
Pietermaritzburg City Hall with
its distinctive red brick and
elaborate ornamentation.

2. In Longmarket Street,
Pietermaritzburg, are the stately
buildings of the old Natal
government Legislative
Assembly and Legislative
Council.

3. Natalia, Natal Provincial
Administration headquarters, as
seen from Churchill Square,
Pietermaritzburg.

4. Another fine example of the
use of red brick with cement
ornamentation is in these
buildings of Maritzburg College,
one of Natal's famous schools,
which dates from 1863.

1

2

3

4

turned into a car-park and renamed Churchill Square to honour the memory of the British Prime Minister.

Rich in their associations of the past, Pietermaritzburg's old churches reveal much of the glorious story. St George's Garrison Church in Fort Napier contains relics of the old colonial days and the years that followed. There are memorials to the famous British regiments stationed there and the Roberts' Window, in memory of Captain the Honourable F. Roberts, V.C., who was killed at Colenso in the Anglo-Boer War. He was the only son of General Roberts who later commanded the British Forces, himself awarded the V.C. in India in 1858. In the adjoining military cemetery there are tombstones of many soldiers of the imperial regiments. The old Presbyterian Church, built in 1852, is in Church Street, close to the Memorial Arch of the Court Gardens. St Mary's Church, which Bishop Colenso had built in 1856 for his black congregation, had to make way for parliament buildings in Longmarket Street and was demolished and rebuilt stone by stone on its present site on the corner of Commercial Road and Burger Street. The Italian Prisoner of War Church, Old Main Road, in the suburb of Epworth, was built by the prisoners during the Second World War from stone available in the area. Most of the churches mentioned are national monuments.

Pietermaritzburg has a number of other national monuments worth visiting and these include: The Voortrekker Museum in Church Street at the east end of Churchill Square. This was the original Church of the Vow dating from 1840 and renovated and opened as a museum in 1912. Its gables, tiled roof and windows are not authentic. Among the many interesting relics to be seen in the museum are an original Voortrekker ox-wagon built in 1824 and used in the Great Trek, a chair carved from the trunk of an ironwood tree and used by Dingaan and the pulpit of the Church of the Vow (itself a national monument), in use in the church for 20 years from 1841. The City Hall on the corner of Commercial Road and Church Street is the largest structural brick building in the southern hemisphere and contains some beautiful stained-glass windows and magnificent pressed ceilings. The 47-metre-high clock tower has a Westminster chiming clock and a carillon of 12 bells. Tatham Art Gallery on the second floor was established with the assistance of Mrs F.S. Tatham in 1903 and contains a small but outstanding collection of French and English paintings, oriental rugs, Chinese, Delft, Dresden and Sèvres porcelain and other objets d'art. The pièce de résistance is the gilded ormolu clock of over 150 years, a replica of one in Buckingham Palace – the moving bell-ringers appearing every half-hour. Macrorie House, on the corner of Loop and Pine Streets was the nineteenth century home of William Macrorie, the Anglican Bishop who was in rivalry with Bishop Colenso during the period when the Anglican Church in South Africa was split on doctrinal matters. The house contains a small museum and chapel. What is known to Pietermaritzburg people as 'the oldest house in town' No. 333 Boom Street is the only remaining homestead of the Voortrekkers; it was built for Petrus Pretorius in 1846 and today is part of the Voortrekker Museum. The charming Publicity House in Commercial Road near the corner of Longmarket Street was built in 1884 as the Borough Police Station. From here there is a free information service, telephone 51348.

The list of historical monuments in Pietermaritzburg is quite extensive and those which generally can be viewed from the street but also visited by appointment are: the Legislative Assembly and Legislative Council buildings in Longmarket Street opposite the General Post Office; Old Government House, the residence of British Governors, now in use as 'part of the Natal Teachers' Training College, where the campus is bounded by Church, Pine and Longmarket Streets at the west end of the city; Clark House and Victoria Hall, Maritzburg College, fine examples of Natal Colonial architecture of the Victorian era; and the acacia tree in the beautiful grounds of Parkside, the Administrator's residence in Topham Road – a magnificent example of the flat-topped species, Acacia woodii – where the members of the Natalia Republic Volksraad met on 15 July 1842 and decided to accept British rule.

Natal's first newspaper, The Natal Witness, first appeared on 27 February 1846. Its editor, David Buchanan, after being imprisoned for contempt of court, continued to write his editorials from the gaol and the address of 'Pietermaritzburg gaol' appeared on a number of early issues of the paper.

The Natal Society was founded in 1851 to provide for the literary and scientific needs of the community. In 1903 the library was separated from the collection of natural history specimens and the Natal government constructed a building for the museum section in Loop Street. This graceful building which today forms part of the Natal Museum, was opened in 1904. The Natal Museum is one of the five national museums of South Africa and is a true general museum. A large modern extension added in 1969 contains a well-equipped lecture theatre and large mammal, marine and cultural history halls as well as a library and offices. The Natal Society Library is now housed in the magnificent modern building on Churchill Square facing Church Street.

Adjacent to the Natal Museum there is another fine old building constructed in 1903 as offices for the Natal Government Railways. It is now the main office of the South African Police. Across the street is the Imperial Hotel. The brass plaque fixed to the old hitching post in front of the hotel commemorates the visits of Louis Napoleon, Prince Imperial of France, who was later killed in an ambush during the Zulu War of 1879.

On the first floor of Harwin's Arcade, Timber Street, the Natal Flyfishers' Club has created a flyfishing museum, the first of its kind in southern Africa, it was opened in June 1983.

Another unusual exhibition is the Chocolate Museum at the Nestlé factory in Victoria Road where a display of beautiful chocolate sculptures can be seen. It is necessary to telephone 2-8731 for an appointment to visit this museum.

Maritzburg's real glory is its gardens and here nature and the citizens have combined to provide generously. Lying to the south of the city astride the

Umzinduzi River, covering an area of 65 hectares, is Alexandra Park, named after the British Queen. The park is notable for a number of features and among these are the lovely roses of the Mayor's Garden, a fine rock garden spread over a wide area, the part riverine setting, a tree-enclosed cricket oval, athletic and cycle track and a lovely swimming pool. Adjoining is Kershaw Park with its public tennis courts.

Wyllie Park, in the suburb of Wembly, covers 8 hectares and was presented to the city by Mrs G.H. Wyllie; it is noted for the number and variety of its azaleas, in full bloom from August.

The Botanic Gardens, three kilometres from the city centre, are highly rated in the botanical world and contain some magnificent trees and shrubs. The azalea collection and the famous avenue of plane trees are particularly noteworthy. The gardens were founded by the Botanic Society in 1872, the site of 41 hectares was donated by the City in 1874 and a pathway (named Mayor's Walk) from town to the garden site was constructed in 1876. The macadamised road to the gardens remains Mayor's Walk today.

The Natal Parks Board has its headquarters in the splendid 105-hectare nature reserve, Queen Elizabeth Park, eight kilometres from the city centre on national road N3 to Johannesburg. It is possible to make a circular drive in this beautifully situated reserve.

Opposite Queen Elizabeth Park is the turnoff to the rocky eminence, World's View, 1 080 metres above sea level, a favourite picnic place near the route the Voortrekkers took over the Swartkop range. The old wagon track, a national monument, is clearly visible.

Below Queen Elizabeth Park is the golf course of the Maritzburg Country Club, in a superb setting. The city has another golf club at Hayfields and there are other recreational clubs such as Wanderers with a clubhouse close to the famous Woodburn Rugby Grounds. Four bowling clubs welcome visiting bowlers and Jan Smuts Stadium in Alexandra Park is the venue for cricket and soccer.

Pietermaritzburg Turf Club has had a number of firsts in South Africa in its enterprising approach to racing. It was the first club to introduce the Place Accumulator, the Jackpot and the International Jockey events. The polo grounds are near the Show Grounds of the Royal Agricultural Society of Natal, the senior show-holding society of South Africa. The Show is held annually in June.

Pietermaritzburg serves a rich agricultural district notable for dairy products, stock breeding, general produce and timber. The City's remarkable industrial development over the past two decades has resulted in the doubling of its population during that period. The considerable advance in manufacturing industries can be attributed to the foresight of a progressive City Council providing attractive conditions for industrial investors, coupled with the resources of transportation, power, water, labour and housing and the geographic, climatic and other appealing natural aspects of this beautiful city. Among the international concerns who have plants here are Deutz, Fiat, Vickers, Gilbeys, Scottish Cables,

Beaulieu, Weltexa and Anchor. Pietermaritzburg's suitability for the location of the footwear industry has long been established whilst the other factories covering a broad spectrum include pharmaceutical and veterinary supplies, gear and conveyor equipment, tool and chain manufacture, textiles and synthetic fibres, plywood and chipboard and the assembly of tractors, heavy vehicles and farm implements. In the six industrial estates the growing list of plants number over 200.

Pietermaritzburg has a proud record as an educational centre. The University of Natal has faculties of Law, Arts, Science, Economics, Education and Agriculture and provides facilities for higher research. The spacious campus is in the suburb of Scottsville. The Natal Teachers Training College, Longmarket Street, provides courses for teaching diplomas. The Allerton Institute for Veterinary Research and the Technical Colleges offer diploma courses and some of the best schools in South Africa are among the 16 high schools.

The Imperial, the Camden and the Capital Towers are all hotels of high reputation in the city. The municipal caravan park is on the eastern outskirts of the city.

The population of Pietermaritzburg is in the vicinity of 180 000 and that of its close neighbour, Edendale (a part of KwaZulu, from where the city draws its major work force), over 200 000.

Pietermaritzburg to Transkei border on route R56

South of Pietermaritzburg route R56 leads to Transkei and to the Cape in superb farming country, where the hills and valleys are interlaced with lush grazing meadows, timber, sugar-cane, maize and citrus. The road passes the Roadside Inn at Thornville, a railway junction, and the Baynesfield Dairies at Nelsrust where Joseph Baynes established the first creamery in Natal, in 1899. Baynesfield Estate was bequeathed to the nation and is today a training centre for black farm labourers.

Richmond

In a picturesque rural setting on the banks of the Illovo River is the little town of Richmond. Its first European inhabitants were of the Byrne Settlers of 1850. They came from Beaullieu, the seat of the Duke of Buccleuch in Richmond, and were the founders of many of the leading families in Natal. Originally the settlement was named Beaullieu, but this name fell into disuse because of the difficulty in pronunciation. Richmond is administered by a Town Board, it has a population of 3 500 and is the terminus of the railway from Thornville Junction. The farming district it serves is engaged principally in dairying, stock, timber and sugar-cane. Richmond has a fine country club and three hotels.

Byrne, Hela Hela and Eastwolds

West of Richmond is the settlement of Byrne with its popular Oaks Hotel, and the beautiful scenic drive to Eastwolds through the Umkomaas Valley, beneath the sandstone cliffs of Hela Hela. The area is inhabited by the Bhaca tribespeople who are

1

2

4

3

5

1. 2. and 3. Hilton owes its perpetual greenness to the fact that it lies in the misty rainbelt at the foot of the Drakensberg escarpment. In this lovely environment are the famous Tudor-style three-star Hilton Hotel, St Anne's Diocesan College and Hilton College.

4. and 5. Howick Falls, one of Natal's best known beauty spots, and Midmar Dam, a beautifully developed public resort, are both in the course of the Umgeni River.

renowned for their immaculate costumes of intricate beadwork. In the valley is the 500-hectare Soada Forest Nature Reserve. This is exciting country to explore on foot, the view from the summit of Hela Hela being superb.

Ixopo

In beautiful hilly countryside, Ixopo is overlooked by the southern Drakensberg. It was laid out in 1878 and given the name Stuartstown, after the magistrate Martinus Stuart, but the Zulu *Ixopo* an anomatopoeic term imitating the squelching sound made by cattle plodding through the marsh (in use before Europeans came to the area) was adopted. The village is in an attractive sylvan setting and has two old English-type wayside inns. Alan Paton's novel, *Cry the Beloved Country,* begins in this area. Ixopo is on the narrow-gauge railway line from Umzinto to Underberg and serves a famous dairy farming district.

Roads to interesting places lead off from Ixopo. To the south-east through Highflats, Dumisa and Umzinto, a road joins with national road N2 near Park Rynie and north-west through Creighton, Donnybrook and Bulwer (in each of which there is an hotel) a road leads to Underberg and the Drakensberg resorts. At Donnybrook, St Marc Camembert cheese is produced.

Weza and Ingeli

Ixopo is only 19 kilometres from the Transkei border village, Umzimkulu (Chapter 7). At its southern end the Province of Natal is shaped in the form of a boot, with territory of the Transkei filling in the instep of the boot. From Umzimkulu trunk road R56 crosses this strip of the Transkei filling in the instep of the boot. From Umzimkulu trunk road R56 crosses this strip of the Transkei and touches the toe of the 'Natal boot'. Here are the magnificent forests of Weza and Ingeli (notable for their population of bushbuck) and the convenient Ingeli Forest Motel just off trunk road R56.

Harding

Near the forests, on national road N2 to the coast, is the small town of Harding at the base of the Ingeli Mountain. The town was named in honour of the first Chief Justice of Natal, the Honourable Walter Harding. It was established in 1877 as a military outpost and was of strategic importance during the short Griqua uprising under Smith Pommer a year later. Harding was declared a township in 1911; it has a population of 3 000 and serves important dairy and timber interests. A narrow-gauge railway links Harding with Port Shepstone and the road down to the coast provides an interesting drive, partly through KwaZulu territory.

Pietermaritzburg to the southern Drakensberg resorts

West of the city a road leads out past an industrial area and the large KwaZulu township and hospital at Edendale. It passes the turnoff to Henley Dam, popular for yachting, boating and picnics, and climbs into hilly country, covered with aloes and overlooking

the Zulu tribal area of the Umzinduzi Valley. Further on it passes the farming area of Boston and then skirts the magnificent Umkomaas Valley.

Bulwer

At 82 kilometres from Pietermaritzburg the road enters the trading and magisterial village of Bulwer, founded during the term of office of the Natal governor, Sir Henry Bulwer, and named after him. Close to the Drakensberg, the village lies in beautiful surroundings at an altitude of 1 578 metres. Nestling on the hillside is the holiday hotel Mountain Park.

From Bulwer the road passes through forest-covered hills into the village of Underberg and the spectacular Drakensberg range, described in the last section of this chapter.

Pietermaritzburg to Colenso via Greytown

North-east of Pietermaritzburg route R33 leads to Greytown through undulating country where the landscape is covered with plantations of wattle, gum and pine with occasional breaks of sugar-cane and sisal. On its way the road climbs out of the city revealing fine views of the built-up area enclosed in lush-green hills. The road passes the turnoff to Albert Falls, a lovely cascade in the Umgeni River, and then passes through the village of New Hanover and the turnoff to Dalton where there are timber mills.

Greytown

At 69 kilometres from Pietermaritzburg (five kilometres out of Greytown) there is a turnoff leading for half a kilometre to the stone cairn which marks the birthplace of General Louis Botha. Born here on the farm Honeyfontein on 27 September 1862, he became Commandant-General of the Republican forces in the Transvaal (1900-1902), Prime Minister of the Transvaal (1906-1910) and first Prime Minister of the Union of South Africa (1910-1919). Venerated and treated with great respect both at home and abroad, he attended the Peace Conference at Versailles in 1919, returned to South Africa in failing health and died in Pretoria on 27 August 1919 at the early age of 57.

Greytown is the principal centre of the rich timber-producing area of Umvoti County. It was laid out on the banks of the Umvoti River in the 1850s and named after the very popular Cape governor, Sir George Grey. It became a borough in 1915 and has a population of 14 000.

Being close to the Zululand frontier, Greytown had its excitement in the early days. During the Bambata Rebellion of 1906 the town was the centre of military operations. Bambata, the chieftain ring leader of the rebellion, was eventually shot and killed and Dinizulu (son of Cetshwayo, the king of the Zulus) was found guilty of harbouring rebels and banished for life to Middelburg, Transvaal.

There is an hotel in the town and at Merthley Lake there is boating, trout fishing and a caravan park with rondavels and all facilities.

At the baSinga rug factory, tribespeople produce a particularly fine all-wool product on hand looms.

On the road from Greytown to Kranskop a turnoff leads to the factory of Natal Tanning Extract Company and to Hermannsburg where the Hanoverian Mission was founded in 1854. The old mission house is a national monument.

Kranskop and the scenic routes of the district

Surrounded by sugar-cane and wattle plantations, Kranskop lies some 34 kilometres to the north-east of Greytown. When it was laid out in 1894 it was called Hopetown and was subsequently renamed after the colossal rock feature 12 kilometres away, that the Zulus call *iTse lika Ntunjambili* (the rock with two openings). Looming over the immense Tugela Valley, this great scenic landmark rises to 1 127 metres. The almost vertical faces of the peak have been scaled only on three occasions; the first in 1879 by Captain A.M. Montgomery of the Natal Native Contingent. Kranskop is the terminus of the railway from Pietermaritzburg. There is an hotel in the village.

Kranskop is at the junction of several roads. Route R74 having started its journey south-east from Colenso continues on a further 75-kilometre-long scenic drive to Stanger at the coast. Another road heads northwards from Kranskop to Qudeni, Nqutu and Dundee on one of the most dramatically spectacular scenic drives on the sub-continent. This road crosses the Tugela (the traditional boundary) into Zululand at Jameson's Drift (after H.B. Jameson, the engineer under whose supervision the road was constructed). There is a spectacular panorama from the viewsite 23 kilometres out of Kranskop.

North-west of Greytown route R33 links with Dundee and national road N3 (at Fort Mistake) through Tugela Ferry, Pomeroy, Helpmekaar and Bonny Doon and makes a delightful alternate route of part of the way from the coast to the hinterland and vice versa. Although tarred this is by no means a fast route, the road winding through undulating country, at times mountainous and wooded with spectacular views of the Tugela River, the landscape studded with tribal huts in amongst the aloes and the tribespeople often in full regalia proceeding to a wedding or some indaba (meeting).

Muden

Between Greytown and Weenen, route R74 passes the village of Muden in the valley of a tributary of the Tugela. The extensive groves of oranges that once covered this valley were uprooted in 1965 but two small citrus farms do remain with their orange wineries. The farm Sonnegold has been operating for four generations and produces 78 000 litres of 'orange wine' per annum. This is marketed throughout South Africa (with a small quantity being exported to Germany) under the label of Sonnegold Nectar.

South of Muden, on the gravel road between Greytown and Mooi River, is the Craigie Burn Dam. It impounds the Mnvamvubu River, a tributary of the Mooi, and is part of an irrigation scheme.

Weenen and Bloukrans Monument

One of the oldest settlements in Natal, Weenen (weeping) was founded by the Voortrekkers in 1838 who named it to commemorate the tragedy of Bloukrans. After Dingaan had seen to the murder of Piet Retief and his party he gave orders to his impis to find and wipe out the remainder of the Voortrekkers. On the hill at Bloukrans and below at Moordspruit in the triangle formed by Chieveley – Estcourt – Weenen, a terrible massacre was carried out on the night of 16-17 February 1838. The Zulus completely surprised the laagers of the Liebenbergs, the Rossouws, the Bezuidenhouts, the Engelbrechts and the Greylings and 41 men, 46 women, 156 children and 200 servants were put to death. From 20 000 to 25 000 head of cattle were driven off. The laagers of Maritz, Sarel Cilliers and the van Rensburgs south of Estcourt successfully defended themselves and beat off the attack. On 16 December 1895 on the instigation of General Piet Joubert the remains of the victims of the great massacre were gathered and solemnly re-interned in a common grave. In 1897 the Bloukrans Monument was erected over the mass grave and in 1937 it was fenced and proclaimed a national monument. The monument can be reached from Weenen and is well signposted between Estcourt and Colenso on national road N3.

Weenen has a population of 3 000 and its small-holding farms, irrigated by the Bushman's River, produce a large vegetable crop, lucerne and groundnuts. There is a small local history museum in the village.

In June 1980 the Natal Parks Board opened the 2 928-hectare Weenen Nature Reserve where antelope, white rhino and giraffe have been introduced. There are picnic sites and walking trails and a promise of a rustic camp and caravan park.

Pietermaritzburg to Van Reenen – National road N3

Hilton

The highway N3 climbs out of Maritzburg's Town Hill overlooking the Country Club and Queen Elizabeth Park on the right and passing the turnoff to World's View on the left and reaches the turnoff to Hilton (formerly Hilton Road and named after the original farm). This little village of country lanes, hedges, gardens and lovely walks is surrounded by pasture lands and gum plantations and backed in the distance by the majestic Drakensberg – snowcapped in the winter. Hilton's bracing climate and charming Tudor-style hotel in its lovely grounds provide ingredients for a relaxing holiday. In the vicinity are two of South Africa's principal schools, Hilton College and St Anne's Diocesan College.

Cedara and Midmar Dam

Beyond Hilton, national road N3 passes Cedara Agricultural College, in the setting of a model farm, and then the turnoff to Midmar Public Resort, Midmar Lake. The dam which was built at the confluence of the Umgeni and Lions rivers was completed in 1964 and covers an area of 1820 hectares with a shoreline of 56 kilometres. With the development by Natal Parks Board of a nature reserve surrounding the dam, the complex is placed among the best inland resorts in the country. The attractions are yachting, power-boating, carp and bass fishing and organised riding

Three-star Sani Pass Hotel, the luxury mountain resort in the southern region of the Natal Drakensberg, has its own 9-hole country golf course, superior bowling greens, all weather tennis courts, jacuzzi, pool and playground, riding stables and a trout stream.

1

1. Himeville Arms Hotel, an all-year-round base for country lovers, trout fishermen, and those exploring the Drakensberg. Here a predominant feeling of friendliness prevails and there is good fare and real comfort.

2. Champagne Castle, Monk's Cowl and Cathkin Peak, under snow, looming over the Injasuti hutted camp of the Natal Parks Board.

and walking trails. Launch trips are also arranged. The accommodation comprises bungalows and chalets and there is a restaurant and a camping ground. The game animals in the reserve include white rhino, zebra, wildebeest, eland, impala, blesbok and reedbuck. An added attraction at Midmar is the 20-hectare open-air museum with its two themes, agriculture and transport.

Howick

On the Umgeni River downstream from the Midmar Dam, is one of the best-known beauty spots in Natal, the Howick Falls. Taking a direct plunge of 94 metres, the falls are particularly spectacular after the summer rains, and are a proclaimed natural monument. Following the course of the Umgeni for 10 km below the falls is the delightful Umgeni Valley Nature Reserve, owned by the Wildlife Society and open to the public. For reservation of cottages and camping sites telephone 03321-3931. Access to the reserve is through Howick village, beyond the Karkloof turnoff.

The municipality of Howick lies at an altitude of 1 021 metres in picturesque rural surroundings and with its fine climate is recognised as a resort for recuperative holidays. There is a good hotel near the falls, municipal caravan park on the bank of the Umgeni River, and a tearoom at the falls. Howick has a well patronised golf course.

BTR Sarmcol (Pty) Ltd, manufacturers of hose, rubber footwear and the like, has its plant and head office in Howick, and after additions in 1983 the plant became the largest of its kind in the world. The population of the town is 18 000.

Karkloof Falls, cascading 105 metres, are 15 km from Howick, and occur on the farm of SAPPI, the plantation owners, who have provided a lovely area for picnics, to which members of the public are admitted free of charge.

Lions River, Dargle, Lidgetton, Balgowan, Nottingham Road and Rosetta

Mooi River can be reached from Howick by a loop road through the rural villages of Lions River (the last lion to be shot in the district was killed in a gully near the river in 1856), Lidgetton (named after the successful immigration leader, John Lidgett, who brought 104 British settlers to the area in 1850), Balgowan (named after the Scottish village in the 1850s by John Ellis, the first owner of the farm), Nottingham Road (first settled in 1850 by the King family, renowned for its trout fishing and named after the Nottinghamshire Regiment stationed in the area in 1856, when Fort Nottingham, 11 kilometres to the south-west of the village, was constructed) and Rosetta (where roses flourish and there is good trout fishing).

The whole area is magnificent upland farming country, especially for stock breeding and dairying. At Lions River there is a turnoff to the farming area of Dargle and to the farm holiday resorts Hebron Haven and Everglades.

The famous South African Diocesan school for boys, Michaelhouse, is at Balgowan. Before reaching Nottingham Road the road passes Rawdon's Hotel, with its thatched roof and miniature lake. Rawdons is famed for its good food and gracious living. New to

the area, opened in 1987, is Granny Mouse, a delightful country house hotel.

Mooi River (bypassed by N3)

The bracing climate, trout fishing, a country club and beautiful farms of dairying and stock breeding attract city dwellers to the Mooi River district.

The built-up area had its start when the railway reached there in 1884 and Alexander Lawrence called his township Lawrenceville; later it amalgamated with three other small townships under the name Mooi River, after the river the Voortrekkers had rightly named Mooirivier (beautiful river). Municipal status was reached in 1959, and the town with its population of 8 000 lies at an altitude of 1 388 metres. Three important industries are Mooi River Bacon, Mooi River Textiles and the cheese factory of National Co-op Dairies. The district is notable for its potteries.

The exclusive and elegant Hartford Country House on the Ellis' 400-hectare stud farm is 5 km along the Hlatikulu road, in the direction of the Drakensberg. Argyll Hotel is in Lawrence Road and Sierra Ranch on the way to Greytown.

Estcourt (bypassed by N3)

An important industrial centre in the heart of a rich stock breeding and agricultural district, Estcourt has a population of 14 000. It lies at the confluence of the Bushman's and Little Bushman's rivers at the commencement of thorn bush country which stretches northwards to Vryheid and Newcastle.

The town was founded in 1851 by an early settler, J.B. Wilks, who named the place after a friend, Thomas Estcourt, a British member of parliament. Originally it was called Bushman's River Post.

Fort Durnford, a substantial stone building and typical mid-Victorian frontier post was constructed in 1875 after the Langalibalele Rebellion of 1873. Designed by Col Durnford of the Royal Engineers, it was built on the site of an outpost of the 45th Regiment who were sent there in 1847 from Fort Napier, Pietermaritzburg, to protect the Boers from marauding Bushmen. The fort commands the Bushman's River crossing.

The obstreperous chief, Langalibalele, of the Hlubi tribe inhabiting the region of the foothills of the Drakensberg below Champagne Castle, rebelled against the Natal Government regulations regarding firearms. After fleeing to Basutoland (now Lesotho), the chief was captured and imprisoned.

Notable manufacturing concerns in Estcourt are Farmers Co-operative Bacon Factory, Burlington Hosiery, Masonite and Nestle.

For the traveller there are two hotels in the town and a municipal caravan park perfectly situated on the bank of the Bushman's River. In the world of recreation the town has golf and bowling clubs and 5 km along the Ntabamhlope road is Wagendrift Dam where the Parks Board controls a public resort and nature reserve. Facilities include campsites, boating, fishing and an 80-bed school education centre.

Estcourt to Colenso (old main road)

There are several points of interest along the old main road from Estcourt to Colenso. Five kilometres out from Estcourt this road crosses the narrow-gauge line to Weenen and 14 kilometres further on there is a branch road to the west to Winterton and the Drakensberg resorts.

One and a half kilometres beyond the Winterton turnoff, a bronze plaque marks the place where the Boers ambushed and wrecked the British Armoured Train on 15 November 1899. This was the action in which the war correspondent for *The Morning Post,* Winston Churchill, was taken prisoner by the Boers. Across the railway line, which runs parallel with the road, is the graveyard of those killed in the action.

A further 1,5 kilometres from the plaque is the turnoff east, leading for 8 kilometres to Bloukrans Monument where the massacre of the Voortrekkers by the Zulus took place on the night of 16-17 February 1838.

At approximately 32 kilometres from Estcourt, 3 kilometres to the turnoff to Colenso, is the Cloustan Military Cemetery. Spread out in the thorn bushes are the graves and tombstones of a number of British soldiers including some of the Natal Carbineers. These graves were removed from the town of Colenso to this more suitable resting place.

Colenso

The municipality of Colenso lies on the banks of the Tugela River and is dominated by the huge cooling towers of the Electricity Supply Commission. The town was founded in 1885 and named after the controversial Bishop Colenso.

The area was the scene of a heavy defeat of the British by the Boers. It was from here that General Redvers Buller made his first attempt to relieve Ladysmith and four Victoria Crosses were awarded in the battle that followed.

Colenso's population is 4 000 and there is an hotel and a caravan park. At Colenso route R74 commences its scenically beautiful journey to Stanger on the Natal north coast.

Colenso to Ladysmith

A few kilometres south of Ladysmith a branch road leads left (west) to Winterton and the Drakensberg resorts and shortly thereafter national road N3 reaches the traffic interchange and the junction with route R23. From here the national road N3 continues its journey through Van Reenen's Pass to Harrismith and then crosses the eastern sector of the Orange Free State before meeting with route R23 south of Heidelberg in the Transvaal. This route through the Free State to the Natal Coast is the popular one for people coming from the Transvaal.

From the interchange, route R23 before entering Ladysmith passes the Andrews Motel at the Ladysmith Aerodrome and a number of signposts mark the whereabouts of the Anglo-Boer War battlefields which lie in amongst the aloes and acacia trees of the veld.

Ladysmith

Dr William Stanger, the first Surveyor-General of Natal, laid out Ladysmith which was proclaimed a township in 1850. It was named in honour of the lady of the Cape governor, Sir Harry Smith, whom Sir

Harry had gallantly rescued from his own men at the siege of Badajoz in the Peninsular War. But this fair lady, one of the most romantic figures in South African history, was not to know that 49 years later Ladysmith was to be associated with a grim and lengthy siege of its own.

Ladysmith holds a strategic position on the map of South Africa. In the closing years of the nineteenth century it was a focal point. The railway from the coast reached it in 1886 when it became the railhead for the rich hinterland with transport riders plying over the Drakensberg to the diamond fields of Kimberley and the goldfields of the Witwatersrand. And of course it was the gateway to Natal itself.

At the outbreak of the Anglo-Boer War the Boers were quick to invest Ladysmith and made no mistake about the strength with which they did so. During the 120 days of siege from 1 November 1899 to 28 February 1900 Ladysmith suffered untold privation. The Boer 'Long Toms' commanded the town and all supplies, including water, were cut off. Some 3 000 died in the defence and eventual relief of Ladysmith. Their monuments and cemeteries surround the town. Of the battlefields, Caesar's Camp and Wagon Hill are within easy walking distance of the town; transport is needed to visit Umbulwana Hill and Lombard's Kop. The museum at the Town Hall (a national monument) has a considerable collection of siege relics.

Ladysmith lies in the Klip River Valley enclosed by flat-topped hills in a district noted for its cattle raising. The town was proclaimed a borough in 1899 and after the war it continued to be an important communications centre. It is the junction of highways and railways and has one of the largest marshalling yards in the country. The amenities include a fine country club, a motel at the aerodrome, two hotels in the town and an all-facility municipal caravan park. The population of the town is 40 000 and that of Ezakheni, a part of the fragmented KwaZulu, 15 kilometres to the east, 50 000.

Bergville

A road from Ladysmith leads south-west for 48 kilometres to Bergville, the railhead centre of a prosperous dairy and beef farming district, situated in a tranquil setting on the banks of the Tugela River. This little municipality of 800 inhabitants with its hotel and caravan park lies close to the northern resort sector of the Drakensberg.

Spioenkop

Seventeen kilometres north-west of Bergville is Spioenkop Dam, completed in 1973. It impounds over 278 million cubic metres of water of the upper Tugela River, enabling the irrigation of thousands of hectares of farmland in the Tugela and Bloukrans valleys and the use of 83 million cubic metres of water for the industrial expansion of the Ladysmith-Colenso-Bergville area. In what is known as the *Drakensberg Scheme* the surplus 250 million cubic metres of water per annum are pumped from the Tugela to the Vaal Basin in a hydro-electric plan, which, in replacing coal fuel, saves the country some R50-million per annum.

1. Realistic life-size Bushmen models at Main Cave site-museum Giant's Castle
Game Reserve.
2. The largest choir school in the world, Drakensberg Boys Choir is on the farm
Dragon Peaks, below Champagne Castle.

232

Positioned in a lovely part of the Berg, facing onto Cathkin Peak and Champagne Castle, is The Nest, the holiday hotel renowned for hospitality, comfort, good fare and first-rate recreational facilities.

Spioenkop Public Resort, created by Natal Parks Board, provides facilities for accommodation, caravan sites, water sports, swimming and angling in the environment of a nature reserve. The yachting and power-boat club is approached via Winterton. Zebra and a variety of antelope have been introduced into the 400-hectare reserve.

The Anglo-Boer War battlefield of Spioenkop (where Botha's commandos defeated Buller's forces on 24 January 1900) is readily accessible from the resort. The peak rises to 2 149 metres.

Woodstock Dam
Fourteen kilometres south-east of Bergville, the huge Woodstock Dam is the largest dam in the *Drakensberg Scheme*. It lies at the confluence of Tugela and one of its tributaries, the Mnjaneni. In full supply its surface area is 2 915 hectares and its capacity 381-million kilolitres (compare Midmar, 1 592 hectares and 190-million kilolitres). This is the main supply dam in the scheme and from here via the small Kilburn Dam and Driel Barrage water is pumped into the Sterkfontein Dam. Woodstock Dam was completed in 1983 and despite the fluctuating level of water (due to pumping operations) it is being considered by the Natal Parks Board for recreational development.

Van Reenen's Pass
Thirty-five kilometres north-west of Ladysmith national road N3 is carried over the Drakensberg by the broad, sweeping Van Reenen's Pass and in so doing the road rises from 1 000 metres to 1 680 metres in fifteen kilometres. At about midway up the pass are the attractive slate-roofed wigwam type chalets of Andrews Motel, and at the summit there is a turnoff to the viewsite known as Windy Corner. A stop is worthwhile; the green clad mountains are a magnificent sight. The pass was first constructed in 1856 and named after the farmer whose lands were at the foot of the pass and who assisted the surveyors in their preliminary work.

A short distance north of the summit is the village of Van Reenen with its hotel and guest-houses. Close to the highway is a beautiful stone oratory, said to be the smallest in South Africa. Beyond the turnoff to the village there are service stations and restaurants on both sides of the highway, virtually on the border of the Orange Free State, which Province is described in Chapter 13.

Natal Coalfields

From Ladysmith trunk road R23 enters the coalfields district of Natal. Although the deposits of Natal are only a fraction of those in the Transvaal, Natal coals are generally of higher calorific value, and anthracitic as well as bituminous coals are found in Natal (notably around Vryheid), whereas with the exception of mines in the Ermelo district, Transvaal deposits are bituminous only. Exploited true coking coals are more or less confined to Natal. According to the 1975 report by the Petrick Commission of Enquiry on the coal resources of South Africa, Natal has minable reserves of 3 000-million tons of which approximately 1 000-million tons are considered to

be technically and economically extractable.

Dundee
In the heart of the Natal coalfields is Dundee, a short deviation east of trunk route R23. It lies in the Biggarsberg range at an altitude of 1 250 metres and was laid out on the farm of its founder, Peter Smith, as a centre for the coal deposits which he had started to work and market in 1862.

Dundee became a borough in 1902 and has a population of 22 000. Its important industries are Beech-Nut Life-Savers Limited and Consolidated Glass Limited. The town has an 18-hole golf course, two hotels and an all-facility caravan park. There is a small museum devoted chiefly to metallurgical and geological material with interesting relics from the history of the local coal mining.

Close to Dundee are the historical battle sites, Blood River, Rorke's Drift and Isandhlwana which are described in Chapter 9.

Coal mining centres near Dundee are Glencoe, Dannhauser, Wasbank and Elandslaagte. There are hotels at Glencoe and Dannhauser.

Newcastle
Founded in 1864, Newcastle was named after the British Secretary for the Colonies, the Duke of Newcastle. It became a borough in 1891 and has a population of 34 000. Madadeni and Osizweni, 12 and 20 kilometres respectively from Newcastle, are KwaZulu townships with a combined population of 175 000.

Newcastle owes its prosperity to its natural resources of water and coal and to the siting there of the third Iscor, South Africa's great steel producer. Red oxide and calcium carbide are also produced and Defy Industries, the largest manufacturer of stoves and baths in the country, is sited here. The Electricity Supply Commission power station, near Chelmsford Dam to the south of the town, is the largest power station in Natal with a capacity of a half-million kilowatts. The Chelmsford Dam delivers over 120 million litres of water a day.

Situated close to the Drakensberg range at an altitude of 1 200 metres, Newcastle enjoys an invigorating climate with an annual rainfall of 900 millimetres. Recreational facilities include trout fishing in the Incandu River, water sport on the Chelmsford Dam and an 18-hole golf course. There are four hotels in the town (including the Holiday Inn) and a municipal caravan park with all facilities.

St Dominic's Academy, founded in 1896, is one of the finest girls schools in the country. Its unusual Pavilion in circular shape with a diameter of 30 meters was constructed (mainly of timber) in 1916 and was proclaimed a national monument in 1977.

Newcastle's other national monuments are Fort Ameil, built by the British soldier, Colonel Ameil in 1876, just prior to the annexation of the Transvaal; the Town Hall, built to commemorate Queen Victoria's diamond jubilee of 1897 and completed a year later, and the Carnegie Library, opened during World War I.

Newcastle was very much involved in the operations of the South African Wars. It was from here that General Sir Pomeroy Colley led his forces to his defeat and death at Majuba, 40 kilometres to the north. In 1889 it became the main stronghold from which the Boers held Northern Natal and besieged Ladysmith and Dundee. Until its reoccupation by the British on 18 May 1900 the name of the town had been changed to Viljoensdorp.

Laing's Nek Pass and Majuba

Laing's Nek Pass carries trunk road R23 over the escarpment onto the highveld, the foot of the pass being reached 24 kilometres north of Newcastle. The 1 676-metre summit lies 16 kilometres ahead. It was in this pass that the ill-fated British soldier and Natal Governor, General Sir George Pomeroy Colley, tried to force a way for his troops against the Boers under Commandant-General Piet Joubert on 28 January 1881 and in so doing was defeated with the loss of a sixth of his force. Eighty-three men, including seven officers, were killed and 111 were wounded. At approximately ten kilometres from the foot of the pass a signpost on the left marks the turnoff to O'Neil's Cottage, a national monument on the farm Mount Prospect. Here, after the second encounter between the forces (described below) the agreement between the British and the Transvaal Republic was signed on 21 March 1881, ending the hostilities variously referred to as the First Anglo-Boer War, the Anglo-Transvaal War and the First Boer War.

Overlooking O'Neil's Cottage is the flat-topped height, Majuba (hill of the doves) from where on the night of 27 February 1881 General Colley sought to avenge his defeat of a month previous. On the same night that General Colley and his forces occupied the commanding feature, storming forces under General Piet Joubert surprised and killed Colley and 92 of his men; 134 were wounded and the British had suffered a second ignominious defeat.

Ingogo

In the Laing's Nek Pass on the left, proceeding northwards, are the Valley Inn and the Inkwelo Motel, and on the opposite side is the village of Ingogo.

Charlestown

Near the Transvaal border, Charlestown was, toward the end of the nineteenth century, a flourishing town and the scene of much activity. In those years this was the terminus of the Natal railway from the coast where trans-shipment from railway trucks to ox-wagons and coaches of the transport riders took place and this was the customs post of the frontier between the British colony of Natal and the Transvaal Republic. Today Charlestown is reduced to a village with one or two small industries and a population of 150. Three kilometres north of Charlestown route R23 enters the Transvaal (Chapter 11).

Drakensberg Resorts

The Drakensberg range which stretches from the Eastern Cape to the North-eastern Transvaal over a distance in excess of 1 600 kilometres, is South Africa's major escarpment. It divides the highveld plateau of the interior from the eastern coastal belt and separates Natal from Lesotho and the Orange Free State.

Along a 139-kilometre semicircle facing the western edge of Natal this mighty 'Mountain of the Dragon' forms a rampart of peaks and pinnacles at an average 3 000 metres above sea level and 1 500 metres above the surrounding country. On the foothills and snuggling below these giant peaks are the famous resorts. A number of excellent hotels and guest farms cater for year-round holiday-makers who come to enjoy the hiking, climbing, trout fishing, trail riding, swimming, golf, bowls and tennis in the crisp air and exhilarating climate amidst the mountain grandeur of what has come to be known as simply 'the Berg'.

Underberg and Himeville

Within 5 kilometres of each other Underberg and Himeville are trading villages in the southern region of the range, situated near the borders of Natal, Transkei and Lesotho. This area is renowned for what is perhaps the finest trout fishing in the country.

For all who seek a retreat from town life the Himeville Hotel can surely be recommended. Ye Olde Himeville Arms pub, The Trout House restaurant and the comfortable guest cottages coupled with the warmth of hospitality of the proprietors, Jonathan and Sylvia Aldous, provide the retreat. The hotel faces the Drakensberg and when the mountains are snow-covered, log fires burn in every hotel room.

The interesting fort museum is across the road from the hotel, and five minutes away is Himeville Nature Reserve with its trout dams, rowing boats, wildfowl and antelope. The hotel is pictured on page 229.

Drakensberg Garden and Bushman's Nek

Six kilometres west of Underberg is the Drakensberg Garden resort hotel dominated by the sandstone mass of Garden Castle, which was renamed by the surveyor, Dr Sutherland, who gave it the maiden name of his mother. The previous name, Giant's Castle (given by Capt Allen Gardiner, the missionary, in 1835) was from then on applied to the feature, further westwards, on the main wall of the range.

Beyond the hotel the road continues to the Garden Castle Forestry Station in the upper valley of the Mlambonja River where the impressive 2 997-metre-high Rhino Horn dominates the area.

Along another road 10 kilometres south-west of Underberg is the Bushman's Nek Hotel in the area where the Bushman's Nek Pass is overlooked by the 3 028-metre Devil's Knuckles. In what is known as the Drakensberg Hiking Trail, (Giant's Cup), a five-day walk of extravagant mountain beauty connects this area with Sani Pass.

Sani Pass

Three kilometres beyond Himeville a turnoff to the north-west leads to the luxury mountain resort, Sani Pass Hotel. The spectacular 10-kilometre drive up to the hotel from the main road is over the foothills into the beautiful valley of the Umkomazana (little

This is Cayley Guest Lodge, on 100 acres in the central section of the Natal Drakensberg, from where you look across a trout lake directly at Cathkin Peak and Champagne Castle — majestically beautiful in all the seasons. Details on page 402.

237

Umkomaas) River with a backdrop of mountain scenery. Apart from the comfort and fine table, the hotel has every amenity for holiday-makers, including a country golf course, bowling greens, tennis courts, riding stables and swimming pools. A trout stream runs through the extensive grounds and the well planned walks lead to beauty spots such as the plateau view and the waterfall and to Bushman paintings, including the famed *Icanti*. All of these attractions at Sani blend with the real magic of the scene – the absolute serenity.

Beyond the hotel a track road leads on for 25 kilometres following the gorge of the Umkomazana River to the Lesotho border post, which is at an altitude of 1 950 metres. Inside Lesotho, on the summit at 2 865 metres, is the Mountaineers' Chalet which claims to be the highest licensed premises in southern Africa. From the summit the track road continues for 55 km to the trading centre, Mokhotlong, over the roof of southern Africa and passes the highest point on the sub-continent, the 3 482-metre Thabana Ntlenyana (nice little mountain), so named by the Basotho because on this elevated plateau of over 3 000 metres it simply protrudes and gives the appearance of a low hill. The track road up the pass is restricted to four-wheel drive vehicles and a passport or identity document is necessary in crossing the border. The hotel arranges daily trips, generally starting at 10 a.m. and returning at 4 p.m. The journey covers some of the most spectacular mountain scenery to be seen in southern Africa.

From national road N3 the recommended route to the southern Drakensberg resorts is by taking the turnoff near Howick, clearly marked 'Merrivale, Bulwer'. From Pietermaritzburg, Bulwer can be reached via Edendale and from Nottingham Road there is a direct gravel road to Himeville, through superb scenery. Visitors approaching from the Cape should take the road Kokstad, Ixopo, Bulwer.

Loteni, Vergelegen, Kamberg and Coleford Nature Reserves

Loteni Nature Reserve (3 984 ha) and Vergelegen Nature Reserve (1 100 ha) both off the Nottingham Road- Himeville Road, Kamberg Nature Reserve (2 232 ha) 40 km west of Rosetta on the Kamberg road and Coleford Nature Reserve (1 272 ha) 27 km from Underberg on the Swartberg road, all provide hutted accommodation for trout fishermen and nature lovers. Game animals and a variety of birdlife can be seen in all of the reserves. Enquiries: Natal Parks Board.

Giant's Castle Game Reserve

This magnificent park is overlooked by a 35-kilometre-long stretch of the Drakensberg – a formidable wall of basalt maintaining a height of 3 000 metres over the whole distance. At Cathkin Peak (3 148 metres) the northern extremity, the range swings back out of view and at the near end an enormous exposed massif, the 3 314-metre Giant's Castle, blocks the view of the continuation of the range in the southerly direction.

The Zulu name for Giant's Castle is iNtabayikonjwa (the mountain at which people must not point). It reacts by bringing on bad weather, so the legend says, and indeed this is the huge corner-stone where storms seem to gather – electric in summer and snow in winter. Other peaks on the main wall have Zulu names typical in their originality: the Njesuthi Twins at the source of the Njesuthi (well-fed dog) River and the KwaMfazo Gaya Mabele (the old woman grinding corn). Easily recognisable shapes have resulted in naming rock faces the Thumb, and Bannerman, after the likeness of the British Prime Minister, Sir Henry Campbell-Bannerman. These and other peaks present challenging climbs and mountain huts are placed at strategic points. The easy climb to Giant's Castle itself, is by way of a twelve to fourteen hour walk along a 35-kilometre path from the main camp to the hut on the summit and an unforgettable view from the roof of southern Africa.

The unspoilt wilderness of 34 284 hectares of grass covered hills and deep ravines of forest was proclaimed a game reserve in 1903 and is the sanctuary of a variety of game animals and bird fauna. Two species closely associated with Giant's Castle are the mountain eland (the bovine antelope in every detail similar to other eland except that the horns are exceptionally straight above the spiral) and the rare lammergeyer (the giant vulture-like eagle, a magnificent bird in the air, gliding at great speed. He relishes the marrow of bones but if unable to crush these after dropping them from great height they are swallowed whole and digested).

In early history Bushmen followed the game; they hunted from the shelter of the caverns in the mountain foothills and there remains today some treasured examples of their rock art in many preserved galleries. Battle Cave and Main Cave have two of the most important displays and at Main Cave the Natal Parks Board has developed a realistic site museum with life-size Bushmen models. The 45-minute walk from the camp is worthwhile.

The visitors camp comprises self-contained huts and cottages set in a delightful garden, a luxury complex built into the hillside and a separate camping ground. Cooks are available but visitors must bring their own food supplies. There is a stable and organised trail riding. The Bushman's River, famed for its brown trout fisheries, has its source here. The game reserve is accessible from Mooi River and Estcourt. Enquiries: Natal Parks Board.

Injasuti Nature Reserve

This intimate chalet camp in a 356-hectare reserve is dominated by the closeness of those magnificent heights, Champagne Castle, Monks Cowl and Cathkin Peak. Well-fitted chalets apart, there are no facilities. This is a camp for those who go for the true outdoor experience and here it is on a grand scale. Injasuti is reached by leaving the N3 at the Estcourt-Loskop interchange and taking the Loskop road for 27 km to the signpost, from where there is a further 30 km. Reservations: Natal Parks Board.

Cathkin Peak and Champagne Castle

Dominating the central region of the Drakensberg is the 3 184-metre Cathkin Peak, a great corner-stone standing detached from the main wall. It received its imported name from David Gray who came to the area to farm in 1858 and called the peak after Cathkin Braes near his Scottish home town, Paisley. The more original and very descriptive Zulu name is Mdedelele, the name they give to a bully and literally means, 'make way for him'. On the main wall is Cathkin Peak's massive campanion, Champagne Castle; at 3 350 metres it is one of the highest points of the escarpment. The name Champagne Castle, for a long time, applied also to Cathkin Peak after David Gray and Captain Grantham R.E. mysteriously lost part of their bottle of champagne during their attempt to conquer the peak. In recent times and to put an end to continual confusion, the name Champagne Castle was applied to the previously unnamed height on the main wall.

In the beautiful Sterkspruit Valley along a good access road to the escarpment are a number of Berg resorts: Cayley Guest Lodge, The Nest, El Mirador, Cathkin Park and Drakensberg Sun, all at an altitude of over 1 200 metres, lie sheltered below the Little Berg; and higher up at 1 526 metres is Champagne, at the foot of the peaks. On the way to the escarpment, on the left, the road also passes, Mountain Splendour Caravan Park and a 9-hole golf course and on the right Dragon Peaks Caravan Park and the famous Drakensberg Boys Choir School.

This central region of the Drakensberg is approached from the north via Olivershoek, Bergville, or Ladysmith, Frere, Winterton, and is approached from the south via Estcourt, Ennersdale and Loskop. Where the roads from Bergville, Winterton and Estcourt form a junction, the tarred access road to the escarpment is well signposted with the names of all the resort properties.

Cayley Guest Lodge is 12 km from the junction and is the first turnoff right from the access road, from where you follow the signposts along district roads D53, D277 and D184. All Scots are good hosts and none more so than the Diack family, who own and personally supervise Cayley Lodge which is positioned on a prime site overlooking Cathkin Peak and Champagne Castle. Architecturally this is a completely fresh concept of Berg accommodation with a delightful atmosphere of warm hospitality along with all the recreational amenities for happy holidays for the whole family. Details appear on page 402 and pictures on page 236 and 237.

The Nest Hotel has for a number of years been under the personal supervision of the owners, Ernie and Edelweiss Malherbe, and it is thanks to them that it has such a good name today. The improvements they have made are remarkable, and here at The Nest you can count on comfort, good table and a wide range of recreational facilities (including the immaculate bowling greens). The hotel has a dramatic scenic aspect no matter where you are. From the garden, the swimming-pool, the luxury bedrooms and the cocktail bar you look directly at Champagne Castle and Cathkin Peak. The Nest is a few kilometres along the access road on the right. Details appear on page 402 and pictures on page 233.

Cathedral Peak

Tucked away on its own beneath great peaks and buttresses is Cathedral Peak Hotel, surrounded by a beautiful garden, situated in the deep valley of the Umlambonja River and overlooked to the north by a ridge of the Drakensberg which projects eastwards from the main wall. The sharp points of the collection of peaks have caused the tribesmen of the region to call this ridge the Umponjwana (place of the small horns).

The main peaks of the protruding ridge are Cathedral peak (3 004 metres), and next to it, easily identifiable, The Bell (2 918 metres). To the left of The Bell and closer to the main wall are Outer Horn (3 009 metres) and Inner Horn (3 017 metres). A network of well-kept paths permits easy access to the wonderful viewsites in this glorious scenery. The return journey to the top of Cathedral Peak takes a full day and the reward is an unforgettable close-up view of the whole of the northern sector of the Drakensberg. There are many other walks ranging from one hour to nine hours to such places as Doreen Falls, Oqalweni Fern Forest, Tryme summit, Blue Pool, Mushroom Rock and Contour Path, and beyond to Sebaaieni Cave on the Ndedema River where there is one of the best galleries of Bushman paintings. The many challenges to climbers include some on the main wall of the range, where the Pyramid (2 914 metres) and the Column (2 926 metres) are two of the testing climbs to be undertaken only by experienced climbers. The summit of the 3 281-metre Cleft Peak (one of the highest points in the main wall) can be reached by way of a footpath in a simple climb, although there are difficult climbs up this face as well.

Ownership and management of Cathedral Peak Hotel has been in the well known van der Riet family for three generations since the resort started on two farms purchased in 1937. Major constructional improvements and refurbishing were completed in 1987 and these include the establishment of a fine convention centre, gymnasium and beauty salon. The outstanding recreational facilities in this dramatically beautiful mountain setting include bowls, tennis squash, horse riding, mini golf, swimming and evening entertainment.

Tarred national and provincial roads lead to Winterton from where there is a good gravel road and a most memorable drive for 39 kilometres to the hotel. At the hotel the road ends in a cul-de-sac. Beyond the hotel closer approach to the escarpment can only be made by foot or horseback. Five kilometres before reaching the hotel there is a turnoff left to Mike's Pass (named after the research officer, Michael de Villiers), a scenic drive to the summit of the Little Berg, under the control of the Cathedral Peak Forestry Station. On the opposite side of the turnoff is the delightful camping and caravan site maintained by the Forestry Department.

Royal Natal National Park — Mont-Aux-Sources

Some of the finest mountain scenery on the African continent can be seen in the 8 000-hectare Royal Natal National Park in the northern part of the Natal Drakensberg.

Pages 240 and 241
A favourite with South African and overseas visitors alike, Cathedral Peak Hotel, in amongst the great peaks and towering buttresses of the Natal Drakensberg. In these pictures from the beautiful hotel-property, Cathedral Peak, The Bell, Outer Horn and Inner Horn are prominent.

In 1836 two French missionaries, Arbrousset and Daumas, set out from what was then Basutoland to explore the massive basalt of this region of the Drakensberg and came upon the plateau summit in the area which the Sotho tribespeople called Phofung (place of the eland). Here the missionaries found the source of many rivers and so the 3 282-metre summit received the French name, Mont-Aux-Sources, and it followed that the name was thereafter applied to the whole region.

It was some years after its discovery that the authorities realised that this was one of the natural wonders of southern Africa and development of a national park was started in the slow process of acquiring farms and other land. Natal National Park came into being by proclamation on 16 September 1916. Administration of the park started with an Advisory Committee that was succeeded by the Natal Provincial Administration and finally, upon its establishment in 1947, the Natal Parks, Game and Fish Preservation Board. During its history the 'hostel' at the park had a succession of lessees and park superintendents, among them in the 1920s and 1930s were Otto and Walter Zunckel. Alan Short was in charge when the British Royal family stayed at the park in May 1947. It was after their visit that the name was changed to Royal Natal National Park.

Keeping abreast with modern times, two star, fully licensed, Royal Natal National Park Hotel maintains a very high standard of comfort, table and service to provide the perfect base for completely relaxed enjoyment of this magnificent scene. From here, under expert guidance, guests can partake of gentle or robust exploration of the entire region and at the hotel itself there are superb recreational facilities.

The Mont-Aux-Sources Amphitheatre is formed by a curve in the main basalt wall, 8 km across, towering 1 220 m above the base (3 000 metres above sea level), flanked by two great peaks, the Sentinel, 3 274 m on the right, and the Eastern Buttress, 3 133 m on the left. The gigantic wall is broken by fantastic pinnacles (such as the Devil's Tooth), deep chasms and narrow ravines. Of the five rivers which rise on the slopes of the Mont-Aux-Sources, the Tugela and the Elands are the largest and provide the most spectacular waterfalls and the most interesting watercourses. The Tugela plunges over the Amphitheatre for 2 000 m in a series of falls and cascades – the drop, 213 m is one of the highest vertical drops in the world. It then traverses a narrow wooded gorge of great splendour before it deepens and broadens into the valley below, and finally flows into the Indian Ocean on the east coast. The Elands has its source quite close to the Tugela but, separated by a ridge, it makes its course in a northerly direction forming its own beautiful waterfall in a series of cascades for 1 200 m. Reaching the valley it eventually flows into the Vaal, joins with the Orange and flows into the Atlantic on the west coast, 1 400 km from the mouth of the Tugela.

Under strict rules of conservation, Natal Parks Board has constructed bridle and foot paths to provide 31 walks and trails with combined outward and homeward walking times ranging from 40 minutes to 11 hours. At least one of two superbly mapped out routes should not be missed by visitors to the Park. In the first a 11 km path follows the Tugela River to the magnificent gorge near the foot of the waterfall and entails no climbing whatsoever. The other route, a distance of 23 km, leads to the Amphitheatre, from where the summit of the Sentinel can be reached by way of two chain-ladders of 100 rungs. Overnight shelter is provided by the Sentinel hut, $1^1/_2$ km from the top of the ladder. From the hut the highest point of Mont-Aux-Sources is 4 km away, and is a simple climb.

Mont-Aux-Sources Hotel, overlooking the Amphitheatre, the Cavern, and Hlalanathi chalets and caravan park are all in the vicinity.

The northern Drakensberg resorts are accessible from a number of points along the N3 between Durban and Johannesburg. There are turnoffs at Estcourt, Colenso and Ladysmith which lead to Bergville from where there is a tarred road to the resorts. The approach from the Free State and Transvaal can be made via Oliviershoek Pass or Van Reenen's Pass (both tarred).

Oliviershoek Pass

The road from Harrismith to Bergville over Oliviershoek Pass is an interesting route with dramatic views of the Drakensberg range.

The road passes the solitary sandstone mountain feature, Kerkenberg (2 090 m) in beautiful sheep-farming country, 30 km from Harrismith. The bulky mountain marks the place where Piet Retief and his followers, with 50 wagons, camped in October 1837. From here Retief and 14 others rode out to visit Dingaan in Zululand. In the vicinity three points of interest are national monuments. Retief Klip, a stone painted with the leader's name by his daughter on the occasion of his 57th birthday; Blijde Vooruitzicht (joyful prospect), the viewsite at the edge of the escarpment from where the trekkers first saw Natal, and Oudeberg Pass which they built.

After crossing the border into Natal 36 km from Harrismith, the Oliviershoek Pass descends from the 1 737-metre-high summit. The pass is an area notable for red bottlebrush protea, masses of mimosa and fields of cosmos. A few kilometres down the pass is a turnoff right to the mountain resort, Little Switzerland. On the way to Bergville the road reveals some splendid views of the Drakensberg, extending from the Sentinel through Cathedral to Cathkin.

CHAPTER 11

Johannesburg, Witwatersrand, Southern and Western Transvaal

Johannesburg

The Witwatersrand, the ridge of white waters, commonly called the Rand or the Reef, is a plateau of from fifteen to nineteen hundred metres above sea level and 650 kilometres from the sea. It forms an important watershed – from the northern slopes the waters are carried by the Limpopo and Crocodile Rivers to the Indian Ocean – to the south the Vaal and the Orange Rivers carry the waters to the Atlantic.

The gold ore is contained in reefs occupying an area of from three to twelve kilometres wide from the West Rand to the East Rand, 130 kilometres long. It spreads at the eastern end to 30 kilometres wide. These reefs run at varying depths and the ore has been mined from surface outcrop to a depth of three kilometres below surface. Covering the area are the flourishing mining and industrial towns where the features of landscape are the huge yellow and white dumps of waste and tall headgears of the mines. Across the central Rand stretches the great city of Johannesburg.

When George Harrison's strike in 1886 proved that the main reef contained payable gold in conglomerate formation, a great human rush of fortune-seekers and adventures surged upon the scene. During the middle of that year the Pretoria Government sent the Surveyor-General, Johann Rissik and Christiaan Johannes Joubert to lay out the town and proclaim the goldfields. Field Cornet Johannes Petrus Meyer was appointed Mining Commissioner. The farm Ranjeslaagte, adjoining the prospecting camps of Ferreira and Meyer, was chosen as the site and the first stands were auctioned during November and December. In a tempo of wild excitement, with no thought of permanence, a mining town shot up immediately. The place had to be named and there was not time or concern for a more imaginative name than the common Christian name of the officials involved in its foundation.

This then was the beginning of what, in the course of a man's lifespan, was destined to become the greatest city in southern Africa, superseding others that were, at its birth, already more than 200 years old. The steps it took to reach this eminence are in themselves quite remarkable. Soon after its establishment, Johannesburg was controlled by a Sanitary Committee; ten years later, in 1897, the Pretoria Government appointed a Burghermeester in control of a council; in 1903, during Lord Milner's British regime, it became a municipality and finally, in 1928 a city.

The natural sequence was that Johannesburg, the richest city in all Africa, should become the financial and commercial capital of the Republic. The capital market of the entire sub-continent is centred on the Johannesburg Stock Exchange. The administrative headquarters of the South Africa Transport Services are here and so are the head offices of the majority of banks, building societies and insurance companies. The population of Johannesburg is 1 739 000. The growth in its building value has been astronomical; in the course of ten years, 1974 to 1983, its net rateable value soared from R2 625-million to R7 643-million. Its capacity for architectural modernisation is extraordinary; great buildings, standing for only a few decades, are almost continuously being demolished to make way for better and taller structures, allowing for open spaces to avoid crowding and to beautify the city. The municipal area is 508 square kilometres.

Symbolic of the progress of this great city is its imposing Civic Centre; built at a cost of over R28-million and completed in 1978, it contains a magnificent Council Chamber (12 800 square metres in area), two handsome administration blocks of 16 and 6 storeys and a 3-level parking garage for 920 cars, the whole complex fronted by a beautiful piazza on an elevated site in Braamfontein, overlooking the city.

Johannesburg enjoys no less than 8,7 hours of sunshine daily, with an average temperature of 16°C. At an altitude of 1 752 metres it has a bracing, invigorating climate with fine weather for the greater part of the year.

Communications

The National Tourist Bureau of the S A Tourism Board is at Carlton Centre, Commissioner Street. Telephone 331 5241.

Johannesburg is the Republic's transportation pivot. Jan Smuts International Airport, with its first-rate passenger handling facilities, comfortable lounges and magnificent restaurant, 24 kilometres from the city, is linked with the world's trunk routes. Adjoining the airport is a technical base, equipped with the most modern facilities for the maintenance of aircraft and the training of aircrews. South African Airways Centre and the Rotunda passenger terminal are adjacent to the railway station.

The 32-kilometre network of soaring express motorways have cost R80-million.

Johannesburg Railway Station covers a surface area of 22 hectares and was built at a cost of R40-million. One of the largest and most modern railway stations in the world, it is used by a quarter of a million passengers daily. The magnificent main concourse, built on an 8-hectare concrete deck slab, covers the suburban and mainline platforms and provides a vast hall 168 metres long, 42 metres wide and 18 metres high. In addition to the usual railway facilities the hall houses attractive rest rooms, restaurant, tearooms, hairdressing salons, shops, private and public bars and bookstalls. Stairways and escalators provide access to and from the concourse and the platforms 6 metres below. The passenger main line reservation office is in the main concourse.

The heart of South Africa's sophisticated microwave radio system carrying simultaneously thousands of trunk telephone calls and teleprinter data communications is the J.G. Strijdom Post Office Tower. Completed in 1971, it rises 269 metres above the street in Hillbrow and is the tallest structure in Africa. Admission to the tower was closed to the public in 1980.

1

2

Pages 244 and 245

Scenically the most magnificent of all South Africa's national parks, Royal Natal National Park, Mount-Aux-Sources, is controlled by the Natal Parks Board and has as its main 'camp' the privately operated two-star Royal Natal National Park Hotel, a first-rate holiday resort.

1. The hotel entrance.
2. Typical thatch roof accommodation. 3 Climbers looking at Mount-Aux-Sources. 4. Tennis and bowls in this majestic setting.

3

4

South African Broadcasting Corporation (SABC)

The SABC radio and television network had its beginning in 1936 when the first national radio service was broadcast in English. Today the radio service broadcasts 2 207 hours a week in 20 languages in 19 different radio programmes. The television service in English and Afrikaans, with parity of both languages, began on 5 January 1976 and presents a weekly 44-hour transmission schedule.

Broadcasting Centre, occupying a site of 15 hectares at Auckland Park to the west of Johannesburg's city centre, is one of the largest broadcasting complexes on one site in the world. The complex includes the 28 storey administrative head office, 48 radio studios and 7 television studios.

The centre point of the frequency modulation system (FM radio transmissions) as well as housing the originating television transmitter, is the SABC Tower. It is 253 metres high and has a 52-metre-high steel antenna mast on top. Admission to the tower was closed to the public in 1980.

Gold Mines and Stock Exchange

The gold mining area of South Africa stretches in an arc of about 560 kilometres from Evander in the Far East Rand to Virginia in the Orange Free State. With the discovery of the Orange Free State Goldfields in 1946, the Witwatersrand was superseded in importance, but in more recent times Far West Rand (also known as the West Wits Line) has come into prominence as the biggest producer. South Africa produces 74 percent of the Free World's gold supply and is one of the world's three largest uranium producers.

The recent dramatic rise in the free market price of gold has caused the country's income from gold to increase by more than 1 200 percent in a decade, notwithstanding a considerable drop in production. The comparison is indeed interesting. In 1970 South Africa produced 1 000 417 fine gold kilograms worth R831-million and in 1980 it produced 673 997 fine gold kilograms worth R10 193-million. Of the 41 mines being worked 27 are in Transvaal and 14 in the Free State.

Up to 130 tons of ore is taken from the earth to get one kilogram of gold, with the result that some of the world's largest man made hills are in this gold-mining area. The mine rock dump at Government Area has more bulk than the Great Pyramid of Cheops. At Randfontein Estates the biggest sand dump of 42 000 000 tons could fill the Kimberley Big Hole and leave a surplus of 17 000 000 tons. The white, golden and yellow colour of the mine dumps is due to the cyanide and other chemicals used in the gold extraction process. A little east of Johannesburg is East Rand Proprietary (E.R.P.M.), the world's deepest mine. Here at a depth of over 5 kilometres miners are confronted with a natural rock temperature of 50°C necessitating the use of refrigeration plants to pump down cold air to make it possible to work at that depth. In the honeycombed underground, trains run along tunnels for distances up to 11 kilometres, vast caverns contain massive winding machinery and great pumping plants. Down in the bowels of the earth 333 000 men go to work each working day.

The R137-million East Rand Gold and Uranium Company (Ergo) is Anglo American's metals-from-waste project, started in 1977. In recovering gold, uranium oxide and sulphuric acid from the mine dumps it will yield considerable profit. With the expectancy of other houses following Anglo's lead, significant generation of foreign exchange will result from the exploitation of the mountains of waste scattered over the Witwatersrand and OFS from decades of gold mining.

All of the gold from the mines is sent for treatment to the Rand Refinery at Germiston, the biggest gold refinery in the world, before it is sold to the Reserve Bank and exported to the world's bullion markets. Chamber of Mines of South Africa is an association of gold, uranium, diamond, platinum, antimony and coal producers, and the large finance groups which administer the mines. Common policy in the industry is formulated through the Chamber.

The claims of the discoverers of the main reef of goldbearing conglomerates at Langlaagte are preserved as a national monument and can be seen at George Harrison Park, five kilometres along West Main Reef Road. There is also an old Stamp Battery of the type first erected in April 1887.

Part of the old workings of Crown Mines (once the richest gold mine in the world, but no longer in production) has been converted by the Chamber of Mines into a Gold Mine Museum. The museum presents an imaginative conversion back to the gold mining scene at the turn of the century with a typical restaurant, steam train ride, gold pouring and underground workings. It is six kilometres out of the city and is reached by taking the southern freeway marked OFS and leaving the freeway at the second turnoff marked Xavier Street, from where there are signposts.

Conducted Tours of underground and surface workings of gold and uranium mines are arranged by the Chamber of Mines. There is a choice of some 26 mines on the Witwatersrand and Orange Free State and visits are made on Tuesdays, Wednesdays and Thursdays. For details telephone the Mine Visits Department, 838-8211.

Johannesburg Stock Exchange (JSE) moved from Hollard Street to the ten-storey, R21-million complex on the corner of Pritchard and Diagonal Streets in December 1978. The U-shaped building has a grand glass-roofed podium and visitors witness trading from two galleries. Conducted tours, held Monday to Friday at 11 a.m. and 2.30 p.m., include two audio-visual programmes – one on the economy of South Africa and the other on the history of JSE – and an explanation of trading, including identification of market-floor parties to a transaction. The Hall of South African Achievement houses a unique exhibition where the most modern techniques have been employed.

Tribal Dances and Black Peoples Townships

Nearly 400 000 black people work on the gold mines. Of these 60 percent come from the African countries beyond the borders of the Republic. These mine workers come from 50 different tribes and most of them direct from the farms of their homelands. Rhythmic dancing is their natural recreation, and so it is that they practise and compete during their leisure. Contrary to popular belief none of the dances are war dances. Visitors to Johannesburg should not miss the opportunity to attend the inter-tribal dances held nearly every Sunday morning at one or other of the mine compounds where the performances are widely representative of all tribes. Nowhere else in Africa will you have such an opportunity. For details and directions telephone the Chamber of Mines at 838-8211 and ask for Mine Visits.

What has come to be known as Greater Soweto comprises the original Soweto township and three others close to Soweto. These Black peoples Townships, some 25 kilometres to the south-west of Johannesburg, cover an area of 63 square kilometres where 101 000 houses (which would cost over R400-million to replace) house a population of over a million. A large proportion of these people work in Johannesburg and other Reef towns. The original housing scheme was undertaken by the Johannesburg City Council after World War II and 60 000 houses were constructed by 1964. In 1973 the administration of this colossal scheme was transferred to the West Rand Administration Board (WRAB), and today authority of administration is vested in three black peoples councils elected by the citizens of Greater Soweto with WRAB acting as agent of the councils and agent of the central government.

Tours of the townships are conducted by the Communications Services. Telephone 932 000 for details.

University of the Witwatersrand

Having descended from the South African School of Mines which came into being at Kimberley in 1896, University of the Witwatersrand, Johannesburg, was formally constituted in 1922 and established at Milner Park on 33 hectares of land donated by the Municipality of Johannesburg. The first chancellor was HRH Prince Arthur of Connaught, the first vice-chancellor, Sir Robert Kotze, and the first principal, Jan H Hofmeyr (at the age of 28), later The Right Honourable, Minister of Finance and Deputy Prime Minister in the Smuts government.

With the acquisition of an adjacent 32 hectares in 1985 (previously the Milner Park Showground, and for 90 years the venue of the Rand Show), the land area of the main campus has been doubled – the newly acquired portion, known as the Western Campus, forming an integral part of the original campus. The Medical School is located opposite the Johannesburg Hospital in Parktown and the Graduate School of Business Administration is housed in St David's Place, Parktown.

Wits, the largest university in South Africa teaching exclusively through the medium of English, has ten faculties (Arts, Science, Medicine, Engineering, Commerce, Law, Dentistry, Architecture, Education and Business Administration), 105 departments and 1 409 courses. Its student enrolment in 1987 was over 18 000.

Noted for its extensive involvement in research, Wits supports some 47 'own staff' organisations operating in a wide variety of areas. Included are the Bernard Price Institutes mentioned below, and others of significant importance are the African Studies Institute and the Nuclear Physics Research Unit. Modern research tools such as electron microscopes, mass spectrometers and the Tandem nuclear accelerator are available for use by staff and students.

Jan Smuts House, in the grounds of the University, is a memorial to General Smuts and contains a replica of the General's library on his farm *Doornkloof*, Irene. The original cross planted by Bartholomew Dias at Kwaaihoek, Algoa Bay, in 1488, stands at the entrance to the University library. It was discovered and reconstructed by Dr Eric Axelson in 1938.

Conducted tours of the University of the Witwatersrand are held every Wednesday morning and it is necessary to make prior arrangements with the Public Relations Department, telephone 716-3162.

Bernard Price Institutes of Palaeontological Research and Geophysical Research

These two famous institutes of the University of the Witwatersrand were named after one of its great benefactors, the electrical engineer and physicist, Dr Bernard Price.

The palaeontological museum, which is situated near the main south entrance to the Showgrounds, accommodates one of the world's largest collections of fossil materials, including the enormous collection of man-like bones recovered from Makapansgat, the huge cave in the Northern Transvaal. The geophysical research institute had as its first director the famous physicist, Dr (later Sir) Basil Schonland. At the institute he did important research on lightning discharge and radio. Persons interested in these fields should communicate with the university.

The Planetarium

Situated in the grounds of the University of the Witwatersrand opposite the main entrance to the Showgrounds, the Planetarium opened to the public in 1960 and has had over a million spectators since then. The main planetarium projector weighs two tons and would cost R2¼ million to replace. A great attraction in recent years has been the introduction of Laserama, a scientific development where the powerful laser beam (in harmony wth music) provides an ultra-dazzling fantasy among the stars.

Rand Afrikaans University

Rand Afrikaans University (RAU) has its spacious campus at Auckland Park. Construction was completed in 1974 at a cost of R42-million and this modern academic centre will match the best in the world. The pre-stressed concrete structure, with pillars 30 metres high, embodies new methods of construction and reinforcing in South Africa and covers 15 hectares of lecture rooms, laboratories, staff offices, administration blocks, library and students' centre. The student enrolment at RAU in 1984 was 6 500 and the six faculties are: Arts, Natural Science,

Indaba Hotel and Conference Centre, Hartbeespoort Dam Road, Fourway Park, 35 km north of Johannesburg — in an atmosphere of relaxation and country elegance with its purpose-built facilities — unrivalled in southern Africa. Details on page 403.

Economics and Administrative Science, Law Education and Engineering. Visitors are welcome to visit this magnificent campus on Wednesdays and Fridays at 2.30 pm. It is preferable to make prior arrangements; telephone 726-5000.

City Hall

Johannesburg's City Hall bounded by Harrison, President, Rissik and Market Streets, is a massive stone building of fine architectural proportions occupying an area of nearly one hectare. Dating from 1915, it is a national monument. The main concert hall has seating accommodation for 2 000 persons. The organ specification was prepared by the late Dr Alfred Hollins, the celebrated blind organist of Edinburgh, and in the completeness of design and absence of duplication of tone colours it stands unique in the world. Concerts by the famous National Symphony Orchestra of the SABC given during the various seasons, are usually held in the City Hall.

Rissik Street Post Office and the Impala Fountain

The only remaining building dating from the South African Republic (Transvaal), this post office has been declared a national monument. Erected in 1897 it was designed by Wierda and built by Meiscke and although dwarfed by the surrounding concrete and glass skyscrapers, it stands alone – a symbol of the days of architectural care and graciousness.

In a small garden immediately behind the Rissik Street Post Office eighteen bronze impalas spring over the water jets where rainbows are often formed in the sunlight. The beautiful fountain was presented to Johannesburg by Harry Oppenheimer, in memory of his father, Sir Ernest Oppenheimer. The work is that of the sculptor, Hermann Wald.

Libraries

The Municipal Public Library was founded in 1889 and the fine central library building is on Market Square, the entrance being in Fraser Street, facing the Library Gardens. Located here is the main lending library; the general reference library (which includes the Seymour Memorial Library on mining, geology, engineering and technology); the famous Strange Africana Library and the Children's Library. Michaelis Art Library, the Music Library and the Gramophone Record Library are in Elizabeth House, Pritchard Street. The municipality has 34 branch libraries and a travelling library. The catalogue office and cuttings collection are in Lewis & Marks Building, President Street, and the Photographic Library is at 17 Empire Road, Parktown. At the Civic Centre, Braamfontein, there is the Municipal Reference Library dealing with local government.

Africana Museum

Housed on the top floor of the central Public Library the Africana Museum contains a wide and interesting variety of exhibits which tell the story of southern Africa. The South Gallery deals with the Non-white peoples and contains some striking examples of original Bushman rock paintings and engravings and also houses Professor P.R. Kirby's unique collection of musical instruments. The North Gallery begins with the Portuguese explorers and in chronological order it deals with the European history of southern Africa. The Central Gallery, the Johannesburg Room, houses a collection which gives a résumé of the growth, of Johannesburg from 1886 to the present day. The Museum is open on weekdays from 9 a.m. to 5 p.m. and on Sundays and Public Holidays from 2 p.m. to 6 p.m. except Christmas Day and Good Friday.

Geological Museum and Harger Archaeological Museum

The Geological Museum is situated on the first floor of the central Public Library. Among the outstanding exhibits are the display of visible gold specimens lent by the Chamber of Mines of South Africa; the Draper Gemstone Collection and the Physical Geology display. The Harger Archaeological Museum which adjoins the Geological Museum, contains a small but excellent collection of South African Stone and Iron Age implements. Both museums are open daily from 9 a.m. to 6 p.m. and on Sundays and Public Holidays from 2 p.m. to 6 p.m. except Christmas Day and Good Friday.

South African Railway Museum

Housed in the old concourse (downstairs) in the railway station complex at the top of Eloff Street, this museum contains a wide collection of scale model locomotives and rolling stock, dating from the first trains in southern Africa. In the comprehensive assembly the other services of the transport administration are represented, including motor transport, harbours, lighthouses and airways. Open Mondays to Fridays 9 a.m. to 4 p.m. Closed Saturdays, Sundays and public holidays.

James Hall Museum of Transport

A remarkable collection of vehicles is displayed at Pioneer Park, La Rochelle, on the banks of Wemmer Pan. This collection includes carts, wagons, old automobiles, steam tractors, tramcars and fire engines. The museum is open Mondays to Saturdays from 9 a.m. to 5.30 p.m. and on Sundays and public holidays from 2 p.m. to 5.30 p.m. Closed Good Friday and Christmas Day.

Bensusan Museum of Photography

One of the foremost of its kind in the world, this museum is named after its founders, Dr and Mrs Bensusan, and is situated at 17 Empire Road, Parktown. The history of photography is told by means of a series of photographs and equipment and there is a comprehensive library covering the many aspects of photography. Open Mondays to Saturdays from 9 a.m. to 1 p.m. and 2 p.m. to 5 p.m., and Sundays and public holidays (except Good Friday and Christmas Day) from 2 p.m. to 5.30 p.m.

Bernberg Museum of Costume

This museum, the only one of its kind in southern Africa, is on the corner of Jan Smuts Avenue and Duncombe Road, Forest Town. Here, in a suburban dwelling, models dressed in period costume make a superb display in rooms authentically furnished. To complete the excellent collection are display cases exhibiting a great variety of accessories such as shoes, shawls, fans, jewellery, parasols and other articles of high fashion. Open weekdays 9 a.m. to 1 p.m. and 2 p.m. to 5.30 p.m.; Sundays and public holidays (except Good Friday and Christmas Day) 2 p.m. to 5.30 p.m.

Harry and Friedal Abt Jewish Museum
On the fourth floor of Sheffield House, corner of Kruis and Main Streets, the Jewish Museum is devoted to religious ceremonial art and the history of South African Jewry. There are some fine examples of cases holding the Torah and pointers used for reading the Torah together with such items as multi-branched candlesticks, seals, signs of the zodiac and precious stones set in silver cases. Open Mondays to Thursdays 9 a.m. to 5 p.m. and Fridays from 9 a.m. to 4.30 p.m. Closed between 1 p.m. and 2 p.m. and on all Jewish and public holidays.

South African National Museum of Military History
Assembled in the Hermann Eckstein Park (east end of the zoo), Saxonwold, is a lavish display of weaponry and military uniforms. In this comprehensive exhibition there are famous aircraft of the first and second world wars, tanks, armoured cars, and a wide collection of machine guns, rifles, pistols, swords, daggers and bayonets; the decorative side includes examples of battle flags, medals, uniforms and insignia and there are paintings, many war photographs and a German one-man submarine. Open daily (except Good Friday and Christmas Day) from 9 a.m. to 5 p.m.

Museum of South African Rock Art
In the zoo grounds and open from 10 a.m. to 1 p.m. and 2 p.m. to 4 p.m. is the open-air museum of rock engravings collected mainly from the Transvaal and Northern Cape areas.

Standard Bank Foundation Collection of African Art
This, the largest public collection of its kind in South Africa, includes masks, headdresses, fetishes, beadwork and Ndebele fertility dolls. It is housed in the Gertrude Posel Gallery, Senate House Concourse, University of Witwatersrand which is open on Tuesdays and Fridays from 10 a.m. to 5 p.m. and Saturdays from 2 p.m. to 5 p.m.

First National Museum
An audio-visual presentation of the history of banking in South Africa is the main attraction at this museum. It takes place at 90 Market Street, corner of Harrison Street, daily at 10.30 a.m. in Afrikaans and 11.30 a.m. in English. The museum contains old furniture, photographs, historical documents, and a model bank in the basement.

Adler Museum of the History of Medicine
Situated in the grounds of the South African Institute for Medical Research, the museum has interesting exhibits of the history of medicine, dentistry and pharmacy with emphasis on South Africa's part in this. Open daily from Mondays to Fridays 10 a.m. to 4 p.m.

Chris Lessing Boxing Museum
On the eleventh floor of Old Mutual Centre, 29 Kerk Street, the boxing museum displays trophies, gloves and a good collection of photographs. Open Mondays to Fridays from 9 a.m. to 4.30 p.m. Closed between 1 p.m. and 2 p.m.

Santarama
Established in 1973, Santarama is the largest and most comprehensive mini-land in Africa. A product of the efforts of Johannesburg City Council and SANTA, it is based on the lines of the famous Madurodam in The Hague and occupies 2,8 hectares at Wemmer Pan. Santarama is open from 10 a.m. to 5 p.m. every day of the year.

Theatre and other night entertainment
The seasons of live theatre, opera and ballet are published in the daily press. Johannesburg supports an array of good theatres. Those in Braamfontein are The Civic, within the complex of the Civic Centre; The Alexander in Stiemens Street; The Academy in Wolmarans Street and The Intimate in Smit Street. The Andre Huguenot is in Kaptain Street, Hillbrow, and The Market is in Bree Street. In Sauer Street (behind the library) is The Library Theatre. The Barnato is in Commissioner Street. The Brian Brooke Theatre is in de Villiers Street. In Rosebank, Pact has The Arena, and the Film Trust Arena in Broadway Extension, Kensington South, is a venue for all the live arts and ice spectaculars. The Carlton Centre Skyrink on the 50th floor is another venue for Ice shows. Live shows are also held in the University of Witwatersrand Great Hall, Milner Park. Ballet, concerts and recitals are occasionally presented in the magnificent settings of the city's parks.

There are numerous first-rate City and suburban Cinemas and Cineramas and as many Drive-in Cinemas including one which has been constructed on the top of a mine dump.

For those who seek entertainment to the early hours of the morning, nightclubs, plus discotheques and restaurants abound – Hillbrow, with its exciting cosmopolitan atmosphere, has a wide and varied selection.

Indaba Hotel and Conference Centre
Situated on Hartbeespoort Dam Road, Fourway Park, 35 km north of Johannesburg, this superb conference centre is unique in southern Africa. Its purpose-built facilities, elegant accommodation and outstanding recreational amenities are detailed on page 403 and pictures appear on pages 248/9.

Rand Show
The Rand Show, held at Easter, is one of the three biggest combined agricultural and industrial shows in the world (the other two are of Sydney and Toronto). This is the show where the townsman can see what the country produces and the countryman what the cities produce. The cattle rate with the finest in the

1. In the mine compounds surrounding Johannesburg the competitive dancing of some 50 different tribes is held on Sunday mornings and draws large crowds of supporters and tourists.

2. Illuminated musical fountains at Wemmer Pan in the suburb of La Rochelle.

3. Bars of **99** percent gold, worth millions of rands, being checked at the head office of South Africa's Reserve Bank.

4. Pouring gold into bars after treatment at the Rand Refinery, the biggest gold refinery in the world.

1

2

3

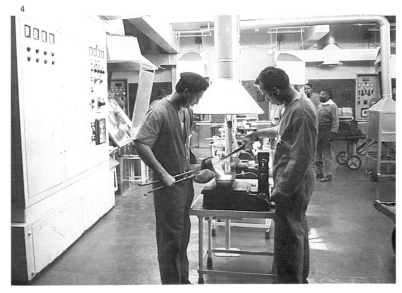

4

world. The grand arena events, overhead gondolas and restaurants provide pleasure and entertainment. The original venue, the showgrounds at Milner Park (now part of the University of the Witwatersrand) was granted to Johannesburg Municipality by President Kruger who opened the first show in 1895. Over 840 000 people visited the last show to be held here which ended on 23 April 1984. The modern venue at Crown Mines, next to the Mine Museum is twice the area of the old venue.

Carlton Centre and other shopping centres

Johannesburg's R88-million Carlton Centre was completed in 1972. This super block of 50 storeys above street level and 7 below is one of the world's tallest concrete buildings. The city within a city shopping centre has six suburbs spread over two enormous levels where there are over 160 different tenants including two department stores. Within the complex is the olympic size ice rink and the 50th floor Panorama outlook. The 31-storey Carlton Hotel has 603 guest rooms and banqueting facilities for 800. The car park takes 2 000 vehicles.

Other notable shopping centres are: The Firs and The Mall in Rosebank; The Mall in Killarney; The Hyperama in Edenvale: The Hypermarket in Norwood; Sandton City in the municipality of Sandton; Oriental Plaza in Fordsburg and Flea Market in Hillbrow.

Johannesburg's parks and gardens and its facilities for sport and recreation

Before the discovery of gold the Witwatersrand was a barren, treeless ridge, inhabited by a few struggling pioneer farmers. Then came the builders and a civic minded people who were determined to beautify. They dammed the waters of the Vaal, 65 kilometres away, to ensure their lifeline and they planted trees and flowers. Suburban Johannesburg today contains some of the most beautiful homes to be found anywhere in the world, and within the municipal area of the city there are 500 parks covering 4 000 hectares. The sporting facilities are also among the world's best.

Joubert Park

The six hectares of lawns, trees and flowers forms a haven near the city centre. It was laid out in 1887 and named after the mining commissioner, Johannes Joubert. This lovely park contains a conservatory, a floral clock, a giant chess board, an open air theatre and an open air art mart. There is a restaurant and bands provide light music on Sundays.

Situated within the park is the Johannesburg Art Gallery and Sculpture Garden. The building, which opened in 1915, was designed by Sir Edwin Lutyens and is a fine example of English classical architecture. The gallery contains one of South Africa's best collections of European paintings and works by famous South African artists. Open daily (except Mondays, Good Friday and Christmas Day) from 10 a.m. to 5 p.m. If a public holiday falls on a Monday the gallery closes the following Tuesday. Tours are held and the gallery opens in the evening during the summer months on Wednesdays, Sundays and public holidays.

Hermann Eckstein Park, the Zoo and Zoo Lake

In the northern suburb of Saxonwold, this magnificent park covers over 100 hectares on both sides of Jan Smuts Avenue and is one of Johannesburg's main recreational attractions.

To the south-east of the Avenue is the Zoological Garden with its collection of over 2 000 mammals, reptiles and birds in beautifully-kept grounds. There are pony and donkey rides for the children and meals and refreshments are served in the restaurants and tea-kiosks. The motor car entrance is in Upper Park Drive, off Jan Smuts Avenue. Open daily 9 a.m. to 5 p.m.

In the north-west portion of this huge area is the Zoo Lake, an unfenced park of shady trees, spacious lawns and a lovely lake for boating and fishing. The amenities include a restaurant and a children's playground. There are swimming baths at the northern boundary of the grounds.

The mining house, Werner Beit and Company, donated the land to Johannesburg in 1903 and the park was named after the deceased senior partner, Hermann Eckstein.

The Wilds

A beautiful 18-hectare reserve of South African flora is laid out on the slope of Houghton Drive, where proteas, ericas and Namaqualand daisies flourish depsite their natural habitat (the Cape) being of a completely different climate. The best time to visit The Wilds is September to December.

Emmarentia and Johannesburg Botanic Garden

In this northern suburb the dam is famed for its boating, yachting, skiing and fishing. The lawned shores provide picnic places. This is the home of the 125-hectare Botanic Garden with its 12 000 tree-rose garden – quite magnificent when in flower. In addition there is the well-known herb garden.

Melville Koppies Nature Reserve

Declared a national monument, the reserve, approached from Judith road, Emmarentia, preserves within its 40 hectares the indigenous plant life and pre-history relics of the Witwatersrand.

Melrose Bird Sanctuary

Over 120 different species of birds have been recorded in the Melrose Bird Sanctuary in Melrose Street, Melrose.

Wanderers Club

One of the world's great sporting clubs, Wanderers Club occupies a large area on both sides of Corlett Drive, in the northern suburbs. The amenities include athletics ground, cricket pitches, golf course, tennis courts, bowling greens and a splendid clubhouse. The Wanderers Cricket Stadium is the venue of provincial and international matches.

Ellis Park

This famous venue for rugby, tennis and swimming is in the suburb of Doornfontein, 3 kilometres to the east of the city centre. It was named after a mayor of Johannesburg, J. Dowell Ellis.

Headquarters of Transvaal Rugby Union, Ellis Park stadium seats 70 000 and has an enormous outdoor television screen which enables spectators to view replays of interesting parts of a game in progress. Inter-provincial and international rugby, as well as professional soccer matches are played here.

All of the important tennis championships and matches of the international grand prix circuit are held at Ellis Park where there are over 20 courts and the centre court stand seats 6 000 people.

The full Olympic-standard swimming pool at Ellis Park is used for all important competitions held in the city, and open air boxing matches are also held here.

Rand Stadium and Wemmer Pan
In the suburb of La Rochelle, southern suburbs, the Rand Stadium is the headquarters of association football. Boxing and wrestling are also staged here.

Wemmer Pan in Pioneers Park is a venue for rowing, boating and water skiing. Within the 88-hectare park there are picnic places, a restaurant and the very popular illuminated musical fountains which play for an hour and a half every evening in summer.

Kyalami Grand Prix Circuit
There is motor racing throughout the year at Kyalami, with three club races, three national events, the Grand Prix, usually staged on the first Saturday of March and the International Six-Hour Endurance race, held in November. Reservations at Book-a-ticket, Carlton Centre.

Witwatersrand Association of Racing Clubs
The Transvaal horse racing calendar occupies nearly twelve months of the year and is arranged by the Association whose six clubs operate from four venues. Turffontein, the main venue, is 3 kilometres south of the city, where meetings are arranged by Johannesburg Turf Club and Transvaal Racing Club. Other meetings are held at Gosforth Park, Newmarket and Vereeniging.

Golf Clubs and Bowling Clubs
Within the Johannesburg area there are some twenty golf clubs. The Municipal Links at Huddle Park are open to visitors. Here, there are three 18-hole courses, a driving range and three practice putting greens. For information as to availability and whereabouts of bowling greens, visitors should contact the Southern Transvaal Bowling Association.

Lion Park
North of Johannesburg on the corner of the main road, Pretoria to Krugersdorp, and the old road to Rustenburg, the Lion Park comprises 360 hectares with a 16-kilometre road circuit and a variety of game animals, especially lions, which may be viewed at close quarters.

Transvaal Snake Park
Situated at Halfway House, between Johannesburg and Pretoria, the snake park has a large variety of reptiles. Regular demonstrations of milking poisonous snakes are held.

Witwatersrand Towns

The mining and industrial towns of the Witwatersrand spread out to the east and west of Johannesburg over a distance of 96 kilometres. The maze of roads and ill-defined boundaries make it difficult for the stranger to determine, from time to time, his exact location. Each of these towns occupies a wide area; each has its separate residential environment and recreational grounds. A feature of the Witwatersrand is the number of man-made lakes.

Other urban areas of pure residential structure have become municipalities administering their own affairs.

Randburg and Sandton
To the north of Johannesburg are the municipalities of Randburg, with a population of 104 000, and Sandton with a population of 64 000. Primarily residential, these towns have developed with amazing rapidity and contain some of the most magnificent homes, gardens, golf courses and other residential amenities in the Republic. Sandton was established in 1969 when Bryanston and Sandown merged and the areas of Morningside, Rivonia and Witkoppen were incorporated. Sandton City is a shopping complex comparable with the finest anywhere in the world.

Midrand
Half-way between Johannesburg and Pretoria is Midrand, a municipality established in July 1981 incorporating Olifantsfontein and Halfway House, and a number of residential developments. The population is 18 000 and within the municipal area (170 square kilometres) is Kyalami with its beautiful homes, country club, riding stables and Grand Prix circuit.

Germiston (East Rand)
Bordering Johannesburg on the East Rand is the city of Germiston with a population of 220 000.

In 1887, August Simmer and John Jack, on their way to the Eastern Transvaal, outspanned on the farm Elandsfontein; they liked the place, decided to buy it and abandoned their trek farther east. About two kilometres from the present Simmer and Jack mine, John Jack laid out a town and called it Germiston after his father's farm, 11 kilometres from Glasgow. Germiston became a municipality in 1903 and a city in 1950. The Simmer and Jack gold mine is now a museum.

With its extensive marshalling yards, Germiston is the largest railway transportation centre in the Republic. It is the third city of the Transvaal and the sixth of South Africa. In Germiston is the largest gold refinery in the world with an annual output of approximately 74 percent of the total gold produced in the Western world (estimated to be 65 percent of the total world production). Among the 600 secondary industries are those of basic metals, machinery, telecommunications equipment, transportation equipment, steel and concrete

Pages 256 and 257

**Three-star Mount Grace
Country House Hotel, an
enchanting retreat 85 km
from Johannesburg, at
the foothills of the
Magaliesberg on the way
to Rustenburg and
Bophuthatswana.**

**Mount Grace
in its 17-hectare
parkland setting
rates with the very best
country hotels in
southern Africa and
is an established
convention centre.**

structures, clothing, textiles, assaying, refining of precious metals, food processing, glass and ceramics, paper and packaging, joinery, furniture, building materials and many others.

Germiston Lake covers a surface of 65 hectares and is surrounded by 40 hectares of parkland with a first-rate caravan park amongst well-established trees. Gosforth Park is the venue for the race meetings of Germiston Sporting Club and Benoni Turf Club. Rand Airport (owned by the Johannesburg City Council) handles a considerable volume of traffic in the Republic and is in the centre of Germiston.

Boksburg

Boskburg was named after W.E. Bok, a friend of President Kruger and Secretary of the National Committee. It was founded in 1887 and became a municipality in 1903. The first railway of the Transvaal called the 'Rand Tram' was built in 1890 and linked Johannesburg with Boksburg. The mining commissioner, Montague White, was responsible for beautifying the town when he planted over 100 000 trees and built a dam across the valley. This today is Boksburg Lake which provides the town with a handsome recreational area. The population of the town is 204 000.

E.R.P.M., the deepest gold mine in the world, is in Boksburg and there is considerable industrial activity, notably in the manufacturing of electric motors, transformers, switchgear, electric stoves and washing machines, high tension insulators, nuts, bolts, nails, veneered boards, edible oils, detergents, railway trucks, cranes, boilers and many other products.

St Dominic's Convent, Boksburg, is acknowledged to be a fine school for girls, however its world fame stems from its Drum Majorettes who took first place and the title 'Miss Drill Squad' in two world championships in the USA; the first in 1982 and again in 1984.

Benoni

Benoni owes its attractive layout, trees, lake and wide open spaces to the foresight of Sir George Farrar, of the mining company that owned the land. The name Benoni comes from the Old Testament and means 'son of sorrow'. Benoni became a municipality in 1907 and has a population of 250 000. The industrial part of the town is extensive and includes steel rolling mills, foundries, die and pattern making, gear manufacturing as well as rubber, textile, chemical and asbestos factories. Korsman Bird Sanctuary is a 60-hectare reserve with a variety of aquatic birds including ibis and flamingoes and a number of antelope. There are two fine golf courses in Benoni.

Brakpan

Brakpan became a municipality in 1919 and has a population of 90 000 and received its name from the brack water pan to the north of the town. Originally it was established in the centre of the gold- and coal-mining district and like other Reef towns has developed a healthy industrial output particularly in the line of foundries and engineering shops. The town's recreational facilities centre around Hosking Park and Jan Smuts Park on the shores of V.F.P. Dam.

Springs

Springs takes its name from the original farm, presumably so named from the fountains there. After the discovery of a good quality coal in the area in 1890 the railway known as the 'Rand Tram' had its terminus extended to Springs (the railway company, Z.A.S.M., mining its own coal). Gradually, coal mining gave way to gold mining and industry. Springs became a municipality in 1904, it has a population of 175 000 and among its industries are food processing and cosmetics, glass and paper manufacturing. Murray Park pleasure resort, laid out next to Alexander Dam, and Davies Drive Lake with its lawns to the water's edge, are two fine assets of the town. P.A.M. Brink Stadium is the home of the Eastern Transvaal Rugby Union.

Nigel

Nigel lies to the south of Springs and is a fast-developing industrial town with a population of 54 000. It became a municipality in 1930. The town took its name from the Nigel Gold Mining Company, formed in the 1880s and so named by its founder, Petrus Johannes Marais, a farmer and storekeeper who, after reading Sir Walter Scott's The Fortunes of Nigel believed that the tale symbolised his own dreams, aspirations and problems. The name of the suburb Glenvarloch is from the book and all of its streets are named after the characters.

Kempton Park, Edenvale and Alberton

To the north of Germiston and Benoni is Kempton Park with a population of 92 000.

Within its municipal boundary is Jan Smuts International Airport and the huge industrial complex of Isando with numerous national manufacturers such as South African Breweries, Barlows, Gordons, Agfa and Siemens.

Kempton Park is the railway junction for Modderfontein Dynamite Factory of African Explosives and Chemical Industries – the largest dynamite factory in the world. Close by, the giant Kelvin Power Station generates electricity for the East Rand and adjoining is the municipality of Edenvale with its knitwear factory, other industries, modern housing schemes and the well-appointed two-star Duneden Hotel. Nearby is the Hyperama, the largest shopping complex in Africa.

South of Germiston is Alberton, one of the most rapidly developed industrial towns in South Africa. Here are the plants of Fiat, Fuchs, Wispeco and many others and within the municipality is the Newmarket Race Course where Wednesday meetings are held.

Roodepoort (West Rand)

On the West Rand the municipality of Roodepoort adjoins Johannesburg. An extensive residential city with a developing industrial sector, Roodepoort was among the pioneer gold mining areas with Fred and Harry Struben working their Confidence Reef; A.P. Marais on Maraisburg and van der Hoven, Bantjies and Lys on Florida. The municipality incorporates the former towns of Roodepoort, Hamberg, Florida and Maraisburg and the population is 166 000. Florida Lake and the adjoining park provide one of the finest recreational and picnic areas on the Witwatersrand.

Krugersdorp

Krugersdorp dates from 1887 when a portion of the farm Paardekraal was laid out as a town which was named after President Paul Kruger. In the days when Transvaal history was being made, Krugersdorp was the scene of drama and action and it was for no mean reason that it became known as the 'fighting town'. The Paardekraal Monument commemorates the meeting of 6 000 burghers in 1880. They met to record their protest against the British annexation of their country and appointed a triumvirate – Paul Kruger, Piet Joubert and Marthinus Pretorius – with power to act.

As a sign of their solemn pledge to stand united, each of the 6 000 men placed a stone on a cairn. In a short, decisive war, independence was restored and the burghers resolved that there be a celebration held at the cairn on 16 December every five years to combine thanksgiving for independence and victory over Dingaan. Krugersdorp has a population of 117 000. It is a mining and industrial town with a busy, modern commercial centre and its whole area is beautified with trees, lawns, flowers and spacious recreational parks (notably Coronation Park and the Wanderers Ground). There are gold mines within the municipal boundaries and rich deposits of manganese, iron, asbestos and dye in the district. South Africa's first uranium recovery plant was opened here in 1952; West Rand Consolidated being the first mine in the world to produce uranium as a by-product of gold. The sand dump from this mine is the largest man-made 'mountain' in the world.

Krugersdorp, 1 740 metres above sea level, is on the summit of the Witwatersrand, close to the western edge of the ridge where fine, rugged scenery falls away to the bush covered land of the lowveld country. The moderate climate, brisk in the lovely autumn and winter months, and the natural scenic beauty of the district has led to the development of attractive pleasure resorts for picnicking, braaivleis, swimming and other recreational pursuits.

Krugersdorp Game Reserve

This interesting reserve occupies 1 400 hectares of undulating grasslands, forest and bushveld, five kilometres west of the town. It contains over a thousand head of antelope in addition to zebra, giraffe, white rhino, lion, leopard, hyena, jackal and numerous bird species. A feature of the reserve is its openness, affording unobstructed photographic possibilities. The reserve provides overseas short-stay visitors to Johannesburg (only 40 km away) the opportunity to see South African wildlife. Luxury hutted accommodation surrounds the filtered, heated swimming pool. Hot meals may be purchased at the kiosk near the tree house. Enquiries and reservations to P.O. Box 94, Krugersdorp. Telephone 660-6611.

Sterkfontein Caves

These famous caves were discovered in 1896 by the Rand pioneer, G. Martinaglia and are situated eleven kilometres north-west of Krugersdorp. Dr Robert Broom (1866-1951) referred to the caves as the anthropological treasure-house of the world. His discovery here in 1947 of a set of bones of the semi-human female ape attracted world-wide scientific attention to the caves. Described as the most perfect pre-human skull ever found, *Plesiantropus transvaalensis* soon took on the jocular name of Mrs Pless.

A proclaimed national monument, the Sterkfontein Caves are under the control of the University of the Witwatersrand and comprise six large caverns connected by smaller chambers and a maze of passages. There are stalactite and stalagmite formations and fossil remains to be seen in the caverns. The bone-bearing breccia deposits have yielded enormous quantities of bones of extinct apes, sabretooth tigers and other carnivores, horses and smaller mammals, all belonging to extinct species. The large underground lake of crystal clear water, the only one of its kind in South Africa, is reputed to flow from Maloney's Eye, 27 kilometres away. The local tribespeople believe this water to have curative powers. Conducted tours of the caves are held daily from 9 a.m. to 5 p.m. and the tour lasts 45 minutes. The Robert Broom Museum adjoins the restaurant near the caves.

Randfontein

South west of Krugersdorp is the goldmining town of Randfontein with a population of 51 000. The famous mining magnate, Sir J.B. Robinson (of Robinson Mine and Robinson Deep) secured options and started the Randfontein Estates mine in 1889. The recreational areas of the town are the Robinson and Riebeeck Lakes.

Western Transvaal

Magaliesburg

The quaint village of Magaliesburg and the handsome eminence known as the Magaliesberg took their names from the perennial Magalies River. Here in the beautiful river valley the chief of the Po tribe, Magali, once lived.

To this rugged region, which lies approximately half-way between Krugersdorp and Rustenburg on the main route to Bophuthatswana, the city dwellers of the nearby Witwatersrand are attracted to relax at weekends and in the holiday seasons.

The environmental attractions are both natural and man-made, and visitors to the area certainly have in the Mount Grace Country House Hotel one of the most enchanting establishments of its kind anywhere in the Republic. Mount Grace occupies a spectacular position to the north of the village; the turnoff, right, is 1½ km along the R24 – it is well marked and is just past the Wicker Tea Garden. The tarred subsidiary road to the hotel passes Camp Caplan of the United Progressive Jewish Congregation, and Boys Town.

To the north of Mount Grace, drives along the Maanhaarrand road to see the Rosalind Rose Farm and the herb garden of Maggie Roberts are really worthwhile. The road to Hekpoort is scenically beautiful, and on the road to the Sterkfontein Caves there is trout fishing at the Rainbow Trout Farm.

Rustenburg

Rustenburg is pleasantly situated near the western end of the Magaliesberg range. When its founders laid out the town in 1851 the name 'town of rest' suited the tree-filled valley. The Transvaal Volksraad sat here in 1852 during the rivalry for leadership between Andries Pretorius and Andries Potgieter. Not far from the town was Paul Kruger's farm Boekenhoutfontein, where the old homestead (restored in 1983) is now a restaurant. There is a statue of the president by the French sculptor, Achard, in the garden of the Town Hall. The British built a fort in Rustenburg after the occupation of 1877. In 1880 it was besieged by the Boers.

Rustenburg became a municipality in 1918 and today has a population of 39 500. It is the centre of a rich citrus, tobacco and cotton farming district (aided by an extensive irrigation system). The United Tobacco Company factory is the largest pipe-tobacco factory in the Southern Hemisphere. Two other substantial organisations in the town are Magaliesburg Milling Company and the citrus concern, Rustenburg Co-operative Packhouse Company Limited.

Rustenburg Platinum Mine is the largest single platinum producer in the world. This mine also produces significant quantities of palladium, iridium, nickel and silver.

Throughout the year but particularly in the winter months, Rustenburg attracts holiday makers to its mild climate and attractive surroundings. The municipality has laid out a pleasant holiday resort in the Rustenburg Kloof where there are furnished rondavels and first rate facilities for caravanners and campers. The delightful swimming pools are watered by the mountain streams. At the southern entrance to the town is the Paul Bodenstein Reserve, a sanctuary for small game and birds. The well-known holiday resort hotels of Rustenburg are Safari, Hunter's Rest, Tambuti Inn, Olifantsnek, Sparkling Waters and The Wigwam.

Northam, Thabazimbi and the Pilanesberg

The road due north of Rustenburg leads through the Republic of Bophuthatswana (Chapter 15) to the platinum mine of Northam and the enormous iron mine at Thabazimbi ('mountain of iron') which supplies the Iron and Steel Corporation (Iscor). In Bophuthatswana, 40 kilometres north-west of Rustenburg, is the Pilanesberg, a unique geological circular formation of volcanic rocks 28 kilometres in diameter. It forms part of the *Bushveld Igneous Complex* described by the distinguished geologist, Dr A.L. Du Toit, as 'one of the most remarkable geological occurrences in the whole world'. The range was named after the Tswana chieftain, Pilane.

Swartruggens

Also known as Rodeon, Swartruggens is on the road between Rustenburg and Zeerust and the main railway line between Johannesburg and Mafikeng. The town has a population of 3 000 and was the scene of the first action involving the Australian contingent in the Anglo-Boer War.

Muzista, South Africa's largest slate producer, has its quarry at Swartruggens from where slate is exported to Australia, Europe, the Far East and the USA.

Groot Marico

The rural centre of Groot Marico, with its intriguing Voortrekker atmosphere, is in the valley of the river with the same name, where there are farms of citrus, tobacco, lucerne and cattle. This is the valley of the tales of that great South African author, Herman Charles Bosman.

Zeerust

Zeerust was named after its founder, D.J. Coetzee, and was originally Coetzeerust (Coetzee's rest). It was founded in 1867 and became a municipality in 1937. Today it has a population of 12 000 and serves a district producing citrus, tobacco, wheat, maize and cattle. Twenty kilometres west of Zeerust, at Mosega (the divider), Hendrik Potgieter's force (which included Gert Maritz and Pieter Uys) attacked Mzilikazi's Matabeles (a tribe of the Zulus) on 17 January 1837. It was not until November of that year that Potgieter and Uys led the main Voortrekker assault on the Matabele in the celebrated 'Nine Days War' at the royal kraal of Kapain to the north of Mosega and scored a resounding victory that resulted in Mzilikazi and his Matabele fleeing into what is today Zimbabwe.

The road south of Zeerust divides at Ottoshoop; the branch to the right leads to Mafikeng (Chapter 15) and the road to the left to Lichtenburg.

Lichtenburg

A striking feature of Lichtenburg is its handsome central square (shadowed by Karee trees) with its magnificent equestrian statue of General Delarey (the Volksraad member for Lichtenburg and brilliant leader in the Anglo-Boer War). It is a pleasant, tranquil town but this has not always been the scene. The discovery, in 1926, of alluvial diamonds by Jacobus Voorendyk on his farm Elandsputte and the following year at Grasfontein, brought a frenzied rush of over 100 000 fortune seekers to the area. Some magnificent stones were found and fortunes were made but the findings petered out in 1935. The museum, which contains relics of the diamond rush days, and the library, are worth visiting. Lichtenburg today has a population of 19 000 and is the centre for an important maize and sunflower seed producing district. White's Portland Cement Works was established here in 1950. At the two-star Elgro Hotel comfort and good food are provided.

Barberspan Nature Reserve

Eighty kilometres south-west of Lichtenburg, on the road to Delareyville, is Barberspan Nature Reserve with its lake, 25 square kilometres in extent. The lake is fed by the Harts River and takes its name from the barber (barbel) which stock the waters. There are also carp and yellow fish and this is a great place for fishing competitions among the neighbouring farmers. The birdlife is prolific and the area has been developed as a resort around the Elgro Hotel, with bungalows, caravan sites, swimming, boating and skiing.

Delareyville

Founded in 1914, Delareyville was named after the famous Boer general. The population of 8 500 is principally engaged in salt production from the natural pans in the area.

Schweizer-Reneke
Schweizer-Reneke was named after two soldiers, Captain Schweizer and Field-Cornet Reneke, who were killed in an expedition against a local tribe in 1885. The town lies on the banks of the Harts River and is the centre of a farming district noted for maize and sunflower seeds. Groundnuts, wool and beef are also produced. The population is 11 000.

Christiana
From Schweizer-Reneke a road leads to the southern-most town of the Transvaal, Christiana, which was named after the daughter of the Voortrekker leader, Andries Pretorius, who crossed the Vaal at this point. Founded in 1870 as diamond diggings, its importance today centres around the agricultural development of the nearby Vaal-Harts irrigation scheme. The population of Christiana is 8 000.

From Christiana route R29 heads north-east. Six kilometres out of the town is the turnoff to the Rob Ferreira Mineral Baths, well developed with accommodation, restaurant and all facilities.

North of the mineral baths in the Orange Free State is the famous prehistoric rock engraving resembling a hippo, on the farm Stowlands-on-Vaal.

Bloemhof
Bloemhof, on the Vaal River, is a maize centre with a population of 6 500. To the north of the town there are still signs of the diamond diggings of the 1870s.

Wolmaransstad
Founded in 1890 Wolmaransstad was named after Jacobus Wolmarans, the South African Republic Volksraad member. There are old diamond diggings in the district and maize is the main crop of the farmers. The population of the town is 9 500.

Klerksdorp
The oldest white settlement of the Transvaal, Klerksdorp was founded in 1837 on the trekker farm of C.M. du Plooy. He gave a number of other trekkers each an erf of ground and communal grazing rights in return for their protection. The settlement was named after the leader of the group, Barend le Clerq. The farming community remained in peace until gold was discovered in 1886. There followed disputes over land rights and in 1887 President Kruger confirmed the ownership of the original settlers.

Initially, vast sums were expended on the gold mines of Klerksdorp. A town sprang up with numerous commerical buildings including a Stock Exhange and no less than 67 bars and beerhalls. Everything looked rosy for Klerksdorp but by the 1890s it was found that production costs did not warrant the continuance of mining and during the Anglo-Boer War the mines closed completely. There was a revival of interest in 1936 but the Second World War intervened. At the end of the war R200 million was invested and with new mining methods

the Klerksdorp mines went ahead and today gold and uranium are produced on a profitable scale. Klerksdorp is also the head office of South Africa's largest grain co-operative, The Central Western Co-operative Company.

Klerksdorp is a modern town with every amenity. It is fast developing industrially and has a population of 86 000. For the visitor there are three hotels. The prehistoric rock engravings at Bosworth, 18 kilometres to the north of the town, have been proclaimed a national monument.

Orkney
The border town Orkney lies south of Klerksdorp on the Vaal River and is the centre of Western Reefs, Vaal Reefs and Zandpan Gold mines. It is a uranium extraction point and Pretoria Portland Cement Company has a factory there. Orkney is the headquarters for Western Transvaal of the Electricity Supply Commission; the great generating station of Vierfontein being 20 kilometres to the south in the Orange Free State. There is a fine pleasure resort with yachting on the Vaal. Orkney has a championship golf course on the South African Sunshine Circuit. There are two hotels. The population is 43 000.

Stilfontein
The model mining town of Stilfontein has a population of 29 000. Its inhabitants are mainly concerned with the gold mines Stilfontein, Hartbeesfontein and Buffelsfontein. The town was laid out in 1949 in a most attractive arrangement of spacious gardens and handsome buildings.

Potchefstroom
The Voortrekkers laid out Potchefstroom in 1838 as the first town north of the Vaal River and as the capital of the South African Republic which they were about to establish. Its foundation followed the return to the area of Andries Hendrik Potgieter with his men after the victory over Mzilikazi and the Matabele in the famous 9 days battle in the Magaliesberg. The town was laid out on the banks of the Mooistroom (pretty stream) and there is one explanation of the name being a combination of 'Pot' in Potgieter, 'chef' acknowledging Potgieter as the chief, and the word 'stroom' (stream). The more likely explanation is that the name is derived from the collection of potsherds (in Dutch potscherf) found near the stream.

Although Pretoria replaced Potchefstroom as the state capital in 1860, to this day the town bears an atmosphere of political authority and culture and is still referred to as 'the old capital'. President Marthinus Pretorius owned a house in Potchefstroom which he often occupied during the years 1860 to 1894.

The remains of the Fort in which the British garrison and civilians were besieged in 1880-1881 and the adjoining cemetery is a proclaimed national monument. At the time that the burghers were having their meeting at Paardekraal, Major R.W.C. Winsloe of the 2nd Battery Royal Scots Fusiliers arrived from Pretoria to take command of the garrison of 213 officers and men. The first shots of the war were fired by Cronje's men in Potchefstroom on 16 December, 1880. Winsloe with his force, and a number of civilians including women and children, 322 people in all, occupied the small fort of 25 square metres for a period of three months. During that time there were assaults from the Boer side, sorties from the British side and bombardments on both sides. The British casualties were 25 killed and died of wounds, 6 died of disease and 54 wounded.

In June 1900 Potchefstroom was again occupied by the British. The garrison brought into existence the famous artillery camp which was later taken over by the South African Defence Force. Near the camp (on the Ventersdorp road) is the impressive Gunners Memorial.

The valley of the Mooi River is one of the most fertile and well-watered regions in the Transvaal and the district is noted for its grain, sunflower seed, lucerne, beef, dairy products, fruit, vegetables and poultry. The abundance of water from the powerful springs of the Mooi River (the strongest yields more than 54 000 000 litres a day) enables the luxury of furrow irrigation of private gardens in the town. King-Korn Malt factory, probably the largest factory of its kind in the world, is established in Potchefstroom; other industries include edible and industrial oils, air and water hoses, chalks and crayons, paint, flour and fertilizer.

Potchefstroom has always been an educational and cultural centre. There are fine schools in both mediums, an agricultural college, Potchefstroom University and an excellent Municipal Museum, with many Voortrekker relics. The town boasts a country club and a pleasure resort at the Mooi River Dam, where there is a restaurant and caravan park. Of the five hotels in Potchefstroom, the two-star Elgro Hotel is very comfortable and has exceptionally good amenities for a country town hotel. Potchefstroom is a venue for national athletic championships. The population is 67 000.

Ventersdorp

Fifty-three kilometres north-west of Potchefstroom, on the Schoonspruit, is Ventersdorp. It was founded in 1887 and named after the original farm. Considered to be of strategic importance during the Anglo-Boer War, it was the meeting place of President Steyn and General Christiaan de Wet, and in 1903 Joseph Chamberlain met General Delarey there. The population is 6 500. Nearby is Schoonspruit Nature Reserve.

Carletonville

Carletonville was founded in 1942, became a municipality in 1959 and has a population of 120 000. It was named after Guy Carleton Jones (the mining engineer, geologist and director of Consolidated Goldfields) who contributed largely to the development of gold mining beyond the previously accepted limits of Randfontein, which resulted in the establishment of mining in the Far West Rand. Also known as the West Wits Line, these are currently the richest gold producing mines in the world. Among these big producers are West Driefontein, East Driefontein, Western Deep Levels, Blyvooruitzicht and Western Areas. Blyvooruitzicht and West Driefontein also produce uranium.

Southern Transvaal

Vereeniging

On national road N1, 58 kilometres due south of Johannesburg, is Vereeniging. Its establishment dates from 1878 when rich coal deposits were discovered by the geologist George Snow. Samuel Marks, the Russian-born South African industrialist and friend of President Kruger, formed the company with the name *De Zuid Afrikaansche en Orange Vry Staatsche Kolen en Mineralen Myn Vereeniging* to exploit the coal and received the President's consent to establish a town in 1892, using the last word of his company's title as the name of the town. From its position on the Vaal River close to the frontier with the Orange Free State, the town soon gained prominence and prosperity was accelerated with the opening of the railway linking the Rand with the Cape through the Free State on 15th September, 1892.

At the end of the Anglo-Boer War, Vereeniging was in the world news when peace negotiations were conducted there; although the actual *Treaty of Vereeniging* was signed in Pretoria.

The establishment in 1909 of large electric power stations in Vereeniging was followed in 1913 by South Africa's first steel ingot being made by Union Steel Corporation, started by Samuel Marks. In modern times Usco became associated with Iscor and is the country's principal nut and bolt producer.

Today Vereeniging, with its population of 123 000, is the major source of electric power for the whole of the Witwatersrand with five giant thermal power stations, Vaal, Vereeniging, Taaibos, Klip and Highveld dominating the scene. Its industrial expansion has been considerable, with the establishment of such substantial industries as Stewarts and Lloyds, Massey-Ferguson, President Windmills, McKinnon Chain, Vereeniging Brick and Tile, African Cables and Thames Wire and Cable.

The Vaal River at Vereeniging is ideal for water sport. Vereeniging has a caravan park on the banks of the Vaal, and 4 hotels.

Vaal River

The Vaal River rises near Breyten in the Eastern Transvaal and journeys some 1 100 kilometres before its confluence with the Orange near Douglas in the north-eastern Cape. And on its long course it is well and truly harnessed at many places. The Vaal Dam, upstream from Vereeniging, was constructed in 1936 and spreads out in a highly irregular shape for a distance of 104 kilometres, bulging at places from 10 to 24 kilometres wide, and is up to 52 metres deep. It controls the flow of the water and feeds the Vaal Barrage (built in 1923) from where the Rand Water Board pumps supply the entire water requirements of the whole of the Witwatersrand, Pretoria and the Southern Transvaal, an area of 11 000 square kilometres, at the rate of 1 040 million litres a day. The Vaal Dam also supplies users lower down the river. The Free State Goldfields take 210 million litres a day and the Klerksdorp gold area 70 million litres a day. This magnificent stretch of water is much used for water sport and is famous for its barbel and yellow fish. An area around the Dam is a nature reserve.

Vanderbijlpark

Laid out in 1942 as the town to house the employees of the second steel foundry of Iscor, Vanderbijlpark was named after the Corporation's chairman Dr H.J. van der Bijl (1887-1948). With its tree-lined streets and magnificent Emfuleni Park on the Vaal River it is a model industrial town. There is a Holiday Inn at the water's edge and in the town there are three hotels. The population is 89 800.

Heidelberg

Travelling south from the Witwatersrand on national road N3 the first town to be reached is Heidelberg. Established by a German immigrant trader in 1866 he named it after the university town of his homeland. It became a municipality in 1903 and has a population of 31 000. During the war of 1880-1881 Heidelberg was the scene of much activity as the seat of the triumvirate government. The Army Gymnasium and several schools are in the town. There is an hotel and a municipal caravan park at the recreational centre, the Kloof.

Standerton and Tutuka Power Station

A.H. Srander was the owner of the original farm where Standerton was laid out. It was proclaimed a township by Sir Theophilus Shepstone in 1879 and became a municipality in 1903. The town is overlooked by the mountainous feature Standers Kop and it was from here that the Boers besieged 350 British soldiers in the war of 1880-1881. The town serves an important agricultural district. There are three hotels and two caravan parks with all facilities.

Tutuka, near Standerton, is one of a number of South African thermal power stations that rate with the largest in the world.

Volksrust

After the Battle of Majuba in 1881 Volksrust came into being as a border town. It was here that the people would rest before crossing into Natal and this is how the name came about. The town serves an agricultural district and has a population of 17 900. There are two hotels in the town and Andrews Motel is on the northern outskirts.

Majuba Power Station, near Volksrust, is another of the world's biggest thermal stations.

From Volksrust national road N3 crosses the border into Natal (described in Chapter 10).

The famous bronze of President Paul Kruger which dominates Church Square was sculptured by Anton van Wouw. Behind the statue is the historic Raadsaal where Kruger presided for ten years.

The Union Buildings on Meintjeskop, designed by Sir Herbert Baker in 1910, stands in a garden of 65 hectares overlooking the city of Pretoria. In the foreground is the statue of General Louis Botha, South Africa's first Prime Minister.

CHAPTER 12

Pretoria, Northern Transvaal, Eastern Transvaal and Kruger National Park

Pretoria

Pretoria is the administrative capital of the Republic as well as the provincial capital of the Transvaal. It was founded in 1855 by Marthinus Wessel Pretorius (the first President of the South African Republic) who named it after his father, Andries Pretorius, the hero of the Battle of Blood River in 1838.

The pioneers of the Great Trek, the Voortrekkers, had been farming along the Apies River at the foothills of the Magaliesberg ever since their arrival in the Transvaal in 1837 and after the death of their leader, Andries Pretorius, in 1853 they decided to build a central capital.

The story of Pretoria's early days is one of excitement and drama. When he was elected First President of the South African Republic in 1857, Marthinus Pretorius sought union with the smaller republics. Although he failed with the Orange Free State, in 1860 he received the unique honour of being elected President of that country as well. He had many opponents and Pretoria experienced turbulent times, with civil war around the corner, until Pretorius resigned in 1871 in favour of the Reverend Thomas Burgers. Burgers, in attempting to relieve the Republic of its financial strain, made overtures in Europe. This, together with the frontier trouble with chief Sekukuni, culminated in a political crisis, the arrival in Pretoria of Sir Theophilus Shepstone and the British annexation of the Transvaal in April 1877. The peace and prosperity that followed ended abruptly when war broke out and the Republicans besieged Pretoria from December 1880 to March 1881. Britain's defeat at Majuba resulted in the re-establishment of the South African Republic with President Kruger in firm control. For nearly two decades he dominated the scene in Pretoria as in fact he did throughout the Republic.

Pretoria prospered, the handsome Raadsaal was built and great excitement followed the discovery of gold in Barberton in 1884 and Johannesburg in 1886. 1896 saw the trial of the Jameson raiders take place in the Raadsaal. The tension between Boer and Briton could not be restrained and culminated in the outbreak of the Anglo-Boer War on 11 October 1899. Pretoria was occupied by the British, as a free city, from June 1900 and the Peace Treaty of Vereeniging was signed here on 31 May 1902.

Pretoria has a population of 802 000, it covers an area of 588 square kilometres (the largest municipal area in South Africa) and is at an altitude of 1 370 metres. It was proclaimed a city in 1931.

Essentially a city of fine buildings, Pretoria is notable for its jacaranda-lined streets and rose gardens. There are some 500 kilometres of jacaranda trees in the city and when these are in bloom in early summer the streets are ablaze with the beautiful mauve flower.

Information and Communications

The Visitors Information Bureau is in Munitoria, corner Vermeulen and van der Walt Streets; telephone 21-2461. The National Parks Board booking office is at Groenkloof National Park, Muckleneuk Ridge, Devenish Street Extension; telephone 343-1991 between 9 am and 3 pm only. South African Airways terminal is in DeBruyn Park Building, Andries Street; telephone 26 7028.

A selection of Pretoria hotels appears in the accommodation directory and these include the Burgerspark, the Boulevard and the Holiday Inn.

Church Square

The famous statue of President Paul Kruger by Anton van Wouw stands in the centre of historic Church Square, a garden in the centre of the city, surrounded by fine buildings. The northern side of the square is in the style of the Place de la Concorde in Paris and the southern side that of London's Trafalgar Square.

Among the buildings that face the square are the Raadsaal and the Palace of Justice, both built in Kruger's time. Filled with the atmosphere of the past, the Raadsaal is worth visiting and is open to the public on weekdays. The construction of the Palace of Justice was nearing completion at the outbreak of the Anglo-Boer War and during the British occupation in 1900 it was used as a military hospital; it is today the Supreme Court of the Transvaal Division.

City Hall and Central Station

The main streets radiate from Church Square. Paul Kruger Street leads past the City Hall, with its massive clock tower and carillon of 32 bells, to Pretoria Station (designed by Sir Herbert Baker) where the old Z.A.S.M. locomotive of 1889 is on view. In the garden of the city hall are the statues of Andries Pretorius and his son, President M.W. Pretorius. Church Street East leads to the principal shopping area.

Union Buildings

In 1910 Sir Herbert Baker was commissioned to design the building which was to become the South African seat of Government. Union Buildings, three kilometres from Church Square, are a remarkable achitectural achievement. Magnificently situated at Meintjeskop overlooking the city, on a site described as one of the finest in the world, the buildings were completed in 1913. The design is modified Grecian style; extensive wings with pillared pavilions flank a colonnaided semi-circular central structure with two domed towers 55 metres high. The approach to the amphitheatre is through a beautiful terraced garden of 65 hectares rising from the frontage on Church Street.

On the terraces are the statue of General Louis Botha, the first Prime Minister of South Africa, the Pretoria War Memorial in the Garden of Remembrance and the Delville Wood Memorial. The tearoom is closed on Saturday afternoons, Sundays and holidays.

Bryntirion

Pretoria is the residence of the State President, the Ministers of the Government, and the headquarters of the Diplomatic Representatives. Most of the official and mininsterial residences are at Bryntirion, the suburb on the ridge adjoining Meinteskop. Here are to be found Libertas, the Prime Minister's official residence, and the State President's House designed by Sir Herbert Baker.

President Kruger's House

This is in Church Street West, a few blocks from Church Square. Home of the President from 1883 to 1900 it is now a museum and national monument. This unpretentious bungalow with its pair of marble lions contains personal relics and is preserved in the same condition as when the President occupied it. Open weekdays (including holidays) 8 a.m. to 5 p.m., Sundays 11 a.m. to 5 p.m.

Old Cemetery

Paul Kruger's grave is in the Old Cemetery not far from the house. Here in Hero's Acre are buried Commandant General Andries Pretorius, Advocate J.G. Strijdom, Dr. E.G. Jansen and Dr H.F. Verwoerd.

Melrose House

This beautiful Victorian home was built in 1886 by George Heys of coach service fame. It is in Jacob Maré Street, off Paul Kruger Street, near Burgers Park. The Treaty of Vereeniging, terminating the South African War, was signed here on 31 May 1902, and this was the temporary home, first of Lord Roberts and then Lord Kitchener. It is now a museum and contains beautiful period furniture, porcelain, works of art and stained glass. Open Tuesdays to Saturdays from 10 a.m. to 5 p.m. and on Sundays from 1 p.m. to 6 p.m. Closed on Mondays and religious holidays. At this lovely venue evening musical recitals are held.

Transvaal Museum

On the east side of Paul Kruger Street, midway between Church Square and the railway station is the Transvaal Museum. Apart from geological exhibits for which it is famous, it houses a natural science collection of mammals, birds, reptiles, amphibians and insects, and noteworthy exhibits of fossils including prehistoric ape-man. Open daily 9 a.m. to 5 p.m., Sundays and holidays 2 p.m. to 5 p.m. Closed New Year's Day, Good Friday and Christmas Day.

National Cultural History and Open Air Museum

This museum adjoins the Zoo in Boom Street and contains relics of the South African Republic (Transvaal), the General Louis Botha collection and replicas of General Hertzog's study and General Smuts's bedroom. Open daily 8 a.m. to 5 p.m., Sundays 10 a.m. to 5 p.m. Closed New Year's Day, Good Friday and Christmas Day.

The Pioneer open-air Museum

An extension of the National Cultural Museum is in Silverton and is open daily from 9 a.m. to 5 p.m.

Janse Entomological Museum

Housed in a building in Malan Street, near the corner of Voortrekker Road (one of the arterial routes to the north), it is necessary to make an appointment to see this world famous collection of a million moths and butterflies. Enquire at the Visitors Bureau.

South African Police Museum

In Compol Building, Pretorius Street, the Police Museum exhibits a revealing collection of the instruments of crime. It is open Mondays to Fridays from 7.30 a.m. to 4 p.m. and Saturdays from 8 a.m. to 12 noon.

Engelenburg House Antique Museum

Once the home of the distinguished Pretoria citizen, Dr F.V. Engelenburg, the building together with the art treasures therein were left to the nation upon his death in 1938. Dr Engelenburg, a great collector and nephew of Marie Koopmans de Wet of Cape Town, was an eminent writer and editor of *Die Volkstem* for 25 years. A confidant of President Kruger and later General Louis Botha, he accompanied the South African delegation to the Versailles Peace Conference. Among his other accomplishments, he designed Pretoria's coat of arms. The museum is in Ziervogel Street, near the corner of Edmund and Hamilton Streets, off Beatrix Street and north of Church Street, and is open Tuesdays from 9 a.m to 12 noon and 2 p.m. to 5 p.m.

Staats Model School

This historical monument is a typical architectural example of a Republican school building. During the Anglo-Boer War it was used for the detention of the British officer-prisoners and it was from here that Winston Churchill made his escape in December 1899 after his capture near Estcourt a month before. The Staats Model School is at the corner of van der Walt and Skinner Streets south of Church street and west of Paul Kruger Street. It is today in use as the Library of the Transvaal Department of Education.

Pretoria Art Museum

The galleries of this museum house the famous Michaelis Collection and many works by South Africa's best known painters. It is situated in Park Street, east of Paul Kruger Street and south of Church Street, and is open Tuesdays to Saturdays from 10 a.m. to 5 p.m., Sundays from 1 p.m. to 6 p.m. and Wednesdays from 7.30 p.m. tp 10 p.m. It is closed on Mondays and religious holidays.

University of South Africa (UNISA)

UNISA was founded in 1873 as the University of the Cape of Good Hope. Simultaneously with its transfer from Cape Town to Pretoria in 1916 the name changed. In 1972, a year before its centenary, UNISA took occupation of its handsome R9,5-million academic block on Muckleneuck Ridge. Since then the prominent complex, on the right of the highway at the entrance to Pretoria from Johannesburg, has grown to include the administrative block and the second academic block, at the cost of R12-million and R7,8-million respectively. Completed in 1987 at

1. *The South African State Theatre, on Strijdom Square, was completed in 1981 at a cost of R47-million.*

2. *An avenue of jacarandas leads to John Vorster Tower on Muckleneuk Ridge.*

3. *The headquarters of University of South Africa on Muckleneuk Ridge.*

3

4

5

*4. and 5. Of fine
architectural proportions with
elegant decor, is Volkskas
Centre on Strijdom Square.
From the observation platform
on the 37th floor, reached by
scenic lift, there are superb
views of Pretoria.*

269

a cost of R34-million the library, housing some four millions volumes, is by far the largest library in southern Africa.

UNISA is the only university of its kind in the world, all of its students (88 466 enrolled in 1987) receive tuition by correspondence or what is known as teletuition. UNISA has six faculties (arts, science, law, education, commerce and theology) and caters for the tuition of a third of the 16 universities in the Republic. Ten percent of UNISA students are from abroad. The postal address is P.O. Box 392, Pretoria, 0001 and there are regional offices in Johannesburg, Durban, Cape Town and Pitermaritzburg.

University of Pretoria
The Afrikaans medium University of Pretoria was founded in 1908 and has its campus six kilometres to the east of the city in Lynwood Road. It is the largest residential university in the Republic with a student enrolment in 1987 of 21 290 in the eleven faculties.

Strijdom Square
On Strijdom Square, a spacious area bounded by Pretorius, van der Walt, Church and Prinsloo Streets, there is a strking memorial to South Africa's fifth Prime Minister, Advocate J.G. Strijdom. The giant bronze bust and group of charging horses is the work of sculptor Coert Steynberg.

On the square is Volkskas Centre, the handsome head office block of Volkskas Limited, the wholly South African owned commercial bank. The 37-storey building was completed in 1979. Volkskas was founded by Joseph Jacobus Bosman and a small group of Afrikaners in Pretoria on 1 February 1935. With its nation-wide system of branches it today ranks among the four largest banks in the Republic.

Adjacent to Volkskas is the South African State Theatre, a grand complex built at a cost of R47-million and opened by State President Viljoen on 23 May 1981.

South African Museum of Science and Technology
The only one of its kind in Africa, this museum is in Skinner Street, between Paul Kruger and Andries Streets. Open Mondays to Fridays 10 a.m. to 4 p.m. Closed at weekends and public holidays.

Provincial Building
Adjacent to the Raadsaal on Church Square, this building is a splendid example of modern South African architecture. Opened in 1963, it cost R10-million and houses a fine collection of modern sculpture and traditional South African art.

South African Mint
Many government departments are housed in extensive modern buildings in the central city area. The South African Mint is at the corner of Visagie and Bosman Streets, four streets south of Church Street and east of Paul Kruger Street. Visits can be arranged by appointment.

South African Bureau of Standards
The testing station for the nation, this national institute is engaged upon setting standards for industry and commerce. It is at No. 1 Dr. Latagan Road, Groenkloof, opposite the National Parks Board, and may be visited by appointment.

Scientia
The headquarters of the South African Council for Scientific and Industrial Research (CSIR) occupies 137 hectares, 11 kilometres east of the city. Ten national research institutes with a staff of 1 800 answer scientific and industrial queries from all parts of the world. Scientia can be visited by appointment.

Iscor
South African Iron and Steel Corporation is among the largest industrial undertakings in South Africa and has one of its plants 8 kilometres west of the city where high-grade steel and iron products are produced. Conducted tours are held on Wednesdays and Saturdays at 2 p.m.

Onderstepoort
The Veterinary Research Institute at Onderstepoort, 11 kilometres north of Pretoria, was established after the rinderpest outbreak of 1896. The first director, Professor Arnold Theiler, was knighted in 1907 for his research work in vaccine controls for a number of livestock diseases including rinderpest and gallamsiekte.

Onderstepoort is one of the largest and most successful institutions of its kind in the world, the research station laboratories occupying some 200 hectares with an adjacent 7 000-hectare farm. It houses the Veterinary Science Faculty of the University of Pretoria.

Pelindaba
A name derived from two Zulu words meaning 'the end of the affair', Pelindaba farm was apparently so named because most of its land was to be submerged by the waters of the Hartbeespoort Dam. Here on the high land of the farm South Africa's atomic research centre was established by the Atomic Energy Board in 1949. In the development of nuclear fuels, radio isotopes are made in the atmoic reactor and enriched uranium is produced.

Premier Diamond Mine
On 26 January 1905 the world's largest diamond was found in Premier Mine and named after Thomas Cullinan, the discoverer of the huge, seemingly inexhaustible diamond pipe.

The Cullinan Diamond, with a mass of 3 106 carats and width measurement of 127 millimetres (5 inches), was sold to the Transvaal Government (then under British colonial control) and presented to King Edward VII (Queen Victoria's son). Amsterdam diamond cutters spent two years cutting it up into over a hundred lesser stones, including the 530-carat Star of Africa, set in the sceptre of the Crown Jewels; the 317-carat Lesser Star of Africa, set in the Imperial State Crown and seven other gems of the British Royal family.

The original open cast workings of Premier Mine have been converted to underground mining. Visits can be arranged.

National Zoological Gardens

Pretoria zoo, with its 3 500 different species of wild animals, is one of the largest in the world. The cableway provides unusual views of the animals and there are picnic places, pony rides and refreshments. The famous zoo is situated in Boom Street near the corner of Paul Kruger Street. Open daily from 8 a.m. to 5.30 p.m.

Fountains

What Pretoria people call Fountains is the Fountains Valley Nature Reserve at the source of the Apies River and the southern entrance to the city where picnic sites, lovely trees and lawns, swimming pool, restaurant, tennis courts, caravan and camping sites, miniature lakes with aquatic birds and a miniature railway with its steam locomotive, attract many visitors throughout the year.

Burgers' Park

During his five years in office as the second president of the South African Republic, Thomas Burgers founded the library, museum and the botanical gardens which were named after him. With the development of the National Botanical Gardens in Brumeria Road, Burgers' Park became more of a recreational park and sanctuary. It is bounded by Andries, Visagie, van der Walt and Jacob Maré Streets. A statue of the president was erected in the park in 1955.

Loftus Versveld and Berea Park

Pretoria is the headquarters of Northern Transvaal Rugby Union and of Northern Transvaal Cricket Association. Its famous rugby ground, Loftus Versveld Stadium (named after Robert Loftus Versveld, an administrator of the game), seats 85 000 and is in Kirkness Street, where tennis championships are also played. Berea Park, near the Pretoria railway station, is the home of professional soccer and cricket is played at Centurion Park, Verwoerdburg.

Austin Roberts Bird Sanctuary

The delightful sanctuary, with its observation hide, in Boshoff Street, off Queen Wilhelmina Avenue, New Muckleneuk, was named after the famed authority on birds of South Africa. A small museum displays birds of the area. Open daily from 9 a.m. to 6 p.m.

Johann Rissik Scenic Drive and Klapperkop

Klapperkop, the one remaining fort of four built by the Republicans to defend Pretoria after the Jameson Raid of 1896, is today preserved as a military museum and national monument, and is a feature of the beautiful Johann Rissik Scenic Drive.

The fort is entered by way of a drawbridge and in the courtyard is a most remarkable curiosity in the form of a nine-seater military cycle built by the British during the Anglo-Boer War. The vehicle is equipped with flanged wheels enabling use on a railway track. There are four sets of pedals and four saddles on either side and a centre saddle for the officer-in-charge. The amazing object was devised to locate booby traps, transport wounded and for reconnaissance purposes.

There are a number of small rooms in the fort and these contain an interesting collection of relics, documents, photographs and dioramas which illustrate the military history of the two Boer republics. The museum is open Mondays to Fridays from 10 a.m. to 4 p.m. and on Saturdays, Sundays and public holidays from 10 a.m. to 6 p.m. It is closed on Good Friday and Christmas Day.

To reach the drive (which was named after the Acting Surveyor-General of the South African Republic who was responsible for the laying out of Johannesburg), take the south-eastern turnoff at the Fountains traffic circle, into Maria van Riebeeck Avenue (leading to Jan Smuts Airport) and after about a kilometre along the avenue, turn left at the signpost.

Wonderboom

The most northerly of Pretoria's suburbs, 13 kilometres from the city centre, is Wonderboom. It takes its name from the 1 000-year-old wild fig tree (Ficus pretoriae) with its phenomenal thirteen trunks spreading over half a hectare, some 23 metres high. An area of 450 hectares surrounding the famed tree has been proclaimed the Wonderboom Nature Reserve and Bird Sanctuary. The Wonderboom was first discovered by Voortrekker Hendrik Potgieter in 1836.

Voortrekker Monument

Opened on 16 December 1949, the Voortrekker Monument is six kilometres from Pretoria off the Johannesburg road, and was completed at a cost of £360 000. This memorial to the pioneers of South Africa is a colossal structure in granite which towers 61 metres above the crest of the hill on which it stands. It is a prominent landmark and from its oberservation terrace there is a vast panorama of Pretoria and the surrounding countryside. The monument was designed by Gerard Moerdjik, the South African architect and specialist in public buildings, and symbolizes the fortitude, courage and indomitable spirit of the Voortrekkers.

A wall around the monument is carved to resemble a Voortrekker laager of 56 wagons – the number in the laager of the Battle of Blood River, scene of the final defeat of Dingaan on 16 December 1838. Massive granite figures of four Great Trek leaders: Piet Retief, Andries Pretorius, Hendrik Potgieter and the Unknown Voortrekker, guard the four corners of the monument, and at the entrance stands Anton van Wouw's outstanding bronze of a Voortrekker woman shielding her two children from the dangers of barbarism. The main chamber is the impressive Hall of Heroes; its marble floor is 30 metres square and is surrounded by a magnificent historical marble frieze. The Alter of Sacrifice, a symbolic cenotaph, and the eternal flame of civilisation are contained in the crypt. Precisely at noon on 16 December a beam of sunlight shines through an aperture in the upper dome onto the cenotaph where the words *Ons vir jou Suid-Afrika* (We are yours South Africa) are engraved.

The museum at the monument houses Voortrekker relics and excellent reconstructions of homes of that period. A beautiful tapestry of fifteen needlework panels containing over three million stitches depicting the events of the Great Trek was presented to the monument in 1960 by the Women's section of the Afrikaans Cultural Society of the South African Railways.

The monument is open Mondays to Saturdays from 9 a.m. to 5 p.m. and on Sundays from 2 p.m. to 5 p.m. Closed on Christmas Day.

Hartbeespoort Dam

Thirty-five kilometres west of Pretoria, Hartbeespoort Dam closes a poort in the Magaliesberg, impounding the waters of the Crocodile River to form a reservoir of 12 square kilometres, forty metres deep. In addition to its use to irrigate approximately 16 000 hectares of farmlands, the lake is one of the most popular recreational areas of the Pretoria district.

A number of boating and angling clubs, including Transvaal Yacht Club, are based here and the lake is used freely by the public. Lovely views are yielded by the road which skirts the lake, passes through a 56-metre-long tunnel and crosses the dam wall. Among the varied amenities are caravan and camping sites, an hotel, lodge accommodation, tearooms, a snake park, a small zoo and what is claimed to be the largest freshwater aquarium in Africa, with a remarkable collection of indigenous and exotic fish, crocodiles, performing seals and aquatic birds. A 1,2-kilometre-long cableway connects the highest point in the Magaliesberg with a station at the dam and provides a thrilling ten minute ride with fine views. The cableway is open daily from 8 a.m. to 6 p.m. and on Saturday nights until 11 p.m.

On the northern shores of the lake is Cosmos, with its holiday cottages enveloped by colourful jacarandas, flamboyants, hibiscus, bougainvillaea, poinsettias and other sub-tropical plants.

Doornkloof farm, Irene

General Smuts's home, 16 kilometres south of Pretoria, is now a national monument. A modest rambling farmhouse constructed of timber and galvanised iron (recovered after the first World War from the large military camp in Middelburg), it contains the original simple furniture and many Smuts relics. The general's ashes and those of his wife, Isie, are scattered on Smuts Kop, at the farm.

The grounds of Doornkloof have become a favourite picnic place. Refreshments, barbecue facilities and caravan sites are available.

Verwoerdburg

The municipality of Verwoerdburg, established in 1964 and named after Prime Minister Dr Hendrik Verwoerd, embraces several townships, including Doornkloof, Irene and Lyttleton. On the eastern side of the town is Waterkloof, the South African Airforce station. Centurion Park, the Northern Transvaal Cricket Stadium, is in Verwoerdburg.

Voortrekkerhoogte

Ten kilometres south-west of Pretoria is the Voortrekkerhoogte Military Centre, encompassing the headquarters of Northern Command, the South African Army College, the Military Hospital, and training depots. The Police Training College and Police Dog Camp may be visited by arrangement.

Northern Transvaal and Eastern Transvaal – National roads N1 and N4 and the area between these highways

National road N1, having traversed the country from Cape Town to Johannesburg and Pretoria, continues northward to the Zimbabwe border as The Great North Road, and in so doing follows the approximate route taken by the Voortrekkers. Meanwhile N4 starts its journey from Pretoria, heading due east to the Moçambique border, following the approximate course of the historic Eastern Line (the first railway from Pretoria to Lourenco Marques, now Maputo) the construction of which, it is said, killed more men than there were sleepers supporting the lines.

Within the region the Drakensberg escarpment gives way to the lowveld of the Eastern Transvaal and the atmospheric environment of a staggeringly beautiful wilderness. This is the country immortalised by John Buchan and Rider Haggard; this is *Jock of the Bushveld* country and this is the entrance to the most famed of all game parks, Kruger National Park. The scenery of the region is rich and varied; breathtaking mountain passes, great forests, silver waterfalls, green gorges, strong flowing streams, orange groves, vast plains of thorn-bush, a profusion of wild flowers, fern and singing birds – a land of peace and tranquillity – profoundly beautiful.

Pretoria to Pietersburg

National road N1 now bypasses places of interest as far as Warmbaths. The old Pretoria-Warmbaths road crosses the Magaliesberg range and passes Wonderboom with its thirteen trunks and then the turnoff to Onderstepoort, the famous veterinary research institute – both described in the Pretoria section of this chapter.

Bon-Accord, Hammanskraal, Papatso and Pienaarsrivier

At Bon-Accord are the Pretoria granite quarries and a large irrigation scheme. Hammanskraal serves a large Balck community and is famed for the Hammanskraal South African Police Training College where 500 to 600 Blacks from South Africa and the Black States undergo an intensive six-month police training course. The gymnastics display team is said to be in world class. In the neighbourhood a pan containing a deposit of sodium carbonate is worked.

Approximately 52 kilometres from Pretoria on the right of the road is Papatso, with its large display of tribal art. At Pienaarsrivier there is a tall grain elevator.

Springbok Flats

From Pienaarsrivier, and lying mainly south-east of the Great North Road, extending some 80 kilometres to the south of Potgietersrus, is the vast plain known as the Springbok Flats. The area, much feared by early travellers from the number of encounters with lions in the thorn-bush, is now highly productive in wheat, groundnuts, maize and tobacco.

Two great 3-star hotels in the Northern Transvaal on the Great North Road: 1. The Park, on the northern outskirts of Potgietersrus and 2. The Ranch, south of Pietersburg. These hotels carry a high reputation for comfort, cuisine and hospitality.

Warmbaths

Renowned for its hot water spring, Warmbaths lies 112 km north of Pretoria and has a population of 11 000. The waters of the spring, rich in sodium chloride, calcium carbonate and other salts, are beneficial in cases of rheumatic ailments.

Of the early Voortrekkers, Carl van Heerden was said to be the first to establish a farm at the hot spring which became known as Het Bad. When Mzilikazi was finally driven from the Magaliesberg, popularity of Het Bad grew and many came to take the waters. Before these times, vast numbers of wild animals fell victim to the death trap of this powerful spring and when the area was eventually drained, skeletons of numerous species, including those of elephants, were found. The site was brought under State control in 1873 by President Burgers after his long struggle to persuade the Volksraad to purchase it. Ten years later the place was developed and named Hartingsburg, after Professor Harting, a prominent scholar at the time. The name fell into disuse and in 1921 the town of Warmbaths was proclaimed.

Beautifully developed by the State owned Overvaal Warmbad, the resort covers 1 040 hectares and comprises: accommodation in self-contained chalets spread over a large area, a luxury apartment block, fully licensed restaurant and cafeteria and a first-rate caravan park. The David Brink spa centre, considered to be in world class, provides for both active and passive treatment under the control of a qualified biokinetician and a registered physiotherapist. With a yield capacity of 28 m^3 the temperature of the mineral water at source is 52^{0}C, in the main swimming-pool 34^{0}C, and in the rheumatism pool 40^{0}C. Some 400 000 persons visit the spa annually; many come, especially in the winter months when the climate is near perfect, for the simple pleasure of swimming in the fine pools. A major part of this Overvaal resort is a game reserve for a variety of antelope and birdlife.

A national monument, and preserved in good condition, is one of the British blockhouses of the Anglo-Boer War. There are three graded hotels in the town and eight blocks of holiday flats. Recreational amenities include golf, bowls, tennis and angling in the municipal dams. The town has a landing strip for small aircraft. The district is notable for citrus, groundnuts, maize, wheat and carnations.

Sixty kilometres west of Warmbaths, in a highly mineralized area, are the Rooiberg and Vellefontein tin mines, which may be visited by arrangement.

Buyskop

Six kilometres north of Warmbaths is Buyskop which marked the mail coach staging post between Pretoria and Pietersburg in the old Republican days. From this hill the beautiful rose-coloured sandstone was quarried and used in Union Buildings, Pretoria. This landmark received its name from the notorius ruffian, Coenraad de Buys, who fled north of the Vaal well in advance of the Voortrekkers. The story is told of his sheer bravado when he and his followers were besieged on the summit of this hill by a hostile tribe, who were convinced that de Buys would be forced to surrender through lack of water. De Buys withstood the siege for eight days and instead of surrendering he chose a time when he suspected that his enemies were themselves suffering from thirst and from a prominent position on the hill he hurled a skin filled with water down at them. The dispirited besiegers, believing he had plenty of water, withdrew.

Nylstroom, Ellisras and Marble Hall

It is said that the Voortrekkers gave Nylstroom its name when they came upon the local stream flowing north in full flood and believed it to be the unknown source of the Nile. The town of 10 500 inhabitants is the principal centre for the highly productive Waterberg district. The town is notable for its peanut butter industry and the district for the substantial groundnut and tobacco crops. There is an 18-hole golf course, an hotel and the J.G. Strijdom House Museum in the town.

Nylstroom lies on a junction of roads. The R517 leads north-west to Ellisras (where there is an hotel and Matimba, the world's largest direct dry-cooled power station) and the Botswana border. In the opposite direction, the R33 leads south-west to Marble Hall where there are valuable deposits of marble in fifteen varieties. From Marble Hall the R33 continues south-eastwards via Groblersdal to Middelburg, thus linking the N1 with the N4 and making a short cut to Natal.

Naboomspruit and Zebediela

The next town on the N1 is Naboomspruit (stream of the euphorbia) situated in a district richly mineralized and notable also for its maize, groundnut and citrus production. In the 1920s it was the site of the first practical use of Frank Dutton's road-rail system, a South African invention to provide cheap transport, it ran for some 35 km linking Naboomspruit and Singlewood.

Today a standard-guage railway links Naboomspruit with Zebediela (the largest citrus estate in the southern hemisphere) founded by I.W. Schlesinger, the South African financier and industrialist, soon after World War I. From 650-thousand trees 3-million cases of oranges are exported in a good season.

In the Waterberg, near Naboomspruit, a number of hot springs have been developed by private enterprise as resorts with rondavel and cottage accommodation, mineral baths, caravan parks and picnic places. There is an hotel in the town and there are some 3 000 white inhabitants.

Via the R520 (turnoff 1 km north of town), 25 km to the north-west is the Trans-Oranje Bird Sanctuary and a large variety of indigenous and exotic birds.

The turnoff from the N1 to Doorndraai Dam Nature Reserve is 16 km north of Naboomspruit. Here the antelope species include tsessebe, sable antelope, kudu, reedbuck, steenbok and duiker. The dam impounds the Sterk River and is open for angling, power boating and water-skiing.

Moorddrif

At the point where the N1 crosses the Nyl stream, 41 km north from Naboomspruit (11 km south of Potgietersrus) is a simple stone monument, a reminder of the dreadful massacre of Voortrekkers that took place in September 1854. Here at Moorddrif (murder drift) and in the vicinity, 33 men, women and children were done to death by the followers of Makapan (a tribe of some 2 000 of mixed Zulu, Barolong and Sotho blood). Most of those murdered were members of the party under Field Cornet Hermanus Potgieter (a brother of the Voortrekker leader Andries Hendrik Potgieter) who had been hunting in the Waterberg. Other victims were Willem Prinsloo, his wife and three children, Jan Breed, his wife and three children, L. Bronkhorst and Flip du Preez who were all in one party travelling from Schoemansdal to Pretoria; Potgieter was skinned alive and the six children of Prinsloo and Breed had their heads smashed against the trunks of the two acacia trees that flank the stone memorial erected at the drift in 1937. This brutality was avenged by the Voortrekkers at Makapansgat a month later.

Potgietersrus

Potgietersrus (originally Piet Potgietersrus) was founded in 1858 and named in honour of Commandant-General Piet Potgieter who was killed at Makapansgat in 1854. A modern, well kept town with tree-lined streets and beautiful sub-tropical gardens, it became a municipality in 1904 and has a population of 10 800 whites. Potgietersrus serves a district famous for tobacco, groundnuts, sunflower seed, maize, cotton and citrus. The Chronomore Mine, south of the town, works the richest chrome deposits in Africa. South-east the R518 leads for 45 km to the famed Zebediela Citrus Estate and north-west into cattle ranching country. Also north-west the R35 cuts through Lebowa on its way to the Botswana border. In Potgietersrus there is a municipal caravan park and the Orinoco Hotel, at 66 Ruiter Street, is acknowledged for its comfort and good table.

On the northern outskirts of Potgietersrus on the left hand side of the N1 to Pietersburg is The Park, a three star hotel in the typical thornbush setting with bars, restaurants, lounges and recreational areas grouped around a crystal clear swimming pool – an obvious stop or base to explore this interesting part of the Northern Transvaal.

Percy Fyfe Nature Reserve

Situated on a plateau where the highest point is 1 500 metres above sea level, occupying the 3 032-hectare farm Lunskip is Percy Fyfe Nature Reserve. Reached by gravel roads (well signposted) the Reserve is 30 km to the north of Potgietersrus and 40 km to the south-west of Pietersburg.

Born in Scotland in 1884, Percy Poynton Fyfe immigrated with his parents and was educated at Durban High School and Weenen Agricultural School. He worked in a Potgietersrus bank for 12 years and saved the equivalent of R4 000 to purchase the farm Lunskop in 1912. A dedicated conservationist, Fyfe donated the farm to Transvaal Province in 1953 and in 1954 Percy Fyfe Nature Reserve was proclaimed.

Under the Conservation Division of the Transvaal Provincial Administration the dedication continues. The primary function of the Reserve is the breeding and relocation of endangered species and to this end there has been singular success. In the ten years

since 1977, 180 tsessebe and 86 roan antelope have been bred and relocated in reserves throughout the Republic and in South West Africa and Swaziland. Some progress has been made with sable antelope and 31 of the rare Addo buffalo have been bred.

The Reserve is also the home of black wildebeest, waterbuck, kudu, eland, reedbuck, steenbok, impala, blesbok, klipspringer, duiker and zebra. The Primates are baboon, vervet monkey and bushbaby, and the predators: leopard, caracal, black-backed jackal and small-spotted genet. Of the 209 bird species recorded, a pair of black eagle have permanent nesting in the Reserve, and the secretary bird and black-breasted snake eagle have been seen.

Game viewing, interest stimulation and education are other objectives of the Conservation Division, and youth camps of up to 500 are arranged in the month of April. The facilities are: showers and toilets laundry, kitchen with electric stoves and refrigeration, one hut with several beds and an interpretation hall where film shows and lectures are held. Tents, equipment and food are not provided. Members of the public are welcome strictly on the basis of prior arrangement. Enquiries: Telephone Potgietersrus (01541) 5678 or write to PO Box 217, Pietersburg 0700.

Makapansgat

On the right (east side) of the N1, 14 km north-east of Potgietersrus, is a turnoff to Makapansgat, the enormous cave (600 metres by 150 metres) that lies in a rugged kloof covered in euphorbia, aloes and thornbush. Under the direct control of the University of the Witwatersrand, the cave is not open to the public.

It is a national monument for two reasons. Explorations have yielded valuable pre-human and sub-human relics. Among these are the remains of *Australopithecus prometheus*, the man-like ape believed to have mastered the use of fire and to have been able to make weapons of bone. The other reason for it having been proclaimed is historical. Makapan and his followers who were responsible for the savage killings at Moorddrif in September 1854 were soon after set upon by a punitive force of two commandos led by Commandant-General M.W. Pretorius (Magaliesberg) and Commandant-General Piet Potgieter (Zoutpansberg and Waterberg). In the face of the advancing commandos, Makapan fled, with his tribe of 2 000, to the protection of the huge cave. The generals realising the futility of attack laid a siege from 25 October 1854. During the siege Commandant-General Piet Potgieter was shot outside the entrance to the cave and it was here that the 29-year-old Field Cornet, Paul Kruger, acted with bravery in recovering the general's body in the face of heavy fire. After 25 days, the commandos stormed the cave to find it in a state of nauseating putrefication with three quarters of the tribesmen dead.

Eersteling

Thirty kilometres north-east of Potgietersrus the N1 reaches the turnoff south-east to Eersteling where there are two historical monuments, namely: the First Gold Crushing Site where the prospectors

1

2

1. and 2. Magoebaskloof Hotel occupies one of the most spectacular sites in Africa and is famous for its hospitality and good fare.

3. Troutwaters Inn and Lakeside Chalets on the same route as Magoebaskloof Hotel, R71, have all the appurtenances for happy holidays.

3

Coach House ★★★★T YYY is placed in the beautiful farmlands of Agatha overlooking the Drakensberg, 15 kilometres south of Tzaneen, and is without doubt one of the finest country house hotels in southern Africa.

Button and Pigg used a rocking boulder for crushing quartz in 1872, and the site of the first Gold Power Plant worked by the same miners. The rocking boulder, with a mass of half a tonne is in the Geological Museum, Pretoria and the tall smokestack of the power plant is still standing. The Aberdeen granite specially imported by Button for the construction of the smokestack, is stated to have cost £20 000, and during the Anglo-Boer War an unsuccessful attempt was made to pull it down with a team of 16 oxen.

In January 1988 Severin Gold Mining Company commenced mining at the Eersteling site and early results indicate a rich gold strike.

Marabastad

Continuing northwards, 46 km from Potgietersrus (14 km south of Pietersburg), the N1 reaches the turnoff east to the old British fort, Marabastad. This was one of seven forts manned by the British during the First Anglo-Boer War (1880-1881) which were situated at Pretoria, Potchefstroom, Rustenburg, Lydenburg, Wakkerstroom, Standerton and this one at Marabastad. Here in 1880 a Boer commando lead by Barend J. Vorster forced a siege of 140 British and Hottentot soldiers and civilians in a confined space of 20 paces square for 105 days. Skirmishes took place during the siege resulting in the British loss of 5 killed and one wounded and one Boer was killed. There is a monument in honour of the British at the site.

Pietersburg

As the Great North Road (N1) approaches the southern outskirts of Pietersburg, on the left hand side of the highway is a landmark of considerable significance, The Ranch, one of the best known hotels in southern Africa, and indeed the complete haven after a day's motoring. The director and host, Tom Shearer, deserves congratulations and his hotel the highest recommendation. See pages 273 and 407.

The principal town of the Northern Transvaal, Pietersburg was founded in 1886 and named after Commandant-General Piet Joubert, victor at Majuba Hill. Municipal status was granted in 1903 and the population today is 40 000. The town lies on what is known as the Pietersburg Plateau, at an altitude of 1 280 metres, and despite its situation on the tropic of Capricorn, the climate is invigorating.

The bustling activity in Pietersburg arises from its being the centre for some of the finest cattle ranches in South Africa and it is a major staging post, being half-way between Pretoria and the Zimbabwe border. It is an attractive town with wide streets lined with jacaranda and coral trees, imposing buildings, colourful parks and gardens and a reliable shopping centre. In the town there is a municipal caravan park and a Holiday Inn. There is also an Information bureau and an airport connecting Jan Smuts with scheduled daily flights. The visitor is provided with most forms of recreation.

Pietersburg has always been the administrative centre for the large community of Black peoples of the district, numbering some 500 000. With the advent of self-government for Lebowa there has been a decentralisation of administration to Black townships.

Pietersburg to Tzaneen

The trunk road, R71, from Pietersburg down to Tzaneen is along a singularly beautiful route with many places of interest on the way. Twenty-four kilometres from Pietersburg the road reaches the University of the North with its modern campus at Turfloop, and 10 km farther on is Zion City Moria, headquarters of the Zion Christian Church, the Black peoples church with the largest following in South Africa. In the region forests of euphorbias, aloes and enormous boulders provide a fascinating change of scenery.

Haenertsburg, Ebenezer Dam, George's Valley and the Wolkberg

Fifty-eight kilometres from Pietersburg the R71 passes the forestry village of Haenertsburg in an area famed for trout streams. The village was at one time the centre of the Woodbush Goldfields, named in 1894 after the discoverer of the deposit, C.F. Haenert. Just outside the village a branch road, R528, leads past the Ebenezer Dam, a fine stretch of water surrounded by forest. The dam impounds the Letaba River stabilising the water for irrigation of the valley and providing for yachting, boating and fishing. Overlooking the dam, 5 km from Haenertsburg is a memorial to author John Buchan who undoubtedly loved this area. Cheerio Halt Nursery is notable for the blaze of colour provided by the azaleas and cherry blossom trees in the spring.

Continuing on the R528, it follows the Letaba River on the slopes of the Wolksberg through George's Valley and on to Tzaneen on an alternate drive. The Wolksberg (cloudy mountain) is notable for the magnificent caves there that are being scientifically explored.

Magoebaskloof

Returning to the trunk route R71, a few kilometres after the branch off to Ebenezer Dam (R528), it crosses a spacious plateau in its approach to Magoebaskloof, one of the great ravines of South Africa, traversed by this splendid mountain road which starts on the edge of the northern escarpment and in reaching down to the great Letaba Valley, drops 600 metres in 5 kilometres.

It was here in the kloof that the obstreperous chief Makgoba ('Magoeba' in the corrupted form) and his tribesmen had their hideout, impregnable to the commandos of the old Republic. Friendly Swazi warriors eventually tracked them down and brought back the head of Makgoba.

In arriving at the edge of the escarpment two hotels have been passed and are well worth recounting; one recently established and the other with a romantic history. Opened in 1986, Troutwaters Inn, as the name implies, is built around a private lake which is filled with trout. The Inn has 16 well-appointed suites, good restaurant and atmospheric bar. Adjoining, the Lakeside Chalets and caravan park provide a choice of accommodation. The setting makes for an ideal family holiday, not only for trout fishermen, there is swimming, boating and tennis on the property. Troutwaters Inn is right at the top of the plateau, 6 km from Haenertsburg on the R71. Another 3 km along this trunk route is Magoebaskloof Hotel, famed for its truly spectacular position at the top of the Magoebaskloof pass, and for the warmth of hospitality it has retained during its 50 years of existence. The site is remembered for an even earlier history, for here it was that John Buchan had his shack, at a time when he was secretary to Lord Milner. Spectacular site and history apart, the Magoebaskloof Hotel has all the attributes of a good hotel: gracious comfort, unobtrusive service, well prepared and presented meals and a good wine list.

Dap Naude Dam and Debegeni Waterfall
Approximately one kilometre from the hotel a signpost on the left of the road directs the motorist along a gravel road to the Dap Naude Dam. This gravel road forks a short distance from the main road; the right hand fork leads to the Debegeni waterfall. In the pine forest (part of the Woodbush Forest Reserve) surrounded by a natural pole fence there is a simple stone monument to Alexander James O'Connor, Director and Conservator of Forestry, famed in this area for the successful introduction of Patula pines by the innoculation of the soil of local nurseries with the soil of the forests of Tokai, Cape. Near here is the lovely glade, known as Limber Lost, the scene of the title of John Buchan's book.

The gravel road to Debegeni Waterfall winds its way through the evergreen De Hoek Forest Reserve, at times reaching down to the floor of the gorge where wild flowers, fern and bracken abound. The spectacular waterfall is in the surroundings of dense vegetation, a place of beauty to relax, swim and picnic. From the turnoff to the waterfall the road continues through beautiful scenery to meet the main road to Tzaneen near the foot of Magoebaskloof.

Tzaneen
In a splendid scenic setting, Tzaneen lies at the foot of the Drakensberg on the banks of the Letaba River at an altitude of 700 metres. The name comes from the Sotho Tsaneng (a gathering place). The population of the town is 7 000 and another 7 000 live in the immediate rural neighbourhood. The climate is sub-tropical and near perfect during the winter months, with an average annual rainfall of 900 mm, mainly in the summer months.

After the Anglo-Boer War the Lord Milner administration established what was known as Tzaneen Estate, an experimental tobacco farm with its own cigarette and cigar processing plant, and it was not until 1920 that the township was laid out, on a different site, and the first plots were sold.

Tzaneen is the commercial centre for the rich Letaba district. It is surrounded by magnificent farms of timber, tea, citrus, nuts, winter vegetables and all kinds of sub-tropical fruit. The 8 000-hectare Westfalia Estate (Hans Merensky Foundation) is the largest producer and exporter of avocado in Africa, and an interesting industry at Westfalia is the manufacture of eucalyptus furniture from timber grown, cut and processed on the Estate. The other large industries of the area include vegetable and fruit juice canning, carpet weaving and bus building. The Sapekoe Tea Estate, on the road to Magoebaskloof, is well worth a visit.

Originally part of Westfalia Estate, the Letaba Country Club, with its fine 18-hole golf course, was donated to the Tzaneen Municipality by the Foundation. It occupies a prime position between Tzaneen and Duiwelskloof near Politsi village, and overlooks the Hans Merensky Dam. The dam was constructed under the supervision of Dr Merensky and in the world of water conservation it is considered to be a masterpiece. Other recreational assets of the area are the Olympic-sized swimming-pool, tennis and squash courts. At the Fanie Botha Dam, to the north of the town, there are opportunities for camping and boating. There is a caravan park at Manorvlei and a two-star hotel in the town. Recommendation of the four-star Coach House, described below, is made without hesitation. From Tzaneen Airport, Letaba Airways has scheduled flights to and from Jan Smuts.

When considering a holiday there are many attractions in and around Tzaneen, and in all of southern Africa there is no better place to stay than the Coach House. It is a credit to its hosts, the owners, Guy and Jane Matthews, that they have succeeded where so many hoteliers have failed. At the Coach House you have a commercial structure infused with a residential atmosphere – the place is timeless pervaded with a sense of home. If a holiday is not possible a short visit should not be missed.

Coach House is at New Agatha, 15 km south of Tzaneen and is easily reached by following Agatha Road out of the town. At 1 100 metres, with a direct view of the Drakensberg, the hotel is situated in a cool region where log fires are lit in the winter. See pages 277 and 408.

In the 1890s New Agatha was a staging post on the coach road to Leydsdorp (of gold rush fame) and the romantic history of the Coach House dates from then. The area around New Agatha is rich in archaeological sites.

Duiwelskloof and the rain queen Modjadji
The village of Duiwelskloof is 17 km north of Tzaneen, and the road, R36, passes Fanie Botha Dam, Magoebaskloof road junction (R71), Politsi village, Hans Merensky Dam and Westfalia Estate. It is a picturesque part of the region surrounded by forests and vividly decorated with exotic blooms such as jacaranda and silver oak in the spring; flamboyant and frangipani in summer; hibiscus, poinsettia, golden shower and bougainvillaea in winter. The high summer rainfall, that ensures the splendour of sub-tropical vegetation (some 1 500 mm), was the cause of much discomfort to the early transport riders when the road through the kloof became a quagmire and the place was suitably named Duiwelskloof (kloof of the devil). The modern traveller may explore this beautiful region with the comfort and safety of tarred roads.

West of the village is World's View, from where there is a spacious panorama of the Letaba Valley and the Drakensberg escarpment.

East of Duiwelskloof, in the valley of the Molototsi River, is the village of the refugee Lovedu tribe, who fled from the disturbances in Zimbabwe with their princess in the 16th century. This princess carried with her the great family secrets of rain-making; surrounding herself in mystique, she wielded her powers to the extent that she was venerated among tribes as far afield as Swaziland. She assumed the dynastic title of Modjadji (rain queen) and withdrew from public view. Presents were sent to her from far and wide. She was considered to be immortal and was always obeyed. This was the character upon whom Rider Haggard based his famous novel *She*. Through the generations successive rain queens of the Lovedu people remain out of sight, and the secret ritual of rain-making continues. Modjadji of today will see only favoured guests.

The forest of cycads on the hillside above the Lovedu village is a national monument and well worth visiting. The majority of specimens are from 3 to 4 metres high, while many reach 6 metres.

Tzaneen to Phalaborwa
From Tzaneen there are a number of routes to Phalaborwa; the direct route south-east is R71. Outside Tzaneen the route passes the huge citrus estates of Letaba and Letsitele. North and south of route R71 several byways lead to interesting places.

Eiland Mineral Bath and Hans Merensky Nature Reserve
After crossing the Letaba River, 28 km from Tzaneen on route R71, a branch road, R529, leads north-east for another 55 km to this beautifully laid out reserve on the Letaba River.

On the farm Eiland (which received its name from the islands of the Letaba River), a thermal spring produces a flow of water (43⁰C at source) at some 18 000 litres an hour, and here Overvaal has developed a very popular resort. The indoor rheumatism pool has jets and there are four hydrotherapy baths and saunas. The large warm water, cold water, and children's swimming-pools are placed in the surroundings of well-kept lawns and indigenous shade trees. Floodlit tennis courts, mini-golf, children's playground and horse-riding are other attractions. Accommodation is of high standard thatched rondavels, and there is a fine caravan park of 420 sites. Enquiries: Overvaal Eiland, P.B. 527 Letsitele 0885. Tel: 015238 667.

The 5 200-hectare Hans Merensky Nature Reserve adjoins the Overvaal resort and is the sanctuary of many species of antelope including sable, tsessebe, kudu, waterbuck, eland, steenbok, klipspringer, bushbuck and reedbuck. There are also giraffe, zebra, crocodile and hippopotamus, and a large variety of birds. Adjoining the reserve is the Tsonga Kraal where interesting demonstrations of the life-style of these tribespeople are held in an open museum.

Ofcolaco and The Downs
Some 45 km south of Tzaneen off the route R36 is Ofcolaco which takes its name from 'Officers Colonial Land Company', a land settlement scheme formed by British army officers after World War I. It lies in a fertile farming area where mangoes and coffee are grown.

From Ofcolaco a very rough road leads to The Downs on the summit of the Drakensberg Escarpment. The Downs was named by the famous prospector Orlando Baragwanath who came from the Surrey Downs. Today the area falls within the Lekgalameetse Nature Reserve where there are attractive mountain chalets available for overnight stops. From here the narrow, steep track (built by Baragwanath) which runs over the Escarpment, down to the Olifants River, is negotiable in 4-wheel drive vehicles only.

South of Ofcolaco is Trichardtsdal, where, in 1837, Louis Trichardt crossed the Drakensberg on his way to Lourenço Marques (now Maputo).

Murchison Range, Leydsdorp, Gravelotte and Mica
James Sutherland and Edward Button found the first gold in this outlier of the Drakensberg in 1870 and they named the range, where the peaks reach 1 800 metres, after Sir Roderick Murchison, the famed geologist. The deposits were mostly refractory and nothing further came of the discovery until 1888 when more gold was found by the well-known prospector French Bob and this started a wild rush. Thousands of claims were pegged and in 1890 the government chose the site for the administration of the gold-fields and named it Leydsdorp, after State Secretary Dr W. Leyds.

The mining area became known as the Selati Goldfields, after the female ruler of the small Tebula tribe, and in 1892 an attempt was made to construct a railway connecting the gold-fields with Komati-poort. At about this time mining activities around Leydsdorp came to an unromantic end.

Despite the early failure in gold-mining the Murchison Range is a highly mineralised area. The Consolidated Murchison Mine, near Gravelotte, is the largest producer of antimony in the world and from the Mica railway station, at the southern end of the range, the mica of several mines is despatched. Other important workings are those of emeralds, feldspar and cinnabar, and some gold is still produced.

Phalaborwa
Translated from the language of the tribespeople, Phalaborwa is 'better than the south', and refers to the place being free of fever as compared with the territory farther south. The whole area is now clear of fever.

The modern town was laid out in 1957 and followed the establishment of Phosphate Development Corporation (Foskor), financed by the State to the extent of R23-million with a view to making South Africa self sufficient in phosphate concentrate, vital in agricultural fertilisers. With the apatite (phosphate) deposits vermiculite and mica are found and Foskor also produces zircon oxide as a by-product. Zircon oxide is used in fire-proofing material where high temperatures are demanded, such as in the glass and ceramic industries and for nuclear reactors.

Palabora Mining Company Limited was launched in 1963 to work the enormous outcrop of copper ore, believed to be more than 300 million tonnes. By-products of the copper operation are magnetite concentrate and sulphur dioxide gas for sulphuric acid which is used in the fertiliser manufacturing. The company also operates a vermiculite deposit.

Bosveld Kunsmis was established in Phalaborwa in 1964. It purchases the rock phosphate from Foskor and with the use of sulphuric acid, which it purchases from Palabora Mining, it transforms the rock phosphate into phosphoric acid and double super-phosphates, both constituents of artificial fertilisers.

The mining companies have provided first-rate recreational amenities in Phalaborwa with a fine golf course at Hans Merensky Club (Dr Merensky's early research proved the mineral wealth of the region), and all weather tennis courts and championship bowling greens at Selati Club.

Phalaborwa has a reliable shopping centre and some very beautiful sub-tropical gardens. The population of the town is 11 000. Comair has scheduled flights connecting Hendrik van Eck Airport, Phalaborwa, with Jan Smuts. The three-star, airconditioned Impala Inn makes the ideal base or stop for visits to the Kruger National Park. The

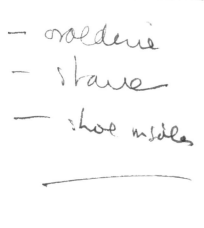

— ordderie
— stare
— shoe msole

Pietersburg to Messina

Continuing on N1 (the Great North Road) where it was left to make the detour from Pietersburg to Phalaborwa through Tzaneen, at 82 km from Pietersburg the road passes Lalapanzi Motel, a popular stop 6 km north of the small centre and hill called Bandelierkop (where the R36, from Tzaneen, Duiwelskloof and Soekmekaar, joins the N1). From here it is a further 30 km to Louis Trichardt.

Louis Trichardt
In 1898 Louis Trichardt was founded as an administrative centre of the Venda tribe. The town occupies a splendid position in a highly fertile region

with the majestic backdrop of the Soutpansberg range. The Voortrekker leader, Louis Trichardt, had in fact farmed in the area for nearly a year after his arrival there in 1837, expecting to join up with Hendrik Potgieter. Finding himself in a grave plight when Potgieter did not arrive, he led his party to Lourenço Marques (now Maputo), arriving there on 13 April 1838, after experiencing fearful hardships. Trichardt and half of his followers died in Lourenço Marques of the fever they had contracted on the way.

The population of Louis Trichardt is 9 000. Following upon the advent of self-government for the homelands, like most other towns of the northern Transvaal, the population of Louis Trichardt has fallen considerably. The town remains the centre of large afforestation undertakings, cattle ranching, citrus estates and groundnut, potato and vegetable farming. South-east of the town is the famous Elim Mission Hospital.

Based at one of the two mountain hotels or one of the two caravan parks, Louis Trichardt makes a convenient centre from which to explore the Soutpansberg and the fascinating tribal life. From here a road leads to Punda Maria, the northernmost gate of the Kruger National Park.

Picnic places have been provided in the beautiful Hangklip Forestry Reserve and an interesting climb to the summit of Hangklip itself (1 718 metres high), is fairly easy. The salt pan, after which the range is named, lies at the western edge. At the summit of the pass over the mountain there is a turn left (west) to Bluegumspoort, a spectacular 15-kilometre drive.

Venda

The famous Verdun Ruins, near Mopane station, and the Dzata Ruins in the Nzhelele Valley, belong to the Zimbabwe Culture, and are held as sacrosanct by the BaVenda who claim these to be the work of their ancestors. Fundizi Lake – said to be bottomless, the BaVenda believe, holds the ghosts of long-dead chiefs and regular offerings of beer and corn are made to appease the spirits.

Thohoyandou (Sibasa), the capital of Venda lies 69 km due east of Louis Trichardt and is the starting point for visits to this very interesting independent state. Full day, and half day luxury bus tours start at the Tourism Office in Thohoyandou from 9 am returning approximately at 5 pm, and picnic lunches are provided. The tour tariff is R45 a day per person (January 1988) and operates provided there are at least three persons.

At Nwanedi Resort, within the game reserve, the hutted and deluxe accommodation is under thatch, and an à la carte restaurant and conference centre are other amenities. The intimate Tshipise Tsha-Sagole Resort has hot springs, and each of the two self-contained cottages has its own mineral-water pool. Ditike is being developed as a craft centre and Venda Sun International hotel and casino is at Thohoyandou.

The Tourism authorities would appreciate it if intending visitors communicate with the Tourism Office at least the day before arrival. Telephone 015581- 21131/6. P.O. Box 9, Sibasa, Republic of Venda.

Wylie's Poort and Tshipise

At approximately 20 kilometres from Louis Trichardt, national road N1 reaches the central valley of the Soutpansberg and then enters the famous scenic pass Wylie's Poort. The two Hendrik Verwoerd tunnels, 457 and 274 metres long (opened in 1961), carry the national road through the mountain, while the old twisting gravel road through the poort still remains open.

Beyond the pass the road enters the land of the baobab trees and passes the turnoff right to the Nzhelele Dam (which irrigates about 1 800 hectares of farmland) and the Tshipise Mineral Baths, administered by Overvaal Resorts. Tshipise is the Venda word for hot spring, and this one yields a consistently strong supply of water at a temperature of 50⁰C. The resort has been developed around two pools and there is hotel and rondavel accommodation.

Messina

Sixteen kilometres south of the Limpopo River is Messina, where the Messina (Transvaal) Development Company Limited operates the largest copper mine in South Africa.

The town, which has a population of 15 000, was founded in 1904 after the discovery of the deposits by Colonel John Grenfell. Long before Europeans reached the area there had been primitive workings of copper and iron, and clear evidence of this was found by the early prospectors. The name Messina is a corruption of 'musina', a word used by the local tribes which referred to the copper 'spoiling' the iron ore which they were smelting.

In addition to copper, asbestos, iron ore and magnesium carbonate are produced in the district. Messina is notable for its magnificent flamboyants and baobabs.

All of the baobab trees (Adansonia digitata) north of the Soutpansberg, including the fine specimens preserved in the streets, public and private gardens of Messina, have been proclaimed national monuments. Described by the famous German scientist, Alexander von Humboldt, as 'the oldest organic monument of our planet', these wood-spongy trees with enormous shiny trunks and disproportionately fine branches can reach the age of many hundreds of years. The tribespeople drink the sourmilk-like juice produced from the pear-shaped fruit. The early European settlers used the fruit as a substitute for cream-of-tartar.

Pretoria to Kamatipoort with a deviation into the coalfields of the South-eastern Transvaal

National road N4 follows the route of the famous Eastern Line linking Pretoria with the coast and Lourenço Marques (now Maputo). The exit from Pretoria for N4 is near the suburb of Silverton with its two popular night stops, Palms Hotel and Oklahoman Motel, and where Sigma Motor Corporation has its giant assembly plant.

Bronkhorstspruit

Heading eastwards, at 56 kilometres, national road N4 reaches Bronkhorstspruit where the British 94th regiment was ambushed by the Boers in the first Battle of the 1880-1881 war. The town has a population of 1 400 and there is an hotel. Eight kilometres south, on the road to Bapsfontein, there is a resort at Bronkhorstbaai on the shores of an eleven square kilometre lake with a caravan park and swimming, boating, yachting and fishing.

Witbank

More than half the coal used in South Africa is produced from the 22 mines of the Witbank area. There are also works for the production of carbide and cyanide of potassium (used in the reduction works of the gold mines), and a major power station of Escom. West of Witbank, on the old Preotria road, is the Highveld Steel and Vanadium Corporation plant. It produces most of the world's vanadium (a metallic element used for strengthening steel) and is one of 200 extractive processing plants in South Africa.

Winston Churchill took refuge in the workings of one of the collieries whilst on his way to Lourenço Marques (now Maputo) after his escape from the Boers in Pretoria.

Witbank takes its name from an outcrop of light coloured stone; it was founded in 1903 and became a municipality in 1910. The population is 60 000. The well-known, airconditioned three-star Hotel Boulevard is adjacent to the golf course in a quiet part of the town. There are two other hotels in the town and at 2 kilometres to the east at Witbank Recreation Resort there are 188 sites at the all-facility caravan park.

South of Witbank a maze of roads connects the numerous rail and road centres of the flat highveld district of the south-eastern Transvaal. The region lies within the famous maize triangle where cattle and potatoes also thrive and where some of the richest coal-bearing deposits of the country are mined. One road linking Witbank with Springs (a distance of 100 kilometres) passes through Clewer, Ogies, Kendal, Delmas and Eloff, all towns with a population of between 5 000 and 10 000 people.

Bethal

A major road and rail junction, Bethal (79 kilometres due south of Middelburg) lies at an altitude of 1 731 metres and became a municipality in 1921. The town has three hotels and a municipal caravan park. The population is 23 000. The original farm was owned by Elizabeth du Plooy and Alidia Naude and the town's name is composed of parts of their first names.

Secunda

West of Bethal are the old-established coal centres, Trichardt and Evander and between these two towns is Secunda, founded in 1977 to house the employees involved in the construction and working of Sasol II and III, the giant oil-from-coal plants which, together with the first Sasol (Suidafrikaanse Steenkool Olie en Gas Korporasie – South African Coal Oil and Gas Corporation) will produce about 50 percent of South Africa's fuel needs. Among the greatest engineering feats in the world, these plants at Secunda use a third of the coal produced in South Africa. The adjacent coal mine, Bosjesspruit, is the largest hard black coal mine in the world, designed to yield an annual output of 25 million tons. Brandspruit Colliery is the largest subterranean coal mine in the world. Sasol II and III have cost R6-billion to construct. There is a Holiday Inn at Secunda.

Kriel

Thirty-two kilometres north-east of Bethal, at Kriel, is one of the largest power stations of the Electricity Supply Commission (Escom) and a major contributor to South Africa's grid system which is based in this part of the Transvaal. Altogether these power stations feed 400 000 volts of electricity to 80 000 kilometres of transmission lines covering the entire country. Kriel generates 3-million kilowatts and two recently completed stations, Duvha and Matla, each supply 3,6-million kilowatts. Two other giant stations of the region (in course of construction), Ilanga and Tutuka, will each generate 6-million kilowatts and will be the biggest thermal power stations in the world.

Ermelo

Named after a town in Holland by its founder, Reverend F.I. Cachet, Ermelo has a population of 26 000. It is in the centre of the eastern highveld in an important coal-mining district. The town is also supported by a prosperous farming area where the chief products are timber, maize, sunflower seed and potatoes, and where cattle, sheep, pigs and horses are reared. At Douglas Dam, ten kilometres from the town, there is a recreational resort with a caravan park and small game reserve.

Ermelo is situated at a very busy junction of roads and has three hotels (including the two-star Holiday Inn) and a caravan park, 6 kilometres out of the town on the main road to Hendrina.

South-east of the town, on trunk route R29, is Camden power station (a major contributor to Escom's grid) and the adjoining Usutu Colliery.

Hendrina and Breyton

Midway between Ermelo and Middelburg (at the junction of routes R65 and R38), Hendrina lies in an extensive coal-bearing area, within the maize belt. Two of Escom's power stations, Arnot and Hendrina, are in the district. The town was named after Hendrina Beukes, wife of the owner of the farm on which it was founded. There is an hotel and caravan park.

North of Ermelo, route 36 links with Breyton, the railhead for Swaziland – to which country SAR road transport operates.

Carolina and Badplaas

Named after Carolina Coetzee, wife of its founder, Carolina was established in 1882 and has a population of 7 000. Between Carolina and Machadodorp (on route R36) is the plant of Feralloys Limited, in an asbestos- and coal-mining district. There is an hotel and a caravan park in Carolina.

On route R38, 52 km east of Carolina, is Badplaas, famed for its mineral spring, it is one of the largest resorts of Overvaal, and is very popular. Its facilities include Badplaas Hotel, rondavels, chalets, caravan park and a huge swimming pool. Details on pages 405 and 420.

Chrissiemeer – Oshoek

On route R39, some 37 kilometres north-east of Ermelo, is Chrissiemeer, a village on the north-western side of Lake Chrissie. This natural lake, with a circumference of 25 kilometres and depth of up to 6 metres, is the habitat of a variety of aquatic birds, including flamingoes. In the surrounding grasslands the farmers breed blesbok for venison. The district is also notable for its forestry plantations. The lake and village were named after Christiana, the daughter of President M.W. Pretorius.

Continuing on route R39, after passing the settlements of Warburton and Lochiel, at 88 kilometres, the road reaches the much used border post between Transvaal and Swaziland, with the unimaginative name of Oshoek (ox glen). The border post is open from 8 a.m. to 11 p.m. Swaziland is described in Chapter 15.

Morgenzon and Amersfoot

South-east of Ermelo route R39 links with Standerton through the village of Morgenzon (morning sun) in the maize triangle. There is an hotel in the village.

Directly south of Ermelo, on its way to Volksrust, route R36 passes through Amersfoort, a town of 4 000 inhabitants in a sheep and maize district.

Piet Retief

South-east of Ermelo, on trunk road R29, is Piet Retief. It was founded in 1883 and named after the Voortrekker leader.

There is extensive afforestation in the area with plantations of large groups such as Huletts, Hunt Leuchars, Rand Mining Timber and Yellowstone Timbers. In the town is the particle board factory of Bisonbord Limited, and the paper mill of Piet Retief Paper Mills Limited. There is also considerable activity in wattle bark. Mica, iron and kaolin deposits are worked and tobacco is grown in the district. The population is 8 000. There are two hotels and a municipal caravan park.

Trunk road R29 continuing south-east enters Natal after passing through Pongola (Chapter 9).

Middelburg

Returning to national road N4 where it was left to describe the country south of Witbank, the next town on the highway is Middelburg. With its population of 33 500 it serves an agricultural district and is near the collieries. It had its start in 1866 as a settlement called Nazareth but the name became unpopular and was changed to Middelburg in 1874; being halfway between Pretoria and Lydenburg.

Outside the town, on the Hendrina road, is the stainless steel plant of Palmiet Chrome Corporation. There are three hotels and a municipal caravan park and rondavels on the shores of Kruger Dam at the southern end of the town.

Fort Merensky and Botshabelo Mission Station

On the Loskop Dam road, 8 kilometres out from Middelburg, is Fort Merensky, built in 1865 by Dr

1. *Where the Eastern Transvaal Drakensberg gives way to the bushveld, near Hoedspruit.*

2. *Tea growing in one of the Sapekoe Estates on the beautiful slopes of the Northern Drakensberg, near Tzaneen.*

Hotel Malaga an irresistible stop across the Elands River on a short turnoff from the N4 at Sycamore, between Waterval-Onder and Nelspruit. A restful retreat where the Mediterranean villa appeal is complimented by fine cuisine and hospitality.

Alexander Merensky (father of Dr Hans Merensky) of the Berlin Missionary Society to protect the Botshabelo Mission Station, it served as a stronghold against the attacks of Sekukuni. It was used by the British forces during the wars 1880-1881 and 1899-1902 and was restored by the Simon van der Stel Foundation in 1962 after which it was proclaimed a national monument.

At Botshabelo Mission Station there is a most attractive presentation of the handcraft of the Ndebele Tribespeople in the form of an open air museum.

Loskop Dam

The resort and nature reserve at Loskop Dam, 55 kilometres north of Middelburg is a Transvaal Board of Public Resorts development of exceptional merit. The dam impounds the waters of the Olifants River providing irrigation for 26 000 hectares of surrounding farms of groundnuts, tobacco, grain, cotton and vegetables. With its fine caravan park, bungalow accommodation and restaurant the resort provides opportunities for boating, fishing and swimming, and a number of game animals are to be seen in the reserve.

The route from here through Groblersdal, Marble Hall, Roedtan to national road N1 is most pleasant and the one popular with Zimbabwians travelling to and from the Natal coast.

Belfast

At 1 970 metres above sea level, Belfast is the highest town in South Africa. It is on the Eastern Line at the junction to Lydenburg. The town was started in 1890, taking the name of the birthplace of R.C.W. O'Neil who owned the original farm. Belfast has a population of 6 500 and the district is notable for its sheep and dairy farms.

Machadodorp

The town of Machadodorp came into being upon the opening of the Eastern Line in 1894 and was named in honour of General J.J. Machado, engineer surveyor of the railway and Governor of Moçambique. Two kilometres from the town are the radio active thermal sulphur baths. There is an hotel in the town and one at the baths. The population is 4 000.

Machadodorp to Nelspruit

Just north of Machadodorp, national road N4 reaches a junction with route R36. From here there are two routes for part of the way to Nelspruit: the route on N4 via Waterval Boven and the Elands River Valley and the alternative route on R36 (left at the junction) via the well-known night stop, Bambi, and the Schoemanskloof.

Schoemanskloof – Crocodile River – Montrose Falls

At fifteen kilometres, just before reaching the Schoemanskloof, R36 divides, the lefthand fork continuing to Lydenburg.

Taking the righthand fork to Nelspruit the road commences its descent from the highveld into the lowveld country through the 50-kilometre-long gateway, known as Schoemanskloof (after an early settler who farmed in the area). In spectacular, evergreen scenery the road loses 700 metres in 50 kilometres to enter the broad wooded valley of the Crocodile River. The picturesque Montrose Falls are at the point where the road crosses the river and at the Montrose Falls Hotel this route joins with national road N4.

Waterval Boven

Returning to Machadodorp, national road N4 leads to Waterval Boven (above the waterfall) with its marshalling yard and railway shops. It had its start when the Eastern Line was opened in 1894. The original line up from Waterval Onder (below the waterfall) taking the course around the cliffs of the waterfall and through the 213-metre long curved tunnel, was worked by the only rack railway in South Africa. The cogs in the line worked with the cogs in the wheels of the rack engines which pushed the trains up the one-in-twenty gradient from the rear. The old Z.A.S.M. tunnel, closed in 1908, is an historical monument. There is a car park close to its entrance and at the other end there is a fine view of the waterfall, in an atmospheric area proclaimed a nature reserve.

Waterval Onder and Krugerhof – Elands River

At the bottom of the Elands River Pass, in the heart of the valley, is Waterval Onder a delightful little settlement with its historic Wayside Inn, the ideal stop over. Krugerhof, an old homestead set in the lovely garden of the Inn, is a national monument. Here President Kruger spent some of his last days in South Africa before he left, by way of Lourenço marques (now Maputo), for Holland. On 29 May 1900 the President moved the seat of Government to Machadodorp (Pretoria being under threat of the British troops) and he lived in a railway carriage there. He moved to the house at Waterval Onder on 30 June, where he remained until 28 August 1900. Executive Council meetings were held there daily during that period. After the Battle of Dalmanutha the seat of government was moved to Nelspruit.

In beautiful scenery the road from Waterval Onder follows the Elands River and after approximately 10 kilometres it reaches a turnoff left which crosses the river into the small settlement of Sycamore. Here on the bank of the Elands is Three-star Hotel Malaga, its authentic Mediterranean style architecture in complete harmony with the tranquil scene.

Continuing, the road passes Ngodwana, the site of Sappi paper mill, completed at a cost of a billion rands in 1983, it is among the most advanced paper mills in the world, its modern technology providing an odour-free operation with affluent disposal being re-employed in agriculture.

Beyond the paper mill is the turnoff right to the old gold diggings of Kaapsehoop. From here N4 passes the wooded village of Elandshoek after which it is joined by the road from Schoemanskloof.

Sudwala Caves

Five kilometres from Montrose Falls, a branch road leads left (north-west) for 10 kilometres up the

Houbosloop Valley (a lovely retreat) to the quite remarkable Sudwala Caves, with the mountainside entrance hidden by indigenous trees and plants such as the wild pear, kaffirboom and aloe, and to the Sudwala Holiday Resort on the banks of the Houtbosloop River.

Once the sanctuary of a tribe of the Swazi, led by their illustrious Captain Sudwala, these caverns are among the largest in southern Africa. The principal chamber, named after the owner of the property, P.R. Owen Hall, is roughly circular in shape with a diameter of 67 metres and a dolomite dome rising to 36 metres above the floor level. The acoustics of the chamber come as close to perfection as possible, and this combined with the sloping terraces of the floor provides excellent opportunities for large gatherings for concerts and folk singing.

A strange phenomenon and priceless asset of the Sudwala Caves is the perpetual current of cool, fresh air, maintaining an even temperature of 20°C. The source of this ventilation is still undiscovered. Guided tours operate daily from 8.30 a.m., and throughout the tourist route of approximately 600 metres there is a rich store of dripstone formations. Some, like the beautiful frozen cascade, known as the Weeping Madonna, are delicately tinted with reds, browns and yellows, caused by iron and manganese oxides. The caves are open throughout the year and restaurant and accommodation facilities are provided at Sudwalaskraal resort. An added attraction at the caves is the impressive museum of dinosaurs.

Nelspruit

A flourishing modern town of even progress over the years, Nelspruit has a population of 19 500. Its ideal situation in the heart of the bounteous lowveld has made it the principal marshalling centre for the vast resources of this territory. Sited on the banks of the Crocodile River it markets a great variety of fruit and produce ranging from export citrus and avocados to bananas, paw-paws, granadillas, mangoes, litchies, nuts, tomatoes, beans, cucumbers, peas and sweet potatoes. The district is noted for its tobacco and there are important forests and a thriving timber industry. The Lowveld Botanic Garden and the Citrus and Subtropical Fruit Research Institute are in Nelspruit.

The streets of Nelspruit are lined with flamboyant and jacaranda trees and these, together with other exotic shrubs, climbers and palms, beautify the homes and lawnswept gardens of the lovely residential areas. The modern commercial area displays a considerable amount of activity and for the traveller it makes a pleasant place for refreshment and replenishment of supplies. The recreational amenities of the town include a country club with golf, bowls, tennis and swimming.

Nelspruit had its beginning with the coming of the railway line in 1892 and was named after the owners of the original farm, the three brothers Nel. Hugh Lanion Hall (1858-1940) came to the district in 1890 and pioneered one of the greatest citrus and subtropical fruit estates in the country, trading today as H.L. Hall & Sons Limited. During the 1930s the eradication of the mosquito in the Crocodile Valley and the whole of the lowveld brought an upsurge in prosperity. In 1940 Nelspruit became a municipality. On the eastern outskirts of the town, N4 passes the magnificent farm of Crocodile Valley Estates where massed flowering shrubs line the verges of the road, providing a spectacular border for the citrus groves.

There are two hotels and a municipal caravan park in Nelspruit and several hotels and parks in the district.

Crocodile Country Inn

For a home from home base to explore the scenic delights of the lowveld, or a night stop, there can be no better recommendation than two-star Crocodile Country Inn. It is situated in a peaceful, picturesque riverine setting on the bank of the Crocodile River just off national road N4, 20 kilometres west of Nelspruit. See pages 289 and 407.

National road N4 follows the eastwards course of the fast-flowing Crocodile River and passes through the Crocodile River Poort in impressive scenery – the huge granite boulders on the hillside mixing with a varied assortment of beautiful indigenous trees, especially spectacular in the autumn with the leaves from pale green through deep yellow to scarlet.

Kaapmuiden and Malelane

Kaapmuiden is a rail and road junction for Barberton to the south. Malelane, the railhead, is the centre for the vast sugarcane plantations that surround it, the sugar mill there, and the banana crop, is one of the largest in South Africa.

The Malelane gate and camp (the most southerly of the Kruger National Park) is 5 kilometres to the north of the village. From Malelane a road leads south to Swaziland, entering at Jeppe's Reef border post.

Komatipoort

Near the Moçambique border, Komatipoort is said to be the hottest town in the Transvaal.

On the Kamati River bank, near the town, the Nkomati Accord between South Africa and Moçambique was signed by Prime Minister P.W. Botha and President Samora Machel on 10 March 1984.

From Komatipoort a road leads north to Crocodile Bridge, the eastern gateway to the Kruger National Park and another road leads south to enter Swaziland at Border Gate.

Having reached the eastern extremity of national road N4, a return to Nelspruit is necessary to explore further interesting regions of the Eastern Transvaal lowveld.

Barberton and its district

From Nelspruit a road leads south to the atmospheric town of Barberton with its 5 000 inhabitants. The broad, green valley in which it lies and the river of the valley have taken the name De Kaap from the imposing headland or kaap (a spur of the Drakensberg) which overlooks the town.

The wild rush of 1884 from the four corners of the

1. Flowering in the winter, magnificent aloes are to be seen on the road between Nelspruit and Barberton.

2. 3. and 4. Within 20 km of reaching Nelspruit on the N4 route is Crocodile Country Inn, a recommended stop for comfort and especially good table. The on-property recreational amenities are tennis, bowls, swimming and fishing.

Elegance, fine cuisine, good cellar, varied recreation, and total relaxation are all to be found at Jatinga — close to White River and Kruger National Park. Details on pages 291 and 407.

earth which shook the veld where Barberton stands today, all happened when the brothers Fred and Harry Barber and their cousin Graham Barber stumbled upon some gold quartz. The find was reported to the Mining Commissioner, David Wilson, who appeared on the scene a few days later to proclaim the prospecting camp he named Barberton.

A boom town shot up with astonishing speed, with its cosmopolitan inhabitants as tough as they come. Shacks mushroomed in an atmosphere of heavy drinking, gambling, brawling and gunplay. With the finding of the famous Sheba Reef a year later, a separate suburb called Eureka City sprang up.

Barberton's population grew to 8 000 whites by the end of 1885 and fortunes changed hands. By the end of 1886 the goldfields boasted two stock exchanges and 200 bars. In an atmosphere of easy fortunes a hectic night life prevailed. The bevy of femine beauties included the celebrated Cockney Liz who held her own auctions! In spite of the rich strikes of some mining undertakings, notably the famed Bray's Golden Quarry, many properties and shareholdings were sold under false pretences. In fact the gold deposits were not as rich as these were boosted to be and the majority were soon worked out. The inevitable decline started with the discovery of gold on the Witwatersrand, the final crash coming in 1888.

Although mining continues, Barberton derives its main prosperity from the surrounding cotton, tobacco, citrus, sisal, sub-tropical fruit and timber estates. The aerial cableway, passing over the mountain to Barberton railway station, serves the Havelock Asbestos Mine in Swaziland, 20 kilometres away.

Barberton is a convenient base from which to visit the interesting district. There are two hotels in the town and a municipal caravan park in Fitzpatrick Park. Here in the park is Ivan Mitford-Barberton's fine bronze of Jock, the famous character of Sir Percy Fitzpatrick's classic, *Jock of the Bushveld*. The two-star Impala Hotel in De Villiers Street contains a fine mural frieze of the Jock of the Bushveld story painted in 1936 by the famous wandering artist, Conrad Genal. Opposite the Phoenix Hotel on the corner of Pilgrim and President Streets, the interesting local museum is housed in the original Kaap Gold Field Stock Exchange, the first stock exchange of the Transvaal and a national monument.

From Barberton there is an especially interesting drive north-west through Noordkaap, Avoca, and Louw's Creek, rejoining national road N4 at Kaapmuiden. Along this road there are turnoffs of short distances to the two working mines Agnes and Fairview, the ruins of Eureka City and Sheba Mines. The road passes Jock's Tree, an umbrella-like acacia that provided shelter for Jock and his master.

Other magnificent drives to be taken from Barberton are to the Havelock Asbestos Mine in Swaziland through the tortuous route revealing breathtaking scenery, and to Kaapsehoop.

Escarpment and Lowveld

To the north of Nelspruit is the Drakensberg escarpment with vast afforestation, and bushveld country with its wild fauna sanctuary – Kruger National Park.

The trunk routes to reach this area are from east to west R40, R37 and R36. Numerous subsidiary roads connect the trunk routes and the whole area is scenically magnificent.

On the way to White River the R40 from Nelspruit passes through the Crocodile River Valley in beautiful countryside of citrus groves.

White River

The R40 is the main thoroughfare of this attractive town and the southern entrance sidewalk is lined with majestic date palms and colourful bougainvillaea; the scene changes in the central business area where the pavements are decorated with jacaranda trees (flowering in the spring).

The town has a population of 4 850 and there are nearly as many people on the smallholding farms that surround the town. Well irrigated from the Witklip, Longmere, Danie Joubert and Da Gama dams (all lying to the north), these farms are prodigious producers of citrus, vegetables, sub-tropical fruit, flowers and timber. The first settlers arrived in the area in 1890 and municipal status was proclaimed in 1932. Today White River has a good shopping and business centre to serve not only the farming district but also the touring public. There is an hotel and a municipal caravan park in the town.

At the traffic lights near the end of the main thoroughfare (where the R40 swings left) there is a huge signpost directing the visitor to the numerous holiday hotels of the game reserve region. Main highways from here lead to the Numbi Gate and to the Paul Kruger Gate. Five kilometres north of the huge signpost the R40 divides, the left-hand R40 is the more direct route to Hazyview and the Paul Kruger Gate, the right-hand, now the R538, the direct route to the Numbi Gate of the Park.

The Winkler

From the point where the two highways divided, if the R538 is taken, after a further 1¹/₂ kilometres a very well-known lowveld landmark is reached – the famed three-star Hotel The Winkler, with its striking architecture. In every respect an excellent base, close to Numbi Gate, it rates amongst the very best country hotels in South Africa. Pictures page 293, details page **408**

Jatinga

Returning to White River, at the last traffic intersection where the huge signpost directs motorists on the R40, should you disregard this signpost and carry on straight past the traffic lights (on what is the continuation of the main thoroughfare through White River from Nelspruit), without turning left or right for approximately 7 km, two sets of railway lines will be reached. 100 metres beyond the second crossing the sand road turnoff right, clearly signposted 'Jatinga' is taken and 2 km along this sand road the imposing entrance to Jatinga is reached.

Inside the entrance to Jatinga the driveway is lined with pines. Here your hosts, Ken and Mike, have

This magnificent male specimen in typical repose bears witness to the fact that lions are indolent by nature.

In a 25-hectare parkland setting near White River and only 25 km from Numbi Gate, Kruger National Park, is 3-star Hotel The Winkler, acknowledged to be among the best hostelries in the country.

created a lovely retreat for gracious living, the cuisine is superb and recreation opportunities include tennis, bowls and swimming. Details on page 408

Mala Mala Game Reserve

From Hazyview a fine road (R536) leads to Paul Kruger Gate and Skukuza. At a point 36 km along this road there is a gravel road turnoff left, where a number of signposts indicate the distances to various properties. Prominent among these are Mala Mala main camp and the other two camps of the reserve, Kirkman's Kamp and Harry's.

Mala Mala Game Reserve boasts the largest privately owned area of big game land in South Africa. This remarkable property lies to the west of the Kruger National Park, with a common boundary of over 35 km, and the Sand River flows through the property giving some 50 km of river frontage.

Heading the list of overseas visitor attractions in the subcontinent of Africa, way out in front are game reserves, and leading the field in the whole continent of Africa, according to no less an authority than *The Hideaway Report,* is Mala Mala Game Reserve.

The well-known South African entrepreneur, Michael Rattray, is the owner and all of his famous camps in this area face the meandering Sand River. His management watchword could well be 'personal service in an atmosphere of complete relaxation' and luxury conditions for the privileged few at Mala Mala are exceptional by any standard. The never-more-than-fifty guests in camp are provided with a staff three times their number. Each of the twenty-four double and two single huts constructed in traditional style under thatch has every modern amenity, featuring oversized single beds, airconditioning, insect screened windows, 'his' and 'hers' bathrooms attached to each double rondavel and a PABX system for room service or to take telephone calls in the privacy of your room. The tastefully decorated buffalo lounge, the bar, diningroom and the swimming-pool overlooking the Sand River are perfect for relaxing between game drives. Dinner in the buffalo boma, where guests are seated around a log fire under a floodlit 900-year-old ebony tree, is in itself an exciting experience.

The Sable suite at the southern end of the camp is a decentralised unit for up to 14 guests. For complete privacy and extra luxury 'the Sable', with its own swimming-pool, lounge, diningroom, viewing deck and boma is a unique amenity fitting unobtrusively into this beautiful camp. Children are not permitted in the Sable unit.

The romantic sounding name *MalaMala* comes from the Shangaans, the local tribespeople, and is their name for the sable antelope. Mala Mala camp is 28,5 km from the R536 turnoff.

Within Mala Mala Game Reserve the two other camps are Kirkman's Kamp and Harry's. Both camps are named in honour of W. Harry Kirkman, the highly respected conservationist whose influence in this area dates back to the 1920s.

Kirkman's Kamp is notable for its authentic Victorian colonial architecture and furnishings. Twenty guests are accommodated in semi-detached two bedroom cottages, each with private verandah and airconditioning. The en suite bathrooms have large baths with claw-and-ball feet and brass fittings. Kirkman's Kamp is a wonderful link with the past and many old photographs and memorabilia complete the atmosphere of nostalgia. Construction of the tennis court dates back to 1922 and today is hard-topped, and there is a fine filtered swimming-pool.

Harry's, a camp for 16 guests, is a very special place. The camp is decorated with Ndebele artwork and the setting is mature indigenous trees with emerald green lawns sweeping down to the Sand River. The boma has openings onto the river (floodlit at night) enabling dining guests to view the game drinking. A lounge, airconditioned bar and a viewing deck compliment the intimate scene. Lunch or dinner at Harry's, at a table overlooking the river is one of the highlights of a trip to Mala Mala Game Reserve. The bedrooms at Harry's are airconditioned and have en suite bathrooms.

Visitors to Mala Mala Game Reserve will marvel at the attractive camps situated in the heart of this lovely wilderness providing comfort and service in a completely unspoilt on-safari atmosphere. Quite remarkable is the table, superb home-cooking (including many vension specialities) and the finest South African wines. It must be said that these are the factors contributing to Mala Mala having received world-wide acclaim.

The secluded sanctuary with its wide variety of wild animals is rich in bird and plant life with many magnificent trees. Guests, in constant care of expert rangers who are dedicated to conservation, experience the thrill of the close-up 'in the bush' contact with game. Your game ranger becomes your personal host and guide; driving an open landrover with an experienced African tracker in attendance, he will take you almost directly to the game you particularly wish to see, and the thrill of it all is that he is not confined to roads or tracks and will invariably cut directly across bushveld. The ranger and tracker combination make an unbeatable team and safaris of not more than 7 guests per landrover are arranged for the best game-viewing times of the day, and again after dark to listen to the magic night sounds of the bush and to discover nocturnal species with the aid of a spotlight. Little is left to chance by the 12 game rangers covering the wilderness, and so it is that their landrovers are equipped with radio, making it possible for any one ranger to beam in to the others to meet at the scene of some drama, like a predator kill. Although the landrovers are linked by radio, rangers use single earphones to avoid guests being disturbed by 'radio talk'.

Should you so wish your ranger will take you into the bush on foot, tracking lion or elephant. Yes, the excitement runs high, and there are always exhilarating experiences such as awakening in the early morning to witness zebra and waterbuck grazing outside your hut, or watching from camp the various species coming down to drink at the river.

All of Africa's most sought after animals, the 'big five' are here, and Mala Mala Game Reserve's 'Big Five Club' entitles you to a certificate when you have seen lion, elephant, rhinoceros, buffalo and leopard. Other species include, cheetah, giraffe, zebra, baboon, warthog, crocodile, hippopotamus, honey badger, hyena, jackal and a large variety of antelope such as wildebeest, kudu, impala, waterbuck, steenbok, duiker and the rare tsessebe.

The large majority of visitors to Mala Mala Game Reserve make use of the excellent air transport facilities. Twin-engined charter aircraft to Mala Mala airstrip takes one hour from Johannesburg and two hours from Durban. Comair have schedule airline flights between Jan Smuts and Skukuza and Citi Air between Louis Botha and Skukuza.

Further particulars of accommodation and reservations appear in the accommodation directory of this guide.

Londolozi Game Reserve

Londolozi lies within the Sabi-Sand Wildtuin on the south-western boundary of Kruger National Park. The Zulu name Londolozi, meaning 'protector of living things', is repeated in the dedication to conservation practised by the brothers, John and David Varty, who own and personally manage this magnificent reserve. A vital project of theirs is the translocation of elephant, cheetah and nyala. And visitors to Londolozi certainly do benefit by the opportunity of authoritative wildlife discussion. All of the big game are here, lion, cheetah, leopard, elephant, buffalo, rhino, hippo, giraffe, apart from a large and varied population of antelope, and a considerable variety in birdlife.

In the 18 000 hectares of bushveld wilderness the two camps occupy prime positions overlooking the Sand River. The main camp, with a maximum capacity of 24 guests at any one time, comprises 8 luxury chalets, en suite, with balconies overlooking the river, and 4 rustic rondavels, each with shower and toilet. There is a lounge/pation, a curio shop, romantic boma and beautiful swimming-pool, and the atmosphere is relaxed and informal. A separate operation is the bush camp where there is accommodation for 8 guests in 4 bungalows, and the accent is on simplicity.

A typical day at Londolozi starts with coffee at daybreak and game spotting in open landrovers (accompanied by white rangers and Shangaan trackers – all highly experienced). A bush breakfast on the banks of the river could be followed by tracking game on foot. Back at the camp for morning tea and relaxation around the filtered pool until lunch, which is served on the patio overlooking the river. The afternoon game-viewing safari continues into the darkness of night with the exciting experience of spotlights to discover nocturnal species. Return to camp for a hot bath, a beer or two or a glass of wine, a delicious dinner (including braai game delicacies) around the boma log fire. Finally a comfortable bed.

Londolozi can be reached by car or aircraft. The best route by car is via Hazyview and Paul Kruger Gate of Kruger National Park. At a point 36 kilometres on route R536 to Skukuza there is a gravel road turnoff left where a number of signposts indicate the distances to various privately-owned game reserves in the Sabi-Sand complex. Follow the Londolozi signs from here and it is 27,8 kilometres to the main camp. Light aircraft can land at Londolozi Airstrip and charters can be arranged. Comair have daily schedule flights between Jan Smuts and Skukuza, and Citi Air between Louis Botha and Skukuza, and transport to the camp can be arranged at the time of booking your accommodation at Londolozi. For accommodation reservations see the accommodation directory of this guide.

Bosbokrand and Acornhoek

Nineteen kilometres north of Hazyview, Bosbokrand (Bushbuck Ridge) is a densely settled tribal area of Lebowa. A further 43 kilometres to the north the road reaches Acornhoek and a turnoff right (east) and a further 43 kilometres to Orpen Gate of the Kruger National Park. A few kilometres north of Acornhoek the road divides, the left branch leading west to Abel Erasmus Pass and the right branch to Hoedspruit (page 281).

Kruger National Park

The famed park covers an area of 19 010 square kilometres, measuring 322 kilometres north to south and an average of 65 kilometres east to west. It is bounded on the south by the Crocodile River, on the north by the Levuba River; on the east the Lebombo range separates it from Moçambique, and the western boundary is determined by the surveyor's line and a veterinary fence.

The enormous tract of flat bush country lies in the lowveld below the escarpment of the Eastern Drakensberg and holds an unchallenged sway over the imagination of the people; known to South Africans simply as the Game Reserve it is an internationally famous park abounding with a selection of game animals unsurpassed in its variety anywhere else in the world.

This magnificent sanctuary began at the instigation of President Kruger in 1895 and was proclaimed in 1898 as The Sabi Game Reserve. In 1902 the British administration under Lord Milner appointed Lieutenant-Colonel James Stevenson-Hamilton, whom the tribespeople called Skukuza (he who has turned everything upside down, referring to his regulations for conservation of flora and fauna) the first warden. It was he, with his unflinching determination, dedication and enthusiasm, who laid the solid foundation of the park. In 1903 the area to the north known as the Shingwedzi Reserve came under the warden's control. The National parks board was instituted by Parliament in 1926 and from then on the reserve was known as the Kruger National Park. The Park was opened to the public in 1927 and during that year only three cars ventured through the gates.

1

2

**Mala Mala Game Reserve —
Eastern Transvaal**

1. Although male hippopotami
can be violent, aggresive
fighters, if left alone they are
good-natured and inoffensive.
2. The luxury Sable suite at the
southern end of the main camp.
3. and 4. Thrilling close contact
with big game — both dangerous
animals — the temperamental
and unpredictable elephant is
gregarious, and the leopard a
solitary, nocturnal hunter with
very secretive habits.
5. and 6. Kirkman's Kamp with
its historical background and
Harry's, an intimate camp with a
special blend of on-safari.

All of the camps at Mala Mala
face the Sand River on a
frontage of 50 km.

3

4

5 6

Punda Maria and Pafuri

In the far north the entrance gate, approached from Louis Trichardt, is Punda Maria. The rest camp is at the foot of the Punda Maria mountain eight kilometres into the park from the gate and within easy distance of the watering place. Part of the northern section is in the tropics and where the rainfall is less than 380 millimetres a year. Here the hardy mopane tree predominates, interspersed with ancient baobabs, while lush gallery forests line the watercourses. Pafuri in the extreme north, near the Limpopo River, is a resting spot in the most densely wooded section of the entire Park.

Shingwedzi

Shingwedzi is a delightful camp with the huts forming a square in amongst the mopane trees and ilala palms, with the fire places and cooking facilities in the centre of the square. The camp is set in magnificent scenery.

Shawo, Letaba and Phalaborwa Gate

Shawo is a resting spot on the way to Letaba, the large camp on the south bank of the Great Letaba River set amidst a luxuriant forest of wild-fig and mbandu trees. Phalaborwa the centre gate of the Park is 53 kilometres west of Letaba camp.

Olifants

Olifants camp lies on the north bank of the Olifants River against the Lebombo mountains where the giant wild-figs dominate the scene.

Balule

This rather primitive small camp attracts those who seek the wild bushveld experience. It lies on the south bank of the Olifants near the road crossing to Olifants camp.

Roodewal

Under the control of Olifants, and roughly half-way on the road to Satara, Roodewal is another intimate camp, in a magnificent region, which must be reserved en bloc, the maximum number of persons being fifteen.

Orpen and Maroela

The Orpen gate and rest camp were named in memory of Mr and Mrs James Orpen, great nature lovers and conservationists, who purchased over 25 000 hecatres of farmlands to enable the extension of the western boundary of the Park, and donated this to the Parks Board. The small camp accommodates up to 28 people. Maroela Caravan Camp, to the north of Orpen, is reached by driving through the Orpen rest camp.

In the central and southern sections of the Park acacia thornbush species and the red bush-willow are dominant; marula and wild-fig flourish near water while sweetgrass and tamboekie provide the grazing.

Satara

Satara camp is situated in good grazing country and is notable for the exceptionally large flat-crowned thorn tree under which tea is served and where glossy starlings and hornbills are prolific.

Nwanedzi and Tshokwane

Nwanedzi, a very popular camp on the river of that name, accommodates only 15 persons and must be reserved en bloc. At Tshokwane there is a tearoom on the east bank of the Nwaswitsonto River where refreshments are taken in the shade of a huge sausage tree.

Skukuza and Paul Kruger Gate

Named after the tribal name given to Colonel Stevenson-Hamilton, the first warden, Skukuza is the largest camp and the headquarters of the Kruger National Park. It is situated on the banks of the Sabi River and despite its commercial atmosphere it remains a very popular camp not only because of its accessibility by road, air and rail, but also its favourable location for game viewing.

The very large administration complex includes the reception office, a licensed restaurant and snack bar, shop, an agency of Volkskas Bank, and a large post office. Here too is the information and conservation education complex centred around the Stevenson-Hamilton Memorial Library. On display are the magnificent tusks of the famed old bull, Mafuyane, that died in the park in November 1983.

At the fuel station the Automobile Association has a well-equipped workshop. Comair has its office at the Skukuza Airport where there are scheduled flights arriving from and departing to Jan Smuts daily. A railway coach restaurant was inaugurated at Skukuza station at the close of 1983.

Skukuza is best reached by road from the fine approach highway to the comparatively new Kruger Gate. Here at the entrance is the striking bust of the park founder, President Paul Kruger, by the sculptor Coert Steynberg.

Pretoriuskop and Numbi Gate

Pretoriuskop, eight kilometres from the Numbi gate, was the first rest camp to be built in the Park. The region is at a considerably higher altitude than the rest of the Park and the camp is a favourite summer resort. It abounds with splendid shade trees such as marula, wild-fig, kaffirboom and mkuhla – especially beautiful in the summer.

Lower Sabie, Crocodile Bridge and Malelane

Lower Sabie, on the Nwaswitshaka River, is a delightfully situated camp of medium size. Crocodile Bridge and Malelane are gate camps in the southern extremity of the Park, and both lie on the bank of the Crocodile River; Crocodile Bridge in the east and Malelane in the west.

Berg-en-dal

Aptly named, Berg-en-dal (mountain and dale) is situated in the wooded hills between Malelane and Pretoriuskop. It is a large camp with luxury accommodation and was opened in 1984 with a view to relieving the ever-increasing demand for accommodation in the Park. An unusual attraction is its filtered swimming pool.

1

2

At Londolozi Game Reserve, a sanctuary in the bushveld:
1. The bull elephant would have no trouble in pushing over the tree. He has a probable mass
of 7 tons and eats 150 kilograms of vegetation in a day.
2. At close quarters, guests watch a pair of lions during mating season.

1

3

4

5

6

7 8

1. and 2. In the vicinity of Shingwedzi camp, a family of elephants take a bath in the Luvuhu River (one of the beautiful watercourses of the Kruger National Park), and a bull elephant, with a probable mass of 6 tons, is about to cross the road.

3. Secretary bird strides majestically, runs with great speed, flies strongly and lands running with wings spread. The reptile is a delicacy of its diet; it despatches the snake with the violent stamping of its bony feet.

4. The bovine eland once roamed the lowveld in great herds.

5. Lilac-breasted roller, particularly beautiful in flight, is a fairly common resident of the bushveld.

6. Burchell's zebra are widely distributed throughout Kruger National Park.

7. The magnificent cheetah is of solitary and retiring disposition.

8. Ebony-coated sable antelope, with its snow-white underparts and boldly curved massive horns, negotiates the thick bush with amazing dexterity.

Game animal species

For variety of species the Kruger National Park is the best stocked game reserve in the world, and for those who love the bush and the sight and sound of wild creatures no experience there can ever be dulled by repetition whether or not high drama, such as a 'kill' is included.

There is little doubt that the biggest attraction is the traditional king of the beasts – the lion. Despite their having occupied the veld of Africa for many thousands of years the extraordinary thing about lions is that they have an intense dislike of the full heat and during the middle of the day they will seldom stir from patches of long grass, bushes or reeds. Most predator hunting is done at night but in the Kruger Park lions are invariably on the prowl or at waterholes up to 10 a.m. and after 3.30 p.m. During times of extreme hunger they will hunt in the full heat of the day. The lion population of about 1 500 is well distributed and lions are mostly seen at Shingwedzi and south of the Olifants River in the area, Satara, Skukuza and Pretoriuskop.

Leopards and cheetahs (magnificent creatures of solitary and retiring disposition) occur throughout the Park, the cheetah being more often seen than the decidedly nocturnal leopard. The leopard is particularly partial to baboon and monkey and despatches its prey by severing the jugular vein or neck vertebrae in a single bite, and is sufficiently powerful to carry a kill heavier than itself up a tree.

Among the smaller species of cat family in the Park are the caracal, serval and civet and other carnivore include hyena, wild hunting dog and jackal.

The ratel or honey badger, a normally peaceful little beast, has great courage and tenancity when riled. Although less than a metre long and a mere 300 millimetres in height, with his tough, elastic skin, strong digging claws and powerful bite he attacks the genital organs of his adversary and is known to have put to death a buffalo. He kills and eats small mammals and snakes, and enjoys honey and the grubs of the bees nest.

The African elephant, the biggest quadruped on earth, lives in family groups of ten to twenty and often bands together into herds of 200 and more, forming a fantastic spectacle.

For tourist popularity it runs the lion a close second. An adult bull weighs up to 7 tons, he eats 150 kilograms of vegetation a day and can push over a tree a metre in diameter. The cow is a devoted mother and is extremely dangerous while rearing her young. There are over 7 000 elephants in the Park, their main concentration being in the Tsende River – Great Letaba River – western boundary triangle. Probably the most exciting and entertaining wildlife experience is to witness the performance of these highly intelligent mighty beasts at drinking and bathing time – early in the morning or late in the afternoon.

The African buffalo, a dangerous customer, conjures up an excitement for that reason. In the Kruger Park there are some 29 000 of these formidable, massive, cunning and vindictive one-time trophy providers. Never found far from water, there are large herds in the Crocodile Bridge – Lower Sabie, Tshokwane and Shingwedzi areas.

The tallest, most polite, gentle and singularly beautiful specimen, is the giraffe. Apparently mute, he does offer a husky grunt when alarmed; his defence is his size, the toughness of his hide and the power of his kick. Plentiful throughout the Park, there are some 4 500 head. Giraffe are frequently seen outside the Park in the thornbush from Acornhoek to Bushbuck Ridge.

The wild horses of Africa are divided into three species. One species, the quagga, is extinct; the mountain zebra is preserved in small numbers in the Mountain Zebra National Park and the Burchell's zebra is well distributed in all game parks. In Kruger Park there are some 8 000 head, 5 500 of which are in the central area. Blue wildebeest are their habitual associates.

The Park contains seventeen species of antelope, ranging from the large eland to the small red duiker.

The eland is of bovine build; the bull standing nearly two metres at the top of the humped shoulder and weighing up to a metric ton. Mainly browsers, they are to be seen throughout the areas north of Letaba.

Roan antelope, mainly grazers, are conspicuous by the black and white face, ridged main, long tufted ears and upward and backward curved horns. They run in small groups in highly wooded, hilly country and can be seen near Punda Maria, Shingwedzi and Letaba.

The ebony-coated sable antelope with its snow-white under parts and magnificent horns swept backwards in an arched curve, is found in large numbers in the north from Punda Maria to Shingwedzi. Great herds once roamed the Newington area.

The majestic kudu with his magnificent spiralled horns, measures 1.5 metres at the shoulder, weighs up to 270 kilograms and is quite capable of jumping over a 2.5 metre-high fence. Essentially browsers they are plentiful and well distributed in the Park.

The heavily maned, robust waterbuck, to be seen all over the Park, is another handsome antelope with his wide lyre-shaped horns and conspicuous white ring around the rump.

The blue wildebeest, (the main prey of the lion), noted for its tenacity and speed, performing strange antics in flight, is probably the most sociable of the animals. They live in large herds in association with other animals, especially the zebra, and are evenly distributed over the Park.

The graceful impala is a close relative of the gazelle and the most plentiful antelope in the Park. The population of some 100 000 is widely distributed with great herds in the area of the Sabi River. With seeming lack of effort an impala can leap a distance of ten metres and clear a height of over three metres. Impala rams are often seen in ferocious combat, their magnificent lyrated horns locked in the duel. They are preyed on mainly by leopard, cheetah and wild hunting dogs, lions finding them too alert and elusive.

Among the other antelope in the Park are the thickset, coarse-haired bushbuck of nocturnal habits; the uncommon reedbuck found in the marshy areas of the north: nyala, often seen with impala, the massive, grey-brown males with their fine lyre-shaped horns and the strikingly lovely females, their orange-coloured coats richly striped and spotted: the exquisite, solitary little steenbok gazing in curiosity; the amazingly agile little klipspringer, racing up a rockface at great speed or balancing motionless with all four hoves tightly bunched together at the edge of a rock ledge, and the tiny red duiker who lives in the dense bush and is seldom seen.

The major rivers of the Kruger National Park are inhabited by hippopotami and in the same waters the crocodiles have their haunts. Mammal and reptile are unconcerned with one another and often bask on the sandbars and rocks together. The hippos live in groups of up to 20. The bull, heavier than the cow, from snout to tail measures four metres and weighs 4 tons. He has an enormous head and his equally large round body is supported by short legs.

Hippos remain completely submerged in the water for as long as 6 minutes before surfacing to breathe. Most of their day is spent in the water or close to the water where they bask on the rocks and sandbars. They are herbivorous and roam the banks of the river and inland, feeding on the luxuriant vegetation of the area in which they live. Generally peaceful creatures unless aroused, a cow hippo has been known to have bitten a human in two when he came between her and her calf: the bulls engage in violent fights between themselves sometimes inflicting mortal wounds with their powerful canines and incisors. The South African whip called the *sjambok* is usually made of the tough hippo hide.

Both species of the rhinoceros have been reintroduced into Kruger Park. The white rhino, the second largest land mammal, is not white but dark grey. It is apparent that the name is a corruption from the Afrikaans 'wyd' referring to the characteristic wide mouth. Better described as the square-lipped rhino, the bull weighs up to 5 tons. He is a grazer and a friendly docile creature unless aroused. The anterior horn measures up to a metre long. The black rhinoceros, also dark grey in colour is characterised by its prehensile upper lip with which it browses leaves. Regarded as short tempered, irritable and aggressive, the black rhino, despite its three tons of bulk, takes off like a sprinter and in a charge can reach 50 kilometres an hour. Both species, quite capable of looking after themselves in their wild state, were, before conservationists took notice, in danger of being shot out by the African tribespeople who crushed the horns into powder form and received high prices from the traders of the East, where it is believed that the rhino horn contains aphrodisiac properties.

Bird species
Birdlife in the Park is prolific, there being over 450 species. Always fascinating the ground birds include ostrich, secretary bird, ground hornbill and bussard. Of the arboreals there are numerous rollers, canaries, weavers, queleas, waxbills, buntings and bishop birds and a varied selection of insectivores such as flycatchers, swallows, larks, tits and many shrike species. In the fine stretches of water are the storks, hammerheads, herons, plovers, kingfishers, geese and ducks. Carnivorous birds are in abundance, the striking bateleur and fish eagles always draw attention and there are numerous species of hawks and large groups of vultures of different kinds.

Accommodation, reservations, regulations
Accommodation in the Park comprises family cottages, self-contained huts and huts without shower and toilet, all fully furnished, with bedding but without cooking or eating utensils. Tents wihout bedding may be hired and caravan and camping sites have all facilities. Most of the camps have restaurants, shops and petrol service stations.

Details of regulations, travelling times, entrance fees and entrance fees and accommodation charges should be obtained from the National Parks Board and accommodation should be reserved well in advance. The Parks Board booking office is at Groenkloof National Park, Muckleneuk Hill, Devenish Street Extension. Telephone 343-1991 between 9 am and 3 pm. Letters should be addressed to P.O. Box 787, Pretoria.

Sabie
In a region of forests and waterfalls is the town of Sabie. It is beautifully situated on a terrace of the Drakensberg at an altitude of 1 109 metres, below Mount Anderson (2 282 metres) and above the Sabi River. The magnificent pine plantations in this region go to make up one of the greatest man-made forests in the world. Sabie had its start as a gold mining camp in the 1880s and is today a big producer of paper pulp and timber. The population is 8 000.

Waterfalls in the mountains and woods provide delightful places to visit on foot, horseback or by motor car. Sabi Falls are within the municipal area, whilst Bridal Veil, Lone Creek, Horseshoe and Mac-Mac falls are within a radius of 14 kilometres of the town. Sabie Country Club welcomes visitors to its golf course, bowling green and tennis courts and there is angling in the Sabi River.

There is an hotel in the town and at 0,5 kilometres along the old Lydenburg road, perfectly situated with a kilometre-long frontage to the Sabi River is the popular two-star Floreat Motel. There are also 2 caravan parks along the old Lydenburg road.

Sabie lies at the junction of a number of roads. The scenic road (R536) east from Sabie follows the course of the Sabi River. Known as the Gorge road, it is from here the best and quickest route to the Kruger National Park.

At approximately 18 kilometres out from Sabie there is a turnoff left leading to Dr de Wet Nel's Tree Breeding Station in a lovely garden setting. To improve the quality of trees the station is devoted to research in cross and artificial pollination, grafting and growth control. The success of the afforestation of the Sabie region is understood when it is realised that the rainfall is in excess of 2 000 millimetres a year.

1

2

The Sabi region is a particularly picturesque part of the Eastern Transvaal.
1. Along the old Lydenburg road. 2. The Lone Creek Falls. 3. Sabi River. 4. and
5. Two-star Floreat Motel, the well-appointed stop-over and base with a river
frontage in a sylvan setting, just outside Sabie, half a kilometre along the old road
to Lydenburg.

2

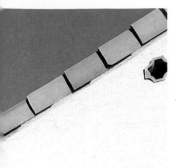

Three-star Hotel Casa do Sol, Sabi River Valley, is in its own 600 ha parkland, off the scenic road (R536) between Hazyview and Sabie — a Mediterranean village with excellent restaurants and an exquisite base from which to explore the wonders of this region.
1. The executive suite.
2. The swimming pools from the Bar Tropique. 3. Part of the beautiful village.

4. The giraffe is the tallest, the most polite and the gentlest of all the animals. In defence he depends on the power of his kick.

1

4

5

6

3

1. **The vastness of the lowveld, an aspect from the escarpment near Graskop.**

2. **The mountains known as the Three Rondavels overlook the Blyde River Canyon.**

3. **Bourke's Luck Potholes, near the confluence of the Blyde and Treur Rivers.**

4. 5. and 6. **Two-star Kowyn Hotel, Graskop, with its poolside rooms, ladies bar and chalets, is well-known for its comfort and good table, and it is right in the heart of the famous Panorama Route.**

Casa do Sol

From the Gorge road (R536) about 5 kilometres before reaching the junction of roads at Hazyview, there is a turnoff right (from Sabie) to Casa do Sol, a Mediterranean village hotel in its own 600-hectare lowveld setting, a unique concept and a dreamworld for a relaxing holiday.

Hazyview and Kiepersol

The largest banana plantations in South Africa are in the district of Hazyview, and at the edge of the banana belt at Kiepersol (named after the tree) is Tartan Farm with its 85 varieties of bougainvillea – of these, 30 varieties are available on the market.

Graskop and Kowyn's Pass

Near the edge of the escarpment, at an altitude of 1 494 metres, is the forestry village, Graskop. From here the scenic drive to the north, known as the Panorama Route (R532), commences, and to the east of the village is Kowyn's Pass, a magnificent mountain road winding up from the lowveld. In the village two-star Kowyn Hotel makes the ideal stop-over or base; its off-licensed chalets being a great help to the budget traveller.

Panorama Route

The circular Panorama Route leads from Graskop to the Blyde River Canyon and Pilgrim's Rest and return to Graskop; in all an 80-kilometre journey of scenic delight.

Close to Graskop, the outstanding features on the route are the Pinnicle and Driekop Gorge (1,5 km); Lisbon Falls (6,5 km) and God's Window (8 km) with its famed view across the lowveld to Moçambique.

A kilometre beyond the detour to God's Window, a road leads to Blyde River swimming-pools, and a further kilometre along the route is the turnoff to the 80-metre-high Berlin Falls. After a journey through the forest, crossroads are reached at Vaalhoek, approximately 35 kilometres from Graskop. From here there is the choice of extending the drive by visiting Bourke's Luck Potholes and the Blydepoort Resort, to the north, or of continuing on the Panorama Route southwards to Pilgrim's Rest.

Pilgrim's Rest

A digger named Pilgrim's Rest in 1873. He had found the gold he believed would enable him to rest after a long pilgrimage, seeking fortune.

The little village of some 1 200 people retains the atmsophere of many romantic associations of early gold mining in the Transvaal, particularly in 1875 with the great excitement of one of the biggest gold rushes ever to be experienced. Thousands of adventurers filled the lovely valley of Pilgrim's Rest where the scene was one of continuous hilarity with the daily discovery of fine nuggets of alluvial gold in the stream that came to be called Pilgrim's Creek.

Fittingly, to preserve this unique relic of buildings, little changed, since the atmospheric gold digging days, the Transvaal Provincial Administration has purchased the entire village and it has been proclaimed an historical monument. The old Royal Hotel (part of which used to be a church in Lourenço Marques (now Maputo) and was brought to Pilgrim's Rest by ox wagon) is administered by Overvaal Resorts. The place undoubtedly has the power of nostalgia and will remain an attraction for all time.

A few years after the rush, as the finds became smaller and smaller, prospecting in the valley went into decline but in the 1890s the Transvaal Gold Mining Estates Limited revived considerable interest with large investment in the area. Mining activities ceased in 1971 and the buildings of the refinery have been converted into a mining museum.

Mount Sheba

From Pilgrim's Rest route R533 leads west through fine scenery for 29 km to join with the main road between Lydenburg and Ohrigstad. The route is over the Blyde River bridge, past the Vaalhoek road junction and the golf course on the right (north) side, then through the Morgenzon Forest Reserve and Rowers Pass.

At approximately 14 kilometres from Pilgrim's Rest, on the left (south) is the Paardekraal road turnoff, which leads for a further, well signposted 11 kilometres to a 1 600 metre-high plateau and Mount Sheba, a three-star hotel within a 1 500-hectare nature reserve; a delightful mountain resort, with a touch of class, romantically positioned in a paradise of indigenous forest and river gorge wilderness. Visitors to the north-eastern Transvaal should not miss an opportunity to visit Mount Sheba Hotel, surrounded by a magnificent nature reserve.

The Berg and Ohrigstad Dam

Returning from Mount Sheba to the Paardekraal turnoff and continuing on the R533 to join the Ohrigstad-Lydenburg road, the delightful little settlement, The Berg, is passed and the turnoff to Ohrigstad Dam, whre the fishing is said to be very good.

Lydenburg and Ohrigstad

The mountain streams that find their way into the warm, sheltered valley where Lydenburg lies are noted for trout.

In 1849 the trekkers under Hendrik Potgieter moved from the fever stricken Ohrigstad (then known as Andries Ohrigstad) to the higher position which they called Lydenburg, referring to the suffering which they had undergone. They chose this as the capital of the small Lydenburg Republic which later united with the Utrecht Republic and was finally absorbed in the South African Republic (Transvaal).

The Old Lydenburg School, erected in 1851, is a national monument. When the Reverend Andrew Murray Jnr. and J.H. Neething visited the town from the Orange Free State in 1852 they resided in the school building.

In 1925 Lydenburg became the centre of a platinum field and today the town serves a large agricultural district. To the east of the town, on the road to Sabie (R37) is the interesting aquarium of the Transvaal Provincial Fisheries Institute that can be visited daily from 8 a.m. to 4 p.m. The Institute is engaged in research of Transvaal freshwater fish.

Three-star Mount Sheba Hotel, positioned in the centre of a nature reserve, off the Pilgrim's Rest — Lydenburg road, is renowned for perfection in hotel-keeping, tranquillity and the profound beauty of its surroundings. For timesharing of cottages ask Ovland.

Two well managed hotels notable for comfort and good table: Lydenburg Hotel, three kilometres from the town on the Burgersfort road and Orinoco Hotel at 66 Ruiter Street, Potgietersrus.

From the hatcheries, comprising 120 dams, the annual output of eggs sold is more than two million, and 100 000 fish are placed in dams and rivers of the country. The population of Lydenburg is approximately 10 000.

Lydenburg Nature Reserve, 2 km to the north of town, is stocked with a variety of antelope and there is a profusion of birdlife. A municipal caravan park and Morgan's Hotel are in the town. On the Burgersfort road (R37) 3 km on the northern side is the two-star Lydenburg Hotel; with its good table, comfort and peaceful setting it makes the obvious stopover or base for the visitor.

Penge

In the rugged country of the Drakensberg, 100 kilometres north of Lydenburg, is the asbestos-mining town of Penge. It lies on the south bank of the Olifants River, and in 1888 it received its name (after the London suburb) from the surveyor, Johann Rissik.

The vast deposit of asbestos of a unique variety which was uncovered during the early 20th century, became known as amosite (from the initials of Asbestos Mines of South Africa – the name of the company which first exploited the deposit). Amosite, with its long, springy fibres, is found nowhere else in the world; its properties provide for excellent insulation and it is used throughout the world, principally for the lining of ships' boilers.

Long Tom Pass

Between Lydenburg and Sabie, Long Tom Pass is the perfect example of fine road engineering in splendid scenery. The pass carries the road (the highest motor road in the Republic) for 46 kilometres over the Drakensberg reaching the summit at 2 149 metres. Points of interest on the old transport road are clearly signposted including the notorious Devil's Knuckles and the site from where the Boers last used their famous field gun, Long Tom.

In this region of the pass there is a particularly good view site overlooking Sabie. Other points of interest are the Old Portuguese Mine, the Old Trading Post, the Old Harbour Road and The Staircase near the top of the pass. There are vast pine forests close to the road and in the spring the open sections of the veld are a profusion of wild flowers.

Mac-Mac
The road north from Sabie linking with Graskop is a garden route of wild flowers in the open spaces of the forests. This road passes the Mac-Mac Pools, a lovely place for picnics and swimming in the crystal clear water fed by the mountain streams. Above the pools is the Mac-Mac Waterfall. The pools and the falls take the name from the number of Scots diggers in the mining camp established there in 1872.

Burgersfort and Gethlane Lodge
From Lydenburg the scenic route R37 leads northwards for 70 km through the Waterval Pass and the beautiful valley of the Waterval River to the small trading town of Burgersfort.

At the turnoff right, marked Fraaiuitzicht, 11 km south of Burgersfort, a farm road leads for 4,6 km through the dense Transvaal bushveld to the entrance gate of Gethlane Lodge – a veritable oasis with an abundance of clear mineral water, birdlife, small fauna and rare plant life. This is an area much loved by the young hunter, Paul Kruger, whom the romancers will have it, later buried the Kruger millions right here! For those who seek a peaceful sojourn, assured of comfort, good fare and excellent holiday amenities in the surroundings of a 180-hectare nature reserve, Gethlane Lodge could well be the answer. The Lodge can also be reached from the south by following the route R555 from Middelburg via Stoffberg and the Steelpoort River valley.

Bourke's Luck Potholes
Returning to Vaalhoek where Panorama road (R532) and the road from Pilgrim's Rest meet; at 41 kilometres from Graskop are Bourke's Luck Potholes (just above the confluence of the Blyde and Treur Rivers), a curious formation of rounded holes in the rock caused by the perpetual swirling waters of the Treur River. The potholes were named after the digger who found gold in considerable quantity in close proximity. The trekkers named the Blyde (joyful) and Treur (sorrowful) following an incident when their sorrow turned to joy.

Blyde River Canyon
Northwards from Bourke's Luck Potholes the splendid road (route R532) skirts the verge of the Blyde River Canyon. Three specially constructed view sites have been provided at points 45, 50 and 57 kilometres from Graskop. The view differs at each site and all three should be visited. For sheer magic in scenic beauty the awe inspiring Blyde River Canyon rates with anything to be seen on the African continent and is especially magnificent at sunset. The Blyde River cuts a zig-zag passage, 16 kilometres long at a depth of 750 metres in the midst of dense vegetation below towering buttresses capped by cliffs of the most remarkable shapes.

Overvaal* Blydepoort (F.H. Odendaal Camp) is one of two resorts developed in the Blyderivierspoort Nature Reserve. It is 14 km from Bourke's Luck Potholes (51 km from Graskop) and overlooks the Canyon mountain feature known as the Three Rondavels. The resort comprises some 70 stone under tile chalets, each completely self-contained and fully equipped. The resort facilities are grand by any standard and include a motor garage, supermarket, liquor store, à la carte restaurant and cafeteria (both fully licensed), swimming pool, all-weather tennis courts, saunas, mashie golf course and full conference facilities. There is a play-park for children, and horses and ponies can be hired. The resort has a small but fine caravan park. Resort reservations telephone (013231) 901.

The second resort within the nature reserve is Overvaal Sybrand van Niekerk, across the Blyde River on the eastern side of the Canyon, and can only be reached by travelling some 85 km. From F.H. Odendaal Camp follow the R532 due west to meet trunk route R36 at the commencement of Abel Erasmus Pass, continue through the pass and the J.G. Strijdom Tunnel and on reaching the intersection turn right into route R531. After 18 km turn right again, following the R531 for a further 12 km, where the access road (right again) leads to the Sybrand van Niekerk resort. Apart from the drive itself being very rewarding, arrival at the resort is an experience not to be missed. The camp is surrounded by the enormous buttresses of the Drakensberg escarpment – this is mountain scenery at its best. Accommodation comprises comfortable, fully equipped bungalows and a large caravan park on the Blyde river bank. Facilities at this resort are equal to those of Blydepoort (described above). By prior arrangement visitors can be fetched from the Hoedspruit airfield, 45 km away. Resort reservations telephone 0020 and ask for Blydedam No. 1.

Echo Caves
From the Blydepoort resort turnoff the R332 leads west to join the R36 and just south of the junction of the roads is the turnoff left to the Echo Caves, a national monument. The caves are so named from the echoes made when the stalactites and stalagmites are tapped.

Abel Erasmus Pass
Continuing north to Tzaneen, route R36 is carried over the Drakensberg by the spectacular Abel Erasmus Pass (named after a pioneer settler from Ohrigstad). From the Ohrigstad River the road rises 335 metres and descends 732 metres to the valley of the Olifants River. In the northern section of the pass the 128-metre J.G. Strijdom Tunnel cuts through the massif.

Out of the Abel Erasmus Pass the road passes the turnoff east (right) to Hoedspruit where there is the Fort Coepieba Motel on the way to Phalaborwa (page 280). Beyond the turnoff the Olifants River is crossed and from here it is 83 kilometres to Tzaneen (page 279).

---

* Overvaal is the statutory body operating the holiday resorts owned by the Province of Transvaal, and until 1 December 1983 was known as the Board for Public Resorts.

Gethlane Lodge, 65 km north of Lydenburg off the scenic route R37, is well worth considering for holidays, conferences, timeshare. Tranquillity, comfort, good cuisine, fine recreational opportunities, are all to be found here in the surroundings of a 180-hectare nature reserve.

CHAPTER 13

Bloemfontein and the Orange Free State

Bloemfontein

Capital of the Province of the Orange Free State, Bloemfontein is also the judicial capital of South Africa. It lies on the highveld plain (often referred to as the great Free State plateau) at an altitude of 1 392 metres, where the climate is dry and bracing to very cold in the winter and warm with cool evenings in the summer, having an average annual rainfall of 500 millimetres. The city is laid out around the flat-topped mountainous feature (of the type characteristic of the Province) known as Naval Hill. The population is 240 000.

Bloemfontein received its name from an early settler, Johan Brits, who found flowers of the veld and a fountain where, in a free wilderness, he pegged his claim to farm in 1840. At this time there were a number of trekkers scattered about in the area who had crossed the Orange River to escape British rule. In 1846 their independence was disturbed when Major Henry Douglas Warden of the Cape Mounted Rifles arrived with orders to establish himself as British Resident of the territory. Warden took a liking to the Brits farm Bloemfontein and purchased it for £87 10s to set up his headquarters. With the help of his Hottentot soldiers a small fort was built.

One of the functions of Warden's office was to find a solution to the border trouble between the Basotho king, Moshesh, and the war-like Sikonyela. Dashing and impetuous as ever, the Cape Governor, Sir Harry Smith, arrived at Bloemfontein in 1848 with what he believed to be the solution; the Queen's sovereignty would cure the ills of Briton, Boer and Basotho. And so the Orange River Sovereignty was proclaimed.

Furious with this development, Andries Pretorius formed a commando of 1 200 burghers and soon put Warden back across the Orange River and then lay in wait at Boomplaats for Sir Harry Smith's force of 850. The battle took place on 29 August 1848 with Smith's well trained and disciplined men proving to be the superior but Pretorius and his commando escaping capture. Bloemfontein was re-occupied by the British and many hundreds of Boers trekked again, this time across the Vaal to join Potgieter in his happy isolation.

The British sovereignty continued for six years by which time there was a distinct change of policy at the Colonial Office, with a strong leaning towards being relieved of the responsibility and expense of maintaining the control of the central and northern regions of South Africa. In 1854, Sir George Clark arrived in Bloemfontein as Special Commissioner for the Colonial Office and on the 23 February of that year he signed the *Bloemfontein Convention* to acknowledge the independence of the Orange Free State.

An intelligent, crippled farmer from Smithfield, Josias Philippus Hoffman who had assisted in the drawing up of the Convention document, was elected first president by the first Volksraad (people's council or parliament) of this diminutive republic. His was no

easy task in a rural state with very little financial means and troublesome Basotho on the eastern frontier. He chose to seek friendship with Moshesh the king of the Basotho people, and left alone, his plan could well have succeeded. It was in fact his undoing. Riot was near to erupting when it was heard that he had presented Moshesh with a keg of gunpowder.

Hoffman resigned and was succeeded in 1855 by Jacobus Nicolaas Boshof, who had been Chairman of the Volksraad of the Republic of Natalia, and after its annexation by Britain, Master of the Supreme Court in the Natal Colonial administration. A capable administrator, President Boshof was confronted with the problems of the warring Moshesh and the efforts of President M.W. Pretorius of the South African Republic in the Transvaal to annex the Free State. Finally he fell out of favour with the Free State burghers when he supported the plan of Governor Sir George Grey to federate South Africa. Boshof's resignation came in 1859 and he was replaced by M.W. Pretorius, who now held the office of President of the two Boer Republics.

As strong a character as President Pretorius was, he soon realised that his idea of the union of the two republics could not be accomplished. The continuous feuds of the rival fractions of the Boers and the bloody battles against the tribespeople ended in his resigning his presidency of the Free State in April 1863.

It was during Pretorius's term of office in August 1860 that Queen Victoria's son, Prince Alfred, visited South Africa. In the *Fehr Collection* paintings, preserved in the Castle in Cape Town, is the scene of "The greatest hunt in history," organised for the prince, when 4 000 head of antelope were slaughtered in one day — only eight kilometres from Bloemfontein.

With the resignation of President Pretorius the Free State Volksraad looked again to another part of South Africa for his replacement, and this time they chose very wisely. Johannes Hendricus Brand, the Cape Town lawyer (who had been admitted to the Bar in England in 1849) and member of the Cape Parliament for Clanwilliam, arrived in Bloemfontein in November 1863, when the little republic, almost bankrupt, was threatened with another invasion by the Basotho. He was to remain in office for 25 glorious years during which time, under the most adverse conditions (including the fighting of losing battles against Moshesh), he succeeded in forming a state which, although small in numbers and wealth, had won political security, integrity and national consciousness. Queen Victoria paid the unique compliment of conferring a knighthood upon him. Having been re-elected for a third successive term, he died in office in 1888. President Sir J.H. Brand will always be remembered by his favourite saying, *Alles sal recht komen mits iedereen zyn plicht doenen* (everything will come right provided that everyone does his duty).

Francis William Reitz who had been called to the Bar at the Inner Temple in England, and who was Chief Justice of the Orange Free State when President Brand died, became the next president.

Although in the face of ill health he resigned in 1895 his public career was by no means over. In 1897, after moving to Pretoria, he was at first appointed Judge of the Supreme Court and then State Secretary of the South African Republic in the Transvaal. As State Secretary he was responsible for the drafting of the famous ultimatum to Great Britain which led to the Anglo-Boer War. After the war he left South Africa for a number of years, returning in 1910 to become the President of the Senate in the first parliament of the Union of South Africa.

During Reitz's presidency the railway for which President Brand had incessantly laboured, came into being. When Reitz left office in 1895 he was succeeded by Marthinus Theunis Steyn, who was previously State Attorney and then Judge of the Supreme Court. He and his wife (born Tibbie Fraser) were adored by the people. President Steyn, a man of wisdom, tact and moderation despite failing health, completely gave himself to his country; even to arranging meetings in Bloemfontein between President Kruger and Lord Milner in a desperate attempt to prevent hostilities. At the outbreak of war he joined the burghers on commando selflessly sacrificing any opportunity of regaining his health. He continued with unfailing efforts to work for Union when the war was over and collapsed and died while addressing a meeting in an attempt to prevent hostilities at the time of the 1914 Rebellion.

Against his background of presidential stalwarts and many other accomplished South Africans, the city of Bloemfontein has emerged a leader in many of the fields of the way of life in this country. Any visitor will sense this atmosphere of historic stability and will want to explore the many fine monuments of the past whilst enjoying the modern amenities of this handsome city.

The First Raadsaal, often called the Old Raadsaal, in St. George's Street, is historically the most important building in the Orange Free State. Built by Major Warden as a school in 1849, it has served as a church, seat of the British Legislative Council, seat of the first sessions of the Volksraad, and again as a school. Under its thatched roof were held many of the meetings which led to the signing of the Bloemfontein Convention. At the south end of President Brand Street, where it merges with Eunice Road, is the stately building of The Presidency, built in 1884 near the end of President Brand's term. It was guarded by the famous Staatsartillerie (State Artillery), the only standing force of the republic. Formed in 1880, its first commander was a German officer, Major R. Albrecht, and the wartime strength was 400. The State Artillery of the South African Republic in the Transvaal was formed in 1890; built with the aid of Austrian and German officers, its strength was 800. Both units emerged from the Anglo-Boer War with high distinction. The First Raadsaal and the Presidency are national monuments.

The Fourth Raadsaal, referred to today as simply the Raadsaal, is on the corner of President Brand Street and Elizabeth Street. This striking building with its sandstone pillars, red brick walls and fine domed tower was designed by Gordon Leith and opened by President Reitz on 5 June, 1893. Here the Volksraad

of the "model republic" sat until 1899. After the Anglo-Boer War it was the seat of the Legislative Assembly of the crown colony, now renamed Orange River Colony, until Union in 1910 when the Province took its original name, Orange Free State, and the Raadsaal became the seat of the Provincial Council.

This council chamber witnessed many bitter debates in the troubled times of the little republic's history. Here the decision was taken not to unite with the South African Republic in the Transvaal and here, some years later, the lot of the Free State was thrown in with the other republic to enter the war against Great Britain and its forces, fought courageously to the bitter end. In this chamber the National Convention which led to the Union of South Africa held its final sittings in May 1909.

Many more fine buildings front President Brand Street, a wide and stately thoroughfare. There is the City Hall noted for the austere beauty of its stinkwood panelling; the Letterkundige Museum (Literary Museum) at Old Government Buildings with its statue of President Brand; the Archives and the Law Courts. All of the buildings mentioned here, with the exception of the Appeal Court, are national monuments.

On the corner of President Brand and Charles Streets is the impressive modern memorial to General J.B.M. Hertzog (Judge of the Supreme Court of the Orange Free State 1895 – 9, founder of the National Party and South African Prime Minister 1924 – 39).

A national monument of unusual charm is the Twin Tower Church (Dutch Reformed), on the corner of Radloff and Hill Streets. At the south end of Church Street is Queen's Fort, built by Major Warden in 1848. Near the fort is a pyramidal monument erected in honour of the burghers who fell in wars against Moshesh, 1865 – 1868.

In Church Street, south of Queen's Fort, is the Women's War Memorial, the highest obelisk in South Africa. When Emily Hobhouse died in 1926, the Afrikaner people bestowed the highest honour they could when she was given a state funeral and her ashes were buried at the foot of the memorial. During the Anglo-Boer War she came to South Africa from England to fight the cause of the women and children in the concentration camps, and at much personal risk she brought about reforms and saved the lives of many. Fifty metres from the memorial is the War Museum with its relics of the two South African Wars 1880 – 1902. Portraits of Boer generals and leaders of the time, and an amazing collection of wood carvings carried out by prisoners in the camps of Ceylon, St. Helena and Bermuda are especially interesting. In the museum is the first wireless set ever intended for use in warfare. President Kruger thought it would be useful and ordered it from Berlin. It arrived in Cape Town after war had broken out and was commandeered by the Royal Engineers. It is a visual reminder of the great strides made in technology since the turn of the century.

The National Museum on the corner of Charles and Aliwal Streets was established in 1877. General in character, the museum has an outstanding anthropological exhibition which includes the unique fossil *Diarthrognatus* forming the link between reptile

1

2

3

5

1. The fourth and final Raadsaal of the Orange Free State, fronted by the equestrian statue of General Christiaan de Wet, a Boer soldier of outstanding ability and courage.

2. Technical College, built in 1894, is on the cnr. of Douglas and Church Streets.

3. Bloemfontein City Hall, within a lovely garden.

4. Dr Verwoerd statue faces the impressive Hendrik Verwoerd Building of the provincial administration; in the rear is the Old Government Building.

5. The exquisite Victorian entrance to one of Bloemfontein's finest hotels — three-star Halevy House Hotel on the corner of Markgraff and Charles Streets.

1

2

1. *Bloemfontein Zoological Gardens — one of many beautiful places in the city.*

2. *Springbok in the Franklin Game Reserve and the Observatory Theatre on Naval Hill.*

*Beautiful land-marks in two Free State towns:
1. In the north, the Dutch Reformed Church in Winburg and 2. In the south, the Dutch Reformed Church in Zastron.*

and mammal, and the Florisbad skull of primitive man. The archaeological section consists of over 400 000 specimens.

A large open area to the west of the city centre contains the President C.R. Swart Park, King's Park, Loch Logan and the Bloemfontein Zoo. The area is perhaps best approached through Selbourne Avenue which runs parallel with the Bloemspruit, where a terrazzo periscope stands in the garden of remembrance at the place where Johan Brits found his fountain of flowers, and adjoining Victoria Park where the City Council has provided a fine caravan park in a splendid setting.

Within President C.R. Swart Park is the Free State Stadium, built to seat 68 000, and the venue for provincial and international rugby matches and athletics meetings. The Olympic standard swimming pool and stadium are also in this park. On the opposite side of the dividing thoroughfare there is a magnificent 3-hectare rose garden in King's Park.

Beyond King's Park is the entrance to the Zoo, beautifully laid out with many fascinating animals in open surroundings, and a particularly fine chimp house. In the natural area of Loch Logan is a popular picnic place where there are facilities for barbecue.

Continuing west along the thoroughfare that separates the zoo area from that of the stadium, across Parfitt Avenue, College Avenue is entered. This avenue passes Grey College on the right and leads to the University. Grey College, one of a number of fine schools in the city, was founded in 1885 on a substantial personal grant by Sir George Grey, Governor of the Cape. President M.T. Steyn and C.G. Fichardt (Mayor of Bloemfontein in 1897 and lifelong friend of General Hertzog), were among the many leading Free Staters to be pupils at Grey. The university graduate side of the college has merged with the University. The University of the Orange Free State, founded in 1950, has an extensive campus and fine modern buildings.

The G.A. Fichardt Public Library was founded in 1875 and is on the corner of Henry Street and West Burger Street and contains some rare Africana. The National Drama Library is housed in the same building. The modern Civic theatre, noted for fine acoustics, is in Markgraaff Street near the Appeal Court.

A great asset of Bloemfontein is its wildlife reserve on Naval Hill – virtually in the middle of the city. Named the Franklin Game Reserve in honour of Mayor J.S. Franklin, it was established in 1928 as the sanctuary for herds of springbok, blesbok, eland, zebra and many wild birds. A perimeter road encircles the 198-hectare wilderness at the summit of the flat-topped hill and provides opportunities for spacious views of the city and the surrounding farmlands. The hill, so typical of the mountainous outcrops on the plains of the Free State, was originally called Bloemfonteinberg. The name was changed during the British occupation in 1900 when Lord Roberts's Naval detachment were posted on the summit with their naval guns.

The clear skies, highveld air and low rainfall are some of the reasons for astronomers being attracted to Bloemfontein. Harvard University started the Boyden Observatory at Mazelspoort in 1927, and University of Michigan established the Lamont-Hussey Observatory on Naval Hill a year later in 1928. Boyden Observatory was incorporated with the Department of Astronomy, University of Orange Free State, in 1976. Its principal instrument is a 152 centimetre aperture reflector. After discovering thousands of binaries, many of great importance, Lamont-Hussey ceased operating in 1975. The observatory with its 17-metre-diameter dome has been converted into a theatre for the Performing Arts Council of O.F.S.

Mazelspoort is 25 kilometres east of the city on the road to Thaba Nchu and here the City Council has constructed a pleasure resort, of the very highest standard, on the banks of the Modder River. Accommodation is provided in the form of furnished bungalows and rondavels as well as first-rate facilities for caravanners and campers. Overlooking the river the modern restaurant is surrounded by well-kept lawns and all along the river are secluded shady spots for fishing, picnicking and barbecue. The recreational amenities include river-boating, tennis and swimming in a gigantic fresh-water pool, 135 metres long.

One of the most sociable clubs to discover in South Africa is the Bloemfontein Yacht Club – its members are sincerely hospitable, even to people who know little about the thrilling sport of yachting. The club is at Rustfontein on a fine stretch of water of the Modder River – 48 kilometres east of the city on the road to Thaba Nchu. The topography surrounding the club allows for excellent winds, and during most weekends in summer regattas and races are held.

Immediately out of the city, on the eastern side (Thaba Nchu road), there is a turnoff left to the Railway Sports Ground (near the railway marshalling yard) and turnoffs right to Schoeman Park golf Club and Bloemfontein Golf Club. Some distance farther on, also on the right, are the turnoffs to Roderick Polo Ground and Bloemfontein Turf Club. Eight kilometres from the city is the turnoff left to J.B.M. Hertzog Airport.

Hoffman Square is a garden in the centre of the city. The Information Bureau is on the square (telephone 8-3636, Saturdays 8-3651), and here on the square is the main Post Office. Maitland Street is the centre of the principal shopping area. S.A. Airways Terminal is in Prudential Assurance Building, St. Andrews Street.

Bloemfontein has several good hotels, including 3-star Halevy House Hotel which has retained the quality characteristics inherited from its Victorian era. It is an hotel of distinction, comfort and fine cuisine and is entitled to recommendation without hesitation.

Southern Orange Free State

National road N1 from the Cape (Chapter 4) crosses the Orange River at Novalspont near the Hendrik Verwoerd Dam where the OFS Provincial Administration has established a pleasure resort. Having crossed the Orange, N1 by-passes a number of towns on its 195 kilometre journey from here to Bloemfontein.

Springfontein

Springfontein, just west of the highway, is an important railway junction with a population of 4 000.

Philippolis

Forty-eight kilometres west of Springfontein is Philippolis, a quaint town of 2 500 inhabitants, named after the Reverend Dr Philip, superintendent in South Africa of the London Missionary Society. In 1826 a section of the Griquas under Adam Kok settled here and remained until 1862 when they trekked over the Drakensberg to *No man's land* which became East Griqualand. The Dutch Reformed Church on the site of the Griqua church is a national monument. Philippolis has an hotel and a caravan park.

Trompsburg

Trompsburg, to the left (west side) of N1, was founded in 1898 and is the centre for an extensive merino sheep farming district. The town was named after Bastian Tromp, the owner of the original farm and has a population of 2 500. In Trompsburg there is an hotel and a caravan park. At this point the road leading north from Philippolis joins N1.

Edenburg

Also on the west side of N1, Edenburg had its start when the Dutch Reformed Church was built in 1862. The population is 3 500. The town has a fine library and other good amenities, including a golf course, swimming pool and an hotel. It serves an area of prosperous cattle and sheep farming.

Jagersfontein

From Edenburg a road leads due west to Jagersfontein, diamond-mining town with a population of 5 000 that had its start in 1870. Although mining over the years has been erratic, there was a period when it rivalled Kimberley for the high quality of its stones.

In 1893 the second largest diamond on record, the Excelsior, was found at Jagersfontein. The town was named after the owner of the original farm, Evert Jager, a Griqua

Fauresmith

Eleven kilometres north-west of Jagersfontein is Fauresmith, where a railway line runs down the main street. The town of 2 500 inhabitants was founded in 1848 – the year of the Battle of Boomplaats and is the second oldest town in the Free State (after Winburg).

Rouxville

Trunk road R30 crosses into the Orange Free State at Aliwal North (Chapter 6) and reaches Rouxville, 35 kilometres from the border. The town of 3 500 inhabitants was founded in 1863 and named after the Reverend Pieter Roux of Smithfield.

Smithfield

Continuing on R30, Smithfield across the Caledon River, was founded in 1848 by Sir Harry Smith. It was the scene of much fighting against the Basotho and here in 1855 Moshesh signed a peace treaty. The first president of the Orange Free State Republic, President J.P. Hoffman, farmed in the district which

today is notable for irrigation farming and wool production. The population is 3 500. To the north-west, beyond Wilcocks Poort, is the Smithfield Dam and Kinderman Park, a fine riverine amenity with picnic sites and a golf course. There is an hotel in Smithfield.

Reddersburg

The last town on R30 before reaching Bloemfontein, 60 kilometres away, is Reddersburg (town of the Saviour); founded by the Dutch Reformed Church in 1859, it has a population of 3 000 and serves a wool-producing district. General Christiaan de Wet captured an entire British column here during the Anglo-Boer War.

Bethulie

From Smithfield a road leads south-west to Bethulie, a farming and railway centre close to the Orange River with a population of 5 000. The town has a beautiful park, a small game reserve, golf course, swimming pool, municipal caravan park (with all facilities) and an hotel.

Zastron

From Rouxville a road leads to Zastron in the extreme south-east of the province near the Lesotho border. Zastron lies at an altitude of 1 607 metres in fine scenery and has a population of 5 500. It was founded in 1876 and named in honour of the wife of President Brand, who was Johanna Sibella Zastron. The town owes its prosperity to the excellent maize, cattle and general farming in the district and to the trading with Lesotho. A famous landmark in the Aasvoëlberg outside Zaastron is the 'eye', a hole in the sandstone cliff, 9 metres in diameter. At Eeufeeskloof, a renowned beauty spot, the municipality has built a fine swimming pool. The area is noted for its caves and Bushman paintings.

Wepener

North of Zastron is Wepener, an agricultural and trading centre with a population of 6 000, lying 5 kilometres east of the Caledon River close to the Lesotho border. Its name commemorates Lourens Jacobus Wepener, killed while leading the attack on the Moshesh stronghold, Thaba Bosiho, on 15 August 1865. Wepener was the southernmost of the settlements which were founded in 1867 by the republican burghers in what was called the *Conquered Territory* (after years of plunder, cattle rustling and losing battles against the Basotho tribes, suffered by both the Sovereignity and the Republic). The territory followed the course of the Caledon River northwards and beyond its source to Fouriesburg, about 160 kilometres long, and taking in an area of over 7 000 square kilometres, including Ficksburg and Ladybrand, and some of the best wheat country in South Africa. When, in February 1869, Britain finally annexed what was then called Basutoland at the pleading of Moshesh and the agreement of President Brand, the present shape of Lesotho was determined. A year later Moshesh died at the age of over eighty. He was the founder of the Basotho nation and one of the greatest men produced by the Black races.

Hobhouse and Dewetsdorp

From Wepener route R26 follows the Caledon River northwards to the village of Hobhouse (named after the Anglo-boer War Concentration camp heroine, Emily Hobhouse), and on to Ladybrand. Another road leads north-west to Dewetsdorp, founded in 1876 and named after the father of the famous General Christiaan de Wet. Pleasantly situated, the streets are lined with trees and there is an hotel. Dewetsdorp is 66 kilometres south-east of Bloemfontein.

Petrusburg and Koffiefontein

Due west of Bloemfontein (on route R48) is Petrusburg on the railway line between Bloemfontein and Kimberley in a farming area noted for potatoes. From here the road swings south and then west, in a semi-circle. At the base of the semi-circle there is a branch to Koffiefontein, a diamond-mining centre established in 1892, with a population of 9 000. To the south-east the Kalkfontein Dam impounds the Riet River. Completed in 1938, it has a storage capacity of over 339 million cubic metres (for a long time second only to the Vaal Dam for capacity) irrigating over 7 700 hectares of 238 private farms producing lucerne, potatoes, ground-nuts and other crops, and providing urban supplies for Koffiefontein and Jacobsdal. For boating and fishing it has a reach of 19 kilometres and a surface area of 4 921 hectares.

Jacobsdal

Continuing northwards, the road from Petrusburg reaches Jacobsdal (in a district of salt pans), to join trunk road R29 at the Cape border town Modderrivier.

Dealesville, Baden-Baden – Florisbad

Trunk route R64 links Bloemfontein with Kimberley (Chapter 14). On the way the road passes through Dealesville in an area of salt pans and mineral springs including the well-known Baden-Baden (14 kilometres from the town) and Florisbad (35 kilometres to the east of the town), famed for its hot springs and the fossils there. The National Museum, Bloemfontein, houses the famous Florisbad skull of primitive man.

Boshof

Boshof was laid out in 1856 and named Vanwykvlei and later renamed to honour President J.N. Boshof. The area is dotted with salt pans, some of which are worked commercially.

Thaba Nchu

Due west of Bloemfontein a road leads for 66 kilometres to Thaba Nchu, a town within a displaced portion of the Republic of Bophuthatswana. From 1846 onwards Thaba Nchu was a rallying point of the Great Trek owing to its situation in relation to the eastern Cape Colony, the goodwill of the Barolong Chief, Moroka, and the help of the Wesleyan Missionary, James Archbell. The trek parties of A.H. Potgieter, Gerrit Maritz, Piet Uys and Karel Landman all camped in this vicinity. The grave and pitso (conference place) of chief Moroka may be seen there. Today there is a casino in Thaba Nchu.

Ladybrand

At the close of the final Basuto War in 1867, Ladybrand was established and named after Lady Catharina Brand, wife of Sir Christoffel Brand, Speaker of the Cape House of Assembly and mother of President Sir J.H. Brand. The town is laid out at the foot of the Platberg and commands fine views of the Maluti Mountains in Lesotho. The population is 9 000. A special feature of the town is the resort laid out by the municipality at Leliehoek. Expertly designed so as not to interfere in any way with the lovely, natural surroundings of fine trees and majestic rocks, there are bungalows, caravan and camping sites, picnic spots with barbecue places and a fitted children's playground. The centre-piece attraction is a magnificent, crystal clear swimming pool. This is a fine area for trail riding and horses may be hired. The Ladybrand district is noted for its beautiful farms of wheat, maize and livestock.

The town is linked with Bloemfontein and Bethlehem by railway and does considerable trade with Lesotho (its capital, Maseru, lies across the Caledon River a few kilometres south-east of Ladybrand where the Holiday Inn and Casino, are a big draw-card to South Africans).

Of tremendous interest to archaeologists, artists and art lovers are the caves and the prehistoric and Bushman paintings in the caves of the Ladybrand district. All of these are proclaimed national monuments; the best known being at Modderpoort, 15 kilometres north of the town.

There is an hotel in Ladybrand itself and the delightful two-star resort hotel, Riverside Lodge at the Maseru Gate.

Clocolan

The rural town of Clocolan has a population of 7 500 and serves a prosperous wheat, maize and livestock district. Among its recreational amenities it boasts a racecourse and golf course. The town has an hotel and caravan park.

Ficksburg

Another of the towns established after the final Basuto War of 1867, Ficksburg was named after a leader of that era, Commandant-General Johan Fick. The town of 11 000 inhabitants is built on the west bank of the Caledon River which forms the boundary with Lesotho, and some of its prosperity is derived from trade with that country. The district is a rich farming area for wheat, maize, livestock (including polo pony and racehorse breeding), and produces the finest crop of cherries in South Africa. A cherry festival is held in Ficksburg each year in November. Ficksburg has a strong polo club, a fine golf course, a racecourse with starting pens, an aerodrome, two hotels and an all-facility municipal caravan park.

The town lies at an altitude of 1 629 metres on the eastern slopes of the forest-crowned Imperani Mountain and has warm summers, crisp in the evening, and very cold winters. The area is notable for its fine scenic views extending to the Maluti Mountains (part of the Drakensberg) in Lesotho, usually snow-capped in winter.

From Ficksburg two roads lead north to join route R49, one meeting at Senekal.

1

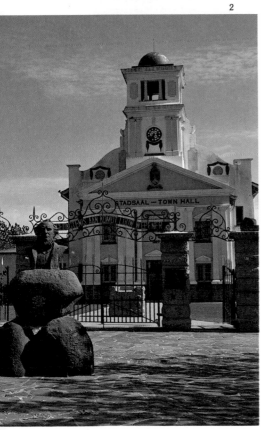

2

3

1. *Willem Pretorius Game Reserve, Allemanskraal Dam, near Winburg.*

2. *Wepener Town Hall and the bronze bust of Commandant Louw Wepener who was killed leading the attack against Moshesh at Thaba Bosiho.*

3. *Kroonpark Holiday Resort, Vals River, Kroonstad.*

Fouriesburg

In scenically beautiful mountainous country, Fouriesburg is close to the Lesotho border. Established in 1892, it is situated 53 kilometres north-east of Ficksburg on route R26 to Bethlehem and has a population of 2 000, an hotel and a caravan park.

Northern Orange Free State

Eighteen kilometres north of Bloemfontein the freeway divides. The right fork, which is national road N1, is the shorter and more direct route to Johannesburg; the left fork which is road R30 leads to Brandfort from where there is more direct route to the Free State Goldfields.

Winburg

The oldest town in the Orange Free State, Winburg (on national road N1), was founded by the Voortrekkers in 1836. It was for a number of years an outpost of the Natalia Republic, its landdrost being appointed by the Pietermaritzburg Volksraad. When the British annexed Natal in 1842, Winburg was the administrative headquarters of the Free State burghers and remained so until Bloemfontein became the capital of the Republic formed in 1854. A pleasantly situated town with two fine Dutch Reformed Churches, it has a population of 7 500 and is the centre for a rich wheat, maize and livestock producing area. There are two hotels and a caravan park in the town.

Willem Pretorius Game Reserve

Immediately north of Winburg, trunk route R49 coming from Harrismith joins with national road N1. Continuing on N1, after 32 kilometres a branch road leads right (west) for 9 kilometres to Allemanskraal Dam and the Willem Pretorius Game Reserve where a holiday resort, with recreational facilities, harmoniously combines with the interesting game reserve.

The game reserve covers 10 900 hectares and the dam which is some 3 400 hectares in extent, impounds the waters of Sand River, irrigating the farmlands of the Goldfields region. Situated as it is in the highveld, almost in the centre of the province, the complex provides the tourist with a fine amenity which is easily accessible.

Since the game reserve was esablished in 1956, and through a process of resettlement, the Provincial Administration has done excellent work in recreating part of the scene of a century ago when great herds of game abounded the province. The game have been re-introduced on the plains bordering the dam and on the slopes and bush-clad kloofs of the Doringsberg. Once practically extinct, over 500 black wildebeest have been re-established (making this the world's largest herd).

Among the wide variety of other antelope there are springbok, blesbok, impala, eland, red hartebeest, steenbok, duiker, mountain, reedbuck, gemsbok, klipspringer and kudu. White rhino were re-introduced from Natal. There are a number of Burchell's and mountain zebra, giraffe, Cape buffalo, baboon and ostrich. Rock rabbits, hares, meercats, small carnivores, monkeys and various reptile species are among the other creatures protected in the reserve. There are no large predators. In the sanctuary more than 200 bird species have been recorded. Spoonbills, pelicans, flamingoes, herons (10 kinds), spurwinged geese, wild duck, hammerheads, secretary birds, eagles, hawks, owls and partridges are all common. The flora is rich and interesting in variety and some of the larger trees along the roads have been numbered to enable identification; these include white stinkwood, barkbrush, kiepersol (umbrella trees), acacia, karoo (sweet thorn), karee and wild olive.

Peculiar to the reserve are the thousands of stone ruins of the small bee-hive type huts in the Doringsberg probably of the lost Leghoya tribe who were in the area before the Matabele invasion from Natal and before the Great Trek.

The reserve was named after Willem Pretorius, Member of the Executive Committee of the Province, who was largely responsible for its establishment.

The pleasure resort, laid out on the koppies overlooking the dam, offers most things for the success of the outdoor holiday. The accommodation comprises rondavels and family cottages and there is an attractive restaurant serving good food, malt and wine. For those who like to prepare their own food in the traditional braaivleis style, outdoor kitchens and grillers are there. The large caravan park has the best facilities. The provision for sport and entertainment is first-rate with swimming, angling (black bass, yellowfish and carp) aquatic speed sports pleasure boat jaunts, tennis, badminton, billiards; bowls and golf.

Enquiries and reservation should be directed to Willem Pretorius Wildtuin, 9451. Telephone 6 (through trunks 0020).

Ventersburg

Continuing on N1, Ventersburg lies at the junction of road R70 to the Goldfields. It was named after the owner of the original farm when it was founded in 1871. It is the centre of a farming district notable for the fertility of its soil, where maize, wheat and livestock flourish. The population is 4 000 and there is an hotel in the town.

Theunissen

North of Ventersburg on national road N1 lies the important large town, Kroonstad, which is described after the journey through the Goldfields has been made. Returning to Brandfort on R30 the first town to its north is Theunissen which was established in 1907. It serves the rural district irrigated by the waters of the 318-million-litre Efenis Dam (impounding the Vet River) which lies to the south-east of the town. This is in the heart of the maize and sunflower producing region and a huge silo dominates the scene. The population is 8 000.

Orange Free State Goldfields

Covering an area roughly 50 kilometres long by 16 kilometres wide, Orange Free State Goldfields stretch from Virginia in the south to Allanridge in the north. It is one of the richest deposits in the world, estimated to contain 8,5-billion rands worth of gold.

The pioneers in the discovery and exploitation of these goldfields had many disappointments over a long period of time before the wealth of the reef was known. The first traces of gold were seen in 1904 by the prospector Archibald Megson on the farm Aandenk (where Allanridge is today). He had to wait until 1932 before he could get anyone interested in financing an exploration.

Allan Roberts and Emmanuel Jacobson were the people he interested and in 1933, in association with Fritz Leonard Marx and Ephraim Benjamin Woolff, they floated the company Wit Extensions Limited. A borehole was sunk but they failed to reach payable gold, about R100 000 being lost in their efforts.

In 1936, Dr Hans Merensky (the famous geologist) carried out drilling in the area and in 1938 Union Corporation Limited, Western Holdings Limited and African and European Investment Company Limited applying geophysical and geological prospecting methods, found the Basal Reef, with high gold values, on the farms Uitsig and St. Helena. Further progress was halted with the outbreak of World War II.

In 1945, Anglo American Corporation of South Africa Limited deepened the borehole drilled by Wit Extensions on the farm Aandenk in 1932 by 122 metres, and struck the rich gold-bearing Basal Reef. During 1945-46 more than R6 000 000 was spent in exploring these goldfields by sinking nearly 500 diamond drill boreholess. The minimum grade required for profitable mining was generally regarded to be 150 inch-dwts. Of the boreholes sunk, 96 gave values over that figure, 15 gave values over 500 inch-dwts and 9 were over 1 000 inch-dwts; with the fantastic news coming from the farm Geduld near Odendaalsrus on 16 April 1946 that a drill intersecting the Basal Reef at a depth of nearly 4 000 feet (1 200 metres) returned a value of 23 037 inch-dwts.

Prior to the discovery of the gold, this flat plain of the Free State was practically featureless. Today the headgear of modern gold mining, the growing mine dumps and the buildings, gardens and playing fields of the boom towns spread out over what was once barren veld. Thousands of flamingoes and strangely enough, seagulls, inhabit the dams of the goldfields.

Virginia

The second largest town in the Orange Free State Goldfields, Virginia was proclaimed in 1954 and has a population of 24 000 (with another 32 000 Black people housed on surrounding mine properties). Planned on modern lines with wide boulevards lined with lawns, trees and flowers, it is a credit to its Town Council and administrators.

Surrounding the town are four gold mines, and at Virginia Gold Mining Company there is a large sulphuric acid plant.

For the holiday-maker there is a fine resort laid out on the south bank of the Sand River, in a parkland setting with lawns, flower-beds and shade trees. The complex consists of a modern, licensed restaurant which overlooks the filtered swimmingpool; ten cottages and 290 rondavels; a separately fenced luxury, riverside caravan park; a section of the Sand River especially dammed for speed boats, water-skiing and rowing; and a 34-hectare game sanctuary.

The sporting clubs of Virginia provide venues for provincial championships; tennis at Harvinia Club and golf at Sand River Golf Club. The mines have stadia for rugby, soccer and hockey, and other recreational amenities in the town are bowling greens, small-bore shooting range and jukskei fields. There are two hotels.

Welkom

With a population of 9 000 (excluding mine workers) Welkom is the largest town in the Orange Free State Goldfields. It was laid out in 1947 on ultra modern lines, spread out over an extensive area with wide, tree-lined American-style boulevards and spacious traffic circles. The central commercial area is planned in the shape of a horseshoe with ample parking and a 4,5-hectare park in the centre. Quite separate is the handsome civic centre. The residential suburbs radiate from the city centre and each has its own shopping complex. Welkom reached municipal status in 1961 and was proclaimed a city on 14 February 1968, 21 years after its establishment.

Welkom serves the six mines which surround the town including St. Helena, the first to be worked in the Free State Goldfields. Excellent accommodation has been provided for the 42 000 Black mine workers and they have a very fine hospital.

A daily air service links Welkom with Johannesburg, the travelling time being one hour. Welkom has a Technological Institute, a Technical College, several primary and secondary schools, three recreation clubs, five swimming baths, four hotels and a municipal caravan park.

Odendaalsrus

Although Odendaalsrus lies in the heart of the goldfields it came into existence long before the gold was discovered. It started with the siting of a Dutch Reformed Church there at the close of the last century and received municipal status in 1912. The town took on a complete transformation following the remarkable gold find at Geduld, five kilometres from the town. The population is 22 000.

Allanridge

Northernmost of the Free State Goldfield towns, Allanridge was named after the unfortunate Allan Roberts who abandoned the borehole drill on the nearby farm Aandenk when it was within 122 metres of one of the richest gold-bearing reefs in the world. Allanridge is another ultra-modern mining town with a population of 12 000. It was established in 1950. The Aandenk Prospecting Borehole is a national monument.

Henneman

Henneman, east of Odendaalsrus, on the main north-south railway, is a rail centre for the northern goldfields (Virginia is also on the line). It has fine Afrikaans medium schools and in the area are the cement factories of Anglo Alpha Cement Limited and Whites Portland Cement Limited.

1. *Lovely liquidambar trees at the entrance to the Loch Athlone pleasure resort, Bethlehem.*
2. *Brandwag rest camp, Golden Gate Highland National Park, beneath the cliff named Brandwag (sentinel).*
3. *South Africa's bird emblem, the blue crane, is fairly well spread throughout the country today but used to be confined to the Central Plains.*

Northern Orange Free State (continued)

Continuing on national road N1, after Ventersburg the road reaches Kroonstad.

Kroonstad

This is a modern bustling town built on the banks of the Vals River. The central position of Kroonstad has led to its becoming a strategic junction and marshalling yard on the main north-south railway (the line reached here in 1892). With its population of 75 000, Kroonstad is an important agricultural, educational and administrative centre. Its establishment dates from the Great Trek and the township from 1855. The town takes its name from Kroon, the famed horse of one of the officials in the early days.

Kroonstad takes on a festive atmosphere during the summer season. Thousands of visitors arrive for the fun and merrymaking at Kroonpark Holiday Resort and the main street is lit up with an array of coloured lights. Kroonpark, laid out on the banks of the Vals River, is a fine inland resort. In the riverine setting with picturesque weeping willows and beautiful lawns and gardens, the visitor is provided with luxury timber bungalow accommodation and first-rate caravan and camping sites. The modern pavilion-restaurant is fully licensed. A motor pleasure boat is operated on the river, row boats may be hired, the swimming pool is filtered and there is a fine putting course. The delightful fairy lights at night provide a romantic scene.

Sporting activities of all kinds are catered for with up-to-date amenities for rugby, tennis, netball, bowls, cricket, hockey, jukskei, water-skiing, swimming, rowing and fishing. There is an 18-hole golf course with a spacious and luxurious country club on the river bank. The South African Jukskei Tournaments are played in Kroonstad; at the headquarters on the Vals River there are excellent playing fields and accommodation for 400 players.

Kroonstad serves a rich maize and livestock producing district and some of its suburbs compare favourably in architecture and landscape gardening with the best in South Africa. The town lies at an altitude of 1 368 metres and enjoys ideal climate with a clear, invigorating atmosphere. There are four hotels. The famous statue of Sarel Cilliers adjoins the garden of the beautiful old Dutch Reformed Church.

Bothaville

From Welkom route R30 leads due north to Bothaville, a town on the Vals River with a population of 12 000. It was founded in 1889 by Theunis Botha and is in the heart of the maize triangle. The town has a racecourse and caravan park, and the Elgro Hotel is a recommended night stop.

Viljoenskroon and Vierfontein

From Kroonstad route R76 heads north-west through Viljoenskroon and Vierfontein to cross the Vaal River at Orkney in the Transvaal (Chapter 11).

Viljoenskroon was named after the famed horse, Kroon, and his master, Hans Viljoen. It lies in a district renowned for its maize, corn and ground-nut production.

At Vierfontein there is the great electrical generating station for the Western Transvaal and Free State gold mines.

Heilbron and Frankfort

Within the 'maize triangle', north-east of Kroonstad, route R34 passes the village of Edenville on its way to Heilbron and Frankfort, busy rail centres and road junctions to the south of Vaal Dam, each with a population of some 10 000 people. As the Afrikaans name implies, Heilbron has mineral springs, and at Langdam Resort there is fishing and swimming with facilities for campers and caravanners. Frankfort, on the Wilge River, has a railway station famed for its model garden. There are hotels in both towns.

Vegkop and the lost Leghoya tribe

Twenty-four kilometres south of Heilbron, on the gravel road to Lindley, is Vegkop, where forty desperate trekkers with their wives and children, led by Andries Hendrik Potgieter and Sarel Cilliers, defeated the Matabele impi of 5 000 warriors on 19 October 1836 (although the Matabele got away with several thousand head of cattle). A memorial gathering takes place here each year on 16 December, and the site of the battle is marked with a monument and buildings used during the memorial service.

The area is also notable for the strange bee-hive stone huts (1,5 metres in diameter and 1,2 metres from floor to ceiling) used by the lost Leghoya tribe. These huts are all proclaimed national monuments.

Lindley

American misionary, the Reverend Daniel Lindley, who ministered to the Voortrekkers, was remembered when Lindley was founded in 1875. A pleasure resort is established on the bank of the Vals River with camping sites under shade trees, swimming pool and fishing amenities. The town has a population of 3 500 and is notable for the manufacture of the protein food Pro Nutro. There is an hotel.

Five kilometres from the town on the Kroonstad road is the monument to the British officers of the famous Imperial Yeomanry, killed in action during the Anglo-Boer War (Lindley was almost completely destroyed during that war). In the district is the historical farm of Sarel Cilliers.

Vredefort

Seventy-six kilometres north of Kroonstad, national road N1 passes through the small town of Vredefort (fort of peace). In 1857, when the presidency of the Free State was in dispute, Transvaal and Free State commandos skirmished here, but after peaceful reconciliation the town was laid out by the Dutch Reformed Church and so named. A goldfield discovered in 1886 petered out after a few years of production.

Parys

Continuing northwards from Vredefort, the N1

reaches Parys.

Parys was named by the German surveyor, Schilbach (who had participated in the siege of Paris during the Franco-Prussian War of 1870-71), because its situation on the Vaal reminded him of Paris on the Seine. Parys acquired municipal status in 1887.

The Town Council has been instrumental in providing fine resort and pleasure amenities in an 8-hectare river-embankment site of the Vaal, and on the large and beatifully wooded islands of the river (one island is 68 hectares in extent). Parys has for long been a highly popular summer resort with its bungalows, restaurant, caravan and camping sites and nine-hole golf course on Long Island (connected to the mainland by suspension bridge). Here on the river-front in a picturesque setting of lawns and willow trees are the two hotels, Riviera and Echoes.

The pleasures to be enjoyed are fishing, golf, tennis, swimming and boating on the 13-kilometre stretch above the weir.

Extensive irrigation is carried out on the Vaal and the principal farming is that of tobacco; Vaalrivier Köoperatiewe Tabakboëre-Vereeniging has its headquarters in the town and handles some 900 000 kilograms of tobacco annually.

Eighteen kilometres north-east of Parys, national road N1 reaches the turnoff east to the border town of Sasolburg. Continuing, N1 crosses the Vaal to enter Transvaal at Barrage (Chapter 11).

Sasolburg

Sasolburg, a modern town with every amenity, was established in 1954 to house the employees of Suidafrikaanse Steenkool Olie en Gas Korporasie – Sasol (South African Coal Oil and Gas Corporation). The siting of the R185-million, Government-sponsored, giant oil-form-coal plant was determined by the occurence of vast deposits of low-grade coal in this northern precinct of the Free State, so close to the Vaal River, able to supply enormous quantities of water required in the conversion process.

This highly sophisticated, intricate installation belching flames, fumes and smoke for twenty-four hours a day, produces 280 000 000 litres of petrol and liquid chemicals annually. Among its considerable list of products are petrol, diesel and fuel oils, liquefied petroleum gas, tar, creosotes, solven benzoles, tar acids, waxes, organic solvents, butadiene, styrene, ethylene, propylene, synthetic ammonia, nitric acid, ammonium nitrate solutions, limestone ammonium nitrate and ammonium sulphate. Fuel gas is supplied to industries of the Witwatersrand by pipeline.

Sasolburg also contains the plants of a number of private enterprise manufacturers where the process is based on Sasol raw materials, such as plastics, solvents, synthetic detergents and fertilisers. In the area, Letaba Power Station rates with the world's biggest.

From Sasolburg the road north into the Transvaal bridges the Vaal River near Vanderbijlpark (Chapter 11).

Eastern Orange Free State

The two principal routes of the Eastern Free State are trunk route R49 from Winburg to Harrismith and national road N3 from Harrismith to Villiers.

Senekal

North-east of Winburg on route R49 is Senekal, a town with a population of 10 000 notable for its production of food. It was named after Commandant-General Frederick Senekal, who fought in the Basuto Wars of the mid-nineteenth century.

Paul Roux

There are a number of old sandstone buildings in this little town of 3 000 inhabitants. It was founded in 1912 and named after the Dutch Reformed minister, the Reverend Paul Roux.

Bethlehem

In 1860 a party of trekkers, believing that they had found their promised land, named the river where they chose to settle, the Jordan, and the settlement Bethlehem. The busy modern town of today has a population of 41 000. Railway workshops, flour mills, a furniture factory and a creamery are the main industries of the town and apart from maize, the district is famed for its sheep, cattle and racehorse stud farms.

For the inland holiday-maker Bethlehem has a very special amenity in its pleasure resort laid out on the banks of Loch Athlone, the dam impounding the Jordan River. The bungalows, rondavels, caravan park, camping sites, swimming pool, golf course and restaurant (built in the shape of the liner, Athlone Castle) are all in a particularly beautiful lakeside setting. The lake provides for skiing, boating, yachting and fishing. Pretorius Kloof, below the dam wall, is a lovely nature sanctuary.

Bethlehem lies in the famous maize triangle and is a major farming, distribution and educational centre of the eastern Orange Free State.

Kestell

Forty-five kilometres east of Bethlehem on trunk route R49 is Kestell with a population of 2 000. It was founded in 1905 and named after the Reverend J.D. Kestell, Dutch Reformed chaplain with the Free State forces during the Anglo-Boer War, and later one of the Secretaries at the Treaty of Vereeniging conference.

From Kestell a road leads south-west through the Golden Gate Highland National Park then passes the village of Clarens before swinging back north-west to meet the trunk road R49 near Bethlehem; the entire journey revealing some of the most spectacular scenery to be seen anywhere in southern Africa.

Golden Gate Highland National Park

Clarens was named after the village in Switzerland where President Kruger died. It is in a beautiful part of South Africa and close to one of the country's scenic wonders, the sandstone mountains of Golden Gate Highlands National Park. The Park was proclaimed in 1963 and covers an area of 4 400 hectares at an altitude of from 1 800 to 2 800 metres on the watershed of the catchment area of the Orange and Vaal Rivers.

The eroded rock formations, unique in the country, show a rich variety of colours – yellow, orange and red being predominant. The hollowed krantzes, dome-shaped promonotories and sheer cliffs create an unusual spectacle, particularly magnificent at sunset.

At the southern entrance is the giant-size cliff, shaped in a remarkable likeness of a human face with a large prominent nose – known as Gladstone's Nose. Near the northern entrance is the turnoff to the Mont-Aux-Sources view site; the massive peak is clearly visible from the Park and a wonderful spectacle after a snow fall.

The two camps are within a kilometre of each other. Dominated by the cliff named the Sentinel is Brandwag Rest Camp, a luxury complex comprising a main building with restaurant, shop, lounges and bedrooms; the nearby special family huts each with two bedrooms, porch, bathroom, toilet and car-port and a recreational area of bowls, tennis, jukskei, golf and trout fishing. The older Glen Reenen Rest Camp has good hutted accommodation with and without private bathroom and provides for caravanning and camping. Fresh produce can be purchased at the shop, and there is a stable of riding horses, and a petrol service station.

A variety of highveld vegetation covers the mountain slopes, the wild flowers being mainly of the bulbous type, like red hot poker and arum lilies. In the sheltered kloofs are the lovely indigenous trees, especially ouhout, while willows and poplars line the banks of the Little Caledon River – the road following its course. Game species which originally occurred in the region have been re-introduced such as black wildebeest, eland, red hartebeest, buffalo, blesbok, springbok, grey rhebok, mountain reedbuck, duiker, reedbuck, zebra and warthog. Ostriches, waterbirds, black eagles, jackal buzzards and other predator birds are also to be seen and the Park is one of the sanctuaries in which the rare lammergeyer, with its 2,5-metre wing span, nests every year.

Reservations: National Parks Board, Box 787, Pretoria. Short notice accommodation telephone Clarens 61 (code 0143262).

Harrismith

Upon its foundation in 1859, Harrismith was named after the hard-riding soldier governor, Sir Harry Smith. Like its sister town, Ladysmith, across the border in Natal (named after the governor's beautiful Spanish wife), Harrismith (as a staging post) experienced substantial boom periods in the old transport days, first with the discovery of the Kimberley diamonds and later with the Witwatersrand gold rush.

Today it serves one of the largest wool-producing districts of South Africa and does considerable trade with nearby Lesotho. Its industries include large cotton and woollen mills and a condensed milk factory.

Harrismith lies in a beautiful setting at the base of the majestic, flat-topped Platberg (2 396 metres) and in the valley of the Wilge River. A very pleasant recreational environment has been established at President Brand Park on the banks of the river. Amongst the willows is the caravan park with opportunities for boating and fishing. Visitors are made welcome at the licensed country club where there is golf, tennis and bowls. The scenic mountain drive to the top of the Platberg is a pleasurable excursion with fine views from the summit. The mountain road is the scene of the annual 13-kilometre cross-country race.

The blockhouse on the commonage was one of the formidable system which stretched across the north-eastern Free State towards the end of the Anglo-Boer War and is a national monument. In the grounds of the Town Hall there is a 30-metre-long petrified tree (coniferae triassio) estimated to be 150 million years old. The health-giving, invigorating air of the Harrismith area has for long attracted people to the town and surrounding guest farms for recuperative holidays. There are four hotels.

Trunk routes R49 and N3 merge at Harrismith. To the south-east N3 passes the villages of Swinburne and Van Reenen and crosses into Natal at the top of Van Reenen Pass (Chapter 10)

Warden, Reitz and Vrede

Following N3 northwards Warden is reached. The town of 3 500 inhabitants was named after the British Resident, Major H.D. Warden of the Sovereignty days, and is the centre of a grain producing district.

Reitz, named after the Free State president and situated due west of Warden, is a town of 7 000 inhabitants (also in the maize belt).

On its way across the Free State plain, intensely cultivated with maize and sunflowers, N3 passes the turnoff to Vrede. Established in 1880, it is today one of the largest cattle markets in the province and has a population of 7 000.

There is an hotel in each of the three towns.

Villiers

Villiers lies on the Vaal River in the great maize triangle and has a population of 3 000. In the pleasant riverine setting there are bungalow and caravan facilities with possibilities of fishing and boating on the Vaal. The town has an hotel. The bridge spanning the Vaal takes N3 into the Transvaal (Chapter 11).

Qwaqwa

The inhabitants of the self-governing territory of Qwaqwa are known as the Basotho ba Borwa (the South Sotho people). They are the descendants of two tribes: the Kwena followers of chief Paulus Mopeli, a brother of the great Moshesh, and the Batlokwa tribespeople whose chief was Wessels Mota (named after Commandant Wessels of Harrismith). With the permission of the Orange Free State government these tribes settled in what was known as the Witsieshoek area during the years 1867 to 1873.

Witsieshoek, once a remote mountain valley sandwiched between the Drakensberg and Maluti, took its name from another chief, Whêtse, who with his followers fled the Zulu holocaust to take refuge here during the 1830s. In the face of starvation Whêtse and his band turned rustlers and were eventually ousted by a Free State commando, but Whêtse made his escape through a tunnel in a huge cave, still to be seen today and known as Whêtse's Cave.

A Dutch Reformed Church mission station was established at Witsieshoek in 1874 and later a theological school and the Elizabeth Ross Hospital (named after the wife of a missionary) were opened.

The name of the country, Qwaqwa (white-white), comes from the name of the flat-topped sandstone mountain (covered in snow during winter) that dominates the mountain valley where the 50 000 Basotho Baborwa are settled. These were the first tribespeople in South Africa to receive local authority; this came about in 1953 and in 1969 self-government was granted. The area of the territory is some 47 000 hectares in extent and the developing capital is Phuthaditjhaba (meeting place of the nations), where the Qwaqwa government and the Qwaqwa Development Corporation have their offices; also in the town is the modern Hotel Qwaqwa with its licensed à la carte restaurant and bars. Phuthaditjhaba, which is south of trunk route R49, is reached by an all-tarred road from Harrismith, a distance of 42 kilometres, and by a good gravel road from Kestell (26 kilometres).

Witsieshoek Mountain Resort

From Phuthaditjhaba a good gravel road crosses the Elands River and leads for 30 kilometres into the Drakensberg range along one of the most spectacular routes in Africa. Five kilometres short of its terminus this road reaches the turnoff to Witsieshoek Mountain Resort superbly situated on a site, 2 100 metres above sea level, developed by the Qwaqwa Development Corporation.

The resort opened in 1972 and comprises comfortable double rooms, chalets and family units with wall-to-wall carpets and private bathrooms, and licensed restaurant where log fires roar in the icy winter nights. It is the haven and meeting place of nature lovers. From here there is by far the easiest access to the summit of Mont-Aux-Sources – the whole exercise an exhilarating experience; in any season the scenery is outstandingly beautiful. The resort borders on and overlooks Royal Natal Park, near the source of the Tugela, and on the other side, appears to be remarkably close to Lesotho's Maluti range.

CHAPTER 14
Kimberley and the Northern Cape

Griqualand West

At the close of the 18th century and the start of the 19th century, the Griquas, a race of mixed origin, European and Hottentot, settled in the area north of the Orange River, extending to the present day Botswana border. Their main settlement was Klaarwater, later renamed Griquatown, and their territory embraced the area of where Kimberley is today.

With the rush of diggers to the alluvial diamond fields at Klipdrift (Barkly West) on the Vaal River early in 1870, Griqualand West suddenly became politically important. Three countries, the Cape Colony, the Orange Free State and the South African Republic in the Transvaal were involved in a dispute of ownership with Nikolaas Waterboer (son of Andries Waterboer, and at the time chief or captain of the Griquas). The Lieut-Governor of Natal, R.W. Keate, a barrister of Lincoln's Inn, was called in to arbitrate and in 1871, in what became known as the *Keate Award*, the matter of ownership went in favour of the Griquas. The diggers themselves were not interested in rightful ownership, took to arms and declared themselves independent with Digger Stafford Parker (who later successfully operated a music hall in Kimberley) elected First President of the Klipdrift Diamond Fields Republic. Their independence was short lived when Britain, in all her imperial glory, simply took cession of Griqualand

West from the Griquas. In 1873 the British proclaimed it a separate colony. Judge Andries Stockenstrom caused an upheaval when he announced from the Bench in 1876 that Britain's possession of the Diamond Fields was illegal. In her predicament Britain ended up having to compensate the Orange Free State (President Brand) in the sum of £90 000. Griqualand West was annexed to the Cape Colony in 1880.

Kimberley

Since its establishment, Kimberley has continuously been the centre of the world's diamond market. It therefore holds a unique place in history. To the peoples of other countries it is probably the best known of all South African cities. The High Court of Griqualand West and the Deeds Office in Kimberley (which remain today), bear testimony of its having been the capital of a separate British Colony.

There have been a number of diamond rushes in South Africa and the greatest of them all, called the New Rush, happened in 1871 when there was a frantic stampede to the area of Colesberg Koppie; today the Big Hole of Kimberley Mine.

Of the rushes in Griqualand West, the first was to the Hopetown district in 1866. In 1869 diamonds were found in the mud walls of a farm-house at Bultfontein; in the gravel bed of the Vaal River at Klipdrift and by children playing on a farm at Dutoitspan. There was a mad rush to the alluvial field at Klipdrift, followed by an even larger one when the "dry ground" discovery took place on the farm of the De Beer family in May 1871 (the name De Beer to remain associated with diamonds forever after). Included in the thousands who were prospecting on

De Beer's farm was the party of Fleetwood Rawstorne. It was their Coloured servant Damon, who, in a state of inebriation, made the first discovery on the famed koppie.

Rawstorne's party hailed from Colesberg and to Colesberg Koppie there rushed thousands from all parts of the world. A seething mass of humanity numbering 50 000 were, within weeks, living in the tents and shacks of the mushroom mining camp which was to become the city of Kimberley – named in 1873 after the Earl of Kimberley, the British Colonial Secretary.

In the individual scramble on Colesberg Koppie in 1871, 700 claims were pegged and in a state of horrible congestion 30 000 men burrowed in the *kimberlite* (blue ground) to make their fortunes. The same sort of thing was going on at Bultfontein and Dutoitspan diggings a few kilometres to the east where the town of Beaconsfield shot up, and was named after Benjamin Disraeli, the Earl of Beaconsfield.

The year 1871 also saw the arrival on the scene of a young genius, destined to make his fortune and take no mean part in the shaping of the history of southern Africa. He was Cecil John Rhodes. At approximately the same time there appeared the dominant and colourful personality, Barney Barnato, vaudeville actor and boxing promoter who also proceeded to make his millions. Rhodes, at the age of 19 years, started out in the mining camp by manufacturing ice and pumping water from the claims, and like Barnato (only a year older than Rhodes), he bought up claims. Rhodes met up with C.D. Rudd, a man ten years his senior, and they each acquired twenty-five percent of the claims of the De Beers farm, and this led to the forming of De Beers Mining Company. In 1880 Rhodes became the Member for Barkly West in the Cape Legislative Assembly, and ten years later he was Prime Minister. One of his great accomplishments was the amalgamation of the interests of the De Beers mine with that of the Kimberley mine in 1888. Barney Barnato's Kimberley Central Diamond Mining Company received a cheque for £5 338 650 and was absorbed in the new consortium, De Beers Consolidated Mines Limited, with Rhodes its chief executive.

At Rhodes's instigation, in 1887 the party, comprising C.D. Rudd, "Matabele" Thompson and Rochefort Maguire, set out from Kimberley for Matabeleland to obtain a concession from chief Lobengula at Bulawayo. Three years later, on 27 June 1890, the pioneer column of the British South Africa Company (incorporated by Royal Charter) left Kimberley for Matabeleland; it comprised 500 police and 200 settlers. This established Rhodes as the founder of the new British territory to the north of South Africa which was later named Rhodesia, and is today Zimbabwe.

Rhodes remained in Kimberley during its 124-day siege by the Boers (commanded by General J.B.M. Hertzog) from 15 October 1899 to 15 February 1900. He arranged the manufacture (in the workshops of De Beers) of *Long Cecil,* a gun firing a 13-kilogram shell. Ironically, its designer, George

Labram, an American engineer, was killed with the direct hit on the Grand Hotel from the Boer *Long Tom* which was brought into action in retaliation. It was Rhodes who organised the shelter for the women and children in the workings of De Beers and Kimberley mines.

The millionaires of Kimberley were largely responsible for the financing of the Witwatersrand goldfields. In 1886 a transport rider whetted their enthusiasm when, in the presence of a number of distinguished people on Kimberley's Market Square, he crushed and washed some gold bearing reef. J.B. Robinson was the first to leave for the Rand and bought the farm Langlaagte for £6 000. His major interests were Robinson Mine, Robinson Deep and Randfontein Estates. Rhodes founded the forerunner of Consolidated Goldfields of South Africa in 1887, and in the same year Werner, Beit & Co. (formerly Jules Porges & Co.) moved from Kimberley to Johannesburg and started what eventually became the Corner House Group (Central Mining). Barney Barnato and his brother Henry established Johannesburg Consolidated Investments in 1889.

Kimberley became a municipality in 1877; its twin town, Beaconsfield rose to that status in 1884. A year later the Seventh Day Adventist Church of South Africa was founded by Pieter Wessels in Beaconsfield. The Kimberley and World Exhibition held in 1892 was the first international exhibition to be held outside London. The Kimberley School of Mines started in 1896, moved to Johannesburg in 1903 and became the University of the Witwatersrand. Before the close of the nineteenth century Kimberley possessed a race course, 84 bars, a Chamber of Commerce, a tramway, streets lighted by electricity, (the first in Africa), a three storey hotel, a Public Library, a rugby field upon which the first Currie Cup game was played and a Stock Exchange which was moved to Johannesburg in 1890.

Rhodes died in Muizenburg on 26 March 1902. *The Shangani,* a private railway coach of De Beers (made by the American Pullman Company) conveyed his body to the Matopos in Rhodesia. It passed through Kimberley on 5 April. In the same year Ernest Oppenheimer arrived in Kimberley as the representative of the famous London diamond merchant, Dunkelsbuhler. He was destined to become the principal figure in South African mining, to gain control of all the diamond fields of southern Africa, to receive a knighthood and to amass a great personal fortune, a large percentage of which he left for the benefit of the nation. It was Sir Ernest who established the now gigantic Anglo-American Corporation of South Africa.

In 1912 Beaconsfield merged with Kimberley; Ernest Oppenheimer became the first mayor of the newly proclaimed City of Kimberley and the Diocese of Kimberley and Kuruman was created with the opening of St. Cyprian's Cathedral.

The first flying school of South Africa started in Kimberley in 1913, with the aerodrome at Alexanderfontein on the outskirts of the city. This was the forerunner to the establishment of the South African Air Force which came into being as the South African Flying Corps in 1915. On the site of the original hangar is The Cradle of Aviation permanent exhibition of photographs covering the history of the South African Air Force.

On the verge of the Big Hole of Kimberley Mine there is a unique open-air museum in the form of a rebuilt street of the glamorous, romantic Kimberley of its Victorian heyday. It contains amongst its interesting items Barney Barnato's Boxing Academy, the oldest house in Kimberley – brought to the diamond fields by ox-wagon, the first Lutheran Church and the historic headgear used after the open cast mining had reached a depth of 366 metres, and during the siege as a conning tower to lower the women and children into the mine. From the observation platform near the museum the Big Hole is an extraordinary sight. It has a circumference of 4 572 metres, a diameter of 1,5 kilometres and an area of 11 heactares. In its 43 years of operation (1871 to 1914) 25 000 000 tons of blue ground were removed from the mine, yielding 14 504 566 carats of diamonds. Water seepage has filled the hole to within 256 metres of the surface.

De Beers Consolidated Mines Limited has its Head Office in Stockdale Steet, housed in a long, solid looking double-storey building erected in 1898. From then until 1974 when the modern high-rise Harry Oppenheimer Building was completed, this was where the diamonds of southern Africa were sorted and dispatched to the markets of the world. Here in the De Beers Board Room is the original paid cheque for £5 338 650 which Barney Barnato received, and from here permits are issued for visits to the Treatment and Recovery Plants of the mines. The one hour excursion commences at 9 a.m.

The De Beers Kennels are probably the best known kennels in the world. Here the De Beers Alsatians are bred and trained for the purposes of protecting mining property and the diamond floors. The kennels may be visited at any time; special performances being held from 10.30 a.m. on the first and third Sundays of each month.

To be seen nowhere else in the world are the street diggers who recover diamonds from the sites of excavated streets and demolished buildings. These areas contain layers of blue ground scattered there during the early days of the Big Hole diggings when recovery methods were primitive.

Kimberley has many fine statues and memorials. The Honoured Dead Memorial, built with stone from the Matopos, was designed by Sir Herbert Baker from a plan selected by Rhodes. It honours those who died in the siege. Nearly sixteen metres high, it is modelled on the style of the famous Nereid Monument of Xanthos and the gun, Long Cecil occupies one of the stylobates. Rudyard Kipling, a lifelong friend of Rhodes, wrote the inscription.

In Dutoitspan Road is the equestrian statue of Cecil John Rhodes, elevated upon a solid pedestal of Scotch granite. It presents Rhodes as the people of Kimberley remembered him, riding up Dutoitspan Road from the Sanatorium Hotel on his favourite horse, which modelled for the statue. He is attired in the clothes he wore at the Matabele indaba in the Matopos. The three panels of the pedestal portray Rhodes receiving his degree at Oxford, as Prime Minister addressing the Cape Parliament and conferring with the chiefs in the Matopos. The sculptor was H. Thorneycroft, R.A.

McGregor Museum, in Chapel Street, was built as a memorial to a former Mayor of Kimberley, Alexander McGregor. Known as the Old Museum, it houses exhibits of pre-hsitory and history of the Northern Cape as well as specimens of minerals and rocks from all over the world. Three extensions of the McGregor Museum are to be found in the fashionable suburb of Belgravia. In Egerton Road is the commodious, rambling Victorian-style building, encircled by its own driveway, it has had quite a checkered history. It was intended by Rhodes that it become a sanatorium but was converted into the luxury hotel of the time, known as Belgrave Hotel; later it became the Lady Oppenheimer Memorial Convent School and finally it was taken over by the McGregor Museum.

Dunlace, the stately residence in Lodge Street, was for 70 years the home of the John Orr family and is now part of the McGregor Museum. Rudd House (also acquired by the McGregor Museum), 5-7 Loch Street, is the so-called bungalow built for the mining magnate, C.D. Rudd. His original 'shack' forms part of the outbuildings.

The Duggan-Cronin Bantu Gallery, also in Egerton Road, has amongst its exhibits an outstanding collection of photographs (some 4 000) of black people, and their way of life, taken by Mr A.M. Duggan-Cronin.

William Humphreys Art Gallery, in the Civic Centre, has a fine collection of South African paintings, including the controversial Kottler nudes.

Kimberley Library, in Dutoitspan Road, houses one of the finest collections of Africana in the world, including Moffat's original translation of the Bible into the Tswana language, and the printing press used in Kuruman to print the work.

St. Cyprian's Anglican Cathedral is in Dutoitspan Road, opposite the Kimberley Hotel. In the cathedral garden is the bronze statue of Sister Henrietta Stockdale. This is the only portrait statue of a nun in the world. Sister Henrietta commenced the registration of nuns in South Africa and started the Kimberley Hospital.

The Sister Henrietta Chapel at Kimberley Hospital, the first Seventh Day Adventist Church, the City Hall (1899), the historic Market Square, the Dutch Reformed Church in the suburb of Newton and the School of Mines (now the workshop of two amateur dramatic societies), in Hull Street, are all national monuments.

Rhodes's office and boardroom in Warren Street, used before the great amalgamation of the mines in 1888, is preserved in the same condition as in the early days and can be visited by arrangement with De Beers.

Among the fine schools are the Kimberley Boys' High School (designed by William Timlin) and Kimberley Girls' High School (attended by Sarah Gertrude Millin) – both founded in 1887. Ten years later the famous Christian Brothers' College opened – the first to be established in South Africa.

Kimberley Club, in Dutoitspan Road, is a famous institution. Established in 1881, the original articles of

1. The Big Hole of Kimberley Mine, around which the city grew.

2. Kimberley City Hall, adjacent to the historic Market Square.

3. At the open-air museum on the verge of the Big Hole is this Victorian bandstand, in perfect condition.

4. Erected to honour those who perished during the siege of Kimberley is the Honoured Dead Memorial, designed by Sir Herbert Baker.

2

3

4

1

association contain the names of several men who influenced the history of South Africa. The imposing club building was erected in 1896 and many celebrated personalities and members of British Royal Family have been in residence there during visits to Kimberley.

Kimberley has a handsome Civic Centre with a lovely Memorial Garden to the late Sir Ernest Oppenheimer, first mayor of Kimberley City.

Griqualand West Provincial headquarters for sporting bodies are in Kimberley. In Kenilworth Road there is the stadium built by De Beers. The large public gardens near De Beers Mine also provide for sports. The 18-hole golf course is in Kamfersdam to the north of the city.

The Visitors Information Bureau is in the City Hall, Market Square, telephone (0531) 2-2241. S.A. Airways Terminal is in Old Mutural Centre, telephone (0531) 511231. J.B. Vorster Airport is 6,5 km from the city centre.

Kimberley has a population of 150 000 and lies at an altitude of 1 198 metres. There are eleven hotels and an all-facility municipal caravan park.

Riverton

This pleasure resort on the Vaal River provided by the City Council of Kimberley adjoins the waterworks and lies 27 kilometres north-west of the city, off the road to Warrenton. The bungalow, rondavel and caravan accommodation is first-rate and there is a restaurant. Fishing, boating, tennis and swimming are the recreational pleasures. This is an extremely popular summer resort with floodlit bathing at night.

Magersfontein

On the outskirts of Kimberley and farther afield there are numerours places of interest marking the Battlefields of the Anglo-Boer War. Near the Modder River is the farm Magersfontein, scene of a bitter battle resulting in a heavy defeat of the British. Here the Boer general, De la Rey, used trench warfare for the first time and the idea was adapted in France during World War I, thirteen years later. At Magersfontein there are several impressive memorials to the Boers, Scottish, English and Scandinavians and the trenches remain in good condition. It was General French with his New Zealanders who eventually relieved Kimberley. Persons interested in visiting the battlegrounds should enquire at the Visitors Information Bureau for directions.

Nooitgedacht and Driekopseiland

At these places, 22 kilometres west of Kimberley (on the road to Barkly West), and on a farm on the Riet River, 64 kilometres south-west of Kimberley, there are appearances of Glaciated Pavements, created during a remote geological epoch. These sites have been preserved by the Monuments Commission.

Territory north of Kimberley

Barkly West

Thirty-five kilometres north-west of Kimberley is Barkly West, on a great bend of the Vaal River; once a convenient crossing place known as Klipdrift. A stone bridge with steel girders (imported from London) was constructed in 1884 and this was the first bridge across the Vaal and is still in use, although a modern birdge completed in 1978 now carries the traffic between Kimberley and Barkly West. On the north bank is the old toll house and Canteen Koppie, once a prominent feature (now completely flattened) which marks the scene of the first alluvial diamond diggings in South Africa in 1869. The old bridge, the toll house and Canteen Koppie (today an archaeological reserve) are national monuments.

The town of 7 000 inhabitants retains much of its diggers-town atmosphere; the museum attached to the office of the Mining Commissioner displaying a unique collection of geological, archaeological and historical relics of the area. On both banks of the Vaal, for 75 kilometres on either side of Barkly West, the landscape is considerably disturbed and lapidaries come from many parts of southern Africa to discover semi-precious stones, of great beauty and variety, exposed by the diggers. In the dry season, June to September, breakwaters and diversion canals are constructed by the diggers, who search the bed of the river for diamonds. The position of these breakwater diggings alter from year to year and the Mining Commissioner in Barkly West should be consulted by those wishing to visit these amazing sites.

Sarah Gertrude Millin grew up in the district and Cecil Rhodes, being the Member for Barkly West in the Cape Parliament, built a house there, which is now owned by the Standard Bank. The first European settlement in the district was at Pniel, founded by the Berlin Missionary Society in 1849 on the south bank of the Vaal. Barkly West has two hotels and a caravan park with all facilities.

Warrenton

Seventy-four kilometres north of Kimberley, on the south bank of the Vaal River is Warrenton. It was named after Sir Charles Warren who led the Expedition to Bechuanaland (now Botswana). Diamonds were first found in Warrenton in 1888. Lying close to the Vaal-Harts Dam and on the Kimberley-Vryburg railway, it is the principal agricultural centre of the Vaal-Harts Irrigation Scheme. The town has a population of 12 000, an hotel and an all-facility caravan park.

Vaal-Harts Irrigation Scheme

It was Cecil Rhodes who first visualised the possibility of the Vaal-Harts Irrigation Scheme but it was not started until 1933 with work on the immense undertaking being completed in 1945. At the time of its construction it was the second largest irrigation scheme in the world. The storage dam, constructed in the Vaal River, 137 metres above the Harts River, has a surface area of 13 000 hectares and a capacity of more than 62 million cubic metres. With its long system of concrete-lined canals the scheme covers 1 200 small holdings and an irrigable area of 41 867 hectares. It has transformed a vast, barren land of vaalbos and kameldoring into lush green fields of lucerne, potatoes, groundnuts and other produce, with wheat as a winter crop.

Jan Kempdorp, Hartswater and Reivilo

The other two centres of the irrigation scheme are Jan Kempdorp (named after the Minister of Agriculture) with a population of 8 000 and two hotels, and Hartswater, with a population of 2 000 and one hotel. At Reivilo (Olivier in reverse) due west of Taung, is the gigantic cheddar-cheese factory.

Kuruman

Eighty-seven kilometres west of Reivilo is the attractive town of Kuruman.

Kuruman has been called the Fountain of Christianity in Africa for the very good reason that the water supply from the famous Kuruman Eye provided Moffat and later Livingstone with a base to commence explorations deep into the territory of Africa – Moffat to Matabeleland and Livingstone first to Lake Ngami and then to the upper Zambesi, where he discovered the Victoria Falls. Later he traced the source of the Nile.

Dr Robert Moffat set up the station of the London Missionary Society in 1826, not far from the Eye, an inexhaustible source of crystal clear water from a dolomite cave, with a continuous rate of flow of 20 million litres a day. The church he started building in 1831 and completed in 1838 was restored in 1938 and proclaimed a national monument. It is constructed of local stone with a reed thatch roof, supported by enormous timbers, brought by ox-wagon some 300 kilometres from the Western Transvaal. The church seats up to 1 000 people and is remarkable for its excellent acoustics. It was in this church building that Moffat printed his translation of the Bible into Tswana. Here too Dr Moffat's eldest daughter Mary was married to David Livingstone in 1845. The marriage register containing the record is preserved at the mission.

Another relic of the Livingstone-Moffat romance is the stump of the old almond tree where the marriage proposal took place.

The Moffat Institute started as a training school of the London Missionary Society, as a memorial to the great man's life; today the original buildings (1870) are used as a boarding school and the name has been retained.

Kuruman is the centre for an exceptionally large cattle ranching district and is the market of a substantial portion of the country's butter. Visitors are invited to inspect the huge plant at the creamery. The area is rich in minerals with asbestos, manganese and iron being exploited on a large scale. The town was laid out in 1886, became a municipality in 1916 and has a population of 8 000. There are three hotels. In the beautiful surroundings of the Kuruman Eye the municipality has provided delightful picnic sites, a caravan park and tearoom.

Sishen

On the road south-west, 51 kilometres from Kuruman is Sishen Mine, the greatest producer in the Republic of high-grade haematite (iron-ore). From here Iscor rail it to Saldanha Bay 1 100 kilometres away. In May 1973, the biggest underground manganese mine in the Southern Hemisphere was opened here.

Postmasburg

The Reverend Dirk Postma, founder of the Dopper section of the Dutch Reformed Church, gave Postmasburg its name. The population is 14 000, and great mineral wealth surrounds this rather drab looking town. Apart from its closeness to Sishen (63 kilometres due south), it has in its vicinity the open cast workings of high-grade manganese mines, the famed Cape Blue Asbestos Mines and the Finsch Diamond Mine.

Whitesand and Roaring Sand

Sixty-five kilometres south-west of Postmasburg are the Whitesand and Roaring Sand phenomena. Here the pure white sand does not mix with the surrounding red sand.

Danielskuil

It is said that the Griquas cast their prisoners into the dolomite sinkhole (kuil) here, and according to legend the 'den' was overrun with snakes and not lions. This is the apparent authentic naming of Danielskuil, the town of 2 000 inhabitants, 56 kilometres to the north-east of Postmasburg.

Within a radius of 25 kilometres of the town, marble, limestone, asbestos and diamonds are recovered.

Vryburg

Market town for a rich beef and dairy product district, Vryburg has a population of 24 000. Its history reads like a fairytale. In 1882 the tribespeople chief, Massouw invited the Boers in the area to assist him oust a rival chief Mankoroane, on the basis that each Boer would be paid 2 500 hectares of land if Mankoroane was defeated. The Boer adventurers numbering 416 went into battle, defeated Mankoroane and with their 1 040 000 hectares formed their own republic. A comet, visible at the Presidential election meeting in 1882, caused them to call the new state the Stellaland Republic. They duly installed Gerrit Jacobus Van Niekerk as President and launched a fully fledged state with a magnificent flag, postal service including a postage stamp series and Vryburg (free town) the capital. Their freedom did not last for long. In the same year another band of Boers had formed their own republic to the north of Vryburg and called their state, Het Land Goshen. President Kruger became alarmed and annexed both states under Transvaal protection. This was not to Britain's liking and in 1885 Sir Charles Warren made his expedition and annexed the territory to Britain without any resistance. It was henceforth British Bechuanaland. The Stellaland flag was sent to Queen Victoria; returned to Vryburg by King George V, it now stands in the Vryburg Town Hall. Vryburg has three hotels and a caravan park.

Stella and Setalgoli

The road to the north links Vryburg with Mafikeng 210 kilometres away. There are hotels at Stella and Setalgoli, two villages on the route.

Mafeking (now Mafikeng)

What used to be the most northerly town of the Cape is now part of the independent state of Bophuthatswana. (Chapter 15).

1. Augrabies Falls — one of the world's great spectacles. The deep granite gorge is 92 metres in diameter and when the Orange River is in full spate 400 million litres of water plunge over the granite every minute.

2. The magnificent gemsbok (oryx) thrives in the arid wastes of the Kalahari. The bull measures up to 122 centimetres at the shoulder and has a mass of 200 kilograms; his rapier-like horns have impaled many a lion.

3. Upington on the Orange River, a veritable oasis bordering the Kalahari Desert.

341

Wondergat

Twenty-nine kilometres south-east of Mafikeng is the *Wondergat* – the wonder hole which owes its origin to the subsidence of the dolomite roof of an underground cavern. It is from 60 to 80 metres in diameter, 75 metres deep and is filled with pure, crystal water.

Slurry

From Mafikeng the road to the north-east crosses the border into the Transvaal and passes Slurry on its way to Zeerust. The Pretoria Portland Cement works at Slurry is one of the largest in the Southern Hemisphere.

Territory south of Kimberley

Griquatown

In a fold of the low range Asbestos Mountains, 158 kilometres south-west of Kimberley is Griquatown. It has the distinction of being the first town to be established north of the Orange River. The story of the Griquas started when the slave Adam Kok (the cook) was given his freedom. He and his half-caste followers left Table Bay, wandered northward, settled first at Piketberg and after much wandering they reached Klaarwater, now Griquatown. The London Missionary Society established a station there, under the care of the Reverends Kramer and Anderson, in 1802. In 1812 the explorer William Burchell recorded the funeral at the mission station of the unfortunate Mrs Kramer, who became the first white woman known to have died north of the Orange. The change of the name to Griquatown came in 1813 at the time of the visit of the Reverend J. Campbell. Dr Robert Moffat arrived at the mission in 1820 and Mary Moffat (who married David Livingstone) was born in the old mission house a year later.

During the Reverend Campbell's visit to the Griquas the catechist, Andries Waterboer, was elected chief (or captain, as these leaders liked to be called). The event caused a split in the clans with Kok and his followers migrating to Philippolis and finally to East Griqualand. Andries Waterboer was in time succeeded by his son Nikolaas who took the brunt of the international dispute over the diamond fields. He eventually received £1 000 a year grant from Britain and retired to Kokstad.

The old mission house, in its original condition, is now the Mary Moffat Museum. The pulpit (a national monument), which Moffat gave to Waterboer, is preserved in the museum. On either side of the memorial over the Waterboer grave are the cannons, *Hans and Griet,* presented to the Griquas by Queen Victoria. Still to be seen in Griquatown is the original Raadsaal and the Execution Tree where cattle thieves were hanged.

Griquatown has a population of 3 000 and it serves a district where asbestos, galena, lime and diamonds are worked and where karakul, merino and dorper sheep thrive on the farms. The area is also notable for tiger-eye and other semi-precious stones.

Campbell

Forty-eight kilometres east of Griquatown is Campbell with its mission station and church, a proclaimed national monument. The site was one of the earliest centres of Christianity north of the Orange River and became the outspan of such early travellers as William Burchell, John Campbell, George Thompson, Dr Andrew Smith, Dr David Livingstone and G.A. Farini. The church was built in 1831 by the Reverend John Bartlett of the London Missionary Society and the station was named in honour of the Reverend John Campbell.

Douglas

On the banks of the Vaal River, Douglas is 14 kilometres east of its confluence with the Orange River. Its establishment dates from 1867 when it was named after Sir Percy Douglas. Municipal status was granted in 1907 and the population is 6 000.

Prior to the town being founded the place was recognised by early travellers as a crossing point of the Vaal. It was at this ford that the Bushmen were routed in a conflict against the Koranna in 1775 and the place became known to the Bushmen as Go Koo Lume (where no mercy was shown).

Today Douglas is the centre of a rich agricultural and karakul sheep district with an extensive irrigation scheme from the large storage dam. The water is taken by canal system through the town to erven beyond and on to the agricultural extension known as Bucklands.

Douglas is possessed of a very beautiful park with a swimming pool; extensive recreation grounds including a golf course and a fine resort on the river bank at Ullswater, where there is a caravan park with all facilities. Fishing in the Vaal is good. The town has two hotels.

Salt Lake

Thirty-two kilometres south-east of Douglas there is a turnoff to Salt Lake, one of South Africa's largest salt producers.

Hopetown

Remembered for the discovery there of the first diamonds in South Africa, Hopetown is situated within 2 kilometres of the south bank of the Orange River, near the junction of trunk road R29, and the road from Douglas. It was laid out in 1854 and named after Major William Hope, Auditor-General of the Cape. Its fame rests with the finding in the district of two gemstones within two years of each other.

In 1866, 15-year-old Erasmus Jacobs, whilst playing on the farm De Kalk, picked up a 21¼-carat diamond. This was the stone that the trader, John O'Reilly, took to the magistrate in Colesberg, who tested it by scratching the letters 'D.P.' on the window. It was later sent to Grahamstown to be identified by Dr W.G. Atherstone and others and was eventually bought by the Cape governor, Sir Philip Wodehouse, for £500.

The magnificent diamond which came to be called The Star of South Africa, weighing 83½ carats, was found in 1868 by a Hottentot witch-doctor. He took it into Hopetown where Schalk van Niekerk bartered a span of oxen and a wagon in its exchange. Van Niekerk sold the diamond to Liliefield Brothers of Hopetown for £11 000, after which it was bought by the Earl of Dudley for £50 000.

Thousands of fortune-seekers rushed to Hopetown after these events but in those early days no further finds were made in the area. Between the years 1924 and 1953 alluvial diggings were worked on the riverside farms near the town.

There is an hotel in Hopetown; the population is 4 500 and the community serves the neighbouring fruit, stock, wheat and potato farms.

P.K. le Roux Dam
South-east of Hopetown, close to Petrusville (a small town with an hotel and serving a farming district) is the P.K. le Roux Dam; named after a former Minister of Water Affairs, it forms part of the Orange River Project, the largest engineering and water conservation project ever undertaken in South Africa.

P.K. le Roux Dam (which completes the major works) was opened by the Prime Minister in November 1977. It has a gross storage capacity of 3 255 million cubic metres and a reservoir surface area of 13 866 hectares. After Hendrik Verwoerd Dam it is the second most important storage dam in the scheme and the main control dam to release water into the Orange for further use downstream and to divert water into the canal system that will irrigate over 100 000 hectares of land, previously mainly arid country. Coupled with the water conservation of the Department of Water Affairs are the important hydro-electric power stations of Escom; the Hendrik Verwoerd Power Station generating 360 megawatts and the Vanderkloof Power Station (constructed underground on the left bank – Cape side – of the P.K. le Roux Dam) generating 240 megawatts; in all a substantial and economical contribution to Escom's national distribution network.

Strydenburg
One of many South African towns to be founded by the Dutch Reformed Church, Strydenburg, a small municipality, 100 kilometres west of Petrusville, lies close to trunk road R29. The first church was built there in 1892. The name, meaning 'town of strife', arose from the disagreement of its founders in the naming and siting of the township. The district is notable for high quality mutton production.

Route R29 meets with R32 near Britstown (Chapter 4) and from here R32 heads north-west to Upington.

Prieska – Upington – Augrabies Falls and Kalahari Gemsbok National Parks

Prieska
Situated on the south bank of the Orange River Prieska has a population of 9 000. Originally Prieskap (the Hottentot word meaning the place of the she-goat) the site of the town is at a fording place much used by early travellers. The town was started in 1878 and today serves a district noted for blue asbestos mining, livestock breeding and intense cultivation on lands irrigated by the Buchuberg Dam irrigation scheme.

North of Prieska the Brak River flows into the Orange and here, during the Anglo-Boer War, the redoubtable General Christiaan de Wet completely outwitted the superior British forces. When cornered at the confluence he escaped through the British lines back to the Orange Free State.

For the visitor Prieska has golf and bowls, two hotels and a municipal caravan park on the river bank. The area is notable for semi-precious stones.

Marydale, Draghoender, Koegas and Westerberg
From Prieska, trunk road R32 passes through the Doringberg range and reaches Marydale, with its railhead, Draghoender, three kilometres to the north. Due east on the opposite bank of the Orange River, is the Koegas Asbestos Mine, the world's largest producer of blue asbestos; it is served by Westerberg, a model mining village where vegetables and fruit, including the finest oranges are produced.

Groblershoop and Buchuberg Dam
At Groblershoop there is a convenient crossing over the Orange River to visit the important Buchuberg Dam. Completed in 1931 it provides irrigation for 24 000 hectares along the river banks, stretching from Prieska to Augrabies.

Upington
Klaas Lucas, the notorious Hottentot river bandit, ruled the lower reaches of the Orange until 1884 when an end was put to his escapades by that famous soldier, Major-General Sir Charles Warren.

Where Upington stands today, a settlement started after the capture of Lucas, and was named Olyvenhoutsdrift, because of the predominence of wild olive trees in the area. The district, previously part of British Bechuanaland and known as Korannaland, was annexed to the Cape in 1895 and renamed Gordonia, after the Cape Prime Minister, Sir Gordon Sprigg. At the same time the town was renamed Upington, after the Attorney General, Sir Thomas Upington.

The real pioneers of Upington were the missionary Schröder and Oom Japie Lutz. In 1890 they erected a pump on the river bank, dug the first irrigation canal (still in existence) and started a pontoon ferry across the river. The story of George St. Leger Gordon Lennox, alias Scotty Smith, adventurer, rustler and highwayman, has been told by F.C. Metrowich in his book, *Scotty Smith*. He died in Upington in 1919 and his grave is in the local cemetery.

Today the urban population of Upington exceeds 45 000. It is a town with every modern amenity, laid out on the north bank of the Orange River. The Kalahari Desert, bordering the town to the north, produces the Republic's richest output of karakul lamb pelts – over 1,7 million reach the London sorting market in a year. Stretching 280 kilometres along the banks of the Orange River at depths varying from 3 to 30 kilometres and bordering directly upon the Kalahari is one of the most intensively cultivated areas in the Republic, where high grade cotton, great quantities of lucerne and the finest sultana grapes are sought after for the markets of the world. The town is close to the Augrabies, one of the five largest

1. This old Bushman, photographed in the Kalahari Gemsbok National Park, claimed to be 104 years old, but it is difficult to judge because the wrinkled skin is a characteristic of the race. His people who controlled the prime lands of the subcontinent for 10 000 years have been driven by other black tribes and the whites into the arid wastes of the Kalahari and northern South West Africa. Only a small percentage of the 30 000 remaining Bushmen (most of them living in Botswana) are still nomad hunter-gatherers, living a life-style unchanged since the Stone Ages. The majority have been absorbed into other African communities, and so the danger of the Bushman becoming extinct is real.
2. and 3. Namaqualand in the spring — an incredible transformation when the desert becomes a vast garden.

3

waterfalls in the world, and is the closest large centre to the Kalahari Gemsbok National Park.

Upington is the obvious base from which to explore these remote and fascinating parts of South Africa – the North-Western Cape cannot be likened to any other region of the Republic. Fine roads, scheduled air and train services link Upington with the principal centres of the country and the amenities of municipal and private enterprises assist adventurers and nature lovers from the world over.

The municipality arranges tours to the Augrabies Falls and the Gemsbok National Park by municipal motor transport or private air charter. The road tours take in visits to a karakul stud farm, a gigantic salt pan and irrigation settlements where, apart from lucerne, sultanas and cotton grown, the visitor is introduced to other significant products of the area such as dried peaches, apricots, hanepoot raisins, wheat, dates, maize, citrus and wine. Salt is produced on a considerable scale from the saline pans in the Kalahari. Among these is Loch Maree, 24 kilometres in circumference and the largest of its kind in the world.

The region is rich in semi-precious stones which attract the attention of experienced lapidaries and amateurs alike. The semi-precious stones polishing works, the cotton ginnery and the wild olive wood occasional furniture factory make interesting excursions.

During the summer months the heat is intense and, notwithstanding airconditioning in hotels and public places, the best time to plan a visit is during the months from April to October, when the weather is absolutely perfect; early morning and late afternoons are crips to chilly and every day is a day of glorious sunshine, free of humidity. Most days end with a dramatically beautiful sunset.

Upington has good hotels; a fine municipal library and attached museum with a fully representative collection of semi-precious stones; amenities for golf, bowls, tennis, boating, swimming, fishing and a holiday resort on Olyvenhoutsdrift Island, where the municipality has provided rondavels, cottages, caravan park and camping sites. Here on the island is the famous date palm avenue, 1 041 metres long, a lovely playground for children, a riverside beach and a good restaurant.

Full details of regional tours, the hiring of rondavels, cottages, caravan sites and tents are obtainable upon application to the Town Clerk, Upington.

Kalahari Gemsbok National Park

Certainly one of the most unusual parks in the world, Kalahari Gemsbok National Park is an area of pure wilderness spread over more than a million hectares. Although the animal population of the Park is restricted to those species adaptable to aridity, there are large numbers of the most magnificent specimens of game.

This is the only park in the Republic where the gemsbok (oryx) is preserved in its natural state. These splendid creatures run in herds of up to thirty. The robust gemsbok of proud bearing is bold and pugnacious and will charge with determination. Many a lion has been impaled on the long, rapier-like horns. There are also herds of springbok, beautiful against the dunes, blue wildebeest, the rare hartebeest, eland, lion, cheetah, jackal and hyena and a great number and variety of ground birds, larks and birds of prey.

There are three rest camps, Twee Rivieren, the southern entrance and where the warden is stationed, Mata-Mata and Nossob through which visitors from the north, that is South West Africa, gain entrance to the Park. The roads in the Park follow the dry river beds of the Auob and Nossob. Breaking the line of the arid landscape, spreading kameeldoring trees provide shade for the game and invariably contain the huge nests of the social weaver.

The southern entrance gate is 320 kilometres from Upington. Enquiries regarding accommodation reservations should be made to the National Parks Board, P.O. Box 787, Pretoria. Special tours of the Park are arranged by the Upington Municipality.

Augrabies Falls

Ranked as one of the world's great spectacles, Augrabies in peak flood is a deeply moving sight. Although the flow of water varies considerably as between a dry winter and a wet summer, the scene is always exciting.

In a setting of harsh and arid landscape the Orange River has cut a gaping wound in a gigantic mass of granite. From the preliminary cascades where the river drops 97 metres, through the impressive main fall of 91 metres to the end of the 240-metre-deep gorge, the wound is 10 kilometres long. Best known of the secondary falls is the Bridal Veil which becomes part of the main fall in flood – cascading down in a mighty crash. Augrabies comes from the Nama word Aukoerebis, meaning 'the place of the big noise', and indeed the roar and rumble of the fall can be heard for a considerable distance.

The Augrabies Falls National Park occupies 8 900 hectares and was opened in 1967. In a fascinating array of wild vegetation – lithops, haworthia, kokerboom (tree aloe), Cape willow, karee, wild olive, Karoo thornbush – there is a large variety of lizards, species of small buck and an abundance of bird life such as wagtails, warblers, water plovers and siskins. The restaurant and curio shop in the Park has been constructed of decorative stonework with an attractive thatch roof.

Augrabies lies 136 kilometres to the west of Upington and is reached by tarred road. There is an hotel five kilometres east of the falls.

Keimoes and Kakamas

Keimoes (population 7 000) and Kakamas (population 4 500) are important irrigation settlements of the Lower Orange River and lie between Upington and Augrabies. There is intense cultivation in the whole of the region including on the large wooded islands in the Orange River. The South African canning peach, the Kakamas peach, originated from here.

Kenhardt

From the Orange River there are roads south to Kenhardt, a wool centre with a population of 3 000.

Verneukpan

South of Kenhardt, in what is known as Bushmanland, there are numerous dry salt pans and the best known of these is Verneukpan, famed as the track used in the 1930s by Sir Malcolm Campbell when he attempted a new world land speed record in his racing car *Bluebird*.

Pofadder

Vanwyksvlei, Brandvlei and Sakrivier are village settlements in the salt pan country, renowned for its extremes of hot and cold weather. Pofadder received its odd name (puffader) from the Koranna chief Klaas Pofadder. It lies to the west of Kenhardt and is a karakul centre with a population of 2 500.

Carnarvon

A road leads south from Vanwyksvlei to Carnarvon which is the junction of many roads, including one from Victoria West (Chapter 4). Carnarvon is a neatly laid out little Karoo town with a population of 6 500 and is the centre for one of the best sheep farming districts. It was named after Lord Carnarvon and became a municipality in 1883.

Williston and the corbelled houses of the district

On the road leading west from Carnarvon is Williston, which had its start with the establishment of the mission station named Amandelboom in 1845. Williston is on the railway line in the heart of sheep country and has a population of 3 000.

On the farms Stuurmansfontein, Gorras, Schuinshoogte, Arbeidersfontein and Grootfontein, situated between Carnarvon and Williston at varying distances from the main road, there are five examples of corbelled houses which the Monuments Commission has proclaimed historical monuments, thus preserving an important landmark in the architectural history of South Africa. When the trekkers reached the area of the vast parched plains of the Northern Cape, there being no timber, they were forced to adapt the corbelling technique of bee-hive shaped rooms constructed entirely of stone and clay. Animal blood was used to bind the clay used for the floors.

Calvinia, Middelpos and Sutherland

Named after John Calvin, the great reformer, Calvinia lies at the foot of the Hantamberg. With its 8 000 inhabitants, it is the largest centre of this great sheep-producing district of the north-west Cape. The town has an interesting local history museum, an attractive aloe garden, three hotels and a caravan park.

Calvinia is the terminus of the branch railway from Hutchinson, and the junction of a number of roads.

Middelpos is 148 kilometres to the south of Calvinia, on the road to Sutherland, a further 82 kilometres to the south-east. There is an hotel at Middelpos.

Sutherland has an hotel, and here at an altitude of over 1 800 metres, is the important CSIR Astronomical Observatory which opened in 1973. Sutherland has the reputation of being the coldest town in southern Africa.

Namaqualand

A broad, arid coastal shelf, Namaqualand extends inland to the Orange River. Swept by the winds of the cold Benguella current, there is no opportunity for moisture evaporation and the shelf is left with a cloudless sky, completely dry. The annual rainfall in Namaqualand varies from 50 to 150 millimetres. For most of the year it is barren of vegetation and appears as an uninviting useless tract of country. But much is hidden, in fact it embraces areas of great mineral wealth, with large copper deposits and rich alluvial diamond diggings on a hundred kilometres of its coastline.

And here in this desert, one of the most remarkable wonders of nature occurs. In the spring, from mid-July to the end of September, provided there has been sufficient winter rain to create the balance of temperature, a most incredible transformation takes place. In an awakening of millions of tiny plants the earth is blanketed with brilliant blooms. The famous wild flowers of Namaqualand are of a wide variety but principally daisies of many colours – white, yellow and orange *Venidium fastuasum;* red Gazanias, purple Cineraria, orange and black spotted Gortevia are a few of the species. The area is also rich in the brilliantly coloured mesembryanthemum.

It is essential that hotel bookings be made prior to proceeding to Namaqualand in the spring. The exact localities of the best displays of the flowers vary each year according to local conditions – especially rainfall, and visitors are advised to be guided by the local people.

From Clanwilliam (Chapter 2) national road N7 in heading north follows the course of the Olifants River and the irrigation canal which gives the life to the magnificent wheatlands, orchards and vineyards in an otherwise barren part of the country.

Klawer and Vredendal

The small town of Klawer, and farther north on a loop road, Vredendal, are the centres for the Olifants River Irrigation Scheme. Vredendal was established in 1945 and has a population of 4 000.

Vanrhynsdorp and district

At the junction of national road N7 and route 27 is Vanrhynsdorp, named after P.B. van Rhyn, first member for Namaqualand in the Cape Parliament. The town has a population of 3 000 and there is an hotel.

Vanrhynsdorp lies at the southern entrance to Namaqualand, and from here there are many interesting drives in the flower region. One of the rewarding routes is along the gravel road, south-east of the town, through Raskraal and Urionskraal to Bottervlei (from where the 121 metre-high waterfall at Ouberg, on the eastern flank of the Matsikama range, is well worth visiting). From here a road leads along the Bokkeveld plateau, past Leeukop and then through the Kobie Valley to Niewoudtville. From Niewoudtville the tarred route R27 can be taken over the Vanrhyns Pass, back to Vanrhynsdorp. Another route leads south-westwards to Lutzville and

Koekenaap and rejoins national road N7 at Nuwerus, 70 kilometres north of Vanrhynsdorp.

Bitterfontein

Continuing northwards national road N7 passes Bitterfontein, the terminus of the railway in Namaqualand, a bleak but nevertheless busy place from where road motor transport serves the rest of the territory.

Garies, Hondeklip Bay and Kamieskroon

Garies is the Hottentot name for a species of local grass. Situated in a very rugged setting, Garies is a centre from which to see the flowers and there is an hotel. From here a road leads north-west to the fishing resort of Hondeklip Bay where there is a fish processing factory and camping grounds much used by local farmers for their holidays. The village of Kamieskroon, 45 kilometres north of Garies, is enclosed by the huge granite masses of the Kamiesberg.

Springbok

The most northerly of the centres from which tourists may visit the wild flowers of Namaqualand, is Springbok. Once a copper mining town of great prominence, it gave way to Okiep, ten kilometres to its north, when the rich copper deposits were discovered there in the 1870s. Despite its early decline, Springbok remains the administrative centre of the district and has a population of 8 000. The town was laid out in 1862 and became a municipality in 1933. There are two hotels and a municipal caravan park.

It was to the Koperberge of the area of Springbok that Simon van der Stel made his historic expedition in 1685. His splendid cavalcade comprised fifteen wagons each drawn by eight oxen and five mule-drawn carts to transport 50 Europeans (soldiers and civilians), a sizeable boat to cross rivers, two cannon for protection, supplies to last many months, Hottentot interpreters and numerous other servants. His Excellency the Governor was conveyed in his magnificent coach. On hoof were hundreds of head of cattle, sheep and horses. The momentous journey began from the settlement at Table Bay on 25 August 1685 and nearly two months later, on 14 October after more than 700 kilometres, the Koperberge were reached. Prospecting shafts were sunk and the ore yield exceeded expectations. After exploring the coast to the west and farther to the north, van der Stel returned to the Cape, arriving at the Castle on 26 January 1686. He had accomplished what he set out to do, but his bitter disappointment was the realisation of the remoteness of the great copper deposits. One hundred and eighty years passed before the discovery was worked by Europeans, but to Simon van der Stel's brilliant leadership goes the kudos for the valuable geographical discoveries which his expedition yielded.

Even in the mid-nineteenth century the would-be copper miners of Namaqualand experienced immense difficulties in so remote an area. Nothing came of the first wild rushes in the 1850s. The Okiep mine (previously O'okiep, a Hottentot word meaning very brackish) of Cape Copper Mining Company and its successors was amongst the world's greatest producers towards the end of the nineteenth century. Today the three main mines, Nababeep, Okiep and Wheal Julia have an annual output of a million tons of ore. The prosperity of these mines is reflected in the built up areas, where the community enjoys the amenities of modern civilisation under the relentless sun in a waterless region. The Monuments Commission has placed two bronze plaques, one to identify a shaft sunk by Simon van der Stel's expedition in 1685 and the other, that of the copper smelting chimney, built by the Cape Copper Company in 1866.

Port-Nolloth – Alexander Bay – Diamond Coast of Namaqualand

North-west of Springbok, 182 kilometres by road is Port Nolloth, an isolated desert port brought into operation for the shipment of copper in the 1850s. Originally known as Robbebaai (seal bay) it was renamed after Commander M.S. Nolloth who had carried out a survey of the coast to find a suitable port. In the 1870s (after many years of oxwagon labour) the copper mines constructed a narrow gauge railway linking Port Nolloth with Okiep and this was in service for some forty years before it was abandoned in favour of heavy road motor transport which carted the ore to the newly established railhead at Bitterfontein. After a period of decline, Port Nolloth revived with the coming of crayfish processing factories. Its real boost came with the discovery of the alluvial diamonds immediately to the north of the port.

The Diamond Coast of Namaqualand consists of the De Beers diggings at Kleinsee on the coast south of Port Nolloth and the State-owned diggings on the strip of coastline (protected by barbed wire entanglements) which runs from Port Nolloth northwards to Alexander Bay. Unless in possession of an authorised permit, visitors are not welcomed in this closed area.

The discovery of these alluvial diamond fields in 1926 brought great excitement to Namaqualand. After the first finds, Hans Merensky (the famous geologist) bought up numerous claims and Ernest Oppenheimer became interested on behalf of De Beers.

The big companies and the Government became alarmed at the possible flooding of the diamond market when the extent of the wealth of the alluvial fields was realised. In 1927 the Government prohibited further diamond prospecting in Namaqualand, took control of the diggings at Alexander Bay and closed off the coast from Port Nolloth to Alexander Bay. The Diamond Syndicate, at that time headed by Ernest Oppenheimer, agreed to purchase the entire output from the Government and these purchases have from then onwards been placed on the world market under strict control, enabling a fair price to be maintained. The Government's decision to close prospecting in Namaqualand was, of course, not popular amongst the thousands of adventurers who had found their way to the Diamond Coast and towards the end of 1928 there was very nearly an armed uprising, but this fizzled out when the mob realised that the heavily reinforced police had no intention of giving way to their demands.

Nababeep, Okiep, Steinkopf and Viioolsdrif

From Springbok, national road N7 heading north, after 6 kilometres, passes the turnoff west leading to Nababeep, the copper mining town with a population of 8 000, and after another 2 kilometres from the turnoff, passes the older mining town Okiep with a population of 3 000.

After a further 44 kilometres N7 reaches Steinkopf, the road junction for Port Nolloth. The Mission Station, Steinkopf, was originally founded for the Nama Hottentots by the Rhenish Mission Society and is now run by the Dutch Reformed Church.

At 114 kilometres from Springbok national road N7 reaches the Orange River at Viioolsdrif in surroundings sharply contrasting with the arid country it has just traversed; with fields of lucerne, citrus, vegetables and other crops very pleasing to the eye and a highline of cliffs to set off the handsome bridge which takes the road across the Orange River into Namibia (South West Africa).

CHAPTER 15

Bophuthatswana, Botswana, Lesotho and Swaziland

Bophuthatswana

The Tswana people of South Africa received sovereign independence with the proclamation of the Republic of Bophuthatswana on 6 December 1977. This brought to fruition the independence of the second Black people's state (Transkei was the first) in the implementation of the South African government policy of multinational development.

Bophuthatswana is a land-locked country of six separate units of which about 90 percent of the land surface area lies in the dry western border with Botswana (the other Tswana country) the whole of Bophuthatswana is surrounded by territory of the Republic of South Africa. Five of the six land units lie close together and were previously part of the western Transvaal and the northern Cape Province. The sixth unit was previously part of eastern Orange Free State and is situated near the Lesotho border.

It is estimated that the population of Bophuthatswana is 1,17 million of which some 75 percent are Tswanas and that approximately one million Tswana nationals live in the Republic of South Africa. Bophuthatswana with an area of 40 330 square kilometres is larger than eight states in Africa.

The Tswana people form part of a large main group, the Sotho, who migrated from Central Africa and settled south of the Zambesi. Little is known of when the migration took place, however the latest conventional acceptance places the time to have been between the 13th and 16th centuries. In more recent times, during the years 1822 and 1837 these people were caught up in the terrible upheaval on the subcontinent that followed the invasion and onslaught of the Zulus under Shaka when the land was devastated by war and famine. A characteristic of the Sotho is its extensive diversity; in the course of history there has been fragmentation into separate tribes and re-unification. Today the three sub-groups are defined as the Western, Southern and Northern Sotho. The Western Sotho are the Tswana of Botswana and Bophuthatswana; the Southern Sotho are of the Kingdom of Lesotho and the RSA homeland Qwaqwa and the Northern Sotho are the Bapedi who occupy the homeland of Lebowa.

The Republic of Bophuthatswana Constitution Bill, tabled in the Bophuthatswana Legislative Assembly (unlike that of Transkei which was tabled in the South African Parliament) is an autochthonical document designed by the Tswana. It provides for a sovereign unitary republic with an economy based on private ownership and enterprise and although it retains traditions exclusively Tswana, it embraces the conventional Western system of democracy.

The National Assembly consists of 99 members; four members designated from each of 12 regional authorities (where there is the retention of the traditional status and powers of the chiefs and headmen); four members elected by popular vote from each of the 12 regional districts and three members designated by the President. The President is elected for a term of five years by an electoral college comprising all members of the National Assembly but excluding the 3 members designated by the President. Executive power is vested in the President who appoints nine ministers from the members of the National Assembly, who together with the President, form the Executive Council. The twelve districts are: Taung, Tlhapping-Tlharo, Ganyesa, Molopo, Ditsobotla, Lehurutshe, Madikwe, Bafokeng, Odi, Moretele and Thaba 'Nchu. Within these regions there are 76 tribes.

Fourteen towns have been proclaimed and the most highly urbanised areas are in the districts of Odi and Moretele which owe their population density to their proximity to the Pretoria/Witwatersrand complex where commuters are employed. By far the two largest towns in Bophuthatswana are Mabopane and Garankuwa. These are residential towns each with an approximate population of 100 000 and both linked with the RSA labour supply of Pretoria and Rosslyn (an industrial growth point on the border). Temba, with a population of 20 000, provides the labour force for Babelegi, the most highly industrialised centre in Bophuthatswana and situated in the Moretele district.

The economic structure of Bophuthatswana is based on agriculture, beef production, mining, tourism, industrial development, commuter income (some 160 000 working in the RSA) and migrant workers in the RSA.

Dry-land crops of maize, wheat and grain sorghum provide a large percentage of agriculture yield. Dry beans and sunflower are also grown with half the maize yield coming from the Ditsobotla district which lies in the fertile maize triangle. Wheat, maize, cotton and vegetables are produced in Taung Irrigation Scheme area (this forms part of the RSA Vaal-Harts Scheme). Citrus comes from the districts of Mankwe, Moretele and Odi and deciduous fruits from the districts of Ditsobotla, Molopo, Mankwe and Taung. Cattle ranching is a development of the traditional ownership of animals and important progress in the marketing of beef is being made throughout the country.

The metal and mineral wealth of Bophuthatswana is spread over all of its districts and is not nearly fully exploited although there are 37 mines in production. *The Merensky Reef* which forms part of the famous *Bushveld Igneous Complex,* is partly within the territory of Bophuthatswana and contains the largest known reserves of platinum in the world. The two mining groups, Rustenburg Platinum Mines and Impala Platinum that have mines in the districts of Odi and Bafokeng (between the RSA towns of Brits and Rustenburg) and in the north of Mankwe district (near Northam mine in the RSA) together contribute nearly one half of Bophuthatswana's Gross Domestic Product. By-products of these mines include palladium, iridium, gold and nickel. Crocidolite asbestos is mined in the Tlhaping-Tlharo district (north of Kuruman in the RSA) and in the Ganyesa district. Low-grade iron ore occurs north-east of Kuruman. In the district of Luhurutshe, north-west of Gopane and close to Botswana, 3 000 tons of manganese is mined per month. Other important exploitations include mines producing vanadium, chrome, granite and limestone. The district of Taung will always be remembered for the prehistoric skull of the *Taung's Man* found in the Buxton limestone works.

Mmabatho and Montshiwa

Montshiwa, a partly industrialised town in the Molopo district and adjoining the RSA town of Mafeking (since 1980 incorporated in Bophuthatswana with the name changed to Mafikeng), was originally developed as the seat of government. However, immediately prior to independence the new capital, Mmabatho (adjacent to Montshiwa) was created. Here at Mmabatho a handsome complex has been constructed to house the High Court, Government Offices and the National Assembly Chamber. Mmabatho Sun, a luxury recreational hotel and casino opened subsequently.

Mafikeng

Mafikeng, previously Mafeking, was transferred from the RSA to Bophuthatswana in 1980. The town was laid out in 1885 by Sir Charles Warren, whose British expeditionary force put an end to the pocket-size republics of Stellaland and Het Land Goshen. Mafikeng is taken from the name of the Baralong tribe who live in the area and means 'the place of the stones or boulders'. Warren made it the administrative centre of British Bechuanaland and it came into prominence as the starting point of the Jameson Raid in 1886. In 1895 British Bechuanaland was annexed to the Cape.

In the year that Mafikeng acquired municipal status, 1896, it was the base for operations in the Matabele Rebellion which lasted for over a year and ended only with the courage of Cecil Rhodes and five others (including two Blacks) who entered the Matopos, the stronghold of the Matabele, unarmed and after lengthy discussion persuaded the Matabele to lay down their arms.

Mafikeng's world fame arose through its having withstood a siege of 217 days (under the command of Colonel Robert Baden-Powell) from the commencement of the Anglo-Boer War. The relief of Mafikeng òn 17 May 1900 (which came from the combined effort of Rhodesian forces from the north and Imperial forces from the south) caused the wildest celebrations in London. During the siege Baden-Powell thought of the idea of training youths in scouting and Mafikeng became the birth-place of the world-wide Boy Scout movement.

There are no less than sixteen churches, and of particular interest is the Anglican Church designed by Sir Herbert Baker and built in memory of those who died in defence of the town. The siege fort at Cannon Koppie has been restored and is a national monument. There are many siege relics preserved in various parts of Mafikeng, especially in the library which was founded in 1894.

Mafikeng is the centre of one of the greatest cattle and dairy farming districts in southern Africa. The town is an important railway centre with extensive workshops. Diamonds have been found in the municipal commonage and on surrounding farms but the discoveries have never been substantial. The population of Mafikeng is 11 000.

Prior to Botswana becoming independent, the British administered the territory, then known as Bechuanaland Protectorate, from Mafikeng. It was the only capital in the world outside the country it governed, and a special part of Mafikeng known as the Imperial Reserve was set aside for the Resident Commissioner and his staff.

There are three hotels in the town and a resort hotel at Rooigrond on the Transvaal border. Rooigrond was the capital of the miniature Goshen republic formed in 1882.

Pilanesberg National Park and Sun City

Bophuthatswana lends itself for development as a tourist attraction for a number of reasons. First, it is a land of year-round sunshine with a low rainfall. It has areas of unspoilt wilderness like the Pilanesberg, a phenomenal volcanic alkaline rock occurrence in a circular group with a diameter of some 28 kilometres. Here the Pilanesberg National Park was opened in June 1980. The park surrounds Sun City, a recreational resort and hotel complex of world class, and certainly unequalled anywhere in Africa.

Unlike other adjoining territories there are no border posts or immigration checks between RSA and Bophuthatswana and this is a blessing for the holiday maker.

Botswana

During his fifteen years of leadership, the first president of Botswana, Sir Seretse Khama, inspired his people to the extent that the country rose from what was once declared to be among the world's poorest countries to a healthy democracy with a viable economy, and certainly one of Africa's most peaceful domains.

Botswana is some 570 000 square kilometres in extent, which is larger than France; it is sparsely populated with only 710 000 inhabitants, and most of its flat surface is the desolate scrubland of the Kalahari, but despite the generally low rainfall and unfriendly climatic conditions, ranging from extremely hot summer days to freezingly cold winter nights, this is great cattle ranching territory (the grass is sweet), there are considerable deposits of copper, nickel, iron ore, manganese and coal, and diamonds have been discovered in several huge pipes. Of importance to Botswana's balance of payments and of interest to tourists is its tremendous wealth in wild animals, particularly elephant, lion and crocodile in the wet northern sector, Ngamiland, where hunting is still the great attraction of adventurers from all over the world.

Before its independence in 1966, Botswana suffered two peculiar encumbrances; as a British Protectorate it bore the name of Bechuanaland, a distinct corruption of the Tswana, and it was governed from Mafeking (now Mafikeng) in South Africa.

Of some seventy tribes of Botswana, the Kwena, Ngwato and Ngwaketse today dominate the political scene. These names derive from the grandsons of Masilo, the legendary king. Sir Seretse Khama was a decendant of the great Khama III (of the Ngwato tribe) who had been baptised in the Christian faith in 1860.

Gaborone

In 1965 the traditional African village of Gaborone was chosen to be the capital of the new state of Botswana. Two good reasons for its choice as the capital were its good water supply and its position on the Vryburg-Bulawayo railway line. The place was originally the headquarters of the Tlokwa tribe and was named after their chief, Gaborone Matlapeng, in 1890.

The town of some 50 000 inhabitants has been laid out on modern western lines with a spacious commercial and shopping mall, government buildings including the house of parliament and a handsome National Museum and Art Gallery. There are three hotels including the Holiday Inn with its casino. On the western outskirts are the airport, national stadium and a large dam used for boating and fishing.

It was from an hotel in the old quarter of the town that Dr Starr Jameson is said to have planned the abortive raid on Johannesburg.

Lobatse

Eight kilometres from the Pioneer Gate border post with South Africa is the cattle town of Lobatse, seat of the High Court of Botswana. The Botswana Meat Commission has its abattoir here and one of the largest meat canning plants in Africa. From the surrounding ranches, some as far away as 500 kilometres, cattle on the hoof are driven into the town in American cowboy-style.

The town is situated in a valley surrounded by rocky hills and has a population of 20 000. There are two hotels.

Kanye

Forty-eight kilometres north-west of Lobatse is Kanye, the oldest tribal settlement in Botswana and the third largest after Gaborone and Serowe. The population of this charming town is 40 000.

Kanye was built by the Ngwaketse tribe with walls around the plateau to form a fortress against marauders from the north. It dates from 1790 and is attractively laid out in two sections.

Molepolole

From Kanye a road leads through the villages of Moshupa and Thamaga for 79 kilometres to Molepolole, the principal centre of the Kwena tribe. This nondescript village is surrounded by a parkland of aloes and acacias. From here there is the access track road to two game reserves, 150 kilometres to the north-west.

Khutse and Central Kalahari Game Reserves

Only part of this vast 54 000 square kilometres of complete wilderness is open to the public. The area consists of sand plains (scattered with pans which hold water only after good rains) partly covered with acacia thorn trees, various grass species and flowering plants.

Vast herds (numbering up to 100 000 at a time) of antelope, such as springbok, gemsbok, eland and hartebeest, migrate in search of water and grass, and these can best be seen during July, August and September.

The Department of Wildlife and Tourism has a camp at Golalabadimo Pan, Khutse, where Bushmen guides can be obtained. The sand tracks of the reserve are suitable only for four-wheel-drive vehicles and there is no accommodation, water or petrol available.

Gaborone to Francistown

The 390 kilometre stretch of road from Gaborone to Francistown, near the Zimbabwe border, has now been tarred. This route passes Mochudi, where the Kgatla tribe with their finely thatched houses have settled; Mahalapye where there is an hotel; and Palapye, named after the impala there, and where there is also an hotel.

Serowe

From Palapye there is a by-road leading for 61 kilometres to Serowe, the headquarters of the Ngwato tribe.

Serowe has 45 000 inhabitants, and with its many

kgotlas (meeting places built of poles in a crescent shape as a protection against wind and sun) and interesting variety of architecture, it is the most picturesque of the Botswana tribal towns.

In 1902 the famed Khama III transferred his headquarters here from Palapye. He and his grandson Sir Seretse Khama are buried in the family burial ground on the tree-covered hill in the town.

There are two small hotels in Serowe.

Selebi-Phikwe
Continuing on the main road from Gaborone, at 80 kilometres from Palapye there is a turnoff eastwards to the modern mining town of Selebi-Phikwe. This is the centre for the copper mine at Phikwe and the nickel mine at Selebi. The population is some 30 000 and there is an hotel.

Francistown
At approximately 90 kilometres from the turnoff to Selebi-Phikwe, the road, having crossed a flat, featureless plain covered with mopane trees, reaches Francistown, surrounded by the derelict workings of gold mines.

This was the scene of a great gold rush in 1869, after the discovery by Henry Huntley, the elephant hunter, of ancient workings. The deposits gradually petered out until the last of the 45 mines, Monarch Mine, closed in 1964. The town was named after a popular prospector, Daniel Francis.

Francistown was the capital of the Tati tribe and lies in amongst the hillocks to the north of the Tati River, and is today an important industrial centre and staging post for Botswana's northern game reserves. Air Botswana operates flights between Johannesburg and Francistown and safari operators have offices here. From here expert taxidermists prepare big game hunter trophies for shipment all over the world. The population is 12 000 and there are two hotels and a caravan park.

Orapa and Lethakane
Due west of Francistown a road leads for 265 kilometres to the diamond mines of Orapa and Lethakane (south of the Makgadikgadi Pans). At Orapa the second largest diamond pipe in the world was discovered by prospectors of De Beers, in 1967, and production started in 1971. The second, smaller pipe at Lethakane came into production in 1976. Twenty million rands worth of industrial diamonds are exported from here annually. De Beers, who are equal partners with the Botswana government in the project, have built a modern town with fine recreational facilities at Orapa.

Makgadikgadi Pans
Commencing at a point some 130 kilometres from Francistown, on the left-hand side of the road to Maun are the twin pans of Sua and Ntwetwe; known collectively as the Makgadikgadi Pans, they form one of the wonders of the world. During the dry season (which is most of the year) the 6 500 square kilometres of the Makgadikgadi is an absolutely flat area of glaring white salt. When it rains and the Okavango Delta fills the Boteti River, the pans are flooded with a shallow depth of water, and this is when countless flamingoes, pelicans and other aquatic birds are attracted to the rich feeding grounds, and great herds of zebra, wildebeest and springbok congregate on the banks and islands of the pan.

Makgadikgadi Pans Game Reserve and Nxai Pan National Park
At the settlement of Nata the road from Francistown divides; the branch due north leads to the confluence of the boundaries of Botswana, Zimbabwe and Zambia – to the Zambesi River and the Victoria Falls. The branch to the west carries on to Maun and in so doing, in turn, divides two wildlife sanctuaries; on the south side of the road is Makgadikgadi Pans Game Reserve and on the north side Nxai Pan National Park – collectively the sanctuaries cover some 10 000 square kilometres, penetrable only in four-wheel-drive vehicles.

Always seeking water and pastures the migratory herds, in vast numbers, move from one area to another – springbok, impala, gemsbok, wildebeest, sable, zebra and giraffe are followed by the predators, lion, cheetah, wild dog, bat-eared fox, hyena and jackal, with elephant and buffalo prominent in the wet season.

Maun
At the fringe of Ngamiland, on the north bank of the beautiful Thamalakane River, lies Maun, the gateway to Lake Ngami, the Okavango Delta and the Moremi Wildlife Reserve. It also lies on one of two routes to the famous Chobe National Park.

From this amiable centre (itself surrounded by a proclaimed wildlife sanctuary) four-wheel-drive vehicles and power-boats can be hired, and within 20 kilometres are the Island Safari Lodge, Crocodile Camp and Okavango River Lodge. Maun is the base of a number of recognised safari operators such as Moremi Safaris, Safari South, Ker and Downey and Selby.

The Thamalakane River is noted for good bream and barbel fishing and birdlife is prolific. Maun is the headquarters of the Tawana tribe and the population includes a number of the colourful Herero people. Because of the intense heat of summer, most tourists visit the region from July to September. After the wet months of January and February the countryside is especially beautiful.

The town is served by Botswana Airways and there is an hotel.

Okavango Delta
The immense network of waterways that make up the Okavango Delta is a phenomenon that occurs each year when the flood waters from the Angolan highlands reach the area via the Okavango River. The flat plains of the delta area extend for some 10 000 square kilometres and during the peak period some of the flood waters reach as far south as Lake Ngami and the Makgadikgadi Pans. Eventually, during the dry season, most of the waters become soaked up by the Kalahari. Except for a few Bushmen and large numbers of crocodiles, hippos, buffaloes and such antelope as lechwe, the delta is uninhabited. Visitors reach the delta (often called the Okavango Swamps

although the waterways are mostly beautifully clear) by boat or canoe and it is essential that anti-malaria tablets are taken well in advance.

Moremi Wildlife Reserve
Covering over 1 000 square kilometres in the north-eastern section of the Okavango Delta, the Moremi Wildlife Reserve is surely among the most beautiful in southern Africa. It was established in 1961 by the Tawana tribe under the direction of their regent, Mrs Pulane Moremi.

The reserve comprises savannah broken by winding water-courses with palm-covered islands, deep forests and lily-covered lagoons. The animal life is as varied as the terrain with great herds of tsessebe, impala, wildebeest, zebra and buffalo, and lesser numbers of the rare lechwe and sitatunga antelope. Notwithstanding the presence of lions, cheetahs and wild dogs, visitors are permitted (at their own risk) to explore the reserve on foot. Herons, ibis, jacanas, spoonbills, storks, geese and waders are among the vast number of birds that inhabit the lagoons.

During the dry season, from May to October, the tracks in the reserve are passable to four-wheel-drive vehicles. In the wet season these tracks become dangerous after flooding. Immunisation is essential, since mosquitoes and tsetse flies infest the region. The famous Khwai River Lodge, on the northern boundary of the Reserve, and the San-Wani Camp on the south-eastern border, cater for the many people who visit Moremi.

Chobe National Park
After the turnoff to Khwai River Lodge in the northern corner of Moremi Wildlife Reserve, the gravel road from Maun continues northwards to enter Chobe National Park, on Botswana's northern border with Zimbabwe.

This magnificent green wilderness of 11 600 square kilometres is established on the banks of the Chobe River, a tributary of the Zambesi, and has its headquarters and main entrance at Kasane in the north-eastern corner, only 80 kilometres from Victoria Falls.

Chobe has the largest concentration of game animals in Botswana and during May to September, the dry months, immense numbers of elephant can be seen along the river banks. This is also the time for large herds of antelope such as sable, roan, eland, kudu, lechwe, tsessebe, eland and impala. The park has numerous predator species, including lion, cheetah and leopard; the waterways are infested with crocodile and hippo and the bird life is prolific. Numerous giraffe, zebra, wildebeest, warthog and baboon populate the plains and forests. There is excellent fishing for tiger-fish, barbel and bream.

The Chobe Safari Lodge is at Kasane and from here boats take visitors some 30 kilometres upstream. There are camping sites in the park and several privately-owned camps of safari operators who hire out boats, four-wheel-drive vehicles, fishing tackle and professional guides. It is necessary to take precautions against sleeping sickness and malaria.

Chartered and private aircraft flights use the nearby Serondela airstrip.

Lake Ngami
The mystery of Lake Ngami (on the fringe of the Kalahari) is understood with the realisation that its existence as a lake is solely dependent upon the rains in the highlands of Angola. In a good season the water penetrates the Okavango Delta; spilling into the Thamalakane and then the Nxhabe River it finally reaches the depression to form a vast lake some 70 × 20 kilometres in size. During severe drought, as in 1965-66, it dries up completely, leaving a sea of reeds. And so it is that the size of the lake varies with the rainfall in the north. In 1849 David Livingstone estimated the huge sheet of water to be more than 170 miles in circumference, and in 1860 Thomas Bain reported the lake to be a fair-sized pond.

In modern times the vast herds of game have made way for the huge concentration of cattle reared in the area, although the huge flocks of aquatic birds, for which the lake is famed, remain, and among their great numbers are flamingoes, pelicans, darters, ducks, geese, tawn, martial and fish eagles with waders and a host of smaller species. Fish that survive the dry periods by hibernation form part of Botswana's important fishing industry which is centred here.

Charter flights to Lake Ngami are run by the safari companies and visitors can reach the area by fair gravel road, 79 kilometres from Maun.

Tsodilo Hills
In the northernmost corner of Botswana, where it is divided from Angola by the Caprivi Strip, and where South West Africa borders on the western side, are the Tsodilo Hills, a strange phenomenon of nature. Here a 20-kilometre-long granite rockface, 400 metres high, rises out of the mopane covered savannah, forming three clusters known to the Bushmen as 'male', 'female' and 'child'. Laurens van der Post described them as the 'mountains of the gods' and in an otherwise featureless landscape they certainly are significant.

World interest in the Tsodilo Hills followed the discovery of the cliff-face galleries of some 2 000 Bushman paintings, some calculated to be more than 4 000 years old. Bushmen (without any of the talents of their ancestors) still live in the desolate area and guide visitors to the paintings. A natural spring provides drinking water and there are pleasant camping sites, but no other facilities. The access is from Maun and the 14-hour journey on a poor desert road is strenuous, but despite the hazards, an increasing number of visitors journey to Tsodilo each year.

Gemsbok National Park
This park in the extreme south-western portion of the country was established in the 1930s to assist the South African authorities in the control of game in the adjoining Kalahari Gemsbok National Park. The easiest access is via the South African Mata Mata gate, although the park can be reached from the Botswana side via the adjoining Mabuasehube Game Reserve which is connected by gravel road with Tshabong to the south and Tshane to the north.

Gemsbok National Park covers some 11 000

1. In the old town hall and library, now the Mafeking Museum, there are many relics of the siege. In the foreground is the memorial to those who fell in the various wars.

2. The siege fort at Cannon Koppie, on the outskirts of present day Mafikeng, is a national monument.

3. Anglican Church opposite the museum is one of sixteen churches in the town; the tower was added to honour those who perished during the siege.

4. Breakfast at Mmabatho Sun, a delightful pleasure resort on the outskirts of Bophuthatswana's capital.

Mashatu Game Reserve

Situated in the north eastern Tuli enclave of Botswana is Mashatu Game Reserve – 40,5 thousand hectares in extent, it is the largest private wildlife sanctuary in southern Africa – a landscape of mopane woodland, centuries-old baobabs, meandering rivers and acacia savannah, inhabited by wildlife of great profusion and diversity.

The elephants of Mashatu, the largest single population in Africa surviving on privately-owned land, are unique, and among the other animals of the reserve are lion, leopard, cheetah, giraffe, zebra, eland, kudu and all common open plain species. Three-hundred-and-fifty species have been recorded in the prolific bird fauna.

Situated within the heart of this remote wilderness is Majale Lodge – intimate and hospitable the camp accommodates twenty-four guests in thatched en suite rondavels. The swimming pool, waterhole bar, curio shop and wildlife library add to the comfort of the camp, Mogorogoro Safari Lodge, the luxury eight bedded tented camp, is in the remote northern precinct of the reserve. Both camps provide full catering and bar service and are managed by experienced field staff.

Game drives are conducted in open, four wheel drive vehicles, normally in the early morning and late afternoon. Walking trails are an exciting experience and extended safaris to the Motloutse archaeological ruin sites and Shashe Limpopo confluence are arranged and should not be missed.

To visit Mashatu Game Reserve by motor car, the convenient crossing of the Limpopo River from South Africa into Botswana is made at Pont Drift, and this is reached from Pietersburg on the tarred R521 via Vivo and Alldays. The distance from Pietersburg to Pont Drift is 213 km. A similar route can be taken further north from Louis Trichardt along the R522. Self-drive guests are personally met at Pont Drift and fly-in packages and individual air charter can be arranged by Mashatu Game Reserve. Anti-malarial precautions are necessary.

Mashatu Game Reserve is owned and directed by Michael Rattray of Mala Mala.

Mashatu Game Reserve, in the north-eastern Tuli enclave of Botswana, is a true African wilderness where the elephants are a unique species.

1

2

1. *A part of Mlilwane, Swaziland's beautiful wildlife sanctuary in the Ezulwini Valley.*

2. *Mantenga Falls, a show-piece of Swaziland, formed by the Little Usutu River.*

3. *On their way to a special function — a Swazi couple in traditional dress.*

356

square kilometres where there are large herds of gemsbok, springbok and other antelope that are able to survive long periods of drought. The famous Kalahari tawny-maned lions move about freely in the open.

Lesotho

When the Basotho people infiltrated the majestic sandstone heights that overlook the beautiful valley of the Caledon River, they were escaping the nineteenth century onslaught of the marauding Zulus, and their continuing security rested with the finding of a fine leader. The modern history of Lesotho commenced in 1824 when Moshoeshoe (Moshesh), from his stronghold, Thaba Bosiho, in these Maluti Mountains, built a nation around his own invincibility, notwithstanding many years of turmoil. After a series of what were called the Basuto Wars, Moshesh pleaded with the British to annexe his country and with the agreement of President Brand of the Orange Free State, this came about in 1869 when the country was named Basutoland Protectorate. A year later, at an age beyond 75 years, Moshesh died. His grave is at the fortress site on Thaba Bosiho.

The country remained a protectorate of Britain for nearly a 100 years. In a gradual process the Basotho was given control. In 1964 a National Assembly was elected with the king, Motlotlehi (also known as Moshoeshoe II) becoming head of state. Final independence was granted the Kingdom of Lesotho on 4 October 1966.

The tiny kingdom covers an area of 30 300 square kilometres and is completely encircled by the Republic of South Africa. Eighty-five percent of the landscape is mountainous mass and no part of the remaining area is less than 1 000 metres above sea-level. Lesotho enjoys a temperate climate with more than three quarters of its rain falling in the summer, October to April. During the winter months, May to September, snowfalls on the Maluti are frequent, with some snow reaching the lower lying areas.

The population of some 2,5 million people are mainly engaged in agricultural activities although there are some important industries, and De Beers Consolidated Mines Limited has a diamond mine of considerable proportions in northern Lesotho.

Maseru

In 1869 Maseru (the place of the red sandstone) became the administrative headquarters ('camp') of Commandant James Bowker, the first British representative of the newly proclaimed protectorate. Today it is the capital of Lesotho and a sizeable town of some 40 000 inhabitants with a royal palace, houses of parliament, a number of interesting industries and eight hotels, including the luxury Lesotho Hilton and the Holiday Inn Casino.

The town lies in the valley of the Caledon River close to the Maseru Bridge and border post with the Orange Free State.

Homecraft industries of Royal Lesotho Tapestry Weavers and Royal Crown Jewellery are in Maseru and are well worth visiting.

Thaba Bosiho

Now a great national shrine of the Basotho, Thaba Bosiho (some 30 kilometres south-east of Maseru) is a unique natural fortress, although this is not apparent at first sight. The intelligent Moshesh assessed the physical locality correctly – the large stronghold became impregnable to any strength of attack of the era.

Thaba Bosiho (or Bosiu) is an enormous eroded flat-topped hill, 5 kilometres by 1,5 kilometres, protruding some 200 metres above the Phuthiatsana River Valley, 1 700 metres above sea level. Its sides are precipitous cliffs and its top is flat and grass-covered with a sufficient water supply from springs. Overlooking the only route of access, Khubelu Pass, Moshesh allowed his many followers to build a village, and he gathered around himself large numbers of refugees seeking protection and offering practical assistance – a British deserter built his personal residence of stone, high on the ridge.

Moshesh commenced the establishment of his stronghold in 1824 (after journeying from the deserted and more vulnerable Butha-Buthe). The first serious attack came from the Ngwaneni tribe of the Zulus in 1827, there followed the attacks of Korana in 1830 and of the Ndebele in 1831 – all three were successfully repulsed and the assailants were well beaten. Within a few years Moshesh's popularity grew as did the numbers of his supporters; he received the French Protestant missionaries, Arbousset and Casalis, European traders, more deserters, gun runners and many others, and yet he never left his mountain stronghold where the population of both people and livestock were increasing considerably.

Moshesh first drew the wrath of the Europeans when he sent his men to rustle the livestock of the settlers on the Free State central plains, and in 1852 this culminated in General Cathcart's 2 500-strong British force attack on the Basotho, but no attempt to storm Thaba Bosiho was made. The incident had no effect on the Basotho and the livestock raids continued. Commandant Senekal and his 1 000-strong Orange Free State force attempted an attack on the fortress in 1858 but soon realised on better judgement that the place, with its large force of Basotho warriors, was impregnable. Meantime Moshesh continued receiving support from many quarters and among these were the Roman Catholics, Allard and Gerard, who established the mission, Roma. In 1865 the Free Staters under command of Commandant-General Fick besieged Thaba Bosiho for two months and then tried to storm the fortress. A handful of the attackers reached the summit but were inevitably repulsed. A few days after the first attack failed the commando, under Commandant Louw Wepener, forced its way up part of Khubelu Pass but the men retreated when their commander was killed. A long and determined siege was then laid by the Free Staters and after hundreds of Basotho cattle had died of starvation and conditions on the mountain became putrid the unsuccessful Peace of the Kaffircorn was called. Although his stronghold remained intact to the bitter end, Moshesh realised that the Free State Boers had effectively captured the rest of his country and it was then that he pleaded with the British to take control.

To visit the site of Thaba Bosiho today is an awe-inspiring experience; the ruin of the great king Moshesh's residence is there and so is his grave and those of a number of his significant followers; the isolated peak of Qiloane guards the sandstone cliffs of the fortress as would a sentinal, and except for the village of Ha Rafutho on the footpath pass which is Khubelu, the place is deserted. There do remain two visibly poignant associations with the scene, one is pleasantly piquant, the other causes sympathy: the first is the ever-remaining dune of fine, red sand which legend says contains the spirit of the great king; the other concerns Maleka, the king's son, who forbidden to marry the girl of his choice, traced his footprint on the stone before jumping from the cliff to his death.

The summit is reached after a moderately strenuous walk from the village of Ha Rafutho, where guides are obtainable.

Roma

The cathedral of the Roman Catholic Church in Lesotho and the National University of Lesotho are at Roma, the site which Moshesh granted to Bishop J.S. Allard and Father Joseph Gerard in 1862.

Roma is reached by taking the road from Maseru to Mafeteng and after 13 kilometres there is the turnoff east which leads for another 19 kilometres to the original mission and the fine complex which is there today.

Matsieng and Morija

After the death of Moshesh, his son Letsie succeeded him and transferred the seat of the Paramount Chief to Matsieng, some 44 kilometres south of Maseru, close to Morija, the French Protestant mission station which was founded in 1833. In fact Letsie had been educated at the mission, and Matsieng has remained the seat of the Paramount Chief (now the king of Lesotho) ever since. The Lesotho Museum is at Morija.

Mafeteng

Seventy-seven kilometres south of Maseru the road reaches the bustling little town of Mafeteng, one of the longest established trading towns in Lesotho. It is said that the name Mafeteng (the place of the fat, unmarried women) goes back in history and has nothing to do with the young ladies of today!

At the foothills of the Maluti, some 35 kilometres to the east of Mafeteng, is the trading station with the peculiar name of Masemouse. The road to the station gives access to spectacular mountain scenery with fine views across the Makhaleng River Valley.

Mohale's Hoek

Named after a brother of Moshesh, chief Mohale, this attractive trading centre, with plenty of trees, was presented to the British by the chief in 1884 for use as an administrative 'camp'. Castle Rock, a fine example of the sandstone cliffs of Lesotho, overlooks the village golf course.

From the cave, 2 kilometres south of Mohale's Hoek, the notorious Motlejoa operated with his cannibal tribe during the 1820s. A visit to the sinister hideout is worthwhile.

Quthing (Moyeni)

In 1877 Moyeni (the place of the wind) was established the Administrative 'camp' for the south-western district of the protectorate and the district was known as Quthing (at the great river); today the village is also called Quthing.

This is in a region much inhabited by the Bushmen with a result that there are good opportunities for seeing their rock paintings. Easily accessible are those in the grounds of the Masitise Mission on the outskirts of the village.

Orange River Valley – Mount Moorosi

At a glance the map of Lesotho reveals that this mountainous country is criss-crossed with rivers. The main watercourse rises near Mont-Aux-Sources in the Natal Drakensberg and crosses Lesotho from the north-east to the south-west; this is the Orange, or as the Basotho knows it, the Sinqua (great river of the Bushmen). It is near Quthing that it crosses the border into the Cape on its tortuous journey to the Atlantic.

From Quthing (Moyeni) a fair gravel road leads northwards for approximately 50 kilometres to Mount Moorosi. This road follows the deep valley of the Orange and the scenery is magnificent. Mount Moorosi, 2 356 metres, completely dominates the rugged landscape and there is no questioning that it commands the surrounding region.

In the year 1850 it was to the summit of this mountain feature that the Baphuthi chief, Moorosi, brought his migrant followers across the mountains from Natal. Within a few years Moorosi built a stone fortress around his lair, encouraged Basotho and Bushmen trackers to join his forces and then proceeded to build up the largest horse and cattle rustling racket on the subcontinent – trading his livestock wealth for guns, ammunition, liquor and the like. He was undoubtedly a bold, shrewd and callous individual, as the events of history proved.

The trouble started after the British authorities established a 'camp' at Moyeni to bring the south-west to a state of law and order. The rustlers were encountered and Doda, son of Moorosi, was arrested and placed in custody. That night Doda's followers broke open the gaol, rescued Doda and fled to the mountain stronghold. The formal police demand for the surrender of Doda was answered with threats and insults. This incident was followed by a 250-strong force of the crack Cape Mounted Rifles launching an attack on the fortress on 8 April 1879. The attack was repulsed with 34 British killed and many wounded. Two Victoria Crosses were awarded for valour in that action.

Fighting continued in the area for many weeks. On 29 May Moorosi's men put to death 21 sleeping soldiers in a surprise attack on an outpost. Later a patrol of yeomanry was ambushed by the rustlers. They captured a man and the following day the captive was decapitated on the mountain top (in full view of his comrades below), his body was thrown over the cliff and his head was impaled on a pole.

June 5 saw the British attempt another attack with no success. There were 14 casualties and the surgeon, Major E.G. Hartley, received the Victoria Cross for risking his life among the wounded.

The matter became so serious that the Cape Prime Minister, Sir Gordon Sprigg, visited the scene and met Moorosi on the mountain slope. This attempt at negotiation was abortive and fighting continued. After a severe winter the British prepared for a decisive attack. Under command of Colonel Bayly heavy artillery bombardment was followed by the now 400-strong Cape Mounted Rifles force attacking at midnight of 19 November 1879. The encounter lasted five hours during which ladders had to be used to scale the final cliffs. As daylight broke the bodies of hundreds of Moorosi's men littered the mountain top, Moorosi himself was riddled with bullets and his son Doda made a miraculous escape but died of wounds soon after the battle. The British losses were 43 killed and 84 wounded. Five hundred of Moorosi's men were killed and ammunition destroyed was estimated to have had a mass of 6 tons. In the tranquil scene of today the Orange twists its way through the mountains.

Qachas Nek

From Mount Moorosi the road makes its complex way in many zig-zags through the valley of the Orange (in the surroundings of dramatic scenery) north-eastwards to reach Qachas Nek, only 2,5 kilometres from the border post with Transkei. The district, where the Orange River forms a great bend, is notable for its wheat and corn production. There is a well-appointed hotel in the village.

The place was named after another of Moorosi's sons who was as notorious as his father in livestock rustling. From Qachas Nek goods are transported across Transkei to and from the railhead at Matatiele in East Griqualand, Natal.

From Qachas Nek a track leads northwards to the 65-square kilometre Sehlabathebe National Park in magnificent mountain scenery.

Teyateyaneng

On Lesotho's western side the Caledon River forms the boundary with Orange Free State for approximately 300 kilometres. North of Maseru the road follows the beautiful valley of the river and at 47 kilometres it reaches Teyateyaneng. This pleasant little town with the strange-sounding name had its start in 1886 as another of the British administrative 'camps' and has since then been called 'TY'. The name refers to the 'shifting sands' of the nearby river and the town will always be remembered for its Anglican mission station, for 50 years in the charge of the much loved Father William Wrenford.

Teyateyaneng is today famous for its interesting craft centres producing carpets and tapestries, table linen, bags, shawls, skirts and the like as well as pottery. In the area there are several galleries, in the caves and rock shelters, of Bushman paintings.

The Blue Mountain Inn is a popular stop-over and has caravan sites adjoining the hotel.

Leribe (Hlotse)

Across the Caledon River from Ficksburg, OFS, lies the busy trading centre, Leribe. The name first applied to the district whereas the village took the name of the river on which its lies, Hlotse. The church, built by Canon Widdicombe in 1876, gave Leribe its start, and is still standing.

Leribe was the scene of heavy attacks against the government forces during the Gun War that flared up in December 1879 and continued for several years. It arose when the Basotho refused to surrender their arms to the Cape Government (which was at the time administering the protectorate for the Imperial Government). During that war the truculent Masupha, a son of Moshesh (who continued to occupy Thaba Bosiho after his father's death), invaded Maseru in October 1880. It was during these years that Leribe received a famous visitor in the person of General 'Chinese' Gordon who made an unsuccessful attempt to arrange a peace settlement. Masupha died in 1897 after being defeated in a civil war against his nephew, Paramount Chief Lerotholi (son of Letsie).

Leribe has an hotel, beautifully situated, overlooking the mountains.

On the road north to Butha-Buthe, 7 kilometres out from Leribe, a turnoff left (west) leads to the old causeway across the Subeng River, 35 metres downstream from which are the pre-historic footprints of 24 five-toed dinosaurs, left in the mud of the river bed and now preserved in the sandstone.

Butha-Buthe – Oxbow – Mokhotlong

Thirty-one kilometres north of Leribe is Butha-Buthe which started as an administrative 'camp' of the British Protectorate days. The name of the village is a corruption of Moshesh's first mountain stronghold Botha-Bothe (the hiding-place), which overlooks the village from the north-east. The village has an inn.

On the road to Joel's Drift is the turnoff right (east) to the famous Sekubu shelters (16 kilometres from Butha-Buthe, so named because the rock formations are shaped remarkably like the 'teats of the hippopotamus'. First occupied by Bushmen, the shelters later became the stronghold of cannibals, and are now used as livestock stables.

From Butha-Buthe a gravel road leads south-eastwards over the basalt roof of southern Africa for 185 kilometres, via Oxbow Camp, to the remote trading station of Mokhotlong. This route is unsurpassed on the subcontinent for sheer magnificence of mountain scenery. It is negotiable by saloon car as far as Oxbow Camp, a distance of 66 kilometres, but even that stretch should not be unertaken by untried drivers. From Oxbow to Mokhotlong the 119 kilometres can be made only in 4-wheel-drive vehicles. On the route to Oxbow the road passes the 2 743-metre Khatibe Mountain, traverses the beautiful valley of the Hololo River, hugs close to spectacular sandstone overhangs such as at Liphofung where Bushmen sheltered and left their fine rock art, and reaching the main wall of the Maluti range it climbs through the Moteng Pass to its 2 834 metre-high summit, descending to the Tsehlanyani River; 66 kilometres from Butha-Buthe it climbs again to look down upon the great Malibamatso River Valley (river of dark pools). Below the confluence of the Malibamatso and Tsehlanyani Rivers, is the site of the gigantic Oxbow Dam Scheme (appropriately named, for here the joining rivers form an ox-bow, in the two meanings – firstly in the formation of a horse-shoe and secondly in the formation of a lake where the one river cuts across the narrow end of the horse-shoe). The joint scheme of the Lesotho and RSA governments will provide Lesotho with much needed hydro-electric power and irrigate its lowlands, and at the same time feed the RSA with over 1 000-million litres of water a day. And here in the valley has developed a fun centre, known as Oxbow Camp; it is the starting base for trout anglers, the Oxbow ski-runs and pony treks into the mountains.

From Oxbow the track continues over the mountains and after 46 kilometres reaches the De Beers workings at Letseng-la-Terai, the world's highest-lying diamond mine. From the mine it is a further 73 kilometres to Mokhotlong, until recently an isolated trading centre and police camp, unreachable except by pony and pack mule.

In 1948 the 56 kilometre track, from Mokhotlong over the Drakensberg and down the Sani Pass to Natal, was improved to enable transportation by 4-wheel-drive vehicles. The area is today a great tourist attraction. The mountaineer's chalet accommodating 22 people is situated at the head of Sani Pass and is the highest licensed hotel on the subcontinent. From here trail riding and walks to the summit of Thabana Ntlenyana are arranged; at 3 482 metres this is the highest point in southern Africa and during the winter there is sufficient snow for ski-runs.

Lesotho Mountain Road

What is to be named the Trans-Maluti Highway starts at Maseru and is constructed as far as Mantsonyane, 124 kilometres due east of the capital. It is to continue down the valley of the Orange and will eventually be connected with the Sehlabathebe National Park, having crossed the centre of the kingdom from west to east. Although the road has not yet been tarred it has a good gravel surface which is nevertheless slippery in wet weather.

This route opens up a new world for the motorist in an area of majestic mountain scenery across the basalt roof of southern Africa.

From Maseru a tarred road leads south-east to Roma: this road is taken for 25 kilometres, at which point, St. Michaels, the mountain road branches eastwards and rises quickly to the summit of a broad plateau with the great bulk of the 2 884 metre Machache ahead. At this point there are fine views back down the southern valley of Roma mission, pro-cathedral and university campus.

Leaving the mountain road at the stream crossing beyond the village of Ha Ntsi, 35 kilometres from Maseru, a by-road leads northwards for 6 kilometres to the world famous Ha Khotso Bushman paintings. The last 3 kilometres to the cave is along a track to the Liphiring River gorge, and it is advisable to take a guide from Ha Khotso village. This is probably the finest example of Bushman rock art to be found anywhere.

Beyond the turnoff to the Bushman paintings the mountain road negotiates three mountain passes in succession over a distance of some 50 kilometres. At the foot of the Bushman's Pass there is the Maluti tearoom and caravan park (with bungalow accommodation). In this pass the road climbs the Thaba Tseka (mountain of the white mark) reaching the summit, 2 268 metres, 47 kilometres from Maseru. Nestled in a delightful wooded glade at the foot of the Molimo-Nthuse Pass (58 kilometres from Maseru) is the Molimo-Nthuse Lodge, a comfortable hide-away with an à la carte restaurant and bar overlooking a cascading trout stream. Pony trekking is popular from here. Appalled at the steep gradient in the pass, early travellers gave it the name Molimo-Nthuse (God help me) which at its summit is 2 318 metres. At about 82 kilometres from Maseru there is a turnoff, northwards which leads for 2 kilometres to Likalaneng trading station, where guides and ponies can be hired to visit Semonkong (the misty place) and the lovely Sinqunyana Falls. The area is notable for aloes and red-hot pokers. The summit of the last of the three passes, Thaba Putsoa (Blue Mountain), is reached at 90 kilometres from Maseru, 2 620 metres above sea level and overlooked by the 3 096-metre-high peak. In spectacular scenery the road descends from here into the cultivated valley of the Sinqunyana (Little Orange). Across the river is Sinqunyana Lodge, where accommodation is provided, however guests must bring their own food. The area is notable for its fishing, riding, swimming, climbing and camping possibilities. From the Sinqunyana River the road ascends once more before dropping into the fertile valley of the Mantsonyane (small black) River, 124 kilometres from Maseru. From here it is not advisable to proceed further, unless by 4-wheel-drive vehicle.

Swaziland

One of the smallest kingdoms of the world, Swaziland measures 144 kilometres at its widest, east to west, and 192 kilometres at its longest, north to south. Its total area of 17 000 square kilometres makes it approximately the size of Wales, half the size of the Netherlands and one fifth the size of Natal. It is completely landlocked by the Republic of South Africa and Moçambique, its eastern border being only 65 kilometres from the port of Maputo. The total population is estimated to be 500 000.

The ancestors of the Swazi people came to this part of the subcontinent with their leader, Ngwane, in about 1750. During a mass migration from the north of Africa at the time, tribespeople moved down the Moçambique coastal belt, some breaking off with Ngwane where Swaziland is today, and the greater mass continuing further south to Zululand. After Ngwane's death the people were led by his grandson, Sobhuza, and in turn Sobhuza's heir was Mswazi, from whom the tribe took its name when he succeeded to power in 1836. The territory, which prospered under Mswazi, was fraught with problems during the remainder of the nineteenth century when Mswazi's son Mbhandeni, at his personal gain, sold concessions to the gold rush prospectors and others who came to exploit the country. These concessions resulted in two-thirds of Swaziland being virtually owned by private concession holders, and when the situation became chaotic in 1895 the Transvaal Republic took control of Swaziland. This authority passed to the British after the Anglo-Boer War and Swaziland became a protectorate in 1902. Sobhuza II, King of Swaziland until his death in August 1982, and grandson of Mbhandeni, became Paramount Chief in 1921 and through his untiring efforts the territory was restored to national ownership. The full sovereign independence of Swaziland was proclaimed on 6 September 1968. In 1987 the young Mswati III was installed as King of Swaziland.

A constitutional monarchy, Swaziland's executive authority is vested in the king and exercised through the cabinet presided over by the prime minister. Matters of Swazi law and custom are authorised by the Swazi National Council – the traditional assembly of all adult male Swazi. Swaziland is one of the few African countries to have a population that is almost entirely homogeneous, sharing a common language, culture and loyalty to their monarch. Without the tribal divisions that have troubled other states, the Swazis have developed their political institutions in a climate of peace, stability and order.

The geographic and climatic regions of the country divide conveniently into four, stepping from west to east from the highlands formed by spurs of the Drakensberg (where the 1 862-metre Emlembe is the highest point), through the midlands to the lowlands, and beyond the Lebombo, a low but nevertheless impressive mountain range separating Swaziland from Moçambique and the Indian Ocean. This is a very well watered country – eight principal trunk rivers cross all four regions on the way to the sea. These are fed by the perennial streams of the highlands and in the summer months by the water courses of the lowlands. The longest river is the Usutu (dark brown) which becomes impressively broad by the time it reaches the lowlands.

A predominantly agricultural country, most of Swaziland's population practises small-scale subsistence farming, but large agricultural estates, co-operative and smallholding schemes have contributed to the development of a diversified agricultural economy which includes such crops as sugar, maize, cotton, citrus, pineapples, potatoes, rice, tobacco and vegetables. Forestry accounts for a large percentage of the export output and there is considerable raising of beef cattle, dairy herds, poultry and pigs. The three major mines of the country produce iron ore, asbestos and coal for export and deposits of barytes, kaolin and pyrophyllite are being exploited. A very healthy tourist industry prevails.

Swaziland has a rich natural flora including species of cycads, aloes, ferns and lilies, some of which are peculiar to the territory. The kloofs of the highlands abound in indigenous trees from which the Swazi obtain materials to fashion various utensils. Bird life is abundant and game such as kudu, wildebeest, waterbuck, impala, duiker and zebra are to be found in the bushveld. More than a century since they were exterminated from Swaziland, in 1987, a herd of 10 elephant was reintroduced to the Hlane National Park – a gift from Dr Anton Rupert. The establishment of large forestry plantations in the highlands has led to a return of some of the smaller antelope to those areas. Crocodiles inhabit the lower reaches of the main rivers while fish such as bream, yellow, tiger, barbel and eel are fairly plentiful.

The Swazis are a friendly courteous people and despite the influence of western civilisation they have retained their colourful traditions and customs. There is preserved for the King of Swaziland (the Ngwenyama – 'the lion') a great loyalty and reverence. Tradition endows the king with mystical characteristics; he is the embodiment of the nation, his health is its prosperity, his fertility its soil. The Ncwala, which heralds the Swazi New Year, is the most sacred of the Swazi ceremonies. It embraces a series of rituals culminating in regiments of warriors dancing before the king and the king dancing with the regiments before his people. The ceremony signifies the reuniting of the nation under the king and permits the first eating of the new crops of the year. The Ncwala lasts for nearly a month and takes place in December-January. The colourful Umhlanga or reed dance lasts a week and takes place in July-August. It is the occasion for the gathering together of Swazi maidens to demonstrate before the Queen Mother, the Ndlovukazi (she elephant) their respect, preservation of chastity and willingness to work together harmoniously. Sibaca dances are held in many parts of the country and take the form of a sport in which teams in distinctive costumes compete.

Ngwenya to Mbabane

Most traffic into Swaziland from the west comes through the Transvaal highveld border post of Oshoek which faces Ngwenya in Swaziland, 27 kilometres north-west of Mbabane. A short distance along this pleasant entry road into Swaziland is the Ngwenya mountain (1 829 metres) and below this the Ngwenya mine of Swaziland Iron Ore Development Company (a subsidiary of Anglo-American). The high grade iron ore which is mined here is sold to Japan under contract and provides Swaziland with its major export income. As a direct result of the contract Swaziland's railway was built in 1964 from the mine railhead. Kadake station, to the Moçambique border at Goba, a distance of 220 km. Of great interest to visitors to the mine are the ancient workings, proved by radio-carbon dating to have produced oxides and red haematite as early as 26 000 B.C., making this the oldest mine in the world.

Twelve kilometres from Ngwenya the road to Mbabane reaches Motsane and the turnoff to Pigg's Peak, described later in this chapter.

Mbabane

The picturesque administrative capital, Mbabane, is surrounded by the Dlangeni hills at the edge of the highlands where the climate is temperate. Trading had been carried on in the locality prior to the arrival of the British who chose the site in 1902 as their administrative headquarters. Like all the towns of Swaziland, Mbabane has retained a village-like atmosphere; the principal thoroughfare, Allister Miller Street, is lined with shops, commercial and official buildings, and tree-shaded pavements. The town has a modern plaza with supermarkets and pavement restaurant, spacious centre of government buildings, hospitals and a broadcasting centre. There are two hotels in the town itself and two on the outskirts.

Mbabane market has a special appeal for the visitor for the reason that the articles offered for sale generally reflect real craftsmanship with a notable absence of spurious rubbish very often offered as souvenirs in other markets. The Swazis are specialists at handcraft and produce especially fine beadwork in which is often incorporated porcupine quills and local bean seeds. Other articles, beautifully displayed, include baskets and mats of sisal, grass and palm leaves; wooden bowls, spoons and carvings; spears, battle axes, shields, knobkerries and walking sticks; pottery, copperware and soap-stone articles; karosses and python skins.

Ezulwini Valley

Down the escarpment, south of Mbabane, is the beautiful Ezulwini Valley (place of the heavens) and one of the most delightful 20-kilometre drives to be had anywhere. The tarred road follows the valley formed by the Little Usutu River and enclosed on the eastern side by the Mdimbza Mountains (with the taboo burial caves of past kings) where the twin peaks of Lugogo, or as the Europeans know them, Sheba's Breasts, dominate the scene. This valley is the heart and soul of Swaziland – in this unspoilt environment are the royal kraals, parliament, the game sanctuary, access to a spectacular waterfall and the fabulous playground for which the kingdom is famous.

On the steep descent after leaving Mbabane, the road passes (on the left) the Highland View Hotel and then the Swazi Inn, both sited on prime positions overlooking the broad valley. At the foot of the descent is the Diamonds Valley Motel and just beyond that is Timbali Caravan Park. At 15 kilometres from Mbabane is the turnoff right to the Royal Swazi Sun, a five star hotel with a fabulous array of entertainment. In addition to the casino are the restaurants, cabaret, theatre, swimming pool terrace, 18-hole golf course, tennis courts, bowling greens, hot springs and the most beautiful parkland garden. Across the highway from the Royal Swazi Sun entrance gate are the Ezulwini Sun and Lugogo Sun, and further along the highway is the Yen Saan Hotel with its authentic Chinese architecture and cuisine.

The beautiful Mantenga Falls are reached by taking the turnoff, right, which leads for 3 kilometres along a gravel road to the parking lot. This turnoff is approximately 17 kilometres from Mbabane and also leads to the Mantenga Hotel and a fine curio shop. Nearby is the Smoky Mountain Village, a private resort in a picturesque setting where chalets surround a restaurant and swimming pool.

Mlilwane Game Sanctuary turnoff is a further 2 kilometres along the highway to Manzini. Occupying some 5 000 hectares, practically the entire park is accessible to the motorist on 22 kilometres of road. This provides excellent opportunities to view a wide range of wild life including zebra, hippo, white rhino, warthog, crocodile, small carnivora such as civet and numerous species of antelope including wildebeest, eland, kudu, waterbuck, impala, springbok and duiker. There is a remarkable abundance of bird life, particularly on and near the lovely stretches of water.

At the delightful rest camp, furnished chalets and beehive huts may be hired. The facilities include baths and showers with hot and cold water, and a caravan park.

Returning to the main Mbabane-Manzini road, after crossing the Little Usutu River, it reaches, on the left, the National Stadium and Houses of Parliament, and then on the right the royal kraals of Lositha and Lobamba (where the Ncwala and Umhlanga ceremonies are held), 21 kilometres from Mbabane.

After the turnoffs to Malkerns, Bhunya and Mhlambanyati the road passes the turnoff to the Matsapa Airport and industrial township (a part of Manzini) before reaching the town of Manzini which is 39 kilometres from Mbabane.

Manzini

The principal industrial town of Swaziland, Manzini, had its name changed from Bremersdorp in 1960. The original name came from the one-time owner of the hotel and trading store, Albert Bremer, who had a flourishing business there during the concession rush of the late nineteenth century, when the enterprising Swazi king, Mbhandeni (who sold his nation) had his royal kraal in the vicinity. During this time the place was the rendezvous of adventurers and horse thieves like the notorious Bob MacNab. Bremersdorp became the capital of Swaziland during the Anglo Boer War and was all but razed to the ground by the Ermelo commando.

Manzini has a number of secondary industries manufacturing a wide variety of goods for domestic consumption and export. It has a Roman Catholic cathedral, three hotels and a caravan park, and is at its best in October when the jacarandas lining the streets are in full bloom. The population is 20 000.

Eight kilometres east of Manzini there is a tarred road leading through a scenic route to Sipofaneni, from where the road continues via Big Bend to Lavumisa and the Natal border, on gravel for most of the way.

Siteki

Situated on the Lebombo ridge, 66 kilometres due east of Manzini, Siteki (the place of marrying) enjoys a cool, pleasant climate in complete contrast with the hot lowland area so close to it. Being only 40 kilometres from the Moçambique border at Goba, the village of Siteki was much used by the livestock rustling renegades of the nineteenth century. There are two hotels, one being a training centre.

Big Bend

For 56 kilometres south of Siteki the road skirts the Lebombo range, in the hot lowlands, to reach Big Bend. The settlement takes its name from the meander of the great Usutu River and is the centre of a large sugar mill where sugar was produced for the first time in Swaziland in 1960.

At the attractive country club visitors are welcomed to the golf course, tennis courts and bowling greens. Yachting, boating and skiing may be enjoyed on the large irrigation dam. A scenic delight is the Usutu gorge in the Lebombo which can be reached on horseback or on foot; the river here is notable for crocodiles, hippos and tiger fish and there is abundant bird fauna. Flamboyants, flowering in the summer, line the main road and golf course. The hotel has airconditioned rooms.

Mhlume and Tshaneni

These neighbouring villages, 84 kilometres north-west of Siteki, are centres of extensive irrigation farms of Colonial Development Corporation where sugarcane, rice and citrus are intensely cultivated. At Tshaneni (the small stone) there is a 16-square-kilometre dam used for water sport, a country club, a small game reserve and an hotel. Mhlumbe takes its name from the *Adina galpini* trees growing there. In this northern lowlands area, close to the Transvaal border post of Border Gate, the summers are hot and humid.

Malkerns, Bhunya and Mhlambanyati

From Mbabane there is an interesting and beautiful 100-kilometre circular drive leading south through the Ezulweni Valley (already described), turning off westwards at the sign to Malkerns (26 kilometres from Mbabane on the Mbabane-Manzini road) and following the road from there to Bhunya and Mhlambanyati, and back to Mbabane. The route is tarred for all but the last 24 kilometres of the drive.

Malkerns got its name from the local trader, Malcolm Kerns Stuart, and is only 6 kilometres from the Mbabane-Manzini road turnoff. It lies in the pineapple-producing district of the midlands where Libby's cannery is conveniently sited. The village has a country club and nearby is the quaint roadside curio shop and nursery of Nyanza Gemstones (Nyanza being the first name of the proprietress) which is well worth visiting. In the vicinity are the Swaziland Agricultural College, University Centre of Elangeni and Malkerns Research Station.

At Bhunya, which is 26 kilometres west of Malkerns, Usutu Pulp Company has its mill. In the centre of a vast pine forest, it produces 100 000 tons of pulp a year.

Mhlambanyati (the buffalo swimming place), 19 kilometres north of Bhunya, is a residential village in the cool, hilly uplands, surrounded by beautiful forests. It was especially laid out for employees of the pulp company and at their Usutu Club there are fine amenities including golf, tennis, bowls, swimming and a charming village-green cricket pitch. The hotel, Foresters Arms, attracts holiday-makers from all over southern Africa.

Although the road down to Mbabane from Mhlambanyati is not tarred, it traverses a scenically spectacular part of Swaziland in the upper valley of the Little Usutu River. At about 9 kilometres from Mhlambanyati there is a turnoff right to Meikles Mount (a holiday resort started by Murray Meikle) from where there are sweeping views of the Ezulwini Valley. The road continues through unspoilt rural country past granite hills to reach Mbabane, 15 kilometres from Meikles Mount.

Piggs Peak

An important forestry centre in the splendid mountain country of north-western Swaziland, Piggs Peak was, for sixty years from its foundation in 1884, a gold-mining camp. William Pigg discovered the gold in what he called the Devil's Reef because of its inaccessibility. Today the plantations of Peaks Forest

and Swaziland Plantations cover the Drakensberg mountainside with gum and pine trees and the village is the starting point for the magnificent scenic drives of the region. The Protea Piggs Peak hotel and casino is located here.

On the road to the border post Ngwenya-Oshoek north west of Mbabane there is a turnoff right which leads along an all-tarmac road for 50 km to Piggs Peak. Of interest along this road at 10 km from the turnoff are the old workings of Forbes Reef which yielded a rich output of gold from the time of its discovery by Alex Forbes in 1884 until it petered out in 1896. The mine and the old hotel there are overgrown with wattles. Beyond the Forbes Reef there is a track leading to a lovely waterfall that occurs in the Maloloja River, a tributary of the Komati.

Piggs Peak village is notable for its handcraft market and the weaving industry started in 1958 by Mrs Coral Stephens. Handwoven materials from here have been exported to many parts of the world with a particular market coming from theatres for the huge curtains which they require.

Piggs Peak lies at an important junction of roads; to the east a gravel road leads to the lowlands irrigated sugar and citrus estates of Tshaneni and Mhlume; to the north the tarmac road leading to the Transvaal border post at Jeppes Reef (40 km away) passes close to the Poponyane Falls, a much visited and photographed beauty spot, about 15 km from Piggs Peak. Due west of Piggs Peak a winding road through the magnificent forest leads for 19 km to Bulembu and the Transvaal border post at Havelock; a most enchanting route during fine weather, it should be avoided in the rain.

Havelock Swaziland Asbestos Mine

The asbestos mine at Bulembu, close to the Transvaal border post is, after the iron ore mine at Ngwenya, the second largest export producer of Swaziland, and one of the five largest asbestos mines in the world.

Although the discovery of asbestos here dates from 1886 when a group of Natal prospectors named their syndicate after the Natal governor, Sir Arthur Havelock, it was not until 1930 that the problem of transporting the chrysotile asbestos from the remote 1 135-metre-high deposit was overcome by the famous Canadian asbestos mining house of Turner and Newall. After paying £240 000 for the prospectors claims, a 20-kilometre-long aerial cableway was constructed from the deposit site, over mountains and valleys, to Barberton in the eastern Transvaal. Since the mine was opened in 1939 its output and all equipment and stores have been transported by this efficient carrier.

Employees at Havelock Mine live in a model village with first-rate recreational facilities including a fine golf course.

From the border post near the mining town the road makes a spectacular descent down the Drakensberg escarpment into the immense De Kaap Valley and just before reaching Barberton it passes the sites of a number of training camps of famous South African regiments of the Second World War.

Hiking Trails and Walks — arranged in the sequence of the chapters of the book

Introduction and Explanation

The National Hiking Way Board functions under the auspices of the Department of Environmental Affairs, Forestry Branch, Private Bag X447, Pretoria 0001. Telephone (012) 310-3839. Since the Board was founded in 1975 organised hiking in South Africa has become very popular and the opportunities are expanding continuously. It is intended, ultimately, that the system of hiking trails will extend from the Cedarberg in the north-western Cape to the Soutpansberg in the northern Transvaal.

The purpose of this schedule of Hiking Trails and Walks is to provide basic information and to direct interested parties to the relevant authority (invariably the regional director or State forester) in order to make necessary reservations and obtain further details. Enquiries should be made about permits, number of persons in the trail and the cost (generally the Walks are free and trails, where hutted accommodation or camps are provided, range from R2,50 to R5,00 per person per night). Most of the authorities sell excellent detailed maps of the regions with route directions, invaluable to the hiker. Relative to most of the hiking trails, hikers must provide their own food, sleeping bags, stoves, cooking utensils and first-aid equipment, and sometimes their own lighting and tents.

1 & 2 — Cape Town and Western Cape

1. **Table Mountain Walks**   A number of walks of unlimited distance and duration. No facilities. Obtain permits at the State Forester, Cecilia State Forest, Cape Town. Tel (021) 77-4642.

2. **Tokai Walk**   Tokai State Forest. Two hours. No facilities. The Regional Director, Western Cape Forest Region. Tel (021) 45-1224.

3. **Braille Walk**   Kirstenbosch. 470 metres. Explanatory labels in braille and large print. Entrance fee. National Botanic Gardens of SA. Tel (021) 77-1166.

4. **Cedarberg Wilderness Area (Walks and Hiking Trails)**   Near Clanwilliam. Take all equipment including tents. No facilities. No fires. Maximum group 12, minimum 3. The State Forester, Cedarberg State Forest, Private Bag X1, Citrusdal 7340. Tel (02682) 3440.

5. **River Bank Walk**   Stellenbosch. Follows the Eerste River for 4 km, starting at the bridge near the Volkskombuis restaurant. Stellenbosch Publicity Association, 30 Plein Street. Tel (02231) 3584.

6. **Vineyard Walk**   Stellenbosch to Kuilsrivier. The whole day, 24 km. No accommodation. Closed during harvesting. Maps available. Obtain permits at Stellenbosch Publicity. Tel (02231) 3584.

7. **Dog Walk**   Sir Lowry's Pass. 7 km. Dogs permitted with hikers. The Regional Director Western Cape Forest Region, Cape Town. Tel (021) 45-1224.

8. **Paardeberg Walk**   Highlands State Forest, near Bot River. 15 km. The Regional Director Western Cape Forest Region, Cape Town. Tel (021) 45-1224.

9. **Boland Hiking Trail (Hottentots Holland section)**   Sir Lowry's Pass or Nuweberg Forest Station, near Grabouw, to Franschhoek Pass. 54 km, 3 days or 25 km, 2 days. Huts equipped with bunks and mattresses. Regional Director, Western Cape Forest Region, Cape Town. Tel (021) 45-1224 or 46-7010. Maximum 30.

10. **Boland Hiking Trail (Limietberg section)**   Hawequas State Forest. Across the Hawequas and Limietberg to tweede Tol, Bainskloof. 34 km, 2 days. Hut equipped with bunks and mattresses. No fires allowed. Maximum group 30. Regional Director, Western Cape Forest Region, Cape Town. Tel (021) 45-1224 or 46-7010.

11. **Swellendam Hiking Trail**   Circular route from Koloniesbos in the Swellendam State Forest. 81 km, 6 days or 50 km, 5 days. Huts equipped with bunks and mattresses. Regional Director, Western Cape Forest Region, Cape Town. Tel (021) 45-1224 or 46-7010. Maximum Group 16.

12. **Boosmansbos Wilderness Area (Walks and Hiking Trails)**   Near Heidelberg. Take all equipment including tents. No facilities. No fires. Maximum group 12, minimum 3. The State Forester Grootvadersbos State Forest. P O Box 109, Heidelberg 6760. Tel (02962) 1812.

3 — The Garden Route

13. **Ruitersbos Walk**   From Eight Bells Mountain Inn, off the R328, 35 km from Mossel Bay, at the bottom of the Robinson Pass. 9 km circular route through Ruitersbos State Forest. 3½ hours, no facilities, no permits, no number restriction. Report at the Eight Bells or Ruitersbos State Forest. Tel: (04441) 5-8589.

14. **Outeniqua Hiking Trail**   From Witfontein Forest Station (off the R29 opposite Blanco village, north-west of George, at the commencement of the Outeniqua Pass) to Diepwalle Forest Station, 18 km north of Knysna. Full course 137 km, 8 days. A choice of starting and ending points provide options of from 2 to 8 days. Huts equipped with bunks and mattresses. Maximum group 30. The Regional Director, Southern Cape Forest Region. PB X12, Knysna 6570. Tel (0445) 2-3037.

15. **Groeneweide Walk**   Groenkop, near Saasveld Forest College, 10 km from George. Two routes of 15 km and 11 km. 6 am to 6 pm, no permits and no restriction of number of participants. Sign the visitors book at the start. The Regional Director, PB X12, Knysna 6570. Tel (0445) 2-3037.

16. **Terblans Walk**   17 km north of Knysna. 7 km Circular route starting at Grootdraai picnic spot, just north of Gouna Forest Station. No permits, no number restriction. Sign the visitors book at the start. The Regional Director, PB 12, Knysna 6570. Tel (0445) 2-3037.

17. **Elephant Walk**   22 km north of Knysna. Circular route starting at Diepwalle Forest Station. Three courses, 18 km, 14 km and 9 km. From 6 am to 6 pm. No permits, no number restriction. Sign the visitors book at the start. The Regional Director, PB 12 Knysna 6570. Tel (0445) 2-3037.

18. **Kranshoek Walk**   32 km east of Knysna. 9 km coastal walk in the Harkerville section of the Kruisfontein State Forest. From 6 am to 6 pm. No permits, no number restriction. Sign the visitors book at the start. The Regional Director, PB 12, Knysna 6570. Tel (0445) 2-3037.

19. **Grootkloof Walk**   Grootrivier Pass. 16 km circular route from the Grootrivier camping site to the top of the plateau at Covie. From 6 am to 6 pm. No permits, no number restriction. Report to The State Forester, Bloukrans State Forest. Tel (04457) 6710.

20. **Otter Hiking Trail**   From Storms River Mouth to Grootrivier Mouth, in the Tsitsikamma Coastal National Park. 48 km, 4$^{1}/_{2}$ days. Huts with bunks and mattresses. Maximum group 12. Very popular, advance booking necessary. The Chief Director, National Parks Board, P O Box 787, Pretoria 0001. Tel (012) Enquiries 44-1171, Reservations 343-1991.

21. **Tsitsikamma Hiking Trail**   From Nature's Valley to Storms River Bridge. Full course 72 km, 5 days. A choice of starting and ending points provide options of from 2 to 5 days. Huts with bunks and mattresses. The Regional Director, Tsitsikamma Forest Region, PB X537, Humansdorp 6300. Tel (04231) 5-1180.

22. **Bushpig Walk, Ferntree Walk, Blue Duiker Walk, The Mouth Walk and Loerie Walk**   These five walks in the Tsitsikamma Forest and Coastal National Park are of 30 minutes each walk and require no permits. Route enquiries from the National Parks Board, Pretoria, the restaurant at Storms River Mouth, or the Tzitzikama Forest Inn.

4 — The Great Karoo

23. **Springbok Hiking Trail**   Circular route, 26 km 3 days, within the Karoo National Park, north-west of Beaufort West. Closed from 15 October to 28 February annually. Huts equipped with bunks and mattresses. Maximum group 12. The Chief Director, National Parks Board, P O Box 787, Pretoria 0001. Tel (012) Enquiries 44-1171 Reservations 343-1991.

24. **Valley of Desolation Walk**   Near Graaff-Reinet, one hour walk in the Karoo Nature Reserve. No facilities. The Senior Officer, Karoo Nature Reserve, P O Box 347, Graaff-Reinet 6280. Tel (0491) 3453.

25. **Spandaukop Walk**   Near Graaff-Reinet, 23 km circular route in the Karoo Nature Reserve – 7 hours. No facilities. Maximum group 10. The Senior Officer, Karoo Nature Reserve. Same as 24.

5 — Port Elizabeth and District and the Settler Country

26. **Bosbok Walk**   25 km west of Port Elizabeth, circular route (16 km) in the Island State Forest. No facilities. The State Forester, Island State Forest, P O Greenbushes 6390. Tel (041) 7-4634.

27. **Groendal Wilderness Area**   Near Uitenhage. Enquiries and reservations: The State Forester, Groendal State Forest, P O Box 445, Uitenhage 6230. Tel (0422) 2-5418.

28. **Alexandria Hiking Trail**   35 km circular route from Alexandria Forest Station across a section of Woody Cape Nature Reserve. Two days. Huts equipped with bunks at starting and overnight points. Maximum group 12. The Regional Director, Eastern Cape Forest Region, PB X7432, King William's Town 5600. Tel (0433) 2-3475.

29. **Mountain Zebra Hiking Trail**   25 km circular route within the Mountain Zebra National Park. Three days. Hut equipped with bunks. Maximum group 12. The Chief Director, National Parks Board, P O Box 787, Pretoria 001. Tel (012) Enquiries 44-1171, Reservations 343-1991.

30. **Kowie River Canoe Trail**   12 km circular route in the horseshoe bend of the Kowie River in the Bathurst Nature Reserve (Waters Meeting). Three hours. Overnight camp with thatched eating shelter, toilets, braai places and fresh water. Hikers provide own tents. Canoes are supplied. Maximum group 12. The State Forester, Bathurst State Forest, Bathurst 6166. Tel (0464) 3876.

31./34. **Ciskei Hiking Trails**   Enquiries and reservations can be made with Ciskei National Tourist Board, P O Box 56, Bisho, Ciskei. Tel (0401) 9-1131, regarding four very interesting trails viz, Amatola Hiking Trail, The Shipwreck Hiking Trail, Double Drift Hiking Trail, and Pirie Hiking Trail.

6 — East London and the Border

35. **Kologha Hiking Trail**   From Isidenge State Forest to Kologha. 35 km, 2 days. Hut equipped with bunks and mattresses. The Regional Director, Eastern Cape Forest Region, PB X7432, King William's Town 5600. Tel (0433) 2-3475.

7 — Transkei and its Wild Coast

36. **Transkei Hiking Trail**   From Port St Johns to Coffee Bay. 60 km, 5 days. Huts equipped with bunks and mattresses. Maximum group 12. The Department of Agriculture and Forestry PB X5002, Umtata, Transkei. Tel (0471) 4322 or 9309.

9 — Zululand and Northern Natal

37. **Mziki Hiking Trail**   Circular routes from Mission Rocks at Eastern Shores Nature Reserve, Lake St Lucia. 38 km, 3 days, 3 circular routes through dune forest and past freshwater lakes. Hut equipped with bunks, mattresses, gas-cooker, lamps, bush shower and toilet. Crockery, cutlery and cooking utensils supplied. Hikers must provide own food and sleeping bags. Maximum 8, minimum 4. Reservation Officer, Natal Parks Board, P O Box 662, Pietermaritzburg 3200. Tel (0331) 5-1514.

38. **Dugandhlovu Hiking Trail**   Circular route starting from Natal Parks Board office at False Bay, 16 km east of Hluhluwe village. Optional 1 or 2 nights, 9 km to the huts. Four huts equipped with beds, cold water shower, gas cooker and bush toilet. Crockery, cutlery and cooking utensils supplied. Hikers must provide own food. Maximum group 16. Reservation Officer, Natal Parks Board, P O Box 662, Pietermaritzburg 3200. Tel (0331) 5-1514.

39./
42. **Umfolozi, Mkuzi and St Lucia Game Reserves and Itala Nature Reserve Wilderness Trails**   From March to November (varying) Natal Parks Board conduct trails in these reserves under the protection and guidance of experienced game rangers. Participants sleep overnight at base camp and tented bush camps and must provide their own food and equipment which is transported for them. These trails last from 3 to 4 days with a maximum of 6 participants and the cost varies between R110 and R165 per person per trail (February 1988) Enquiries and Reservations: Natal Parks Board, P O Box 662, Pietermaritzburg 3200. Tel (0331) 5-1514.

43. **Bosbok Walk, Remedies & Rituals Walk and Ngamanzi Walk**   Three walks ranging from 2 km to 7 km start at the Harold Johnson Nature Reserve camping site near Darnall. The Officer-in-Charge, Harold Johnson Nature Reserve, P O Box 148, Darnall 4480. Tel (0324) 6574.

44. **Ntendeka Wilderness Area near Vryheid**   For information and reservations apply: The State Forester, Ngome State Forest, P B 21306, Vryheid 3100. Tel Hlobane (0386) ask for 883.

10 — Pietermaritzburg, Natal Midlands and Drakensberg

45. **Cedara Forest Walk**   In Cedara State Forest. 10 km, 5 hours. No facilities. The Regional Director, Natal Forest Region, PB 9029, Pietermaritzburg 3200. Tel (0331) 42-8101.

46. **Bushbuck, Dassie and Hoepoe Walks**   From 5 to 10 km, 2 to 5 hours. Circular routes in Weza State Forest from Lorna Doone Forest Hostel – equipped with bunks, tables, benches, stove and ablution facilities. Hostel maximum 30 persons. The Regional Director, Natal Forest Region, PB 9020, Pietermaritzburg 3200. Tel (0331) 42-8101.

47. **Ngele (Ingeli) Hiking Trail**   Circular route in Weza State Forest (near Harding). 50 km, 4 or 5 days, 30 km 3 days. Converted farm houses equipped with bunks and mattresses. Hikers must provide own equipment (including stoves and lighting) and food. Same as 46.

48. **Holkrans Hiking Trail**   Circular route in Drakensberg approximately 25 km south of Newcastle. 18 km, 2 days. Base camp has beds, mattresses, shower, toilets, drinking water, braai facilities, firewood, iron pots and electricity. Holkrans overnight stop has toilet, firewood, iron pots, water in rainy season. Maximum group 30. R5 per day. Mr & Mrs D C P van Niekerk, P O Box 2734, Newcastle 2940. Tel (03435) 600.

49. **Drakensberg, Giant's Cup Hiking Trail**   From Sani Pass to Silver Streams. 63 km, 5 days. 2, 3 or 4 day hikes can also be made. Huts equipped with bunks and mattresses. Maximum group 30. The Regional Director, Natal Forest Region, PB X9029, Pietermaritzburg 3200. Tel (0331) 42-8101.

50./
51. **Drakensberg, Mkhomazi and Mdedelelo Wilderness Areas**   For information and reservations apply: The State Forester, Mkhomazi State Forest, PB X105, Nottingham Road 3280. Tel (033312) ask for 1902, or The State Forester, Monk's Cowl State Forest, PB X2, Winterton 3340. Tel (03682) 2204.

52. **Drakensberg, Mzimkulu Wilderness Area**   For information and reservations apply: Either to The State Forester, Cobham State Forest, P O Box 116, Himeville 4585. Tel (03392) ask for 1831, or The State Forester, Garden Castle State Forest, P O Box 90 Underberg 4590. Tel (3372) 1722.

11 — Johannesburg, Witwatersrand, Southern and Western Transvaal

53. **Bloubos Walk**   Circular route south of Johannesburg. 19 km, 1 day. No facilities. Dr Reid, Klipriviersberg Nature Reserve, P O Box 990140, Johannesburg 2053.

54. **Braamfontein Spruit**   Starts at the source of the Braamfontein Spruit in Hillbrow, then continues through the suburbs of Johannesburg, Randburg and Sandton – forming part of the open space system, linking rivers and ridges throughout the metropolitan area. Total distance 27 km. Send for booklet R2,50 each (plus 20c postage) also maps of Braamfontein and Sandspruit in colour, 50c each. Sandton Civic Foundation, P O Box 78095, Sandton 2146. Tel 784-0317. Sandton Civic Centre, cnr West and Rivonia Roads, Sandown, Sandton.

55. **Suikerbosrand Hiking Trail**   Routes in the Suikerbosrand Nature Reserve, near Heidelberg. 66 km network, 6 days. Six huts equipped with mattresses, cooking pots, kettles, basins, gaslamps, barbecue facilities and firewood. Maximum group 10. The Officer-in-Charge, Suikerbosrand Nature Reserve, PB H616, Heidelberg 2400. Tel (0151) 2181.

56. **Bokmakierie Nature Trail**   Two routes, 10 or 17 km. No facilities. In the Suikerbosrand Nature Reserve. The Officer-in-Charge, Suikerbosrand Nature Reserve, PB H616, Heidelberg 2400. Tel (0151) 2181.

57. **Cheetah Interpretative Trail**   In the Suikerbosrand Nature Reserve. 4 km, 2 hours. Guided by officer or guidebook. The Officer-in-Charge, Suikerbosrand Nature Reserve.

58. **Krugersdorp Game Reserve Trail**   At Krugersdorp. Guided tours on Saturdays and Sundays. 4 km, 4 hours. Six persons per day. Full details from Mrs P A de Winton-Jewers, Tel (011) 665-1473 after 2 pm.

59. **Rustenburg Hiking Trail**   A circular tour in the Rustenburg Nature Reserve from the Koedoe hut to the Hartbees hut on the plateau of the Magaliesberg range. 22 km, 2 days. 2 huts with mattresses. The Officer-in-charge Rustenburg Nature Reserve, P O Box 511, Rustenburg 0300. Tel (01421) 3-1050.

60. **Peglerae Interpretative Trail**   Rustenburg Nature Reserve. 4½ km, 2 hours. Guided tour.

61. **Morelettaspruit Walk**   Pretoria Municipality area. 15 km. No facilities. The City Council of Pretoria, Parks and Recreation Department, P O Box 1451, Pretoria 0001. Tel (012) 21-3411.

62./
63. **Magoebaskloof Hiking Trails**   The two routes, **Dokolewa** and **Grootbosch** both start at the De-Hoek Forest Station and follow the same route for 10 km. Dikolewa, 36 km, 2 to 3 days follows a course through indigenous forest, mountain valleys and past waterfalls and has huts equipped with bunks and mattresses, and the maximum group is 30. Grootbosch, 28 km, 2 days, and the route is through the largest indigenous forest in Transvaal, the ending point being Christnarus, 7 km from Duiwelskloof. For Grootbosch, hikers must provide own tents. The Regional Director, Northern Transvaal Forest Region, PB X2413, Louis Trichardt 0920. Tel (01551) 2202.

64. **Rooikat Walk**   New Agatha State Forest, 18 km south of Tzaneen (near the Coach House). 11 km circular route. Permit required. The State Forester, New Agatha State Forest, PB 4009, Tzaneen 0850. Tel (01523) 2-2347.

65. **Wolkberg Wilderness Area near Tzaneen**   For information and reservations apply: The State Forester, Serala State Forest, Private Bag Haenertsburg, 0730. Tel (0152222) ask for 1303 or New Agatha (01523) 2-2347.

66. **Giraffe Hiking Trail**   In the Hans Merensky Nature Reserve. From the visitors centre to the overnight huts, and circular route returning to same huts the second night and then return to visitors centre. 35 km, 3 days. Three huts equipped with bunks and mattresses. The Officer-in-Charge, Hans Merensky Nature Reserve, PB X502, Letsitele 0885. Tel Lapariza (015238) 632.

67. **Mopanie Interpretative Trail, Letaba Nature Trail and Waterbuck Nature Trail**   1, 5, and 15 km respectively. Circular routes from the visitors centre at Hans Merensky Nature Reserve. The Officer-in-Charge, Hans Merensky Nature Reserve, PB X503, Letsitele 0885. Tel Lapariza (015238) 632.

68. **Soutpansberg Hiking Trail**   From Hangklip Forest Station (3 km from Louis Trichardt) to Entabeni Forest Station. 91 km, 5 days or circular route 21 km, 2 days or 36 km, 2 days. Huts equipped with bunks and mattresses. The Regional Director, Northern Transvaal Forest Region, PB X2413, Louis Trichardt 0920. Tel (01551) 2202.

69. **Ben Lavin Nature Reserve — Tabajwane, Fountain, Waterbuck and Tshumanini Springs Walks**   8, 4, 3, and 5 km respectively. Resort camp near Louis Trichardt, can accommodate 60 persons. P O Box 782, Louis Trichardt 0920. Tel (01551) 3834.

70. **Mabudashango Hiking Trail (Venda)**   54 km, 4 day circular route. Hikers must take own tents. The Director General, Department of Agriculture and Forestry, PB X2247, Sibasa Venda. Tel Venda Tourism: (015581) 21131/6.

71. **Botshabelo Klein Aasvogelkrans Walks**   Two circular routes of 4 hours and 8 hours. From Youth hostel (6 am to 6 pm) near Middelburg. Mrs Ina van Rensburg, Botshabelo, P O Box 141, Middelburg 1050. Tel (01321) 2-3897.

72. **Cycad Hiking Trails — Cycad, Suikerbos, Baboon, Tarentaal**   of 14, 18, 26, and 8 km respectively (2 to 5 days). Thatched huts, field toilets, limited water. Directions: from Middelburg 15 km on Loskop Dam road to left turnoff 'Slaghoek' and further 10 km on gravel road to Cycad Trail signboard, left 2 km to farmhouse. P O Box 1326, Middelburg 1050. Tel (01321) 2-3764.

73. **McManus Walk**   From Sappi's Elandshoogte Plantation (between Machadodorp and Ngodwana). Circular route skirts the edge of the escarpment for half the course. 19 km, half to full day. No facilities. Maximum group 20. The Management Forester, Sappi, P O Box 141, Machadodorp 1170. Tel (013242) 1630.

74. **Elandskrans Hiking Trail**   From Waterval-Boven to Waterval-Onder and by train back to Waterval-Boven. One or two days. One hut. Guided tours. The Manager, Elandskrans Holiday Resort, P O Box 53, Waterval-Boven 1195. Tel (013262) 176.

75. **Gold Nugget Hiking Trail**   From the parking area opposite Barberton Police Station and back to Barberton, following the route of the early miners in their search for gold. 37 km, 2 days, or 44 km, 3 days. Huts equipped with bunks and mattresses. Maximum group 20. Makhonjwa Conservation Foundation, P O Box 221, Barberton 1300. Tel (01314) 2-3373.

76. **Fotuna Mine Walk**   Circular route through Barberton's indigenous tree park and through 600-metre-long tunnel. Whole route 2 km. Barberton Publicity Association. Tel (01314) 3373.

77./
79. **Kruger National Park Wilderness Trails — Wolhuter and Boesman**   (both between Pretoriuskop and Malelane in the south), **Olifants** (near Letaba in the central area) and **Nyalaland** (near Punda Maria in the north) – are four fascinating trails under the protection and guidance of experienced game rangers, lasting for 3 nights sleeping in tents in the bush. All equipment and food is supplied and transported by the National Parks Board. The cost per person per trail is R130 (1988), and there is an age restriction, between 12 and 60 years, with a maximum group of 8 persons per trail. The Chief Director, National Parks Board, P O Box 787, Pretoria 0001. Tel (012) Enquiries 44-1171, Reservations 343-1991.

80. **Fanie Botha Hiking Trail**   The first hiking trail to be opened by the Department of Forestry (in 1973). It covers a beautiful portion of the Eastern Transvaal escarpment and was named after the Minister of Forestry at the time. The trail starts from Ceylon State Forest, near Sabie and close to the Bridal Veil Falls. It follows a route through the pine forest to the first hut, Maritzbos, and then winds up Mount Anderson (2 286 m) and then on past the Mac-Mac Falls to the Graskop hut and God's Window. 79 km, 5 days or 2 circular routes of 3 days each. Huts with bunks and mattresses. The Regional Director, Eastern Transvaal Forest Region, PB X503, Sabie 1260. Tel (0131512) ask for 307. Maximum group 30.

81. **Blyderivierspoort (Blyde River Canyon) Hiking Trail**   From God's Window to Swadini in the Sybrand van Niekerk Holiday Resort (Overvaal) 65 km, 5 days or 32 km, 2 days. Huts with bunks and mattresses. Maximum group 30. The Regional Director, Eastern Transvaal Forest Region, PB X503, Sabie 1260. Tel (0131512) ask for 307.

82. **Loerie Walk**   Starting at Ceylon Forest Station (same as for Fanie Botha Hiking Trail) near Sabie. 14 km walk. No facilities. No reservation, report to the State Forester. Tel (0131512) ask for 659.

83. **Prospector's Hiking Trail**   From Mac-Mac via Pilgrim's Rest to Bourke's Luck Potholes. 69 km and 55 km, 5 days each, shorter circular routes optional. Huts equipped with mattresses. Maximum 30. The Regional Director, Eastern Transvaal Forest Region, PB X503, Sabie 1260. Tel (0131512) ask for 307.

84. **Forest Falls Walk**   From Mac-Mac Forest Station, 4 km circular walk between Sabie and Graskop. No facilities. Report to State Forester, Mac-Mac State Forest Station. Tel (0131512) ask for 2002.

85. **Eerste Liefde Hiking Trail**   From Bourke's Luck Potholes to Eerste Liefde and return. 24 km 2 days. Bourke's Luck has 4 stone huts equipped with bunks, mattresses, braai places, firewood, toilet and open-air shower. Eerste Liefde has one hut with bunks and mattresses. Maximum group 20. Information Section, Blyderivierspoort Nature Reserve. P O Bourke's Luck 1272. Tel trunks 0020 and ask for Bourke's Luck 15.

86. **Op-de-Berg Hiking Trail**   From Bourke's Luck Potholes via Muilhuis to Op-de-Berg near Devil's Window and return to Bourke's Luck. Bourke's Luck facilities see Eerste Liefde above. Muilhuis has a primitive cottage with beds and mattresses. Op-de-Berg has log cabin with beds and mattresses. Maximum group 10. Information Section, Blyderivierspoort Nature Reserve, P O Bourke's Luck 1272. Tel trunks 0020 and ask for Bourke's Luck 15.

87. **Bushman's Nature Trail**   From Bourke's Luck. 5 km, 4 hours. No facilities. Officer-in-Charge Blyderivierspoort Nature Reserve, Tel trunks 0020 and ask for Bourke's Luck 15.

88. **Nature Trails from F H Odendaal Resort, Blyderivierspoort Nature Reserve**   Kadishi 5 km, Potholes 1 km, Leopard 5 km, 4 hours, Loerie 3 km, 2 hours, Tarentaal 4 km up to 3 hrs, Tufa 2 km, 1½ hours. Sycomorus Interpretative Trail 2 km, 2½ hours. Tel (0020) Bourke's Luck 15.

89. **Nature and Interpretative Trails from Sybrand van Niekerk Resort, Swadini Nature Reserve**   Marieps 1 km, 3 hours, Skiereiland 2 km, 3 hours, Waterval 2 km, 2 hours. Tel (0131732) 4904.

90. **Mount Sheba Walks**   A number of short trail routes in and around the indigenous forest of the Mount Sheba Nature Reserve. Accommodation at the hotel. Maps, brochures and information at reception desk. Mount Sheba Hotel, P O Box 100, Pilgrim's Rest 1290. Tel 0131532 ask for 17 or 64.

13 — Orange Free State

91. **Rhebok Hiking Trail**   Golden Gate Highlands National Park circular route starting at Glen Reenen Rest Camp. 30 km, 2 days. One hut equipped with beds. Maximum group 18. Bookings within 3 days of intended participation: Tel Clarens (0143262) ask for 61. Postal enquiries: The Chief Director, National Parks Board, P O Box 787, Pretoria 0001. Tel (012) Enquiries 44-1171 Reservations 343-1991.

92. **Brandwater Hiking Trail**   A five day circular route near Fouriesburg. 68 km, 5 days. Overnight in open caves or sandstone house. Maximum group 30. Write the Town Clerk, Fouriesburg 9725. Tel (014332) 14, 88, or 185.

93. **Korannaberg Hiking Trail**   A circular route near Marquard. 34 km, 2 days. Hut at starting point for first night and second night in open cave. Maximum group 25. The Secretary, Wildlife Society, P O Box 140, Marquard 9610. Tel (05272) 1930.

94. **Tussen-die-Riviere Game Farm**   6 to 18 km walks near Bethulie and Aliwal North. Open between 1 September and 30 April annually. No facilities. The Director, Nature Conservation OFS, P O Box 517, Bloemfontein 9300. Tel (051) 7-0511.

14 — Northern Cape

95. **Klipspringer Hiking Trail**   Circular route in the Augrabies National Park, starting at the Augrabies Falls caravan park, via Twin Falls, Oranjekom and Echo Corner and return. Huts equipped with bunks and fireplaces. Maximum group 12. The Chief Director, National Parks Board, P O Box 787, Pretoria 0001. Tel (012) Enquiries 44-1171 Reservations 343-1991.

15 — Bophuthatswana

96. **Pilanesberg Game Reserve at Sun City**   Guided Trails, 3½ days. Return to tent camp each night. Eating and cooking facilities available. Maximum group 6. Cost per trail R100. The Tourist Officer. P O Box 1201, Mogwase 0302. Bophuthatswana. Tel (014292) 2405.

Distance Table

Approximate Distances in Kilometres	Bloemfontein	Cape Town	Durban	East London	Gaborone	Grahamstown	Johannesburg	Kimberley	Maputo	Maseru	Mbabane	Port Elizabeth	Pretoria	Welkom	Windhoek
Beaufort West	544	471	1192	605	1042	492	950	504	1352	609	1129	501	1008	697	1629
Bloemfontein	–	1015	648	584	622	601	406	177	900	157	677	677	464	153	1593
Britstown	398	722	1046	609	791	496	725	253	1298	555	1075	572	783	551	1378
Cape Town	1015	–	1776	1100	1513	920	1421	975	1915	1172	1692	790	1479	1168	1500
Colesberg	226	789	874	488	848	375	632	292	1126	383	903	451	690	379	1573
De Aar	346	774	994	557	843	444	752	305	1246	503	1023	520	810	499	1430
Durban	648	1776	–	676	993	856	602	825	625	604	562	986	660	578	2240
East London	584	1100	676	–	1206	180	990	780	1301	630	1238	310	1048	737	1985
Gaborone	622	1513	993	1206	–	1223	358	538	960	702	719	1299	350	479	1735
George	773	447	1329	653	1361	473	1197	762	1673	913	1450	343	1237	926	1887
Graaff-Reinet	424	681	944	395	1012	282	830	490	1324	599	1101	291	888	577	1697
Grahamstown	601	920	856	180	1223	–	1007	667	1481	692	1418	130	1065	754	1856
Harrismith	328	1343	320	834	673	929	282	505	652	284	468	1068	340	258	1921
Johannesburg	406	1421	602	990	358	1007	–	472	602	438	361	1083	58	266	1801
Keetmanshoop	1088	995	1736	1482	1230	1351	1296	911	1898	1245	1657	1445	1354	1205	505
Kimberley	177	975	825	780	538	667	472	–	1074	334	833	743	523	294	1416
Klerksdorp	288	1283	659	872	334	889	164	308	766	368	525	1009	222	145	1693
Kroonstad	211	1226	551	795	442	812	195	339	745	247	522	888	253	71	1724
Ladysmith	410	1425	238	752	755	932	364	587	570	366	385	1062	422	340	1497
Mmabatho	468	1359	839	1039	154	1069	291	384	894	549	653	1145	299	325	1069
Messina	953	1968	1149	1537	696	1554	547	1019	706	985	808	1630	489	813	2348
Nelspruit	760	1777	712	1228	392	1361	358	830	244	716	173	1437	344	642	2159
Oudtshoorn	743	506	1304	712	1241	532	1190	703	1708	959	1420	402	1207	896	1828
Pietermaritzburg	567	1695	81	595	912	775	521	744	706	523	643	905	579	497	2160
Pietersburg	742	1757	938	1326	485	1343	336	808	586	774	515	1419	278	602	2137
Port Elizabeth	677	790	986	310	1299	130	1083	743	1611	822	1548	–	1141	830	1950
Pretoria	464	1479	660	1048	350	1065	58	523	586	496	372	1141	–	324	1859
Queenstown	377	1307	678	207	999	269	783	554	1303	423	1240	399	841	525	1829
Umtata	570	1335	441	235	1192	415	881	747	1066	616	1003	545	939	718	2066
Upington	588	894	1236	982	730	851	796	411	1398	745	1157	945	854	669	1005
Welkom	153	1168	578	737	479	754	266	294	816	249	451	830	324	–	1679
Windhoek	1593	1500	2240	1988	1735	1856	1801	1416	2403	1750	2162	1950	1859	1679	–

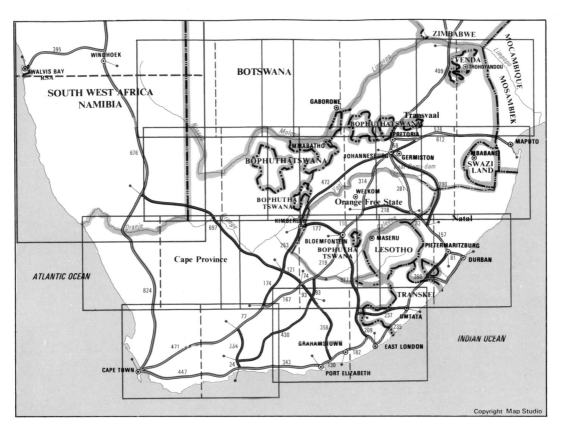

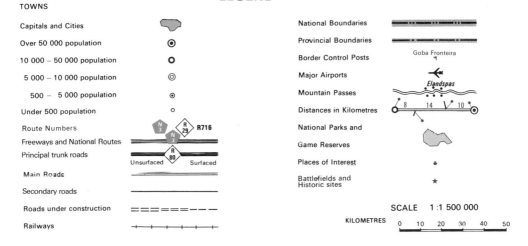

LEGEND

TOWNS

Capitals and Cities

Over 50 000 population

10 000 – 50 000 population

5 000 – 10 000 population

500 – 5 000 population

Under 500 population

Route Numbers

Freeways and National Routes

Principal trunk roads

Unsurfaced   Surfaced

Main Roads

Secondary roads

Roads under construction

Railways

National Boundaries

Provincial Boundaries

Border Control Posts

       Goba Fronteira

Major Airports

Mountain Passes

      Elandspas

Distances in Kilometres

   8   14   10

National Parks and

Game Reserves

Places of Interest

Battlefields and
Historic sites

SCALE   1 : 1 500 000

KILOMETRES   0   10   20   30   40   50

NATIONAL ROUTES – Declared national routes and roads which form part of such routes, pending completion of the National Freeway System.

MAJOR ROUTES – Inter-regional routes, generally connecting reasonably sized towns and consisting of fairly high standard roads.

MINOR ROUTES – Local routes connecting smaller towns or tourist areas.

A new route numbering system is being introduced on a phased basis. Motorists are therefore advised that during this transition period, the route numbers appearing in this publication may not always coincide with the numbers shown on the roads themselves.
The latest route numbers are featured on these maps, but it may take some time before the authorities have erected the correct numbers or changed the existing ones, on the roads themselves.

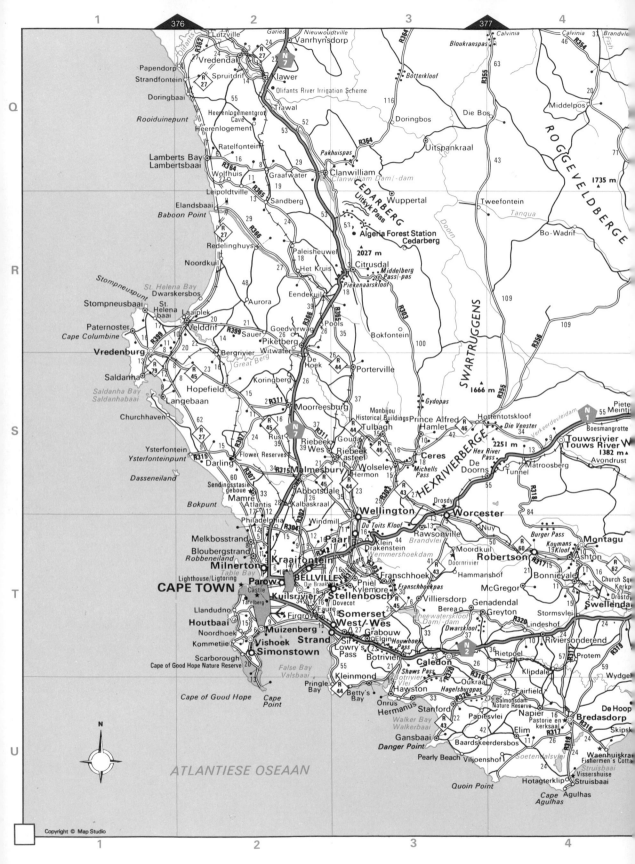

1	2	3	4

Q

Lutzville
Gariep
Nieuwoudtville
Calvinia
Calvinia
Brandvlei
Fish
Vanrhynsdorp
Bloukranspas
Vredendal
Papendorp
Spruitdrif
Klawer
Strandfontein
Olifants River Irrigation Scheme
Botterkloof
Die Bos
Middelpos
Doringbaai
Heerenlogementgrot
Cave
Trawal
Doringbos
Heerenlogement
Rooiduinepunt
Ratelfontein
Pakhuispas
Uitspankraal
1735 m
Lamberts Bay
Lambertsbaai
Wolfhuis
Clanwilliam
Clanwilliam Dam/-dam
Graafwater
Wuppertal
Tweefontein
Leipoldtville
Sandberg
Uitkykpas
Doorn
Tanqua
Bo-Wadrif
Elandsbaai
Baboon Point
Redelinghuys
Algeria Forest Station
Cedarberg
Paleisheuwel
2027 m
Noordkuil
Het Kruis
Citrusdal
Middelberg
Pass/-pas
Piekenaarskloof
Stompneuspunt
St. Helena Bay
Dwarskersbos
Eendekuil
Stompneusbaai
St. Helena baai
Aurora
Paternoster
Laaiplek
Velddrif
Goedverwag
Pools
Bokfontein
Cape Columbine
Sauer
Piketberg
Vredenburg
Bergrivier
Witwater
Saldanha
De Hoek
Porterville
Hopefield
Koringberg
Saldanha Bay
Saldanhabaai
Langebaan
Moorreesburg
Gydopas
1666 m
Churchhaven
Monbijou
Historical Buildings
Prince Alfred
Hamlet
Hottentotskloof
Piete
Meintj
Ysterfontein
Tulbagh
Die Venster
Touwsrivier
Touws River
Ysterfonteinpunt
Darling
Riebeek
Wes
Riebeek
Kasteel
Wolseley
Ceres
Michells Pass
De
Doorns
Avondrust
Dasseneiland
Flower Reserves
Malmesbury
Hermon
Hex River
Pass
Tunnel
Matroosberg
Bokpunt
Sendingstasie
geboue
Abbotsdale
Drosdy
HEXRIVIERBERGE
Mamre
Atlantis
Kalbaskraal
Wellington
Worcester
Philadelphia
Windmill
Du Toits Kloof
Rawsonville
Nuy
Burger Pass
Montagu
Melkbosstrand
Paarl
Klein
Drakenstein
Wemmershoekdam
Brandvlei
Moordkuil
Koymans
Kloof
Ashton
Bloubergstrand
Robbeneiland
Franschhoek
Doornrivier
Robertson
Bonnievale
Milnerton
Table Bay
Pniel
Kylemore
Franschhoekpas
Hammanshof
Church Sq
Kraaifontein
Kuilsrivier
Stellenbosch
Villiersdorp
McGregor
Drostd
CAPE TOWN
Parow
BELLVILLE
Die Braak
Dovecot
Berea
Genadendal
Greyton
Stormsvlei
Swellenda
Castle
Tafelberg
Faure
Somerset
West/-Wes
Theewaterskloof
Dam/-dam
Dwarskloof
Lindeshof
Llandudno
Firgrove
Grabouw
Houtbaai
Muizenberg
Sir
Lowry's
Pass
Elgin
Houwhoek
Pass
Riviersonderend
Noordhoek
Strand
Botrivier
Rietpoel
Protem
Kommetjie
Botrivier
Caledon
Klipdale
Scarborough
Vishoek
Simonstown
Kleinmond
Shaws Pass
Oukraal
Fairfield
Wydge
Cape of Good Hope Nature Reserve
False Bay
Valsbaai
Pringle
Bay
Hawston
Hagelsburgpas
Salmonsdam
Nature Reserve
De Hoop
Cape of Good Hope
Cape
Point
Onrus
Hermanus
Stanford
Napier
Pastorie en
kerksaal
Bredasdorp
Skipsk
Papiesvlei
Elim
Gansbaai
Baardskeerdersbos
Waenhuiskra
Danger Point
Soetendalsvlei
Vissershuise
Struisbaai
Pearly Beach
Viljoenshof
Hotagterklip
Struisbaai
Quoin Point
Cape
Agulhas
Agulhas

ATLANTIESE OSEAAN

N

Copyright © Map Studio

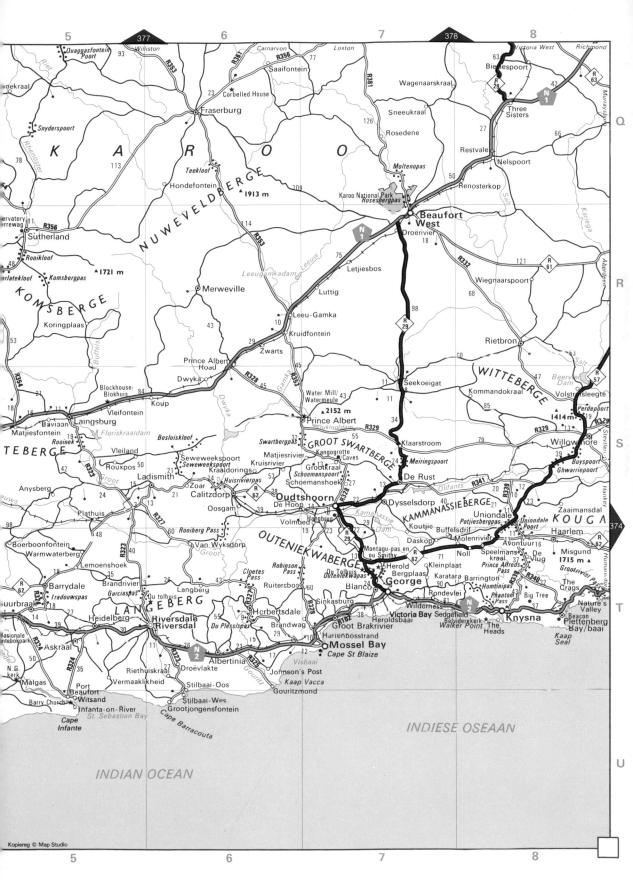

377

378

Riet

Quaggasfontein
Poort

93

Williston

Carnarvon

Loxton

Saaifontein

R356

77

Victoria West

Richmond

63

Bienesport

42

R63

nekraal

R353

R397

R381

Wagenaarskraal

N1

Three
Sisters

Q

23

Corbelled House

Fraserburg

Sneeukraal

126

Rosedene

27

66

Snyderspoort

78

K A R O O

113

Teekloof

Hondefontein

109

1913 m

Restvale

Nelspoort

Renosterkop

Moltenopas

Karoo National Park
Rosesbergpas

50

Beaufort
West

Droërivier

18

R332

121

R61

servatory
rreweg

R356

Sutherland

114

N U W E V E L D B E R G E

R353

N1

75

Letjiesbos

Leeugamkadam

Leeuw

R

Rooikloof

48

1721 m

Komsbergpas

rlatekloof

Merweville

Luttig

68

Wiegnaarspoort

Beervlei
Dam

47

K O M S B E R G E

Koringplaas

53

R354

10

Leeu-Gamka

98

R
29

Rietbron

R57

43

29

Kruidfontein

Buffels

18

16

11

R328

45

Zwarts

Prince Albert
Road

Dwyka

45

Gamka

Water Mill/
Watermeule

43

Seekoeigat

11

Kommandokraal

60

W I T T E B E R G E

Salt

Volstruisleegte

Perdepoort

19

R329

Vleifontein

84

Blockhouse/
Blokhuis

Koup

2152 m

11

34

85

1414 m

Baviaan

R353

Laingsburg

Prince Albert
Oukloofdam

R329

13

Willowmore

R

Floriskraaldam

Matjiesfontein

19

Rooinek

Bosluiskloof

Swartbergpas

32

R329

Klaarstroom

79

39

Buyspoort

Ghwarriepoort

T E B E R G E

Groot

Vleiland

42

Seweweekspoort
Seweweekspoort

Kraaldoringos

Matjiesrivier

Kruisrivier

GROOT SWARTBERGE

Kangogrotte
Caves

Grootkraal

55

24

Meiringspoort

Olifants

R341

De Rust

Anysberg

24

Ladismith

R323

50

Groot

Schoemanspoort

Schoemanshoek

53

27

13

R339

20

12

Zaaimansdal

R374

Plathuis

R327

21

Calitzdorp

R
62

De Hoop

R328

Oudtshoorn

Dysselsdorp

40

KAMMANASSIEBERGE

21

K O U G A

Uniondale

R62

Oosgam

39

Hangbrug

13

Uniondale
Poort

Haarlem

98

Boerboonfontein

R323

Rooiberg Pass

60

Volmoed

23

22

Koutjie

Buffelsdrif

Avontuur

16

1715 m

Grootrivier Pass

Warmwaterberg

40

Van Wyksdorp

19

*Kamanassie
Dam*

29

R
62

Daskop

Molenrivier

71

Noll

Speelmans
kraal

*Prince Alfreds
Pass*

37

De
Vlug

The
Crags

Lemoenshoek

OUTENIEKWABERGE

Montagu-pas en
ou Smithy

Herold
Bergplaas

R339

R340

R62

Barrydale

Iradouwspas

Brandrivier

Garciaspas

3

L A N G E B E R G

26

43

Langberg

Du Tolhuis
Outeniekwapas

Blanco

George

Karatara

Barrington

90

Homtinipas

*Phantom
Pass*

Big Tree

57

Nature's
Valley

Beacon

uurbraak

18

27

Heidelberg

55

Robinson
Pass

*Cloetes
Pass*

Ou tolhuis

Ruitersbos

R328

Sinkasburg

24

Rondevlei

Kleinplaat

61

N2

Wilderness

Sedgefield

Belvidererk

Knysna

Plettenberg
Bay/baai

14

R323

39

Riversdale
Riversdal

Langbergy

Du Plessispas

Herbertsdale

R102

38

Victoria Bay

Walker Point

*The
Heads*

*Kaap
Seal*

30

11

26

21

15

Brandwag

Groot Brakrivier

Heroldsbaai

R314

Askraal

R324

35

Riethuiskraal

27

R322

N2

Albertinia

R325

17

12

Mossel Bay
Cape St Blaize

Visbaai

50

Malgas

Port
Beaufort
Witsand

Vermaaklikheid

Stilbaai-Oos

Droëvlakte

Gouritz

Johnson's Post

Kaap Vacca

Gouritzmond

N G
kerk

Barry Church

Infanta-on-River

Stilbaai-Wes

Grootjongensfontein

*Cape
Infante*

St. Sebastian Bay

Cape Barracouta

INDIESE OSEAAN

INDIAN OCEAN

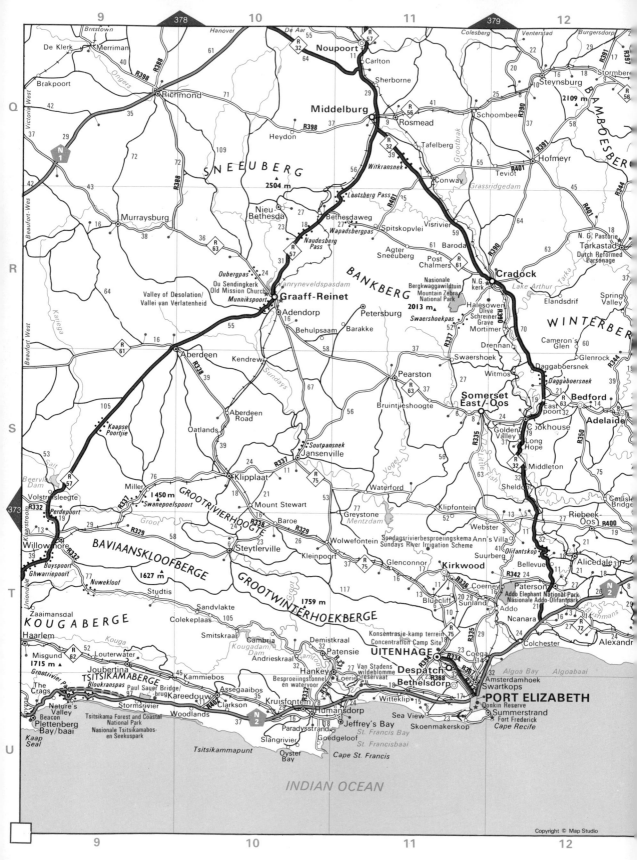

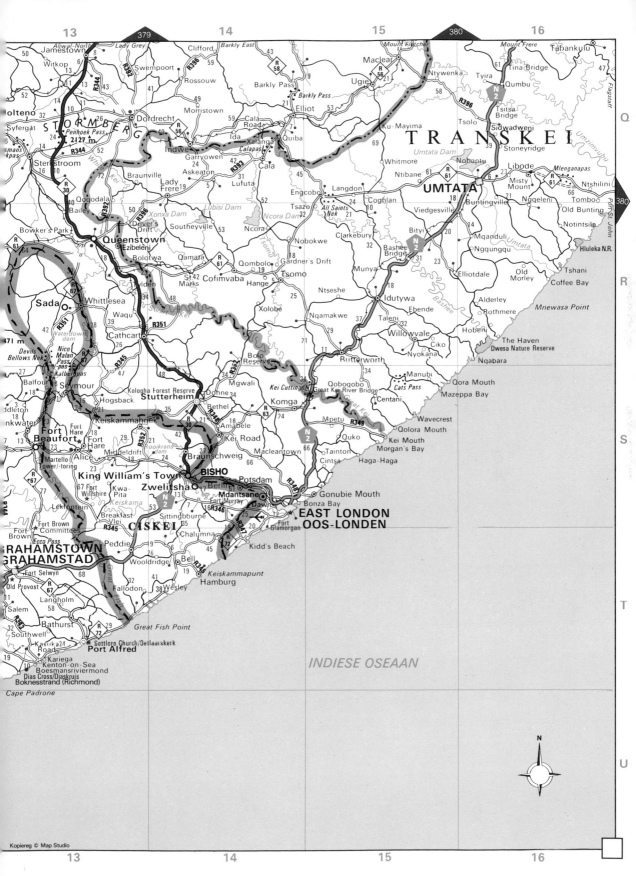

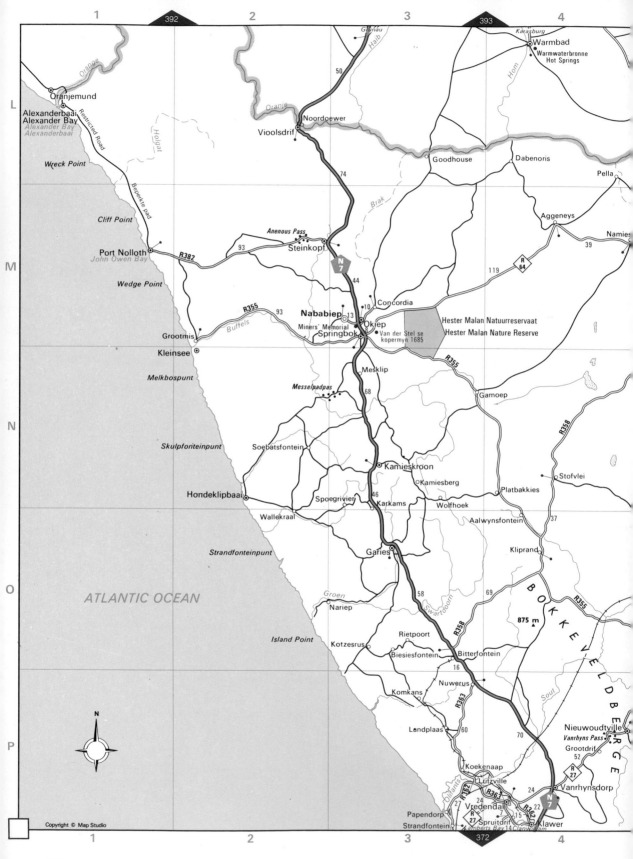

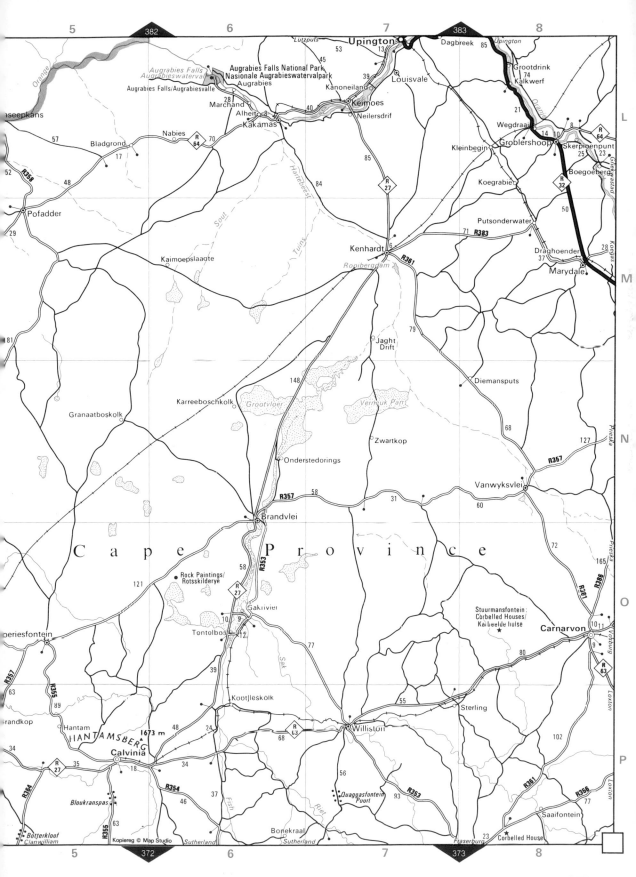

Orange

Lutzputs
53
Upington
13
Dagbreek   85   Upington
Grootdrink
74
Kalkwerf

Augrabies Falls National Park
Nasionale Augrabieswatervalpark
Augrabies Falls/Augrabieswaterval
Augrabies Falls/Augrabiesvalle
Augrabies
45
39
Louisvale
Kanoneiland
Marchand
28
Alheit   8
Kakamas
Keimoes
Neilersdrif
21
Wegdraai
14 10
R 64
seepkans

Nabies
R 64
70
57
Bladgrond
17
Harteheest
Kleinbegin
Groblershoop
Skerpioenpunt
25   23
L

52   R358
48
Sout
85
Koegrabie
R 32
Boegoeberg

Pofadder
29
84
R 27
Putsonderwater
50

81
Kaimoepslaagte
Tuins
Kenhardt   6
R361
71   R383
Draghoender
37
Marydale
28
Kongas

Rooibergdam 2
Jaght
Drift
79
Diemansputs

148
Karreeboschkolk
Grootvloer
Verneuk Pan
68
127
N

Zwartkop
R367

Onderstedorings
Vanwyksvlei
60

R357   58
31
72
165
R368
Priska

Brandvlei
Granaatboskolk
Cape   Province
Rock Paintings/
Rotsskilderye
58
R353
R 27
121
Stuurmansfontein:
Corbelled Houses/
Karbeelde huise
Carnarvon
Vosburg
10 11
O
R 63
9

oeriesfontein
Gakrivier
10   9
Tontolbos
12
77
80
R 63

R357
R355
63
89
Sak
39
Kootjieskolk
55
Sterling
102
P

randkop
Hantam   1673 m
HANTAMSBERG
48
24
R 63
68
Williston
R353
93
Saaifontein
77

34
Calvinia
R 27
35
18
34
56
R361
R366

R364
R354
37
Fish
46
Quaggasfontein
Poort
Corbelled House

Bloukranspas
R355
63
Botterkloof
Clanwilliam
Kopiereg © Map Studio
Sutherland
Bonekraal
Sutherland
Fraserburg
23
Loxton

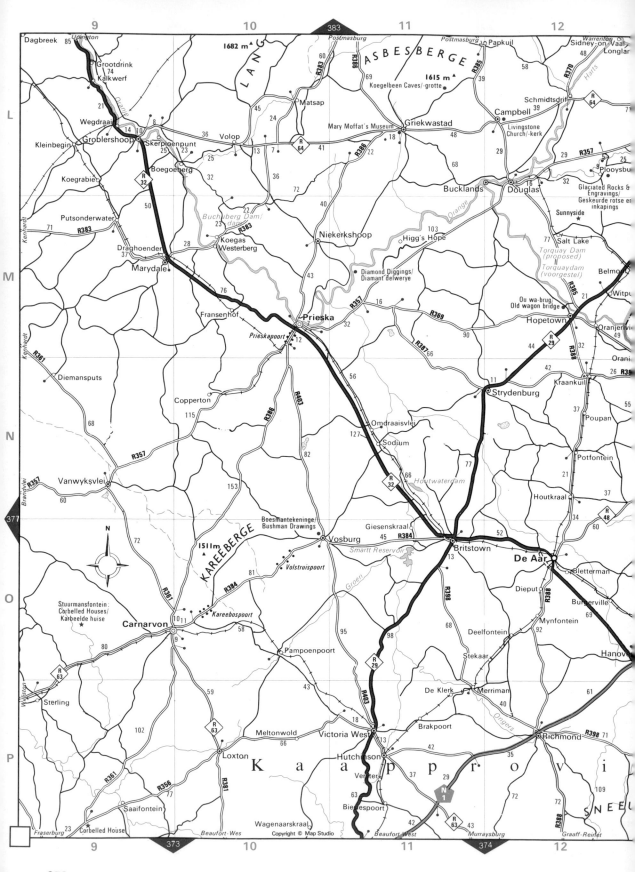

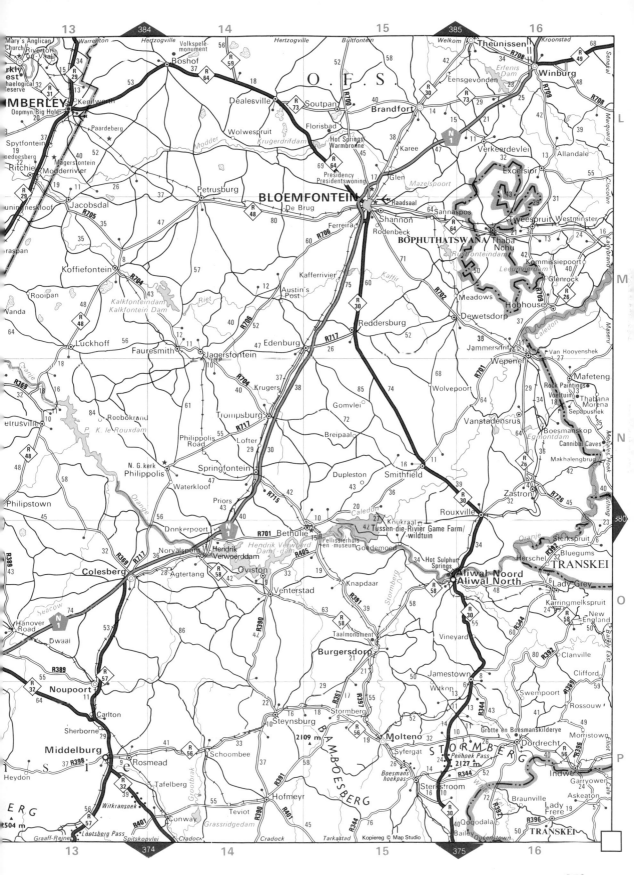

17 **18** **19** **20**

Welkom Kroonstad
Theunissen Senekal Harrismith Swinburn
R708 R49 68 23 Kestell Swinburn
Erfenis R707 Sehlaba ROOIBERGE Golden Gate Highlands Van Reenen 31
Eensgevonden Dam Winburg 45 71 Rosendal National Park Pass/-pas Wyfe
R30 R73 48 26 51 Clarens Nasionale Golden 61 Phuthaditjhaba Geluksbur
14 29 Marquard 2408 m 2477 m Gate Hoooglandpark QWAQWA
L 15 Fouriesburg Rotstekeninge
Verkeerdevlei 39 R711 10 Hendrick's The Cavern Oliviershoekpas
47 11 8 53 19 7 Drift Libono Hotel
32 13 Allandale Gumtree R26 Joel's Drift Qhobela Witsieshoek Mont-Aux- R616
Excelsior Clocolan Ficksburg Caledonspoort Butha-Buthe Mountain Resort Sources Bergville
55 23 18 31 Hlotse Prehistoric Footprints 3285 m Royal Natal National Cathedral
BOPHUTHA- 16 Peka Fort (Leribe) Khabos Woodstock Dam Park Peak
TSWANA Pekabrug 17 Corn Matlameng 3277 m Cathkin
64 Sannaspos 35 Kolonyama Exchange Mothae Letseng-la-Terai Park
R64 Tweespruit Westminster Rotsskilderye St. Theresa Pitseng Kao Champagne
Thaba Rock Paintings Mamates Mapoteng Lejone Castle
Nchu Ladybrand Teyateyaneng Giant's Cast
13 Kommissiepoort Maserubrug Mohatlanes Moletsane Tlokoeng Mokhotlong Game Reser
50 Glenrock MASERU Sefikeng MALUTI
M Leeuwrivierdam Thaba Bosiu 3482 m Loteni Natu
Meadows Moshoeshoe's Matelas Boesmans Pass Reserv
Dewetsdorp R26 Mountain Fortress Roma Blue Mountain Pass Sehonghong Boesmansnek Sani Pass/-pas
33 Mazenod Makhaleng Marakabei Mantsonyane Thaba Mashai Sanipass
Jammersdrift Institute 77 Tseka Sani
Wepener Van Rooyenshek Tlalis Himeville Hotel
R701 Mafeteng Matsieng L E S O T H O Drakensberg
Rock Paintings Morija Raleqheka Linakeng Garden
Wolvepoort Voeltuin Thabana Malealea 3096 m Underberg
64 Sepapushek Morena Sehlabathebe Coleford
Vanstadensrus Boesmanskop THABA PUTSOA Mokopung Sehlabathebe National Park -natuurreservaat
Egmontdam Cannibal Caves Patlong Coleford
R26 Makhalengbrug Mohales Hoek Seforong Tsoelike Kingscote R394
Zastron Kubung Qacha's Nek Ramatselisohek 29
Cutting Camp Paul Kruger-Inskripsie Mafube Swartberg
Rouxville Mekaling Mt. Chief Moorosi's Lehlohonolo 18 New 16 Franklin
379 Sepapala Moorosi Mountain Fortress Ongeluksnek 34 Amalfi 21
Warm Swawel Moyeni (Quthing) Tosing Roamer's 38 10 R56 Adam Kok
bronne Palmietfontein Rock Thaba Rest Cedarville Bonny se laer/
Hot Sulphur Sterkspruit Tellebrug Paintings Chitja Matatiele Ridge Laager
Aliwal-Noord Herschel Bluegums Sigoga 11 Kokstad
Aliwal North TRANSKEI Kiniraoport 61 Colonanek N2
R58 Lady Grey 2771 m Lundean's Mount 66 Brooks Nek
Karringmelkspruit Nek Naudesnek Fletcher 12 Rode Fort
Vineyard R393 Rhodes R396 Lower Tina 35 Donald
55 New Mosheshs Ford Elands Pitseng Lahlangubo Mount
60 England Height Moordenaarsnek Ayliff
Jamestown Clanville Barkly 58 Katkop Tabankulu Magusheni
80 East Halcyon Triple Streams
Witkop Clifford Drift Mount Frere 18
R344 Swempoort Rossouw Maclear Ntywenka Tyira Tina Bridge Flagstaff
Barkly Pass Ugie Qumbu N2
Vineyard Morristown Barkly Pass Ntibane Tsitsa Palmerto
Elliot Ku-Mayima Bridge R61
STORMBERG Penhoek Pass Indwe Ida Xalanga Quiba Tsolo Sidwadweni Lusikisiki
2127 m Garryowen Calapas Stoneyridge Rock of Execution/ Port
R344 Askeaton Cala Whitmore Nobantu Rots van eksekusie St. Johns
Braunville Lufuta Ntibane Libode Mlenganapas Gemvale
Lady Langdon UMTATA Misty Ngqeleni Ntshilini
Oqodala Frere Engcobo Coghlan Mount Tomboo Port
Bailey Queenstown R396 Tsazo Buntingville Viedgesville Mt Thesiger N R Old Bunting St. Johns
Lubisi Dam Ncora Dam Cofimvaba Tsomo All Saints Idutywa Copyright © Map Studio
Nek

17 **18** **19** **20**

L

M

N

INDIAN OCEAN

INDIESE OSEAAN

O

Aliwal Shoal

N

P

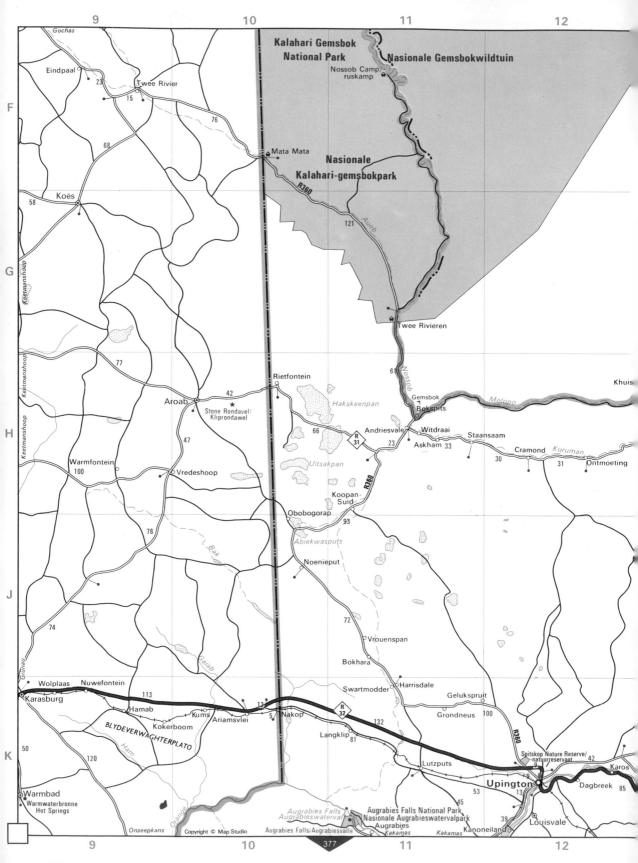

Gochas

Kalahari Gemsbok
National Park

Nasionale Gemsbokwildtuin

Nossob Camp/
ruskamp

Eindpaal

23

Twee Rivier

15

F

76

68

Mata Mata

Nasionale
Kalahari-gemsbokpark

R360

58

Koës

Auob

121

G

Keetmanshoop

Keetmanshoop

Twee Rivieren

61

77

Nossob

Molopo

Khuis

Rietfontein

42

Haskeenpan

Gemsbok
Bokspits

Aroab

Stone Rondavel/
Kliprondawel

66

Andriesvale

Witdraai

Staansaam

H

47

R
31

23

Askham 33

Cramond

Kuruman

Warmfontein
100

Vredeshoop

Uitsakpan

30

31

Ontmoeting

R360

Koopan-
Suid

Obobogorap

93

78

Abiekwasputs

Bak

Noenieput

J

72

74

Vrouenspan

Giriau

Bokhara

Wolplaas

Nuwefontein

Swartmodder

Harrisdale

Gelukspruit

113

12

Karasburg

Hamab

Kums

Ariamsvlei

5

Nakop

R
32

132

Grondneus

100

R360

Kokerboom

Langklip

81

BLYDEVERWAGHTERPLATO

Ham

Spitskop Nature Reserve/
natuurreservaat

42

K

50

120

Lutzputs

9

Karos

Warmbad

53

45

Upington

13

Dagbreek

85

Warmwaterbronne
Hot Springs

Orange

Onseepkans

Copyright © Map Studio

Augrabies Falls
Augrabieswaterval

Augrabies Falls National Park
Nasionale Augrabieswatervalpark
Augrabies

39

Louisvale

Augrabies Falls/Augrabiesvalle

Kakamas

Kakamas

Kanoneiland

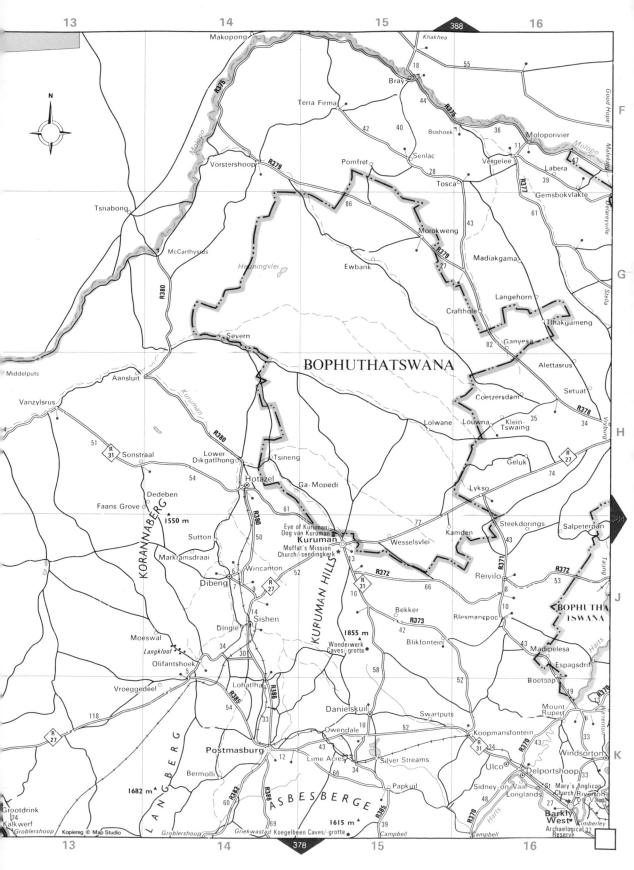

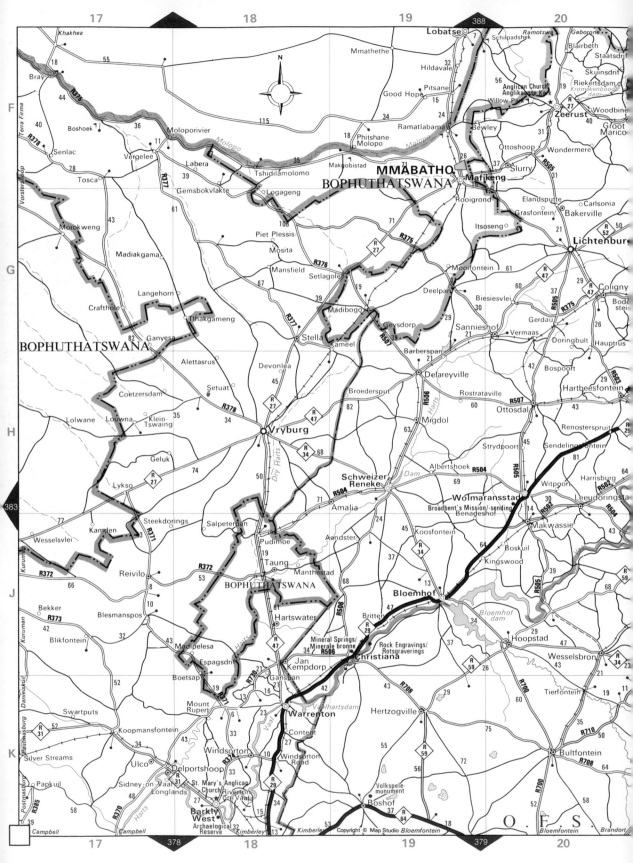

Khakhea

Lobatse 388

Mmathethe

Hildavale

Ramotswa Gaborone

Bray 18 55

R375

44 Good Hope Pitsane 56 Anglican Church/
Anglikaanse Kerk

Schiladshek Blairbeth

Staatsdrif

Skuinsdrif

Riekertsdam

Willow Park 19 Kromellenboog
dam Woodbine

40 Boshoek 36 Moloporivier 34 Ramatlabama Bewley R27 Zeerust 40 Groot
Marico

Senlac 11 18 Phitshane
Molopo 26 Ottoshoop 31 Wondermere

Terra Firma

R378 Vorstershoop

Vergelee 28 Labera 35 Makoobistad Mafikeng 37 Slurry R505 31

Tosca 39 Tshidilamolomo MMABATHO Elandsputte Carlsonia

Gemsbokvlakte BOPHUTHATSWANA Rooigrond Grasfontein Bakerville

Logageng 71 Itsoseng 21 50
R52 Lichtenbur

Morokweng 43 61 108 Piet Plessis R375 Mooifontein 61 R47 29 Coligny

Madiakgama R376 Setlagole R27 Deelpan 60 R505 R375 Bode
stei

Langehorn 67 39 19 Biesiesvlei 30 Gerdau 26

Crafthole Madibogo Geysdorp 29 Sannieshof 21 Vermaas Doringbult Hauptrus

BOPHUTHATSWANA 82 Ganyesa Stella Kameel R507 39 Barberspan 21 42 Bospoort

Alettasrus Devonlea 45 Delareyville R506 Rostrataville R507 Ottosdal 43 Hartbeesfontein R503

Coetzersdam Setuat R27 Broedersput 82 Harts Migdol 60 Renosterspruit R29

Lolwane Louwna Klein-
Tswaing 35 R378 47 63 Strydpoort 45 Sendelingsfontein 81 R502

Kamden R371 Steekdorings Salpeterpan Pudimoe Schweizer-
Reneke Dam Albertshoek R504 69 Witpoort Harrisburg 64

Geluk 74 50 71 Amalia R504 Wolmaransstad Broadbent's Mission/-sending Benadeshof 14 30 Leeudoringsta

Lykso R27 Reivilo 53 Taung Manthestad 68 45 Koosfontein R34 Boskuil Kingswood 39

Wesselsvlei R372 66 8 10 19 Bloemhof 13 Makwassie R505 68

Bekker R373 Blesmanspos 32 43 Hartswater R506 Britten R29 Bloemhof
dam 34 Hoopstad 29 R59

Blikfontein Madipelesa R47 Mineral Springs/
Minerale bronne R506 Rock Engravings/
Rotsgraverings 37 Wesselsbron R34 23

52 Espagsdrif Boetsap 19 16 Jan
Kempdorp Christiana R59 26 R700 21 11

Swartputs Mount
Rupert R371 13 Ganspan 42 43 R708 60 Tierfontein 19

Koopmansfontein 23 Warrenton Hertzogville 75 R710 50

R31 52 34 33 Content 27 55 R708 64

Silver Streams Ulco Windsorton 10 Windsorton
Road R59 56 72 Bultfontein

Papkuil Delportshoop 33 64 Volkspele-
monument 58

R385 58 R31 Sidney-on-Vaal Longlands 48 St. Mary's Anglican
Church Riverton
on Vaal 27 64 Boshof 37 R34

39 Campbell Barkly
West Archaeological
Reserve 32 15 13 53 Kimberley Copyright © Map Studio Bloemfontein 18 O. F. S. Bloemfontein Brandort

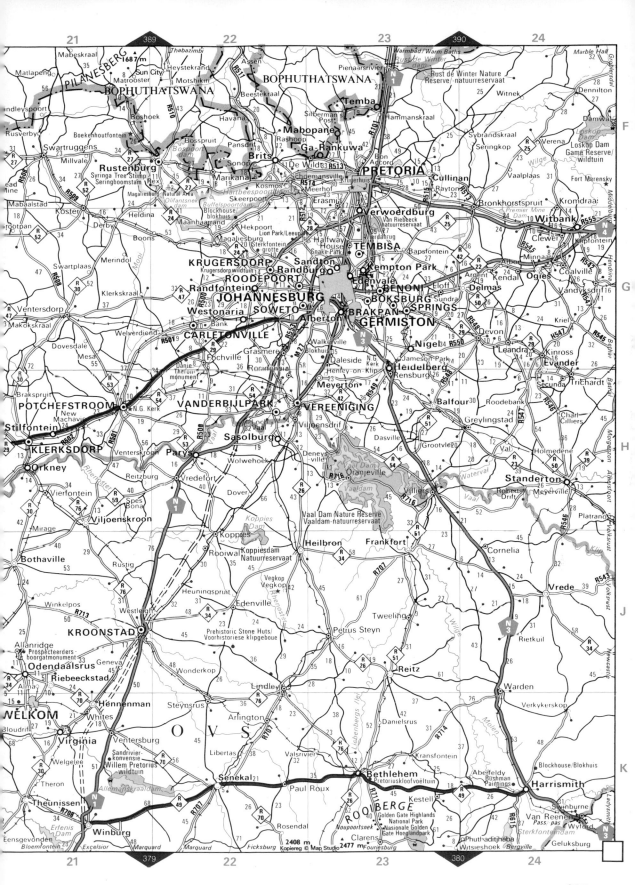

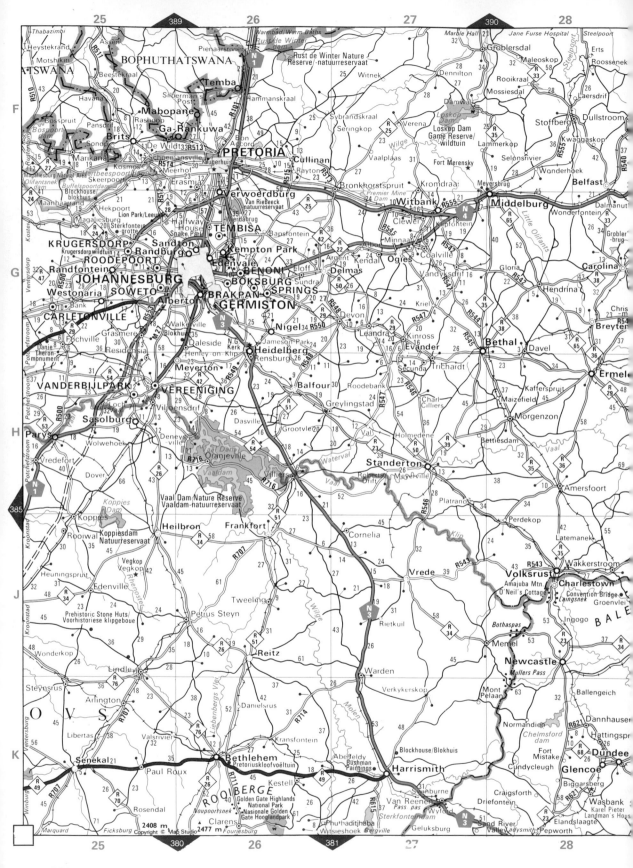

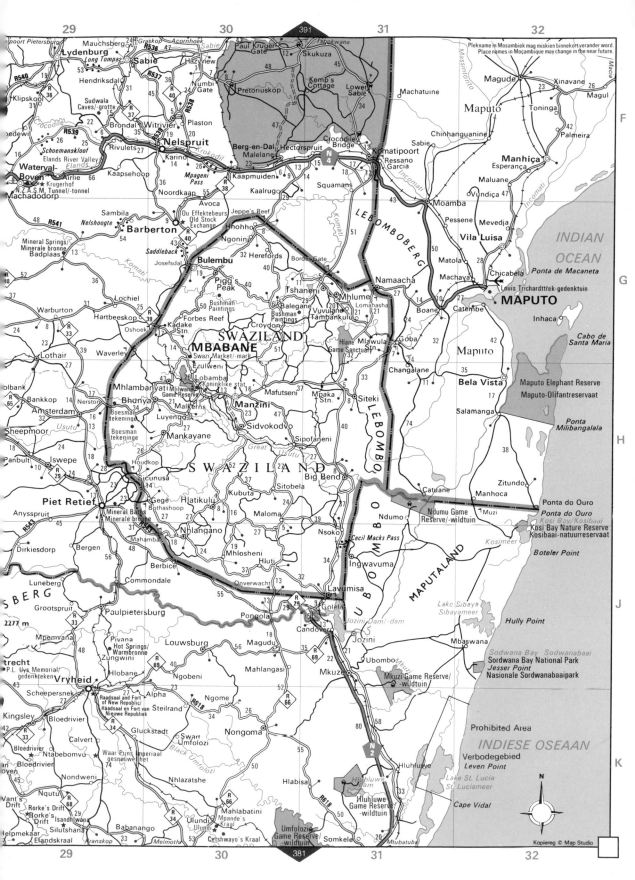

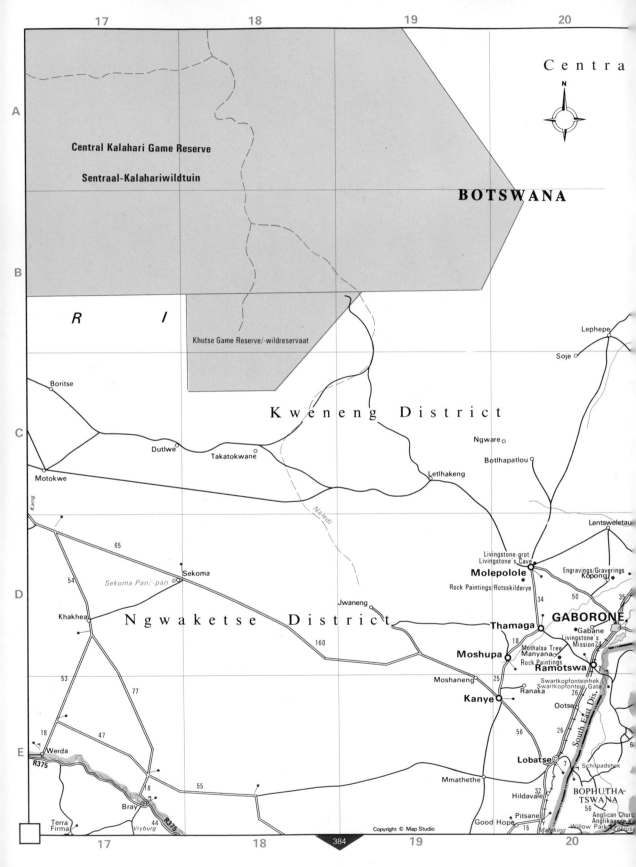

Central Kalahari Game Reserve
Sentraal-Kalahariwildtuin

BOTSWANA

Khutse Game Reserve/-wildreservaat

K w e n e n g   D i s t r i c t

Boritse

Dutlwe
Takatokwane
Motokwe
Letlhakeng

Ngware
Botlhapatlou

Lentsweletau

Livingstone-grot
Livingstone's Cave
Engravings/Graverings
Kopong
Molepolole
Rock Paintings/Rotsskilderye

N g w a k e t s e   D i s t r i c t

65
Sekoma
54
Sekoma Pan/-pan

Jwaneng

34
50
35

GABORONE

Khakhea

Thamaga
Gabane
Livingstone's
Mission

160
18
Mothalsa Tree
Moshupa
Manyana
Rock Paintings
Ramotswa

53
Moshaneng
25
Ranaka
26

77
Swartkopfonteinhek
Swartkopfontein Gate

Kanye
Ootse

18
47
56
26

E
Werda
R375
Lobatse
Schilpadshek
7

55
Mmathethe
Hildavale
32
**BOPHUTHA-
TSWANA**

18
56

Bray
Anglican Church
Anglikaanse K
Willow Park
Good Hope
Pitsane
16

Terra
Firma
Vryburg
R375

Lephepe
Soje

Kang
Naledi

South East Dis.

Copyright © Map Studio

384

388

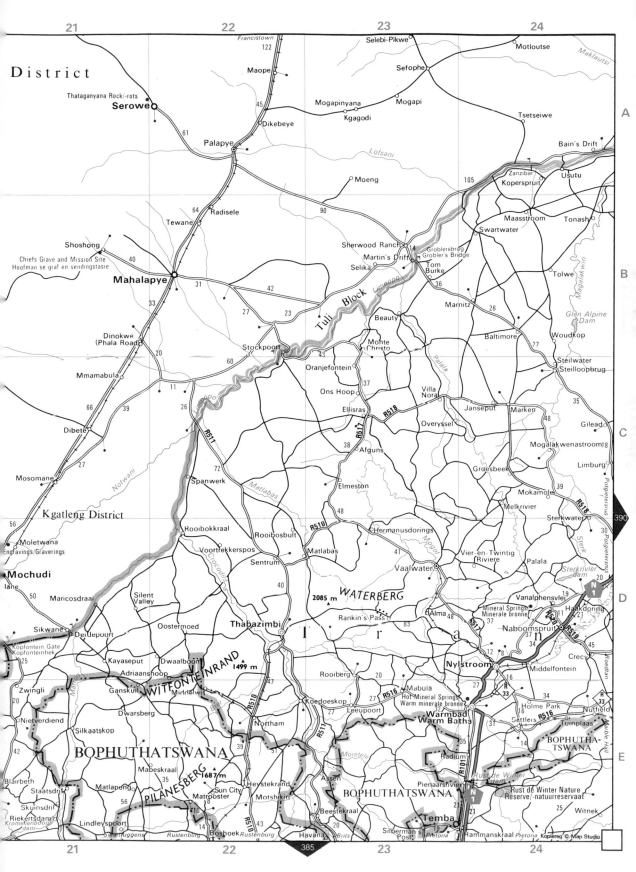

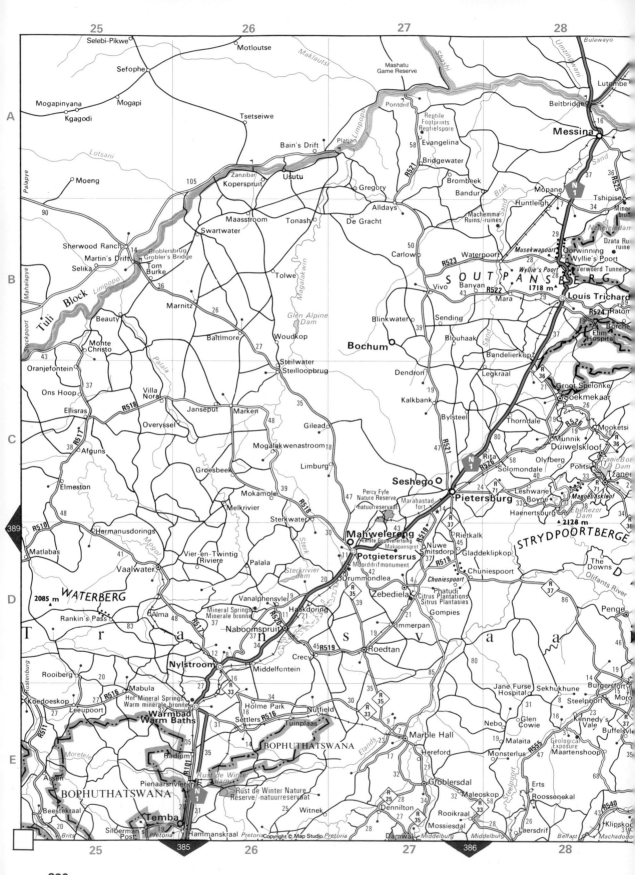

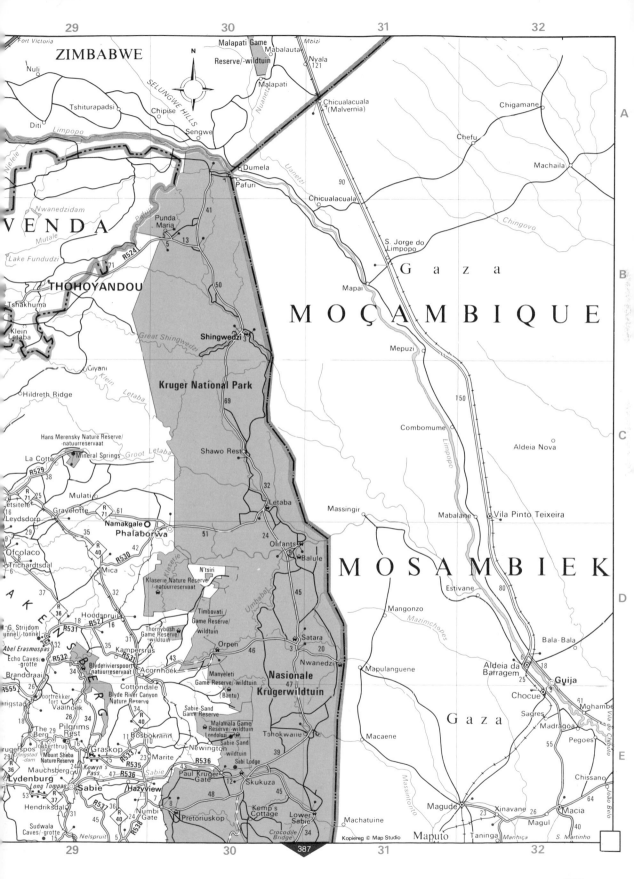

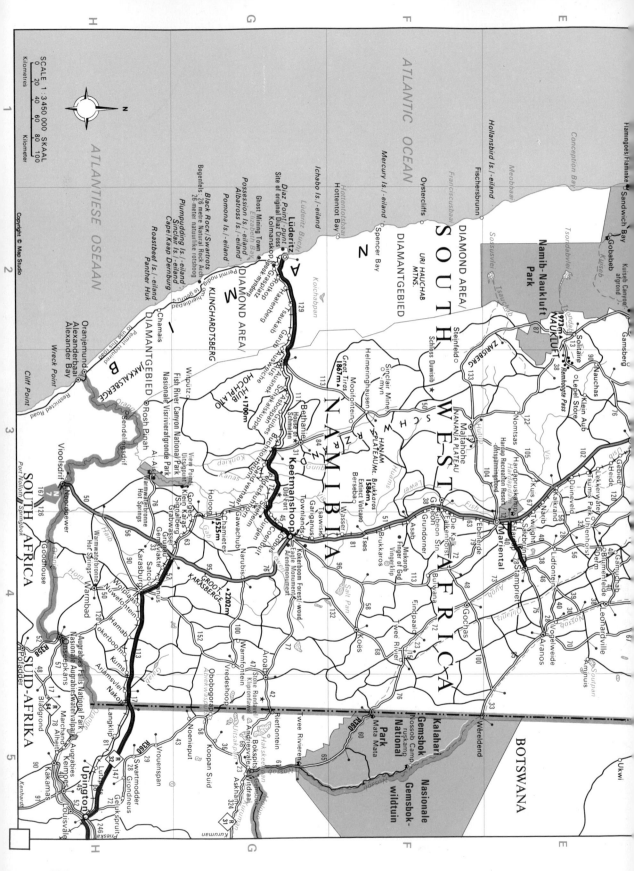

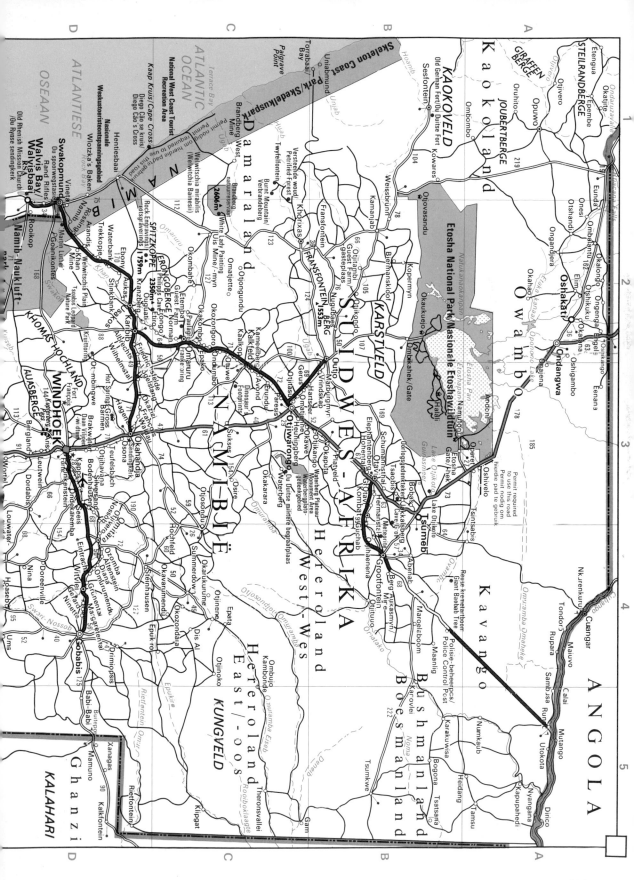

Accommodation Directory — arranged in the sequence of the chapters of the book
HOTELS — a selection of graded hotels and other accommodation

1 — Cape Town, Cape Peninsula and Cape Flats

CAPE TOWN CENTRAL AND GARDENS 021

Cape Sun Hotel ★★★★★TYYY, Strand Street. Tel 23-884.

Heerengracht Hotel ★★★★★TYYY, St George's Street. Tel 21-3711.

Mount Nelson Hotel ★★★★★TYYY, Orange Street. Tel 23-1000.

Capetonian Hotel ★★★★TYYY, Pier Place. Tel 21-1150.

De Waal Sun Hotel ★★★★TYYY, Mill Street. Tel 45-1311.

Inn on the Square ★★★TYYY, Greenmarket Sq. Tel 23-2040.

Town House Hotel ★★★TYYY, 60 Corporation Street. Tel 45-7050. P O Box 5053 Cape Town 8000. Telex 520890. 104 bedrooms en suite. Television, PABX telephone, airconditioning. Mostert's Hoek Bar, Pierneef Lounge, Town House Restaurant with its old world ambience, fine fare and wine, and unobtrusive service. Gymnasium, swimming-pool, whirlpool, squash courts and sauna. Conference facilities. Garaging. A first-rate base for visitors exploring the Cape and an obvious choice of business people. See page 16.

Carlton Heights Hotel ★★TYYY, 88 Queen Victoria Street. Tel 23-1260.

Garden Village Hotel ★★TYYY, Union Street. Tel 24-1460.

Pleinpark Travel Lodge ★★T, Cnr Barrack and Corporation Streets. Tel 45-7563.

Tudor Hotel ★T, Greenmarket Square. Tel 24-1335.

BANTRY BAY 021

Ambassador by the Sea Hotel ★★★TYYY, 34 Victoria road. Tel 49-6170.

BELLVILLE 021

Holiday Inn ★★★TYYY, Cross Street. Tel 97-8111.

Boston Hotel ★★TYYY, Boston and Voortrekker Roads. Tel 97-0911.

BLOUBERGSTRAND 021

Blue Peter Hotel ★★TYYY, Popham Road. Tel 56-1956.

CONSTANTIA 021

Alphen Hotel ★★★TYYY, Alphen Drive. Tel 74-1011.

The Cellars Country House, Hohenort Avenue, Constantia 7800. Tel 74-3468 and 74-1771. Telex 524842. 9 bedrooms en suite. Set high above the Constantia Valley with views on to Table Mountain – here you are offered a peaceful refuge, indeed country tranquillity with city convenience. Converted from a winery built in circa 1700 into a gracious country house, guests can be sure that Lyn and Jonathan Finnis, the owners, are happy to share the pleasures of this historic country home, and bring a sincere personal touch to all aspects of your stay. The Cellars Country House is famed for its cuisine (advance reservations for dining may be made), its rooms are exquisitely furnished, it is positioned in beautiful grounds and has a lovely swimming pool. See pages 31 and 32.

FISH HOEK 21

Avenue Hotel ★T, First Avenue. Tel 82-6026.

Outspan Hotel ★T, 16 Kommetjie Road. Tel 82-3578

GLENCAIRN 021

Clencairn Hotel ★TYYY, Glen Road. Post Office Simonstown. Tel 82-1122.

GOODWOOD 021

Goodwood Hotel ★★TYYY, 44 Voortrekker Road. Tel 591-2285.

GREEN POINT 021

Claridges Hotel ★★★TYYY, 47 Main Road. Tel 44-1171.

HOUT BAY 021

Flora Bay Bungalows, Chapman's Peak Drive. Tel 790-1650.

Hout Bay Hotel ★★TYYY, Main Road. Tel 790-1060.

KOMMETJIE 021

Kommetjie Hotel ★TYYY, Main Road. Tel 83-1706.

MUIZENBERG 021

Marine Hotel ★★TYYY, 125 Main Road. Tel 88-1162.

NEWLANDS 021

Newlands Sun Hotel ★★★★TYYY, Main Road. Tel 61-1105.

Vineyard Hotel ★★★TYYY, Protea Road, Newlands. Tel 64-4122. P O Box 151, Newlands 7725. Telex 522954. 108 Bedrooms en suite. Television, PABX telephone, airconditioning. The decor is traditional Cape country antique. A la carte restaurant, live piano music, coffee shop, Swiss patisserie, hairstylist, antique shop, gift shop, swimming-pool. Set in 6 acres of parkland through which the Liesbeek River runs. Spectacular view of Table Mountain. Conference facilities, on-property parking. A gracious hotel with elegant comfort, a fine cuisine and excellent cellar. In one of the most stunning settings in all the Cape, and once the home of Lady Anne Barnard. See page 16.

PAROW 021

New National Hotel ★★TYYY, 358 Voortrekker Road. Tel 92-7140.

ST JAMES 021

St James Hotel ★★★TYYY, Main Road. Below the Muizenberg Mountain and opposite the Indian Ocean, False Bay. P O Box 93 Muizenberg 7951. Tel 88-8931. Telex 524429 SA. Wide range of bedrooms all en suite – standard, deluxe, suite, duplex and cottage. All accommodation has television and video, touch dial telephone, many rooms have private balconies or verandahs. St James Restaurant – continental cuisine, La Terrasse Continental Expresso Bar, Pizzeria, Red Parrot English Pub. First rate conference and functions facilities. Heated swimming-pool in the hotel garden, sun room and lounge bar. Tennis court. Ample secure parking. The hotel has its own private beach huts on St James beach and tidal pool directly opposite the property. See pages 34 and 36.

SEA POINT 021

President Hotel ★★★★TYYY, Beach Road. Tel 44-1122.

Arthur's Seat Hotel ★★★TYYY, Arthur's Road. Tel 44-3344.

Century Hotel ★★★TYYY, Main Road. Tel 49-1181.

Winchester Mansions Hotel ★★★TYYY, Beach Road. Tel 44-2351.

Regency Hotel ★★TYYY, 90 Regent Road. Tel 49-6101.

Surfcrest Hotel ★★T, 327 Beach Road. Tel 44-8721.

Kings Hotel ★TYYY, 94 Regent Road. Tel 49-6040.

SIMONSTOWN 021 see also GLENCAIRN

Lord Nelson Hotel ★RYYY, 58 St George's Street. Tel 86-1386

TABLE VIEW 021

Blaauberg Hotel ★TYYY, Marine Circle. Tel 57-1191.

THREE ANCHOR BAY 021

Carnaby Hotel ★T, Main Road. Tel 49-7410.

WOODSTOCK 021

Holiday Inn ★★★TYYY, Melbourne Road. Tel 47-4060.

2 — The Western Cape

ALBERTINIA 02952

Albertinia Hotel ★★TYYY, Main Street. Tel 30.

ARNISTON 02847

Arniston Hotel ★★TYYY, P O Box 126, Bredasdorp. Tel 640.

ASHTON 0234

Olympic Hotel ★TYYY, Main Road. Tel 51108.

BARRYDALE 02972

Valley Inn ★TYYY, Van Riebeeck Street. Tel 26.

BETTY'S BAY 02823

Sea-klip Hotel ★TYYY, P O Box 27 Betty's Bay. Tel 8700.

BONNIEVALE 02346

Bonnievale Hotel ★TYYY, Main Road. Tel 2155.

BOT RIVER 02824

Bot River Hotel ★TYYY, P O Box 2. Tel 640.

BREDASDORP 0284

Standard Hotel ★TYYY, Long Street. Tel 4-1140.

Victoria Hotel ★TYYY, Church Street.
Tel 4-1159.

CALEDON 0281
Alexandra Hotel ★TYYY, Pioneer
Road.
Tel 2-3052.

Overberg Hotel ★TYYY, Prince Alfred
Road. Tel 2-1128.

CERES 0233
New Belmont Hotel ★★TYYY, Porter
Street. Tel 2-1150.

CITRUSDAL 02662
Citrusdal Hotel ★TYYY, Voortrekker
Street. Tel 82.

CLANWILLIAM 02682
Clanwilliam Hotel ★TYYY, Main Street.
Tel 61.

DARLING 02241
Nemesia Hotel ★TYYY, Main Street.
Tel 2263

DE DOORNS 02322
Hex Valley Hotel ★TYYY, Station
Road. Tel 2090.

DU TOIT'S KLOOF 0231
(Worcester)
Protea Park Hotel ★TYYY,
P O Box 144, Rawsonville. Tel 9-1092.

EENDEKUIL 02624
Eendekuil Hotel ★TYYY, Main Street.
Tel 660.

ELANDS BAY 0265
Elands Hotel ★TYYY, P O Elandsbaai.
Tel 640.

FRANSCHHOEK 02212
Swiss Farm Excelsior Hotel ★★TYYY,
P O Box 54, Franschhoek 7690. Tel 2071.
Forty-five bedrooms en suite with
bathroom or shower, fitted carpet, airconditioning, radio and telephone. Television
available. Full health centre. Wine farm *Le
Moutonne* with wine tasting in *Die Binne-
hof,* on the Franschhoek Wine Route.
Three-roomed, fully equipped convention
centre, 24 to 80 persons. On-property
bowling green, tennis court, squash court,
swimming pool. Set in magnificent mountain scenery in the heart of wine country.
See pages 69 and 70.

Huguenot Hotel ★TYYY, Huguenot
Road. Tel 2092.

GANSBAAI 02834
De Kelders Hotel ★TYYY, P O Box 80.
Tel 4-0421

GORDON'S BAY 024
Van Riebeeck Hotel ★★★TYYY, Beach
Road. Tel 5-61441.

GOUDA 0020
Gouda Hotel ★TYYY, Main Street. Tel
4.

GOURTISMOND 02952
Gourtiz River Mouth Hotel ★TYYY
P O Gourtismond. Tel 5313.

GRAAFWATER 026722
Graafwater Hotel ★TYYY,
Station Road.

GRABOUW 0240
Forest Hotel ★TYYY, Main Road.
Tel 4429.

GREYTON 02822
The Post House, Main Road, Greyton
7233. Tel 9995. Once the village post office,
the original 1860 building having been restored and remodelled, The Post House
provides country house accommodation at
its best. Original rough-hewn yellowwood
ceilings remain and huge fireplaces add to
the comfort of attractive lounges, diningroom, and a really authentic Old English
Pub. The furniture is country cottage
interspersed with Edwardian antique, and
the personal collection of *objet d'art* and
memorabilia enhance a warmth not found
in 'run of the mill' places. The 15 en suite
bedrooms (bearing the names of the
delightful Beatrix Potter characters) have
individual decor and each has its own verandah, many have own fireplaces and all
face the courtyard and swimming pool.
Here in Greyton there are opportunities
for walking, riding, bass fishing, tennis and
croquet, in this gentle rural setting below
the majestic Riviersonderend range. As
important as the excellent preparation and
presentation of the country cooking is the
personal touch and efficient management
of James and Gailo Borland, the owners.
Remote from noises of the urban area, The
Post House will provide a holiday or short
stay carefree and cared for. See pages 89
and 90.

HEIDELBERG 02962
Esperanza Hotel ★TYYY, Niekerk
Street. Tel 87.
Heidelberg Hotel ★TYYY, Van
Riebeeck Street. Tel 47.

HERMANUS 02831
Marine Hotel ★★TYYY, Marine Drive,
P O Box 9, Hermanus 7200. Telephone
2-1112. Re-opened in December 1985 after
four years of extensive renovations, and
what a remarkable job David Rawdon has
done for the historic Marine Hermanus –
started by the Luyt family in 1902. The
meticulous care in the refurbishing has
provided the enchantment of grace and
ease (generally hopelessly neglected in
present day hotels), and with this atmosphere, it is hardly necessary to say, goes
unobtrusive service, traditional hospitality
and the best of everything in food and
wines. Each of the individually decorated
suites, bedsitters and bedrooms (45 in all)
has en suite bathroom with shower, towel-
warmer and hairdryer, and each has colour
TV set and small refrigerator. Two of the
suites have spa-baths. Many of the rooms
overlook the beautiful Walker Bay as does
the Mediterranean-style Diningroom, on
two levels, extending to the courtyard. On
a lovely day meals are served al fresco in
the open area close to the Diningroom and
during winter months the magnificent Public Bar, with tables near the fireside, is used
for bar lunches and Sunday night suppers.
The Residents Lounge overlooks the spectacular seascape and the Billiard Room
also faces the sea. On the first floor is the
Pool Room with its jacuzzi, heated swimming pool and tiled sun deck. There is also
an outdoor pool and a tidal pool amongst
the rocks below the hotel. See pages 85
and 86.

HERMON 0224
Hermon Hotel ★TYYY, Main Street.
Tel 220.

HOPEFIELD 022822
Commercial Hotel ★TYYY,
Voortrekker Road. Tel 106.

HOUW HOEK 02824
Houw Hoek Inn ★TYYY, national road
N2, near the summit of Houw Hoek Pass.
Tel 646. Site of historic coaching inn.

KLAPMUTS 02211
Klapmuts Hotel ★TYYY, Old Main
Road. Tel·5215.

KLEINMOND 02823
The Beach House ★★TYYY, Beach
Road. P O Box 14, Kleinmond 7195. Telephone (02823) 3130. At the Kleinmond
lagoon and facing 8 km of magnificent
ocean beach, this comfortable, well-
appointed hotel has 27 bedrooms all en
suite with private bathroom, telephone,
and TV available. À la carte restaurant,
exclusive ladies bar and swimming pool.
Under the personal supervision of owners
James and Gailo Borland of The Post House,
Greyton.

LAMBERT'S BAY 026732
Marine Hotel ★TYYY, Voortrekker
Street. Tel 49. Overlooking the pictu-
resque bay.

LANGEBAAN 02287
Panoramic Hotel ★TYYY, Main Road.
Tel 2144. In the village at the head of the
lagoon.

MALMESBURY 0224
Swartland Hotel ★TYYY,
Voortrekker Street. Tel 2-1141.

MONTAGUE 0234
Avalon Hotel ★★TYYY, Market Street.
Tel 4-1122.

Montagu Hotel ★TYYY, Bath Street.
Tel 4-1115.

MOORREESBURG 02642
International Hotel ★TYYY,
Main Street. Tel 1154.

Samoa Hotel ★TYYY, Royal Street.
Tel 201 and 885.

NAPIER 0284
Napier Hotel ★TYYY, Sarel Cilliers
Street. Tel 64.

PAARL 02211
Mountain Shadows, Klein Drakenstein.
P O Box 2501, Paarl 7620. Tel 62-3192
Telex 521147 SA. Guests (not exceeding 12
at any one time) enjoy a true Cape hospitality life-style on a lovely wine farm. The
dining and reception rooms are in the
Manor House which was built in 1823 and
is a national monument, and the bedrooms
(all en suite) are in the Jonkershuis and the
converted wine cellar. The scene is traditional Cape Dutch in an atmosphere of
gracious living, warmth, comfort and relaxation. There is a beautiful garden and
delightful pool terrace. Well worth partici-
pating in are the Cape safaris (including
deep sea fishing), an optional extra to
accommodation. Aircraft met at D F Malan
Airport by arrangement. By road from
Cape Town, proceed along national road
N1 towards Worcester. After bypassing
Paarl and before ascending Du Toit's Kloof
the N1 crosses the Berg River. A short distance beyond the crossing take the turnoff
left marked 'Klein Drakenstein' and proceed 300 metres to take the turnoff right to
Drakenstein Noord. Follow this road for 2
km to reach Mountain Shadows signboard
on the right. See pages 73 and 78.

Picardie Hotel ★TYYY,
158 Main Street. Tel 2-3118.

PATERNOSTER 02285
Paternoster Hotel ★TYYY,
Main Street. Tel 703.

PIKETBERG 02612

Boland Hotel ★TYYY, Church Street. Tel 3-1154.

Nederberg Hotel ★TYYY, Voortrekker Street. Tel 3-1465.

PRINCE ALFRED'S HAMLET 0233

Hamlet Hotel ★TYYY, Voortrekker Road. Tel 3290.

RAWSONVILLE 0231

Rawsonville Hotel ★TYYY, Van Riebeeck Street. Tel 9-1080.

RIVERSDALE 02932

President Hotel ★★TYYY, Main Street. Tel 192.

RIVIERSONDEREND 0286

Garden Route Hotel ★TYYY, Main Street. Tel 364.

ROBERTSON 02351

Grand Hotel ★TYYY, Barry Street. Tel 3272.

ST HELENA BAY 02283

Steenberg's Cove Hotel ★TYYY, Main Street. Tel 750.

SALDANHA 02281

Hoedjiesbaai Hotel ★★TYYY, Main Street. Tel 4-1271.

Saldanha Hotel ★★TYYY, Main Street. Tel 4-1201.

SIMONDIUM 02211

Simondium Hotel ★TYYY, Main Road. Tel 4-1046.

SOMERSET WEST 024

Alexandria Hotel ★RYYY, 147 Main Road. Tel 2-1735

STANFORD 02833

Stanford Hotel ★TYYY, Queen Street. Tel 710.

STELLENBOSCH 02231

Lanzerac Hotel ★★★TYYY, Jonkershoek Road. P O Box 4. Tel 7-1132. The stately old Cape Dutch homestead and ancillary buildings (built in 1830 and a national monument) converted into an hotel. Forty-two bedrooms/suites all en suite with bathroom. Outstanding decor, furnishing and setting. Several restaurants, cocktail bar, coffee shop, beautiful swimming pool. See pages 61 and 63.

Devon Valley Hotel ★★TYYY, opposite Bertrams Winery in Devon Valley. Tel 7-0211.

D'Ouwe Werf Country Inn ★★TYYY, 30 Church Street. Tel 7-4608. Telex 520706. To discover an inn of high rating standards and unique appointments and decor tucked-away in a quiet corner right in the heart of historic Stellenbosch, is to find D'Ouwe Werf. It has 26 individually furnished en suite bedrooms, each containing a refrigerator, tea and coffee maker, direct dial telephone and radio. D'Ouwe Werf is expressive of all that is best in traditional Cape hospitality, comfort and service. Nothing is too much trouble for the owner, your host, Gerhard Lubbe, and an added bonus is his knowledge of Stellenbosch. D'Ouwe Werf operates on the bed and breakfast system and breakfast is served on the terrace or in the Coffee Shop. Lunches of salads, pâtés, quiches and a dish of the day are served, and in the evenings there are light suppers. Gerhard will gladly introduce you to the restaurants of Stellenbosch. See pages 52/53 and 59.

Stellenbosch Hotel TYYY, 162 Dorp Street. Tel 7-3644.

STILBAAI 02934

Bellevue Hotel ★TYYY, Osler Street. Tel 41505.

STORMSVLEI 0286

Stormsvlei Hotel ★TYYY, off N2 between Riviersonderend and Swellendam. Tel 289.

STRAND 024

Da Gama Hotel ★★TYYY, Beach Road. Tel 3-7400.

Metropole Hotel ★★TYYY, Beach Road. Tel 3-1501.

STRUISBAAI 02846

Struisbaai Motel ★TYYY, Minnetonka Street. Tel 625.

SWELLENDAM 0291

Swellengrebel Hotel ★★TYYY, 91 Voortrek Street, P O Box 9, Tel 4-1144. Fifty-one bedrooms (one executive suite) all en suite private bathroom, telephone, radio, television, airconditioning, fitted carpet. Voortrekker à la Carte restaurant and cocktail bar. Table d'hôte, functions room (10 to 300 persons). Swimming pool, sauna and whirlpool, children's playground. Car park. Centre of town. Overlooked by beautiful Langeberg range. See page 93.

Ten Damme Hotel ★TYYY, 27 Voortek Street. Tel 4-1179.

TULBAGH 02362

Tulbagh Hotel ★TYYY, Van der Stel Street. Tel 71.

Witzenberg Hotel ★TYYY, Piet Retief Street. Tel 159.

VELDDRIF LAAIPLEK 022882

Laaiplek Hotel ★TYYY, Jameson Street. Tel 15.

Riviera Hotel ★TYYY, Voortrekker Road. Tel 37.

VILLIERSDORP 02252

Keerom Hotel ★★TYYY, Main Road. Tel 3-1110.

Boland Hotel ★TYYY, Main Road. Tel 3-1107.

VREDENBURG 02281

North Western Hotel ★TYYY, Main Street. Tel 3-1291.

Vredenburg Hotel ★TYYY, Main Street. Tel 3-1110.

WAENHUISKRANS SEE ARNISTON

WELLINGTON 02211

Commercial Hotel ★TYYY, 101 Main Street. Tel 3-2253.

Langham Park Hotel ★TYYY, Denne Street. Tel 3-3023.

WITSAND 0020

Lucky Strike Hotel ★TYYY. Tel 31.

WOLSELEY 023232

Waverley Hotel ★TYYY, Eeufees Street. Tel 113.

Wolseley Hotel ★TYYY, Solomon Street. Tel 240.

WORCESTER 0231

Cumberland Hotel ★★TYYY, Stockenström Street. Tel 7-2641.

Brandwacht Hotel ★TYYY, Napier Street. Tel 2-0150.

3 — The Garden Route, the Little Karoo and the Long Kloof

CALITZDORP

Queens Hotel ★TYYY, Queen Street. Tel 332.

CAPE ST FRANCIS SEE ST FRANCIS BAY

DE RUST 04439

De Rust Hotel ★TYYY, Schoeman Street. Tel 2001.

GEORGE 0441

Hawthorndene Hotel ★★TYYY, C.J. Langenhoven Road, Heatherlands. Tel 7-1160.

Mayfield Park Hotel ★★TYYY, National road N2, 8 km east of George. Tel 7-1023.

Garden Route Hotel ★TYYY, C.J. Langenhoven Road. Tel 3600

Outeniqua Hotel ★TYYY, 123 York Street. Tel 7-1428.

HARTENBOS 04441

Riviera Hotel ★TYYY, P O Box 7. Tel 5203.

Sea Shells Motel ★TYYY, P O Box 1. Tel 5103.

HEROLD'S BAY 0441

Seale's Inn ★TYYY, P O Box 138, George. Tel 4528.

HUMANSDORP 04231

Grand Hotel ★TYYY, 52 Main Street. Tel 5-1805.

Royal Hotel ★TYYY, Main Street. Tel 5-1558.

Transvia Motel ★TYYY, Voortrekker Road. Tel 5-1070.

JEFFREY'S BAY 04231

Savoy Hotel ★★TYYY, Da Gama Street. Tel 3-1106.

Beach Hotel ★TYYY, Da Gama Street. Tel 3-1104.

JOUBERTINA 04272

Kloof Hotel ★TYYY, Main Street. Tel 34.

KAREEDOUW 04233

Assegaaibosch Hotel ★TYYY, on the P.E. road, 3 km from Kareedouw. Tel 700.

KEURBOOMS RIVER 04457

Frederick Hotel ★TYYY, National road N2. Tel 9609.

KEURBOOMSTRAND 04457

Keurboomstrand Hotel ★TYYY, at the beach. Tel 9818.

KNYSNA 0445

Leisure Isle Hotel ★★TYYY, P O Box 19, Knysna 6570. The Leisure Isle is connected to the mainland by motor road causeway and occupies a tranquil position near the water's edge of the Knysna Estuary. Fifty metres from the hotel, at Bollard Bay, bathing is perfectly safe, conditions are ideal for windsurfing and there are opportunities for fishing, boating and sailing. Close at hand are the bowling greens, tennis courts and golf course. The hotel has its own swimming-pool. Positioned in a garden setting, the bedrooms are en suite with either private bath or shower. They are fully carpeted and have PABX system telephone, and radio – many have colour television. Leisure Isle is renowned for its country style comfort, good table, and hospitality where the emphasis is on relaxation – pub lunches in a convivial atmosphere. Knysna is half-way between Cape Town and Port Elizabeth on national road N2. Make Leisure Isle your base whilst you explore the celebrated Garden Route. A leisurely setting for all kinds of functions and conferences. On site parking.

Knysna Protea Hotel ★★★TYYY, Main Street. Tel 2-2127.

Brenton Hotel ★TYYY, Agapanthus Avenue, Brenton-on-sea. Tel 2-1160.

LADISMITH 02942
Dinnies Hotel ★TYYY, Van Riebeeck Street. Tel 56.

Royal Hotel ★TYYY, Queen Street. Tel 37.

LAKE PLEASANT 04455
Lake Pleasant Hotel ★★TYYY, P O Box 2, Sedgefield. Telephone 313. Few hotels are as pleasantly placed as this one – in the surroundings of a bird sanctuary and nature reserve at the water's edge of Lake Pleasant (otherwise known as Groenvlei). In this peaceful setting of the Garden Route Lake District it is situated off national road N2 between Sedgefield and Knysna. Each of the 21 tastefully furnished bedrooms is en suite with private bathroom, and each has telephone and radio. Attractive furnishing and decor, happy atmosphere, convivial pub, TV viewing, excellent table and wine cellar, make this the ideal base from which to explore the whole Garden Route; and the lake bass fishing, boating, tennis court, swimming-pool, delightful walks, coupled with congeniality, provide the ingredients for a happy, carefree holiday. Close by there are ocean beaches and opportunities for sea fishing. See pages 103 and 105.

LITTLE BRAK RIVER 04441
Little Brak River Motel ★TYYY, off national road N2. Tel 6262.

MISGUND 0020
Roddekrantz Motel, P O Box 41. Tel 81.

MOSSEL BAY and ROBINSON PASS 04441
Eight Bells Mountain Inn ★★TYYY, P O Box 436, Mossel Bay 6500. Tel 5-8155 and 5-8480. Situated at the foot of the Robinson Pass (Outeniqua range), on the R328 between Mossel Bay (35 km) and Oudtshoorn (50 km). Placed in an attractive country garden setting, there are 23 comfortably furnished double rooms, rondavels and family suites, each with its own bathroom, radio and intercom telephone. The important attribute of Eight Bells is in its positioning on a 170-hectare farm, permitting extensive recreational facilities – the fine riding stables, swimming-pool, all-weather tennis courts, full-sized bowling green and glass-back squash court are all maintained in top condition (particularly the bowling green and for this reason there is a separate beginners rink). And then there are the delightful hiking trails and climbs into the surrounding Outeniqua mountains, not to mention the actual farmyard thrills – chickens, ducks, geese, turkeys, cows, pigs, sheep, horses, donkeys, cats and dogs. Inside the inn the pleasures continue

– you can enjoy country hospitality whilst you relax on the wide verandah or play billiards, watch television, sit around a log fire, or savour a drink in the Eight Bells Pub. Preparation and presentation of excellent meals rounds up the reason for Eight Bells Mountain Inn being very popular for holidays for the whole family – and it is convenient for all the attractions of the Garden Route. See pages 99 and 100.

Golden Rendezvous Hotel★TYYY, south of the town, near national road N2. Tel 3641.

Santos Protea Hotel ★TYYY, George Road. Tel 7103.

OUDTSHOORN 04431
Holiday Inn ★★TYYY, Baron van Rheede Street. Tel 2201.

Kango Protea Inn ★★TYYY, Baron van Rheede Street. Tel. 6161.

Queens Hotel ★★TYYY, Baron von Rheede Street. Tel 2101.

PLETTENBERG BAY 04457
Beacon Island Hotel ★★★TYYY, PB 1001. Tel 3-1120.

The Plettenberg ★★★TYYY, P O Box 4. Tel 3-2030.

Formosa Inn ★★TYYY, National Road. Tel 3-2060.

PRINCE ALBERT 04436
Swartberg Hotel ★TYYY, Church Street. Tel 332.

ST FRANCIS BAY 04231
St Francis Hotel TYYY, at the marina on the beach. Tel 4304.

SEDGEFIELD SEE LAKE PLEASANT

STORMS RIVER 04237
Tzitzikama Forest Inn ★TYYY, P O Storms River. Tel 711. Off the national road, in the heart of the indigenous forest. Twenty-five bedrooms all have private bathroom and wall-to-wall carpeting. Good table, comfortable lounges, TV viewing, Hunter's Inn Pub. Log fires in winter. Picnics provided for. Swimming-pool, spa bath and sauna, tennis, indoor games. Numerous trails in the area. See page 113.

WILDERNESS 0441
Holiday Inn ★★★TYYY, off the national road, north of the village. Tel 9-1104.

Wilderness Hotel ★★★TYYY, in the village opposite the lagoon. Tel 9-1110.

Fairy Knowe Hotel ★TYYY, on the river. Tel 9-1100.

4 — The Great Karoo

ABERDEEN 049212
Aberdeen Hotel ★TYYY, Hope Street. Tel 62.

BEAUFORT WEST 0201
Oasis Hotel ★★TYYY, Donkin Street. Tel 3221.

Masonic Hotel ★TYYY, Donkin Street. Tel 2332.

Royal Hotel ★TYYY, Donkin Street. Tel 3241.

Wagon Wheel Motel ★TYYY, North End.

BETHESDA ROAD 04923
Good's Motel, P/Bag Graaff-Reinet. Tel 718.

BRITSTOWN 05732
Trans Karoo Hotel ★★TYYY, Market Street. Tel 27.

COLESBERG 05852
Central Hotel ★★TYYY, Church Street. Tel 90.

Merino Inn ★★TYYY, National road bypass. Tel 265.

Torenberg Hotel ★TYYY, Church Street. Tel 315.

Van Zylsvlei Motel ★TYYY, on the road to Philippolis. Tel 1513.

DE AAR 0571
De Aar Hotel ★TYYY, Friedlander Street. Tel 2181

Walter Hotel ★TYYY, Church Street. Tel 2541.

FRASERBURG 02072
Central Hotel ★TYYY, Voortrekker Street. Tel 330

GRAAFF-REINET 0491
Drostdy Hotel ★★TYYY, 28 Church Street (a national monument facing Parsonage Street). P O Box 400, Graaff-Reinet 6280. Telephone 2-2161. Telex 242711. Forty-six bedrooms/suites, in historical Stretch's Court, all have private bathrooms, telephone, radio, airconditioning. Suites with television on request. Candle lit Table dhôte Dining Hall. De Camdeboo à la Carte Restaurant for dinner and buffet lunches. Cocktail bars. De Wijnkamer for private dinner parties. Conferences and receptions in fully equipped auditorium (up to 200 persons), and The Marquee swimming pool area for outdoor functions. See pages 125 and 127.

Panorama Hotel ★★TYYY, Magazine Hill. Tel 2-2233.

Graaff-Reinet Hotel ★TYYY, Market Square. Tel 2-4191.

HANOVER 057212
New Grand Hotel ★TYYY, Market Street. Tel 19.

LAINGSBURG 02372
Laingsburg Hotel ★★TYYY, Voortrekker Street. Tel 9.

Grand Hotel ★TYYY, Station Street. Tel 38.

LEEU-GAMKA 02082
Leeu-Gamka Hotel ★TYYY, P O Box 1. Tel 1.

MATJIESFONTEIN 0020
Lord Milner Hotel ★★TYYY, P O Matjiesfontein 6910. Telephone 3. Thirty-six bedrooms all have private bathroom, radio and intercom telephone. Unique setting redolent of the Victoria era and notable for fine cuisine. Laird's Arms English country pub. Swimming-pool, tennis, croquet, coffee shop, gift shop. Film shows Fridays and Sundays. Chapel services on Sunday. See pages 120 and 121.

MIDDELBURG 0483
Country Inn ★★TYYY, Loop Street. Tel 2-1126.

Middelburger Hotel ★TYYY, Meintjies Street. Tel 2-1100.

MURRAYSBURG 049222
Murraysburg Hotel ★TYYY, Leeb Street. Tel 119.

NORVALSPONT 0020
Glasgow Pont Hotel ★TYYY,
P O Box 5. Tel 22.

NOUPOORT 05742
Naauwpoort Hotel ★TYYY,
Andries Pretorius Street. Tel 69.
Imperial Hotel ★TYYY, Murray Street.
Tel 71.

PETRUSVILLE 057232
Transkaroo Hotel ★TYYY,
Market Square. Tel 33.

PHILIPSTOWN 057222
Disa Hotel ★TYYY, Church Street.
Tel 53.

RICHMOND 05752
Belsana Hotel, Pienaar Street. Tel 36.
Richmond Hotel, Loop Street. Tel 61.

ROSMEAD 0483
Rosmead Hotel, Tel 2-1426.

STEYNSBURG 04842
Grand Hotel ★TYYY, Kerk Street.
Tel 133.

TOUWS RIVER 02382
Loganda Hotel ★TYYY, off national
road N2. Tel 130.

UNIONDALE 04462
Royal Hotel ★TYYY,
Voortrekker Street. Tel 9904.

VICTORIA WEST 02042
Halfway House Hotel ★TYYY,
Church Street. Tel 129.

WILLOWMORE 04942
Royal Hotel ★TYYY, Knysna Street.
Tel 225.

5 — Port Elizabeth and District and the Settler Country

PORT ELIZABETH 041
Algoa Protea Hotel ★★★TYYY,
7 Lutman Street. Tel 2-1558.

Beach Hotel ★★★TYYY, Marine Drive,
Humewood, Port Elizabeth 6001.
Telephone 53-2161. Telex 243142. Situated
directly opposite the famous Hobie Beach,
the ideal launching pad for windsurfers,
hobie-catters, surfers and fishermen – and
a gently sloping, safe bathing beach. The
64 bedrooms, many sea facing, are all en
suite with private bathroom (some have
showers in addition), and all have direct
dialling telephones and colour television
with second channel. Two comfortable
lounges, two bars, a first-rate dining room,
and The Bell à la Carte Restaurant and
cocktail bar – famed for the excellence of
its cuisine and wine cellar – where the ever
popular Gino is in attendance. There is
safe parking. With its helpful and friendly
service, 'The Beach' is the first choice for
holidays in Port Elizabeth; business people
will relax here and there are all the facilities
for conferences and weddings. See pages
135 and 136/7.

Edward Hotel ★★TYYY, Belmont
Terrace, Port Elizabeth 6001. Telephone
56-2056. Telex 243136. Commanding fine
views of the city, harbour and Algoa Bay,
Edward Hotel faces onto Donkin Reserve
in the historical quarter of the city, and is

in fact part of that history – it was built
around 1900. Architecturally the
Edwardian flavour is retained, the Art
Nouveau decoration (popular in the era)
having been preserved through the years
of careful maintenance. Inside the hotel the
atmosphere of those gracious-living days
persists – first in The Palm Court (once an
interior carriage-way), with its terracotta
fountains, and then Edd's Inn, a character
pub, The Terrace and Place Belmont, two
social bars, and finally in The Causerie, an
extensive black-and-white tiled diningroom, seating 130 persons. The Edward
has 111 bedrooms en suite with private
bathrooms and all provided with colour
television and video, and direct dialling
telephones. Accommodation varies from
Master suites to standard room with tariffs
scaled to assist differing budgets. There
are also 16 rooms without private
bathrooms. Conference and functions
facilities at The Edward are of an
exceptionally high standard, catering in a
range from 10 to 600 persons in eight
functions rooms. See pages 131 and 136/7.

Elizabeth Hotel ★★★★TYYY,
La Roche Drive, Humewood. Tel 52-3720.
Humewood Mansions ★★TYYY,
Beach Road, Humewood. Tel 2-8961.
Hunter's Retreat Hotel ★★TYYY,
Old Cape Road. Tel 30-1244.
Marine Holiday Inn ★★★TYYY,
Marine Drive, Summerstrand. Tel 53-2144.
Walmer Gardens Hotel ★★TYYY,
10th Avenue, Walmer, Port Elizabeth 6001.
Tel 51-4322. Telex 243579. Situated in the
garden suburb of Walmer in an
atmosphere of peacefulness and serenity,
far removed from the humdrum of city life,
yet only 1½ km from the airport, 3 km
from the city, the harbour and the sea. The
hotel is on the city bus route and only two
blocks away from a shopping centre. It is
well appointed and is placed in a garden
setting with a lovely swimming-pool. All
rooms have bathrooms, colour TV/video
and are tastefully furnished. Twin Palms
cocktail bar provides light snacks, and Pine
Inn Restaurant and cocktail bar caters for
both table d'hôte and à la carte.

ADDO 04252
Zuurberg Inn ★TYYY, 16 km north of
the Addo Park. Box 12. Tel 109.
Commando Kraal Hotel ★TYYY, in the
village. Box 22. Tel 34.

ADELAIDE 04662
Commercial Hotel ★TYYY, Market
Square. Tel 155.
Midgley's Hotel ★TYYY, Market
Square. Tel 119.

BATHHURST 0464
Pig & Whistle Hotel ★TYYY, Kowie
Road. Tel 3673.

BEDFORD 04632
Bedford Hotel ★TYYY, 36 Donkin
Street. Tel 110.

CRADOCK 0481
New Masonic Hotel ★TYYY,
Stockenstroom Street. Tel 3115.
Victoria Hotel ★TYYY, Market Square.
Tel 3020.

FORT BEAUFORT 043512
Savoy Hotel ★★TYYY, 53 Durban
Street. Tel 62.

GAMTOOS FERRY 0421
Camtoos Ferry Hotel ★TYYY,
P O Loerie. Tel 758.

GOLDEN VALLEY 0424
Golden Valley Hotel ★TYYY,
P O Golden Valley. Near Cookhouse.
Tel 7-1155.

GRAHAMSTOWN 0461
Cathcart Arms Hotel ★★TYYY,
5 West Street. Tel 2-7111.
Graham Hotel ★★TYYY,
123 High Street. Tel 2-2324.
Grand Hotel ★★TYYY, 23 High Street.
Tel 2-7012.
Settlers Inn Motel ★★TYYY, 2 km west
of city on N2 to Port Elizabeth. Tel 2-7313.
Stone Crescent Hotel ★TYYY
Howiesons Poort, on N2 to Port Elizabeth.
Tel 2-7326.

HANKEY 04236
Hankey Hotel ★RYYY, Box 30, Tel 322.

HOFMEYR 04852
Victoria Hotel ★TYYY, Molento Street.
Tel 111.

HOGSBACK 0020
Hogsback Inn ★TYYY, Box 63
Hogsback 5312. Tel 6. Situated 47 km from
Cathcart and 33 km from Alice in the
Amatola Mountains, Hogsback Inn can be
reached via Cathcart without traversing
any part of the Ciskei. Twenty-nine
bedrooms all en suite with private
bathroom. An historic wayside inn
established in the 1850s – the oldest
occupied site on the Hogsback with the
upper Tyumie River dividing the grounds
of the inn, over 7 hectares in extent. All of
the rooms have a garden view. Ladies bar
and television viewing lounge. Country
cooking and a private cellar of specially
selected and matured estate wines. Games
room. Natural rock swimming pool
supplied by own pure spring. The inn
adjoins the government forest and forest
walks and trails are marked. Fully
equipped conference centre (60 persons).
Personal management of the proprietors.
See pages 156, 157 and 158. In the grounds
of the Hogsback Inn bordering on the
forest are the Hogsback Mountain Cabins,
completely self-contained and fully
equipped.

Kings Lodge Hotel ★TYYY,
P O Hogsback. Tel 24.

JANSENVILLE 04932
Angora Inn ★TYYY, Main Street. Tel 243.

KENTON-ON-SEA 0464
Kenton Hotel ★TYYY, Box 6. Tel 81333.

KIRKWOOD 04262
Kirkwood Hotel ★TYYY, 185 Main
Street. Tel 294.

MIDDLETON 0424
Middleton Hotel ★TYYY, Tel 7-1250.

MPEKWENI (CISKEI) 0403
Mpekweni Marine Resort (licensed
hotel) P O Box 2060, Port Alfred 6170.
Tel 61-3126. 40 km from Port Alfred on the
R72 to East London, 130 km.

PATENSIE 04232
Ripple Hill Hotel ★TYYY, Box 68.
Tel 9902.

PATERSON 04282
Sandflats Hotel ★TYYY, Bruton Street.
Tel 12.

PEARSTON 0424
Pearston Hotel ★TYYY,
Voortrekker Street. Tel 6-1103.

PORT ALFRED 0464
Kowie Grand Hotel ★★TYYY,
cnr Princes Avenue and Grand Street,
Port Alfred. P O Box 1 Kowie West
6171. Telephone 4-1150/1. Situated high
above the Kowie River mouth and
within easy walking distance of the main
beach, the Kowie Grand Hotel provides
every comfort in a delightful holiday
environment, and in so doing it meets
the needs of every member of the
family. Each of the 24 bedrooms is en
suite with private bathroom and is
equipped with radio, telephone, coffee
maker and television, and enclosed
balconies offer commanding views of
the river and Indian Ocean. The Grand
has a reputation for excellent fare –
snacks in the Ladies Bar, carvery and
table d'hôte in the dining room, à la
carte in Granny's Restaurant are all well
prepared and presented. Drinks are
served in the View Lounge and on the
Sun Terrace. Ask about Kowie Grand
Timeshare, it is so easy to participate.
Pictures on pages 144 and 145, text on
pages 143 and 146.

Victoria Hotel ★★TYYY,
High Street, East Bank. Tel 4-1133.

Langdon Hotel ★TYYY, Beach Road,
West Bank. Tel 4-1122.

SOMERSET EAST 0324
Royal Hotel ★TYYY, Worcester Street.
Tel 3-2045.

STEYTLERVILLE 04952
Karoo Hotel ★TYYY, 2 km from the
town on the Vaalheuwel road. Box 5.
Tel 10.

THORNHILL 04212
Thornhill Hotel ★TYYY. Tel 653.

UITENHAGE 0422
Crown Hotel ★TYYY, 142 Caledon
Street. Tel 2-4417.

Rose & Shamrock Hotel ★TYYY,
21 John Street. Tel 2-1351.

Waterford Hotel ★TYYY,
127 Durban Street. Tel 2-8016.

6 — East London, the Border, North-eastern Cape and East Griqualand

EAST LONDON 0431
Kennaway Hotel ★★★TYYY,
Esplanade. Tel 2-5531.

Kings Hotel ★★★TYYY, Esplanade.
Tel 2-2561.

Dolphin Hotel ★★TYYY,
Nahoon Beach. Tel 5-3314.

Esplanade Hotel ★★TYYY,
Clifford Street. Tel 2-2518.

Holiday Inn ★★TYYY, Esplanade.
Tel 2-7260.

Osner Hotel ★★TYYY, Esplanade.
Tel 43-3433.

Weavers Hotel ★★TYYY, Esplanade.
Tel 2-3186.

ALIWAL NORTH 0551
Balmoral Hotel ★★T, Somerset Street.
Tel. 2452.

Juana Maria Hotel ★★TYYY, Barkly
and Smith Streets. Tel 2475.

Umtali Motel ★★TYYY, Dan Pienaar
Avenue, Spa. Tel 2400.

Aliwal Health Springs Hotel ★TYYY,
Duncan Street, Spa. Tel 3311.

Somerset Hotel ★TYYYY,
Somerset Street. Tel 2861.

Spa Hotel ★TYYY, Dan Pienaar Avenue,
Spa. Tel 2772.

BARKLY EAST 04542
Drakensberg Hotel ★TYYY,
Greyvenstein Street. Tel 277.

BEACON BAY 0431
Bonza Bay Hotel ★TYYY,
Kingfisher Avenue. Tel 47-2401.

BERLIN 04235
Berlin Hotel ★TYYY, Oxford Street.
Tel 2210.

BISHO (Ciskei) 0433
Amatola Sun Hotel & Casino, 6 km
from King William's Town on route R63 to
Kei Road. Tel 2-2516.

BURGERSDORP 055312
Jubilee Hotel ★TYYY, Smit & Coligny
Streets. Tel 101.

CATHCART 04562
Royal Hotel ★TYYY, Box 2. Tel 145.

DOHNE 04362
Tiptop Hotel ★TYYY, Box 265.
Tel 7720.

DORDRECHT 045512
Highveld Hotel ★TYYY, Grey Street.
Tel 81.

ELLIOT 045312
Merino Hotel ★TYYY, Maclear Road.
Tel 45.

Standford Hotel ★TYYY, Voortrekker
Street. Tel 90.

Mountain Shadows Hotel ★TYYY, in
the Barkly Pass. Dial 0020 and ask for
Barkly Pass 3, through Elliot.

FRANKLIN AND SWARTBERG 0374
Franklin Hotel ★TYYY. Tel 219.

Swartberg Country Club, Swartberg.
Tel 242.

GONUBIE 0431
Gonubie Hotel ★TYYY, 141 Main Road.
Tel 94-2591.

HAGA HAGA 04372
Haga Haga Hotel ★TYYY, Tel 6302.

INDWE 045522
Blue Crane Hotel ★TYYY, Barkly and
Graham Streets. Tel 116.

New Indwe Hotel ★TYYY,
Voortrekker Street. Tel 66.

KEI MOUTH 0020
Florence Hotel ★★TYYY, Neptune
Drive. Tel 11.

Kei Mouth Hotel ★TYYY,
Beach Road. Tel 17.

KEI ROAD 04337
Hangman's Inn ★TYYY, Main Street.
Tel 678.

KIDD'S BEACH 04323
Kidd's Beach Hotel ★TYYY,
Main Road. Tel 715.

KING WILLIAMS TOWN 0433
Central Hotel ★★TYYY, Market
Square. Tel 2-1440.

Commercial Hotel ★TYYY,
Downing Street. Tel 2-1578.

Crown Hotel ★TYYY,
Woodhouse Street. Tel 2-3025.

Grosvenor Hotel ★TYYY,
Taylor Street. Tel 2-2311.

Masonic Hotel ★TYYY,
Smith Street. Tel 2-2611.

KOKSTAD 0372
Ingeli Forest Motel ★★TYYY,
on routes N2 and R56 between Harding
and Kokstad. Tel dial 03942 and ask for
225. A first rate stop-over.

Balmoral Hotel ★TYYY, Hope Street.
Tel 3602.

Mount Currie Motel ★TYYY,
National road. Tel 2378.

Royal Hotel ★TYYY, 84 Main Street.
Tel 2060.

KOMGA 04372
Royal Hotel ★TYYY, 15 Main
Street. Tel 29.

LADY GREY 05552
Mountain View Hotel ★TYYY.
Botha Street. Tel 112.

MACLEAR 045322
Central Hotel ★TYYY,
Van Riebeeck Street. Tel 5.

Royal Hotel ★TYYY, Royal Road.
Tel 9907.

MATATIELE 0373
Royal Hotel ★TYYY, 103 Main Street.
Tel. 3100.

MOLTENO 04572
Central Hotel ★TYYY, Brownlee Street.
Tel 20.

Phoenix Hotel ★TYYY,
Brownlee Street. Tel 121.

MORGAN BAY 0020
Morgan Bay Hotel ★TYYY,
Tel Kei Mouth 62.

QUEENSTOWN 0451
Hexagon Hotel ★★TYYY,
The Hexagon. Tel 3015.

Central Hotel ★TYYY,
139 Cathcart Road. Tel 3150.

Gardens Hotel ★TYYY, Robinson Road.
Tel 3008.

Grand Hotel ★TYYY, 41 Cathcart Road,
Tel 3017.

Queens Hotel ★TYYY,
12 Calderwood Street. Tel 3138.

Royal Hotel ★TYYY, 104 Cathcart Road.
Tel 4004.

Windsor Hotel ★TYYY,
22 Cathcart Road. Tel 3119.

STERKSTROOM 04592
Premier Hotel ★TYYY, John Vorster St.
Tel 57.

STUTTERHEIM 04362
Scoonie Hotel ★TYYY, Maclean Street.
Tel 42.

Stutterheim Hotel ★TYYY, 49 Hill Street.
Tel 45.

TARKASTAD 04582
Royal Hotel ★TYYY, Murray Street.
Tel 58.

VENTERSTAD 055332
Union Hotel ★TYYY, Kruger Street.
Tel 50.

7 — Transkei and its Wild Coast

UMTATA 0471
Holiday Inn, off national road N2, at the
south end of the town. Opposite the
University of Transkei. Tel 2-2181.

QOLORA MOUTH 04341
Seagulls Hotel, Box 204, Butterworth.
Tel 3287.

Trennery's Hotel, P/Bag 3011,
Butterworth. Tel 3293.

WAVECREST 04341
Wavecrest Hotel, Box 81, Butterworth.
Tel 3273.

MAZEPPA BAY 04341
Mazeppa Bay Hotel, P/Bag 3014,
Butterworth. Tel 3278.

QORA MOUTH 0020
Kob Inn, P O Qora Mouth, Willowvale.
Tel ask for Qora Mouth No. 2.

**BASHEE MOUTH — THE HAVEN
0020**
The Haven Hotel, Bashee Mouth,
P O Elliotdale. Tel ask for The Haven
No 3.

COFFEE BAY, NQANDULI 0020
Ocean View Hotel, P O Nqanduli.
Tel ask for Nqanduli No. 59.

Lagoon Hotel, P O Nqanduli. Tel ask for
Nqanduli No. 50.

UMNGAZI MOUTH 04752
Umngazi Bungalows Hotel, P O Box 75,
Port St Johns. Tel 747.

PORT ST JOHNS 04752
Cape Hermes Hotel, Box 10. Tel 35.

CASINO 0471
Wildcoast Sun Hotel and Casino,
Box 23 Port Edward. Tel 5-9111. Central
Booking Durban (031) 304-9237.

8 — Durban and District and the Natal Coastal Resorts

DURBAN 031
Maharani Hotel ★★★★★TYYY,
Marine Parade. Tel 32-7361.

Royal Hotel ★★★★★TYYY,
267 Smith Street, Tel 304-0331.

Edward Hotel ★★★★TYYY,
Marine Parade. Tel 37-3681.

Elangeni Hotel ★★★★TYYY,
Marine Parade. Tel 37-1321.

Tropicana Hotel ★★★★TYYY,
Marine Parade. Tel 37-6261.

Albany Protea Hotel ★★★TYYY,
Smith Street, Tel 304-4381.

Blue Waters Hotel ★★★TYYY,
Snell Parade. Tel 32-6877.

Four Seasons Hotel ★★★TYYY,
85 Gillespie Street. Tel 37-3381.

Holiday Inn ★★★TYYY,
Sol Harris Crescent. Tel 37-1211.

Malibu Hotel ★★★TYYY,
Marine Parade. Tel 37-2231.

Athlone Hotel ★★TYYY, 10 Northway,
Durban North. Tel 84-1251.

Beach Hotel ★★TYYY, Marine Parade.
Tel 37-5511.

Belgica Hotel ★★TYYY, 74 St George's
Street. Tel 31-1064.

Lonsdale Hotel ★★TYYY, West Street.
Tel 37-3361.

Balmoral Hotel ★TYYY, Marine Parade.
Tel 37-4392.

Killarney Hotel ★TYYY, 21 Brickhill
Road. Tel 37-4281.

Palmerston Hotel ★TYYY,
Palmer Street. Tel 37-6363.

Pavilion Hotel ★T, Old Fort Road.
Tel 37-7366.

AMANZIMTOTI 031
Beach Hotel ★TYYY, 9 Beach Road.
Tel 93-5328.

Lagoon Hotel ★TYYY, 1 Beach Road.
Tel 93-2346.

BALLITO 0322
La Montagne, 100 Compensation Beach
Road. Tel 6-2121.

BOTHA'S HILL 031
Rob Roy Hotel ★★★TYYY,
Old Main Road, P O Box 10, Botha's Hill
3660. Telephone 777-1305. Telex 6-25226.
Thirty-seven luxury bedrooms and suites
all have private bathroom, radio, television
(with video channel), telephone and central
heating. MacGregor's Bar, the popular
rendezvous. The elegant Caledonia Dining
Room for superb carvery, and the
Clansman à la carte with its own intimate
ladies bar. Six functions rooms (5 to 150
persons), all visual aids and personal
attention. Indoor heated swimming-pool,
squash court and sauna bath. Sightseeing,
invigorating climate. Magnificent position
overlooking the Valley of a Thousand Hills.
See page 204.

Botha's Hill Hotel ★TYYY,
Old Main Road. Tel 777-1508.

CAMPERDOWN 03251
Camperdown Hotel ★RYYY, Shepstone
Street. Tel 5-1215.

Mandalay Farm Hotel ★TYYY, off
route R78 which leads from Umlass Road
to Kingsburgh on the South Coast.
Tel 5-1120.

CATO RIDGE 03251
Cato Ridge Hotel ★TYYY. Tel 2-1551.

CHAKA'S ROCK 0322
Chaka's Rock Hotel ★★TYYY,
P O Box 121 Umhlali. Tel 5015.

DRUMMOND 03251
Thousand Hills Hotel ★TYYY, Old
Main Road, Drummond. Tel 4343.

**GLENMORE BEACH SEE
VOORTREKKERSTRAND**

HIBBERDENE 0399
Alexander Hotel ★TYYY, Baracouda
Boulevard. Tel 2309.

HILLCREST 031
Hillcrest Hotel ★TYYY, Old Main Road.
Tel 75-2616.

ILLOVO 031
Illovo Hotel ★TYYY, 4 Walsh Place. Tel
96-2900.

KLOOF 031
Field's Hotel ★RYYY, Old Main Road.
Tel 74-1313.

Tina's Hotel ★TYYY, 14 Beryldene
Road. Tel 74-1325.

MARGATE 03931
Margate Hotel ★★TYYY, Marine Drive.
Tel 2-1410.

Palm Beach Hotel ★TYYY, Duke Road,
Beach front. Tel 2-1612.

MARINA BEACH 03931
Marina Beach Hotel ★TYYY, Marine
Drive. Tel 3-0022.

MTWALUME 03230
Mtwalume Hotel ★TYYY, Old Main
Road. Tel 783.

NEW GUELDERLAND 0324
New Guelderland Hotel ★TYYY,
Tel 2-2467.

ORIBI GORGE 0397
Oribi Gorge Hotel ★TYYY, P O Box
575, Port Shepstone. Tel 753.

PARK RYNIE 03231
Oceanic Hotel ★TYYY, Main Street. Tel
2-0080.

Park Rynie Hotel ★TYYY, Main
Street. Tel 2-1993.

PINETOWN 031
Rebel Inn ★RYYY, Underwood Road,
Sarnia. Tel 78-4232.

Park Lane Hotel ★TYYY, Park Lane.
Tel 72-3541.

PORT SHEPSTONE 0391
Bedford Inn ★★TYYY, Colley Street,
Tel 2-1085.

Marine Hotel ★TYYY, Bisset Street.
Tel 2-0281.

Port Shepstone Hotel ★TYYY, Bisset
Street. Tel 2-1378.

RAMSGATE 03931
Crayfish Inn ★★TYYY, Marine Drive.
Tel 4410.

ST MICHAEL'S-ON-SEA 03931
St Michael's Sands Hotel ★★TYYY,
No 1 Marine Drive, P O Box 45, St
Michael's-on-Sea 4265. Telephone 5-1230.
Holiday-wise St Michael's Sands has many
attributes and its most exciting feature is
its positioning. The hotel fronts northwards
directly onto the charming Umhlangeni
estuary, on its eastern boundary is one of
the safest and most beautiful beaches in
Natal, and on the western side, on its own
property, a near perfect 9-hole golf course.
To the south is a shopping centre and
further afield Margate and its divers
attractions. All bedrooms are tastefully
furnished with bathroom en suite and are
equipped with telephone, radio alarms,
colour television with video, coffee maker
and hairdryer. The Colonial Room à la
carte restaurant, Tartan Tavern bar with
live entertainment. Apart from the famed
golf course, there is a swimming-pool with
pool bar and coffee shop and a bowling
green. Mikes Kitchen on the premises. Ask
Ovland about timesharing. See pages 192
and 196.

SALT ROCK 0322

Salt Rock Palms (Salt Rock Hotel and Timeshare Resort) with its luxury apartments, bars, restaurants, swimming-pools, gym, sauna, bowls, tennis and squash, is due to be opened during December 1988. See page 201, and ask Ovland Timesharing for further details.

SAN LAMEER 03931

P O Box 78, Southbroom 4277. Telephone 3-0011. Telex 649217. A unique 134-hectare sub-tropical resort on coastal route R102 between Southbroom and Port Edward. Deluxe hotel accommodation and luxury self-contained villas. Langeler Room Restaurant, famed for its seafoods and international cuisine. Lagoon Coffee Shop serving breakfast and light meals. Two cocktail bars. Conference facilities up to 300 persons. The outstanding recreational facilities include a private ocean beach, golf, bowls, tennis, squash, horse-riding, boating, fishing, windsurfing, canoeing, and two swimming-pools. Owned by Sanlam and managed by Protea. See pages 193 and 198.

SCOTTBURGH 03231

Blue Marlin Hotel ★★TYYY, 180 Scott Street. Tel 2-1214.

Cutty Sark Hotel ★★TYYY, coastal route R102. Tel 2-1230.

Golf Inn Hotel ★★TYYY, Scott Street. Tel 2-0913.

SEZELA 03231

Sezela Hotel ★TYYY, P O Sezela. Tel 5-1330.

SHELLY BEACH 0391

Dawn View Hotel ★TYYY, coastal route R102. Tel 4841.

SHONGWENI 031

Polo Pony Hotel ★★TYYY, off national road N3. Tel 7-9729.

SOUTHPORT 0391

Southport Hotel ★TYYY, coastal route R102. Tel 3319.

STANGER 0324

Stanger Hotel ★★TYYY, Reynold Street. Tel 2-1291.

UMDLOTI BEACH 031

Umdloti Strand Hotel ★★TYYY, North Beach Road. Tel 5-8611.

UMHLALI 0322

Umhlali Hotel ★TYYY, Main Street. Tel 7-1557.

UMHLANGA 031

Beverly Hills Hotel ★★★★★TYYY, Lighthouse Road. Tel 561-2211.

Cabana Beach Hotel ★★★TYYY, 10 Lagoon Drive. Tel 561-2371

Oyster Box Hotel ★★★TYYY, 2 Lighthouse Road. P O Box 22, Umhlanga Rocks 4320. Telephone 561-2233. Ninety-five bedrooms/suites all en suite with private bathroom, equipped with telephone, radio, television (with video channel). The Oyster Box Grill famed for oysters and crayfish. The Pearl Room and The Green Room for functions and conferences of every description. Two cocktail bars. Beautiful 2-hectare tropical garden, all weather tennis court, filtered swimming-pool. The hotel at the water's edge. See page 200.

Umhlanga Sands Hotel ★★★TYYY, 44 Lagoon Drive. Tel 561-2323.

Breakers Resort Complex ★★TYYY, 88 Lagoon Drive. Tel 561-2271.

Edge of the Sea Hotel ★★TYYY, Lagoon Drive. Tel 561-1341.

Umhlanga Rocks Hotel ★★TYYY, Lagoon Drive. Tel 561-1321.

UMKOMAAS 03231

Lido Hotel ★★TYYY, 1 McLean Street. Tel 3-1002.

Ocean Park Hotel ★RTYYY, 53 Harvey Street. Tel 3-0181.

UMLAAS ROAD 03251

Van der Merwe Hotel ★TYYY, Old Main Road. Tel 96-3810.

UMTENTWENI 0391

Umtentweni Hotel ★TYYY, 222 Commercial Road. Tel 5-1138.

Venture Inn ★RYYY, Commercial Road. Tel 5-0110.

UMZINTO 03231

Archibald Hotel ★TYYY, Ixopo Road. Tel 4-2434.

Plough Hotel ★TYYY, Main Road. Tel 4-1990.

UMZUMBE 0391

Pumula Hotel ★TYYY, Steve Pitts Road. Tel 6717.

UVONGO BEACH 03931

La Crete Hotel ★★TYYY, Beach Front. Tel 5-1301.

VOORTREKKERSTRAND 03938

Glenmore Sands Hotel ★★TYYY, 1 Boulder Road. P O Box 10, Voortrekkerstrand 4279. Telephone 312. Twenty-two bedrooms all en suite with private bathroom and telephone, and completely equipped for self-catering. Nightingale à la carte restaurant. Turtles ladies bar, open till late and entertainment nightly. Filtered swimming-pool. The hotel is magnificently positioned, fronting onto the beach and Indian Ocean. See pages 192 and 198. Ask Ovland about timesharing.

WARNER BEACH 031

Seaward Hotel ★TYYY, 175 Kingsway. Tel 96-3333.

WESTBROOK BEACH 0322

Westbrook Beach Hotel ★★TYYY, at the beach. Box 48, Tongaat 4400. Tel 4-2021. Famed for sea foods and hospitality.

WESTVILLE 031

Westville Hotel ★★★TYYY, 124 Jan Hofmeyr Road. Tel 86-6326. Excellent restaurant, comfort and service.

WINKLE SPRUIT 031

Park Beach Hotel ★TY, Beach Road. Tel 96-2524.

9 — Zululand and Northern Natal

BABANANGO 03872

Babanango Hotel ★TYYY, Justice Street. Tel 34.

EMPANGENI 0351

Royal Hotel ★★TYYY, Turnbull Street. Tel 2-1601.

Imperial Hotel ★TYYY, Maxwell Street. Tel 2-1522.

ESHOWE 0354

George Hotel ★TYYY, Main Street. Tel 4-1124.

Royal Hotel ★TYYY, Osborn Road. Tel 4-1111.

GINGINDLOVU 035312

Imperial Hotel ★TYYY, Main Road. Tel 20.

HLOBANE 0386

Hlobane Hotel ★TYYY, Box 2. Tel 481.

Kongolana Hotel ★TYYY, Box 45. Tel 781.

HLUHLUWE 03562

Zululand Safari Lodge ★★★TYYY, Tel 64.

Hluhluwe Protea Hotel ★★TYYY, Tel 46.

JOZINI 0020

Jozini Ho-Motel, Tel 81.

MELMOTH 03545

Melmoth Inn ★TYYY, Reinhold Street. Tel 2074.

MKUZE 0020

Ghost Mountain Inn ★★TYYY, Box 18. Tel 18.

MTUBATUBA 03552

Safari Motel ★★TYYY, off national road N2 north. Tel 107.

Sundowner Hotel ★TYYY, Riverview Road. Tel 153.

MTUNZINI 035322

Trade Winds Hotel ★★TYYY, Hutchison Street. Tel 1.

Forest Inn Hotel ★★TYYY, National road N2 north. Tel 95.

NATAL SPA 03852

Natal Spa ★★TYYY, P O Box 122 Paulpietersburg. Telephone 03852 and ask for 4, 350 or 356. Telex 648327. Fifty-six bedrooms/suites en suite with private bathroom and equipped with TV/video and telephone. The diningroom serves a sumptuous carvery or à la carte, and can seat up to 350 people. The Koffiehuis serves light snacks, coffee and tea and is open all day. There is a ladies bar and the hotel has fully equipped conference rooms. The spa has nine hot and cold mineral spring pools ranging from cold to 44°C. The pools contain carbonates, chlorides, sulphates and magnesium. The riding school boasts fine horses and a fully qualified riding instructor for supervised outrides on the lovely 300-hectare farm. The other recreational amenities are: hiking trails, bowls, tennis, squash, fully equipped gymnasium, fishing in the Pivaan River, badminton and chess. There is a children's creche and a library on the premises. Ample parking. See page 217.

NKANDLA (KWAZULU) 0020

Nkandla Hotel, Tel 16.

PAULPIETERSBURG 03852

Dumbe Motel ★TYYY, High Street. Tel 131.

PONGOLA 03841

Pongola Hotel ★TYYY, Tel 3-1352.

RICHARDS BAY 0351

Richards Hotel ★★★TYYY, Hibberd Drive. Tel 3-1301.

Bayshore Inn ★★TYYY, The Gulley. Tel 3-2451.

ST LUCIA ESTUARY 03592

Lake View Hotel ★★TYYY, McKenzie Road. Tel 6.

Estuary Hotel ★TYYY, McKenzie Road. Tel 9.

ULUNDI (KWAZULU) 0358

Holiday Inn, Tel 2-1121

UTRECHT 03433

Grand Hotel, Tel 3028.

VRYHEID 0381

Stilwater Motel ★★TYYY, Vryheid-Dundee road. Tel 6181.

President Hotel ★TYYY, Church Street. Tel 5201.

10 — Pietermaritzburg, Natal Midlands, Natal Coalfields and Drakensberg Resorts

PIETERMARITZBURG 0331

Camden Hotel ★★★TYYY, 99 Pietermaritz Street. Tel 3-8921.

Capital Towers Hotel ★★★TYYY, 121 Commercial Road. Tel 94-2761.

Imperial Hotel ★★TYYY, 224 Loop Street. Tel 2-6551.

Royal Hotel ★★TYYY, 301 Burger Street. Tel 2-8555.

BALGOWAN 03324

Granny Mouse's Country House, Tel 4071.

BALLENGEICH 03431

Status Hotel Ballengeich ★TYYY, 15 km from Newcastle on route R23 to Ladysmith. Tel 7822.

BERGVILLE 03642

Walter Hotel ★TYYY, Tatham Road. Tel 12.

BULWER 033822

Bulwer Hotel ★TYYY, Cecil Street. Tel 9.

Mountain Park Hotel ★TYYY, Boast Street. Tel 26.

COLENSO 0362

Battlefields Hotel ★TYYY, St George's Street. Tel 2242.

CREIGHTON 0020

Creighton Hotel ★TYYY, 1 Clarke Road. Tel 10.

DALTON 033512

Dalton Hotel ★TYYY, Jacaranda Street. Tel 24.

DANNHAUSER 0344

DNC Hotel ★TYYY, Trunk route R23. Tel 2210.

DONNYBROOK 033812

Donnybrook Hotel ★TYYY, Tel 23.

DRAKENSBERG — SOUTHERN SECTION

Drakensberg Garden Hotel ★★TYYY, P O Underberg. Tel 0020 and ask for Drakensberg No 1.

Bushman's Nek, P/Bag 137, Underberg. Tel 033712 and ask for 103.

Sani Pass Hotel ★★★TYYY, P O Himeville 4585. Telephone 033722 and ask for 29. In recent times the accommodation and facilities of Sani Pass Hotel have been considerably up-graded and this together with natural attributes and the long standing experience of its directorate, places it in an enviable position as a leader among holiday hotels in the Berg. It is well known for the high standard of comfort, cuisine and hospitality. The accommodation comprises one hundred bedrooms in all, made up of 21 suites (3 executive) and 7 double rooms in the main building and 72 double and single rooms in the cottages and rondavels, all have private bathroom/shower, wall-to-wall carpeting and telephone. Candle-light dinner dances, evening entertainment, film shows. N'taba and Pipe and Hat Ladies bars, billiards. Trout fishing, horse riding, 9-hole country golf course, bowling greens, tennis courts, squash court. Filtered swimming-pool, sauna, jacuzzi and massage facility. Pool bar and snack lunches. Children's paddling pool and playground. Walks and climbs, landrover drives to the top of Sani Pass and into Lesotho. Bushman paintings in the surrounding mountains. Air strip. Shop. Fully equipped conference centre. See pages 228, 235 and 238.

DRAKENSBERG — CENTRAL SECTION

Cayley Guest Lodge, P O Box 241, Winterton 3340. Telephone 03682 and ask for 2722. Cayley is from the Gaelic *Ceilidh* which means 'a happy gathering' which is in every way true to the atmosphere provided by the owners, the Diack family, who personally supervise the Lodge. The 24 tastefully furnished bedrooms, each en suite with private bathroom and dressing room, command superb views of Cathkin Peak, Champagne Castle and the surrounding countryside. These suites are named after famous clans of Scotland and the Scottish theme is carried through the Lodge. Excellent home-cooked meals are served in the *Haggis Pot,* and although the premises are not licensed, you take your drinks to the convivial pub, the *Deoch-an-Doris.* Ever thoughtful of guests' comfort, log fires are lit in the comfortable lounge in winter, there is a super billiard room, separate TV viewing lounge, games room with table tennis and a wide verandah overlooking the majestic mountain scene. A filtered swimming-pool, all-weather tennis court, fishing, fine stables and forest walks make up the outdoor recreational opportunities. See pages 236, 237 and 239.

The Nest Hotel ★TYYY, Private Bag X14, Winterton 3340. In accommodation there is a choice of the tastefully furnished new luxury rooms each with private patio and breathtaking views of the mountains, or standard rooms in thatched rondavels. All rooms are en suite with private bathroom, fitted carpet, telephone and radio. The Nest is famed for wholesome home-cooked meals and well stocked wine cellar. There are two pubs, the large Cocktail Bar from where there is the stunning view of Champagne Castle and Cathkin Peak, and the very casual pub with its dart board and pool table. Guests have a choice of three lounges, including one for TV viewing from where videos are shown regularly. Other evening entertainment includes Saturday candlelight dinner and disco. The billiard room has a full size table and table tennis is played on the verandah. The Nest is known far and wide for its three

championship bowling greens (novices and informal games are encouraged), there are two all-weather tennis courts, a swimming-pool and a croquet lawn. The hotel has a fine stable of horses and the neighbourhood is renowned as ideal riding and walking country. You can expect warm hospitality from your hosts, the owners, Ernie and Edelweiss Malherbe. See pages 233 and 239.

El Mirador ★T, P O Winterton 3340. Tel 03642 and ask for El Mirador No 1.

Cathkin Park Hotel ★TYYY, P O Winterton 3340. Tel 03642 and ask for Cathkin Park No 1.

Drakensberg Sun Hotel ★★★TYYY, P O Winterton 3340. Tel 03642 and ask for Cathkin Park No 11.

Champagne Castle Hotel ★TYYY, P O Winterton 3340. Tel 03642 and ask for Champagne Castle No 3.

Cathedral Peak Hotel ★★TYYY, P O Winterton 3340. Telephone 03642 and ask for Cathedral Peak. Telex 646066. If ever a place has developed a personality Cathedral Peak Hotel has, and this has been brought about by its thrilling situation, so close to the peaks and pinnacles of the mountains, combined with the strong influence of the van der Riet family's hospitality. These assets cannot be bought at any price and Cathedral Peak will remain the first choice of many holiday visitors to the Natal Drakensberg. The hotel is renowned for its excellent table and wine cellar. There are 85 bedrooms each en suite with private bathroom, fitted carpet, radio and telephone. Ladies bar, TV viewing lounge, dancing and other evening entertainment. Beauty salon, hairdressing salon. Fully equipped gymnasium, squash court, sauna. Filtered swimming pool, children's paddling pool, playground and playroom, pony rides. Horse riding, all-weather tennis courts, bowling greens, mini golf, croquet lawn, deck quoits. Snooker room, table tennis. Trout fishing. Network of paths for mountain walks to viewsites and mountain climbing. Shop and petrol bowser. The complete conference centre. See pages 239, 240 and 241.

DRAKENSBERG — NORTHERN SECTION

Royal Natal National Park Hotel ★★TYYY, Private Bag 4, Mont-aux-Sources 3353. Telephone 03642 and ask for Mont-aux-Sources No 1. Positioned as it is in the most magnificently beautiful of all South Africa's national parks, this hotel bears a standing unmatched in the Drakensberg for the long list of its important visitors from all over the world, and with this credit is coupled its reputation for warm hearted hospitality. The accommodation ranges from luxury cottages to the traditional rondavels and all of the 68 bedrooms are en suite with private bathrooms and are equipped with fitted carpet, radio and telephone. Fine table, comfortable lounges (log fires in the winter) Pink Panther speciality bar and the Sentinel Inn, television viewing lounge. Snooker room. Evening entertainment includes dancing, film shows and games. Tennis courts, bowling greens, horse riding, swimming-pool. Year round trout fishing in hotel dam. Guided hikes every day – 200 km of marked walks and trails. Shop and petrol bowser. See pages 239, 242, 244, 245.

Mont-Aux-Sources Hotel ★TYYY, P/Bag 1, MXS. 3353. Tel 03642 and ask for MXS 7.

Cavern Berg Resort, P/Bag 626, Bergville 3350. Tel 03642 and ask for 172.

Little Switzerland Hotel ★TYYY, P O Box 200, Bergville 3350. Tel 03642 and ask for Robbers Roost 2.

DUNDEE 0341

El Mpati Hotel ★★TYYY, Victoria Street. Tel 2-1155.

ESTCOURT 03631

Lucey's Plough Hotel ★★TYYY, Harding Street. Tel 2-3040.

Estcourt Hotel ★TYYY, Harding Street. Tel 2-3043.

Willow Grange Hotel ★TYYY, on the old road to Mooi River. Tel 2-4622.

FAWN LEAS 033542

Fawn Leas Hotel ★TYYY, P O Fawn Leas. Tel 19.

FORT MISTAKE 0344

Andrew Motel ★TYYY, Box 1035, Ladysmith. Tel 2052.

GLENCOE 0341

Glencoe Hotel ★TYYY, Biggar Street. Tel 3-1157.

GREYTOWN 0334

Umvoti Hotel ★TYYY, Voortrekker Street. Tel 3-2018.

HARDING 03942

Southern Cross HOtel ★TYYY, Hawkins Street. Tel 70.

HIGHFLATS 033622

Highflats Hotel ★TYYY, Main Road. Tel 13.

HILTON 0331

Hilton Hotel ★★★TYYY, Hilton Road (off national road N3). P O Box 35, Hilton 3245. Telephone 3-3311. Telex 6-43206. Forty-one bedrooms individually decorated, en suite with private bathroom, fitted carpet, telephone, heating, radio and colour television. Three restaurants: The Copper Kitchen à la Carte, Lien Wah Chinese cuisine and the Hampton Room for the more informal meals and Sunday buffet. Ladies Bar (open fires during winter months). Three functions rooms. Tudor Room for conferences and receptions up to 300 persons; Hilton Room for private parties and meetings up to 36 persons and the Henry Room for intimate get-togethers up to 25 persons. In a beautiful 3-hectare garden setting, the on-property amenities include bowling greens, tennis court, a lovely swimming-pool and garden braai complex. Car park, undercover parking and lock-up garages. See pages 224 and 227.

Crossways Hotel ★TYYY, Box 16, Tel 3-3267.

HIMEVILLE 033722

Himeville Arms Hotel ★★TYYY, P O Box 105, Himeville 4585. Telephone 033722 and ask for No 5. The road to the Sani Pass runs through the delectable little village of Himeville, close to the Drakensberg. About half-way through the village it reaches the Himeville Arms. Whatever you do, don't be put off by the front façade - inside, the old village inn has been refurbished by your hosts the owners, Jonathan and Sylvia Aldous, and they have created an enviable ambience.

This is a really comfortable stop and base to explore the area. Accommodation comprises 13 guest rooms in a garden setting facing the mountains, these are all en suite with private bathroom. Ye Olde Himeville Arms pub, The Trout House à la carte Restaurant and the table d'hôte dining room beckon you to enjoy the comfort, service, fine fare and warm hospitality. The hotel has a lovely swimming-pool and within five kilometres there is trout fishing, golf, tennis and bowls. See pages 229 and 235.

HOWICK 03321

Howick Falls Hotel ★TYYY, Main Street. Tel 2809.

INGOGO 03434

Inkwelo Motel, Mount Prospect, route R23. Tel 737.

Valley Inn Hotel ★TYYY, route R23. Tel 721.

IXOPO 033612

Off Saddle Hotel ★TYYY, Margaret Street. Tel. 27

Plough Hotel ★TYYY, Margaret Street. Tel 80.

KRANSKOP 03344

Kranskop Hotel ★TYYY, Main Street. Tel 739.

LADYSMITH 0361

Crown Hotel ★★TYYY, Murchison Street. Tel 2-2266.

Royal Hotel ★★TYYY, Murchison Street. Tel 2-2176.

Andrew Motel, at the aerodrome, south of the town. Tel 2-6908.

LIONS RIVER 03324

Hebron Haven Farm Hotel ★TYYY. Tel 4431

MOOI RIVER 0333

Hartford Country House ★★★TYYY, P O Box 31. Tel 3-1081

Argyll Hotel ★TYYY, Lawrence Road. Tel 3 1106

Sierra Ranch Hotel ★TYYY, Mooi River – Greytown road. Tel 3-1073.

MUDEN 03346

Golden Valley Hotel ★TYYY, Main Road. Tel 611.

NEWCASTLE 03431

Holiday Inn ★★TYYY, Victoria and Hunter Streets. Tel 2-8151.

Kings Hotel ★TYYY, 15 Harding Street. Tel 2-6101.

NOTTINGHAM ROAD 0333

Rawdon's Hotel ★★★TYYY, Old Main Road (off national road N3) Tel 3-6044. A distinguished hotel, famed for its comfort, cuisine and tranquil setting.

Nottingham Road Hotel ★TYYY, in the village. Tel 3-6151.

RICHMOND 03322

Central Hotel ★TYYY, Shepstone Street. Tel 2164.

Richmond Hotel ★TYYY, Shepstone Street. Tel 2166.

The Oaks Hotel ★TYYY, at Byrne. Tel 2324.

THORNVILLE JUNCTION 03325

Thornville Hotel ★TYYY, Main Road Tel 300.

UNDERBERG 03372

Underberg Hotel ★TYYY, Main Road. Tel 22.

VAN REENEN 014364

Andrew Motel ★TYYY, national road N3, in the pass. Tel 741.

Green Lantern Inn ★TYYY, Wragg Street. Tel 691.

WARTBURG 033532

Wartburger Hof ★★★TYYY, Noodsberg Road. Tel 268.

WASBANK 0345

Waschbank Hotel ★TYYY, Box 2, Tel 336.

WINTERTON 03682

Bridge Hotel ★TYYY, Springfield Road. Tel 54.

11 — Johannesburg, Witwatersrand, Southern and Western Transvaal

JOHANNESBURG 011

Carlton Hotel ★★★★★TYYY, Main Street. Tel 331-8911.

Johannesburg Sun and Towers ★★★★★TYYY, Jeppe Street. Tel 482-2327.

Sandton Sun Hotel ★★★★★TYYY, Sandton City. Tel 783-8701.

Rosebank Hotel ★★★★TYYY, Tyrwhitt Avenue, Rosebank. Tel 788-1820.

Braamfontein Hotel ★★★★TYYY, De Korte Street. Tel 725-4110.

Protea Gardens Hotel ★★★★TYYY, O'Reilly Road, Berea. Tel 643-6610.

Holiday Inns, all ★★★TYYY:-
Down Town Tel 28-1770
Jan Smuts Tel 975-1121
Milpark Tel 726-5100
Sandton Tel 783-5262

Indaba Hotel and Conference Centre ★★★TYYY, Hartbeespoort Dam Road, Witkoppen. P O Box 67129, Bryanston 2021. Telephone (011) 465-1400. Telex 4-30132. The complex comprises 6 specialised lecture theatres each with projection room supported by 24 small syndicate rooms, highly developed audio visual in-situ includes Betamax, VHS and Umatic video systems, visual display unit, 35mm, 16mm and overhead projection, on-line computer facilities, a 200-seater audittorium and a 225-seater banqueting room make Indaba the premier conference centre in the country. Amenities include 2 sparkling swimming pools, 2 floodlit tennis courts, two airconditioned squash courts with saunas. The Ndaba, a self-contained executive wing, boasts its own reception area, 2 lecture rooms, 8 syndicate rooms, and 30 bedrooms. A luxurious lounge and dining room, both of which lead onto a resplendent pool and braai terrace. With good food and wines, personalised service and comfortable rooms in an atmosphere of relaxation and country elegance, Indaba Hotel and Conference Centre offers the ideal venue for both business and holiday maker with easy accessibility from Johannesburg, Pretoria and airports. There is ample parking and a helipad. See pages 248, 249, 251.

Johannesburger Hotel ★★★TYYY, Twist Street. Tel 725-3753.

Mariston ★★★T, Claim and Koch Streets. Tel 725-4130.

Moulin Rouge Hotel ★★★TYYY, Claim Street. Tel 725-4840.

Southern Sun Airport Hotel ★★★TYYY, Jan Smuts Airport. Tel 974-6911.

Sunnyside Park Hotel ★★★TYYY, 2 York Street. Tel 643-7226.

Ambassador Hotel ★★TYYY, 52a Pretoria Street, Hillbrow. Tel 642-5051.

Dawsons Hotel ★★TYYY, 117 President Street. Tel 337-5010.

Diplomat Hotel ★★T, Klein and Bree Streets. Tel 29-2161.

Quirinale Hotel ★★TYYY, 27 Kotze Street. Tel 724-1725.

Victoria Hotel ★★TYYY, 25 Plein Street. Tel 28-1530.

Alba Hotel ★TYYY, 90 de Kotze Street. Tel 339-1361.

Constantia Hotel ★TY, 35 Quartz Street. Tel 725-1046.

Oxford Hotel ★TYYY, 165 Oxford Road, Rosebank. Tel 442-9216.

ALBERTON 011

Alberton Hotel ★★TYYY, 34 Voortrekker Road. Tel 869-4618.

Newmarket Hotel ★TYYY, Voortrekker Road. Tel 869-6251.

BALFOUR 01562

Balfour Hotel ★TYYY, 20 Stuart Street. Tel 259.

BAPSFONTEIN 011

Bapsfontein Hotel ★TYYY, Box 7092, Petit. Tel 964-1305.

BARBERSPAN 0144322

Elgro Hotel ★TYYY, Sandvlei. Tel 28.

BENONI 011

The Prospector Hotel ★★★TYYY, 2 Voortrekker Road. Tel 54-9911.

Van Riebeeck Hotel ★★TYYY, Great North Road. Tel 849-8917.

BLOEMHOF 018022

Bloemhof Hotel ★TYYY, 49 Prins Street. Tel 211.

BOKSBURG 011

Transvaal Hotel ★TYYY, 14 Kerk Street. Tel 52-7487.

BRAKPAN 011

Dunswart Hotel ★TYYY, 4 Main Reef Road. Tel 54-5454.

Savoy Hotel ★RYYY, 241 Prince George Avenue. Tel 55-1226.

CARLTONVILLE 01491

Carltonville Hotel ★TYYY, Gold Street. Tel 3305.

President Hotel ★TYYY, Annan Road. Tel 6771.

COLIGNY 014462

Coligny Hotel ★TYYY, Voortrekker Street. Tel 88.

DELAREYVILLE 0144312

Elgro Hotel ★TYYY, General Delarey Street. Tel 25.

DELMAS 0157

Delmas Hotel ★TYYY, Sarel Cilliers Street. Tel 3002.

DEVON 01582

Devon Hotel ★TYYY, Derwig Street. Tel 52.

DUNNOTTAR 011

Dunnottar Hotel ★TYYY, 50 Nigel Road. Tel 734-2551.

EDENVALE 011

Duneden Hotel ★★TYYY, 46 Van Riebeeck Avenue. Tel 53-8610.

EIKENHOF 011

Lido Travelodge ★TYYY, Old Vereeniging Road. Tel 948-9049.

ELANDSFONTEIN 011

Delmont Hotel ★TYYY, North Reef Road. Tel 974-1066.

ELOFF 0157

Mimosa Hotel and Pleasure Resort ★TYYY, 21 km from Springs on the road to Delmas. Tel 9661.

ELSBURG 011

Republic Hotel ★RYYY, Voortrekker Street. Tel 827-2212.

FLORIDA 011

Killarney Hotel ★TYYY, 42 Hull Street. Tel 672-5301.

Lake Hotel ★TYYY, Fourth Avenue. Tel 672-0540.

FOCHVILLE 01492

Flamingo Hotel ★TYYY, Losberg Street. Tel 2065.

Kraalkop Hotel ★TYYY, 55 km from Potchefstroom on the Johannesburg road. Tel 2958.

GERMISTON 011

Caledonian Hotel ★RYYY, 1 Main Reef Road, Primrose. Tel 825-6120.

Clarendon Hotel ★RYYY, 72 Webber Road. Tel 825-1610.

Primrose Hotel ★TYYY, Rietfontein Road. Tel 58-9061.

GREYLINGSTAD 015082

Grand Hotel ★TYYY, Main Street. Tel 9904/59.

GROOTVLEI 015092

Merino Hotel. Tel 124.

HALFWAY HOUSE 011

Halfway House Hotel ★TYYY, Old Pretoria Road, Midrand. Tel 805-3048.

HARTBEESFONTEIN 018122

Transvaal Hotel ★TYYY, Voortrekker Road. Tel 11.

HEIDELBERG 0151

Heidelberg Hotel ★TYYY, Box 3. Tel 6201.

HONEYDEW 011

Honeydew Motel ★TYYY, D.F. Malan Drive. Tel 795-3641.

KEMPTON PARK 011

Kempton Hotel ★TYYY, Pretoria Road. Tel 975-2961.

KLERKSDORP 018

Constantia Hotel ★★TYYY, Emily Hobhouse Street. Tel 2-4501.

Klerksdorp Hotel ★★TYYY, Anderson Street. Tel 2-3521.

Van Riebeeck Hotel ★★TYYY, Plein and Kok Streets. Tel 2-9451.

KOSTER 0142412

Koster Hotel ★TYYY, Brink Street. Tel 400.

KRUGERSDORP 011

Witpoortjie Hotel ★★TYYY, Main Reef Road, Luipaard Street. Tel 664-6009.

Bacchus Inn ★RYYY, 33 Ockerse Street. Tel 660-6027.

Luipaard Hotel ★TYYY, Luipaard and Monument Streets. Tel 665-1167.

LEEUDORINGSTAD 01813

Leeudoringstad Hotel ★TYYY, George Street. Tel 2045.

LICHTENBURG 01441

Elgro Hotel ★★TYYY, Republic and Scholtz Streets. Tel 2-3051.

Langrish Hotel ★TYYY, Scholtz Street. Tel 2-5041.

LOCH VAAL 016

Loch Vaal Hotel ★TYYY, Vanderbijlpark/Barrage Road. Tel 87-2006.

MAGALIESBURG 01382

Mount Grace Country House Hotel ★★★TYYY, off route R24 outside Magaliesburg village on the way to Rustenburg. P O Box 251, Magaliesburg 2805. Telephone – dial 01382 and ask for 119. Forty bedrooms/suites all en suite with private bathroom, fitted carpet, telephone, radio, television, heater. Thatchstone à la carte Restaurant (buffet lunch on Sunday). The Copperfield Restaurant for breakfast and light meals. Hartley's intimate pub. Swimming-pool, tennis court, evergreen bent grass bowling green, volley-ball, paddle tennis, trampoline. Opportunities for hiking and picnics. Conference centre with every modern visual aid – three venues accommodating from 8 to 150 persons. Protestant inter-denominational church services are held every Sunday at 10.30 am. The hotel property is 17 hectares in extent and there is a large macadamised carpark and covered parking. See pages 256, 257 and 259.

Happy Valley Hotel ★TYYY, Box 13. Tel 93.

Magaliesburg Hotel ★TYYY, Rustenburg Road. Tel 26.

MAKWASSIE 01811

Makwassie Hotel ★★TYYY, Potgieter Street. Tel 4237.

MARAISBURG 011

Delarey Hotel ★RYYY, 635 Ontdekkers Road. Tel 673-5091.

Maraisburg Hotel ★RYYY, 16 Tenth Avenue. Tel 672-5338.

MEYERTON 01612

Meyerton Hotel ★TYYY, Loch Street. Tel 2-1448.

MULDERSDRIFT 011

Beau Valley Hotel ★TYYY, Swartkop Road. Tel 659-1324.

NIGEL 011

New Goldfields Hotel ★TYYY, 50 Springs Road. Tel 739-3300.

Noycedale Hotel ★TYYY, Heidelberg Road. Tel 739-2005.

ORKNEY 018

Reefway Hotel ★TYYY, Kingley Avenue. Tel 3-1731.

Riesling Hotel ★TYYY, Patmore Road. Tel 3-1471.

PERDEKOP 013362

Perdekop Hotel ★TYYY, Durban Street. Tel 95.

POTCHEFSTROOM 0148

Elgro Hotel ★★TYYY, 60 Wolmarans Street. Tel 2-5411.

Impala Hotel ★TYYY, Church Street. Tel 2-3954.

Royal Hotel ★TYYY, Lombard Street. Tel 4219.

RANDBURG 011

Ridgeway Hotel ★★TYYY, 158 Hendrik Verwoerd Drive. Tel 787-1000.

RANDFONTEIN 011

Central Hotel ★RYYY, 50 Main Road. Tel 693-3068.

Rand Hotel ★RYYY, 7 Main Road. Tel 693-2086.

ROODEPOORT 011

Bacchus Inn ★RYYY, 8 Burger Street. Tel 763-6187.

Roodepoort Hotel ★RYYY, 17 President Square. Tel 763-3923.

Savoy Hotel ★RYYY, Burger Street. Tel 763-3293.

RUSTENBURG 01421

Belvedere Hotel ★★TYYY, Box 1298. Tel 9-2121.

Cashane Hotel ★★TYYY, 66 Steen Street. Tel 2-8541.

Hunter's Rest Hotel ★★TYYY, 13 km from the town off route R24. Tel 9-2140.

Safari Hotel ★★TYYY, 7 km from town opposite the Kloof. Tel 3-1053.

Sparkling Waters Hotel ★★TYYY, off route R24. Tel 9-3240.

Wigwam Holiday Hotel ★★TYYY, off route R24. Tel 9-2147.

Ananda Holiday Resort ★TYYY, 6 km from town on Swartruggens Road. Tel 2-2332.

Olifantshoek, 17 km from town off route 24. Tel 9-2208.

Cynthiana Hotel ★TYYY, 4 km from town off route 24. Tel 9-2361. (Previously Tambuti Inn.)

Toeriste Hotel ★TYYY, 4 Pretorius Street. Tel 2-2470.

Transvaal Hotel ★TYYY, 7 Prinsloo Street. Tel 2-9351.

SANDTON 011

Sandton Sun Hotel ★★★★★TYYY, Sandton City. Tel 783-8701.

Balalaika Hotel ★★★TYYY, Maud Street. Tel 884-1400

Holiday Inn ★★★TYYY, Rivonia Road. Tel 783-5262.

Indaba Hotel and Conference Centre ★★★TYYY, Box 67129, Bryanston 2021. Tel 465-1400. Full details listed under Johannesburg on page 403.

Sleepy Hollow Hotel ★★TYYY, 11th Avenue, Rivonia. Tel 803-1005.

SANNIESHOF 014472

Sannieshof Hotel ★TYYY, Spoor Street. Tel 104.

SCHWEIZER-RENEKE 018012

Therese Hotel ★TYYY, 18 Delport Street. Tel 5.

SPRINGS 011

New Casseldale Hotel ★RYYY, 36 Ermelo Road Casseldale. Tel 56-8123.

Park Hotel ★RYYY, 124 Nigel Road, Selection Park. Tel 818-5115.

Veld and Vlei Hotel ★TYYY, 114 Third Avenue. Tel 812-2514.

Vossie's Royal Hotel ★RYYY, Fourth Avenue, Geduld. Tel 812-2658.

STANDERTON 01331

Masonic Hotel ★TYYY, 26 Charl Cilliers Street. Tel 2-1366.

Toristo Hotel ★TYYY, 20 Piet Retief Street. Tel 2-5371.

STILFONTEIN 018

Three Fountains Hotel ★TYYY, Box 55. Tel 4-1771.

SWARTRUGGENS 014262

Swartruggens Hotel ★TYYY, 541 Aletta Street. Tel 82.

THABAZIMBI 01537

Kransberg Hotel ★★TYYY, Deena Street. Tel 21-207.

VANDERBIJLPARK 016

Riverside Holiday Inn ★★★TYYY, Kemmon-Wilson Drive, 5 km from town at the Vaal River. Tel 32-1111.

Killarney Hotel ★TYYY, Siemens and Jenner Streets. Tel 33-4021.

Park Hotel ★TYYY, Shakespeare and Ferraday. Tel 33-4821.

Van Riebeeck Hotel ★TYYY, 8 Jean Street. Tell 33-4461.

VENTERSDORP 01480

Ventersdorp Hotel ★TYYY, Carmichael Street. Tel 2033.

VEREENIGING 016

Riviera International Hotel and Country Club, Vaal River. Tel 22-2861.

Central Hotel ★TYYY, 21 Beaconsfield Avenue. Tel 21-1778.

Hilton Hotel ★TYYY, Voortrekker Street. Tel 21-3957.

VOLKSRUST 01333

Andrew Motel ★★TYYY, 8 km from town on Standerton Road. Tel 2150.

Transvaal Hotel ★★TYYY, 57 Joubert Street. Tel 2078.

WESTONARIA 011

Main Shaft Hotel ★★TYYY, Box 990. Tel 753-2206.

Golden West Hotel ★TYYY, Codrington Street. Tel 753-2621.

WOLMARANSSTAD 01811

Wolmaransstad Hotel ★TYYY, Kruger Street. Tel 2-1160.

ZEERUST 01428

Marico Hotel ★TYYY, 5 Church Street. Tel 2-1164.

Transvaal Hotel ★TYYY, 22 Church Street. Tel 2-2003.

12 — Pretoria, Northern Transvaal, Eastern Transvaal and Kruger National Park

PRETORIA 012

Burgerspark Hotel ★★★TYYY, Minnaar and van der Walt Streets. Tel 28-6570.

Boulevard Hotel ★★★TYYY, 186 Struben Street. Tel 26-4806.

Holiday Inn ★★★TYYY, Church and Beatrix Streets. Tel 341-1571.

Karos Manhattan ★★★TYYY, 247 Scheiding Street. Tel 28-6061.

Palms Hotel ★★★TYYY, 682 Pretoria Road, Silverton. Tel 86-1014.

Protea Hof ★★★TYYY, Pretorius and Van der Walt Streets. Tel 28-6900.

Arcadia Hotel ★★TYYY, 515 Proes Street. Tel 26-9311.

Continental Hotel ★★TYYY, 152 Visagie Street. Tel 323-2241.

Hamsin Hotel ★★TYYY, 675 Pretorius Street. Tel 42-5154.

New Union Hotel ★★TYYY, 573 Church Stret. Tel 42-5001.

Assembly Hotel ★★TYYY, Van der Walt and Visagie Streets. Tel 323-3075.

New Summerhill Hotel ★TYYY, Bon Accord. 14 km from city on old Warmbaths Road. Tel 5-9215.

ALLDAYS 01554

Alldays Hotel ★TYYY, Box 46. Tel 405.

AMSTERDAM 013421

Amsterdam Hotel ★TYYY, 102 President street. Tel 255.

BADPLAAS 013482

Badplaas Hotel ★★TYYY, at Overvaal Resort. Box 15. Tel 7/41.

BANDERLIERKOP 0020

Lalapanzi Hotel ★TYYY, Tel 13.

BARBERTON 01314

Impala Hotel ★★TYYY, De Villiers Street. Tel 2108.

Phoenix Hotel ★TYYY, Pilgrim Street. Tel 4211.

BELFAST 0132512

Belfast Hotel ★TYYY, Vermooten Street. Tel 60.

BETHAL 01361

Christo Hotel ★★TYYY, Lakeside Avenue. Tel 5970.

Douglas Hotel ★TYYY, 100 Main Avenue. Tel 2469.

Selborne Hotel ★TYYY, 52 Mark Street. Tel 2358.

BREYTON 013452

Breyton Hotel ★TYYY, Steyn Street. Tel 5.

BRITS 01211

Overberg Hotel ★★★TYYY, 8 Church Street. Tel 2-4270.

Molani Hotel ★TYYY, 32 Church Street. Tel 2-0518.

BRONKHORSTSPRUIT 012121

Park Hotel ★TYYY, 18 Church Street. Tel 2-3105.

CAROLINA 013442

Carolina Hotel ★TYYY, Voortrekker Street. Tel 356.

CHRISSIESMEER 0134232

Chrissies Hotel ★TYYY, King Edward Street. Tel 64.

CULLINAN 01213

Premier Hotel ★RYYY, Hotel Street. Tel 3-0204.

La Château. A delectable retreat in the farming district of Cullinan, half an hour from Pretoria. Quite unusual in South Africa. Comfortable suites, excellent restaurant. Tel 3-1411 or 3-1474.

DENNILTON 0020
Bundu Inn ★TYYY, on the R25. Tel Simpkinsvale No 2.
DUIWELSKLOOF 015236
Imp Inn ★TYYY, Both Street. Tel 3253.
DULLSTROOM 0132522
Dullstroom Inn ★TYYY, Box 44. Tel 11.
ELANDSHOEK 0020
Montrose Falls Hotel ★TYYY, national road N4, 30 km west of Nelspruit. Tel Montrose Falls No 3.
ELLISRAS 01536
Ellisras Hotel ★TYYY, Main Street. Tel 3-2140.
ERMELO 01341
Holiday Inn ★★TYYY, Kerk and Fourie Streets. Tel 2315.
Libertas Hotel ★★TYYY, 25 De Clerque Street. Tel 2234.
Merino Hotel ★TYYY, Joubert Street. Tel 2321.
GRASKOP 0131522
Kowyn Hotel ★★TYYY, Main Road. P O Box 64. Telephone 44. Twenty-nine bedrooms all have private bathroom/shower, telephone, radio and wall-to-wall carpeting. Ladies Bar. Television lounges. Steak Bar (fresh trout). Swimming-pool and braaivleis. Indoor games, film shows and music. Special attraction for families and budget holiday-makers are the 15 well-equipped chalets (with private bathroom), and five self-contained luxury log cabins on the off-licensed section of the property. The hotel is 52 km from Numbi Gate, Kruger National Park and 62 km from Paul Kruger Gate (Skukuza entrance). See page 309.
GRAVELOTTE 0152332
Casa Creda Hotel ★TYYY, Antimony Road. Tel 35.
GROBBLERSDAL 01202
Grobblersdale Hotel ★TYYY, Van Riebeeck Street. Tel 2057.
Loskop Hotel ★TYYY, Van Riebeeck Street. Tel 2081.
HARTBEESPOORT 01211
Hartbeespoort Lake Hotel ★TYYY, Monica Street. Tel 3-0001.
HAZYVIEW 0131242
Casa do Sol Hotel ★★★TYYY, 4 km from Hazyview on the Sabie road (R536). P O Box 57, Hazyview 1242. For all reservations telephone (011) 880-2000 or telex 431005. To reach the hotel dial 0131242 and ask for 22. Of all the lovely places to stay, Casa do Sol will remain the favourite of a great many people who visit the eastern Transvaal – the answer to the question 'what is the attraction' is surely the whole ensemble. Casa is under the personal direction and care of the owners, the Bailey's – Wellesley with his wizardry in constructional imagination and Odette with her natural aptitude in garden landscape have combined to produce this uniquely beautiful Mediterranean village in 600 hectares of parkland, where game animals such as antelope, zebra and giraffe are being introduced. In this enchanting setting are the holiday amenities, hospitality, comfort and fine cuisine for which Casa is famed. There is a wide range of accommodation available: casas, villas, luxury suite villas on ground or upper floor, double-storeyed executive suite, and self-contained, 3-bedroom guest-house. All accommodation is en suite with private bathroom and has TV, telephone, airconditioning, cocktail cabinet and bar fridge. The executive suite and the guest-house each has its own swimming-pool and jacuzzi. Chiquitas bar is close to the table d'hôte restaurant, A Cozinha Velha (cozy and intimate), where you'll find a fabulous 24 item breakfast menu. The quaint stable restaurant O Estábulo à la carte has its own bar and a separate kitchen. Recreation includes film shows, dancing, swimming-pool with poolside Bar Tropique, tennis court, horse riding, bass fishing, canoeing and game trails. Casa is only 25 km from Kruger National Park. Fully equipped conference centre. Exclusive opportunity for past guests to participate in timesharing. See pages 306, 307 and 310.

Sabie River Hotel and Coutry Club ★★★TYYY, Hazyview – Sabie road. Tel 12.
Don Carlos Hotel ★★TYYY, Box 105, Tel 51.
Numbi Hotel ★★TYYY, Main Road. Tel 6.
Böhm's Zeederberg Gastehaus, Hazyview-Sabie road. Tel 1111. A delightful place to stop awhile.
HECTORSPRUIT 013161
Buffalo Hotel ★TYYY, First Street. Tel 834.
HENDRINA 013282
Hendrina Hotel ★TYYY, Scheepers Street. Tel 39.
HOEDSPRUIT 0131732
Fort Coepieba Motel ★TYYY, Box 35. Tel 35.
River Lodge ★TYYY, Box 53 Tel 5813.
KINROSS 01363
Werda Hotel ★TYYY, Voortrekker Road. Tel 7-1181.
KLASERIE 0131732
Cheetah Inn ★TYYY, 6 km from Klaserie on Thorny Bush/Hoedspruit Road. Tel. 6.
KOMATIPOORT 013163
Doeane Motel ★TYYY, national Road N4. Tel 3237.
Komati Hotel ★TYYY, 5 Hutton Street. Tel 1333.
LOSKOP DAM (NEAR GROBLERSDAL) 01202
Kloof Motel ★TYYY. Tel 4016.
LOUIS TRICHARDT 01551
Clouds End Hotel ★★TYYY, 3 km north of town. Tel 9621.
Mountain Inn ★★TYYY, 6 km north of town. Tel 9631.
Ingwe Motel ★TYYY, 15 km north of town. Tel 9687.
LYDENBURG 01323
Lydenburg Hotel ★★TYYY, Burgersfort Road (R37) 3 km from the town. P O Box 660 Lydenburg 1120. Telephone (01323) 2091. Telex 4-24004. Eighteen bedrooms all en suite with private bathroom, fitted carpet, telephone and radio (8 rooms have television). Die Ou Dae à la carte restaurant, Plough Inn ladies bar. Functions room for 200 persons. Open parking. Swimming-pool and 5 hectares of garden. Trout fishing by arrangement. See pages 310, 312 and 313.
Morgan's Hotel ★★TYYY, Voortrekker Street. Tel 2165.
LYDENBURG — BURGERSFORT 013230
Gethlané Lodge ★★★TYYY, P O Box 28 Burgersfort 1150. Telephone and Fax (013230) 827 and 865/6. Central reservations (011) 339-5979. Telex 488784 SA. As the name implies this is a 'place of tranquillity', but indeed it is more than that – on arrival here you immediately experience the feeling of well-being and carefree comfort, and this surely is what holidays are all about. Gethlané has it all, particularly in the fields of relaxation and recreation – three swimming-pools (each different in size and beautiful aspect, filled with mineral water 29°C at source), jacuzzi, sauna, tennis courts, croquet, target golf, volley ball. Placed as it is in a 180-hectare nature reserve, the opportunities abound for game trails, bird trails, nature walks and horse riding. The children have not been forgotten with their playground, farmyard and aviary. Indoors there's pool table, darts, table tennis, videos, board games. In the main building the Izinyoni à la carte restaurant leads off the large reception area and on this level is the TV viewing lounge (2nd channel video). On the upper level there is a comfortable lounge and the Lowveld Loft ladies bar.
In the garden is the Summer House open air restaurant and The Hut pool bar. The accommodation consists of 3 deluxe chalets, 10 family chalets, 5 twin-room chalets and 6 rondavels. All rooms are en suite with private bathroom, airconditioning and heating, fitted carpet, telephone, radio and hair dryer. The luxury rooms have TV and trouser press. The fully equipped conference centre has controllable airconditioning and can seat up to 60 delegates. Under cover parking and registered airstrip.
Ask about timesharing of new duplex accommodation.
Gethlané is personally supervised by owners Keith and Marian Lodewick. Road directions on page 313 and photographs on pages 314/315.
MACHADODORP 013242
Bambi Motel ★★★TYYY, 23 km from town on Schoemanskloof Road (R539). Tel 101.
Hydro Baths Hotel ★TYYY, in the town. Tel 114.
MAGOEBASKLOOF 0152222
Magoebaskloof Hotel ★★TYYY, spectacularly situated at the top of the Magoebaskloof pass (route R71). P O Magoebaskloof 0731. Telephone 0152222 and ask for 82 or 83. The 52 spacious bedrooms (including the honeymoon suite) all have a lovely aspect (with views down the kloof or over the garden to the hills and forests) and each is en suite with private bathroom and TV. The hotel is notable for its good table and is able to draw on the abundance of sub-tropical fruit, fresh farm produce and mountain trout for which the district is renowned. On property squash, bowls, billiards and swimming-pool, and nearby fishing, tennis, yachting, boating, hiking and golf. See pages 276, 278 and 279.

Troutwaters Inn ★★TYYY and Lake-side Chalets, are situated on route R71, at the edge of the escarpment on the Help-mekaar River which flows into the Ebe-nezer dam, P O Magoebaskloof 0731. Tel (0152222) ask for 53 or 80. The Inn has 16 delightful suites, each comprising one or two bedrooms, bathroom and lounge (accommodating families of 4 of 6 persons). Each suite has its own refrigerator, TV (with video channel), radio and telephone. The à la carte restaurant caters for meals at reasonable prices, and there is the Dry Fly ladies bar (open fires in the winter). Lakeside Chalets and caravan park are on the adjoining property. The chalets and bungalows are self-contained, comfortably furnished and serviced daily. All facilities, tennis, trout fishing, boating, trampoline and swimming-pool available to residents. Squash, bowls and golf nearby. Provision shop on the premises. See pages 276 and 278.

MALELANE 0131622
Lelane Hotel ★★TYYY, Impala Street. Tel 13.

MARBLE HALL 012082
Marble Hall Hotel ★TYYY, Government Square. Tel 21.

MESSINA 01553
Impala Lily Motel ★TYYY, national road N1. Tel 2197.

Limpopo Inn ★TYYY, national road N1. Tel 2300.

MIDDELBURG 01321
Midway Inn ★★TYYY, national road N4. Tel 2-7283.

Towers Motel ★★TYYY, national road N4. Tel 2-6186.

Middelburg Hotel ★★TYYY, 22 Long Street. Tel 2-2116.

MOOLMAN 013431
Moolman Hotel ★TYYY, Box 20. Tel 731.

MORGENZON 013642
Marnico Hotel ★TYYY, Steyn Street. Tel 108 or 106.

NABOOMSPRUIT 01534
Naboom Hotel ★TYYY, Hans Van Rensburg Street. Tel 3-0321.

NELSPRUIT 01311 — District 0131232
Crocodile Country Inn ★★TYYY, off national road N4, 20 km west of Nelspruit. Telephone, dial 0131232 and ask for 30 (alternate business hours number direct dialling 01311 – 28214). Telex 335056. P O Box 496, Nelspruit 1200. Set in a delightful sub-tropical garden on the banks of the Crocodile River. Much has been accomplished in recent times by the owners, Barry and Shirley Sergay, in the refurbishing of the Inn; they have a good understanding of tone in decor and have provided comfort in a peaceful, happy atmosphere. A log fire burns in the lounge on a cold winter's night and drinks can be taken in the intimate, convivial pub. Breakfast and light meals are served in the diningroom. Crocodile Inn is famed for its country cuisine, so well prepared and served in the candle-lit restaurant at night. There are 32 bedrooms all en suite with private bathroom, telephone, airconditioning, radio and television (with

video). There is a functions room as well as a swimming-pool, floodlit all-weather tennis court, bowling green and fishing – all on the property. Close to Kruger National Park and the other interesting attractions of the lowveld. See pages 287 and 289.

Drum Rock Hotel ★★★TYYY, 6 km from town on White River road (R539). Tel 2-2154.

Paragon Hotel ★★★TYYY, 19 Anderson Street. Tel 2-2283.

NOORDKAAP 01314
Bouganvillea Hotel ★TYYY, Delightful setting in the old gold-minding district of Barberton on the R38 to Kaapmuiden. Box 9. Tel 9681.

NORTHAM 0153812
Northam Hotel ★TYYY, Box 14. Tel 14 or 41.

NYLSTROOM 01531
Nylstroom Hotel ★TYYY, Potgieter Street. Tel 2491.

OGIES 0135312
Ogies Hotel ★TYYY, Main Road. Tel 93.

PHALABORWA 01524
Impala Inn ★★★TYYY, 52 Essenhout Street. Tel 5681.

Andrew Motel ★★TYYY, Mila Road, 12 km south-east of the town. Tel 2381.

PIETERSBURG 01521
Ranch Hotel ★★★TYYY, P O Box 77, Pietersburg 0700. Telephone (01521) 7-5377/8. Telex 331320. The hotel is situated in 5 acres of garden on the Great North Road N1, 17,6 km south of the town, and offers a variety of first-rate accommodation for holiday-makers, families and business people. There ar 80 rooms all en suite with private bathroom, telephone, radio and television (2nd channel video). The luxury rooms have hairdryers and trouser presses, and the executive suites have, in addition, private courtyards with spa pools. There are two restaurants, The Armoury à la carte offers a fine cuisine, entertainment and dancing in a sophisticated, mediaeval atmosphere; and The Buttery, in a light, colourful atmosphere, serves breakfast and light meals all day until ten in the morning and light meals all day until ten in the evening. There are bars in plenty: The Georgian, a sophisticated bar for private functions, The Milking Shed, a unique bar for a drink, a chat and a dance; The Cockpit; the intimate mens bar with its collection of badges, and The Pool Bar in the swimming-pool complex (here there is a main pool, a children's pool and 15 seater open-air jacuzzi). Also on the property are tennis and squash courts, sauna, golf driving range, and children's playground (with baby sitter service). Functions and conferences up to 200 persons. Fully licensed, 1 200-metre airstrip. See pages 273 and 278.

Holiday Inn ★★TYYY, Vorster Street. Tel 6584.

Great North Road Hotel ★TYYY, 47 Mare Street. Tel 7-1031.

PIET RETIEF 01343
Imperial Hotel ★★TYYY, 31 Church Street. Tel 4251.

Central Hotel ★TYYY, 77 Church Street. Tel 4251.

PILGRIM'S REST 0131532
Mount Sheba Hotel ★★★TYYY, P O Box 100, Pilgrim's Rest 1290. Telephone

0131532 and ask for 17 or 64. Telex 335638. Central Reservations (011) 788-1258. Situated in the heart of a 1 500-hectare nature reserve on a mountain plateau between Pilgrim's Rest and Lydenburg. Accommodation, finished and appointed to the highest standards, is available in two styles: Luxury Suite – with private bathroom, a king size bed and separate sitting area which includes an open fireplace, and Duplex Suite – consisting of twin-bedroom upstairs, a bathroom, spacious lounge (with open fireplace) and patio downstairs. In the main building there are two comfortable lounges (open fires in the winter), the Candalier restaurant (Sheba is renowned for the excellence of its table and cellar), the Potted Owl bar (built for congeniality), the billiard room and the library. Hackett's pool deck restaurant, open from 7.30 am to 6 pm, serves breakfast, luncheon and light snacks throughout the day, and the adjoining Propecter's bar offers full service in the recreation area: barbecue, tennis and squash courts, swimming-pool, sauna, solarium and children's playground. The purpose-built Sheba Room conference centre, seating 80 delegates, is equipped with every modern facility. There is an on-property petrol bowser. Mount Sheba's pièce de résistance is the magic of its surroundings – here in the bowl of the Eastern Transvaal Drakensberg are indigenous forests, mountain waterfalls and pools, fauna and flora, as beautiful as anywhere else in the world. Full road directions to the hotel on page 310 and aerial picture on page 311. For details of timesharing 13 perimeter cottages, ask Ovland Timesharing.

Royal Hotel TYYY (Overvaal Resort) Main Street. Tel 4.

POTGIETERSRUS 01541
The Park Hotel ★★★TYYY, P O Box 1551, Potgietersrus 0600. Telephone (01541) 3101/2, Telex 321847. Conveniently and peacefully situated half a kilometre north of the town on the left hand side of the Greeat North Road N1, in a typical Northern Transvaal thornbush setting, this distinguished hotel is notable for its comfort, hospitality and fine fare. The 100 tastefully furnished bedrooms are all en suite and each is equipped with airconditioning, TV (with 2nd channel video), radio, direct dialling telephone, hairdryer, trouser press, tea and coffee maker. Baby-sitter service is available. Grouped in a semi-circle around the lovely swimming-pool are: Gysie's Koffie Huis – the breakfast and light meal restaurant (open from breakfast to late night), the sophisticated Squirrels ladies bar, the Veld Express – an action bar with its 'wild-mail-coach-era' decor and live music, and Brambles, a top-of-the-line à la carte restaurant with dancing, live entertainment and famed speciality dishes. The Park specializes in conferences with 4 airconditioned venues accommodating from 20 to 300 persons. See pages 273 and 275.

Orinoco Hotel ★TYYY, P O Box 339, Potgietersrus 0600. Telephone (01541) 5487. Telex 424004. Situated in the town at 66 Ruiter Street, The Orinoco has 36 well-appointed bedrooms all en suite with private bathroom, radio, telephone, TV, inhouse video, fitted carpet. An attractive, comfortable hotel with its Steak House, action bar and beer garden, and good food and service are the other credentials which make it so popular.

Fiesta Park Motel ★TYYY, 26 km south of town on N1 to Naboomspruit. Tel 5641.

ROEDTAN 015442

Roedtan Hotel ★TYYY, Main Road. Tel 49.

ROOIBERG 015334

Rooiberg Hotel ★TYYY, Box 1. Tel 604.

SABIE 0131512

Floreat Motel ★★TYYY, P O Box 150, Sabie 1260. Telephone 391. Situated just outside the town, half a kilometre along the old road to Lydenburg. Surrounded by the beautiful forests of the area, the motel has a kilometre-long frontage to the Sabi River. Forty bedrooms all en suite with private bathroom, fitted carpet, airconditioning, telephone and radio. À la carte restaurant and ladies bar, TV viewing. Swimming-pool. See pages 303, 304 and 305.

SECUNDA 01363

Holiday Inn ★★TYYY, Horwood Street. Tel 4-1121.

SETTLERS 015332

Settlers Hotel Tel 694.

SYCAMORE 013262

Malaga Hotel ★★★TYYY, P O Box 136, Waterval-Boven 1195. Telephone 431. Situated in a beautiful garden on the bank of the Elands River, off national road N4 between Waterval-Onder and Monttose Falls. Fifty bedrooms/suites all en suite with private bathroom (with shower), fitted carpeting, radio, TV, telephone, airconditioning, central heating. Esmeraldos Restaurant and Algheros ladies bar. Swimming-pool, tennis court, trout fishing. See pages 285 and 286.

TINMYNE 015424

Tinmyne Hotel ★TYYY, Box 12. Tel 661. 32 km west of Potgietersrus.

TSHIPISE 015539

Overvaal Tshipise TYYY, Box 4. Tel 624.

TZANEEN 015236

Coach House ★★★★TYYY, P O Box 544, Tzaneen 0850. Telephone (015236) 2-0100 and 2-0170/1. Telex 3-21831. Situated at New Agatha, 15 km south of Tzaneen, overlooking the Drakensberg, this is an enchanting place to relax and unwind, and with the peaceful environment goes comfort, the best food and wine, unobtrusive service and hospitality. Each of the 34 en suite bedrooms has an uninterrupted view of the mountains, all are well-appointed with handcrafted kiaat furniture; the custom made beds are two metres long. Each room has a TV set with video channel, 4-station radio and a telephone. The double rooms have wood burning fireplaces. The bathrooms all have showers, bidets, hair dryers and more than enough space. The excellent meals served in the dining room are the more enjoyable because of the presentation in lovely surroundings and the use of fresh farm produce and such delicacies as Drakensberg brook trout and thick country cream. Helping to create the right atmosphere in the delightful Buchan's Bar are the seligna wall panels of scenes from the stage coach days. The sparkling swimming-pool faces the fabulous view and from the open deck and pool-side terrace, drinks and luncheons are served. Coach House farms comprising 560 hectares, are mostly planted to macadamia, pecan nuts and seligna and these lands together with the nearby Rooikat Forest Trail and New Agatha Forest Reserve, provide guests of the hotel unique opportunities for both leisurely walks and energetic trails. See pages 277 and 279.

Karos Tzaneen Hotel ★★TYYY, Danie Joubert Street. Tel 2-1056.

WARMBATHS 015331

Overspa, part of Overvaal Warmbaths. Box 75. Tel 2200. See page 274.

Bonnehof Hotel ★★TYYY, 31 Sutter Road. Tel 2102.

Floyd's Valhalla Motel ★TYYY, Box 222. Tel 2320 or 2330.

New White House Hotel ★TYYY, Pretoria and Voortrekker Roads. Tel 2404.

WATERVAL-ONDER 013262

Malaga Hotel ★★★TYYY See SYCAMORE

Wayside Inn ★★TYYY, national road N4. Tel 12 or 425.

WHITE RIVER AND PLASTON 01311

Hotel The Winkler ★★★TYYY, P O Box 12, White River 1240. Telephone (01311) 3-2317/8/9. Telex 335678. Five kilometres from White River on the Numbi road (R538), this hotel, of the highest reputation, is placed in a 25-hectare country estate only 20 minutes by car from the Numbi Gate of Kruger National Park. A veritable landmark of the Lowveld the intriguing architecture is a combination of Japanese and African styles – the sweeping pagoda-roofed central building confirming the Japanese influence, and the long, curving wings relating to the formation of an African kraal – the whole complex embraces a peaceful outlook onto the vast area of rolling lawns, with a swimming-pool centre-piece; and beyond, the backdrop of the eastern Transvaal Drakensberg. Inside the hotel, in the immense atrium, a fountain cascades beneath the open pagoda roof where the arboretum displays its ferns and shrubs. From here the public rooms of the hotel lead off – the front office screen and reception desk are beautifully carved, directly opposite, the boutique has a fine display of arts and crafts; facing the garden, the lounge (with deep English country style chairs) where two log fires burn in the winter, and the adjoining well-appointed bar; and the restaurant with its pleasing decor and excellent table d'hôte and à la carte menus.
The luxury accommodation in the two wings of the hotel comprises 44 rooms all en suite with private bathroom and shower, fitted carpeting, airconditioning, telephone, radio and television (with video channel). Family and interleading rooms and two luxury suites. Bass fishing, tennis, bowls and swimming as well as own vegetable and fruit gardens on the estate. Reduced rates over weekends, children welcome. Garaging and ample open parking. Conference facilities. Golf, squash, cricket and hockey at White River Country Club, 5 km from hotel. See pages 291 and 293.

Jatinga, Jatinga Road. P O Box 77, Plaston 1244. Telephone White River (01311) 3-1932. Exquisite and exclusive, this private resort is positioned on a 12-hectare farm in a lovely part of the eastern Transvaal lowveld. Although close to the Kruger National Park and the other places of interest, many guests visit Jatinga for the sheer pleasure of the immediate environment – it is such a delectable place in which to unwind, with the attractions of a beautiful, sub-tropical garden, the two-kilometre-long river frontage and the swimming-pool, tennis court and bowling green. The accommodation comprises 16 double rooms in thatched bungalows with en suite bathrooms. In the main building is the graciously furnished and comfortable lounge (open fires in the winter) and one of the most inviting, intimate restaurant's to be found anywhere, and its cuisine is the crème de la crème. If you do nothing else, before you leave the Lowveld, book your table for dinner at Jatinga – enjoy the 7-course gourmet meal and the warm hospitality of your hosts, the proprietors, Ken and Mike. Very important to the high standard of preparation of meals is the garden fresh produce, grown on the estate, and the culinary expertise of Ken. Photographs appear on page 290 and route directions on page 291.

Pine Lake Inn ★★★TYYY, 8 km from White River on R40 to Hazyview. Tel 3-1186.

Karula River Hotel ★TYYY, Old Plaston Road. Tel. 3-2277.

Petra Mountain Inn ★T, 14 km from White River on the R538 to Numbi.

White River Hotel ★TYYY, Theo Kleynhans Street. Tel 3-2241.

WHITE RIVER DISTRICT 01311

Cybele Forest Lodge, off route R40 between White River and Hazyview. P O Box 346, White River. Tel 3-2791.

WITBANK 01351

Boulevard Hotel ★★★TYYY, 167 Jellicoe Street. Tel 2424.

Athlone Hotel ★TYYY, Eadie Street. Tel 6-2451.

Carlton Hotel ★TYYY, Main Street. Tel 2805.

13 — Bloemfontein, the Orange Free State and Qwaqwa

BLOEMFONTEIN

Bloemfontein Sun Hotel ★★★TYYY, East Burger Street. Tel 30-1911.

Halevy House Hotel ★★★TYYY, Cnr Charles and Markgraaff Street. P O Box 1368, Bloemfontein 9300. Telephone 8-0271. Twenty-two bedrooms all en suite with private bathroom, fitted carpet, airconditioning, telephone, radio and television. Leviseur's à la carte restaurant (restored to its Victorian elegance), St Claire's Place (elegantly appointed ladies bar) and Sophies Terrace (a convivial beer garden). De Raadzal (the complete conference centre). See pages 319 and 322.

Holiday Inn ★★★TYYY, 1 Union Avenue. Tel 30-1111.

Cecil Hotel ★★TYYY, 69 Andrew Street. Tel 8-1155.

Fontein Hotel ★TYYY, Zastron Street. Tel 8-4791.

Fourways Hotel ★TYYY, Heatherdale Road. Tel 32-4775.

Boulevard Hotel ★TY, 61 Peet Avenue. Tel 7-7236/7.

BETHLEHEM 01431

Green's Hotel ★TYYY, 13 Muller Street. Tel 3-5120.

Park Hotel ★TYYY, 23 Muller Street. Tel 3-5190.

Royal Hotel ★TYYY, 9 Boshoff Street. Tel 3-5448.

BETHULIE 05862

Royal Hotel ★TYYY, Voortrekker Street. Tel 154.

BOSHOF 053232

Boshof Hotel ★★TYYY, Jacobs Street. Tel 91.

BOTHAVILLE 014141

Elgro Hotel ★TYYY, Van Lingen Street, Tel 2097.

Enkel Den Hotel ★★TYYY, President Street. Tel 4341.

BRANDFORT 05222

Elgro Hotel ★TYYY, Voortrekker Street. Tel 73.

Walmay Hotel ★TYYY, 36 Voortrekker Street. Tel 410.

BULTFONTEIN 0525

Elgro Hotel ★TYYY, President Swart Street. Tel 3-1158.

CLARENS 014326

Maluti Lodge ★★TYYY, Naauwpoort Street. Tel 661.

CLOCOLAN 05652

Clocolan Hotel ★TYYY, 1st Street South. Tel 19.

DEALESVILLE 05292

Olien Hotel ★TYYY, Church Street, Tel 20.

DENEYSVILLE 01618

Vaaldam Hotel ★TYYY, Pier Avenue. Tel 201.

DEWETSDORP 052112

De Wet Hotel ★TYYY, 25 Kerk Street. Tel 92.

EXCELSIOR 05672

Harvest Inn ★TYYY, Church Street. Tel 145.

FAURESMITH 05822

Phoenix Hotel ★TYYY, Voortrekker Street. Tel 19.

FICKSBURG 0563

Commercial Hotel ★TYYY, Voortrekker Street. Tel 2411.

Ficksburg Hotel ★TYYY, Voortrekker Street. Tel 2214.

FOURIESBURG 014332

Fouriesburg Hotel ★TYYY, 17 Reitz Street. Tel 30.

FRANKFORT 01613

Central Hotel ★TYYY, 46 Brand Street. Tel 3-1071.

HARRISMITH 01436

Holiday Inn ★★TYYY, McKechnie Street. Tel 2-1011.

Grand National Hotel ★TYYY, Warden Street. Tel 2-1060.

Sir Harry Motel ★TYYY, King and McKechnie Streets. Tel 2-2151.

HEILBRON 01614

Commercial Hotel ★TYYY, Longmarket Street. Tel 2-2055.

Tucker's Hotel ★TYYY, Longmarket Street. Tel 2-2080.

HENDRIK VERWOERD DAM 0020

Hendrik Verwoerd Dam Motel ★★TYYY, Tel 60.

HENNEMAN 0173

Henneman Hotel ★TYYY, Crescent Street. Tel 3-1131.

HOOPSTAD 01742

Hoopstad Hotel ★TYYY, Van Zyl Street. Tel 58.

KESTELL 014392

Mount-aux-sources Hotel ★TYYY, Blignaut Street. Tel 50.

KOFFIEFONTEIN 05372

Central Hotel ★TYYY. Tel 69.

Koffiefontein Hotel ★TYYY, Groot Trek Street. Tel 64.

KOPPIES 016152

Friesland Hotel ★TYYY, Noord Street. Tel 178.

KROONSTAD 01411

Toristo Hotel ★★TYYY, Rautenbach Street. Tel 2-5111.

Selborne Hotel ★TYYY, 36 Cross Street, Tel 2-4269.

Zeederberg Hotel ★TYYY, 17 Market Street. Tel 2-2137.

LADYBRAND 0561

Riverside Lodge Hotel ★★TYYY, Maseru Bridge, Box 112. Tel 2681.

New Central Hotel ★TYYY, 19 Joubert Street. Tel 2.

LINDLEY 0141512

Clarendon Hotel ★TYYY, Pretorius Street. Tel 135.

LUCKHOFF 0020

Luckhoff Hotel ★TYYY, Dr Bosman Avenue. Tel 12.

MARQUARD 05272

Marquard Hotel ★TYYY, 34 Union Street. Tel 80.

MEMEL 013322

Memel Hotel ★TYYY, Voortrekker Street. Tel 197.

ODENDAALSRUS 0171

Commercial Hotel ★★TYYY, Steyn Market Streets. Tel 4-1299.

Outspan Hotel ★TYYY, Waterkant Street. Tel 4-3201.

President Hotel ★TYYY, 70 Josias Street. Tel 4-1256.

PARYS 01601

Riviera Hotel ★★TYYY, De Villiers Street, Tel 2143.

Parys Hotel ★TYYY, 17 Phillip Street. Tel 3555.

PETRUSBURG 05282

Petrusburg Hotel ★TYYY, East Street. Tel 4.

PETRUS STEYN 10432

Masonic Hotel ★TYYY, Church Street. Tel 3410.

PHILIPPOLIS 05872

Oranjehof Hotel ★TYYY, 72 Voortrekker Street. Tel. 8.

REDDERSBURG 052122

Sarie Marais Hotel ★TYYY, Van Riebeck Street. Tel 138.

REITZ 01434

Royal Hotel ★TYYY, 32 Church Street. Tel 3-2561.

ROUXVILLE 05572

Criterion Hotel ★TYYY, Morgan Street. Tel 55.

SASOLBURG 016

Indaba Hotel ★TYYY, 47 Fichardt Street. Tel 6-8111.

SENEKAL 014351

New Free State Hotel ★TYYY, 19 Long Street. Tel 2232.

Senekal Hotel ★TYYY, Dreyer Street. Tel 2380.

SMITHFIELD 05562

Smithfield Hotel ★TYYY, Brand Street. Tel 46.

SPRINGFONTEIN 05882

Springfontein Hotel ★TYYY, Pres. Brand Street. Tel 56.

STEYNSRUS 014122

Steynsrus Hotel ★TYYY, Van Riebeeck Street. Tel 84.

SWINBURNE 014364

Montrose Motel ★TYYY, National Road. Tel 601.

THABA 'NCHU (BOPHUTHATSWANA) 05265

Thaba 'Nchu Sun Hotel and Casion, Box 114. Tel 2161/3.

THEUNISSEN 01752

Elgro Hotel ★★TYYY, Retief St, Tel 338.

TROMPSBURG 05812

Commercial Hotel ★TYYY, Jan Street. Tel 93.

TWEESPRUIT 05682

Harvest Inn ★TYYY, Ash Street. Tel 18.

VENTERSBURG 01734

Ventersburg Hotel ★TYYY, 4 Voortrekker Street. Tel 4045.

VIERFONTEIN 018142

Vierfontein Hotel ★TYYY. Tel 77.

VILJOENSKROON 014132

Mahem Hotel ★TYYY, Voortekker Street. Tel 211.

VILLIERS 016134

Toeriste Hotel ★TYYY, Pieter Street. Tel 2732.

VIRGINIA 01722

De Bonheur Hotel ★★TYYY, Sand River and Virginia Roads. Tel 2-2211.

Doringboom Hotel ★TYYY, Berea Avenue. Tel 2-5124.

Harmony Hotel ★TYYY, 52 Harmony Way. Tel 7-4624.

Virginia Park Hotel ★TYYY, Highlands Avenue. Tel 2-3306.

VREDE 013342

Balmoral Hotel ★★TYYY, 54 Church Street. Tel 21.

VREDEFORT 016022

Vryst-a-a-a-t Hotel ★TYYY, Voortrekker Street. Tel 142.

WARDEN 014372

Warden Hotel ★TYYY, Piet Retief Street. Tel 133.

WELKOM 0171

Holiday Inn ★★★TYYY, Tempest Street. Tel 7-3361.

Golden Orange Hotel ★★TYYY, Stateway. Tel 2-5281.

147 Hotel ★★TYYY, Stateway. Tel 2-5381.

Welkom Hotel ★★TYYY, Koppie Alleen Road. Tel 5-1411.

Dagbreek Hotel ★TYYY, 96 King Street. Tel 2-4269.

WEPENER 05232

Wepener Hotel ★TYYY, 17 Church Street. Tel 87.

WESSELSBRON 01762

Wesselsbron Hotel ★★TYYY, Pres. Steyn Street. Tel 26.

WINBURG 05242

Winburg Hotel ★TYYY, Brand Street. Tel 160.

ZASTRON 05542

Maluti Hotel ★TYYY, Main Street. Tel 107

QWAQWA

PHUTHADITJHABA 01432

Qwaqwa Hotel, Box 5581, Tel 9032.

WITSIEHOEK 014382

Witsieshoek Mountain Resort Licensed Hotel. P/Bag 828, Witsieshoek 9870. Tel No. 5.

14 — Kimberley and the Northern Cape

KIMBERLEY 0531

Kimberley Sun Hotel ★★★★TYYY, 120 Dutoitspan Road. Tel 3-1751.

Savoy Hotel ★★★TYYY, 15 De Beers Road. Tel 2-6211.

Colinton Hotel ★★TYYY, 14 Thompson Street. Tel 3-1471.

Horseshoe Motel ★★TYYY, Memorial Road. Tel 2-5267.

Kimberlite Hotel ★★TYYY, 162 St George Street. Tel 2-6661.

New Grand Hotel ★★TYYY, Southey Street and Transvaal Road. Tel 2-6251.

Crescent Hotel ★TYYY, D'Arcy Street. Tel 2-2413.

Halfway House Hotel ★TYYY, 229 Dutoitspan Road. Tel 2-5151.

Phoenix Hotel ★TYYY, Market Square. Tel 2-7101.

Queens Hotel ★TYYY, Stockdale Street. Tel 2-3299.

AUGRABIES 0020

Augrabies Falls Hotel ★TYYY, Box 34. Tel 18.

BARKLY WEST 05352

Grand Hotel ★TYYY, Campbell Street. Tel 38.

Queens Hotel ★TYYY, Campbell Street. Tel 85.

BITTERFONTEIN 02752

Bitterfontein Hotel ★TYYY, Spoorweg. Tel 42.

BRANDVLEI 02702

Brandvlei Hotel ★TYYY, Main Street. Tel 2.

BRAY 0020

Bray Hotel ★TYYY. Tel 15.

CALVINIA 02772

Calvinia Hotel ★TYYY, Hope Street. Tel 491.

Hantam Hotel ★TYYY, Church Street. Tel 512.

Holdens Commercial Hotel ★TYYY, Water Street. Tel 20.

CARNARVON 02032

Astoria Hotel ★TYYY, Victoria Street. Tel 110.

Carnavron Hotel ★TYYY, Pastorie Street. Tel 95.

DANIELSKUIL 053872

Commercial Hotel ★TYYY, Rhodes Avenue. Tel 19.

DELPORTSHOOP 0020

Delportshoop Hotel ★TYYY. Tel 14.

DOUGLAS 05362

Douglas Hotel ★TYYY, Arnot Street. Tel 20.

Frederick Hotel ★TYYY, Barkly Street. Tel 168.

GARIES 02792

Garies Hotel ★TYYY, Main St. Tel 42.

GRIQUATOWN 05962

Louis Hotel ★TYYY, 1 Main St. Tel 84.

GROBLERSHOOP 05472

Grootrivier Hotel ★TYYY, Main Road. Tel 14.

HARTSWATER 05332

Hartswater Hotel ★TYYY, Smuts Street. Tel 4-1117.

HOPETOWN 05392

Radnor Hotel ★★TYYY, Church Street. Tel 15.

JACOBSDAL 053212

Jacobsdal Hotel ★TYYY, Bouw Street. Tel 38.

JAN KEMPDORP 0533

Border Hotel ★TYYY, Main Road. Tel 6-1532.

Jan Kemp Hotel ★TYYY, D.F. Malan Street. Tel 6-1621.

KAKAMAS 05442

Waterwiel Hotel ★TYYY, Voortrekker Street. Tel 250.

KAMIESKROON 0257

Kamieskroon Hotel ★TYYY. Tel 614.

KEIMOS 05492

Keimos Hotel ★TYYY, Hoof St. Tel 29.

KENHARDT 05462

Kenhardt Hotel ★TYYY, Main Street. Tel 32.

KLAWER 02724

Klawer Hotel ★TYYY, Main Street Tel 6-1032.

KRAANKUIL 057222

Kraankuil Hotel ★TYYY. Tel 601.

KURUMAN 01471

El Dorado Motel ★★TYYY, Main Street. Tel 2-2191.

Grand Hotel ★TYYY, 15 Beare Street. Tel 2-1148.

Savoy Hotel ★TYYY, Beare Street. Tel 2-1121.

LIME ACRES 053882

Finsch Hotel ★★★TYYY, Diagonal Street. Tel 121 and 129.

LOERIESFONTEIN 02762

Loeriesfontein Hotel ★TYYY, Main Street. Tel 1.

LUTZVILLE 02725

Lutzville Hotel ★TYYY, Malan Street. Tel 7-1513.

MADIBOGO 01451

Madibogo Hotel ★TYYY, Box 2. Tel 2.

MARYDALE 05482

Marydale Hotel ★TYYY, Snijman Street. Tel 44.

MIDDELPOS 0020

Middelpos Hotel ★TYYY. Tel 7.

MODDERRIVIER 053222

Crown and Royal Hotel ★TYYY, Box 2. Tel 22.

NABABEEP 0251

Nababeep Hotel ★TYYY, Main Road Tel 3-8151.

NIEKERKSHOOP 05922

Hay Hotel ★TYYY, Fourie St. Tel 74.

NIEWOUDTVILLE 0020

Niewoudtville Hotel ★TYYY, Voortrekker Street. Tel 46.

OKIEP 0251

O'okiep Hotel ★TYYY, Main Street. Tel 4-1000.

OLIFANTSHOEK 059512

Kalahari Hotel ★TYYY, 22 Van Riebeeck Street. Tel 7.

PAPKUIL 053882

Papkuil Hotel ★TYYY. Tel 16.

POFADDER 02532

Pofadder Hotel ★TYYY, Voortrekker Street. Tel 43.

PORT NOLLOTH 0255

Scotia Inn Hotel ★TYYY, Beach Road. Tel 8353.

POSTMASBURG 0591

Postmasburg Hotel ★TYYY, 37 Main Street. Tel 7-1166.

PRIESKA 0594

Border Hotel ★TYYY, Victoria Street. Tel 3-1149.

Prieska Hotel ★TYYY, Church Street. Tel 3-1129.

REIVILO 014572

Cecil Hotel ★TYYY, Voortrekker Street. Tel 91.

RICHMOND 05752

Beisana Hotel ★TYYY, Pienaar Street. Tel 36.

Richmond Hotel ★TYYY, Box 9. Tel 61.

SETLAGOLE 014542

Setlagole Hotel ★TYYY. Tel 994.

SPRINGBOK 0251

Springbok Hotel ★TYYY, Van Riebeeck Street. Tel 2-1161.

STELLA 014542

Stella Hotel ★TYYY, Main Road. Tel 49.

STRYDENBURG 05762

Excelsior Hotel ★TYYY, Church Street. Tel 106.

SUTHERLAND 02392

Sutherland Hotel ★TYYY, Piet Retief Street. Tel 96.

UPINGTON 0541

Extension Inn ★★TYYY, Hoop Street. Tel 5731.

Oranje Hotel ★★TYYY, Scott Street. Tel 4177.

Upington Protea Inn ★★TYYY, Schröder Street. Tel 5414.

VANRHYNSDORP 02712
North Western Hotel ★TYYY, Voortrekker Street. Tel 3.

VANWYKSVLEI 0020
Vanwyksvlei Hotel ★TYYY, Hoof Street. Tel 1.

VANZYLSRUS 01474
Gemsbok Hotel ★TYYY. Tel 238.

VREDENDAL 0271
Maskam Hotel ★TYYY, 26 Van Riebeeck Avenue. Tel 3-1336.

Vredendal Hotel ★TYYY, Voortrekker Street. Tel 3-1064

VRYBURG 01451
Central Hotel ★★TYYY, 101 Market Stret. Tel 3926.

Grand Hotel ★★TYYY, 104 Market Street. Tel 3861.

International Hotel ★TYYY, 41 Market Street Tel 2235.

WARRENTON 05333
Warrenton Central Hotel ★TYYY, Uys Street. Tel 3131.

WILLISTON 02052
Williston Hotel ★TYYY, Lutz Street. Tel 5.

WINDSORTON ROAD 053252
Rand Motel ★TYYY. Tel 9903.

WITPUT 0020
Witput Hotel ★TYYY. Tel 108.

15 — Bophuthatswana, Botswana, Lesotho and Swaziland

HOTELS, GAME LODGES & CAMPS, CARAVAN PARKS

Bophuthatswana

MAFIKENG 01401
Crewe's Hotel, Carrington Street. Tel 3-2364.

Surrey Hotel, Shippard Street. Tel 3-2349.

Cookes Lake Municipal Caravan Park, 1 km from town on Lichtenburg Road. Tel 3-2531.

MMABATHO 01401
Mmabatho Sun Hotel and Casino. Tel 2-11424.

Molopo Sun Hotel, in the capital Mmabatho. Tel 2-4184.

PILANESBERG 104651
Pilanesberg National Park
Kwa Maritane Game Lodge, 4 km from Sun City. P O Box 39, Sun City 0316. Tel 2-1820/9. 46 time-share units of cabanas and chalets (with cooking facilities), restaurant, swimming pool, tennis courts, sauna. 200-metre-long tunnel conects lodge with game hide at water hole. Game ranger for safaris by vehicle or on foot. Hourly shuttle service bus to Sun City. Accommodation and facilities available to the public upon reservation.

Sun City Hotel and Casino. Tel 2-1000.

ROOIGROND 01448
Fish Hoek Hotel. Tel 644.

Botswana

From RSA the dialling code for all towns in Botswana is 09267. To reach places where no telephone number is given below dial 0903 for enquiries and 0900 to book calls.

CHOBE NATIONAL PARK — KASANE
Chobe Safari Lodge, in town centre. P O Box 10. Tel 25-0336. 2 suites, 13 double rooms, 12 rondavels. Set menu, cocktail lounge, bar and bottle store. Swimming-pool, boat and canoe hire, fishing, game-viewing, curio shop. Camping site.

Chobe Game Lodge, in Chobe National Park, 12 km from Kasane on Chobe river bank. (Sun International) Tel 2-50340. Box 32 Kasane. 50 double airconditioned rooms en suite and 4 with own private pool and verandah, à la Carte, cocktail bar. Swimming-pool, river cruises, boats and fishing rods for hire. Game-viewing with experienced guides.

CHOBE NATIONAL PARK (WESTERN) AND LINYANTI RIVER
Allan's Camp and South Camp, on the Savuti Channel in the Mababe Depression. Reservations: Gametrackers. Tel (011) 886-1810. 2 luxury camps each accommodates 12 guests in luxury safari tents. Ablution block, bar and radio telephone. Rates include all meals, game-viewing by 4-wheel drive vehicles and air transport from Johannesburg.

Lloyd's Camp, on the Savuti Channel in the Mababe Depression. Reservations: Lloyd Wilmot Safaris, Box 37. Tel 26-0205 Maun. Camp accommodates 12 guests in luxury safari tents. Ablution block. Rates include all meals and game-viewing by 4-wheel drive vehicle.

Linyanti Camp, on Linyanti River north of Savuti. Reservations: Gametrackers. Tel (011) 886-1810. Camp accommodates 12 guests in luxury safari tents. Ablution block, bar and radio telephone. Rates include all meals, game-viewing by 4-wheel drive vehicles and special boats, use of hides, fishing and air transport from Johannesburg.

Linyanti Explorations, on Linyanti River west of Savuti. Reservations: Box 11, Kasane. Radio Tel A2RC338. Camp accommodates 14 guests in luxury safari tents. Ablution block, diningroom, bar. Rates include all meals, game-viewing by 4-wheel drive vehicles and special boats, use of hides, fishing. Own airstrip. Wildlife films.

FRANCISTOWN 09267
Grand Hotel, opposite railway station. Box 30 Tel 21-2300.

Marang Motel, 5 km south of town on road past golf course. On the bank of Tati River. Box 807. Tel 21-3991.

Thapama Lodge, south of the Mall near the circle. Tati Hotel, opposite railway station. Box 15. Tel 21-3872.

GABORONE 09267
Gaborone Sun, Nyerere Drive next to golf course. Casino. P/Bag 0016. Tel 35-1111.

Gaborone Hotel, on the railway station. Box 5. Tel 35-3991.

President Hotel, Botswana Road, the Mall. Box 200. Tel 35-3631.

GABORONE DISTRICT
Morning Star Motel, on Zeerust Road 5 km east of town. Tel 35-2301.

Oasis Motel, on Zeerust Road 3 km east of town. Tel 35-3671.

Mogo Motel, on Molepolole Road 5 km west of town. Tel 35-2733.

GHANZI
Kalahari Arms, in the town.

KANYE
Kanye Hotel, in the village

LOBATSE 09267
Cumberland Hotel, in town centre. Box 135. Tel 33-0281.

Lobatse Hotel, near railway station. Box 93. Tel 33-0319.

MAHALAPYE 09267
Mahalapye Hotel, on Mahalapswe River bank. Box 256. Tel 41-0200.

MAUN 09267
Riley's Hotel, in the village on Thamalakane River bank. Box 1. Tel 26-0204.

Ngami Sands, camp site with ablution blocks, restaurant, bar. Adjacent to Riley's Hotel. Box 369. Tel 26-0357.

MAUN DISTRICT (at Matlapaneng, 12 km north of Maun) 09267
Crocodile Camp, on east bank of Tamalakane River. Box 46. Tel 26-0265. Thatched chalets, restaurant, bars. Camp site. Swimming-pool, game-viewing by boat, truck or plane. Professional guides and boatmen.

Island Safari Lodge, on west bank of Thamalakane River. Box 116. Tel 26-0300. Chalets, restaurant, bars. Camp site. Swimming-pool, game-viewing by boat, truck or plane. Professional guides and boatmen.

Okavango River Lodge, on east bank of Thamalakane River next to Crocodile Camp. Rooms and facilities as offered by Island Safari Lodge (under same ownership). Box 32. Tel 26-0298.

OKAVANGO DELTA — MOREMI WILDLIFE RESERVE 09267
Camp Okavango, on island south of Qugana Lagoon. Res: Desert/Delta Safaris, Box 448, Maun. Tel 26-0205. 12 guests in luxury safari tents. Diningroom. Game-viewing trips by boat to heronries in Moremi.

Delta Nyogha Camp, on north shore of Chief's Island. Res: Box 233, Maun Tel 26-0205. 12 guests in thatched reed cottages with showers, toilets etc. Boat game-viewing, fishing.

Khwai River Lodge, 10 km east of North Gate of Moremi on Khwai River. Thatched chalets en suite. Diningroom, bar, swimming-pool, radio telephone. Rate includes flight from Johannesburg, meals, boating, fishing and game walks. Res: Gametrackers, Tel (011) 886-1810.

Nxamaseri Camp, at junction of Nxamasere and Okavango Rivers south of Shakawe. Res: Box 250, Maun 26-0205. 8 guests in luxury safari tents. Diningroom. Boats and fishing tackle for hire, guides available.

Okavango Fishing Safaris, on west bank of Okavango River, 12 km south of Shakawe. Box 446, Francistown. Radio Tel A2RC137. 12 guests in luxury safari tents. Diningroom and bar, showers, toilets. Power boats for hire with experienced boatmen. Fishing tackle, visits to Tsodilo Hills and on the river with professional guides.

San-Wani Safari Lodge, on lagoon 12 km south of Moremi South Gate. Res: Gametrackers, Tel (011) 886-1810.

12 guests in brick and thatch chalets with separate showers, toilets etc. Diningroom and bar. Rate includes flight from Johannesburg, meals, game-viewing, boating, fishing.

Tsaro Lodge, on Khwai River, 2 km west of Moremi North Gate. Box 448, Maun. Tel 26-0205. 4 luxury brick and thatch chalets en suite. Diningroom and bar. Game-viewing, boating, fishing. Experienced guide. En bloc occupation.

Xugana Lodge, on Qugana Lagoon at west of Moremi. Res: Okavango Explorations, The mail bag 048, Maun. Tel 26-0205. 6 guests in luxury safari tents. Diningroom and bar. Game-viewing by truck and boat, fishing and walks. Power-boat hire, water-skiing, skin-diving and snorkel gear. En bloc occupation. Separate accommodation on The Situtunga river boat, with 3 double cabins, diningroom, bar and third deck for game-viewing over reeds – also en bloc occupation.

Xaxaba Camp, on west bank of Boro River, 10 km west of Chief's Island. Res: Box 147, Maun. Tel 26-0205. 6 thatched chalets with bathrooms. Diningroom and two bars. Swimming-pool. Power-boats, dugouts (mokoro), fishing tackle for hire. Experienced guides and boatmen available. Game-viewing by truck or plane. Charter air service.

PALAPYE 09267

Palapye Hotel, in centre of village on railway station. Box 1. Tel 42-0277.

SELEBI-PHIKWE 09267

Bosele Hotel, in the centre of town. Box 117. Tel 81-0675.

SEROWE 09267

Serowe Hotel, in centre of village on main road. Box 150. Tel 43-0234.

Tshwarangano Hotel, in centre of village near turnoff to Kgotla. Box 102. Tel 43-0377.

NORTH-EASTERN TULI ENCLAVE

Mashatu Game Reserve, the largest private wildlife sanctuary in southern Africa. By road approached from Pont Drift. Majale Lodge – 24 guests in thatched en suite rondavels. Swimming-pool, waterhole bar, curio shop, wildlife library. Mogorogoro Safari Lodge – luxury 8-bedded tented camp, full catering and bar service. Game drives. Extended safaris to Motloutse and Shashe Limpopo confluence. Reservations: Mala Mala, Box 2575, Randburg 2125. Telephone (011) 789-2677/8/9. Telefax 8864382. Telex 4-24807 SA. See page 355.

TULI BLOCK

Limpopo Inn, on Limpopo River bank, about 60 km north of Sherwood Ranch.

Camp, fishing, game-viewing. Box 26, Selebi-Phikwe. Tel Sherwood Ranch 505 (0900).

Limpopo Safari Lodge, on Limpopo River bank, about 15 km north of Buffels-drift. Game-viewing with experienced guides. Pan African Travel, Box 2, Gaborone. Tel 35-2321 (09267).

Stevensford Safari Lodge, on Limpopo River bank, 16 km north of Sherwood Ranch. 4 rooms two with bath. Cooking facilities, swimming-pool, game-viewing and fishing. Horses, vehicles, boats and guides can be hired. Res: American Express, Box 1188, Gaborone. Tel 35-2021 (09267).

Tuli Lodge, on the Limpopo River bank near Pont Drift. Res: Box 184, Bergvlei 2012. Tel (011) 788-1748. 26 guests in thatched chalets en suite. Diningroom and bar. Swimming-pool and curio shop. Game-viewing, drives and fishing.

Zanzibar Hotel, on the Limpopo River bank at Zanzibar. Res: Box 26, Selebi-Phikwe. Tel Sherwood Ranch 420 (0900). 15 rooms, diningroom, bar and bottle store. Fishing and game-viewing. Camping.

Lesotho

From RSA the dialling code for all towns in Lesotho is 09266.

MASERU 09266

Lesotho Sun Hotel Tel 31-3111.

Victoria Hotel Tel 32-2002.

Lakeside Hotel Tel 31-3646.

Lancers Inn Tel 32-2114.

Maseru Casino Hotel Tel 31-2434.

Tollgate, Mountain Road. Box 212. Tel 32-2002. Caravan and camping stands.

BUTHA-BUTHE 09266

Crocodile Inn Tel 4-6233.

LERIBE 09266

Leribe Mountain View Hotel Tel 4-0242.

MAFETENG 09266

Mafeteng Hotel Tel 7-0236.

MOHALES HOEK 09266

Mount Maluti Tel 8-5224.

MOLIMO-NTHUSE PASS — LESOTHO MOUNTAIN ROAD

Molimo-Nthuse Lodge Tel 6-6010.

QACHAS NEK 09266

Qachas Nek Lodge Tel 9-5224.

QUTHING 09266

Orange River Hotel Tel 8-0297.

SEHLABATHEBE NATIONAL PARK 09266

Sehlabathebe Lode. Res: Lesotho National Parks, Box 24 Maseru. Tel 32-2002. Single

and double rooms, and 50 camping stands.

TEYATEYANENG 09266

Blue Mountain Inn Tel 50-2362.

Swaziland

From RSA the dialling code for all towns in Swaziland is 09268. A few places are reached through international trunks, 0900.

MBABANE AND EZULWINI VALLEY 09268

Listed from north to south

In the town

Tavern Hotel Tel 4-2361.

Jabula Inn Tel 4-2406.

Overlooking the valley

Swazi Inn Tel 4-2235.

In the valley

Diamonds Valley Motel Tel 6-1041.

Royal Swazi Sun Hotel and Casino Tel 61001.

Ezulwini Sun Tel 6-1201.

Lugogo Sun Tel 6-1101.

Yen Saan Hotel Tel 6-1051.

Smoky Mountain Village Tel 6-1291.

Happy Valley Motel Tel 6-1061.

Milwane Wildlife Sanctuary, Box 33 Mbabane. Caravan and camping stands and rest camp huts.

BIG BEND 09268

Bend Inn Tel 3-6111.

HLATIKULU 09268

Assegai Inn Tel 7-6128.

LAVUMISA 0900

Lavumisa Hotel Tel 7.

MANKAYANE 09268

Inyatsi Hotel Tel 8-8261.

MANZINI 09268

George Hotel Tel 52061.

MHLAMBANYATI 09268

Foresters Arms Hotel Tel 7-4177.

Meikles Mount, 8-cottage holiday resort between Mhlambanyati and Mbabane. (Take your own liquor). Tel 7-4110.

NHLANGANO 09268

Nhlangano Sun Hotel and Casino Tel 7-8211

PIGGS PEAK 09268

Piggs Peak Hotel and Casino (Protea) Tel 7-1144.

TSHANENI 09268

Impala Arms Hotel Tel 31244.

Accommodation Directory — arranged in the sequence of the chapters of the book CARAVAN PARKS, PUBLIC RESORTS, NATIONAL PARKS, GAME AND NATURE RESERVES

1 — Cape Town, Cape Peninsula and Cape Flats

BELLVILLE 021

Caravans Cape, at exit 10 of N1 and Old Oak Road (3 km from town). Box 298. Tel 99-4814. Caravan and camping stands.

Hardekraaltjie, Voortrekker Road. Box 2. Tel 97-2818. Caravan and camping stands.

FISH HOEK 021

Fish Hoek Municpal, Foreshore. Tel 82-5503. Caravan stands. No bookings.

Sunnyacres, Box 50. Tel 85-1070. Caravan and camping stands. Bungalows.

KOMMETJIE 021

Imhoff Park, Wireless Road, Box 18. Tel 83-1634. Divisional Council. Caravan and camping stands.

KUILSRIVIER 021

Kuilsrivier, Van Riebeeck Road. Tel 903-3113. Caravan and camping stands.

MELKBOSSTRAND 02224

Ou Skip Parke, Otto Du Plessis Drive, Box 13. Tel 2058. Caravan and camping

stands.

MILLER'S POINT 021

Miller's Point, 8 km south of Simonstown, Box 44. Tel 86-1142. Divisional Council. Caravan stands.

MUIZENBERG 021

Zandvlei, The Row. Box 298, Cape Town (8000). Tel 210-2507 or 885215. Caravan stands. Cottages.

PAROW 021

Parow, off Hendrik Verwoerd Drive, Plattekloof. Box 274. Tel 92-1913. Caravan stands.

SIMONSTOWN 021

The Aloes Holiday Resort, Boulders Place off Bellvue Road. Tel 81-1758.

Blue Lantern Holiday Cabins, Main Road. 2 km from town (on the Fish Hoek side). Fully equipped cabins. Tel 86-2113.

Oatlands Holiday Village, Main Road, Froggy Pond. 2 km on the Cape Point side of town. Rondavels and chalets. Caravan and camping stands. Tel 86-1410.

2 — The Western Cape

AGULHAS (See BREDASDORP)
ARNISTON (See BREDASDORP)

BAIN'S KLOOF PASS 02324

Tweede Tol Nature Camp (C.P.A. Nature Conservation), in the pass (R303) north-east of Wellington and north of the summit. Tel 607. Caravan and camping stands.

BONTEBOK NATIONAL PARK (See SWELLENDAM)

BREDASDORP 0284 District 02846 and 02848

Agulhas Caravan Park, Main Road close to Agulhas lighthouse. Caravan and camping stands, Tel (02846) 615. Bungalows, Tel (0284) 4-1126.

Suikerbossie Caravan Park, 2 km from town on the coastal road exit to Agulhas and Arniston. Tel (0284) 4-1135.

Die Dam, at the coast, 55 km south-west of the town on route R317. caravan and camping stands. Tel (02848) 710.

Waenhuiskrans (Arniston) Caravan Park, on the beachfront. Caravan and camping stands. Bungalows. Tel (0284) 4-1126.

CALEDON 0281

Caledon (Municipal), to the north of the town off Nerina Avenue. Tel 2-2060. Caravan and camping stands, rondavels/huts.

CEDARBERG, CITRUSDAL DISTRICT 02682

Algeria Camp (Department of Forestry), on the banks of the Rondegat River, Cedarberg wilderness area, 30 km north of Citrusdal on the gravel road between Nieuwoudts Pass and Cedarberg Pass. Box 203, Citrusdal. Tel 3440. Camping and caravan stands, chalet and bunkhouse.

Cedarberg Recreation Area, Sanddrif, Dwarsrivier farm, Cedarberg, on the gravel road approximately 25 km south-east of Algeria Camp (see above). P.O. Citrusdal. Tel 1521. Camping and caravan stands, cottages, chalets.

Cedarberg Tourist Park, on the gravel road approximately 48 km south-east of Algeria Camp (see above). P/Bag Kromrivier, P.O. Citrusdal. Tel 1404. Caravan and camping stands, cottages.

CITRUSDAL 02662

Hennie van Zyl Tourist Camp (Municipal), Oewer Street, close to Olifants River. Box 57. Tel 81. Caravan and camping stands.

The Baths, 18 km south of town. Box 133. Tel 3312. Caravan stands, apartments, bungalows, cottage. Closed 1 June to 31 August.

CERES 0233

Pine Forest Holiday Resort (Municpal). Tel 2-2060. Caravan and camping stands, cottages, rondavels.

CLANWILLIAM 02682

Clanwilliam Dam Resort (Municipal), Old Cape Road. P.O. Box 5. Tel 26. Caravan and camping stands

DE HOOP NATURE RESERVE See STRUISBAAI

FRANSCHHOEK DISTRICT 02212 (See also PAARL)

Hollandsche Molen, on Paarl/Wemmershoek Dam road (R303). Box 535 Suider Paarl. Tel 2704. Caravan and camping stands. Bungalows. Tearoom.

GANSBAAI (see UILENKRAALSMOND)

GORDON'S BAY 024

Hendon Park Holiday Resort (Municipal), Beach Road. Tel 56-2321. Caravan and camping stands, cottages.

Panorama, Disa Street. Box 346 Strand (7140). Tel 56-1730. Caravan and camping stands.

Sea Breeze, Water Way. Box 38. Tel 56-1400. Caravan and camping stands, bungalows.

Steenbras Dam Rondavels. Cape Town Municipality, Box 298 Cape Town 8000. Tel (021) 210-2507. Rondavels.

Steenbras Holiday Resort, Steenbras River Mouth. Box 143. Tel 41-8097. Caravan stands, bungalows.

GOURITSMOND 02952

Gouritsmond, at the coast, 35 km south of Albertina on route R325. P.O. Gouritsmond. Tel 5630. Caravan stands, rondavels.

GOUDINI 0231

Goudini Spa, 6 km north-west of Rawsonville. Facilities adjoining the 1-star hotel. Box 47 Rawsonville. Tel 9-1100. Caravan stands, rondavels, bungalows. Licensed restaurant.

GROOT-JONGENSFONTEIN 02934

Jongensfontein Resort, at the coast 10 km west of Stilbaai. Tel 4-8015. Caravan stands, bungalows.

HEIDELBERG 02962

Heidelberg (Municipal), Box 12. Tel 11. Caravan and camping stands.

Siesta, Eksteen Street. Tel 475. Caravan and camping stands

HERMANUS 02831

De Mond (Municpal). On the banks of the Kleinriviervlei, cor. 10th Street and 17 Avenue, Voëlklip. Tel 2-1617. Caravan and camping stands.

KLAPMUTS 02211

Oukraalpark, Bungalows and rondavels. Tel 5282.

KLEINMOND 02823

Kleinmond Caravan Parks (Municipal). Caravan and camping stands at Main park and Palmiet River park. Tel 4050.

LAMBERT'S BAY 026732

Lambert's Bay (Municipal). On the beach 500 m from town. Tel 588. Caravan and camping stands

LANGEBAAN 02287

Langebaan (Municipal), lagoon beachfront. Brëe Street, Box 11. Tel 2752. Caravan stands, cottages.

MOORREESBURG 02642

Amos Lambrecht (Municipal) on Hooikraal Road. Box 3. Tel 414. Caravan and camping stands.

ONRUS RIVER 02831

Onrus River Municipal Camping Ground. De Villiers Street. Box 23. Tel 6-1610. Caravan and camping stands.

Paradise Park Holiday Camp, Hermanus Main Road. Tel 6-1007. Caravan and camping stands, rondavels.

Sherwood Park, Main Road. Box 50. Tel 6-1230. Caravan and camping stands, cabins.

PAARL DISTRICT 02211 (sse also KLAPMUTS)

Campers Paradise, 5 km from Paarl on Simondium/Franschhoek Road (R45). Tel 63-1650. Caravan and camping stands. Bungalows. Café.

Safariland Game Park. Box 595 Suider-Paarl. Tel 4-2110. Cottages.

Wateruitjiesvlei (Municipal) 5 km from Paarl on the Wemmershoek Dam Road (R303). Tel 63-1250. Caravan and camping stands.

PEARLY BEACH 02834

Pearly Beach Holiday Resort, between Gansbaai and Aghulhas. Tel 9613. Caravan and camping stands, cottages, rondavels.

PIKETBERG 0261

PW Koorts (Municipal), Main Road. Tel 3-1684. Caravan stands.

RIVERSDALE 02932

Takkieskloof Tourist Camp (Municipal). Tel 704. Caravan and camping stands Rondavels and fully equipped cottages. In residential area adjoining sports grounds.

RIVIERSONDEREND 0286

Riviersonderend (Municipal) Main Road. Box 31, Tel 360. Caravan and camping stands.

ROBERTSON 02351

Silverstrand Holiday Resort (Municipal), 3 km from the town, on the banks of the Breede River. Tel 3321. Caravan and camping stands. Chalets and rondavels. Restaurant.

SALDANHA 02281

Blouwaterbaai Holiday Resort, Camp Street extension, 2 km east of town on the bay front. Fully equipped cottages. Tel 4-2400.

Vredenburg-Saldanha Municipal Holiday Resort, Saldanha Bay coast. Saldanha, Tel 4-1525. Caravan and camping stands, bungalows, luxury cottages.

SOMERSET WEST 024

Cloetenberg, on the national road N2. Tel 2-2778. Caravan and camping stands.

STANFORD 02833

Salmons Dam Nature Reserve (Divisional Council), off route R326. 17 km due east of Stanford. Tel 789. Caravan and camping stands, bungalows.

STELLENBOSCH DISTRICT 02231

Bergplaas Holiday Ranch, Helshoogte Road (R310), north-east of the town. Tel 7-5119. Caravan stands, cottages.

Drie Gewels Holiday Resort, 9 km south-west of the town on route R310. Tel 630 (02234). Caravan stands, bungalows.

STILBAAI 02934

Ellensrust (Municipal), Main Road East. Tel 4-1034. Caravan and camping stands, rondavels/bungalows.

Riverside Farm, on the banks of the Kafferkuils River. Main Road 5 km north of Stilbaai. Tel 4-1608. Caravan and camping stands.

STRAND 024

Kays, cor. Woltemade Street and Lourens River Road. Close to beach. Tel 53-1129. Caravan and camping stands. Restaurant.

Voortrekker Park (Municipal), Hofmeyr Street. Close to beach. Box 35. Tel 3-2316. Caravan and camping stands, chalets.

STRUISBAAI 02846

Struisbaai (Divisional Council), on the beachfront, near De Hoop Nature Reserve. Box 35, Bredasdorp. Tel 820. Caravan and camping stands, bungalows.

SWELLENDAM 0291

Bontebok National Park, on the breede River, 6 km south-east of Swellendam, off national road N2. Overnight caravan stands. Shop. Tel 4-2735.

Die Stroom (Municipal), 6 km to the north fo the town on the Breede River. Tel 4-2705. Caravan and camping stands.

Swellendam Municipal, Glen Road. Tel 4-2705. Caravan and camping stands, bungalows.

TULBAGH 02362

Tulbagh Municipal, Van der Stel Street. Box 3. Tel 20. Caravan stands.

UILENKRAALSMOND 02834

Uilenkraalsmond (Divisional Council), at the sea 7 km east of Gansbaai. Tel Gaansbaai 8700. Caravan and camping stands, cottages. Restaurant.

VELDDRIF LAAIPLEK 022882

Kingfisher Heads, on the banks of the Berg River 2 km from Velddrif. Tel 500. Holiday Flats.

Stywelyne (Municipal), adjoining Laaiplek harbour area. Tel 408. Caravan and camping stands.

VILLIERSDORP 0225

Villiersdorp (Municipal), near Theewaterskloof Dam, 1 km from town. Tel 3-1130. Caravan and camping stands.

WELLINGTON 02211

Katryntjiesdrif, near the berg River, 3 km to the west of the town. Box 517. Tel 3-1625. Caravan and camping stands.

Pinnie Joubert (Municipal), Addy Street. Tel 3-2603. Caravan and camping stands.

WITSAND 0020

Barry's. Chalets. Tel 62.

Witsand (Divisional Council), near the mouth of the Breede River. Tel 27. Caravan and camping stands.

WORCESTER 0231

Burger Park (Municipal), De La Bat Road. Tel 7-1992. Caravan and camping stands.

Rustig, 8 km to the north of the town on the foothills of the Brandwagberg, off national road N1. Tel 7-0081 or 2-7245. Caravan and camping stands, chalets. Club hall for youth groups.

YSTERFONTEIN 02245

Ysterfontein (Divisional Council), Tel 211. Caravan and camping stands.

3 — The Garden Route, the Little Karoo and the Long Kloof

BRENTON, LAKE BRENTON, BRENTON-ON-SEA AND BUFFALO BAY (See KNYSNA)

CALITZDORP 04437

Calitzdorp Spa (Divisional Council), hot springs near Olifants River, 15 km from Calitzdorp on the old road to Oudtshoorn. Tel 371. Caravan and camping stands, chalets. Dance hall, restaurant, shop.

CAPE ST FRANCIS (See ST FRANCIS BAY)

GEORGE 0441 (See also GLENTANA, HEROLD'S BAY, VICTORIA BAY AND WILDERNESS)

George Municipal Tourist Camp, at the Cape Town end of York Street (the main thoroughfare), 2 km from the centre of town and 10 km from the sea. Tel 7-2205. Caravan and camping stands, rondavels/bungalows/huts, cottages.

Mayfield, 6 km from George on national road N2 to Wilderness, 5 km from the sea. Tel 4490. Caravan and camping stands, one cottage. Adjoining two-star Mayfield Park Hotel.

Overdale Country Cottages, 3 km from George off N2 to Knysna. Tel 3469. Cottages and chalets.

Sea Breeze Cabanas, Victoria Bay road. Tel 4661.

GLENTANA 0441

Glentana, on the coastal road 26 km west of George (10 km east of Great Brak River). Tel 7-2553. Caravan and camping stands.

GREAT BRAK RIVER 04442

Souwesia (Municipal) Tel 2100. Caravan and camping stands.

Pine Creek, Box 80. Tel 2434. Caravan and camping stands.

HARTENBOS 04441

Afrikaans Taal- en Kultuurvereniging (ATKV) Holiday resort. On the beachfront, 10 km east of Mossel Bay. Tel 5107. Caravan stands, camping stands, apartments, cottages, rondavels. Restaurant.

HEROLD'S BAY 0441

Dutton's Cove Holiday Resort, 18 km west of George, 8 km from P.W. Botha Airport. Tel 76-9205. Caravan stands, cottages, chalets, rondavels. Games room.

Herold's Bay (Divisional Council), 15 km west of George. Tel 74-4040. Caravan and camping stands.

HUMANSDORP 04231

Ben Marais (Municipal), Main Street Tel 5-1111. Caravan and camping stands, rondavels, cottages, chalets.

JEFFREYS BAY 04231

Jeffreys Bay Holiday Resort, Goede Hoop Street. Tel 3-1330. Caravan and camping stands, cottages, chalets, rondavels.

Kabeljoes-on-Sea Holiday Resort (Municipal), Tel 3-1775. Caravan and camping stands, cottages.

Jeffreys Bay Municipal, Tel 3-1111. Da Gama Street. Caravan and camping stands.

KEURBOOMS RIVER 04457

Arch Rock, 8 km east of Plettenberg Bay. Tel 9309. Caravan stands and cottages.

Keurbooms River Public Resort, in the Cape Provincial Council riverside nature reserve, 7 km east of Plettenberg Bay. Tel 9828. Caravan and camping stands, cabins.

Lagoon Holiday Resort, Keurbooms River Mouth, 10 km east of Plettenberg Bay. Tel 9830. Caravan and camping stands, cottages, bungalows, chalets, TV lounge.

San Marino, near river, 7 km east of Plettenberg Bay. Box 413, Plettenberg Bay 6600. Tel 9700. Caravan and camping stands, chalets.

KNYSNA 0445

Ashmead Holiday Park, off the road to Knysna Heads (George Rex Drive). Tel 2-2985. Caravan and camping stands, timber chalets, cottages, apartments. TV room.

Buffels Bay, 19 km west of Knysna. Tel 2-2205. Caravan and camping stands. (Divisional Council).

Knysna, Main Road (east end) Tel 2-2011.

Lagoonside, Main Road (east end) Tel 2-1751. Caravan stands, rondavels, cottage, hire vans.

Lake Brenton Holiday Resort, near Brenton-on-sea, 16 km from Knysna town. Tel 2-1501. Caravan and camping stands, rondavels, chalets. TV and games room.

Lightleys Holiday Cruisers, fully equipped luxury cabin cruisers on Knysna Lagoon. Tel 2-3071/2.

Monk's, Main Road (east end) Tel 2-2609. Caravan stands, bungalows.

Waterways Holiday, Holiday Park Crescent. Tel 2-2241. Caravan stands, cottages.

Woodbourne Holiday farm, George Rex Drive. Tel 2-3223. Caravan stands, cottages.

LITTLE BRAK RIVER 04441

Riverside, 5 km north of Little Brak River. Tel 6316. Caravan and camping stands, cottages.

MOSSEL BAY 04441

Mossel Bay Caravan Parks (Municipal). The 3 parks, all on the seafront are:
Bakke, out of season Tel 2915, in season (1 Dec to 20 Jan) Tel 2043.
Santos, open only in season, Tel 2043.
Point, out of season Tel 3501, in season (1 Dec to 20 Jan) Tel 2043.

NATURE'S VALLEY 0441

Groot Rivier Camping Site, National Parks Board, George. Caravan and camping stands. Tel 74-6924.

OUDTSHOORN 04431

Kleinplaas Holiday Resort, Cnr Baron van Rheede and Noord Streets. Fully equipped chalets. Camping and caravan stands. Vans hired. Tel 5811.

NA Smit Tourist Camp (Municipal), Park Road North. Tel 2224. Caravan and camping stands, chalets, rondavels.

Schoemanspoort (Divisional Council), on the banks of Grobelaar River, Rietkloof, 20 km north of the town. Caravan and camping stands, rondavels. Tel 2241.

OYSTER BAY 04231

Oyster Bay, Caravan and camping stands, cottages, rondavels. Tel 5-2626.

PARADISE BEACH 04231

Paradise Beach, Tel 5-2559. Caravan and camping stands.

PLETTENBERG BAY 04457
(See also KEURBOOMS RIVER)
Piesang River, Beacon Island Drive. Tel 3-1634. Caravan and camping stands.

Plettenberg Bay, Keurbooms Lagoon (Lookout Beach). Tel 3-2567. Caravan and camping stands.

Robberg Caravan park. Tel 3-2571.

ST FRANCIS BAY 04231
Cape St Francis, Da Gama Road. Tel 4211. Caravan and camping stands.

SEDGEFIELD 04455
Cloverdale, at Swartvlei on road to George. Box 21. Tel 903. Caravans stands.

Jooris, Swartvlei on road to George. Tel 905. Caravan and camping stands, vans for hire, cottages, rondavels.

Lake Pleasant, 4 km from Sedgefield on road to Knysna. Tel 985. Caravan and camping stands, vans for hire.

Landfall Holiday Resort, Kingfisher Drive, Swartvlei. Tel 840. Caravan and camping stands, cottages, chalets, rondavels. Vans for hire.

Pine Lake Marina, at Swartvlei on road to George. Tel 742. Caravan and camping stands. Luxury bungalows.

Trail's End, west bank of Swartvlei. Box 31. Tel 914. Caravan stands, bungalows.

STORMS RIVER 04237
Tsitsikamma Coastal National Park, Storms River Mouth. Tel 607. Caravan and camping stands, cottages, luxury apartments. Restaurant.

Tsitsikamma Forest National Park, Paul Sauer Bridge over Storms River. National Parks Board as above. Caravan and camping stands. Restaurant.

VICTORIA BAY 0441
Victoria Bay (Divisional Council). Tel 74-4040. Caravan and camping stands.

VLEESBAAI 04441
Karmosyn, 18 km west of Mossel Bay. Tel 3837. Caravan stands.

WILDERNESS 0441
Ebb and Flow Nature Reserve (Divisional Council), 3 km east of Wilderness. Tel 74-4040. Caravan stands, rondavels.

Island Lake, 4 km east of Wilderness. Tel 9-1194. Caravan and camping stands, rondavels.

The Lakes, 2 km from Wilderness off the road to Knysna. Tel 9-1101. Caravan and camping stands.

Wilderness Rest Camp, National Parks Board. On the banks of Touws River (in nature reserve) 4 km east of Wilderness. Caravan and camping stands, cottages, chalets, caravans for hire. Tel 9-1197.

4 — The Great Karoo

ABERDEEN 049212
Aberdeen Municipal, Hope Street. Tel 14. Caravan and camping stands.

BEAUFORT WEST 0201
Beaufort West Municipal, Danie Theron Street, at the south end of town. Tel 2800 or 2121. Caravan and camping stands.

BRITSTOWN 05732
Britstown Municipal, on the south side of town on the R29 to Victoria West. Tel 3. Caravan stands.

COLESBERG 05852
Colesberg Municipal, on the south side of town on the N1 to Hanover. Tel 20. Caravan stands.

DE AAR 0571
Van der Merwe (Municipal), 2 km from town on the R32 to Hanover. Tel 2131. Caravan stands.

GRAAFF-REINET 0491
Urquhart Park (Municipal), Murraysburg Road. Tel 2-2121. Caravan and camping stands, bungalows.

HANOVER 057212
Hanover Municipal, 1 km from town on the N1 to Colesberg. Tel 53. Caravan and camping stands.

LAINGSBURG 02373
Sit-en-rus, Voortrekker Street Wimpy Bar. Tel 93. Caravan stands.

MIDDELBURG 0483
Middelburg Municipal, Heuwel Street. Tel 2-1133. Caravan and camping stands.

MURRAYSBURG 049222
Murraysburg Divisional Council, Voortrekker Street. Box 331. Tel 19. Caravan stands.

PHILIPSTOWN 057222
Philipstown Municipal, Venter Street. Tel 94. Caravan and camping stands.

RICHMOND 05752
Richmond Municipal, Market Street. Tel 1. Caravan and camping stands.

STEYNSBURG 04842
Steynsburg Municipal, Hendrik Potgieter Street. Tel 34. Caravan and camping stands.

TOUWS RIVER 02382
Oom Loots, national road N1. Tel 49. Caravan and camping stands, rondavels, cottages.

UNIONDALE 04462
Nietgenaand Nature Reserve (Divisional Council). Tel 1903 (between 1 and 2 pm) Beyond the town 20 km along the R57 to Willowmore. Near the foot of the eastern Swartberg. Caravan stands, apartments. Hot springs and baths.

VICTORIA WEST 02042
Victoria West Municipal, Muggelstone Avenue. Tel 26. Caravan and camping stands.

WILLOWMORE 04942
Willowmore Municipal, Knysna Street. Tel 4. Caravan stands.

5 — Port Elizabeth and District and the Settler Country

PORT ELIZABETH AND DISTRICT 041
Parks and resorts under control of Algoa Regional Services (C.P.A.) Tel 56-1000.

Beachview Holiday Resort, in St Francis Bay, 31 km west of the city (beyond Seaview). Caravan and camping stands, chalets. Restaurant. Tel (041) 74884.

Gamtoos River Mouth, in St Francis Bay, 56 km west of the city (beyond Thornhill) Camping stands. Tel (0422) 5649

Maitlands Camping Ground, on the Maitland River, close to Beachview (above), 33 km from the city. Camping stands.

Van Stadens River Mouth, in St Francis Bay, 41 km west of the city. Caravan and camping stands, rondavels. Tel (0422) 5990.

Willows Holiday Resort, 18 km from the city along the Marine Drive past Summerstrand. Caravan and camping stands, cottages, chalets, rondavels, vans. Restaurant. Tel (041) 36-1717, 36-1734.

Brookes Hill, at Humewood Beach. Tel 2-5400. Caravan stands.

Sea Acres, at Humewood Beach. Tel 53-3095. Caravan and camping stands, chalets and rondavels.

St George's Strand. At the beach in Algoa Bay, 25 km north of the city (off the N2). Tel 61-1163.

ADDO 04252
Addo Elephant National Park. Tel 140. Reservations (021) 419 5365 or (012) 343-1991. Caravan and camping stands, rondavels, chalets. Restaurant.

ADELAIDE 04662
Dunvegan, Princess Street. Tel 180. Caravan stands.

ALEXANDRIA 04652
Alexandria Municipal, Stephanus Oosthuizen Street. Tel 56. Caravan and camping stands.

Boknes (Divisional Council), approximately 30 kilometres along the circular drive from Alexandria to Bushmans River Mouth. Tel 5131. Caravan and camping stands.

Cannon Rocks, approximately 25 kilometres along the circular drive from Alexandria to Bushmans River Mouth. Tel 3612. Caravan stands, chalets. Restaurant.

BATHURST 0464
Newton Walker Municipal, Tel 3639. Caravan stands.

BUSHMAN'S RIVER MOUTH 0020
Bushman's River Mouth Municipal. Tel 27. Caravan and camping stands.

COLCHESTER 041
Pearson Park, at the mouth of the Sundays River. (2 situations). Tel 61-1150. Caravan and camping stands. Restaurant. Rondavels.

FORT BEAUFORT 0435
Fort Beaufort Municipal, Durban Street. Tel 3-1136. Caravan stands.

GRAHAMSTOWN 0461
Grahamstown Municipal, Mountain Drive, off the N2 to Port Elizabeth, 1 km from town. Tel 2-2043 day 2-4366 night. Caravan and camping stands, chalets, rondavels.

HANKEY 04236
Yellowwoods (Municipal), Kleinrivier Road. Tel 302. Caravan and camping stands.

HOFMEYR 04852
Hofmeyr Municipal, Tel 97. Caravan and camping stands.

MOUNTAIN ZEBRA NATIONAL PARK

Reservations Tel (021) 419-5365 or (012) 343-1991. Further details of facilities appear on page 160.

JANSENVILLE 04932

Jansenville Municipal, Tel 21. Caravan stands.

PATENSIE 04232

George Rautenbach Park, (Municipal). Tel 257. Caravan and camping stands.

PORT ALFRED 0464

Medolino, Steward Road, West Bank. Tel 4-1651. Caravan and camping stands, cottages, chalets.

Riverside, Mentone Road, West Bank. Tel 4-2230. Caravan stands, chalets.

SOMERSET EAST 0424

Max Clarke, (Municipal), Bestershoek, adjoining Bosberg Nature Reserve, 2 km from town. Caravan and camping stands, vans for hire. Tel 3-1333.

UITENHAGE 0422

Two caravan parks under the control of the Municipality, Box 45. Tel 2-6011 and 2-5574:

Magennis Park, High Street. Caravan stands.

Springs Pleasure Resort, 8 km from town on the R75 to Jansenville. Caravan stands, rondavels.

6 — East London, the Border, North-eastern Cape and East Griqualand

EAST LONDON 0431

Blue Bend, at Nahoon Mouth, Beacon Bay. Tel 47-1537. Caravan stands, apartments.

Marina Glen. Adjoining Marina Glen at Eastern Beach. Tel 2-8753. Caravan and camping stands.

Nahoon Beach (Municipal), at the mouth of the Nahoon River, East London. Tel 5-7569. Caravan and camping stands.

Verina, Settlers Way, Greenfields. On the West Bank, 12 km from the city. Tel 46-1069. Caravan and camping stands.

EAST LONDON DISTRICT 0431

Resorts north-east of city

Cefani Mouth, 43 km from the city. Tel 95-1169. Caravan stands, cottages, bungalows, rondavels.

Cintsa Bay, 40 km from the city, East London. Tel 95-1178. Caravan and camping stands, cottages, rondavels.

Cintsa West, 40 km from the city, Beacon Bay. Tel 95-1176. 60 caravan and camping stands, 4 cottages.

Four Seasons. Beacon Bay. Tel 95-1276. Caravan and camping stands, cottages.

Glen Navar, 32 km from the city. East London. Tel 95-1329. Caravan and camping stands, chalets.

Gonubie (Municipal), Meier Street, 20 km from the city. Box 20 Gonubie. Tel 94-1313. Caravan and camping stands, chalets.

Gwenshaw, Arum Road, Gonubie. 16 km from the city. Tel 94-1710. Caravan and camping stands.

P.S.A. Holiday Resort, Gonubie. 14 km from the city. Tel 95-1022.

Pirates Creek, at the Quinera lagoon, Bonza Bay. 10 km from the city. Tel 47-1160. Caravan and camping stands, cottages.

Queensberry bay, 24 km from the city. Tel 95-1277. Caravan stands, cottages.

Quinera Lagoon, 19 km from the city. Tel 95-1462. Caravan and camping stands, cottages.

Rainbow Valley, 25 km from the city at Sunrise-on-Sea. Tel 95-1519. Caravan stands and chalets.

Xanadu, at Cintsa River Mouth. Tel 95-1159. Caravan and camping stands, chalets.

Yellow Sands, at Kwelera Mouth, 29 km from the city. Tel 95-1336. Caravan and camping stands.

EAST LONDON DISTRICT 0431 AND 04323

Resorts south-west of the city

Aqualea, 24 km from the city off the R72 to Kidd's Beach. Tel (04323) 858. Caravan and camping stands.

Christmas Rock, 38 km from the city, 11 km beyond the turnoff to Kidd's Beach. Tel (04323) 899. Caravan and camping stands.

Lincott Manor, Main Road, Kidd's Beach; Tel (04323) 643. Caravan and camping stands, bungalows, cottage.

Palm Springs, Umbele Lagoon, Kidd's Beach. Tel (04323) 879. Caravan and camping stands, cottages.

Welcomagain, 13 km from the city, at Hickmans River. Tel 46-1080. Caravan and camping stands, bungalows.

ALIWAL NORTH 0551

Aliwal North Spa Holiday Resort, at the Spa, 2,5 km south of the town. Tel 2951. Caravan stands, cottages.

BARKLY EAST 04542

Barkly East Municipal, Tel 158. Caravan and camping stands.

BEACON BAY (SEE EAST LONDON)

BURGERSDORP 055312

Shorten Park (Municipal), President Swart Road. Tel 14. Caravan and camping stands.

CATHCART 04562

Cathcart Municipal, Robinson Street. Tel 22. Caravan stands.

DORDRECHT 045512

Hofmeyer (Municipal), Overnight stops only, at the rugby ground. Tel 17. Caravan and camping stands.

ELLIOT 045312

Elliot Municipal, Maclear Road. Tel 11. Caravan and camping stands.

GONUBIE (SEE EAST LONDON DISTRICT)

HAGA HAGA (MOOIPLAAS 04372)

Bosbokstrand, 72 km north-east of East London. At Mooiplaas (on N2) take turnoff

east to the coast. Tel 4512 or (011) 696-1442. Caravan and camping stands, chalets. On a private nature reserve.

JAMESTOWN 05521

Jamestown Municipal, on outskirts of town on Aliwal North Road. Tel 641. Caravan and camping stands.

KEI MOUTH 0020

Kei Mouth. Tel 4. Caravan and camping stands, rondavels, chalets, cottages.

Whispering Waves. Tel 30. Caravan stands, cottages, rondavels.

KIDD'S BEACH (SEE EAST LONDON DISTRICT)

KING WILLIAM'S TOWN 0433

King William's Town Municipal, Cathcart Street. Box 2-3160 caravan and camping stands.

KOKSTAD 0372

Kokstad, Hawthorn and Barker Street. Tel 3389. Caravan and camping stands. Vans hired.

Mount Currie Motel, national road N2. Tel 2178. Caravan and camping stands.

KOMGA 04372

Komga Municipal, Main Street. Tel 28. Caravan stands.

LADY GREY 05552

S J Schlebusch (Municipal), Murray and Burnett Streets. Tel 19. Caravan and camping stands.

MATATIELE 0373

Haig Park (Municipal), Tel 3786. Caravan stands.

MORGAN BAY 0020

Double Mouth Camping Site (Department of Forestry), Tel (0431) 46-3532. In the indigenous forest 6 km from Kei Mouth. Caravan and camping stands.

Morgan Bay, at the edge of the lagoon. Tel Kei Mouth 62. Caravan and camping stands, cottages.

QUEENSTOWN 0451

Queenstown Municipal, on river bank, 3 km from the town. Tel 3131. Caravan and camping stands.

STUTTERHEIM 04362

Stutterheim Municipal, Tel 9. Caravan stands.

VENTERSTAD 055332

Venterstad Municipal, near Hendrik Verwoerd Dam. Tel 24. Caravan and camping stands.

7 — Transkei and its Wild Coast

UMTATA 0471
Umtata Municipal, Eli Spilkin Street, at the southern end of the town, near the hospital, University and Holiday Inn, and close to the N2. Tel 2-2253. Caravan sites.

PORT ST JOHNS 04752
First Beach Holiday Camp (Municipal). Tel 75. Caravan and camping stands, bungalows and cottage.

Second Beach Holiday Camp (Municipal). Tel 31. Caravan and camping stands, bungalows, rondavels and cottage.

Second Beach Holiday Resort. Tel 61. Caravan and camping stands, and cottages.

WILD COAST CAMPING SITES
There are a number of proclaimed camping sites along the Transkeian Wild Coast. Some of these have been provided with ablution blocks, and others have no facilities at all. Camping sites administered by the Department of Agriculture and Forestry are marked with an asterisk, and contact should be made with the department at Private Bag X5002 Umtata, telephone (0471) 2-4930 or 2-4928 before proceeding to sites.

Bashee Mouth. The Magistrate, Elliotdale. No facilities.

Cebe Mouth. Department Agriculture and Forestry, Butterworth. Ablution blocks.

Coffee Bay*. Ablution blocks.

Mdumbi Mouth *. No facilities.

Msikaba. Officer in charge, Lusikisiki. Ablution blocks.

Pressley Bay*. No facilities.

Qolora Mouth*. No facilities.

Qora Mouth*. No facilities.

Xhora Mouth. The Magistrate, Elliotdale. No facilities.

Dwesa Nature Reserve*. Ablution blocks. Permit required.

Hluleka Nature Reserve*. Bungalows and ablution blocks. Permit required.

Mkambati Game Ranch. Dial 0020 ask for 89 Flagstaff. Safaris, game hunting and viewing.

8 — Durban and District and the Natal Coastal Resorts

DURBAN 031
Ansteys, 6 Anstey Road, Brighton Beach. Tel 47-4061. Caravan stands.

Durban, 55 Grays Inn Road, Bluff. Tel 47-3929. Caravan and camping stands.

ANERLEY 0391
Banana Beach. Tel 3043. Caravan and camping stands, rondavels, chalets, cottages.

Bendigo. Tel 3451. Caravan and camping stands, cottages, vans for hire.

Ilanga Banana Beach. Tel 3280. Caravan and camping stands.

Marlon Sunwich Port. Tel 3596. Caravan and camping stands, cottages, vans for hire.

Saame Park, Sunwich Port, Box 39. Tel 3325. Caravan stands, cottages.

Villa Siesta. Tel 3343. Caravan stands, chalets.

BALLITO 0322
Dolphin, Compensation Beach Road. Tel 6-2187. Caravan stands, chalets, cottages.

Lala Lapha, Ocean Drive into Gazelle Street. Tel 6-1430. Caravan, camping stands, vans for hire.

BAZLEY BEACH 03239
Bazley Beach, Tel 863. At the mouth of the Ifafa River. Caravan and camping stands, cottages.

BLYTHEDALE BEACH 0324
Blythedale Beach, Umvoti Drive. Tel 2-3613. Caravan and camping stands.

CLANSTHAL 03231
Ciansthal, off coastal road R102, 5 km south of Umkomaas. Tel 3-0211. Caravan and camping stands.

DOONSIDE 031
Pot Luck, 5 Topham Road. Tel 903-6498. Caravan and camping stands.

HIBBERDENE 0399
Carousel, Woodgrange Street. Tel 2406. Caravan stands, cottages, apartments.

Happy Days, Marlin Drive. Box 1. Tel 2310. Caravan and camping stands, chalets.

Hibberdene, Umzimai river. Tel 2308. Caravan and camping stands.

Rondalia. Tel 2123. Caravan stands, rondavels. Restaurant.

Umzimai. Tel 2507. Caravan and camping stands. Restaurant.

IFAFA BEACH 03239
Club Marina, P/Bag Ifafa Beach. Tel 611. Caravan and camping stands, chalets

ILLOVO 031
Illovo Beach, Elizabeth Avenue, Box 19. Tel 96-3472. Caravan and camping stands, cottages.

Natalia, A.T.K.V. Elizabeth Avenue. Tel 96-2626. Caravan stands, apartments.

Plett-Haven, Elizabeth Avenue. Tel 96-3055.

Villa Caravan Spa, Elizabeth Avenue. Tel 96-2139. Caravan and camping stands, cottages, vans for hire.

KARRIDENE 031
Karridene Holiday Resort, coastal road R102. Tel 96-3321. Caravan and camping stands. Flats.

KELSO 03231
Happy Wanderers, on the beach off the old south coast road. Tel 5-1104. Caravan and camping stands, cottages and chalets.

Kelso Valley, Cod Crescent. Tel 5-1805. Caravan and camping stands, vans hired.

MARGATE 03931
Constantia, Tel 2-0482. From South Coast Road, westward – along Collins Road and right (northwards) into Valley Street. Caravan and camping stands.

De Wet, St Andrews Road. Tel 2-1022. Caravan, camping stands, cottages and vans for hire (near Palm Beach Hotel).

Margate, Valley Road. Tel 2-0852. Caravan and camping stands.

MARINA BEACH 03931
Belle Vista. Tel 3-0755. Caravan and camping stands. Restaurant.

Sherwood Forest, 100 m off the R61. Caravan and camping stands. Tel 3-0971.

MTWALUME 03230
Vergesig A.T.K.B. Holiday Resort, Tel 641.

Long Beach. Tel 711. Caravan and camping stands, cottages and rondavels, vans for hire.

Mtwalume, Tel 719. Caravan and camping stands.

MUNSTER 03938
Leisure View, Blackpool Avenue. Voortrekkerstrand. Tel. 367. Caravan and camping stands.

Mittenwald. Tel 347. Lower South Coast Road. Caravan and camping stands.

ORIBI GORGE NATURE RESERVE
Natal Parks Board, Box 662, Pietermaritzburg. Tel (0331) 5-1514. The approach road is off the N2 between Port Shepstone and Harding. Hutted camp.

PALM BEACH 03938
Greenhart, at the beach. Tel 285. Caravan and camping stands, cottages.

PARK RYNIE 03231
Caravan Cove, Marine Drive. Tel 2-1215. Caravan stands, chalets, cottages, vans for hire.

Paradys, off Coastal Road R102. Caravan and campings stands, chalets, vans for hire. Tel 2-1336.

Rocky Bay, Marine Drive. Tel 2-0546. Caravan and camping stands.

PENNINGTON 03231
Pennington, Old Main Road. Tel 5-1107, caravan and camping stands, vans for hire.

Umdoni, Old South Coast Road. Tel 5-1261. Caravan and camping stands, chalets, vans for hire.

PORT EDWARD 03930
Koelwaters, at the seafront. Tel 675. Caravan and camping stands.

Pont, (Municipal), Bannersrest. Tel 211. On the bank of the Umtamvuna River, close to nature reserve. Caravan and camping stands.

S.A.P. Holiday Resort, at the beach. Tel 333. Caravan stands, cottages, chalets and rondavels.

QUEENSBURGH 031
Queensburgh, Haslam Road. Tel 44-5800. Caravan stands.

ST MICHAEL'S-ON-SEA AND SHELLY BEACH 0393
Blue Seas, Shelly Beach. Tel 5-1049. Caravan and camping stands.

Kingfisher, Spink Road, St Michael's. Tel 5-0272. Caravan and camping stands, vans for hire.

Surf Bay. St Michael's. Tel 5-0233. Caravan and camping stands.

Karapark, Main Road, Shelly Beach. Tel 5-1226. Caravan and camping, vans for hire.

SALT ROCK 0322
Salt Rock, off Basil Hulett Drive (adjoining the hotel). Tel 5025. Caravan and camping stands.

SCOTTBURGH 03231

Scottburgh (Municipal), at the beachfront. Tel 2-0291Caravan and camping stands.

SOUTHBROOM 03931

Ooteekalia. Tel 6080. Caravan and camping stands. (Seasonal).

Paradise, Marine Drive. Tel 3-0655. Caravan and camping stands, vans for hire.

TRAFALGAR 03931

Port-O-Call, Trafalgar Square, Tel 3-0511. Caravan and camping stands, vans for hire.

TUGELA MOUTH 03245

Tugela Mouth North-Bank. P O Mandini. Tel 3641. Caravan and camping stands.

UMHLANGA ROCKS 031

Umhlanga, Weaver Crescent. Tel 561-3217. Caravan and camping stands, vans hired.

UMKOMAAS 03231

Widenham, off coastal road R102, south of the town. Tel 3-0351. Caravan and camping stands, vans for hire, chalets.

UMTENTWENI 0391

Umtentweni, on the Umtentweni River bank, off the N2. Tel 5-0531. Caravan and camping stands, chalets.

UMZUMBE 0391

Hideaway, Tel. 6283. Caravan and camping stands, cottages, chalets, vans hired.

UVONGO BEACH 03931

Oasis, Falcon Road. Tel 5-0778. Caravan and camping stands, chalets.

Uvongo, Colin Street. Tel 5-0424. Caravan stands.

Uvongo River, Tel 5-1156. Caravan stands.

VOORTREKKERSTRAND 03938

Leisure View, Tel 367. Caravan stands (with tents), vans hired.

Transvaal Onderwysstrand. Tel 729. Caravan stands and cottages.

WINKLE SPRUIT 031

Karavana, Tel 96-2929. Caravan stands (with tents).

Mount Carmel, Camp Road. Tel 96-1720. Caravan stands.

Ocean Call, Murray-Smith Road. Tel 96-2644. Caravan and camping stands, vans hired.

Uitspan, off coastal road R102, Tel 96-1677. Caravan and camping stands, vans hired.

Winklespruit, Eastern Glen Road. Tel 96-2318. Caravan and camping stands, cottages.

ZINKWAZI BEACH 0324

Zinkwazi. Tel 3344. Caravan stands, cottages, chalets.

9 — Zululand and Northern Natal

ESHOWE 0354

Eshowe Municipal, Saunders Street, adjacent to the Dlinza Forest Nature Reserve. Tel 4-1141. Caravan and camping stands.

MTUNZINI 035322

Forest Inn, overlooking Ngoye Forest Reserve off N2, 22 km south of Empangeni. Tel 95. Caravan stands

Umlalazi River Resort, off N2 to Empangeni, Caravan and camping stands, vans hired, chalets. Tel 340.

Umlalazi (Parks Board). See below.

Xaxaza. Tel 140. Caravan and camping stands.

PAULPIETERSBURG 03582

Paulpietersburg Municipal. Tel 10. Caravan stands.

RICHARDS BAY 0351

Richards Bay Municipal, Tel 3-1971. Caravan and camping stands.

ST LUCIA ESTUARY 03592

St Lucia Travel Lodge, Tel 36. Caravan stands, furnished rooms.

VRYHEID 0381

Swart Umfolozi River Resort, 39 km from Glückstadt, 74 km from Vryheid. Caravan and camping stands, chalets. Nearby swimming-pool, café). Tel (03824) 793.

Vryheid Municipal, Utrecht Street. Tel 2106. Caravan and camping stands.

WEENEN 03632

Weenen (Municipal). Tel 711. Caravan stands.

ZULULAND GAME AND NATURE RESERVES

All enquiries for accommodation at these reserves should be made to Natal Parks Board, P O Box 662, Pietermaritzburg 3200. Telephone (0331) 5-1514. In cases where the officer-in-charge of the camp may be contacted direct the telephone number is given.

Charters Creek. Tel (03552) 1431. Hutted camp.

False Bay Park. Tel (03562) 2911. Caravan and camping stands.

Fanies Island. Tel (03552) 1431. Hutted camps, caravan and camping.

Harold Johnson Nature Reserve. Tel (0324) 6-1574. Limited camping facilities. Tugela River, adjacent to Fort Pearson.

Hluhluwe Game Reserve. (Tel (03562) 7. Hutted camp.

Kosi Bay Nature Reserve. 4-wheel drive vehicles only Camping stands.

Mapalane Nature Reserve. Tel 03592 ask for St Lucia Estuary 20. Log cabins and camping stands.

Mkuzi Game Reserve. Tel 0020 ask for Mkuzi Reserve. Caravan and camping stands, rondavels, cottage, bungalows.

Ndumu Game Reserve. Tel 0020 ask for Ingwavuma 32. Rondavels. No camping or caravans.

St Lucia Resort. Tel 03592 ask for St Lucia Estuary 20. Caravan and camping stands.

Sordwana Bay National Park. Tel 0020 ask for Jozini 1102. Open campsites.

Umfolozi Game Reserve. Reservations Officer Pietermaritzburg. Two hutted camps.

Umlalazi Nature Reserve. Tel (035322) 136. Caravan and camping stands, log cabins.

Malachite Camp, a private game reserve in the Mala Mala group (see pages 210 and 213), 8 km south-east of Mkuze village. Reservations (011) 789-2677. Enquiries (031) 75-3325.

10 — Pietermaritzburg, Natal Midlands, Natal Coalfields and Drakensberg Resorts

PIETERMARITZBURG 0331

Pietermaritzburg Municipal, Cleland Road, Hayfields. Tel 6-5342. Caravan and camping stands.

BERGVILLE 03642

Bergville Municipal, on the Tugela River bank, 1 km from the village. Tel 36. Caravan and camping stands, chalets.

COLENSO 03622

Colenso Municipal, Botha Road. Tel 2-1111. Caravan and camping stands.

CRAMOND 03393

Albert Falls Public Resort (Natal Parks Board). Tel 612. Chalets, rondavels, caravan and camping stands, 2 camps in the nature reserve.

DRAKENSBERG GAME AND NATURE RESERVES

All enquiries for accommodation at these reserves should be made to Natal Parks Board, P O Box 662, Pietermaritzburg 3200. Telephone (0331) 5-1514. In cases where the officer-in-charge of the camp may be contacted direct the telephone number is given.

Coleford Nature Reserve. Hutted camp and rustic camp.

Giant's Castle Game Reserve – general booking, cottages, bungalows, rondavels, mountain huts (0331) 5-1514. hillside campsite booking (03631) 2-4435. Giant's Lodge luxury accommodation, Director's Secretary (0331) 5-1221.

Himeville Nature Reserve. Tel (033722) 36. Caravan and camping sites.

Injasuti (near Giant's Castle). Tel Loskop 1311. Cabins, caravan and camping sites.

Kamberg Nature Reserve. Hutted camp, rustic cottage.

Loteni Nature Reserve. Hutted camp, rustic cottage. Tel (033722) 1540. Hutted camp, caravan and camping sites.

Royal Natal National Park. Tendele Camp. Cottages, rondavels. Mahai Camp Site. Tel (03642) 3. Caravan stands. Rugged Glen Nature Reserve. Tel (03642) 7104. Caravan stands.

Spioenkop Public Resort. Cottages. Tel (03682) 78, regarding caravan stands.

Vergelegen Nature Reserve. Cottages.

DRAKENSBERG, DEPARTMENT OF FORESTRY AND PRIVATE PARKS

Cathedral Peak State Forest. Tel (03682) Cathedral 3621. Caravan and camping stands.

Dragon Peaks, Tel (03642) Dragon Peaks No. 1. Caravan and camping stands, cottages, chalets, vans hired.

Drakensberg Garden. Tel 0020 ask for Drakensberg Garden No. 1. Caravan and camping stands adjacent to hotel.

Monk's Cowl State Forest, Winterton. Tel (03682) 2204. Caravan stands.

Mountain Splendour, in the Cathkin Valley. Tel (03682) 3503. Caravan and camping stands, chalets.

DUNDEE 0341

Dundee Municipal, Union Street. Tel 2-2121. Caravan and camping stands.

ELANDSLAAGTE 03621

The Cabins. Tel 738. Cabins and caravan stands.

ESTCOURT 03631

Estcourt Municipal, Lorne Street, off the N3, on the Bushman's River bank. Tel 2-3000. Caravan and camping stands.

Wagendrift Public Resort (Natal Parks Board), at the dam, 5 km to the east of the town. Tel 2550. Caravan stands.

GREYTOWN 0334

Lake Merthley, 7 km from town on the Dundee road. Caravan stands, camping stands, chalets. Tel 3-1171 (Municipal).

HIMEVILLE 033722

Cobham State Forest, caravan and camping ground. Tel 1403.

Highland Nook, Private Park. Tel 1611 Mr J.D. Mclean.

HOWICK 03321

Howick Municipal, Tel 2124. Caravan and camping stands.

Midmar Public Resort and Nature Reserve (Natal Parks Board), Reservations Box 662, Pietermaritzburg 3200. Tel (0331) 5-1514 for chalets and cabins. Tel (03321) 2067 for reservation of caravan and camping stands.

LADYSMITH 0361

Ladysmith Municipal, Harrismith Road. Tel 2-6804. Caravan and camping stands.

MOOI RIVER 0333

Riverbank, off the Greytown road on the river bank. Caravan and camping stands.

NEWCASTLE 03431

Chelmsford Public Resort Nature Reserve (Natal Parks Board) 26 km and 13 km from Newcastle on the Ladysmith/Newcastle Road. Booking for chalets at Leokop and Richgate Park (0331) 5-1514. Campgrounds at Leokop, Sanford and Richgate Park (03431) 7715.

Newcastle Municipal, Hardwick Street. Tel 8-1273. Caravan and camping stands.

WINTERTON 03682

Kelvin Grove. Tel 2502. District road 277 on Estcourt/Bergville route. Caravan and camping stands, cottages, rondavels.

Spioenkop Resort Nature Reserve (Natal Parks Board), 15 km from Winterton. Tel (03682) 78. Caravan and camping stands, chalets. Restaurant.

11 — Johannesburg, Witwatersrand, Southern and Western Transvaal

JOHANNESBURG 011

Barden, 10 km from city on road to Vereeniging. (Near Uncle Charlie's). Tel 942-2600. Caravan stands.

Bezuidenhout Park, 180 Third Avenue, Bez Valley. Tel 648-6302. Caravan stands.

Blossom Valley, south end of Gordon Road, Kibler Park. Tel 943-1508. Caravan and camping stands.

Meredale Pleasure Resort, 10 km from city on road to vereeniging. Lark Street, Meredale, off M1 south. Tel 942-2100. Caravan and camping stands.

Panorama, 14 km from city on road to Little Falls. Tel 679-1225. Caravan stands.

Rivonia, 186 Rietfontein Road, Rivonia. Tel 803-2501.

Willow Grove, Adrian Avenue, Rembrandt Park. Tel 608-2491. Caravan stands.

ALBERTON 011

Elandia, adjacent to N3 Freeway, Alberton, 15 km from Johannesburg. Tel 902-3917. Caravan and camping stands.

Werda, 11 km from town on old road to Vereeniging. Tel 868-2098. Caravan and camping stands.

BAPSFONTEIN 011

Bapsfontein Pleasure Resort, Main Delmas/Bronkhorstspruit road. Tel 964-1305. Caravan and camping stands.

BARBERSPAN 0144322

Elgro, Sandvlei. Tel 28. Caravan and camping stands. Adjacent to hotel.

BENONI 011

Fairwinds, 10 km from town on road to Pretoria. Tel 848-1819. Caravan stands.

Cairngorm, 1 km from Petit on Benoni/Bapsfontein Road. Tel 965-1007. Caravan and camping stands.

BOKSBURG 011

Fun Park City, Jan Smuts Avenue, between the R22 and North Rand Road. Adjacent to Wild Waters. Caravan and camping stands, chalets, restaurant, conference facilities, tennis coach. 4 km from airport.

BOKSBURG WEST 011

Adventure, 119 Madeley Road. Tel 826-1074. Caravan and camping stands.

BRAKPAN 011

Jan Smuts Park (Municipal) Escom Avenue. Tel 55-7711. Caravan stands.

CHRISTIANA 0534

Rob Ferreira Mineral Baths (Overvaal) 4 km from town on the R29 to Bloemhof. Tel 2244. Caravan and camping stands, chalets.

DALESIDE 01612

Kareekloof (Overvaal), in the Suikerbosrand Nature Reserve 10 km from Daleside. Tel 5334. Caravan stands. Restaurant. Shop.

EIKENHOF 011

Lion Rampant, near Lido Hotel. Tel 943-4230. Caravan stands.

ELOFF 0157

Mimosa Hotel Pleasure Resort, 21 km from Springs on the road to Delmas. Tel 9661. Caravan stands.

FLORIDA 011

Florida Lake, (Municipal), Westlake Road. Tel 472-1400. Caravan stands.

HONEYDEW 011

Honeydew, on DF Malan Drive between Eastwood and Dalelace Streets, 16 km from Johannesburg. Tel 795-2031. Caravan stands.

KLERKSDORP 018

Water Paradise, 8 km from town on Ventersdorp Road. Tel 2-0160. Caravan and camping stands.

KRUGERSDORP 011

Krugersdorp Game Reserve (Municipal), 6 km from town on the road to Magaliesburg. Tel 660-1076. Caravan stands. Cottages and rondavels.

The Pines Resort, Ivan Smuts Avenue, Silverfields (3 km from town). Tel 664-4613.

LICHTENBURG 01441

Fanie Labuschagne Resort 30 km from town on Zeerust road, Tel (014287) 710. Caravan and camping stands, rondavels.

Lichtenburg Municipal, adjacent to a small game reserve and swimming pool, 3 km from town. Tel 2-4349. Caravan and camping stands.

MAGALIESBURG 01382

Lovers Rock, beyond the village on main road to Rustenburg. Tel 87. Caravan and camping stands, rondavels, chalets, cottages.

MULDERSDRIFT 011

Syringa Spa, Tel 957-2314. Caravan and camping stands. Restaurant.

ORKNEY 018

Orkney-Vaal Holiday Resort, (Municipal) Tel 3-3228. Caravan and camping stands. Rondavels, chalets. Restaurant.

POTCHEFSTROOM 01481

Potchefstroom Dam Holiday Resort, Tel 2-5144. Caravan and camping stands, rondavels, chalets, family houses. Restaurant.

RANDFONTEIN 011

Riebeeck Lake Park, Tel 693-5219. Caravan and camping stands.

ROODEPOORT 011

Little Falls, Hendrik Potgieter Road. Tel 475-1433. Caravan and camping stands.

RUSTENBURG 01421

Ananda, 8 km from town on the road to Swartruggens, adjacent to hotel. Tel 2-2332. Caravan stands.

Bergheim, 16 km from town, off Pretoria Road. Tel 9-2363. Caravan and camping stands, rondavels.

Jacaranda West, Tel 2-2077. Caravan stands.

SCHWEIZER-RENEKE 01801

Wentzel Dam (Municipal) Tel 3-1331. Caravan and camping stands.

419

SPRINGS 011

Murray Park (Municipal), 5 km from town on Paul Kruger Highway. Tel 816-1104. Caravan and camping stands..

STANDERTON 01331

Standerton Municipal, Tel 2-5200. Caravan and camping stands.

THABAZIMBI 01537

Ben Alberts Nature Reserve, 7 km from town. Tel 2-1509. Caravan and camping stands.

VAAL DAM 016

New Aloe Fjord, Vereeniging-Villiers Road. Tel (01618) 781. Bookings (011) 683-7320. Caravan stands, cottages and rondavels.

Vaaloewer, at Loch Vaal. Tel (016) 87-1787. Caravan stands.

VANDERBIJLPARK 016

Vanderbijlpark, on the Vaal River. Tel 32-3683. Caravan stands.

VEREENIGING 016

Dickinson Park (Municipal), Lewis-Avenue, at the Vaal River. Tel 22-2251. Caravan and camping stands.

VOLKSRUST 01333

Volksrust Municipal, Tel 2141. Caravan and camping stands.

WOLMARANSSTAD 018112

Wolmaransstad Municipal, Tel 412. Caravan and camping stands.

ZEERUST 014282

Krans Resort, 2 km from town on road to Rustenburg. Tel (01428) 2-2008. Caravan stands, rondavels.

12 — Pretoria, Northern Transvaal, Eastern Transvaal and Kruger National Park

PRETORIA 012

Fountains Valley (Municipal), south of the city. Tel 44-7131. Caravan and camping stands.

Hengelaarsvriend, at Roodeplaat Dam. Tel 82-1056. Caravan and camping stands, cottages, rondavels.

Joos Becker, Apies River Road, Mayville, at northern entrance to the city. Tel 75-4029. Caravan and camping stands.

Magalieskloof, 30 km west of the city on Pretoria North/Hartbeespoort Dam Road. Tel (01204) 707.

Pretoria, 26 km north of city on N1. Tel 5-1808. Caravan stands, camping stands.

Roodeplaat Dam Nature Reserve, 9 km on the Moloto road. Tel 82-2185. Caravan and camping stands.

BADPLAAS 013482

Badplaas Mineral Baths (Overvaal) Tel 7. Caravan and camping stands, rondavels, chalets.

Therons, 3 km east of Badplaas. Tel 24. Caravan stands.

BARBERTON 01314

Barberton, Tel 3323, General Street. Caravan and camping stands, chalets.

BELFAST 0132512

Belfast Municipal, at the dam. Tel 291. Caravan stands.

BETHAL 01361

Bethal Municipal, at the town dam. Tel 2031. Caravan and camping stands.

BLYDEPOORT 013231

Blydepoort Resorts (Overvaal), overlooking the Blyde River Canyon – 2 camps – FH Odendaal Camp at the southern end of the canyon, and Sybrand van Niekerk Camp at the northern end of the canyon. Caravan stands at each situation and luxury chalets and rooms at both. Each camp has a licensed restaurant. See page 313.

BROEDERSTROOM 01205

Winsome Valley Holiday Resort, on the Crocodile river bank, south of Hartbeespoort Dam, off route 512 between Pretoria and Johannesburg. Tel 741. Caravan and camping stands.

BRONKHORSTSPRUIT 013121

Bonamanzi at the dam, 8 km from the town on the road to Delmas. Tel 2-1631. Caravan and camping stands.

Bronkhorstbaai Pleasure Resort, at the dam 12 km from town on the Bapsfontein Road. Caravan stands, chalets, rondavels. Tel 2-2202.

Clover Hill, on the banks of the dam. Tel 2-0951. Caravan and camping stands, vans hired. Restaurant.

CAROLINA 013442

Joubert Park, Voortrekker Street. Tel 52. Caravan and camping stands.

DUIWELSKLOOF 015236

Duiwelskloof Holiday Resort. Tel 3651. Caravan and camping stands, rondavels. Restaurant.

ERMELO 01341

Republic Park, 6 km from the town on road to Hendrina. Tel 4093. Caravan stands, rondavels.

GRASKOP 0131522

Municipal Tourist Park, Louis Trichardt Avenue. Tel 126. Caravan and camping stands. Chalets, cottages, rondavels. Restaurant.

Panorama Rest Camp, 2 km from the town. Tel 91. Caravan and camping stands, chalets.

GROBLERSDAL 01202

Groblersdal Municipal, 23 van Riebeeck Street. Tel 3056. Caravan and camping stands.

HARTBEESPOORT DAM

Hennops Pride, Hennops River Road. Tel (012) 78-3638, 78-2721. Caravan stands, rondavels.

Iscor Angling Resort, on the road to Cosmos. Tel (01211) Y 3-1035. Caravan and camping stands, cottages, rondavels.

Lakeside Lodge, alongside the dam on the road to Skerpoort. Tel (01205) 671. Caravan stands, chalets.

HAZYVIEW 0131242

Aan de Vliet Holiday Resort, Hazyview/Sabie Road. Tel 70. Caravan stands, cottages, chalets, rondavels. Restaurant.

Numbi Garden, Adjacent Numbi Hotel. Caravan stands and bungalows. Hotel facilities.

Sabie River Mineral Baths, 3,5 km from village on road to Skukuza. Tel 94. Caravan and camping stands, rooms.

HENDRINA 013282

Van Riebeeck Square Municipal, Tel 1. Caravan and camping stands.

HOEDSPRUIT 0131732

Manousta Park, 3 km north of Strijdom Tunnel along route R36. Tel 4623. Caravan stands.

HOEDSPRUIT GAME LODGES 0131732

Chi Mani Mani Safaris, 25 km north of Klaserie. Box 178. Tel 2613. Hunting and photographic safaris. Chalets, rondavels.

Motswari-M'bali Game Lodges, 58 km from Hoedspruit in the Umbabat Nature Reserve, adjoining Timbavati and Kruger National Park. Reservations and enquiries: (011) 463-1990 or (0131732) 2140. Bungalows and habitents. On the banks of the Timbavati River. Landrover and foot game tracking, boma, swimming pool. Air strip.

Thorny Bush Game Lodge, 20 km north of Klaserie in the Timbavati Reserve. Tel 2602. Thatched bungalows.

Tunda Tula Game Lodge, P O Hoedspruit. Tel 2322. In the Timbavati Reserve. Rondavels.

KOMATIPOORT 013163

Komatipoort Municipal, on the Komati River bank. Tel 3301. Caravan stands.

KRUGER NATIONAL PARK 012

Enquiries and reservations, National Parks Board, Box 787, Pretoria 0001. Tel Reservations 343-1991.

Balule, 10 caravan and camping stands, 5 rondavels.

Berg-en-Dal, luxury camp, huts, cottages, caravans and camping stands. Restaurant, shop, pool, conference facilities.

Boulders, family cottage (for en bloc reservation).

Crocodile Bridge, caravan and camping stands, rondavels. Shop.

Jock of the Bushveld, thatched huts (for en bloc reservation).

Letaba, caravan and camping stands, bungalows. Restaurant, shop.

Lower Sabie, caravan and camping stands, 94 bungalows. Restaurant, shop.

Malelane, rondavels (for en bloc reservation).

Maroela, caravan and camping stands.

Nwanedzi, family cottage, 2 huts (for en bloc reservation).

Olifants, 108 rondavels. Cottages, restaurant, shop.

Orpen, huts, shop.

Pretoriuskop, caravan and camping stands, bungalows, cottages, rondavels. Restaurant, shop, swimming pool.

Punda Maria, 25 caravan and camping stands, cottages, rondavels. Restaurant, shop.

Roodewal, cottage, 3 luxury huts (for en bloc reservation).

Satara, 30 caravan and camping stands, rondavels, cottages, restaurant, shop.

Shingwedzi, caravan and camping stands, bungalows, restaurant, shop, swimming-pool.

Skukuza, caravan and camping stands, bungalows, cottages, rondavels. Restaurant, shop, bank, airport, conference facilities.

LETSITELE 015238

Eiland Mineral Baths (Overvaal). Tel 667. Caravan and camping stands, rondavels. Restaurant. (See page 280).

LONDOLOZI GAME RESERVE

Central booking telephone (011) 726-7360, telex 4-24618 SA. Main camp, luxury chalets, en suite, with balconies, and rustic rondavels, with shower and toilet. Lounge/patio, curio shop, boma, swimming pool. Bush camp, bungalows with an accent on simplicity.
See pages 295 and 299.

LOSKOP DAM 01612

Loskop Dam Resort (Overvaal) Tel 5334. Caravan and camping stands, cottages, chalets, restaurant.

LOUIS TRICHARDT 01551

Ben Lavin Nature Reserve, 12 km south-east of town. Tel 3834. Owned by the Wild Life Society. Caravan and camping stands, vans hired, cottages.

Louis Trichardt Municipal, Grobler Street. Tel 2212. Caravan and camping stands..

LYDENBURG 01323

Krugerspos, 24 km from town on road to Byldepoort. Tel 3871. Caravan and camping stands, bungalows.

Uitspan south of the town, (Municipal) Tel 2914. Caravan and camping stands, rondavels, cottages.

MAGOEBASKLOOF 0152222

Lakeside Chalets, adjoining Troutwaters Inn (fully licensed) at the lake off route R71. Caravan stands, bungalows and chalets, restaurant, swimming pool, tennis courts, boating, trout fishing. See pages 276 and 278. Tel 53 or 80.

MALAMALA GAME RESERVE

Central Reservations (011) 789-2677/8/9, telex 424807, fax 8864382. P O Box 2125, Randburg 2125. Enquiries (031) 75-3325/6/7/8/9.

MalaMala main camp has 24 double and 2 single luxury huts. Here are the buffalo lounge and buffalo boma, the bar and swimming-pool, and a shop. At the southern end of the main camp is the exclusive **Sable Unit** (maximum 14 guests) with its own facilities.

Kirkman's Kamp, where up to 20 guests are accommodated in cottages, and **Harry's,** a camp for 16 guests (accommodated in huts) have their own attractive facilities. Full details and pictures appear on pages 294, 296 and 297.

MARBLE HALL 012020

Caravan's Rest, at Moses River, 6 km from town. Tel 2987. Caravan and camping stands.

MARIKANA 0142222

Mountain Sanctuary, caravan and camping stands, chalets. Tel 1430.

Omaramba, at Buffelspoort Dam, caravan stands, cottages, rooms. Tel 27.

Buffelspoort, at the dam, caravan stands, rondavels. Tel 42.

MESSINA 01553

Messina Municipal, southern entrance of town. Tel 2210. Caravan and camping stands.

MICA 0020

Hippo Pools Resort, Tel 811. Caravan stands, cottages, restaurant.

MIDDELBURG 01321

Kruger Dam Municipal, Coetzee Street. Tel 2-2551. Caravan and camping stands, rondavels, chalets.

Uitkyk, 25 km from Middelburg on the Belfast road. Tel 2-3810 (Jan Marais). Caravan and camping stands.

NABOOMSPRUIT 01534

Constantia Spa, 13 km north-west of town. Tel 3-0487. Caravan and camping stands, rondavels, restaurant.

Lekkerrus Baths, 24 km north of town. Tel 3-2264. Caravan and camping stands, rondavels, restaurant.

Libertas Spa, 20 km west of town. Tel 3-0351. Caravan and camping stands, rondavels, cottages, restaurant.

Maroela, 5 km west of town. Tel 3-0327. Caravan and camping stands, rondavels.

Rhemardo Holiday Resort and Mineral Spa, 16 km west of town. Tel 3-0612. Caravan stands, rondavels.

Rondalia Die Oog, 14 km west of town. Tel 3-2257. Caravan stands, rondavels. Restaurant, fully licensed.

NELSPRUIT 01311 — DISTRICT 0131232

Come Together, 16 km from town on N4 to Pretoria. Tel (0131232) 2831. Caravan stands, rondavels, chalets.

Montrose Falls, 30 km from town on N4 to Pretoria. Tel 0020 ask for Montrose Falls 3. Caravan and camping stands. Adjacent to hotel.

Nelspruit Municipal, on the bank of the Crocodile River, adjacent to the Falls, 3 km from town on the road to White River. Caravan and camping stands. Cottages. Tel 5-9111.

Sudwala Caves, 34 km from town off N4 to Pretoria. Tel (0131232) 3913. Caravan stands, restaurant.

NYLSTROOM 01531

J G Strijdom Park, (Municipal) on the river bank. Caravan and camping stands, restaurant.

Stokkiesdraai Holiday Resort, 6 km north of town. Tel 4005. Caravan and camping stands. Chalets, restaurant.

PIETERSBURG 01521

Fynbos Holiday Resort, Chunnelspoort. Caravan and camping stands, vans hired, cottages, rondavels, chalets, restaurant. Tel 2737.

UNION PARK

Union Park (Municipal), adjoining local game reserve, 2 km from the town. Tel 6468. Caravan and camping stands, rondavels.

PIET RETIEF 01343

Piet Retief Municipal, Tel 2211. Caravan and camping stands.

PILGRIM'S REST 0131532

Pilgrim's Rest (Overvaal), Tel 36. Caravan and camping stands, cottages, restaurant.

POTGIETERSRUS 01541

Fiesta Park, 26 km south of town on the N1 to Naboomspruit. Tel 5641. Caravan and camping stands.

Potties Pride, Bloemhof Farm, Tel 5516. 10 km from town. Caravan stands, rondavels, restaurant.

SABIE 0131512

Castle Rock (Municipal), off old Lydenburg Road to Lone Creek Falls. Tel 203. Caravan and camping stands.

Jock of the Bushveld, Main Street. Tel 541. Caravan stands and bungalows.

Merry Pebbles, 1 km from town on old Lydenburg Road. Tel 326. Caravan and camping stands, chalets, cottages, restaurant.

TRICHARDTSDAL 0152302

Makutsi Spa, on the Lydenburg Road R36, near the Strijdom Tunnel. Tel 2402. Caravan and camping stands, rondavels.

TSHIPISE 015539

Tshipise Mineral Baths (Overvaal), Tel 624. Caravan and camping stands, rondavels. Restaurant.

TZANEEN 015236

Fairview, 2 km from town at Manorvlei. Caravan stands.

Fanie Botha Nature Reserve and Caravan Park, Tel 5641. Caravan and camping stands.

VAALWATER 015352

Lapalala Wilderness, in the Waterberg. 74 km from Vaalwater. Three bush camps close to rivers with basic requirements. Guests bring own food and liquor and hire entire camp. Tel 2813.

Waterberg Natuurpraal, Tel 2712. Cottages, rondavels, caravan and camping stands.

VERWOERDBURG 012

Doornkloof, Smuts House, Irene. Tel 6-5476. Caravan and camping stands.

Polkadraai, near Voortrekkerhoogte. Tel 666-8710. Caravan and camping stands.

WARMBATHS 015331

Klein-Kariba Mineral Baths, 6 km north of town on the N1. Tel 2388. Caravan and camping stands, apartments.

Ronwill, 4 km north of town on the N1. Tel 2350. Caravan and camping stands, chalets, cottages.

Overvaal Warmbad, Sutter Road. Tel 2200. Caravan and camping stands, chalets. Site of the famous mineral baths.

WATERVAL BOVEN 013262

Elandskrans Holiday Resort (Municipal), Tel 176. Caravan and camping stands, chalets.

WHITE RIVER 01311

White River Municipal, Hennie van Til Street. Tel 3-1176. Caravan and camping stands.

WITBANK 01351

Witbank Recreation Resort, 4 km east of town. Tel 7-0147. Caravan and camping stands, rooms and cottages.

13 — Bloemfontein, the Orange Free State

BLOEMFONTEIN 051

Johan Brits (Municipal), opposite the free State Stadium and Swimming Bath. Tel 8-3636. Caravan stands.

Maselspoort Holiday Resort (Municipal), on the banks of the Modder River 24 km from the city on the Thaba Nchu Road. Tel 3-7848. Caravan and camping stands. Cottages, rondavels.

Pitstop, on western bypass at Bultfontein/Eeufees Road offramp. Tel 33-2129. Caravan and camping stands.

Toms Place, 40 km from Bloemfontein on N1 to Colesberg (take Koppieskraal turnoff), adjacent to Kaffer River Dam. Caravan stands and cottages. Restaurant. Tel (05215) 680.

BETHLEHEM 01431

Loch Athlone Holiday Resort (Municipal), 2 km from town on the road to Ficksburg. Tel 3-5732. Caravan and camping stands, cottages, rondavels, chalets, restaurant.

BETHULIE 05862

Bethulie Municipal Holiday Resort, at the municipal dam. Box 7, Tel 2. Caravan and camping stands, cottages, rondavels.

BOTHAVILLE 014141

Bothaville Municipal, alongside the river, south of the town. Tel 2017. Caravan stands.

BRANDFORT 05222

Brandfort Municipal, behind the town hall. Tel 2. Caravan stands.

BULTFONTEIN 05252

Bultfontein Municipal, Diamant Street. Caravan stands.

CLARENS 014326 (see also Golden Gate)

Clarens Municipal, Malherbe Street. Tel 605. Caravan and camping stands.

Greenlands Resort, off the Clarens/Golden Gate road. Caravan stands, cottages, rondavels, chalets, mountain huts. Tel 850.

CLOCOLAN 05652

Ikebana Mountain Resort, on a farm 12 km south of town (gravel road sign posted.) Caravan and camping stands, cottages, rondavels, chalets, restaurant. Tel 3604.

Steunmekaar, 2 km from main road at Steunmekaar Dam. Tel 24. Caravan and camping stands.

FICKSBURG 0563

Thom Park (Municipal) McCabe and Bloem Streets. Tel 2122. Caravan stands.

FOURIESBERG 014332

Fouriesburg Municipal, Kosmos Street. Tel 14. Caravan and camping stands.

Meringskloof (Municipal), 3 km from town. Tel 14. Caravan and camping stands, cottages.

FRANKFORT 01613

Dorpoewerpark, on the bank of the Wilge River. Tel 3-1610. Caravan and camping stands, rondavels.

Jim Fouché Holiday Resort, (Provincial Administration), 16 km from Oranjeville, near the inflow of the Wilge River into the Vaal Dam. Tel (01616) 804. Caravan and camping stands, rondavels, restaurant.

GOLDEN GATE HIGHLANDS NATIONAL PARK 012

Enquiries and reservations, National parks Board, Box 787, Pretoria 0001. Tel 343-1991. There are two camps, 19 km east of Clarens.

Brandwag Rest Camp (luxury accommodation and facilities). Single and double rooms in the main building, and self-contained chalets. Restaurant and coffee shop.

Glen Reenen Rest Camp. Caravan and camping stands. Rondavels. Tel (014326) 711.

HARRISMITH 01436

President Brand Park (Municipal), on the Wilge River. Tel 2-1061. Caravan and camping stands.

HEILBRON 016142

Langdam Resort (Municipal), at the municipal dam. Tel 10. Caravan and camping stands.

HENDRIK VERWOERD DAM 0020

Hendrik Verwoerd Dam Resort, 42 km north-east of Colesberg. Tel 45. Caravan and camping stands, rondavels.

KROONSTAD 01411

Kroon Park Resort, on the Vals River bank. Tel 2-5670. Caravan and camping stands, rondavels, chalets, restaurant.

LADYBRAND 0561

Leliehoek Resort (Municipal), 2 km south of the town. Tel 2261. Caravan and camping stands, cottages, chalets, rondavels, restaurant.

LINDLEY 0141512

Lindley Municipal, Tel 4. Caravan and camping stands.

ODENDAALSRUS 0171

Mimosa, Tel 4-1940. Caravan and camping stands.

ORANJEVILLE 01616

Jim Fouché Resort see Frankfort.

PARYS 01601

Mimosa (Municipal), Boom Street, on Vaal River bank. Tel 2711. Caravan stands, cottages, restaurant.

Rusoewer, 4 km south of town off the N1. Caravan and camping stands, Tel 3902.

SASOLBURG 016

Abrahamsrust Resort (Municipal), 6 km north of the town on route 568. Tel 60-1909. Caravan and camping stands, chalets.

SENEKAL 014352

Senekal Municipal, on Sandspruit bank, in the town off main road. Tel 30. Caravan and camping stands.

SWINBURNE 0020

Montrose, off national road N3 between Van Reenen and Harrismith. Tel 19. Caravan stands. Restaurant. Near hotel.

VILLIERS 016134

Villiers Municipal Resort, on the banks of the Vaal River. Tel 2484. Caravan stands, rondavels.

VIRGINIA 01722

Virginia Park, on the banks of the Sand River. Tel 3-2306. Caravan and camping stands, rondavels, bungalows, also hotel accommodation, licensed steak house.

VREDE 013342

Vrede Municipal, at the municipal dam. Tel 2193. Caravan and camping stands.

WELKOM 0171

Welkom Municipal, Disa Street. Tel 2-1455, caravan and camping stands.

WEPENER 05232

Geyer Park (Municipal), Spes Street. Tel 31. Caravan stands.

WILLEM PRETORIUS GAME RESERVE 01734

Willem Pretorius Camp, at the Allemanskraal Dam off the N1 between Kroonstad and Winburg. P O Willem Pretorius Game Reserve, 9451. Tel 4229. Caravan and camping stands, luxury flats and luxury rondavels, huts and rondavels. Restaurant.

WINBURG 05242

Winburg Municipal, Prince Edward Street. Tel 54. Caravan and camping stands.

ZASTRON 05542

Zastron Municipal, at municipal dam. Tel 397. Caravan and camping stands.

14 — Kimberley and the Northern Cape

KIMBERLEY 0531

Kimberley, Hull Street, at the Showgrounds, 3 km from the city centre. Tel 3-3581. Caravan and camping stands.

Riverton Resort (Municipal), on the bank of the Vaal River, 27 km north of the city. Tel 2-2241. Caravan and camping stands. Rondavels, villas.

AUGRABIES FALLS NATIONAL PARK 012

Enquiries and reservations, National Parks Board, Box 787, Pretoria 0001. Tel 343-1991. Caravan and camping stands, bungalows. Restaurant. Klipspringer threeday hiking trail down the ravine. Tel (0020) Augrabies 4.

BARKLY WEST 05352

Barkly West Municipal, at the southern entrance to the town, near the Vaal River and Canteen Koppie, Tel 17. Caravan and camping stands.

CALVINIA 02772

Calvinia, Station Road. Tel 633. Caravan and camping stands.

CARNAVON 02032

Voortrekker (Municipal), Hospital Avenue. Tel 397. Caravan and camping stands.

DANIËLSKUIL 053872

Daniëlskuil Municipal, Park Road. Tel 13. Caravan and camping stands.

GARIES 02792

Garies, High School Sports Ground. Tel 3. Caravan and camping stands.

GRIQUATOWN 05962

Griquatown Municipal, Market Square. Tel 19. Caravan and camping stands.

HARTSWATER 05332

Hartswater Municipal, Viljoen and Strydom Streets. Tel 126. Caravan and camping stands.

KAKAMAS 05442

Kakamas Municipal, Van der Walt Road. Tel 102. Caravan and camping stands.

KALAHARI GEMSBOK NATIONAL PARK 012

Enquiries and reservations, National Parks Board. Box 787, Pretoria 0001. Tel 343-1991. There are three camps:

Mata Mata, 2 cottages, 3 rooms, 10 caravan stands.

Nossob, 3 cottages, 6 rondavels, 10 caravan stands.

Twee Rivieren, 1 cottage, 14 rondavels, 10 caravan stands.

Prior permission is required of persons wishing to use the air landings trips. The Town Clerk, Upington, Box 17. Tel (0541) 2-2241, arranges visits to the Park by motor vehicle.

KEIMOS 05492

Keimos Municipal, Tel 26. Caravan stands.

KURUMAN 01471

Kuruman Municipal, Voortrekker Street. Tel 2-1479. Caravan and camping stands.

OLIFANTSHOEK 059512

Olifantshoek Municipal, Tel 2. Caravan and camping stands.

POFADDER 02532

Pofadder Municipal, Springbok Street, Tel 46. Caravan and camping stands.

PORT NOLLOTH 0020

Port Nolloth, McDougal's Bay. Tel 1521. Caravan stands, rondavels.

PRIESKA 05942

Prieska Municipal, Main Street. Tel 235. Caravan stands.

SPRINGBOK 0251

Kokerboom, off the N7, 6 km from the town. Tel 2-2785. Caravan stands, rooms.

STRYDENBURG 05762

Strydenburg Municipal, Tel 16. Caravan stands.

UPINGTON 0541

The Island Municipal Holiday Resort, on the Orange River. Tel 6911. Caravan and camping stands, rondavels, bungalows, cottages.

VRYBURG 01451

Boereplaas, 18 km from town on road to Mafikeng. Tel 3223. Caravan and camping stands, cottages.

Swartfontein Resort, adjacent to Taljaard Nature Reserve, 6 km from town on the road to Ganyesa. Tel 2241. Caravan and camping stands, rondavels.

WARRENTON 053332

Warrenton Municipal, Tel 1. Caravan stands.

WILLISTON 02052

Williston, Muller Street. Tel 3. Caravan and camping stands.

INDEX

Folios in parenthesis thus (384 H18) refer to atlas page and grid square. Folios in square brackets thus [394] [412] refer to accommodation directory pages. All other folios refer to text pages.